STUDIES IN
SYMBOLIC INTERACTION

Volume 2 · 1979

REVIEWERS for Volume II

Bennett Berger
Fred Block
Herbert Blumer
Patricia Bourne
Catherine Daubard
Lawrence E. Cohen
Lewis Coser
Carl Couch
Una Creditor
Jesse Delia
William Erbe
Frank Falk
Ira Gerstein
Jan Gorecki
Sharon Guten
Robert Hintz
Mike Katovich
Frank Kohout
J. David Lewis
Bruce MacMurray

Jeffrey Maitland
Peter K. Manning
Peter Maris
Michal McCall
Cary Nelson
Daniel O'Keefe
Martha A. Ramos
Joel Rudd
Mary Jo Rudd
Calvin O. Schrag
Gayle Scriven
David Seibold
Gregory P. Stone
Peter Storkerson
Anselm Strauss
David Swanson
Ann Swidler
Richard Travisano
Glenn Vernon
Mark Wardall

STUDIES IN SYMBOLIC INTERACTION

A Research Annual

Editor: NORMAN K. DENZIN
Department of Sociology
University of Illinois

VOLUME 2 · 1979

 JAI PRESS INC.
Greenwich, Connecticut

CONTENTS

THE SOCIAL SERVICES AND
LABELING THEORY

POLITICS, PRESIDENTS, AND
POWER

SOCIABILITY, INTERACTION AND
SOCIAL EXCHANGE

OVERVIEW

The essays in Volume II are organized under four headings. Section One contains three papers in what may be loosely termed the sociology of knowledge. Harvey Farberman explores the theoretical and philosophical foundations of University of Chicago sociology during the years 1915–1932 and 1940–1960. In the work of Chicago sociologists, Park in particular, Farberman finds an emphasis on the ecological perspective in the study of urban social life. Neo-Chicago sociologists, Farberman argues, sought to discover enclaves of primacy in the alienating urban milieu. Absent from their conceptual framework was any consideration of economic and class forces. An overall view of social structure was not present. Farberman traces the Chicago perspective back to Park's use of the Continental theorists, especially Durkheim, Weber and Simmel. The analysis is illuminating and sheds additional light on this perplexing department of sociology. Of particular interest to symbolic interactionists because it was the home of symbolic interactionism until the early 1950's, the Chicago Department will undoubtedly be studied by generations to come. Whether the department was unique in its philosophic and theoretical stand, remains to be documented. Certainly there is some evidence to support this contention of uniqueness (for instance, while statistics swept through sociology in the 1920's Chicago formally resisted the fad until 1927, and here Chicagoans parted company with the other major departments of the time). Of little argument is the influence the Chicago school of sociology wielded over the discipline. Certainly mainstream American sociology, as it appeared in the pages of the *American Journal of Sociology* through 1936, reflected at least in part the dominance of the Chicago perspective. Farberman's essay will be welcomed by all sociologists interested in their intellectual roots.

Reynolds, Reynolds, and Bowden analyze the social networks that exist within a sample of symbolic interactionists. Their data indicate that unconventional interactionists, those who do not hold with consensual definitions of certain basic concepts, are more likely to be caught up in a series of interpersonal relationships with other like-minded symbolic interactionists. This finding could no doubt be generalized to variant perspectives within other disciplines and suggests that social networks are basic to the growth of scientific specialities.

Glenn Jacobs' essay on economy and totality brings Charles Horton Cooley alive and discovers in Cooley's work a theory of pecuniary valuation. Interactionists have tended to ignore economic issues, and Cooley's perspective provides a point of departure for future theory work. Jacobs has performed an important service for the symbolic interactionist community by bringing Cooley's views into clearer focus.

Four papers in this volume deal with methodological and theoretical innovations, or developments within the interactionist-interpretative paradigm. Norbert Wiley, in a pathbreaking essay, addresses the "I-me" problem in social psychology. In particular he asks how it is that the "I" appears in the consciousness of the young child. Mead posited an "I", in response to a "me", but never developed the processes that brought the "I" experience into the child's thought-stream. Wiley explores the works of James and Schutz, and joins symbolic interactionism with phenomenology. This merger of perspectives is long overdue. Wiley proposes that the child's sense of "I" emerges after a "we" relationship has been formed with the significant other. The child experiences the "I" in the mirror of the intimate other. Genesis of self, then, flows from the "me" experience, to the "we" relationship to the sense of "I".

Wiley's insight is critical and should significantly advance studies in the social psychology of self, socialization and interaction. He makes specific applications to the ritual theory of self, to mental illness, to the "object-relations" psychoanalysts, the existential psychoanalysts, to Durkheim, Weber, and modern historians of the family. These fields are ready for conceptual reordering and Wiley offers a compelling set of suggestions concerning future development. His essay warrants a close and careful reading.

Irwin Deutscher and Margaret Gold present a bold and frank account of a program evaluation research project. Their analysis is insightful and basic; it reconceptualizes the very act of evaluation research. Conceiving their project as "a process within an ongoing process," they suggest that conventional canons of research are barriers or obstacles to meaningful evaluation research.

Movidas, the term employed by Mexican-Americans to describe their interactional strategies, is the topic of Reyes Ramos' essay. By examining the actual interactional strategies of the Trujillos and Faustos families, Ramos exposes current sociological stereotypes of the Mexican-American family. He furthermore reveals how a study of everyday taken-for-granted conduct can become a sociological method in its own right. The relevance of ethnomethodological investigations for the study of social order are stressed in Ramos' discussion, and his suggestions are to be recommended to future researchers.

Lawrence Grossberg addresses a major problem in the human sciences: language and its conceptualization. His six-fold category system distinguishes objective and subjective theories of meaning, and he subtlely clarifies the conceptual differences that separate structuralism from hermeneutic analysis, interactionism, and phenomenology. The distinctions that he makes are important and basic. Their explication should serve to stimulate and structure future empirical activity on the organization of meaning and linguistic conduct in everyday life.

Susan Krieger, in "Research and the Construction of a Text," presents a methodological account of the strategies she utilized in analyzing a life history of radio station KMPX in San Francisco during the years 1967–72. Her text and her methods share an affinity with the narrative styles of Virginia Woolf and certain of the "new" journalists. They are sociologically unconventional, quite insightful and moving. The reader catches a sense of drama and authenticity in her writing. Krieger's work is innovative and suggests new avenues for organizational, life history research.

Carole Joffe and William C. Cokerham deal, in turn, with a symbolic interactionist analysis of social services and with the labelling theory of mental disorder. Their essays attest to the viability of interactionism in the applied fields. Joffe challenges conventional views of social service delivery systems and applies the views of Herbert Blumer to an analysis of abortion services in American society. Client-service conflicts are stressed, as are the meanings given the service itself. Joffe observes that the new social service institutions proliferate new occupations and new occupational identities. Her discussion takes the application of symbolic interactionism directly into the institutional structure of society and reveals the power of the perspective in this arena.

William C. Cockerham opens new avenues of research and inquiry for the labelling theory of mental illness. This perspective, he argues, holds the promise of consolidating psychiatric, genetic and physiological processes within a life event approach. His explication of the life history method should be compared to Krieger's development of the same technique.

Symbolic interactionists have not developed a political sociology, nor have they dealt in any detail with the politics of power. Peter M. Hall is one of the interactionists who has examined these issues. In "The Presidency and Impression Management," he offers a method and a metaphor for studying presidential administrations. He compares the Kennedy and Nixon White Houses in terms of the impression management techniques utilized by each president. These recent presidents have symbolically manipulated the American public. They have attempted to create illusions of consensus when consensus was absent. They manipulated war, politicized publics and managed minorities in ways that tore at basic values in the larger society. Hall's method is powerful, his sensitizing concept is penetrating, and his conclusions are sobering.

The American social structure is characterized by unequal distribution of power, wealth, influence and prestige. Multinational corporations dominate in the economic arena and the legal system increasingly favors the corporate power structure. Julian Roebuck and Stanley Weeber apply these observations to the study of political crime in the United States. They offer a typology of American political crime and distinguish crimes committed to maintain the government from crimes against the government. They treat crimes of intervention, surveillance, confrontation and evasion. The crimes of the multinational corporations are examined. Statutes which clarify the legal (and illegal) conduct of these acting units need to be written and *enforced.*

The second essay by Susan Krieger details the life history of the strike which occurred at station KMPX in San Francisco from March to May of 1968. The politics of protest, the co-optive force of corporate structures, the interplay of private (and public) moral careers and the shifting worlds of relational involvement are all apparent in her account. A radio station that stood (at one level) in opposition to the Nixon administration is corrupted by the very forces it originally sought to expose and dethrone. The three essays in this section point to a disquieting feature of American society, perhaps of all modern industrial states—namely, the crippling, corruptive influence of corporate structures over public morality, private trust and personal senses of worth, integrity and influence.

Sociability, interaction, and social exchange are familiar topics to the social psychologist. The final four papers in Volume II examine these social processes. Patricia Clough's essay, based on intensive ethnographic observations of the drinking behaviors of middle class patrons in a bar she calls the Lantern, questions the hypothesis that middle class social relations are equalitarian in nature. Her materials reveal segmentations in the middle class as well as vertical cleavages which rely upon reputations and social appearances. An unstable status hierarchy was observed. Circumstances, stituations, personal identities and public reputations interact in the drinking establishment. While sharing public identities, the members of the middle class may well be moving toward a more personalized, segmented set of self-other relationships. Recognizing their commonalities, they work together to achieve personal uniqueness. Sociability, its forms and its pursuits, deserves greater empirical attention. Clough's conclusions challenge current pictures of the middle class and their stratification systems.

Carl J. Couch takes conventional exchange theory to task for its failure to seriously consider the place of selves, minded behavior, dyads, and cooperative conduct in the exchange act. Before humans can engage in exchange activities they must be able to think and communicate. They must be capable of becoming objects of their own activity. Exchange acts flow from this fundamental feature of the human actor. Couch traces the development of civilizations and democratic political institutions out of the emergence of economic exchanges (on a routine basis) among individuals in a group context. His discussion is mindful of Simmel and clearly challenges the narrowness of current exchange theory.

Individuals have multiple identities and these are often divided among the many spheres that make up their lives. Thus, they can be seen as identifying themselves along religious, political, family, work and perhaps recreational lines. Saul Feldman adds complexity to this topic. He suggests that persons may have multiple identities with the *same* sphere of social interaction. Within the work sphere, one may be, for instance, a symbolic interactionist, a reader of G.H. Mead, a scholar of Cooley, an officer in a symbolic interactionist society, and an author of interactionist materials. Feldman calls these *nested identities.* Such identities are situational in nature, they are evoked as shared identities, some are more salient than others, and some are more complex than others. Feldman calls attention to a neglected component in "identity theory," and his observations readily lend themselves to future empirical inquiry.

The concluding essay in Volume II, by Schmitt, Gorshe and Lindberg, undertakes an empirical study of organizational careers and dying as a status passage. By stressing the complexity of organizational environments and the negotiated meanings given death and other status passages, the authors point to the bonds that knit personal and public careers into those complex bundles sociologists call persons.

Together these essays point to the diversity of thought characteristic of contemporary symbolic interactionists. No single paradigm dominates current theory or research. Rather, an avowed commitment to confront and study, perferably qualitatively, the empirical world in all its variations, commands the attention of the contemporary symbolic interactionist.

It is hope that readers of Volume II will build upon these research and theoretical papers. Volume III will contain studies of mood, emotion, ritual, social situations, the phenomenology of self, alienation, social worlds, and the production of pure sociability. The growth and development of symbolic interactionism is the means and end of this series.

Norman K. Denzin
Series Editor

THREE STUDIES IN THE
SOCIOLOGY OF KNOWLEDGE

THE CHICAGO SCHOOL:
CONTINUITIES IN URBAN SOCIOLOGY*

Harvey A. Farberman, SUNY AT STONY BROOK

Publications of the Heritage of Sociology series by the University of Chicago Press, under the general editorship of Morris Janowitz, in part, has stimulated a renewed interest in the "Chicago School" (1915–1932) of urban sociology. Leading sociologists of sociology have reviewed the contributions of the Chicago School and have begun to render initial historical judgments. Robert Friedrichs (12, p. 73), for example, characterizes the leading figures of the school as prophetic seers dedicated to the progressive *amelioration* of social ills, while Alvin Gouldner (14, pp. 20–21) characterizes them as academic status seekers who declined to point a finger at vested interests. My aim here is twofold: 1) to review the nature and grounds of Gouldner's sociology of knowledge analysis; and 2) offer an alternative metatheoretical analysis which discloses the underlying paradigmatic continuity of the pre-Chicago, Chicago, and post-Chicago tradition of urban sociology.

Studies in Symbolic Interaction—Volume 2, 1979, pages 3–20
Copyright © 1979 by JAI Press Inc.
All rights of reproduction in any form reserved.
ISBN: 0–89232–105–9

A SOCIOLOGY OF KNOWLEDGE ANALYSIS

Gouldner (14) contends that the Chicago School of urban sociology explained the quality of city life in terms of the size, density, and heterogeneity of the generic urban community without regard to the position any given community occupied in the national class system. In consequence, the school overlooked the effect that imposed property institutions and stratification arrangements had on the quality of life. Gouldner attributes this neglect of transcendent economic and political variables to expediency. After all, sociology sought admittance to the academy at a time when society was in economic and political depression. To search for the noneconomic sources of integration took attention away from the economic sources of alienation and did not tread on the toes of powerful interests whose financial sponsorship was necessary for the survival of the academy. Thus, to invoke demographic, morphologic variables instead of transcendent, political, economic variables was to play it safe. In this section, I wish to (a) review the supporting evidence for Gouldner's characterization, (b) sketch the larger historical context in which the school functioned, and (c) demonstrate the weakness of Gouldner's analysis.

R.E.L. Faris (10), son of Ellsworth Faris, one of the school's leading figures, observes—in a rather deprecatory fashion—that Lester F. Ward and especially his disciple, James Q. Dealy, nearly ran sociology into the ground at Brown University by formulating doctrinaire assaults on the ruling interests—particularly John D. Rockefeller, "who had made important gifts to the university and who, it was hoped, was willing to make more." Faris also casts aspersions on E.A. Ross (of Wisconsin) who relished making frontal attacks on those "malefactors of wealth" who controlled railroads, communications, and utilities. During the depths of the Depression, these impassioned reformers had little sympathy for plodding, disinterested research. Faris assures us that this was not the case at the University of Chicago. For, despite the progressive *personal* dispositions of Robert E. Park, the muckraking reporter who served as Booker T. Washington's secretary, or Ernest Burgess, the philosophical materialist, who had an earlier interest in social work, or Louis Wirth, the avowed socialist, the prevailing *institutional* attitude at Chicago was one of disinterested, objective, scientific research. Faris (10, p. 130) observes that:

> The Chicago attitude was essentially that of pure science . . . the restriction of scholarly attention to the search for immediate alleviation of present problems may and generally does fail to solve such problems and also delays the development of the organized and tested knowledge which could be effective.

The consequence of adopting a pure-science approach and avoiding a social-problems approach has been commented on by the eminent epigone of the Chicago School. Ralph Turner (31, p. xvii) in his Introduction to Robert Park's selected papers, remarks that:

> ... it is striking that the achievement of social and economic equality never emerges as a dominant goal in Park's thoughts ... Park took no substantial steps towards developing a theory of stratification.

Morris Janowitz (17, p. ix), moreover, in his recent Introduction to Park and Burgess's classic textbook concludes that

> They did not highlight the structures and the mechanism by which the parts related to the whole. The absence of an explicit macrosociology was a source of intellectual and analytic weakness.[1]

Some insight into why the Chicago School tended toward an objective, pure-science approach may be gleaned by placing the school in its larger historical context. At its inception, in 1885, under the leadership of Albion Small, the Chicago department was hardly insensitive to the larger political economy of emerging industrial capitalism. In fact, H.E. Barnes (quoted in Carey, (3, p 57) reports that Small was an outspoken critic of the system. Both in his classroom lectures and in his book *Between Eras,* Small delivered ". . . as relentless a criticism of our conventional unmitigated capitalism as can be found in Veblen . . . Tawney . . . or Webb."

Small railed against the enormous concentration of capital that emerging corporations could engage in during a period of unregulated economic growth. Lack of government intervention permitted lopsided growth—concentration of *corporate* capital but disarray among farmers, workers, and consumers. Yet, this unfettered, unregulated corporate growth reflected the privileged position that American business had, and was a manifestation of deeply held philosophical and political convictions integral to the American experience.

The idea of laissez-faire, as H.S. Commager (4) notes, was imprinted on those who fled the Old World. Government there was synonymous with oppression; it was the enemy of liberty and justice; it meant a king, court aristocracy, army, church, inquisition, and burdensome taxes levied on the poor to support a system which dispensed justice only for the rich. In the Old World, the hierarchy of social honor and prestige ran from crown to church, to aristocracy, to army—and business merchants quickly married into the landed gentry to escape the stigma of a commercial background. In the New World, there were no such institutional obstacles to business and businessmen. Instead of shame and dishonor, supplication and conformance, the businessman in America set the standard, was the leader. The special position and power of American business and the subordinate role of American government was a central pillar of the American experience. In America, what business did was not merely *in* the public interest, it *was* the public interest. Business was a bulwark against tyranny.

By 1870–1880, business began to fashion its own ideological justification for accumulation of power and privilege. The doctrine known as Social Darwinism contained the key rhetorical elements. Jeffersonian agrarianism and Manchester liberalism provided the idea that least government was best government. The "religious" principle that the ability to make money was a signal of divine approbation coupled with the sanctity of private property provided a moral patina. The notion of white, Nordic supremacy gave warrant not only to the exploitation of ethnic immigrants and southern blacks, but also to the imperialistic forays identified as the "white man's burden." Finally, Spencer's doctrine of the "survival of the fittest" capped off an impregnable philosophical justification for the American business establishment.[2] And American business moved quickly to translate its philosophical advantages into legal precedents; in the process, it evolved from a bulwark against crown tyranny into a bulwark against class equality.

The dual federalism of the American political system left large areas of civil behavior without clear-cut supervening governmental authority. Often, where the jurisdiction of the federal government ended and state government began was not entirely clear. Seizing on this ambiguity, corporate initiatives, on the one hand, persuaded *federal* courts to take a very strict and narrow view of the "commerce and tax" clauses of the Fourteenth Amendment to the Constitution, while on the other, persuaded *state* courts to take a very broad interpretation of the "due process" clause. In either case, governmental intrusion and regulation of corporate business was kept to a minimum.

Often, the legal reasoning, especially behind the "due process" appeals, which overturned and nullified labor and welfare laws were tortuous. For example, the Fourteenth Amendment forbids the suspension of an individual's liberty and property without the "due process" of law. Since no labor or welfare reform could possibly take place without impairing someone's liberty or property, the courts systematically nullified these reforms. According to H.S. Commager (4, p. xiv), a New York act which established working hours for a municipal contract was nullified since it "created a class of statutory workers." An act setting working hours in a Colorado smelting plant was overturned because it constituted an infringement on liberty of contract. And an Illinois court struck down a statute which set limits on the number of hours women could work in sweatshops since women had the same right to work as many hours as men!

The skill and perseverance that the corporate business establishment displayed in beating back any and all reforms that might compromise its position of power and privilege probably culminated between 1915 and 1920, when, according to Carey (3, pp. 11–13), the Supreme Court ruled that the 1916 Child Labor Act and women's minimum wage standard were unconstitutional. Yet, the previous year, 1915, the Court upheld the so-called "yellow dog" contract which stipulated that workers must agree not to join unions as a condition of employment. In 1919, the court approved assessment of triple damages against the United Mine Workers Union under the Sherman Anti-Trust Act, and, in 1921, held that union-led picketing and boycotting were illegal.

These blows to progressive development were concurrent, moreover, with an upsurge of nativism of all sorts. Thus, the Palmer raids and red scare of 1919–1920, the execution of Sacco and Vanzetti, the Ku Klux Klan, the Scopes trial, and the massive rejection of Wilson's international foreign policy and his highly progressive domestic tax reforms—all of these assaults against progressive developments in labor, education, welfare, ethnic assimilation and domestic and foreign policy may be seen against the background of the emergence of an urban-centered, business-dominated society. Successive waves of immigrants from abroad as well as the northern migration of rural blacks provided the industrial army that the rapidly developing nationally coordinated corporate structure required in order to consolidate its position of dominance. Keeping this work force constrained, divided, and impotent, while keeping corporate wealth concentrated clearly served the interest of the emerging corporate sector.

With the proliferation of national corporate coordination came the need for an army of managers, professionals, and white-collar workers, thus setting the stage for the appearance of an upwardly mobile middle class.[3] But, even more importantly, there was a need for accumulation of technical knowledge which professional managers could use for making rational decisions. The accumulation of such knowledge was the motor force of the bureaucratic-technological principle of organization. There was a need to get beyond apocalyptic, passionate politics based on inflexible ideologies, and to dispassionate, objective, research-based knowledge in order to improve operating efficiency—and all of this *within* the moral-political-economic framework of industrial capitalism. Although this was a national imperative, it became most clearly operational on the local level in the city of Chicago in a fashion which touched and influenced the Chicago sociologists.

According to Edward Shils (27), the Chicago School sociologists showed the same apprehension and alienation that most intellectuals had toward a business-dominated society; nevertheless, they, unlike their more stand-offish contemporaries in literary criticism, decided to influence the direction of growth by joining hands with business-initiated efforts to "depoliticize" knowledge. They came to share the view that the best route to enduring change lay in the disavowal of partisan politics. Indeed, in 1928, the Rockefeller Foundation created the Spelman Fund whose aim, according to James Carey (3, pp. 31–33) was crystal clear, namely,

> . . . to separate the social from the political . . . it separated those who were interested in the national welfare, national social control, and objectivity from those whose interests were partisan. . . .

Its intent was to sponsor and fund investigators who adopted a professional apolitical stance—that is, those who did not challenge the political-economic framework of an emerging industrial society. As Carey (3, p. 35) indicates, those who participated in this effort: ". . . were largely indifferent to or uninterested in facets of urban life that were problematic from a Marxian perspective." The culmination of this apolitical, professional, objective approach occurred when Herbert Hoover formed the President's Commission on Recent Social Trends and appointed William F. Ogburn research director, who, in turn, relied on Robert E. Park as a key adviser.

Thus, the heyday of the Chicago School occurred during a period of societal conservatism, when nationally coordinated business structures were settling in place and seeking to use objective research as a means toward eliminating inefficiency and increasing rational decision making, all the while lobbying for legislative and judicial acts that would stem the tide of progressive developments in labor and welfare.

The Chicago School's inclination to throw in with these tendencies in order to influence policies from the inside paid off handsomely. As Faris (10, p. 132) observes rather pridefully:

> In an ever-growing reward for adherence to the search for reliable knowledge, sociology gained acceptance, not only from other departments in the University, but also very gradually from a wider public whose support is necessary for a subject to flourish. The eventual inclusion of the social sciences (including sociology but not social work) as one of the major divisions of the National Science Foundation could not have been achieved without understanding and support from the educated general public and the Congress of the United States.

It would apear then, on the surface, that Gouldner's characterization of the Chicago School is accurate. Yet, there is room for challenge in that Gouldner's assessment clearly rests on two historical conditions: 1) a period of economic instability leading toward conservative reaction; and 2) sociology's simultaneous struggle for academic and financial acceptance. And it is on this point that we may confront Gouldner's sociology of knowledge analysis, for we may hypothesize that, once these historical conditions had passed, sociologists identified with the Chicago tradition would turn to a conceptualization of transcendent variables. This, however, is not the case.

Herbert Gans (13, pp. 625–648), in an essay which modifies Louis Wirth's classic summing up of the Chicago tradition, observes that urban sociologists working in the Chicago tradition during the period from 1940–1960 still had not begun to appreciate the ultimate effect that national policy and system-wide economic and occupational distributions have on ways of life in either urban or suburban milieu. Thus, Form et al. (11) and Greer (15) engaged in area analysis; Axelrod (1) as well as Bell and Force (2) examined participation in local neighborhoods and formal associations: Dewey (6) and Reiss (25) compared, contrasted, and generally rejected the assertion that urban and rural life styles were radically dissimilar: and Janowitz (17) and Stone (29) reported that, for some people, the local community press and the local business establishment were a mediative link which facilitated psychological identification with the local community.[4]

While everyone challenged the alleged consequence on quality of life of Wirth's ecological perspective, *no one directly challenged the pervasive ecological paradigm itself.* No superseding explanatory paradigm replaced the proposition that size, density, and heterogeneity of population caused impersonal, anonymous, segmented relationships. In their haste to discover enclaves of primacy, neo-Chicago sociologists too readily minimized the existence of urban alienation and paid no attention whatever to the transcendent political and economic causes of that alienation. Consequently, Gan's (13, pp. 641–42) declaration that

A causal analysis must trace . . . back to the larger social, economic and political systems . . . [since] these systems determine income distribution, educational and occupational opportunities. . . .

still stands as an open invitation for future inquiry.

Hence, during a historical period when American society was economically robust and sociology secure both academically and financially, post-Chicago urban sociologists were still searching for the noneconomic sources of social integration and far from *challenging* the basic structure of the system were not even recognizing its impact on the quality of life in urban milieu. Even though the historical conditions had changed, the tendency to neglect the importance of transcendent variables remained. Consequently, Gouldner's sociology of knowledge explanation misses the heart of the matter.

A META-THEORETICAL ANALYSIS

As a result, an alternative approach may be proposed to account for the Chicago School's persistent and ongoing neglect of transcendent political-economic variables. In contrast to Gouldner's extrinsic sociology of knowledge analysis, I shall offer an intrinsic meta-theoretical analysis which points toward an underlying paradigmatic continuity which runs through the formulations of the pre-Chicago (or Continental School) of urban sociology as well as the Chicago and post-Chicago Schools. In this section, I shall (a) interpret the contributions of both the French and German wings of the Continental School, (b) indicate their impact on the works of Robert E. Park and Louis Wirth, and (c) in turn, note the influence that Park and Wirth as well as Mead had on the post-Chicago School.

The Continental theorists, including Durkheim in France and Tonnies, Weber, and Simmel in Germany, were still reacting to the passing of traditional society and the emergence of industrial capitalism—albeit in contrary ways.[5] As Nisbet (22) suggests, disintegration of the bonds of feudal community was shocking in its effects. On this, both radicals who were looking ahead to equalitarianism and conservatives who were looking back toward feudalism, could agree. All were anxious over the breakdown of the extended family, the traditional status order, the prevailing morality schema, the deterioration of working conditions, the emergence of child labor, and the overcrowding of cities. Relations among men had suffered a body blow. Societal stability was in jeopardy. The salience of primary-type involvements was diminished. How could collective life continue if the sentiment that bound men together had been wiped away with the destruction of community? The pre-eminent question was: can society survive?

Unlike his contemporaries, Durkheim viewed the admixture of Calvinist theology, which spiritualized labor, and Hobbesian materialism, which sanctified property, as a godsend, if not a necessary evolutionary adaptation. For, not only did this admixture give rise to the principle of exchange (which transforms labor into property) and thus assured the material survival of the collectivity, but also, in its fullest elaboration, as a rationally coordinated division of functions, served as the institutional bedrock of an organic secular morality. The principle of exchange, heart of the division of labor, itself the skeleton of industrial capitalism, killed two birds with one stone—material survival and moral integration. Yet, for all his concern with material survival, Durkheim did not have a very expansive view of *whose* survival was in question. For nowhere, as Gouldner (14) points out, does Durkheim, in his study of the causes, nature, and consequences of the division of labor, consider or argue for an equitable distribution of products and profits. The result is that the overarching political economy of the public sphere *and those who control it* are beyond surveillance.

In fact, any apprehension Durkheim might have had about industrial capitalism came from another quarter entirely—namely, that ordinary workmen might experience untoward impulses for gratification in the face of attractive and tantalizing products spun off by a high-powered technology. And, although it is true that Durkheim never developed a full-blown social psychology, he was confident that the individual, through socialization and internalization of the morality structure, would have his desires defused and impulses curtailed.[6] The upshot of Durkheim's position, then, is that although material survival and moral integration appear as two sides of the same coin, in fact, moral integration works in the service of material survival. Moral constraints integrate (regulate) the individual so that industry and technology can advance. Social order must occur *within* the framework of industrial capitalist growth.

The result of this position is that the political economy of the public sphere is taken as given. Instead, attention focuses on the moral manipulation of the untoward individual, that is, the noneconomic sources of integration (regulation). Thus, Durkheim not only accepts and encourages the emergence of capitalist political economy, but he makes it the very embodiment and mechanism of the common purpose; the overarching organizational principle which integrates complimentary functional differences. The public sphere of the division of labor is the very fiber of organic solidarity which Durkheim seeks to protect against escalating and potentially ruinous expectations of the ordinary citizen through a defusing socialization process.

The leading theorists of the German School take a contrary stance. Tonnies, Weber, and Simmel, unlike Durkheim, observed the emergence of industrial captialism with a sense of foreboding and made a deliberate effort to break away from the (then) current doctrine of transcendent economic determinism which interpreted what went on in the local community solely as an outcome of what went on in the larger society [Sennet (26)]. To be sure, this was an attempt to re-establish the local community as a potent political and economic force *in its own right* in the face of an absolutistic state—but it was more than that. For the theorists of the German School, each in his own way, were in dialogue with Marx and also riding the crest of nineteenth-century German Romanticism. This meant that each sought to reconstitute the integrity and autonomy of the discrete individual lest he be reduced to an epiphenomenon in the wake of societal massification, collectivization and bureaucratization. In this respect, the classical liberalism of the German sociologists paralleled the irrational idealism of certain of their philosophical predecessors and contemporaries—notably Schopenhauer and Nietzsche. The common concern was to protect the individual in a post-revolutionary world where, on the Hegelian model, the state, which was supposed to guarantee individual sovereignty was, in its rush to consolidate on an industrial base, about to crush the individual. Thus, to place the individual outside the public sphere of transcendent political economy and to search for the possible bases of personal autonomy within the private sphere of family, friends, neighborhood and local community, was to preserve him. Indeed, the preservation and reconstitution of the individual was translated into methodological terms in Weber's principle of "Subjective Interpretation," where the investigator must initially view the world from the perspective of the individual.

In consequence, while the French turned away from the public sphere with a sense of wellbeing, the Germans did so with a sense of foreboding; and where the French turned to the private sphere to constrain the individual, the Germans did so to liberate him. Behind both schools, however, is the underlying assumption that, *it is outside the realms of transcendent economic and political forces that the individual can express his impulses, gratify his desires, and, generally, pursue his destiny.* For

Durkheim, this presented a threat; for the Germans, a relief. In any event, this convergence of concern for the status of the individual—both negatively and positively—made inevitable the leading issues of Chicago and urban sociology: (1) identification of the noneconomic sources of integration (regulation), and (2) the possibility of personal autonomy in the urban milieu.[7]

A deeper understanding of what the leading members of the Chicago School were up to may be achieved if we approach their work in terms of these two issues. I shall attempt to put various pieces of Park's rather unsystematic formulations together by examining his views on social control, the repression of man's natural impulses and desires, the process of symbolic expression in "moral regions" and the power of "psychic compensations." Similarly, I will consider the dilemma embodied in Wirth's view concerning the sources of personal autonomy.

Park and Burgess (24, pp. 27–29) in their effort to answer the questions,

> How does a mere collection of individuals succeed in acting in a corporate and consistent way? How in the case of specific types of social group . . . does the group control its individual members: the whole dominates the parts? What are the mechanisms—physical, psychological, and social by which the group imposes its control. . . ?

reveal a clear interest in how society achieves social control. Note well that Gouldner states the Chicago School was interested in searching for the noneconomic sources of societal integration. In using the term "integration" rather than "social control," Gouldner is less bold than Park and Burgess—but, more importantly, blurs and distorts the exceedingly toughminded, unvarnished problematic that Park (and Burgess) were confronting. What Park wanted to discover were the physical, social, and psychological mechanisms through which society tamed its members. In attempting to delineate the *social* mechanisms of control, he leaned heavily on Durkheim's conception of collective representation and Cooley's notion of the primary group; for the *physical* mechanism, he drew on the perspective of ecology; for the *psychological* mechanism, on Thomas and Znaniecki's view of personal evolution as well as Sigmund Freud and Alfred Adler's notion of sublimation and compensation.

At the outset, Park and Burgess (24, p. 30) take a rather tough-minded view of the human species when they say that

> Men act as they do . . . from motives they do not fully comprehend in order to fulfill aims of which they are but dimly or not at all conscious. Men are activated . . . not merely by interests in which they are conscious of the end they seek, but also by instincts and sentiments, the source and meaning of which they do not clearly comprehend.

Given this state of affairs, how, indeed, do men achieve joint functional actions? Park and Burgess (24, pp. 33–34) approvingly refer to Durkheim, who insists that the social group has real corporate existence and that . . . men act together not because they have like purposes but a *common purpose*. Their common purpose imposes itself upon the individual members of a society at the same time as an ideal, a wish and an obligation. . . . Out of the fermentation which association breeds, a new something *(autre chose)* is produced . . . that is not the sum of, and not like, the sentiments and opinions of the individuals from which it is derived. This . . . imposes itself upon the individuals . . . as something more or less external to them. . . . This fact of control . . . is the fundamental social fact.

And this prior, external, constraining purpose begins to be imposed, par excellence, in the primary group. Park and Burgess (24, p. 56) remark that

The intimate face-to-face association of primary groups, i.e., the family, neighborhood, and the village community, are fundamental in forming the social nature and ideals of the individual . . . the relations between men and women under the influence of the sexual instinct. These are the associations in which . . . lasting affections and . . . violent antipathies are formed.

But, in alluding to the imposition of collective representations through primary group socialization, Park was only pointing to the social mechanism. As is well known, he believed that social mechanisms were pervaded, cross-cut, and penetrated by physical or ecological mechanisms. And the ecological forces themselves operated through four basic forms of interaction. The process of competition—universal, yet unintentional and unconscious—would determine the nature and form of the overall market nexus and one's relationship to it. Such competition eventually would give way to passionate *conflict* which would establish an overall political order and our place in it. Through a process of *accomodation,* groups and individuals in them would defend, transmit, and reconcile their own customs, habits, and traditions with those of others until a workable social order developed. And finally, *assimilation* might occur when individuals and groups penetrated one another's personal styles and cultural heritages and began to share an overall universe of discourse.

Thus, where an individual lives, what part of town his parents and family came from, what kind of jobs his father had, what kind of education and job he could expect to have, what part he might play in the political process, how much of his cultural heritage he might expect to retain, what kind of personality he would develop were largely determined by forces and processes over which he had but faint awareness and little control. Consequently, in a variety of cross-cutting ways, individuals and groups would be moved, manipulated, and mandated—in a word, controlled. Citing Thomas and Znaniecki, Park and Burgess (24, p. 52) agree that

The individual living in society has to fit into a pre-existing world. . . . There is no pre-existing harmony whatever between the individual and the social factors of personal evolution, and the fundamental tendencies of the individual are always in some discordance with the fundamental tendencies of social control. Personal evolution is

always a struggle between the individual and society—a struggle for self-expression on
the part of the individual for his subjection on the part of society—and it is in the total
course of this struggle that the personality . . . manifests and constructs itself.

But, if the individual is thus subordinated to the common purpose, what
price does he or she pay? In the most empirically grounded piece of
speculation available in Park's writings—that is, his work in juvenile
delinquency—Park (23, p. 100) provides an answer:

> So ill-adapted is the natural, undomesticated man to the social order into which he is
> born, so out of harmony are all the native impulses of the ordinary healthy human with
> the demands which society imposes, that it is hardly an exaggeration to say that if this
> childhood is spent mainly in learning what he must not do, his youth will be devoted
> mainly to rebellion. As to the remainder of his life—his recreations will very likely turn
> out to be some sort of vacation and escape from this same social order to which he has
> finally learned to accomodate, but not wholly reconcile himself.

In point, man's natural wishes and impulses will be suppressed and they will
mobilize a residue of rebellion or displaced expression.

Note well that Park's view of the loving struggle is an image of natural
man as impulsive, wishful, and creative. This view is inherited largely from
W.I. Thomas's theory of the four wishes—the underlying motivational
imperative of men's action. Thomas—under the influence of Freud's
doctrine—had postulated, and Park agreed, that man acted in order to
fulfill four fundamental wishes. Summarizing Thomas's views, Park (24,
p. 442) states that

> The wish for security . . . new experience . . . for response and . . . recognition are the
> permanent and fundamental unconscious motives of the person which find expression
> in the many and changing concrete and conscious wishes.

And, when these wishes are stifled, obstructed, suppressed, controlled, or
subordinated to the common purpose—as they must be—the individual will
somehow seek to express them. Park (23, p. 44) says that

> . . . men are brought into the world with all the passions, instincts and appetites,
> uncontrolled and undisciplined. Civilization, in the interests of the common welfare,
> demands the suppression sometimes, and the control always of these wild, natural
> dispositions . . . [yet] . . . much . . . finds . . . vicarious expression in forms that are so-
> cially valuable, or at least innocuous. It is at this point that sport, play, and art function.
> They permit the individual to purge himself by means of symbolic expression of these
> wild and suppressed inpulses. This is the catharsis of which Aristotle wrote in his *Poetic,*
> and which has been given new and more positive significance by the investigations of
> Sigmund Freud and the psychoanalysts.

Park thus speculates that the imposition of social control which modifies or
suppresses the wishes and impulses are sublimated or displaced through a
process of "psychic compensation." In using the term "psychic compensation," Park (23, p. 101) refers to Alfred Adler's work on inferiority
complexes.

... an individual who is conscious of his inferiority inevitably seeks to compensate himself for his lowered self-esteem by greater concentration and effort ... or he may find compensation for failure in one field by success in another. ...

I believe Park suspected that individuals who found themselves manipulated and controlled, moved and modified, stifled and frustrated by a society which seeks to subordinate them to the "common purpose" often feel ineffective, powerless, alienated, and inferior. Suffering from low self-esteem, they either redouble their efforts to fight back or find a space within society to seek psychic compensation. As for fighting back, Park (23, p. 14) speculates that "strikes, wars, popular elections and religious revivals' embody such retaliation. Yet, he writes:

[In] the modern democratic state, the classes have as yet attained no effective organization. Socialism, founded as an effort to create an organization based on "class consciousness" has never succeeded, except perhaps in Russia, in creating more than a political party.

In effect, Park implies that retaliation through class organization simply hasn't yet come about in America and, if Russia is any example, it won't amount to much if and when it does come about. As for "psychic compensation," Park speculates that people who share the same passions, tastes, and temperaments—who are like-minded—come together in "moral regions" to symbolically, if innocuously, find compensation. Thus, horse-racing fans, sports enthusiasts, art lovers, and others associate in the private sphere of recreational arenas to pass their leisure time in enjoyable escapes. Park thus finds that what Franklin Giddings called "consciousness of kind" (a derivative of Adam Smith's notion of "moral sympathy") occurs in recreational spheres where it is innocuously expressed, rather than in the public, market, occupational sphere where it might become politically subversive.

Park here implies a bipolar view of the institutional bedrock of society. The public sphere of the division of labor which extracts and coordinates man's labor into hierarchies that transcend his interests and goals and the private sphere which operates as a safety valve so that he may vent his bottled-up passions and resentments. Put another way, in the public sphere, man is under control, while in the private sphere, man approaches the possibility of being in control—even if in an innocuous fashion. If man has any desire at all of finding an institutional base for building personal identity—and, through it, a sense of fulfillment—it is in the private sphere.

Park's image of man, society, and their interaction is not terribly sanguine. By and large, man is buffeted about by a society which seeks to impose its common purpose upon him. This purpose is imposed through the agents and agencies of socialization, and through ecological processes. Yet, despite this press toward control and conformity, man's creative, inceptive capacities resist, and, although direct retaliation usually is blunted, man can achieve some measure of psychic compensation in spheres of interest and activity which *reinforce* rather than challenge the common purpose, the common overarching political-economic framework. In many ways, Park's meta-theoretical image of society reflects those of his continental predecessors—resignation in the face of an imposing transcendent public sphere and residual personal fulfillment in the private sphere.

If Park's answer to the question "What are the noneconomic sources of social integration" led him to a rather grim view of things, Wirth's conjectures on the possibilities of personal autonomy in the urban milieu were hardly more buoyant. In his classic summary of the theoretical and empirical work of the Chicago School, Wirth (33) asserted that warm, intimate, face-to-face primary relationships were being replaced by impersonal, segmented, contacts. Yet, the one redeeming feature of this was that the urban dweller could find a large measure of autonomy in such anonymity. There is a certain irony in this formulation in that the nonconscious, collective substructure of the community, that is, its ecologic, demographic, and morphologic processes became the inevitable behind-the-backs-of-men dynamic that guarantees the new freedom. Neither history, nor state, nor class, nor status group is the vehicle of freedom. The freedom of autonomy based on *anonymity* is grounded in the evolutionary processes of ecology—the species being re-emerges.

Accordingly, the Chicago School killed three birds with one stone. It established the generic urban community as a unit of analysis in its own right, bounded it off from transcendent political and economic contingencies by accounting for the quality of life within it in demographic-morphologic terms, and secured the autonomy of the individual by associating that autonomy with the inevitable escalation in magnitude of demographic-morphologic features. In point, German Romanticism was vouchsafed by French morphology and propelled forward by American ecology.

This complex paradigm was the burden inherited by the neo- or post-Chicago School—a paradigm partially at odds with the newly emergent brand of American social psychology propounded by G.H. Mead and C.H. Cooley. For Cooley and Mead insisted that the initial building blocks of self-identities were warm, intimate, face-to-face relationships and with this contention laid down an axiomatic challenge to the urban sociologists. *Identity needs primacy but primacy is disappearing.* And this axiomatic stand-off became the point of departure for the post-Chicago School (1940–1960). Under the tutelege of the new social psychology and against the claims of the urbanists, the post-Chicago School set out to demonstrate the existence of primary relationships in the urban milieu. Family, friends, neighbors, civic associates, organizational affiliates, local politicians, local business merchants, and the local press—all were shown to be resilient enclaves of primary relationships.

Of paramount interest, however, is the plain fact that the very evidence which indeed humbles Wirth's proposition comes from research sites located in the private sphere of life. For, without exception, these sites form a web of relationships and institutions which lie within the bounds of the residential community and which people enter into as a spin-off from their nuclear families. Thus, factual evidence notwithstanding, implicit concern with the private sphere lifts into relief, once more, the essential paradigmatic continuity between the pre-Chicago, Chicago, and post-Chicago Schools. All schools presuppose in their meta-theoretical imagery an underlying split between the public sphere of necessity, which is coterminous with an overextended division of labor, and the private sphere of freedom, which is coterminous with an overextended kinship system.

In the private sphere, the individual can engage in those integral and significant social relationships that are the building blocks of personal identity. Through these relationships, the individual can build a sense of moral worth, strive for self-transcendence, and gain control of his/her destiny. The public sphere imposes a regime of functional and specific contacts which extract contributions that are rationally coordinated into a hierarchical structure whose goals transcend the individual's own destiny. Accordingly, the private sphere connotes freedom and autonomy, while the public sphere, constraint and alienation. In the private sphere, the individual is *in* control, while in the public sphere the individual is *under* control. In one, he or she prevails; in the other he or she survives.

Yet, the fact remains, as Gans reminds us, that the post-Chicago urban sociologists and social psychologists, in their desire to refute Wirth, confine their inquiries to the private sphere of life in order to search out those enclaves of primary relationships which permit the development of personal identity—an identity grounded in integral relationships rather than anonymous contacts. Despite the salutary efforts of the post-Chicago investigators, they still did not provide a terminology for the conceptual and empirical apprehension of transcendent political and economic variables. In this respect, they continue to work within the same meta-theoretical framework of their predecessors in the Continental and Chicago Schools.

Throughout the history of modern urban sociology, the underlying paradigm envisions a deep-lying structural cleavage in modern society which through time has grown progressively wider. Successive generations of scholars have tapped into this split more or less consciously as they articulated the traditional dichotomies or antinomies of urban sociology. Be it status and contract, passion and reason, sameness and difference, folkness and urbanity, localities and cosmopolitans—throughout, whatever else these distinctions imply, they also capture the public-private split. Apparently, the train of events set in motion by the demise of feudal community and the separation of job from home is still playing itself out. And from both a theoretical and practical point of view, this structural dissociation has meant an ever increasing withdrawal of the individual into the private sphere which virtually insures the predominance of the public sphere.

Simmel (28, p. 336) noted that "general affairs became ever more public and individual affairs ever more secret." And John Dewey (5, pp. 8–9) predicted that eventually there would be a complete severance of public and private life in the most critical way possible. Morals would be driven

> inwards from the public open out-of-door . . . into the obscurities and privacies of an inner life. . . . The cost . . . is almost complete severance of ethics from politics and economics.

The withdrawal of the individual into the private sphere and ultimately into the inner recesses of his own mind and body would insure the dominance of the public sphere.

Thus, Gouldner's sociology of knowledge analysis of the Chicago School's neglect of transcendent variables, which focuses on societal economic disintegration and sociology's drive for academic and financial acceptance, misses the underlying meta-theoretical paradigm which runs through three "schools" of urban theorists over a relatively extended time frame. A more complete analysis must attempt to elaborate the dialectical relationship between the long-term, progressive structural cleavage between the public and private sphere and the meta-theoretical paradigm which reflects and possibly reinforces this process. And at some point, an alternative paradigm which gives serious consideration to transcendent political and economic variables must be advanced in order to overcome the meta-theoretical dispositions of the current paradigm.

FOOTNOTES

*I presented an earlier version of this paper at the third annual special symposium of The Society for the Study of Symbolic Interaction held at the University of Missouri, Columbia, April 5–7, 1976. I wish to thank Herbert Blumer, Norman K. Denzin, and Gregory P. Stone for helpful critiques.

1. Indeed, the Chicago School's inability to develop a macroperspective of any sort but especially within the area of urban ecology has led Claude Levi-Strauss (19) to the following lament. "Much might have been expected from the researcher of the so-called 'Chicago School' dealing with urban ecology, and the reasons for the gradual loss of interst in this line of research are not altogether clear." Levi-Strauss contends that morphological studies (having to do with qualitative, non-measurable distributions through space) are entirely susceptible of transcendent structural analysis.

2. For excellent coverage of the ideological and structural transformations in American society during the turn of the century transitional period, see, respectively: R. Hofstadter (16) and R.H. Weibe (32).

3. According to C. Wright-Mills (21, part 1), this aggregate of upwardly mobile managers, professionals, and white collar workers comprised the natural constituency of American pragmatic philosophy. Both the philosophers—Pierce, James, and Dewey—and their audiences were interested in technological-social amelioration rather than transcendent political, economic reformation.

4. For empirical work which casts doubt on some of these assertions see: H.A. Farberman (8), H.A. Farberman and E.A. Weinstein (9).

5. Although Sir Henry Summer Maine (20) of England also should be included among the continental theorists, I will not deal with his contributions as his examination of the historical evolution of the law did not, in my view, have as direct an impact on the Chicago School as the French and German theorists. In many ways, however, Maine's distinctions between "status" and "contract" is foundational.

6. An explanation of why Durkheim never quite developed a full-blown social psychology may be found in G.P. Stone and H.A. Farberman (30).

7. Sennet (26) also sees these as the leading questions in urban sociology, but he does not offer any explanation as to why they are so.

REFERENCES

Axelrod, Morris, "Urban Structure and Social Participation." *American Sociological Review* 21 (February 195): 13–18.

Bell, Wendell and Maryanne T. Force, "Urban Neighborhood Types and Participation in Formal Associations." *American Sociological Review* 21 (February 1956): 25–34.

Carey, James, *Sociology and Public Affairs: The Chicago School.* Sage Publications, Beverly Hills, Ca. 1975.

Commager, H.S., (ed.), *Lester Ward and the Welfare State.* Bobbs-Merrill, Indianapolis, 1967.

Dewey, John, *Human Nature and Conduct.* New York: Everyman Library, 1922.

Dewey, Richard, "The Rural-Urban Continuum: Real but Relatively Unimportant," *American Journal of Sociology* 66 (July 1960): 60–66.

Duncan, Otis D. and Albert J. Reiss, Jr., *Social Characteristics of Rural and Urban Communities, 1959.* New York: John Wiley, 1956.

Farberman, Harvey A., "A Study of Personalization in Low Income Consumer Interactions and Its Relationship to Identification with Residential Community." Unpublished Ph.D. thesis, Department of Sociology. University of Minnesota, 1968.

————— , and E.A. Weinstein, "Personalization in Lower Class Consumer Interaction." *Social Problems* 17 (Spring 1970): 449–457.

Faris, Robert E.L., *Chicago Sociology.* Chicago: The University of Chicago Press, 1967.

Form, William H., et al., "The Compatibility of Alternative Approaches to the Delimitation of Urban Sub-Areas." *America Sociological Review* 19 (August 1956): 434–440.

Friedrichs, Robert W., *A Sociology of Sociology.* New York: The Free Press, 1970.

Gans, Herbert, "Urbanism and Suburbanism as Ways of Life: A Reevaluation of Definition," in A.M. Rose (ed.), *Human Behavior and Social Processes,* pp. 625–648 Boston: Houghton Mifflin, 1962.

Gouldner, Alvin, *The Coming Crisis of Western Sociology.* New York: Basic Books, 1970.

Greer, Scott, "Urbanism Reconsidered: A Comparative Study of Local Areas in a Metropolis." *American Sociological Review* 21 (February 1956): 19–25.

Hofstadter, R., *Social Darwinism in American Thought.* Boston: Beacon Press, 1945.

Janowitz, Morris, *The Community Press in an Urban Setting*. Glencoe, Ill.: The Free Press, 1952.

————— , "Introduction" to R.E. Park and Ernest W. Burgess, *Introduction to the Science of Sociology*. Chicago: University of Chicago Press, 1969 [1921].

Levi-Strauss, C., *Structural Anthropology* (trans. C. Jacobson and B.G. Schaepf). Garden City, N.Y.: Doubleday, 1967.

Maine, Henry S., *Ancient Law*. New York: Henry Holt, 1906.

Mills, C.W., *Sociology and Pragmatism*. New York: Oxford University Press, 1964.

Nisbet, Robert A., *The Sociological Tradition*. New York: Basic Books, 1966.

Park, Robert E., "Community Organization and Juvenile Delinquency," in R.E. Park and E.W. Burgess, (eds.), *The City*, pp. 99–112. Chicago: University of Chicago Press, 1967 [1925].

————— and Ernest Burgess, *Introduction to the Science of Sociology*. Chicago: University of Chicago Press, 1969 [1921].

Reis, Albert J., Jr., "Rural-Urban and Status Differences in Interpersonal Contacts," *American Journal of Sociology* 65 (September 1959): 182–195.

Sennet, Richard, (ed.), "An Introduction," in *Classic Essays on the Culture of Cities*. New York: Appleton-Century-Crofts, 1969.

Shils, Edward, "The Calling of Sociology," in T. Parsons et al. (ed.), *Theories of Society*, pp. 1405–48. New York: The Free Press, 1961.

Simmel, Georg, *The Sociology of Georg Simmel* (ed. and trans. K. Wolf). New York: The Free Press, 1964.

Stone, Gregory P., "City Shoppers and Urban Identification: Observations on the Social Psychology of City Life," *American Journal of Sociology* 60 (July 1954): 36–45.

————— , and H.A. Farberman, "On the Edge of Rapprochement: Was Durkheim Moving toward the Perspective of Symbolic Interaction?," *Sociological Quarterly* (Spring 1967): 149–164.

Turner, Ralph H., (ed.), *Robert E. Park: On Social Control and Collective Behavior*, University of Chicago Press, 1967.

Wiebe, R.H., *The Search for Order: 1877–1920*. New York: Hill and Wang, 1967.

Wirth, Louis, "Urbanism as a Way of Life." *American Journal of Sociology* 44 (July 1938): 1–24.

VARIETIES OF THEORETICAL EXPRESSION AND INFORMAL PATTERNS OF INTERACTION:
A SAMPLE OF SYMBOLIC INTERACTIONISTS

Janice M. Reynolds, CENTRAL MICHIGAN UNIVERSITY

Larry T. Reynolds, CENTRAL MICHIGAN UNIVERSITY

Charles Bowden, CENTRAL MICHIGAN UNIVERSITY

ABSTRACT

The present study builds upon a series of previous works concerned with the relationship between patterns of formal, institutional relationships and the degree of conventionality-unconventionality of one's theoretical orientation. Previous studies of a sample of symbolic interactionists have strongly suggested that the more unorthodox one's theoretical stance, the more extensive and multibonded are one's formal, institutional ties to other

Studies in Symbolic Interaction—Volume 2, 1979, pages 21–38

sociologists of similar persuasion. The study reported here, using this same sample of interactionists, examines the relationship between the conventionality-unconventionality of theoretical orientations and one's informal, personal ties. The results parallel those of earlier studies and suggest that the more unorthodox one's theoretical perspective, the more one is bound up in a series of personal and friendship relationships with other like-minded symbolic interactionists.

VARIETIES OF THEORETICAL EXPRESSION AND INFORMAL PATTERNS OF INTERACTION: A SAMPLE OF SYMBOLIC INTERACTIONISTS

In a series of articles (Vaughan and Reynolds, 1968; Reynolds et. al., 1970; Reynolds and Reynolds, 1972; Reynolds and Meltzer, 1973) we reported discovering certain patterns of association between one's adherence to selected varieties of symbolic interactionism and one's participation in a particular network of institutional affiliations. In a more detailed article (Reynolds and McCart, 1972), we summarized the results of these earlier studies, presented additional data supporting the previous findings, and reached a general conclusion concerning the relationship between theoretical orientations and the patterning of institutional ties among those sharing similar orientations. The conclusion reached was as follows (Reynolds and McCart, 1972:37):

> . . . a strong multibonded net of supportive relationships is a necessary condition for the creation and development of an unconventional theoretical perspective if that paradigm is going to have a significant impact . . . interactionists loosely tied together become concerned with refining those aspects of interactionism which are both compatible with and supportive of the dominant and conservative paradigm in present-day American sociology.

The pattern was clear: the more unorthodox one's theoretical orientation, the "tighter" one's formal, institutional ties to others of similar theoretical persuasion. But what about informal ties? What is the nature of the relationship between one's theoretical stance and one's informal ties with other like-minded sociologists? Is there a discernable relationship between theoretical orientations and informal linkages, and if so, does this patterning conform to or deviate from the type of patterns recorded between theoretical positions and formal, institutional ties? Fortunately, the same questionnaire which originally provided data on formal affiliations also provides the information necessary to unearth any relationships which may exist with respect to informal ties and theoretical orientations. As the larger questionnaire, from which the data to be presented here is drawn, is described in detail elsewhere (Reynolds and McCart, 1972:17–23), we will restrict our description of the questionnaire to those portions which are immediately applicable. It is, however, perhaps best to first present a description of the sample.

The Sample

The sample for the present investigation was selected in the following fashion:

1. Thirty-one symbolic interactionists who served as subjects in a pilot study for the current investigation were listed.

2. Sociologists who authored theoretical chapters in the major published symposium on interactionism were added to the original list of thirty-one.

3. Several authors of articles appearing in the only book of readings on interactionism available at the time of the study were selected for listing.

4. Authors of major manuscripts or basic texts written from an interactionist's perspective were also listed.

5. An additional list of sociologists whom we personally considered to be closely associated with the interactionist perspective was added to our working list.

From this composite list, and in consultation with three self-professed and well-known symbolic interactionists, a final list of 124 potential subjects was selected. A questionnaire mailed to these sociologists elicited seventy-four usable replies; these seventy-four symbolic interactionists comprise the present sample.

NATURE OF THE DATA

The data analyzed in this paper consist of seventy-four symbolic interactionists' replies to the two-section questionnaire discussed below.

The Questionnaire: Theoretical and Conceptual Diversity

The first section of the questionnaire was composed of a series of statements, all taken directly from the symbolic interactionist literature, which represent a wide diversity of opinion concerning the essential nature and scope of several conceptual and substantive areas within sociology.[1] Respondents were presented a series of alternate ways of defining what a given area or concept "was all about." The concepts and accompanying definitions offered our sample of interactionists were as follows:

Self

1. " . . . Think of self as: (1) *a set of* more or less consistent and *stable responses* on a conceptual level, *which* (2) *exercise a regulatory function over other responses* of the same organism at lower levels."

2. "The magnitude of the self . . . is measured by the society it in-

corporates; the magnitude of the society . . . is measured by the selves that it unites. 'The Society' is the name for the 'unity,' but 'the selves' are that in which the unity is seen as multiple. There are *as many societies* as there are *selves,* and *as many selves* as there are *societies.* It is as *idle to ask which is prior or preponderant,* or which influences the other and how, as to ask the same question of the life and the living, the breathing and the breath."

3. ". . . we may practically say that he (the individual) has *as many* .different social selves as there are distinct *groups* of persons *about whose opinion he cares.* He generally shows a different side of himself to each of these different groups."

4. "As a body of orientation, the theory is well over half a century old, but only within the last four or five years have research methods appropriate to it been employed. . . . But now that the major difficulty—lack of agreement about the class of phenomena to be investigated—has been resolved by the growing consensus that *'the self' is a set of attitudes,* we are able to bring to bear on our investigations of the self the techniques for studying attitudes in general. . . ."

5. "The people who communicate with any one person are not in communication with each other, and so they cannot come to any common understanding regarding him and his behavior. Therefore the reflection of himself which each individual gets from his communication is different for each group of which he is a member. He has *as many selves* as there are *groups to which he belongs.* . . ."

6. *"The self,* as that which can be an object to itself, is essentially a *social structure,* and it arises in social experience. After a self has arisen, it in a certain sense provides for itself its social experiences, and so *we can conceive of an absolutely solitary self."*

Social Control

1. "Self-control refers to behavior that is redirected in the light of the manner in which it is imagined to appear from the standpoint of other people who are involved in a cooperative task. *Once a person defines a situation and locates himself within it in terms of a conventional role, he becomes* cognizant of expected patterns of behavior both for himself and for the other participants . . . *social control rests largely on self-control."*

2. "A central interest for sociologists in the study of human relations is to examine *the ways in which people,* as members of a society, *influence one another. The collectivity of these ways is called 'social control'.* . . . Mutual expectation is the way in which people control each other's behavior in their day-to-day relationships."

3. *"Social control is the expression of the 'me' over against the expression of the 'I'.* It sets the limits, it gives the determination that enables the 'I', so to speak, to use the 'me' as the means of carrying out what is the undertaking that all are interested in."

4. *"Social control [refers to] any means, or the sum total of means, by which a group influences or directs its individual members."*

Culture

1. "The important idea in the concept of culture is that there are common understandings as to how individuals are to behave toward one another. . . . The people who have this culture, or common understandings, are a society, and they are a society because they have this culture, not because they live together . . . or anything else."

2. "The term *'culture'* is generally used to *refer to behavior* patterns. . . ."

3. "The totality of norms upon which the various transactions in any collectivity rest may be *referred to as* the *culture* of that group."

4. "A culture consists of shared meanings and values that the members of a group share in common."

Socialization

1. *"Socialization is a product of a gradual accumulation of experience with* certain people, particularly *those with whom we stand in a primary relation, and significant others* are those who are actually involved in the cultivation of abilities, values, and outlook. . . . Since primary relations are not necessarily satisfactory, however, the reactions may be negative."

2. "A person's total system of definitions, his integrated configuration of meanings, constitutes his world; and no other world exists for him unless, and until, other selectors emerge. . . . *The implanting and incorporation of selector-systems* is called the process of socialization."

3. "Socialization, broadly, refers to the process by which the human organism acquires the characteristic ways of behavior, the values, norms, and attitudes of the social units of which he is a part."

4. "Socialization [refers to] the process by which the individual acquires his human behavior patterns—*the learning process.*"

Social Organization

1. "Social organization: (1) the structure of common meanings and values of a society (since meanings and values are often structured into institutions, the social organization is the totality of institutions), (2) a condition of society in which the members have most of their meanings and values in common."

2. "The term 'social organization' refers to a *social relation in which the individuals* so behave as to *prevent* the *disruption* of their *mutual influences by extraneous events."*

3. "From a structural point of view the framework of *social organization consists in the members of the group and their cultural relationships.* While the introduction of any new culture trait produces problems of readjustment and disorganization, it is also true that social orgnaization is a result of

cultural integration. That is, the attitudes, the folkways, mores, laws, and institutions make up a system of social controls which the group imposes on its members. *In a sense, the social structure seems to be synonymous with culture, since culture affects the framework of social organization. On the other hand, social organization is at once the product of the total culture and a part of it,* rather than the sum total of man's achievements."

4. *"The unity of the social mind consists not in agreement but in organization,* in the fact of reciprocal influence or causation among its parts by virtue of which everything that takes place in it is connected with everything else, and so is an outcome of the whole . . . this differentiated unity of mental and social life present in the simplest intercourse, but capable of infinite growth and adaptation, is what I mean. . . by social organization."

Methodology

1. ". . . in spite of all the word play of recent centuries, the physical and the existential remain different orders methodologically. *If sociology studies existential experience, no form of empirical operationalism whatsoever can directly define and handle this subject matter."*

2. *"If an operational definition cannot be established, this should cause the scientist to question* seriously the utility of *such terms for his research,* and should lead to the conclusion that perhaps many of the commonly accepted concepts are not usable in scientific endeavors."

3. "The most complete form of the sociological datum, after all, is the form in which the participant observer gathers it: an observation of some social event, the events which precede and follow it, and explanations of its meaning by participants and spectators, before, during, and after its occurrence. Such a datum gives us *more information* about the event under study *than data gathered by any other sociological method. Participant observation can* thus *provide us with a yardstick* against which *to measure the completeness* of data gathered in other ways. . . ."

4. "While the symbolic interactionist frame of reference unavoidably entails complicated methodological procedures, it does not imply a return to introspection and speculation as the methods of sociology. Rather it implies *that in sociology, empiricism must be combined with types of interpretive operations not required in the physical and biological sciences."*

Social Change

1. ". . . symbolic interactionism fills a void left by most other efforts to explain social change. Specifically it provides a framework for analyzing the collective behavior that intervenes between the first signs of breakdown of old norms, values, and institutions and the establishment of new ones. Thus it deals with the process of social change from unrest to institutionalization."

2. "I have not found SI theory helpful in looking at the process of social change. Most of its concepts were developed in the context of short episodes of interaction at best, or with respect to phases of socialization. Processes of social change require wider contexts and longer-term time spans."

3. "The position of symbolic interaction . . . views human group life not as having a preestablished organization in fixed forms, but as being continuously involved in a process of formation. . . . Symbolic interaction presupposes that society is involved in the continuous process of meeting situations; the emphasis is on process rather than on expression of established organization and structure. This view of human group life, as involved in a process of meeting situations, signifies that change is indigenous to it. It also implies that instead of regarding social change as something which is unusual, in the sense of being a departure from established ways of living, social change is seen as a natural occurrence in the life of people. . . . Let me conclude by declaring that quite contrary to any charge that symbolic interaction is unsuited for dealing with social change, it provides, in my judgment, the proper framework for handling social change."

4. "I feel that symbolic interactionist theory can handle change rather well from a social psychological view, but only in limited fashion from a sociological standpoint. . . . It emphasizes change in the individual actors and stresses face-to-face, small group situations. As a social psychological theory, the view of change is adequate. . . . It is less adequate, however, as a sociological view of change, particularly because of its weakness on the macrolevel. Its eschewing of structural and cultural variables, or levels, and its denial of analytic significance to anything outside the person-person interaction surely limits the relevance of SI theory."

Respondents were given the opportunity to select, from among the alternative definitions offered, the single definition which either matched or closely approximated their own working definition of the area or concept.

Among the definitions presented for each concept or area was at least one definition which mirrored, given the state of American sociology since 1950 (J.T. Sprehe, 1967), a conventional viewpoint—which is to say a definition which could have just as easily been taken from the structural-functionalist literature as from the interactionist literature. Likewise, among every set of definitions offered was found at least one definition representing an unorthodox, anti-functionalist view. Each respondent was assigned a score of one for each conventional definition and a score of two for each unorthodox definition preferred.[2]

Let us briefly comment on the alternative definitions offered for each concept. The six alternative ways of conceptualizing *self* range from the 'multiple self" definition, which argues that a person has as many selves as there are groups to which he or she belongs (alternative 5), to the definition which depicts an absolutely solitary, or single, self (alternative 6). Alternatives 2 and 3 are similar to alternative 5 in that they, too, conceive of self as being multiple in nature. Alternatives 1 and 4 approach alternative 6 in that they see the self as being a unitary rather than a multiple entity. One can assume, given the context of contemporary American sociology, that alternatives 1, 4, and 6 constitute the more unconventional way of visualizing self. By viewing self as multiple in nature, alternatives 2, 3, and 5 imply an image of people as passive objects, objects which merely react rather than initiate action. Such a conception of human nature, once characterized by Dennis Wrong (1961:187–193) as an "over socialized" conception, has been a dominant assumption of functionalists from Durkheim to Parsons. As functionalism is still the dominant or orthodox orientation in American sociology, the multiple self definitions are more conventional than the unitary self statements.

With respect to the topic of social control, two of the definitions (alternatives 2 and 4) are similar in that they equate social control with control by others. Alternatives 1 and 3, however, make social control synonymous with self control. A definition which equates social control with control by others is more in line with American sociology's theoretical *status quo* than is a definition which visualizes social control as resting on self control. As Lenski has argued, ". . . conservatives have generally maintained that evil has its origin in the egoistic drive of the individual and that the function of society is to restrain and redirect these harmful tendencies . . ." (Lenski, 1966:25). Hence, for conservatives, social control means nothing more than control by others, an attempt to control people's "evil nature" in order to serve the common good. Sociologists opposed to this mainstream image of people have argued that the control of people's behavior for the attainment of collective goals not only can but should rest on self control.

Of the four statements on the nature of *culture* offered respondents, alternatives 3 and 4 are conventional definitions in that they view culture normatively, that is, as shared norms and values. Alternatives 1 and 2 see culture not in normative but in behavioral terms; they approach culture as a series of "behavior patterns." As functionalists employ a nonbehavioral, normative conception of culture, then alternatives 1 and 2, the behavioral definitions, are the more unorthodox statements.

Of the four alternative definitions of *socialization* presented to our sample of interactionists, alternatives 3 and 4 are conventional in nature. They view socialization as a process by which individuals simply acquire norms, values, and behavior patterns. These definitions imply that people are merely objects created and conditioned by the social system, empty cups to be "filled" with culture. Seeing people as something which merely reacts to external stimuli or forces is a functionalist view, and hence is the more conventional of the two sets of definitions. Alternatives 1 and 2, however, imply that socialization involves an accumulation of definitions and experiences which come to constitute the individual's world. Socialization is seen as the selective incorporation of one's experiences. The individual participates in the selecting process; he or she selects from countless stimuli those experiences and objects which make up his or her symbolic environment. Alternatives 1 and 2 are the more unorthodox of the definitions offered.

Looking at the four definitions of *social organization* utilized here, we see that alternatives 1 and 3 define social organization as many sociologists would define culture. Functionalists habitually equate culture and society, and they usually use a normative conception of social organization. Alternatives 2 and 4, while dissimilar, constitute unorthodox definitions of social organization if one assumes, as we do, that functionalism, while weakened, is still the reigning theoretical orthodoxy in present day American sociology. Alternative 2, instead of equating social organization with culture, specifies that the concept pertains to human relationships. Alternative 2 also incorporates the acting individual into its working definition. Alternative 4 also represents an unconventional definition of social organization by conceiving it not in cultural terms, but in mentalistic ones.

Of the four conceptions of *social change* presented in the questionnaire, two of the statements (alternatives 1 and 3) actually convey the same message. Alternative 2, which argues that symbolic interactionism is not helpful in looking at the process of social change, was only selected by three respondents and hence will concern us no further here. We are concerned rather with the following two basic response categories:

Category I (alternative 1 and 3): An unqualified endorsement of interactionism's ability to deal with social change as a generic phenomena; that is, the interactionist perspective is viewed as a general theory of behavior within which all forms of social change can be dealt with.

Category II (Alternative 4): A qualified endorsement of interactionism's ability to treat social change. The interaction framework is found wanting at the macrolevel but is seen as adequate for treating microchange, for example, through socialization; that is, the framework is conceived of as being a social psychological theory largely concerned with the cultural transformation of individual behavior.

Thus, while nearly all respondents subscribed to the idea that interactionism can handle the topic of change, their differences lie in the extent of comprehensiveness assigned to symbolic interaction theory in this connection. Leaving aside any value judgement which may be made with reference to these two positions, one position, the unqualified endorsement category, is much more unorthodox in the context of American sociology of the last few decades.

With respect to the topic of *methodology,* the alternatives offered ranged from a blanket condemnation of empiricism (alternative 1) to a whole-hearted endorsement of the necessity of the operational definition (alternative 2). In fact, however, three basic conceptions of proper methodology are found in the four statements. Alternative 1 implicitly and alternative 3 explicitly propose participant observation as the methodological stance *par excellence*. Alternative 2 favors the cause of empiricism and the operational definition. Lastly, alternative 4 favors an approach which combines logical empiricism with interpretive operations and procedures. Alternative 4, which favors combining empiricism with other methodological techniques, is the most conventional of the three basic stances. It mirrors the methodological concerns of the "theory-method" people in sociology. While some have argued that this school is now breaking apart, it still appears to be the dominant view in contemporary American sociology (Warshay, 1971: 25). Therefore, alternatives 1, 2, and 3 are the more unorthodox conceptions.

In the original analysis of the relationship between degree of theoretical conventionality and "tightness" of institutional, formal patterns of association (Reynolds and McCart, 1972), we divided respondents into three groups based upon the total scores they amassed on all seven areas and concepts. Roughly a third of the sample fell into each of three groups—groups we labeled "conventional," "semiconventional," and "unorthodox" respectively. We will keep this same three-part division of the sample for purposes of reporting the results recorded when examining the relationship between theoretical conventionality and patterns of informal associations.

The following statement encapsulates the nature of the differing theoretical positions held by respondents in the "unorthodox" and "conventional" groups, with the "semiconventional" group being an admixture of the conventional and unorthodox positions.

Those interactionists whose responses . . . were highly unorthodox in the context of contemporary American sociology . . . tend to view the self as being unitary in nature, to equate social control with self-control, to define culture in a behavioristic fashion, to select an individualistic definition of socialization, to employ either a mentalistic or structural conception of social organization, to give an unqualified endorsement of interactionism's ability to treat social change due to its being a general theory, and to prefer either participant observation or empiricism as a methodological stance. These interactionists tended to have an image of man as either subject or as both subject and object. By equating social control with self-control, these respondents also reject the conservative view of man as "essentially bad". . . . Those interactionists whose responses were orthodox or *conventional in character* tended to view self as being multiple in nature, to define both culture and social organization normatively, to view socialization as merely pouring culture into passive recipients, to offer a qualified endorsement of interactionism's utility in handling social change due to its being only a social psychological theory, and to prefer as their methodological stance a position which favors combining empiricism with interpretive operations. These interactionists tended to have an image of man as mere object. By equating social control with control by others, these respondents seem to harbor an image of man which sees him as being "basically bad." (Reynolds and McCart, 1972: 34–35.)

The Questionnaire: Informal Ties and Personal Associations

This section of the questionnaire was designed to elicit information on respondents' informal relationships and interpersonal ties. The following two questions were utilized for this purpose:

1. Please list the names of persons (if any) to whom you send your books and/or articles for comment and criticism prior to submitting them to journals or publishers.
2. Which sociologists (if any) do you count among your closest friends?

In the basis of responses to these two questions, the patterning of informal relationships among respondents was determined.

Mode of Analysis

Sociometric style diagrams were constructed in an attempt to illustrate the nature of the relationship between respondents' patterns of informal linkages and the degree of conventionality of their theoretical orientations. An additional nongraphic measure of connectivity is also utilized. This measure simply indicates what percentage of the total number of possible connections among respondents has actually been realized in a given sociogram.[3] The nature of both questions asked respondents concerning their informal ties is such that sociologists not in the present sample were also likely to be listed as best friends and/or manuscript reviewers. Therefore, a panel of three judges, all well known symbolic interactionists, examined the lists of sociologists named as friends and/or manuscript advisors by our respondents, and they classified those so named on the basis of whether they were symbolic interactionists or whether they were representatives of other theoretical perspectives. It was then possible to ascertain what percentage of the total number of sociologists listed by each of our three "theory groups" were symbolic interactionists.

FINDINGS

Manuscript Advisement and Theoretical Orientation

It will be recalled that respondents were asked to list those persons to whom they sent their manuscripts for review prior to submitting them to journals or publishers. Replies to this question allowed us to measure informal professional communication ties among symbolic interactionists. As can be seen in Figure 1, those respondents in the conventional and semiconventional categories have few ties among themselves with respect to the manuscript reviewing process; however, members of the unorthodox category do indeed rely heavily on other category members as manuscript critics and commentators.[4] It is worth noting, however, that of all the ties recorded in the total sample, only five involved a reciprocal exchange of manuscripts. One such exchange occurred between two members of the *conventional* response category, yet within this reciprocal exchange are to be found two of only three ties recorded between members of this response group. These three ties represent 1.2 percent of the number of total linkages required for maximum connectivity. Members of the semiconventional group, recording just two nonreciprocal connecting links among themselves, realized only .99 percent of maximum possible connectivity.

Among "unconventional" respondents are to be found four sets of reciprocal manuscript exchanges plus a fairly large number of single direction connecting links. Of the total number of links needed to establish maximum connectivity, 5.7 percent are realized by the unconventional response group. Thus with respect to one dimension of informal ties, manuscript reviewing, we see an emerging pattern similar to that recorded with respect to formal, institutional relationships—namely, the more unorthodox the theoretical stance, the closer and more numerous the ties binding together representatives of that viewpoint.

Since many of the sociologists listed by our respondents as manuscript critic-commentators were not found to be in our sample, we submitted to a panel of interactionists the names of all sociologists listed by our subjects. The panel in turn classified all manuscript referees listed into "interactionists" and "noninteractionists." Only seven of the reviewers listed could not be so classified.

As Table 1 reveals, there is a marked difference between the three response groups with respect to the proportion of symbolic interactionists who serve as referees for potentially publishable books and articles. Among those commenting on manuscripts by conventional and semiconventional respondents, only 39.6 percent and 34.6 percent respectively were symbolic interactionists. However, fully 67.5 percent of the manuscript reviewers utilized by unorthodox respondents were symbolic interactionists. If it can be argued that sending one's manuscripts to fellow interactionists is one possible measure of the extent to which one identifies with the perspective, then members of the conventional and semiconventional groups appear to be much less closely identified with the interactionist perspective than members of the unorthodox category.

Theoretical Orientation and Friendship Patterns

Of the many possible types of informal associations and relationships, perhaps friendship is the most obvious. As previously mentioned, respondents were asked: "Which sociologists (if any) do you count among your closest friends?" Figure 2 illustrates the nature and extent of friendship ties among members of the three theoretical categories. Again, among

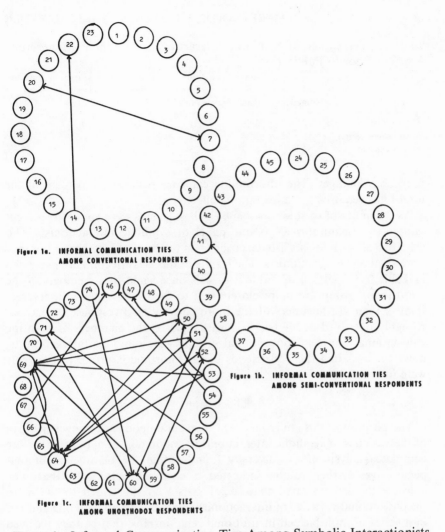

Figure 1a. INFORMAL COMMUNICATION TIES
AMONG CONVENTIONAL RESPONDENTS

Figure 1b. INFORMAL COMMUNICATION TIES
AMONG SEMI-CONVENTIONAL RESPONDENTS

Figure 1c. INFORMAL COMMUNICATION TIES
AMONG UNORTHODOX RESPONDENTS

Figure 1   Informal Communication Ties Among Symbolic Interactionists

members of the conventional and semiconventional groups, exceedingly few friendship ties are recorded. Both groups recorded less than one percent of the number of links necessary to establish maximum connectivity.

However, as was the case with manuscript exchanges, among the unorthodox coterie an extensive network of friendship relationships was observed. Eight members of the unorthodox group named two or more members of the group as close friends. There was one reciprocal choice between respondents 64 and 69, who, it should be noted, along with respondent 60, were selected by numerous other subjects as close friends. There were only eleven interactionists among the twenty-nine unorthodox respondents who were not involved in some manner in the network of

Table 1. Percentage of Symbolic Interactionists to Whom Manuscripts Are Sent Prior to Publication

Group	S.I. Named	Percent of Total	Non– S.I. Named	Percent of Total	Un- classi- fiable	Percent of Total
Conventional	22	39.6	31	54.4	4	6.0
Semi-conventional	18	34.6	34	65.4	–	–
Unconventional	54	67.5	23	28.8	3	3.7

friendship linkages. The unorthodox category realized 7.1 percent of the total links required for maximum connectivity.

As a number of sociologists named as best friends were not in the present sample, we again turned to our panel of symbolic interactionists who classified all sociologists listed as friends on the basis of whether or not they were symbolic interactionists. The results of this classification are presented in Table 2. Inspection of Table 2 reveals once again that members of the unorthodox group are more closely tied to their fellow symbolic interactionists than are members of the more conventional response categories. Roughly one-third of the best friends named by the members of both the conventional and semiconventional groups were symbolic interactionists; however, over half the best friends of the unorthodox group respondents were interactionists.

Discussion

The purpose of this study has been to expand upon earlier investigations of the varieties of symbolic interactionism, and in doing so, to offer a more complete analysis of the diversity found within the parameters of that perspective. Earlier results indicated a clear-cut pattern in that they consistently demonstrated that sociologists who subscribed to the more unconventional varieties of interactionism were bound up with one another in a series of multifaceted institutional relationships, that is, they received their Ph.D.s from a small number of universities, they had a large number of faculty-student ties with other like-minded interactionists, and they often served together on the same faculties in fairly large numbers and over long periods of time. Conversely, those sociologists subscribing to interactionism's more conventional forms shared very few institutional ties with other similarly inclined interactionists.

Table 2. Percentage of Symbolic Interactionists Named as Friends

Group	S.I. Named	Percent of Total	Non– S.I. Named	Percent of Total	Un- classi- fiable	Percent of Total
Conventional	26	29.5	57	64.8	5	5.7
Semi-conventional	31	33.3	57	61.3	5	5.4
Unconventional	74	54.0	55	40.1	8	5.9

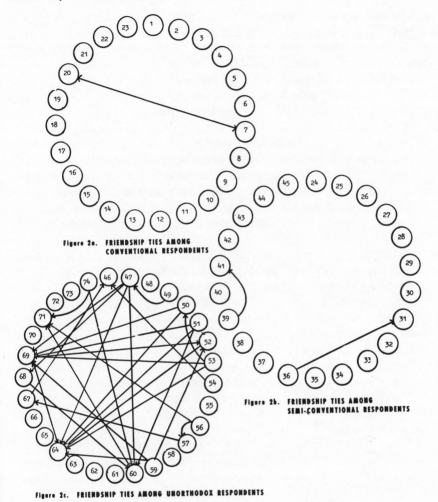

Figure 2a. FRIENDSHIP TIES AMONG CONVENTIONAL RESPONDENTS

Figure 2b. FRIENDSHIP TIES AMONG SEMI-CONVENTIONAL RESPONDENTS

Figure 2c. FRIENDSHIP TIES AMONG UNORTHODOX RESPONDENTS

Figure 2   Friendship Ties Among Symbolic Interactionists

As Mullins (1973:79) correctly points out, in this early research it was implicitly assumed that patterning in any of the informal relationships which may develop after institutional ties are established would follow or parallel the patterning recorded for formal, institutional relationships. Current results would tend to support this earlier assumption: they reveal that as formal, institutional relationships go, so too go informal, or interpersonal, ties. Those interactionists who adhere to an unorthodox theoretical position are indeed bound together in an extensive net of informal relationships, while those of more conventional persuasion are not parties to any such extensive network.

The findings with respect to informal relationships suggest a number of things. They tend to confirm the earlier conclusion we reached with respect to formal affiliations, namely that a strong, multi-bonded net of supportive relationships is a necessary condition for the creation, development, and maintenance of an unconventional theoretical perspective. As Gouldner (1970:46) notes, in speaking of the informal relationship structure of theory groups, the "infrastructure" plays a vital role in the creation and development of any social theory, especially if that theory is going to successfully challenge the reigning theoretical orthodoxy. An underdeveloped infrastructure retards the development of an unconventional theory. The infrastructure of the unorthodox variety of symbolic interactionism, however, is apparently relatively well developed, which may in part account for the fact that interactionism's challenge to American sociology's theoretical *status quo* has been so persistent that one recent text refers to the symbolic interactionists as "the loyal opposition" (Mullins, 1973:75). The symbolic interactionists' perspective has always been a minority viewpoint *within* American sociology, and perhaps the term "*loyal* opposition" is an appropriate one for describing this framework, for, unlike the radical sociologists, they have kept their attack of sociology's theoretical orthodoxy within the parameters of professional, academic sociology. So while symbolic interactionism has been, and continues to be, a minority viewpoint in American sociology, it is a "somewhat successful" minority position.

Because the unorthodox respondents in our sample are parties to an extensive network of both formal and informal relationships, our findings, on the surface, would seem to suggest that persons who closely associate with each other in numerous settings and over lengthy periods of time are apt to think at least somewhat alike. However, such an explanation, which could perhaps partially explain the unorthodox group, could in no way explain the homogeneity of thought observed among our more orthodox respondents. The more conventional respondents were not placed together because they rejected the conceptual and substantive stance of the unorthodox respondents; rather, they were placed together because they selected a whole different set of their own definitions which mirrored what they felt these conceptual and substantive issues "were all about." Because our three sets of interactionists are quite comparable with respect to internal consensus, the differences observed, in terms of the patterns of both formal and informal relationships characteristic of each, simply cannot be explained by recourse to a "flocking together makes birds of a feather" analysis.

If the mutual influence thesis cannot explain the relationships we have observed, what can explain the rather clear patterning of both informal and formal ties we see in our sample? We would simply restate our earlier observation that " . . . the structure of human relationships is associated with the structure and nature of theoretical arguments. That is, certain associational patterns are conducive to the development of certain types of sociological reasoning" (Reynolds and McCart, 1972:36). However, since the 1950s, sociology departments have undergone important shifts in their distribution and structure, and, as has been noted elsewhere:

> Not only have departments grown in size and specialization, but there has been a scattering of sociologists to many major universities instead of their concentration at a few places. This proliferation and fragmentation may betoken a demise of the kind of setting in which creative, unorthodox social thought is produced (Vaughan and Reynolds, 1968:214).

In light of the fact that those institutional settings in which the unconventional varieties of interactionism were produced may well have broken up, it would behove the unorthodox interactionists to keep their strong infrastructure viable, for, as Alvin Gouldner informs us, "Some kind of group support is helpful to those striving to elude conventional ways of looking at human behavior" (Gouldner, 1965:177).

FOOTNOTES

1. Alternative conceptions of social change were gathered in a different fashion. As a fairly large number of prominent interactionists' views on social change were gathered in the pilot study of the present investigation, a number of representative statements were simply selected from among them. As was the case with the definitions selected for most other concepts, these definitions embrace a wide range of response.

2. In the case of the topic of methodology, it was possible for a respondent to score from one to three points on the assumption that a clear preference for participant observation, as one's favored methodological stance, was more unconventional than a stance supporting postitivism and the operational definition; but that a stance favoring operationalism was also a more unconventional posture than a stance which favors combining empiricism with interpretative techniques.

3. The following formula has been used in computing the number of total possible connections: $C_{ma} + \frac{n(n-1)}{2}$ where C_{ma} = the degree of maximum possible connectivity, and n = the number of persons in a sociogram. For a detailed discussion of measures of connectedness, see W.L. Garrison, "Connectivity of the Interstate Highway System," Papers and Proceedings of the Regional Science Association, VI, 1960: 121–137.

4. As respondents were promised anonymity, subjects are identified by number rather than name in the sociograms.

REFERENCES

Gouldner, Alvin W., *Enter Plato*, New York: Basic Books, 1965.
———— , *The Coming Crisis of Western Sociology*, New York: Basic Books, 1970.
Lenski, Gerhard, *Power and Privilege*, New York: McGraw-Hill, 1966.
Mullins, Nicholas, *Theories and Theory Groups in Contemporary American Sociology*, New York: Harper and Row, 1973.
Reynolds, Larry T., et. al., "The Self in Symbolic Interaction Theory," in Larry T. Reynolds and Janice M. Reynolds, *The Sociology of Sociology*, New York: David McKay, 1970.
Reynolds, Larry T. and Carol L. McCart, "The Institutional Basis of Theoretical Diversity," *Sociological Focus* V, No. 3 (1972a): 16–39.

Reynolds, Larry T., and Janice M. Reynolds, "Interactionism, Complicity, and the Astructural Bias," *Catalyst* VII (1972b): 76–85.

Reynolds, Larry T. and Bernard N. Meltzer, "The Origins of Divergent Methodological Stances in Symbolic Interactionism," *Sociological Quarterly,* 14 (1973): 189–199.

Sprehe, J.T., "The Climate of Opinion in Sociology: A Study of the Professional Value and Belief Systems of Sociologists," Unpublished Ph.D. Dissertation, Washington University, 1967.

Vaughan, Ted R. and Larry T. Reynolds, "The Sociology of Symbolic Interactionism," *American Sociologist* III, 3 (1968): 208–214.

Warshay, Leon H., "The Current State of Sociological Theory: Diversity, Polarity, Empiricism, and Small Theory," *Sociological Quarterly,* 12 (1971): 23–45.

Wrong, Dennis, "The Oversocialized Conception of Man in Modern Sociology," *American Sociological Review,* 26 (1961): 187–193.

ECONOMY AND TOTALITY:

COOLEY'S THEORY OF PECUNIARY

VALUATION*

Glenn Jacobs, UNIVERSITY OF MASSACHUSETTS–

BOSTON

Science, unlike other architects, builds not only castles in the air, but may construct separate habitable stories of the building before laying on the foundation stone.
—Karl Marx, *A Contribution to the Critique of Political Economy* (1859, 1970, p. 57)

INTRODUCTION

There now exists a growing body of literature (Furner, 1975; Smith, 1965; Schwendinger and Schwendinger, 1974; Sutherland, 1977; Oberschall, 1972) on the development of the social sciences in the United States. This literature details the dilemmas and contradictions sociology and its parent disciplines faced as they struggled to establish themselves amid the consolidation of corporate capitalism and the expansion of the university prior to (1880–1900) and during the Progressive Era (1900–1915). As it turns out,

Studies in Symbolic Interaction—Volume 2, 1979, pages 39–84
ISBN: 0-89232-105-9

the roots of SI also lie within that period; but by the time Mead had developed a full-blown theory of the self, Cooley had already passed that point and fashioned a whole theory of social organization, social classes and political economy, or if you will, economic sociology.

Charles Horton Cooley (1864–1929) turns out to have developed a full-fledged economic sociology (1919, pp. 283–348) which represents an *institutional* analysis of the economy. A sociologist whose doctorate was in economics, Cooley was a major architect of a point of view in sociology which aided it in establishing itself as a departmental discipline (Sutherland, 1977) in the emerging university of the Progressive Era (1900–1915). This view contained the central concept of the group (Furner, 1975, pp. 305–308; Cohen, 1968). Thus, in addition to a social psychology, Cooley crafted the building blocks of social organization. Society is depicted as a sometimes harmonious and sometimes antagonistic unity; a union, and, perhaps, metaphysically an *identity,* of opposites. It evolves meanderingly, tentatively and adaptively, that is, sympodially. Its medium is public opinion, and it is crystallized into institutions. Indeed, the differentiated social unity served Cooley as an ideal and as a model of progressively evolving democracy based on the revised and adapted principle of competition—a principle which appeared to be fought but never totally expunged from any side that debated it in the academic-economic controversies of the 1880s. This was a period of intensive corporate consolidation, hence a period dramatizing a quintessential contradiction of United States capitalism—monopoly versus competition (Weinstein, 1968; Kolko, 1963). Nearly all of the first generation of academic economists were exposed to, influenced by and shared an intellectual configuration which was to become, along with the social thought whose tenets it nourished and shared, the paradigm of liberal economic ideology of the twentieth century: neoclassical microeconomics. The prototype, consisting of an amalgam of reformist doctrines and neoclassical (marginal utility) economics, served to create an image of consolidation and professionalization for the discipline. It provided its membership with expertise, hence credentials for technically assisting American business, government and labor in their attempts to devise working relationships for the emerging era of full-blown international capitalism.

Within this context, Cooley's theory of pecuniary valuation is an attempt to systematize political economy with the aid of sociology. Cooley thus bears inclusion among the so-called institutional economists. Because he alone among the institutionalists had already developed a general sociology, in addition to a social psychology, his economic thinking bears special notice, if only for a reconnaissance of his acknowledged (Clark, 1927; Dorman, 1949, pp. 401–407) contribution to the economics of the time.

An assessment of the significance of Cooley's economic sociology requires: an examination of the "subtext" of his thought, that is, the underlying historical and philosophical context; a critical analysis of the work itself as it is articulated with its academic-historical context; and an outline of the ramifications of work and context for contemporary social theory.

For the time being, let us say that Cooley was unique among the *sociologists* of his time (e.g., Ross, Small, Giddings) in having developed a recognizable economic sociology. It was derived from a sociology *sui generis* as opposed to an eclectic synthesis or mosaic. As we shall see, his economic sociology was based upon a normative theory of value presupposing a philosophical and historical frame of reference as well as several taken-for-granted economic assumptions. In brief, Cooley's commitment to American transcendentalism and the doctrine of competition shaped the following view of economy and society: (1) human nature is mediated by the social; (2) human nature or "primary" values is nourished in primary groups; (3) human nature cum primary values is mediated by social institutions; (4) the economy is an institution; (5) economic values are human nature or primary values expressed through the economic institution of the market or the pricing, distribution (circulation) or consumership components thereof; (6) through this mechanism, the upper class, via its consumer advantage, controls the market; (7) despite its abuses, competition remains the best social sorting and equilibrium-maintaining mechanism of society and the market; and (8) government regulation and the diffusion of the (upper class) service ethic are the best ways of reforming the economy.

In this respect, the determination of whether Cooley was a prediscoverer of scientific "insight," a theoretical deadend, or a link in the development of scientific truth, seems puerile. Science and society do not develop linearly, but dialectically, that is, in the unfolding of their contradictions.

Cooley represents a moment within the growth and proliferation of the social sciences during a time of crisis of American capitalism (the Progressive Era, 1900–1915). This was a crisis of growth, anarchy and consolidation, a development, which, like a recurrent dream, replays itself with contemporary significance as our capitalist society is beset by new and habitual contradictions.

Cooley (Jacobs, 1976, pp. 375–383) was part of a contingent of Progressive academics, the genteel men of letters, whose romanticism and philosophical idealism prompted him, in part, to derive his formulations about society from a type of romantic anachronism. This, mind you, does not merely shelve Cooley as some kind of eccentric. Rather, as Mead tells us in *Movements of Thought in the Nineteenth Century* (1936, pp. 66–152), it typifies the dialectical-reflexive strain in romanticism which culminated in philosophies such as pragmatism and Marxism. Cooley thus dramatizes the basic issues of economics and social thought of the nineteenth century as they continue to emerge and metamorphosize today. It is my contention that Cooley's framework represents the crystallization of a paradigm of political economy which provided the working method for modern day welfare or micro-economics, that is, neo-classical economics. The danger, as I see it, is that contemporary sociologists may leap too fast into the realm of political economy before questioning these methods and the assumptions that underlie them. While "institutionalism" in economics, then as now, seems so plausible to sociologists searching for the social foundations of the economy, they have not paused to consider the way in which neo-classical economics has already been bootlegged into their sociology. In seeking the "re-embedment," to use Polanyi's term, of economy in society, we inadvertently embed the economy in the economy!

Consequently, before I begin the task of exploring Cooley's economic sociology, I will briefly discuss these issues from the standpoint of the most trenchant criticism levelled at symbolic interactionism—its "astructural bias." From there I will move on to the *structural* biases on symbolic interactionism's horizon. Consistent with my preceding remarks, I will opt for one variety of these—the Marxist. Then I shall (a) detail the connections between Cooley's philosophy and economic sociology; (b) survey that economic sociology; (c) discuss the affinities of it with the professional-academic economics of Cooley's time; and (d) note the relevance of early and contemporary institutional economics to the reconciliation of symbolic interactionism and political economy.

For the present, a review and analysis is justified by our efforts to seek new avenues for the expansion and adaptation of symbolic interaction to a set of societal conditions bespeaking retrenchment, economic stagnation and intermittent crises. Also, it is timely that symbolic interaction be accused of "astructural bias" (Reynolds and Reynolds, 1973) because, having left behind the ferment of the sixties which merely opened our eyes to the structural contradictions and emergent crises of late capitalism, symbolic interactionists are in danger of falling prey to the complacency of hip imagery and/or the arid crotcheting of the perspective into its minutest conclusions, that is, it is endangered of becoming mannerism.

The charge of astructural bias is incisive because it teases out unexamined assumptions which can be summarized by symbolic interactionism's inability to challenge the material bases and standard operating procedures of contemporary capitalist society. However, critiques of the perspective (e.g., Reynolds and Reynolds, 1973; McNall and Johnson, 1975; Huber, 1973) do little more than point an accusing finger. To wit, they contend that SI does not study such and such (economic development, war, imperialism, the ruling class), that liberalism or conservatism is implicit in it, or that studies of institutional settings and public places are bereft of considerations of power and privilege. These are important indicators but fail to get to the heart of the matter. More fundamentally, *symbolic interactionism defines the very foundations of social reality out of existence.* This is the antinomy upon which these putative derelictions rest—society is autogenerative.

The weakness "of symbolic interactionism lies in its failure to answer the question as to the source of these 'definitions of the situation' or 'social constructions of reality' " (Reynolds and Reynolds, 1973, p. 78). Fine (1977) brings us closer to the source of this failure in his analysis of labelling theory. He suggests that viewing the labelling process (social definition) as the sole totality of deviance renders the caveat (Blumer, 1969, pp. 22–23) about the "obdurate character of the empirical world" perfunctory. Thus, when symbolic interactionists eschew positivism, their perspective prompts them to do it for the wrong reason insofar as it extirpates the phenomenon from its determinative historical context (the productive process and social relations of capitalism). The definitional process itself is seen as the objective ground of deviance; subject and object are inverted. Grounding social phenomena in common sense leaves us only the presumed objectivity of the theorist. The phenomenon (in this case deviance) is sociologically defined as an illusion which only the theorist's consciousness can pierce. Thus the suspension of common sense in order to realize the essence of social reality represents "a leap from morality to science" (Fine, 1977, p. 173). As far as positivism is concerned, this is a leap from the frying pan into the fire because a central assumption of positivism is the externality of science to the universe it studies. Fine says that there is available the less facile alternative that

> "common sense" can investigate the historical character of the processes of deviance *and* of labelling; that it can investigate the *conditions* of their emergence, reproduction and disintegration; that it, therefore, can develop a practice to realize this disintegration [italics mine] (1977, p. 189).

However, it is also true that SI's shortcomings are still largely nascent. The dialectical character of SI can still be turned to more creative uses, if what a recent survey of "creative sociology" (Morris, 1975, p. 176) says is true,

> symbolic interaction and its allied perspectives (phenomenology, ethnomethodology) make no political statement [as such]. Rather they are *interpreted* as "potentially" and "inherently" revolutionary, or, quite the opposite, are "serving the power elite."

Already there are signs that these possible *structural* biases are being actualized in the attempts to reconcile Parsonianism with symbolic interactionism (Turner, 1974; Blumer, 1975a; Parsons, 1975; Turner, 1968; Tiryakian, 1975, pp. 26–31), and oppositely, with Marxism (Ropers, 1973; Lichtman, 1970). Finally we must add to the list another *process* or circulation bias: a rapprochement is being sought with exchange theory (Singelman, 1972; Schaffer, 1974). Significantly, the hallmark of all these influences is that they involve economics, substantively or metaphorically, as methods (Marx) or models (exchange theory, Parsons) of economic society. My contention is that it is neither possible nor desirable to avoid bias, but imperative to own up to it. Moreover, it is scientifically contradictory to take the economics of our society-as-constituted as a *model* for its very understanding. The Parsonian case uses money as its root metaphor. Money (the symbolic embodiment of utility) is simultaneously the medium of the economy and of symbolic communication—"actually a language." Money can be used as *the* model for the understanding of the operations of the "generalized media" of the other institutional subsystems: the polity, kinship, etc. Society is grounded in money[1] and money is the detached first member of an imaginary series (Parsons, 1969, pp. 311–316). So, too, "social" exchange reifies commodity exchange as a model of social relations.

In contrast to Parsons, Marx insists that "Money is *not* a symbol" of or for social relations, but is the "perverted appearance" of social relations:

[It is] this prosaically real, and by no means imaginary, mystification that is characteristic of all social forms of labor positing exchange-value. This perverted appearance manifests itself merely in a more striking manner in money than it does in commodities (1859, 1970, p. 49).

From the standpoint of Marxism, the Parsonian notion of "generalized media" is a topsy-turvy conception only bearing a mnemonic or superficial resemblance to Marx's definition of money as a universal equivalent: for Marx, society is the measure of money, not money of society! And society is quintessentially humans producing and reproducing their collective means of subsistence and planetary existences. In contrast to exchange theory, Marx sees exchange as the last, though necessary, issue of the social relations of production, whereas the former apprehends it as the first and only ground of social relations. Indeed, both the Parsonian and exchange views are simply modern, more abstract reified successors to the models and formulations examined herein: Cooley, the reform and institutional economics of progressivism. Call the ruling paradigm marginal utility theory, neo-classical economics, micro-economics, welfare economics, "price theory," or what have you, it comes to the same thing: an economics centered on demand or consumption. Dress it up in sociological jargon and it still comes to the same economic conclusions, namely those evinced in everyday life by the ethics and practice of contemporary business. If this is the paradigm symbolic interactionists shall make theirs, they must be prepared to face up to being intellectual ornamentalists and reproducers of the status quo.

Marxism does use the economy to understand social reality, but not metaphorically. It does so for the purpose of showing how a "distinct mode of production determines the specific mode of consumption, distribution, exchange and the specific relations of these different phases to one another." Furthermore, "Production in the narrow sense . . . is in its turn also determined by the other aspects" (Marx, 1857, 1972, p. 205). Thus, for Marx:

. . . the social relations within which individuals produce, the social relations of production, are altered, transformed, with the change and development of the material means of production, of the forces of production. The relations of production in their totality constitute what is called the social relations, society, and, moreover, a society at a definite stage of historic development, a society with peculiar, distinctive characteristics [author's italics] (Marx, 1847, 1933, pp. 28–29).

The labor process *is* the social basis of capitalism but this is not apparent to either the participants or the participant-intellectuals under the capitalist system of commodity production. The process of circulation is taken to be the dominant level; exchange relationships are the *apparent* locus of social relations. Thus, common sense and scientific thinking inevitably fasten onto (fetishize) circulation (exchange) because it is the most accessible and distinguishing, and hence, the most plausible level within the capitalist system. Exchange relations or market appearances can only be understood, "and the 'fetishes' or 'mystifications' to which these had been subject could only be removed, if they were seen as the expression of these more fundamental relations at the basis of society—of labor as the social activity *par excellence* and of the social division of labor" (Dobb, 1970, pp. 9–10).

The attempts (Lichtman, 1970; Ropers, 1973) to reconcile symbolic interaction with Marxism have, quite naturally, confined themselves to ironing out the difficulties presented by the former's pragmatic understanding of the self, the object world, and consciousness, so that symbolic interactionism can become critical. For this, the idealist elements of pragmatism are seen as removable obstacles. My aim here is not to review these laudatory efforts. I will work with the assumption that the reconciliation has been satisfactorily made. However, I question the efficacy of making symbolic interactionism itself a perspective on political economy. I will say at the outset that this is perhaps possible but not desirable, except as an exercise, for it will only be redundant. This does not say that there cannot be any mutual benefit—indeed, there already has been. I am only questioning the scientific feasibility of turning one into the other; which is not to belittle the necessity of making them compatible. This has a pragmatic as much as a Marxist inclination because they are approaches designed to deal with different scalar levels of reality; mutual conversion is valuable if one completes the trajectory to one's starting point of sociological psychology or political economy. But if we only begin with one to try and convert it into the other, much time will be wasted and perhaps dilution will occur.[2] In short, I am *insisting* that symbolic interactionism should be made compatible with political economy. This is due to the fact that in the contemporary situation it is almost impossible to divorce matters of academic political economy from social policy. Whereas, earlier, symbolic interactionists may have been content to let the matter of social policy rest, the mere fact that we entertain the possibility of investigating political economy forces us to make our covert inclinations overt. Symbolic interactionism must come out of the closet!

SI's debt to Cooley has been acknowledged, albeit cursorily (Martindale, 1960, pp. 344–347; Rose, 1962, passim; Manis and Meltzer, 1972, passim; Rose, 1962, passim; Shibutani, 1961; Strauss, 1959; Farberman and Stone, 1970; Karpf, 1932, pp. 291–307). Elsewhere I and others have detailed the sources of Cooley's sociology (Jacobs, 1976; Cohen, 1968; Jandy, 1942). However, outside of this literature there is virtually no mention or recognition made of the fact that Cooley developed a comprehensive economic sociology, although a major history of American economic thought does do so (Dorfman, 1949, V.3, pp. 401–451). This is remarkable considering the fact that Cooley and most of the early American sociologists (Sumner, Small, Ross, and Giddings) began their academic careers as political economists (Furner, 1975, passim). This oversight is an artifact of SI's "astructural bias" and more importantly, of sociology's "hidden history" as it emerged from the nineteenth century social science movement (Furner, 1975; Bernard and Bernard, 1965) and economics in the United States. Moreover, it is symptomatic of sociology's schizoid mania to examine itself "reflexively" while at the same time ignoring its late nineteenth and early twentieth century American origins. It was, in fact, a discipline that, more than most other social sciences, "venerated 'great thinkers,' " and European ones at that (Furner, 1975, pp. 292–293, 311).[3]

Below, I explain how this tendency articulated with Cooley's rootedness in the philosophy of transcendentalism with its emphasis on the emblematic quality of nature, language, society, and the representative man as universal-social exemplar. Also, I explain how these notions provided a basis for the development of the idea of competition. Finally, the following section demonstrates how this idea undergirds both Cooley's social psychology and his approach to social organization. It is the leitmotif of Cooley's notion of totality or the organic view.

Cooley's Philosophy: The Subtext of Totality

The veneration of great thinkers is especially salient in Cooley's case. I have argued (Jacobs, 1976) for viewing Cooley's contributions to sociology as in large part a product of his participation in the essay tradition.[4] This is objectified in Cooley's "invisible college" or self-styled reference group of literary heroes, especially the American transcendentalist, Emerson. In line with Furner, I also attribute this to the insecurity and newness of the discipline and its membership, and to Cooley's own felt sense of disciplinary marginality vis-a-vis his intentional personal-evolutionary development (Jacobs, 1976, pp. 164–165, 255–284). Cooley conceived of his intellectual reference group as a

larger society of men who live for the ages as well as for the hours and, by virtue of their representative minds, speak to one another from century to century. Of these I imagine

I am one: at any rate I can hear what they say, whether I myself am audible or not (Journals, Vol. 21, 1913-1919, p. 161).

This assignation of transcendental intersubjectivity is neither humanly (Marx, 1947) nor historically idiosyncratic. It is entirely consistent with the Emersonian intellectual tradition (transcendentalism) Cooley took personally and intellectually to heart. Its precepts and corollaries echo throughout his thinking. Moreover, it represents an attenuated but still identifiable aspect of Puritanism. We must recall here Emerson's depiction of property as the "surface action of internal machinery, like the index on the face of a clock" in his famous essay, "Nature," which sets forth the principles of the transcendentalist philosophy. These principles include: (1) idealism: the senses give us representations of things which themselves are emblematic of spiritual facts; nature is the symbol of spirit—it is emblematic; (2) language consists of the signs of natural, hence spiritual, facts; (3) man is placed in the center of things, and human transcendental mediators—*representative* men —are the amplifiers and reproducers of the oversoul or spirit (Emerson, 1929, pp. 1-47).[5]

The representative man is the hieratic (transcendentally emblematic) man. The theme is a prominent one in Cooley's journals and it appears, clearly stated in, his first major work, *Human Nature and Social Order* (1902, rev. ed 1922, pp. 293-357), and *Social Organization* (1909, pp. 15-16).

Thus we may say of all famous and admired characters that, as personal ideas, they partake of the nature of gods, in that the thought entertained of them is a constructive effort of the idealizing imagination to create a personal symbol of its own tendency (1902, rev. ed. 1922, p. 341).

. . . conspicuous men serve as symbols through which the higher structure may either be supported or undermined. We must have heroes, and perhaps villains. . . . In short it makes a difference whether we judge a man with reference to his special history and 'lights' or to the larger life of the world. There is certainly a right for every man . . . while there are some whose right is representative like that of Jesus (1909, pp. 15-16).

Emerson's representative man[6] *par excellence* was the scholar whom he eulogized in the "American Scholar" (1929, pp. 25-36). Thus the scholar represents, within the division of labor (1929, pp. 25-26), "the delegated intellect whose role is to see truth and pierce the spectacle of nature to its core." In Emerson's quasi-Hegelian style this represents "the inexplicable continuity of the Web of God, but always circular power [i.e., the oversoul] returning to itself." The scholar delivers us from alienation.[7] In Cooley's terms, the representative scholar speaks *"sub specie aeternitatis"*—under the aspect of eternity. Herein is the source of the "I" which Cooley joins with the pragmatic "me" to form the looking glass self. The intricacies of this need not concern us here.[8] What is of concern is how this figures as the subtext of his economic sociology. It does so in Cooley's amalgamation of the transcendental "I"—the oversoul—with the pragmatic (William

James's) definition of the self as "mine." This amalgamation is inextricably tied to the notion of competition.

In *Human Nature and the Social Order* (1902, rev. ed. 1922, pp. 168–210), Cooley establishes the "I" as an observable fact of language and interaction: "The 'I' of common speech always has more or less distinct reference to other people as well as the speaker" (p. 168). Its origins are found in instinctive self-feeling, and this feeling is "the my-feeling or sense of appropriation" (p. 169). Thus it is an "aggressive self" identified

> most conspicuously in an appropriativeness of objects of common desire, corresponding to the individual's need of power over such objects to secure his own peculiar development, and to the danger of opposition from others who also need them. And this extends from material objects to lay hold, in the same spirit, of the attentions and affections of other people, of all sorts of plans and ambitions, including the noblest special purposes the mind can entertain, and indeed of any conceivable idea which may come to seem a part of one's life and in need of assertion against some one else" (p. 180).

This instinctively rooted self-feeling and its association with the exercise of power, by the same token, "is always the shadow, as it were, of the common life" (p. 181). Competition is thus rooted in both human nature and society: "Self-feeling has its chief scope *within* the general life, not outside of it" (p. 179). And it is here where we see how Cooley wove together human nature, the self, society and economy into a holistic view. The premise of competition is built into human nature as is the proneness of that nature to sympathy and communication. In fact, sympathy and opposition or competition are a unity of opposites:

> Opposition between one's self and some one else is also a very real thing; but this opposition, instead of coming from a separateness like that of material bodies, is, on the contrary, dependent upon a measure of community between one's self and the disturbing other, so that the hostility between one's self and a social person may always be described as hostile sympathy. And the sentiments connected with opposition, like resentment, pertain neither to myself, considered separately, nor to the symbol of the other person, but to ideas including both (pp. 130–131).

From here Cooley is free to build a conception of society as a totality sublty premised by competiton. This premise is not so much deliberately hidden as it is taken for granted, as we have seen in Cooley's discussion of the "I". But this premise also allows Cooley to work in two directions simultaneously, that is, from the oversoul and universal values *down* through social organization to the individual, or, again from the oversoul cum the "I" *up* through human nature, the looking glass itself and sympathy, communication, and the primary group back to social organization. Hence: "Self and society go together, as phases of a common whole" (1909, pp. 8–9).

Self-consciousness ramifies through social organization "in the fact of reciprocal influence or causation among its parts, by virtue of which everything that takes place in it is connected with everything else, and so is an outcome of the whole" (1909, p. 4). As in the case of the self's development through personal ideas, communication is the glue holding social organization together. On the societal level this is expressed in public opinion which does not unify through agreement but in the crystallization of diverse but related ideas. Cooley's commitment to transcendentalism and the idea of evolution thus permitted him to articulate his conspectus of social organization in moral terms. Hence, public opinion is the "public phase of larger consciousness . . . we call Democracy." It makes "institutions express the higher impulses of human nature, instead of brutal or mechanical conditions" (1909, p. 118). Thus it enlarges individual sympathy and induces "that spiritual identification of the member with the whole, which is the ideal of organization" (p. 116). Finally,

> Society, then, as a moral organism, is a progressive creation, tentatively wrought out through experiment, struggle, and survival. Not only individuals but ideas, institutions, nations, and races do their work upon it and perish. Its ideals, though simple in spirit, are achieved through endless elaboration of the means.
>
> *It will be my further endeavor to throw some light upon this striving whole by considering certain phases of its organization,* such as Communication, Public Opinion, Sentiment, Classes, and Institutions; *always trying to see the whole in the part, the part in the whole, and human nature in both* [italics mine] (1909, pp. 56–57).

Thus, totality is the motif of society and the social self, but its *leitmotif* is competition. Competition is the deeper theme of personal and social organization. As such, it provides a basis for a metatheoretical understanding of Cooley as a theorist of social psychology, social organization *and* economic sociology.

Society "is a vast machine the purpose of which is to organize goodness and power" (Journal, unnumbered, 1889–1891, p. 27). This was written when Cooley was seeking his vocation, actually his calling. It is consonant with Emerson's hieratic emphasis that "Every man's condition is a solution in hieroglyphic. . ." and, moreover, that work represents "God's education . . . he can only become a master, who learns the secrets of labor, and who by real cunning extorts from nature its sceptre" (1929, pp. 1, 74). The fact of one's position in the division of labor is the last issue of spirit.

Thus we find Cooley blending the hierarchical with the hieratic:

> Those who think govern those who toil because government *is* thought. And, for a like reason they must control commerce and finance—because production in its complexity is also thought (Journal, Vo. 16, 1902–1903, p. 99).

Notice here that production is consigned to thought. It only moves one notch, in the mature thinking on pecuniary valuation, to the ideal of artisanship, but never to abstract labor, that is, never to theoretical primacy. Production is the preserve of the scholar and craftsman. Those who toil become refractory.

The conceptions of the government of thought and society-as-detective-agency are prototypes of competition wherein an invisible hand adjusts the division of labor vis-a-vis market values so that all find their vocational slot. This is augmented, individually, by the Emersonian virtues of self-relaince, ambition, and the organizing abilities of representative men.

In "Personal Competition" (1899 in 1930, pp. 163–226), Cooley attempts to reconcile laissez-faire with the critique of competition as brutalizing by arguing that the competitive or "selective" processes themselves are not so intrinsically brutal as they are imperfect: they demand improvement by opening opportunity chiefly through industrial regulation and education. There we find the notion of society-as-detective-agency appearing as the competitive process and its "selective agents." The "status principle" (caste) is the foil for competition because it is given as the sole alternative to it. Competition is bailed out with the suggestion that its nefarious occasions are not intrinsic, but rather are the properties of local groups and conditions, vices associated with other abilities of successful men, and the only temporary success of speculator types. In other words, "competition simply enforces the conditions, *as a whole,* upon all competitors. It levels down or up, just as may happen" (p. 199).

Competition, regulation and totality (the organic view) are the intellectual foundation of Cooley's economic sociology. For example, in his doctoral dissertation in economics, "The Theory of Transportation" (1894 in 1939, pp. 17–118), transportation—"the most organic of all industries"—is established as "the means of material communication between one place and another" as society evolves, differentiates and develops mechanisms through which structural interdependence is effectuated (p. 40). Transportation and communication of thought often share facilities although the two are not synonymous. Nonetheless, "transportation is a highly organic activity . . . a distinct social function. . . . It is an agency by which every part of society is brought into relation with every other, and interdependence, specialization, in a word, organization, made possible." It is the highest example of social organization "in the lower or physical form" and the "political state is the most conspicuous instance of social unification in its higher or moral form. . ." (p. 104). Here the differentiation of higher and lower imposes the imprimatur of morality-as-totality on the state. As the most organic of industries, "the business of transportation unites the requirements of the widest unity with that of very great complexity of detail' (p. 111). This unity is to be achieved by government regulation as a complement to business' ability to "secure the most economical and profitable adjustment of capital and labor power to industrial conditions" (p. 110). Thus, in the case of railroad rates, private enterprise engages in competition which is hostile to any adjustment of rates consistent with public policy. *Both corporate consolidation and public control are* natural *outcomes of the increase of industrial and societal scale and complexity:*

... competition is the best regulating force in most kinds of industrial activity, but ... it is not necessarily nor always good, and may require either to be altogether suppressed in certain cases or more or less stringently regulated for the public good. Individual enterprise is chiefly to be relied upon for progress, and those who propose to substitute government control for it must show a probability of benefit from the change; but where the probability is tolerably clear it ought to be acted upon. As economic organization becomes more complicated and the various parts more interdependent, it constantly happens that the securing of general freedom demands particular regulation (pp. 103–104).

What we have here is Cooley's abstract sublimation of the general state of economy and society in the United States wherein the crisis of corporate anarchy, as a manifestation of the capitalist contradiction between monopoly and competition, demanded a solution in policy and practice. It was up to the academic economists, by way of resolution of their doctrinal and disciplinary struggles, to provide ideological support and practical guidelines as American business, emergent big labor, and the public, responding to the social upheavals of the 1880s, sought to chart a modus operandi for the decades ahead. Cooley's economic sociology influenced a rising group of liberal economists. "While Cooley was less heretical in detail than some of his broad propositions might indicate, their very breadth and his emphasis on social change within the framework of the existing system helped to feed the stream of liberal economic thought" (Dorman, 1949, p. 407).

The Theory of Pecuniary Valuation

The explicit formulation of Cooley's economic approach appears in three papers published in 1913, reprinted as three chapters in *Social Process* (1918, pp. 293–348), including a fourth chapter (pp. 283–292) and a paper published the same year as *Social Process,* "Political Economy and Social Process" (1918 in 1930, pp. 251–289).

The analysis commences with the social basis of value. Values are part of the ethos, the mores, "or whatever you choose to call the collective state of mind" (1918, p. 289). They are thus part of organic mental life; valuation "is only another name for tentative organic process." Hence, an "organic mental life has for one of its phases an organic system of values" (pp. 285, 288). Values can be distinguished according to whether they stem from human nature ("human values") and primary ideals (love, fear, ambition, honor, loyalty), or from the realm of institutions which transform them. All human values are "mediated by social conditions" (p. 287). The process that generates values is mental but not conscious: "it works by suggestion, influence, and the competition and survival of ideas" in a tentative manner (p. 290).

However, institutions have precise methods for the appraisal of values (e.g., tests of membership, creeds, sacraments, exhibitions, medals, titles, academic chairs, etc.). The pecuniary estimates made by people are determined by suggestion and discussion and vary with the group and time. They are products of the same social forces creating other phases of tradition and sentiment (pp. 293–294). Social complexity is interwoven with the value process: "the study of value-making institutions becomes, then, the principal means of arriving at practical truth" (p. 296). In this regard the market is as much an institution as the state or church and should "by no means be understood from a merely individual point of view" (pp. 296–297). The weakness of contemporary political economy is that it is not cognizant of the idea of institutions in its emphasis on demand as its root datum (see also 1930, pp. 252–254).[9] The result has been to plant the market institution in human nature, thereby divorcing it from society (1918, pp. 7, 65, 72–73, and passim). Cooley wishes to "re-embed" the economy in society.

This approach to value reflects his understanding of institutions as crystallized phases of the "public mind," hence, as "phases of a common and at least partly homogeneous body of thought. . ." (1909, p. 314). Institutions are "human nature formulated, cut-and-dried. That which is fresh and forward cannot be formulated. So to the progressive mind institutions are ever commonplace, tyrannical and disgusting" (Journal, Vol. 16, 1902–1903, p. 118). While Cooley was critical of planting the market institution in human nature, he nevertheless hewed to that idea and eschewed the particular view of human nature shared by economists, that is, utilitarian hedonism which individualized market (consumer) motives.

The transcendentalist (Emerson and Thoreau) aversion to conformity thus makes its way into sociology via Cooley's distrust of, actually ambivalence toward, institutions: "whether the service of an institution belittles a man depends upon whether he or the institution is the master" (Journal, Vol. 13, 1898–1899, p. 80). Thus: "The original can hardly be institutional," and, likewise, "specialization and narrow professionalism cut us off from the larger life" (Journal, Vol. 16, 1902–1903, pp. 99, 16–17; Vol. 13, 1898–1899, p. 9). This forces us to lose the thread that connects what we do with what we are, which is to say, estranges us from our own original nature.

Cooley grounds his approach in the pragmatist's conception of plastic human nature, that is, it is a teachable nature (1922 rev. ed., pp. 3–34). He shares with that tradition, too, the emphasis on psychological liberalism and "individualistic piety," thus romanticism as well:

Romanticism as it flowered in America in the Transcendentalist movement, one of [William] James' circles, not only stressed the individual but conceived of him as 'the vehicle of all creative spirit.' Emerson . . . may have spiritualized the individual, but he was still left an individual. Institutions were still *men's* shadows. . . . Through him [James] flowed urgently the individualism that has been a very central current in American life and thought (Mills, 1964, p. 271).

Institutions are eschewed when their mediation of human nature becomes over-formalized or transformed into a dead mechanism (1909, pp. 342–355). Cooley's discussion of institutions, comprising Part V of *Social Organization,* explicitly makes the individual-institution dialectic its focus and the particularities of that relationship the basis of Cooley's judgements about them. So, with respect to values, economic and otherwise, "An institution . . . seldom or never corresponds so closely to a phase of human nature that the institutional values and the immediately human values on the whole coincide" (1918, pp. 288–289). Yet, as we shall see, this dialectic is truncated by a conception of totality that idealized production—its root—and which takes the individualism of representative men as its yardstick. Institutional formalism is evil when "it interferes with growth and adaptation, when it suppresses individuality and stupefies or misdirects the energies of human nature" (1909, p. 342). So the apparent uniformity of the market is due to the molding of individual estimate by that institution, at first loosely and then in the process of price-fixing. Thence the individual and the market reciprocally interact: the market is a continuous institution. It is no more a summation than fashion is a summation of individual ideas about dress. As man conforms to other institutions he does so in a general way to pecuniary ones. He also has a certain individuality in his choices and thus can depart from the norm and initiate new tendencies.

In material anticipating the essays on pecuniary valuation (Journal, Vol. 16, 1902–1903, pp. 95–96), we see reflections on the marketplace that evince an ambivalence about the competitive system. This ambivalence is instructive because it reveals how Cooley's conceptions of value and the market-as-institution run into a *cul de sac:*

Market Value, or Power in the Market is expressive of the whole social order, in all that grandeur and confusion with which nature everywhere presents herself to the finite mind. Most values, perhaps, are vital or organic, springing from the very nature of life, and such as are jusitifed as we come to understand that life, like the commercial power of men of organizing genius. Other values or powers we must regard as parasitical, like that of the clever speculator, or the law-abiding swindler. Others again are secondary, incidental, like those of diamonds or first editions. Yet among the incidental values, derived from the taste or caprice of a few, are the values—so far as they have any in the market—of men of genius in art, letters and pure science. In general the values of the market are those of the actual world, in all its grossness: *spiritual values in the higher sense:* the values of the future or of the finest minds of today, are little felt in it; *they are not organized* [italics mine].

The ambivalence about the market possibly reflects the instability of idealism as it runs up against the actual world. The venality of the market cannot measure up to the higher values Cooley prefers. But his antipathy toward the market is strained—*ex nihilo*. The transcendental formula is evoked at the outset; the Market is emblematic. Higher spiritual values are depicted as offshoots of other, secondary, incidental, often "whimsical," yet "worldly" market values: *antinomianism and its object stem from the same source*. And, appropriately, in this connection I move on to Cooley's treatment of money:

> The money [*sic*] is rather a derivative than an original motive, except as we may come to love it for its own sake; it is a mechanism indispensible to the organization of life. . . . But this sort of motivation is wholly inadequate to the higher incitement of human nature. It takes hold of us, for the most part, in a somewhat superficial way, and if allowed to guide rather than follow the deeper currents of character, it degrades us into avarice and materialism (1918, p. 129).

Here we see the ambivalence reappear. The pecuniary motive is derivative but can become primary-like. It is a mundane necessity and fails to "incite" the higher aspects of human nature. Character is the bulwark against it: idealism toe-to-toe with materialism.

The distinctive function of money is "to generalize or assimilate values through a common measure," thereby giving them reach and flexibility (1918, p. 309): it transcends any special sort of value. *Money thus resembles language since it furnishes a medium of communicative growth,* just as language and social organization are extended in scope by cheap printing, mails, telegraphy, telephones, etc. The function of pecuniary valuation is effectuated by uniform currency and devices of credit and transfer. It is an expression of the total life of society (p. 310). This makes it supple and appears to be automatic.

Money permits the weighing of one value against another, for example honor may call for the saving of money to pay a debt, and friendship righteousness and beauty are guaged in terms of it. If there is "anything attractive about a man he soon learns to collect pay for it" (p. 313). Hence the values we think of as absolute are only "relatively absolute":

> Life itself is not an absolute value, since we constantly see it sacrificed to other ends; chastity is sold daily by people not radically different in nature from the rest of us, and as for honor it would be hard to imagine a kind which might not, in conceivable situations, be renounced for some other and perhaps higher aim (p. 313).

Hence we have the notion of money as a leveller, the economic *lingua franca* but there is a gap as to its origin and the relationship between value, price and profit.

Values are expressions of organization and also are motives: we weigh one kind of value against another and our conduct is guided by the decision. So "apart from any definite medium of exchange there is a system of mental barter . . . by which values are compared definitely enough to make choice possible" (p. 332).[10] Pecuniary valuation supplements this psychic barter by making it communicable and uniform. In effect, a *social* marginal utility mechanism (see footnote 10) is being substituted for the doctrinaire, individual, mechanism of Cooley's colleagues in economics.

Pecuniary standardization ignores or depreciates some kinds of value otherwise held in high esteem and exaggerates others which may appear to have merit—it warps life (p. 333). This is due to the fact that two types of institutional conditions mediate the expression of psychical value via pecuniary ones: (1) those operating within exchange after pecuniary demand is formed; (2) those operating antecedently to actual demand. The first is illustrated by the case of the artist who cannot sell his/her product according to its merit because of his/her ignorance of the market. The artist may lack contact with buyers, and, as in the case of the second, a buying segment may be absent to begin with because of a "low state of taste."

As to the considerations underlying pecuniary demand, a technical class is involved which stands "in the same relation to the pecuniary institution as the clergy, politicians, lawyers, doctors do to other institutions." (pp. 34–335). Their intimate knowledge of the system enables them to guide its working in partial independence of the rest of society. This they do partly in public service and partly for personal aggrandizement, so that the commercially ascendent class possesses, in addition to tangible power, prestige and initiative which enables them to set fashions and control the market in addition to their concentrated buying power. This repudiates the cherished notions of the economists concerning economic freedom "and makes it necessary to look for pecuniary recognition of values to the goodwill of the class that has the most pecuniary power" (p. 336). Unfortunately, Cooley shares this tendency with them.

In addition to this commerical establishment, there is the fact that market value translates into pecuniary terms values which have already become institutionalized, that is, the institutions the market serves, for example, the artist and circles of connoisseurs, wealthy amateurs, other consuming, taste-making and manufacturing networks and publics which establish values translated into pecuniary terms (pp. 337–338). Values which are innovative, non-conformist, and righteous may pay least "not because moral value is essentially non-pecuniary . . . but because pecuniary valuation is essentially an institution, and values which are anti-institutional naturally stand outside of it" (p. 338). To be well-paid, initiative and originality must have power to enhance established market values. Thus the problem in this case is to provide a standard of originality which shall not become conventional. 'The higher values remain . . . untranslated" (p. 321). In the final analysis this is resolved by the concentration of actual buying power of the "richer class, which is largely the same as the commercial class" (p. 335).

In short, the institution of the market is administered by a class. Class control is exerted through control of purchasing power (demand) and through actual administration of the business system giving that class opportunities to increase its power. Note: demand is shifted, not extirpated! The ideals of the controlling class consist of acquisitive commercialism (including the pecuniary display noted by Veblen) and caste ideals. The class in power "is for many purposes a real historical organism acting collectively for its own aggrandizement" (pp. 305–306). Cooley comes very close to developing a notion of the power elite in the following:

> We are all, especially in pecuniary matters, ready to join forces with those whose interest is parallel to our own: bankers unite to promote the banking interest, manufacturers form associations, and so on. The whole business world is a network of associations, formal and informal, which aim to further the pecuniary interest of the members. And while these groups, or members of the same group, are often in competition with one another, this does not prevent a general parallelism of effort as regards matters which concern the interest of the business class as a whole. The larger the group the less conscious . . . is its cooperation, but it is not necessarily less effective and it can hardly be denied that the captialist-manager class . . . acts powerfully as a body in maintaining and increasing its advantages over other classes.

In this fashion the ruling class controls the actual adminstration of the market in the same manner as a powerful political party controls offices with the influence of patronage. From this point the persons having access to opportunities have enhanced market value:

> They are enabled by their advantageous position to draw from the common store salaries, fees, and profits not at all explicable by natural ability alone. This effect is multiplied by the fact that limitation of the number of competitors gives an additional scarcity value to the services of the competent. . . . And the same principle is quite generally required to explain the relatively large incomes of the class in power, including those of the more lucrative professions (1918, p. 307).

Finally, although such a situation does not bespeak a closed upper class or caste, and while partly free from the hereditary character of the European upper classes, "it is yet a true historical successor to the latter, and dominates the weaker classes in much the same way as stronger classes have always done" (p. 308). The powerful classes are still free to use their power for their individual and class advantage.

This description is hard-hitting and still contemporary. So, too, apparently, is Cooley's criticism of the political economists of his time. But in his excoriation of their fixation on demand we actually find a *shift* of the demand function rather than a fundamental critique. Thus, he accuses them of failing to view demand as an expression of economic power, that is, as a class phenomenon responsible for "all the vices and degeneracy of the actual social system" (1930, p. 254). Which is to say that the economists "assume productivity as judged on the market as the righteous or approximately righteous basis of distribution, and in so doing of course accept demand . . . as the standard of economic justice" (p. 254). This affords "no basis for a judgement of the social value of the present distribution of wealth" (p. 255).

Moreover, they abstract competition, "the very heart of the economic process," from other aspects of society; it has been isolated and idealized. As for combination, it has been treated as a disturbing condition. Contemporary political economy presupposes competition as a static condition, but it is, in fact, a static condition which "must destroy free competition and give rise to a rigid and non-competitive kind of organization" (p. 256). Free competition is actually "a phenomenon of social change." In the tendency of competitors to "get together,"[11] monopolistic enterprise is created. Thus the economists are inconsistent, writes Cooley. He is right on both counts; for himself and for the economists. In effect he is positing economic revisionism. The marginal utility paradigm, about which I will have more to say later, posited a static equilibrium of/by competition. He tells us that free competition can only be ensured under present monopolizing conditions by government regulation (pp. 256–257).

Cooley is saying that free competition always was and always will continue to be free only under dynamic conditions. In his mind he makes the assumption that the idealized past will be preserved by social change via government regulation. Neither he nor the economists were able to face squarely the contradiction of monopoly and competition; the one because he assumed the coexistence of the best of both worlds, the latter because they persisted in promulgating the myth of perfect competition and, at best, treated monopoly as exceptional or pathological. In actuality, Cooley's formulation exactly represents the compromise economics was working out as it became a liberal social science. He was at its vanguard. In this connection, he believed he was incorporating a byproduct of sociality, ethics, into economics. He opted for a social science which was ethical science as well, a science affording a basis for the "social value of the present distribution of wealth" (p. 255).

Cooley is actually criticizing political economy from the standpoint of political economy. This has been illustrated by his treatment of demand as a function of institutional valuation. While he accused the economists of taking demand for granted, he did little but emend the limitations of their thinking. His discussion of class control and determination of demand does little to clarify the real source of domination of the ruling class (control of the means of production) except through consumership and taste-making. This is evident in the following:

> Pecuniary value provides a motive to serve the pecuniary organism, a motive that penetrates everywhere, acts automatically, and adjusts itself delicately to the conditions of demand and supply. . . . Thus there is everywhere an inducement to supply these goods and services which the buying power in society thinks it wants, and this inducement largely guides production (1919, p. 310).

Production remains a function of supply and demand. While Cooley understands that profit begets profit ("Commercialism tends to fix attention rather on the acquisition than the use of wealth"), he concludes that there is another sphere of production inaccessible to the market. *In other words, a romantic image of production is defined outside of pecuniary valuation.* Hence, the pecuniary motive

can serve as an effective guide only in the case of deliberate production, for the sake of gain, and with ownership of the product. The production must be deliberate in order that *any* rational motive may control it, and the pecuniary motive will not control it unless it is for the sake of gain and protected by ownership. These limitations exclude such vast provinces of life that we well may wonder at the extent of trust in the market process.

They shut out the whole matter of the production and development of men, of human and social life; that is, they indicate that however important the pecuniary process may be in this field it can never be trusted to control it, not even the economic side of it. This is a sphere in which the market must be dominated by other kinds of organization (p. 317).

The production of commodities is incidental to that of men, and because the market stunts the latter, production is trivialized. On the one hand, the market is a part of a whole which the political economists have unduly circumscribed. On the other, this institution which alienates people from their common human nature can have its rationality augmented so that "the method of reform may be put to restrictions upon demand" (1919, p. 318). Personal and social development may then go on unhampered "through rational organization having a far wider scope than the market, though cooperating with that in every helpful way, and including, perhaps, radical reforms in the pecuniary system itself" (p. 318). Why outside the market? Because these "high goods do not really come within the economic sphere" (p. 319). These higher, ideal values "remain for the most part untranslated, even though translatable, and the material and technical aspects of the process have acquired an undue ascendancy" (p. 321). Commercial ascendancy represents the split between the ideal and the material, thus stifling the self-expression of "the artist, the poet, the skilled craftsman in wood and iron, the born teacher or lawyer" (p. 321). Hence "the pecuniary motive may be said to be an extrinsic one, as compared with the more intrinsic character of those others which I have called motives of self-expression" (p. 322). How could one who saw competition as the design for social structure think otherwise in his idealistic moments?

Self-expression, an ideal, becomes the quintessence of production: "When I say that self-expression is a regulator of productive activity I mean that like the pecuniary motive, though in a different way, it is the expression of an organic whole, and not necessarily a less authoritative expression" (p. 322). And from here on production qua self-expression is mystified further

Self-expression springs from the deeper and more obscure currents of life, from subconscious, unmechanized forces which are potent without our understanding why. It represents humanity more immediately and its values are, or may be more vital and significant than those of the market; we may look to them for art, for science, for religion, for moral improvement. . . . The onward things of life come from men whose imperious self-expression disregards the pecuniary market (p. 323).

Production is sublimated into an ideal. As such, it becomes the preserve of those with the leisure to cultivate the inner life, and it is not the province of the ordinary factory laborer. "At the present time," however, "producers . . . are guided by no ideals of group function and service. . . . This attitude is anti-progressive" (p. 342). "Producers" here refers to the skilled craftsman or the *owner* of the means of production: "A shoe manufacturer is no more justified in making the worst shoes he can than an artist in painting the worst pictures" (p. 342). Yet production has not always lacked ideals, "nor does it everywhere lack them at present" (p. 343).[12]

Cooley's solutions to the rapacity of capitalism are both "progressive" and anachronistic (e.g., rejuvenation of the service ideal among the rich). The corporation of his time was well on its way toward achieving the cooperation of labor leaders, politicians and academicians in forming a new, "responsible," business ethic (Weinstein, 1968). Cooley, like his French counterpart, Emile Durkheim, wished for a new solidarity, a new spirit of cooperation between producing groups. His ideal, like Durkheim's (1933, pp. 1–31; Gerstl and Jacobs, 1976, pp. 10–14; Bowen, 1947), was the syndicate and the guild. The ideals of production

come when the producing group gets a corporate consciousness and a sense of the social worth of its function. The medieval guilds developed high traditions and standards of workmanship, and held their members to them. They thought of themselves in terms of service, and not merely as purveyors to a demand. In our time the same is to some extent true of trades and professions in which a sense of workmanship has been developed by tradition and training. . . . The same principal ought to hold good throughout society, each functional group forming ideals of its own function and holding its members to them. Consuming and producing groups should cooperate in this matter, each making requirements which the other might overlook. The somewhat anarchical condition that is now common we may hope to be transitory. The general rule is that a stable group has a tendency to create for itself ideals of service in accord with the ruling ideals of society at large (p. 343).

This "liberal-syndicalist" motif (Schwendinger and Schwendinger, 1974, pp. 124–129) might represent the corporativist tinge developed as a necessary outcome of capitalist ideology when it seeks a nostalgic return to community without a surrender by the ruling class of the means of production. This is why incipient fascism often gets the support of romantics: non-conformist individuals seeking collectivism within capitalism, seize upon the idea of the 'olk' as a *deus ex machina,* and simultaneously expect the charismatic man and/or the state to conjure it. For Cooley, the puritan ideals of function and service should be embodied "in a system of appealing images by the aid of art." Likewise, we "need to *see* society—see it beautiful and inspiring—as a whole and in its special meaning for us, building up the conception of democracy until it stands before us with the grandeur and detail of great architecture. Then we shall have a source of higher values from which the pecuniary channels, as well as others, will be fed" (1918, p. 344).[13]

Let us turn now to the drift and trend of the economics of Cooley's era. It will be clear that Cooley's formulations were well within the current of the liberal thinking that developed as both product and strategy for the capitalism's most advanced form.

From Reembedment to Retrenchment: the Economics of Cooley's Time

Cooley took his doctorate in economics (with a minor in sociology) at Michigan (1894) under the tutelage of Henry Carter Adams, a moderate reformer who had a brief romance with socialism during the labor conflicts of the mid-1880s, but who, because of threats to his position at Michigan, soon recanted and became "a pioneer in search of ways for scholars in a technological, interest-oriented society to influence traditional values and policies without arousing resistance" (Furner, 1975, p. 142).[14] Cooley's early work on transportation and competition attest to his sharing of his teacher's views, especially with respect to the relations between government and business. As Adams put it: "Both governmental activity and private enterprise are essential to the development of a highly organized society, and the purpose of constructive thought should be to maintain them in harmonious relation" (quoted in Dorfman, 1949, p. 168). The state does not curtail competition but determines the manner in which it operates. By outlawing undesirable practices, it "raises the plane of competition." The state might interfere in business "to secure to the public the benefits flowing from the inevitable organization of those 'natural monopolies' which were the outgrowth of modern industrial development" (Dorfman, 1949, p. 168). Both Adams and Cooley favored government control as opposed to government ownership (Dorfman, 1949, p. 171), and both preferred the expansion of municipal and local state powers as opposed to federal powers on the grounds that "responsibility should be as close as possible to those upon whom it is exercised" (p. 171).

From the time that economics in the United States left its amateur phase (1870s), the key doctrinal issue that characterized it was the conflict between laissez-faire and the positive state (reform). This issue was fought collaterally with that of deduction versus induction. The reformists were led by Richard T. Ely who championed the "new," inductive, historical and ethical approach. The issues American economists confronted were in part a reflection of the German training of a sizable contingent of the first generation of social economists, many of whom studied under the exponents of the German historical school, the *Verein fur Sozialpolitic* ("Union for

Social Policy") or *Kathedersozialisten* ("Socialists of the Chair")—Roscher, Kneis, Wagner, Conrad, Hildebrand and Schmoller. These German political economists, some of them advisors to Chancellor Bismark, replaced the laissez-faire premises of English classical economics with a conception of the positive state, which was envisioned as guiding the evolution of the economy and spreading the benefits of industrialism to all classes (Furner, 1975, p. 48; Herbst, 1965; Dorfman, 1949, pp. 87–96; Hutchison, 1953, pp. 130–37, 180–86; Schwendinger and Schwendinger, 1974, pp. xvii, 86–95).

Despite their nickname (owing to their academic affiliations and liberal reformist policies), they eschewed Marxian-socialist economics, advocating instead "the piecemeal study and preparation of practical immediate measures of reform in relation to hours and conditions of work, social insurance, factory legislation, and the like" (Hutchison, 1953, p. 181). While their historical focus led them to study economic institutions, classes, and economic progress, they rejected utopian plans of wholesale social reorganization—socialist or liberal—and "regarded as premature historical generalizations, and the attempt to promulgate laws of historical development" (Hutchison, 1953, p. 182).

These social technicians who were organically involved with the state, were sometimes affiliated with, occasionally fought, and sometimes overlapped the "Austrian School." This school (Bohm-Bawerk, von Wieser, Menger) developed and shared the marginal utility perspective of Jevons (and later Marshall) in England, Walras in France and J.B. Clark in the United States (Breitan and Ransom, 1971, pp. 1–30; Furner, 1975, pp. 185–89; Dorfman, 1949, pp. 83–87, 190–205; Hutchison, 1953, pp. 32–49, 138–79, 197–215, 251–62). Essentially, the approach was a consumer- or price-based economics beginning with demand or the "final degree of utility" rather than the cost of production as in the case of the classical school. The value of commodities is seen as established by the individual buyer's cost-benefit psychology. Hence:

value was determined by the amount that a consumer would pay for the final unit of a particular good or service that he would add to his supply before switching his consumption to some other item. In any series of increments there was constantly diminishing return. Thus the value (or wages) of labor was determined by the final increment added to the total output of an enterprise such as a farm or factory by the last laborer who could profitably be added to the force. That was what an employer would pay for the last laborer he would hire, and what the last laborer would take before he would offer his services somewhere else. The value (rent or interest) of capital was determined by the amount added to industry by the last unit of capital (land, tools, machines, building) that could be profitably invested in a given industry. That was the amount of interest or rent that an entrepreneur would pay on the last land or other instrument of production he acquired, and the lowest amount that the capitalist would accept before he switched his investment to some other enterprise (Furner, 1975, p. 187).

According to this scheme of consumer sovereignty, cost is ultimately determined by consumer evaluations or the rationally calculating human who balances marginal expenditures and marginal utilities. Commodity production serves consumption. Since an increase in production (serving demand) of a given commodity involves a withdrawal of resources from the production of another commodity, an increase in cost (or decreased consumer benefit utility) results for the alternate commodity. Appropriate or "ideal" production for the economy is achieved when neither an expansion or contraction of output can increase welfare. Such a situation presupposes the equilibrium of perfect competition (Breit and Ransom, 1971, pp. 10–11). With respect to labor, if "the market were perfectly free, both capital and labor would constantly follow the highest possible return," and each would get what it *deserved* (Furner, 1975, p. 187). Economic, moral and social equilibrium are thereby attained: equilibrium in the system obtains when there is perfect competition and when supply and demand are equal.

The doctrine of perfect competition is the required corrollary of marginal utility theory via consumer sovereignty: only under perfect competition is there a guarantee that the entrepreneur will submit to the will of the consumer; perfect competition assures ideal output, that is, marginal benefit is always equated with marginal cost. The rationality of the consumer will always induce him/her to measure the use value of the commodity by its price and producers will adjust their prices to demand. "With consumers and producers so motivated, the conditions of competition create an equilibrium where marginal costs always equal marginal benefits" (Breit and Ransom, 1971, p. 12).

However, supply and demand is no more than the static average of the real condition of ups and downs which concretely and historically demonstrate the non-equilibrium of society (Marx, 1847,1933, p.24). The neoclassicists relocated the economic root, production, shall we say, displaced it behind the illusion of household economy (Furner, 1975, p. 188). Cooley's criticism was correct: disturbances of demand—insufficient demand—are automatically interpreted as the fault of human (consumer) nature; all the evils of the economic system fall to the consumer (1918 in 1930, pp. 252–253). By sleight of hand, productivity as judged on the market was the assumed righteous basis of distribution, hence the standard of economic justice. Thus, this class phenomenon becomes obscured as such. The result was a patchwork affair (Cooley, 1918 in 1930, pp. 255–256). However, Cooley never ventured toward the surplus value theory of production as the foundation of this class *exploitation*. It was seen by Cooley as the upper class's unfair ability to appropriate consumer goods, whom he expected to democratize by appeal to the successor to chivalric service. He simply posited a counter morality to the immorality posited by economists. We must, however, grant Cooley the wisdom of intuition at having at least smelled a rat. But his analysis was limited by his retention of the centrality of demand.

Thus, economists became micro-oriented and pleasantly shifted the focus of economics away from distasteful matters of class exploitation and class struggle. Its macro-side was corporate-liberal social policy. The reified, or conventional way of characterizing this diversion is to say that the advent of neo-classical economics marks the true emergence of economics *sui generis* from political economy. And it did. The reification of the economy by the economists became as abstract and segmental as the economy itself! It became the paradigm of the contempory "free world" economy.

Neo-classical economics became the paradigm of first and last resort for reformists such as Ely, Commons, Adams, and other moderate-to-left centrists who had ventured out into the sticky wickets of social criticism and debate, then took their lumps, if not in the name of, then as leading actors in academic freedom cases. With the exception of Beamis, virtually all of the reformers (see Furner, 1975, passim) who had been fired from their academic positions surrendered their pro-labor, anti-capitalist, quasi-socialist, even bi-metalist views for the sake of academic respectability. For the sake of job retrieval and professional acceptance as civic and government economic advisors and consultants, it was not difficult to swallow one's pride. Amidst a career crisis, job rescue accomodated an alternation in ideology as insurance for biography! As a result, most of the ex-dissidents fled to the more respectable realm of applied marginal utility economics. After all, they had always assumed that the very notion of fair share was sacrosanct no matter where one stood. The fair share approach was the moral supernumerary of perfect competition. Since the chief attribute of economic morality was centered on demand and distribution, the solution of social problems could never entail more than vociferous dickering, at most, about who was getting their rightful due. The very relations of production stood undisturbed. In their graduate training, the reformists seldom went outside the standard texts for their economic methods. Why not, as respectability demanded, make this higgling *formal* and deal with labor conflict, for example, as an anomalous disturbance? Or for that matter, why not simply forget the whole thing, as many did. As for socialism, what the reformists had entertained was a vague political animus. Few read and fewer understood Marx. Socialism was a fuzzy term which was freely used as invective and with little precision by those who nodded to it always as an outside doctrine. As with the Socialists of the Chair, socialism was translated into social engineering and the framing of legislation.

Formalization is implicit in reform, if only logically, as a position which maintains fealty to the premises of the system, which is to say, the prevailing mode of production. Thus, reformists who had strayed were simply guilty of incivility, not treason, though its spectre was frequently raised by the "nattering nabobs" of reaction. Finally, marginalism served reform because it "eventually provided the programming capability and much of the inspiration for welfare economics and supplied the means to welfare capitalism" (Furner, 1975, p. 189).

In sum, because the reformers acted from the same premises that sustained marginal utility economics, there was little discomfort in oscillating between the two, especially when faced with career upset. Marginal utility theory, like statistics and methods in sociology, became the unquestioned method of economic analysis. As the reformers abandoned "their pretensions to a role as arbiters of public policy, they established a more limited goal: recognition as experts with extraordinary technical competence in a highly specialized but restricted sphere" (Furner, 1975, p. 8, also pp. 105–107, 124, 141–146, 160–162, 203–204, 257–259, 273).

INSTITUTIONAL ECONOMICS

Institutional economics is actually a congeries of approaches attempting to tunnel back to society in a manner similar to but less sociologically than Cooley. As in Cooley's case, the institutionalists refracted the socioeconomic totality. The term promises a societal touchstone for economics. However, besides Cooley, Veblen is the only one of the institutionalists who took more than an abstract premise or two from sociology. Yet, it would be arbitrary to separate institutional economics from the reformists among whom it should—with qualifications—be included. For example, John Commons' institutional economics is largely a euphemism for ameliorative legislative reform and social engineering (Dorfman, 1949, pp. 276–299; Gruchy, 1972, p. 72, pp. 34–42; Weinstein, 1968, pp. 172–213). J.M. Clark, son of J.B., later sought a synthesis of marginal utility theory with the pragmatic view of motivation and value of Dewey and Cooley (Gruchy, 1972, pp. 52–55), viz market prices are good measures of social as well as personal utility.

Veblen represents the most interesting case because he earned his reputation for radicalism by his personal lifestyle and the individuality of his thinking, but not for his political activity or crusading. A marginal man, he attained the status of grand academic maverick. It is not so much the sociological content of Veblen that interests me here as it is the way it figures in his economics, which places him the closest to Cooley.

The irrevocable split he perceived between "pecuniary and industrial employments" induced him to idealize production anachronistically as craftsmanship. As with Cooley, production becomes a phantom by segregation.

Veblen saw technology as the institution responsible for material progress. The "industrial arts; their transmission and evolution are the clockwork of society. Businessmen appropriated this process through control of funds. In their mad competition to outdo each other crises, depressions and industrial disorganization result" (1904, 1932).

The marginal utility theorists are seen as classicists in modern dress (1909 in 1947, pp. 231–251). They have taken for granted the institutional roots of industrial and pecuniary employments. Their static approach had "nothing to say to the growth of business usages and expedients or to the concomitant changes in the principles of conduct which govern the pecuniary relations of men, which condition and are conditioned by these altered relations of business life or which bring them to pass" (p. 233). As Cooley noticed a few years later, "pecuniary accountancy . . . extends . . . to many facts which properly have no pecuniary bearing and no pecuniary magnitude, as for example, works of art, science, scholarship and religion" (pp. 245–246, 247).

As for the unskilled operative, it was not always the case that the craftsman was denuded of his pecuniary function: specialization has now *exempted* him from it (n.d. in 1945, pp. 315–316). In Veblen's distinction between industrial and pecuniary employments, production gets lost in the shuffle. On the one hand, "the pecuniary employments do not properly fall under . . . Production." On the other, the laborer was only mechanically engaged in the production of goods and was "primarily occupied with the phenomena of material serviceability [use value], rather than those of exchange value" (n.d. in 1945, pp. 293–295). So, both labor and production become refractory to Veblen's theory. Thus he was to conceive the movement that promised restoration of totality by praxis, socialism, as the "most insidious and most alarming malady, as well as the most perplexing and unprecedented that threatens the modern social and political structure. . ." (p. 319).

The institutionalists, including Cooley, produced a foreshortened analysis of economy and society. All took the market as the locus of the economy for granted. Society was inserted into the process as the source of pecuniary values. The relations of production are evaporated into the halcyon spirit of the past as an idealized form of feudal artisanship. Because the modern unskilled laborer seemed such a sorry sight, how could *he* be the foundation of the economy? The spawn of the cities, rough, improvident, occasionally militantly violent—this was no economic bedrock for the nation. It was only a source of social problems.

Thus, institutionalism in its early forms did little to clarify capitalism itself as *the* social problem. Its pretension about unifying economy and society produced its opposite, fragmentation and obfuscation, by dividing that totality into pecuniary and industrial sectors (Veblen), or by merely extending utilitarianism by the metaphor of social institutions (Clark,

Commons, Anderson and Cooley). Nor can we seek solace in *neo*-institutionalists such as Ayers and Dalton. They simply carry the obfuscations further. Their premises are descendants of the culturalists' mystiques. Let us examine these successor mythologizations before turning to the illusions of sociologism.

C.E. Ayers developed an "instrumental economics" based upon the philosophies and economic theories of John Dewey and Thorstein Veblen. Using Dewey's pragmatic problem-solving epitomizing of human nature and intelligence and his conclusions concerning the inhibitory effects of institutionally derived habits on the creative potential of technology, Ayers conveniently adapts Veblen's distinction between pecuniary and industrial employments to the fashioning of modern welfare economics. However, this aim is more distant. Ayers' immediate goal is to construct a conception of value.

Culture is employed in a negative sense, as an inhibitor of economic development and social justice; it is restrictive, backward looking and preserves existing class arrangements (Ayers, 1944, p. 112). Like Cooley, he decries *homo economicus,* the isolated calculating individual actor of classical and neo-classical economics. Quoting Cooley ("A separate individual is a phenomenon unknown to experience"), he asserts that human beings are culturally conditioned and that all human wants are social or cultural in origin. But unlike Cooley, he does not extend this value derivation into a monistic conception of economy and society, but fashions a dualistic one along the lines of Veblen's. The economy is really two economies, the "price economy" and the "industrial economy."

The price economy is an institutional complex (as with Cooley), based on "ceremonial behavior." It is both a reflection and conditioner of human wants. As such, the kind of values established in the market place (price values) are quantified versions of the judgements people made prior to their price transactions (1944, pp. 226–227). These are pseudo-values because they are grounded in myth and traditional belief.

"Real values," as opposed to price or consumer superfluities, are technological, that is, rooted in science and the technological process. The technological criterion is a pragmatic one, grounded in turn in the life process: "For every individual and for the community the criterion of value is the continuation of the life process—keeping the machines running" (1944, p. 230).

Economic abundance, equality, freedom, security and excellence are technological values because they are socially life-sustaining. Yet they are compromised by the price system, that is, the market system of finance capitalism reflecting institutional arrangements, traditional mores, money-power and so on. Ayers does not wish to wipe away the price system, but to make prices reflect "real," technological values. He wishes to obliterate the lag between technology and the institutional superstructure, and he proposes to rectify the disequilibrium between the price and industrial systems by economic planning.

Economic planning manifests the technological process (1952, p. 190). Ayers promotes a "reasonable society" shorn of privilege, class distinctions, inequality and injustice. Government regulation is invoked as a way-station toward this end. Far from rejecting the neo-classical principle of the marginal productivity of distribution, he finds it useful as an explanation of the behaviors of producers and consumers. He only wishes to correct the model's institutionally-based excesses so that the distribution of income will truly, and scientifically, reflect the input of the community into the society. This can be accomplished by taxation and transferred income from the rich to the poor. Thus:

> We favor the Welfare State because it tends to give the whole community what the whole community creates, and in doing so gives the community the greatest possible encouragement to create more, so that all of us taken together will be better off than anybody has ever been before (quoted in Gruchy, 1972, p. 119).

Ayers has substituted vulgar materialism and pragmatism for the earlier Progressive idealism that typified Cooley and some of the institutionalists. In one sense, this can be interpreted as a "step forward" for what it does is rationalize and legitimate both human and economic engineering. Welfare economics is therefore crystallized. In taking the neo-classicists to task for their outmoded utilitarian psychology, not only has the modicum of economic choice via consumerism been wrested from the individual, it has vested economic stewardship in the State. Technology is conjured to juxtapose "scientific" values such as abundance, equality, freedom, security, and excellence. By fiat, science and government will mollify the classes. Meanwhile, the masses are left to play tag between business and the State. The logical conclusion, it seems, is to go fight city hall when the going gets rough!

Let us pass to the more redoubtable George Dalton (1961). Whereas Ayers represents an obfuscation by fragmentation, Dalton makes the more subtle error of relativism—more subtle, that is, for contemporary sociologists and anthropologists, because cultural relativism is by now a widely shared assumption in these fields. Although Dalton does not use the term, it undergirds his thinking on the inapplicability of contemporary market economics (neo-classicism) to primitive societies. However, this relativism conceals the economistic assumptions that prevent Dalton from coming to grips with the central issues pertaining to primitive economics. My contention is that Dalton's relativism is a two-edged sword: while he abstains from applying neo-classicism to primitive societies, he also abstains from questioning its relevance to his own. While this presumably leaves him free to search for the "substantive" economies of pre-capitalist societies, there is an inadvertent bootlegging of capitalist and imperialist notions into his model of them.

It is Dalton's belief that the historical advent of Western market economies allowed classical, and later, neo-classical economists to devise economism "to focus on economy as separate from society, to regard economy as having such an inner consistency and autonomy as to allow the derivation of distinct economic laws which seemed to operate independently of social institutions" (1969, p. 3). These laws constitute the principles of market exchange, wherein *"Everyone derives his livelihood from selling something on the market"* [Dalton's italics] (p. 1). The utilitarian (neo-classical) embroidery on this theme inserted "the condition of 'natural scarcity' . . . [which] necessitated marginal choice if maximum fulfillment of material wants was to be attained" (p. 4). This addition of the rationally calculating consumer in the service of material wants presumed an atomistic society or an aggregate of self-interested individuals. The *homo economicus* of the 19th century "was not a myth, but a succinct expression of . . . institutional fact" (p. 2). This *economistic* model constitutes one of the two different meanings of the concept "economic." It is only applicable to "market-organized industrialism" (p. 7).

The other definition, which Dalton states is the appropriate one for primitive societies, is "substantivism." This refers to the provision of material goods which satisfy biological and social wants, and is the sole meaning applicable to primitive society. It is "perfectly general in applicability," even to industrial societies, "because all communities, regardless of differences in natural environment, production techniques, or cultural traits, are composed of human beings whose bio-social existence depends upon the sustained provision of material items" (pp. 6-7). Moreover, this implies some type of systematic economic structure. Yet, we are told that substantivism "is not analytically informative in the investigation of specific economies because of the diversity of technical and institutional structure which exists" (p. 6).

In industrial societies the substantive economic facts are that material wants satisfaction is augmented by a special set of economizing practices. Needing material goods to survive, the denizens of industrialism enter the market. The institutional complex which integrates the system "is the supply-demand-price complex" (p. 8). Thus the neo-classical model serves capitalism as both its economistic and substantive descriptor.

Dalton seems to have overlooked the fact that the foundation of his two models is the same—the material wants hypothesis, which at bottom is a consumership model based on functionalism. This automatically shunts the productive process. All societies "regardless of differences in production techniques are composed of human beings whose bio-social existence depends upon the sustained *provision* of material items" [italics mine] (1961, p. 6). There is no mention of human *producers* satisfying their needs; *needs are provided for.* This point of view is central to demand (read neo-classical) economics! From within this perspective, society must become an abstraction; this model of economism has been trans-substantiated into sociologism. Significantly, b\th economism and substantivism are repeatedly described as "integrative patterns" (pp. 8–9). But this is only the beginning. At the point where Dalton begins his extended discussion of substantive economies, he calls the curtain on economism with the following quote from W.E. Moore:

> A considerable body of evidence runs contrary to the notions that human wants are unlimited [the utilitarian motive force behind demand], that financial incentives will transfer labor from nonindustrial to industrial pursuits and thus that the potential worker may be viewed as welcoming release from traditional restraints. Some of this evidence can be interpreted in terms of "rational conduct," but not in terms of economic maximization. The *potential worker* in underdeveloped areas is typically required to give up traditional forms of organization and reciprocal obligations that have combined to offer him security—both material and affective. *The kinship system in any nonindustrial society is likely to provide a major barrier to individual mobility, because it is a social security system,* because it is the focus of positive values and advantages, and because extended kin obligations are likely to reduce the effective appeal of individual rewards [italics mine] (p. 8).

There is scarcely any need to analyze this material, so clearly does it speak for itself. The people of underdeveloped countries are "potential workers"; their kinship systems are "barriers to individual mobility," since they serve as systems of "social security." Doubtless the idiom of imperialism has impressed itself on sociological analysis.

Dalton's approach is bound up with the idiom of functionalism. He exhorts us to follow Malinowski at the end of his essay ("not Ricardo"), "in order to choose the transformations to industrialization which entail only the unavoidable social costs" (p. 21). Malinowski founds society on basic needs and tells us how the "commissariat" provides primitive nourishment.

I take functionalism to be a corollary of neo-classicism because here, too, production serves demand; but in this case the word is not used—"society" is. And society has become an abstraction in the service of concrete need. This is how the Marxist anthropologist Godelier (1977, p. 38) can call functionalism "a case of 'reductionist' materialism" without wincing. The population demands, the technology provides. Society is refracted into pure connective tissue—*integration.* As a result, Dalton equivocates on the matter of structure.

Earlier we referred to Dalton's contradictory position regarding the general applicability of substantivism. The menu of primitive economies are a veritable "non-Euclidian universe." It is admitted that "the poverty of our terminology is a source of built-in ambiguity" (p. 20). It seems the inner logics of these economies must remain ephemeral, their derivations "reciprocity" and "redistribution" notwithstanding.

The deficiencies of Dalton's approach are traceable to his taking-for-granted the neo-classical premises of contemporary capitalism. He seems to say, "I will let the matter rest on economism so far as capitalism is concerned, and will proceed with my analysis of primitive economies as though I shan't use neo-classical economism to analyze them." Putting it another way, facing one's own ethnocentrism is the categorical imperative of cultural relativism. If one hasn't bothered to examine one's background assumptions, the claim to suspend economic judgement in studying other cultures must ring hollow. Borrowing the functionalist idiom, I suggest that this maneuver is a moral sinkhole. The mere verbal magic of reciting the relativist litany helps integrate morality and exploitation. "When the primitives are no longer satisfied with their traditional restraints, we shall provide." Indeed, is this not a "technique of neutralization"? What end does it serve? To put one's morality in one's back pocket, like the theater-of-the-absurd playwright Albert Jarry's Pere Ubu ("I can then consult it when I need it"). Sociology is now free to do missionary service for underdevelopment, whose memory is now in pawn.

The institutionalists bring capitalism to the end of its logical tether. Embedded in the social reality of the welfare state, institutionalism, in its consummated form, hangs on its own petard (firecracker, bomb). If I may digress, further nonchalance on the part of symbolic interactionists will prove equally disastrous. After all, the symbolic universe, integration, "ether," and phlogiston are not so far apart! It can well turn out that interaction and integration are part of the same ocean. As we shall see below, even interaction in our mundane world can be construed as a dance of phantasms in the topsy-turvy world of commodities. For the functionalists, alienation is an ailment of morale; for the Marxist, it is society *sui generis.*

Marxism versus Institutionalism

Like it or not, the productive relations of any society *are* fundamental *social relations.* Life and work are a totality. We symbolic interactionists might add play to this list, for isn't this part of our socialization? Alas, we grow old and the division of labor asserts itself, and so work and play must part. Historians (Gutman, 1976, pp. 3–78) tell us that the early industrial proletariat in England and the United States often fought their labor struggles, in the period 1843–1893, without the benefit of unions, over the rights to observe traditional artisan-worker holidays and leisure pasttimes on and off the job. Our institutions are embedded in our productive relations. In primitive societies, production is not for a market, but that does not mean that there is no production. It means that production is for *use;* for the use designated by the object's maker.

In primitive societies untouched by capitalism (a rarity nowadays) there are no commodities, hence no commodity exchange. There may be an exchange of *use values* alone (i.e., of intrinsically useful natural resources, food or wrought objects); there may be ritual exchange; or, in our own society, "swapping" (Stack, 1974, pp. 32–44). However, as soon as production-for-trade begins, either as a result of colonialism, tribute, slavery or trade with other primitives, exchange value enters the picture and objects become commodities alienated from those who produced them by their *labor.* At that very point, the social relations of a society are being transformed:

> A commodity appears, at first sight, a very trivial thing, and easily understood. Its analysis shows that it is, in reality, a very queer thing, abounding in metaphysical subtleties and theological niceties. So far as it is a value in use, there is nothing mysterious about it, whether we consider it from the point of view that by its properties it is capable of satisfying human wants, or from the point of view that those properties are the product of human labor. . . . But so soon as it steps forth as a commodity, it is changed into something transcendent. It not only stands with its feet on the ground, but, in relation to all other commodities, it stands on its head, and evolves out of its wooden brain grotesque ideas, far more wonderful than 'table-turning' ever was.
>
> . . . In all states of society, the labour-time that it costs to produce the means of subsistence must necessarily be an object of interest to mankind, though not of equal interest in different stages of development. And lastly, from the moment that men in any way work for one another their labor assumes a social form (Marx, 1906, pp. 81–82).

In any society where exchange value begins to predominate, the exploitation of labor comes to characterize social relations. As Marx says (1906, p. 260), in a society where use value predominates, *surplus labor* (unpaid labor, the source of profit) will be limited "by a set of wants which may be greater or less, and . . . here no boundless thirst for surplus labor arises from the nature of the production itself."

Neither use nor exchange values constitute the root value of objects rendered into commodities: "In my opinion, the 'value' of a commodity is neither its use-value or its exchange value" (Marx quoted in Godelier, 1977, p. 155). Exchange value is always a value in quotation marks, because it is created only *in appearance* in the exchange process, that is, in the marketplace. It appears to be born in circulation and assume its value in that process. Its true origin is in the *labor process.* The institutionalists largely take exchange value at its face value. Even the vulgar materialists among them take this for granted—for them, "technology" holds magical functional autonomy as though it were alive. This is how society, too, is abstracted into a ventriloquist's dummy speaking the voice of exchange. Society becomes reified; human relations become more fragmented and simplified; the relations between objects, more complex, as if working by their own laws. This may seem close to Dalton's point, and indeed it is.

There is something wrong, but we do not know what it is, so we turn again to the presence or absence of markets, not the productive process, for the answer.

It is to the credit of Marx that he discovered the fundamental mystification of capitalism, and it is to him that we owe its intellectual demystification. Without this demystification, one will never be able to examine the protocols of society in anything but the most naive way, because theory as well as everyday consciousness is elementally rooted in productive relations and in the social formations of capitalism. It must, therefore, mirror the inverted social reality reflected in it:

> It is not man who deceives himself, it is reality deceiving him, by inevitably appearing in a concealed form [commodity exchange as congealed labor] and presenting itself upside-down in the spontaneous awareness of people living in the market world. This mode of appearing upside-down thus constitutes the necessary starting point made spontaneously by people when dealing with economic relations. These representations and the ideological developments consolidating them, created as much by the 'vulgar' economists as other ideologues, constitute in people's awareness *a more or less coherent domain of spontaneous phantasms and illusory beliefs referring to the social reality in which they happen to live.* Now we can understand why such illusory representations and notions cannot become the starting point for a scientific analysis of social reality [author's italics] (Godelier, 1977, p. 159).

Marx's analysis of commodities (1906, pp. 41–96) takes us through the looking-glass of a world turned upside down. He shows us how the labor expended in production—coagulated, crystallized labor time—is expressed in the disguise of exchange value, money and circulation. Money, expressing as a universal equivalent the *relative* value of commodities (including the labor commodity), gives them a false appearance. Market relations originate in the relations of production. The institutionalists could not crack that code.

The worker sells his/her labor power as a commodity measurable as the labor time socially necessary for the production of a commodity, including the production of the material means required for labor's training, maintenance, and reproduction. But the worker creates something more than equivalence of the wage. It is unpaid work, the origin of surplus value.

Wages make unpaid labor appear to be paid labor and profit appear like the product of capital. Hence, "each social class appears to draw its rightful revenue from the production and circulation of goods" (Godelier, 1977, p. 162). Here is the source of another mistake made by the institutionalists— the "rightful" share of the national product. *Ceteris paribus,* the laboring class and the bourgeoisie *already* receive their rightful share. No amount of "transfer," "welfare," or reform will ever change this in its essentials. Only revolution will. This is fundamental to Marxism. Restoring labor's fair share means eliminating surplus value. Even understanding this is insufficient, for it will not do away with the spontaneous consciousness people have for capitalist social relations. It modifies the role and effects of this consciousness on their behavior, but it does not abolish it, so ubiquitous and strong is the power of commodity fetishism, which makes the relations between people assume "the fantastic form of a relation between things." The world is indeed topsy-turvy, for things assume the quality of social relations:

> It is an *enchanted, perverted,* topsy-turvy world in which Monsieur le Capital and Madame la Terre do their ghost-walking as social characters and at the same time directly as mere things (Marx, quoted in Godelier, 1977, p. 163).

In the humanist tradition, Marx has underscored the folly of the race.

Having thus pointed to the roots of "the social problem," let us turn to the myth of sociologism; in a word, good versus bad totality.

The Ruins of Totality

We can say that the guiding concern of the institutionalists and reform economists was to make economics a total social science. Looking back it is easy to pick apart their work, but from today's perspective, is it possible to build an approach that doesn't suffer from the defects we have discussed? For example, do the attempts by social scientists following the lead of Marcel Mauss (1967) represent any truer grasp of socio-economic totality? Mauss's work certainly seems to offer a more mature sociological grasp of totality. Speaking of archaic gift exchange, he tells us:

> In these total social phenomena ... all kinds of institutions find simultaneous expression: religions, legal, moral, and economic. In addition, the phenomena have their aesthetic aspect and they reveal morphological types (p. 1).

Thus, in archaic gift exchange Mauss claims to have found the deep structure of economy and society. In the manner of Durkheim, he sought to adduce the elementary forms of the economic life. The obligation to give, receive and repay constitute a reenactment of society, and, consequently, its reproduction. Morality reproduces society, society reproduces morality. The giveness and oughtness of society mutually establish each other. In line with this, the task of the sociologist is to reconstitute the whole, "to observe and understand the whole group in its total behavior" (p. 79).

Yet defects soon appear. Mauss tells us that the link between archaic society and civilization, i.e., those societies immediately preceding ours (the Romans, classical Hindus, Germanic societies), contain the seeds of capitalism: "We believe we can demonstrate that our own economic institutions have arisen from ones of the type just reviewed" (p. 46). These midway stages transmit the form which achieves consummation in the present. Yet Mauss laments that the form is "not to be found in the cold reasoning of the business man, banker or capitalist." For a long time man was something different "and it is not so long now since he became a machine—a calculating machine" (pp. 73, 74). Totality's consummation in civilization awaits the payment of a *moral* debt: "It appears that the whole field of industrial and commercial law is in conflict with morality" (p. 64). *Totality stops at the door of pecuniary valuation yet lies at its foundation.* Labor awaits its fair share. Totality is yet to be realized, but the state and social legislation will deliver us from our debts. We are witnessing the return to group morality in the "dawn and realization of professional morality and public law" (pp. 65–67). Now satisfied, Mauss proclaims the proper study of reconstituted man to be " 'civility,' or 'civics' " (p. 81). The civil state redeems capitalism; totality's lein on society is perforce removed.

Sociologism can only reify the economy by culture. Cooley, who followed Emerson's minting of the emblem of property, made this exact mistake. Mauss, positing the elementary form of the economic life, wishes to call exchange something else, something less calculating. Capitalism remains stuck fast in its self-created immediacy, and the phenomena of reification are severed from their economic base. History is no more than a receptacle for the absolute.

Despite its plausibility, Mauss's structuralist reembedment of the economy in society contains serious pitfalls in the form of idealist and culturalist obfuscations. These (a) turn us away from the root of the economic institutions, that is, the historically grounded productive relations of society, and therefore from the problems of class exploitation and class struggle nationally and internationally; and (b) perpetuate the sociological short-circuiting typified by symbolic interactionism's astructural bias. Maurice Godelier's assessment of Mauss's successor, Lévi Strauss, aptly sums up my point:

> Lévi-Strauss confines himself to extracting from concrete facts a "formal system" . . . a system which he then studies in its internal logic and compares with other types, either similar or different, but belonging even in their differences, to the same group of transformations.
>
> In this connection, it could be said that Lévi-Strauss . . . never studies real societies and does not try to account for their diversity or internal complexity.

Is socioeconomic totality, then, a worthwhile aspiration for sociology? Yes, if it is not shrouded in idealism, and if critical inquiry is not confined to devising alternatives to the dehumanizing effects of a given system of production while leaving its basic premises otherwise intact. Otherwise, "there remains nothing but the weapon of moralizing," and we are left with the same contradictions we intend to counteract (Mészáros, pp. 60, 126).

In the *Poverty of Philosophy* (1913, p. 120) Marx posits socio-economic totality: "The relations of production form a whole." This is not merely the early Marx discussing the alienation of the subject from its essence. It is the "mature Marx," indeed, who prepares the way for a social science of the whole. The Preface to the *Critique of Political Economy* builds the scaffolding of this study (1859, 1970, pp. 20–21):

In the social production of their existence, men inevitably enter into definite relations, which are independent of their will, namely relations of production appropriate to a given stage in the development of their material forces of production. The totality of these relations of production constitutes the economic structure of society, the real foundation, on which arises a legal and political superstructure and to which *correspond* definite forms of social consciousness. The mode of production of material life *conditions* the general process of social, political and intellectual life. It is not the consciousness of men that determines their social existence, but *their social existence that* determines their consciousness [italics mine].

Now it may be objected that this statement does, in fact, make a case for economic determinism. Perhaps, but in the broad sense of a socioeconomic whole, and not by reductionism. Note that the social relations of production are *appropriate* to a definite stage of the development of the material forces of production. Social consciousness and the superstructure *correspond* to the economic foundation, and the mode of production *conditions* social, political, and intellectual life. The economic structure prescribes limits but does not presuppose causation. "Rather, it suggests a determination of the limits of variation of the superstructure by the economic structure and says nothing about the *causation* or *origin* of superstructural forms or the ideologies which correspond to them" (Hirst, 1972, p. 36).

Before the superstructure can be understood, however, the historically specific economic foundation must be made explicit or else we fall into the structuralist fallacy of *ex nihilo* totality, morality, and "values." As Marx put it:

The most modern and the most ancient epochs will have [certain] determinations in common. Production without them is inconceivable; but although the most highly developed languages have laws and characteristics in common with the least developed ones, it is precisely the divergence from these general and common features which determines their development. It is necessary to differentiate those determinations which apply to production in general in order not to forget the essential dissimilarites in view of the unity that follows from the very fact that the subject, mankind, and the object, nature, are the same (1902–03, 1976, p. 11).

Put another way, to reduce totality to a single principle, to reduce all the elements that make up the concrete life of historical epochs to one principle of unity, is merely to enunciate that epoch's most abstract ideology. Thus, totality, properly speaking, is a "decentered structure in dominance" (Althusser, 1969, pp. 103, 204–218, 256), or, in Marx's terms, differences within a single unity. Hypostasizing the whole as such, making it eternally recur and favoring it above its facts obviates those facts and mythologizes the whole (see Kosík, 1976, pp. 17–32).

Cooley and the reformist and institutional economists saw the contradictions of capitalism in moral terms, having left the concrete foundations of its structure unexamined: the market remained the market; pecuniary institutions merely translated institutional and human nature values; production was anachronistically idealized as craftsmanship, then banished; the appropriation of labor was seen as improvidence or an exemption from pecuniary concerns; government regulation and service will set capitalism/competition right; exploitation is a departure from competition; exchanges are unequal and must be made right; labor and capital are due their right share of the national product; "reasonable capitalism." All this is the flotsam and jetsam of misapplied totality, of the study of society come to inform economics. False totality is ethereal totality. It is not enough to reject economic formalism for the sake of substantivism. The latter is not mistaken so much as it is inadequate. Once the proponents of reembedment (Polanyi, 1968) leave the realm of pre-capitalist economics, they continue to accept the premises of market economics thought to underlie capitalism, attaching only moral disclaimers to its dehumanization (Godelier, 1977, p. 21).

This brings me to the specific matter of symbolic interactionism and economics, especially Marxian economics, which I consider to be the only non-reified way of understanding the capitalist system. It is the most powerful "outside" perspective available, because it gives us the opportunity to understand the unity and meaning of our capitalist society. Since symbolic interactionists are taking this matter seriously, they cannot run away from its implications; which is to say that while it would be cumbersome and redundant to transform SI into political economy, this shouldn't stop symbolic interactionists from transforming their perspective *as* a social psychology, or from pursuing questions pertaining to political economy. It is no longer possible to continue work in this perspective as though political economy did not exist. We are at the point of necessary choice: politics has re-entered social science. It was always there but now is overt, i.e., has become a proper scientific question. The juxtaposition of scale has forced the matter upon us, my contention being that the framing of macro-questions presupposes conservation or rejection of the premises underlying capitalism.

Symbolic interactionism is a social psychology in the best sense of that expression—in its pragmatic presupposition of intellectual praxis; in its unity of theory and practice; and in its understanding that people produce their world. Important, too, is the fact that symbolic interactionism is *open* methodologically; at times it is *radically* methodological in its opposition, by doctrine and practice, to the positivist hegemony that rules sociology.[15] The kind of sociology abstracted empiricism has fostered is akin to the micro-economic or neo-classical paradigm in economics, namely, manipulative and technocratic sociology.

However, there is a danger that without attention given to the implications of political economy for sociological theory, the methodological integrity of symbolic interaction will suffer. This is regrettable, for already on the Marxist side (Sève, 1975, pp. 46–52) a serious line of thought in psychology is being promoted which is moving in the direction of symbolic interaction. To wit, Marxist psychology is on its way to conceiving its proper data "the social relations between acts (relations *supported* by mental relations between behavior patterns but which differ from them fundamentally) . . ." (Sève, 1975, pp. 47–48). This study of the expanded reproduction of activity is "In a sense the whole *humanist* (I use the term deliberately) aim of a real science of personality of biography . . ." (p. 48). I am suggesting that much of this apparatus has been ready-made by our perspective. However, it has not been *grounded* explicitly in a viable political economy. It is, *de facto,* grounded in a shaky phantom of one. "Grounded theory" can mean nothing more than abstracted empiricism if it is not rooted in something more than a fetishized conception of the mundane world, the world of Monsieur le Capital and Madame la Terre. To qualify the opening statement of the last paragraph, symbolic interaction may not be a perspective *on* political economy, but it is, like it or not, a perspective *of* political economy. The choice is ours as to *which,* shall we say, *whose* political economy it will be.[16]

FOOTNOTES

*The author would like to express his thanks to Peter Storkerson and Ira Gerstein for their valuable advice, comments and "debriefing" as this paper was being written.

1. Let us put this matter of money as a generalizable medium to rest. Even within the restricted orbit of economics, Marx tells us that:

> Money emerges thus as a mere *medium of exchange* of commodities, not however as a medium of exchange in general, but a medium of exchange adapted to the process of circulation, i.e., a *medium of circulation* [Marx's italics] (1859, 1970, pp. 95–96).

2. Peter M. Hall (1972) has developed a symbolic interactionist approach to politics which confessedly seeks to "determine the balance between Marxian and Parsonian positions," a view predicated on the notion of society as a negotiated order ("Joint action . . . now seen as a complex process involving all the manifestations of bargaining and negotiating—strategy, tact, threat, and exchange"). Not only does it distort Marxism, despite its closing quote of Lukács on totality, but, more important, it perfectly illustrates, again, a view based on the fetishism of exchange and exchange categories. Such a view does not and cannot question the underlying basis of society; it can only reproduce it.

3. In this connection I find Gouldner's remarks (1970, p. 88) somewhat misplaced. In his concern "with the historical development of sociology's shared infrastructures, its intellectual and social organization, 'its' division of intellectual labor . . . and the historical periods or stages in which these structures crystallized or changed," he has ignored most of sociology's history as an academic discipline in the United States. His apotheosis of the "historically sensitive critic" and the sociological representative man embedded in the "classics," who does not "treasure the coin of the realm, but values other, rather different kinds of fulfillments," bespeaks this tendency to put oneself "in the company of greatness" so typical of American sociology. Cooley believed in his membership in a "society of men speaking across the ages," and, therefore, his ability to speak *sub specie aeternitatis* (under the aspect of eternity). This interesting phenomenon is probably an aspect of the American tradition of the orator-scholar,

most notably represented by Emerson and then self-consciously taken up by Cooley in sociology (Jacobs, 1976, pp. 155–189, 216–253; Bode, 1956). Furner (1975, pp. 292–293) attributes this veneration of great thinkers on the part of the first generation of sociologists, to their insecurity at having "never really found a center," that is, in being left with the detritus of the other social sciences. Thus, for all Gouldner's efforts, one may wonder, for example, what the unanticipated consequences of having devoted more than two hundred pages criticizing Parsons will be on the sociological tradition.

4. *Intellectually* this was the case. *Existentially* his sociology is a product of transplanted Yankee puritans who formed the elite of a small midwestern university town (Jacobs, 1976, pp. 344–347, 155–158, 180–181, 221–235, 257–260, 264–265, 270–271, 279).

5. These principles are stated in Emerson's three well-known essays, "Nature," "The American Scholar," and "An Address" delivered before the senior class at the Harvard Divinity School. Property is clearly emblematic of the oversoul, as attested to by the following excerpt from his essay, "Nominalist and Realist" (1929, p. 307):

Money, which represents the prose of life, and which is hardly spoken of in parlors without an apology, is, in its effects and laws, as beautiful as roses. Property keeps the accounts of the world, and is always moral. The property will be found where the labor, the wisdom and the virtue have been in nations, in classes and . . . the individual also. How wise the world appears, when the laws and usages of nations are largely detailed, and the completeness of the municipal system is considered! Nothing is left out. If you go into the markets and the custom houses, the insurers' and notaries' offices, the offices of sealers of weights and measures, of inspection of provisions,—it will appear as if one man had made it all.

No doubt much may be made of this Emersonian transmission of the Puritan ethic. Lest we think that this fits the *Weberian* theme, we should be reminded that Marx (1853, 1970, pp. 55–57) was the first to employ Benjamin Franklin's writing (in this case not his maxims but his text on money, *A Modest Inquiry. . .*) as representative of the maturation of capitalism. Weber's essay, first published in 1904–05, significantly, quotes the maxims on money. Marx, commenting on Franklin's text, notes that Franklin "for the first time deliberately and clearly (so clearly as to be almost trite) reduces exchange value to labour-time" (p. 55). However, Franklin is faulted for only viewing money as a technical device introduced into exchange from outside.

6. In his journal this motif appears as "man verifying," the "superior man," "antique man," "efficient man," the "sensitive man," the "man of character," and, of course, Emerson's "man thinking." For the way in which this theme articulates with Cooley's belletristic orientation, see Jacobs (1976, pp. 155–202). Emerson's use of the notion makes the line between philosophy and religion hazy. Thus, in his essay, "Uses of Great Men" (1929, p. 327), representative men are sanctified: "Our religion is the love and cherishing of these patrons." Following suit, Cooley tells us: "Common men study the law externally; try to imitate successful actions . . . Great men feel the law in themselves; do not imitate but *are;* and know that things must follow them" (Journal, Vol. 6, p. 23).

7. Emerson literally uses the theme of the division of labor-as-alienation in connection with the apotheosis of the representative scholar. He laments the fragmentation of the One Man "present to all particular men only partially through one faculty; . . . you must take the whole society to find the whole man" (1929, p. 25). Thus, the division of labor has alienated "this original unit, this fountain of power, [which] has been so . . . minutely subdivided and peddled out, that it is spilled into drops, and cannot be gathered." Hence, society is like a dismembered body (p. 25). Similarly, Emerson's fellow transcendentalist and friend Thoreau, exclaims (Bode (ed.), 1964, p. 301): "Where is this division of labor to end? And what object does it finally serve? Thus, Emerson:

Man is not a farmer, or a professor, or an engineer, but he is all. Man is priest, and scholar, and statesman, and producer, and soldier. In the divided or social state those functions are parceled out to individuals, each of who aims to do this stint of the joint work, whilst each other performs his. The fable [that the gods divided Man into men] implies that the individual, to possess himself, must sometime return from his own labor to embrace all the other laborers (1929, p. 25).

Man may be all, but in his divided state he "is thus metamorphized into a thing, into many things" (p. 26). Hence:

> The planter, who is Man sent out into the field to gather food, is seldom cheered by an idea of the true dignity of his ministry. He sees his bushel and his cart, and nothing beyond, and sinks into the farmer, instead of Man on the farm. The tradesman scarcely ever gives an ideal worth to his work, but is ridden by the routine of his craft, and the soul is subject to dollars. The priest becomes a form; the attorney a statute-book; the mechanic a machine; the sailor a rope of the ship (p. 26).

8. What is of interest here is the trajectory from Hegel's idealist dialectic of the self in the *Phenomenology of Mind* (1807, 1970, pp. 218-240) as encapsulated in the relationship of lordship and bondage, to Emerson's view. Both are idealist, but already in Emerson the dialectic is lost: the oversoul no longer struggles for itself, no longer realizes itself through struggle. In Cooley, as I have shown (1976, pp. 297-345), struggle reenters vis-a-vis his inner work on vanity, the subtext of the looking glass self. As such, Cooley's architectonics are quite innovative because his concept is the resultant of struggle with his own emotions as much as an intellectual product. Mead's is an intellectual process only, and his concept stresses more the cognitive aspects of the self, although it retains a dialectical emphasis. The looking glass self, with the greater emphasis on the "I," in addition to the "me" and its derivation, thus also is a concept of identity. This has been attenuated, however, in subsequent treatments (Foote, 1951; Shibutani, 1961, pp. 213-246, 324, 505, 565, 592; Strauss, 1959) which largely follow the more cognitive approach of Mead. For an analysis of the implications of this kind of forgetting for social science and society, see Jacoby's *Social Amnesia* (1975). There is much fertile material vis-a-vis its contextual grounding—in Cooley's amplification of William James's *appropriative* self viz the identification of "I and mine" (1922 rev. ed., pp. 168-196).

9. The economist B.M. Anderson (1911), developed a theory of social value stemming largely from Cooley's organic approach (pp. 72-89) in *Human Nature and the Social Order* and *Social Organization*. Anderson took courses from Giddings at Columbia but criticized his emphasis on an *identity of content* for a definition of social mind (p. 82). He preferred Cooley's conception because it included "the dissenters." Anderson may be considered an institutional economist who derived his approach directly from sociology. As such, he dropped the eighteenth century notion of the economic man and made "goods reflect the habits of men" (Dorfman, 1949, p. 418). As I mention below, this was more a revision than a revolution.

10. In separating mental barter from exchange, Cooley assumes he is making elbow room for the separation of the social, but actually it is the *mental* social or the individual as homonucleus of the social. In either case, the result is a congruence with the motivation theory of the marginal utility economists he criticizes, that is, their theory of demand.

11. Cooley first uses this expression (to "get together") in discussing in *Personal Competition* (1899 in 1930, pp. 176-177) the relationship between competition and the mitigating factor of association or industrial combination; "getting together" produced a tendency away from the desirable state of "symmetry" or organizational growth balanced by regulation. He felt that there was no great danger posed by this modern organizing tendency and that, if properly regulated, organization and competition could peacefully coexist. Cooley's discussion of social class in *Social Organization* (1909, pp. 209-309) represents the liberal extension of his ideas on

competition. So, for example, he tells us: "All solid betterment of the workers must be based on and get its nourishment from the existing system of production, which must only gradually be changed, however defective it may be" (p. 277). Strangely enough, production gets its due here.

12. Cooley's ideal is not reprehensible as such. It is commendable to value the productive development of people above commodities, but the hypothetical matrix of activity it is anchored in—the medieval past and the managerial capitalist present and future—render this ideal chimerical.

13. This is not idiosyncratic to Cooley. See Tiryakian's essay (1975) which characterizes Mead and Parsons as exemplars of the American Puritan ethos linking voluntarism and service: "let me boldly assert that I consider George Herbert Mead the most important native-born contributor to micro-sociology and Talcott Parsons the most important contributor to macrosociology . . . both express, at a high level of abstraction, central sociocultural realities and value orientations of American society; . . . finally, . . . the existential foundations of Parson's approach to social reality are as consonant with, if not as rooted in, Puritan culture, as Mead's" (pp. 26, 28). This essay is a program for the integration of complementary micro- and macrosociological perspectives to aid in the task of clarifying "this core ambiguity as to the meaning of the collective enterprise" (p. 31). Thus, "I do mean to imply that the Puritan cultural system is of the utmost importance for the sociological analysis of American modernization and modernity" (p. 30). I leave the reader to form his own conclusion.

14. Furner (1975, pp. 124–142) provides an excellent account of Adams' career. From 1881 to 1887 he divided his time teaching alternate semesters at Cornell and Michigan. Beginning in 1885, President Angell and the trustees at Michigan began to have doubts concerning his sympathies for the Knights of Labor and his views on private property, inheritance and socialism. In 1886, following termination of his contract by the Michigan trustees, rather than publicize this abridgement of his academic freedom, "he did his best to suppress the story," reversed his commitment to 'ethical economics,' and "disavowed all that he had written in support of the Knights." With the admission that his prolabor remarks in 1886 had been premature, "Angell, of course, was delighted. He immediately recommended Adams for a permanent professorship, and the repentant economist was appointed without objection" (Furner, 1975, pp. 137, 138, 139). All through this, however, Adams never relinquished his abiding support of the doctrine of competition. He became a staunch supporter of public regulation of industry and in 1888, Cooley's father, the eminent jurist, Thomas McIntyre Cooley appointed him chief statistician of the Interstate Commerce Commission, which the elder Cooley chaired (p. 140). Prior to his graduate work, Cooley, at his father's urging, worked at the Commission and later for the Census Bureau, 1889–1890 (Jandy, 1942, pp. 29–30).

15. Two studies that bear witness to this contention are Stack's (1974) ethnography of the political economy of a black community and Farberman's qualitative analysis of the criminogenic structure of the automobile industry (1975). The spare 129 page text of Stack's book dramatically reconstructs (Cooley, 1930, pp. 283–339) the linkages between poverty (the black industrial labor reserve army) and the social networks of use value circulation; the absence of the bourgeois nuclear family, and the structuring of domestic kinship and its components of multiple parenting (collective responsibility); extended bilaterality; male-female ties and the authentic extensions of kinship (contra Liebow!) through non-marital *affinal* ties. A striking aspect of this study is that there are no Marxist texts in its bibliography. Its accuracy is a product of assiduous fieldwork and uninterrupted fealty to the economic bottom line.

Similarly, my earlier point about compatibility versus convertability is illustrated by Farberman's research trajectory as he studied the structural sources of consumer fraud in a vertical analysis of the automobile industry. The author writes that his original intention was to follow up an hypothesis concerning consumer bargaining tactics, but during his participant observation, serendipitously shifted his orientation when he discovered the "short sale" transaction on the used car lot: "I began deliberately to observe the 'write-ups' " (1975, p. 441).

At that point a new research problem emerged, namely, the analysis of how capitalist accumulation induces illegal activity from the new car dealer through the used car lot. There occurs a transformation in which the emphasis is shifted from symbolic interactionist conceptualizing to political economy. Here the unity and meaning of the capitalist system of production and exchange is translated into situational imperatives. Yet there is no sacrificing of symbolic interactionism. In a footnote (p. 442), we are told that "the new problem actually links to the old problem so that my understanding of the dynamics of customer/salesman interaction is enlarged by my understanding of the systemic dynamics of 'short sales.' "

16. It was not until this paper was completed that I learned of a doctoral dissertation (1978) by David Schulter, Brandeis University, which has come to conclusions similar to my own. Schulter's *Morality from Consumption: the Theory of Consumer Market Conduct in American Sociological Thought, 1894-1901,* attempts to show how the first generation of sociologists in the U.S. attempted to derive a theory of social value out of the language and syntax of the economists via a theory of social consumption. This stressed the themes of personal character development and the quality of life. Schulter's excellent treatment provides much fruitful material for sociologists willing to examine the origins of their traditions beyond the mythological ones usually stressed in "theory" courses.

BIBLIOGRAPHY

Althusser, Louis, *For Marx,* London: Allen Lane, the Penguin Press., 1969.

Anderson, B.M., *Social Value: A Study in Economic Theory Critical and Constructive,* Boston: Houghton Mifflin, 1911.

Ayers, C.E., *The Theory of Economic Progress,* Chapel Hill: the University of North Carolina Press, 1944.

———— , *The Industrial Economy, Its Technological Basis and Institutional Destiny,* Boston: Houghton Mifflin, 1952.

Bernard, L.L. and Jessie Bernard, *Origins of American Sociology: The Social Science Movement in the United States,* New York: Thomas Y. Crowell, 1943, 1963.

Blumer, Herbert, *Symbolic Interaction: Perspective and Method,* Englewood Cliffs, NJ: Prentice-Hall, 1969.

———— , "A Note on Symbolic Interaction," *American Sociological Review* 38 (December 1973): 797-798.

———— , "Comments," *Sociological Inquiry* 45 (1975a):59-62.

———— , "Reply to Parson's Comments," *Sociological Inquiry* 45 (1975b):68.

Bode, Carl, *The American Lyceum,* New York: Oxford, 1956.

———— , (ed.) *Selected Journals of Henry David Thoreau,* New York: Signet Press, 1967.

Bowen, Ralph H., *German Theories of the Corporative State.* New York: McGraw-Hill, 1947.

Breit, William and Roger L. Ransom, *The Academic Scribblers: Economics in Collision,* New York: Holt, Rinehart and Winston, 1971.

Clark, John M., "Recent Developments in Economics," In *Recent Developments in the Social Sciences,* Charles A. Ellwood et al. (eds.), 1927.

Cohen, Marshall J., "Self and Society: Charles Horton Cooley and the Idea of the Social Self in American Thought," Unpublished doctoral dissertation, Department of History, Harvard University, 1967.

Cooley, Charles Horton, MSS, Michigan Historical Collections, University of Michigan.

———— , *Human Nature and the Social Order,* New York: Charles Scribner's Sons, 1902 (rev. 1922; reprinted 1956, with *Social Organization,* in *The Two Major Works of Charles H. Cooley,* Glencoe, IL: Free Press; also reprinted 1964, New York: Schocken.

————— , *Social Organization*, New York: Charles Scribner's Sons, 1909; reprinted 1956 with *Human Nature and the Social Order* in *The Two Major Works of Charles H. Cooley*, Glencoe, IL: Free Press; also reprinted 1962, New York: Schocken.

————— , *Social Process*, New York: Charles Scribner's Sons, 1918; reprinted 1966, Carbondale, IL: Southern Illinois University Press.

————— , *Sociological Theory and Social Research: Being Selected Papers of Charles Horton Cooley*, New York: Henry Holt, 1930.

————— , "Personal Competition," *Economic Studies* (American Economic Association) IV (April 1899); reprinted in *Charles Horton Cooley, Sociological Theory and Social Research*, New York: Henry Holt, 1930.

————— , "Political Economy and Social Process," *Journal of Political Economy* XXV (April 1918): 366–374; reprinted in *Charles Horton Cooley, Sociological Theory and Social Research*, New York: Henry Holt, 1930.

————— , "The Theory of Transportation," *Publications of the American Economic Association* IX (May 1894); reprinted in *Charles Horton Cooley, Sociological Theory and Social Research*, New York: Henry Holt, 1930.

Dalton, George, "Economic Theory and Primitive Society," *American Anthropologist* 63 (1961): 1–25.

Dobb, Maurice, "Introduction" to *Karl Marx, A Contribution to the Critique of Political Economy*, New York: International, 1970.

Dorfman, Joseph, *The Economic Mind in American Civilization, Volume Three: 1865–1918*, New York: Augustus M. Kelley, 1949.

Durkheim, Emile, *The Division of Labor in Society*, New York: Free Press, 1933.

Emerson, Ralph Waldo, *The Complete Writings of Ralph Waldo Emerson*, 2 volumes, New York: William H. Wise, 1929.

Farberman, Harvey A., "A Criminogenic Market Structure: The Automobile Industry," *Sociological Quarterly* 16 (Autumn 1975): 438–457.

Fine, Bob, "Labelling Theory: An Investigation into the Sociological Critique of Deviance," *Economy and Society* 6 (May 1977): 166–193.

Furner, Mary O., *Advocacy and Objectivity: A Crisis in the Professionalization of American Social Science, 1865–1905*, Lexington: University of Kentucky Press, 1975.

Gerstl, Joel and Glenn Jacobs (eds.), *Professions for the People: The Politics of Skill*, Cambridge: Schenkman, 1976.

Godelier, Maurice, *Perspectives in Marxist Anthropology*, London: Cambridge, 1977.

————— , *Rationality and Irrationality in Economics*, New York: Monthly Review, 1972.

Gouldner, Alvin W., *The Coming Crisis of Western Sociology*, New York: Basic Books, 1970.

Gruchy, Allan G., *Contemporary Economic Thought: The Contribution of Neo-Institutional Economics*, New York: Macmillan, 1972.

Gutman, Herbert G., *Work, Culture and Society in Industrializing America*, New York: Random House, 1976.

Hall, Peter M., "A Symbolic Interactionist Analysis of Politics," *Sociological Inquiry* 42 (1972): 35–75.

Hegel, G.W.F., *The Phenomenology of Mind*, London: George Allen and Unwin, 1807, 1970.

Herbst, Jurgen, *The German Historical School in American Scholarship: A Study in the Transfer of Culture*, Port Washington, New York: Kennikat, 1965.

Hirst, Paul Q., "Marx and Engels on Law, Crime and Morality," *Economy and Society* 1 (February 1972): 28–56.

Horton, John, "Combatting Empiricism: Toward a Practical Understanding of Marxist Methodology," *Insurgent Sociologist* III (Fall 1972): 24–34.

Huber, Joan, "Symbolic Interaction as a Pragmatic Perspective: The Bias of Emergent Theory," *American Sociological Review* 38 (April 1973): 274–284.

Hutchison, T.W., *A Review of Economic Doctrines 1870–1929*, London: Oxford, 1953.

Jacoby, Russell, *Social Amnesia*, Boston: Beacon, 1975.

Jacobs, Glenn, *Cooley's Journals: A Study of Sociological Theory Building*, Unpublished doctoral dissertation, Department of Sociology, Temple University, 1976.

Jandy, Edward C., *Charles Horton Cooley: His Life and His Social Theory*, New York: Dryden, 1942; reprinted 1969, New York: Octagon.

Johnson, Harry M., "The Generalized Media in Parson's Theory," *Sociology and Social Research* 57 (January 1973): 208–221.

Karpf, Fay Berger, *American Social Psychology: Its Origins, Development, and European Background*, New York: McGraw-Hill, 1932.

Kolko, Gabriel, *The Triumph of Conservativism*, Chicago: Quadrangle, 1963.

Kosík, Karel, *Dialectics of the Concrete: A Study on Problems of Man and World*, Dortrecht, Holland: D. Reidel, 1976.

Lichtman, Richard, "Symbolic Interactionism and Social Reality: Some Marxist Queries," *Berkeley Journal of Sociology* 15 (1970): 74–94.

Lukács, Georg, *History and Class Consciousness: Studies in Marxist Dialectics*, Cambridge: MIT, 1971.

Manis, Jerome G. and Bernard N. Meltzer (eds), *Symbolic Interaction: A Reader in Social Psychology* (2nd ed.), Boston: Allyn Bacon, 1972.

Martindale, Don, *The Nature and Types of Sociological Theory*, Boston: Houghton Mifflin, 1960.

Marx, Karl, *Wage-Labor and Capital*, New York: International, 1847, 1933.

————— , "Introduction" to *A Contribution to the Critique of Political Economy*, Peking: Foreign Languages Press, 1857–1858, 1976.

————— , "Preface" to *A Contribution to the Critique of Political Economy*, Peking: Foreign Languages Press, 1859, 1976.

————— , *Value, Price and Profit*, New York: International, 1865, 1935.

————— , *Capital*, Volume 1, translated from the Third German edition by Samuel Moore and Edward Aveling, New York: Modern Library, 1906.

————— , *The Poverty of Philosophy*, Chicago: Charles H. Kerr, 1913.

Marx, Karl and Friederich Engels, *The German Ideology*, New York: International, 1947.

Mauss, Marcel, *The Gift*, New York: W. W. Norton, 1967.

Mead, George Herbert, *Movements of Thought in the Nineteenth Century*, Chicago: University of Chicago Press, 1936.

Mészáros, Istvan, *Marx's Theory of Alienation*, New York: Harper and Row, 1970.

Mills, C. Wright, *Sociology and Pragmatism*, New York: Oxford, 1966.

Morrione, Thomas J., "Symbolic Interactionism and Social Action Theory," *Sociology and Social Research* 59 (April 1975): 201–218.

Morris, Monica B., " 'Creative Sociology': Conservative or Revolutionary?" *American Sociologist* 10 (August 1975): 168–178.

Oberschall, Anthony, "The Institutionalization of American Sociology," in Anthony Oberschall (ed.), *The Establishment of Empirical Sociology*, New York: Harper and Row, 1972.

Parsons, Talcott, "Comments," *Sociological Inquiry* 45 (1975): 62–65.

————— , *Politics and Social Structure*, New York: Free Press, 1969.

Polanyi, Karl, *Primitive, Archaic, and Modern Economics: Essays of Karl Polanyi*, edited by George Dalton, Boston: Beacon, 1968.

Reynolds, Janice M. and Larry T. Reynolds, "Interactionism, Complicity and the Astructural Bias," *Catalyst* #7 (1973): 76–85.

Ropers, Richard, "Mead, Marx and Social Psychology," *Catalyst* #7 (Winter 1973): 42–61.

Rose, Arnold, (ed.), *Human Behavior and Social Processes*, Boston: Houghton Mifflin, 1962.

Sahlins, Marshall, *Stone Age Economics*, Chicago: Aldine, 1972.

Schafer, Robert B., "Exchange and Symbolic Interaction: A Further Analysis of Convergence," *Pacific Sociological Review* 17 (October 1974): 417–434.

Schwendinger, Herman and Julia Schwendinger, *The Sociologists of the Chair: A Radical Analysis of the Formative Years of North American Sociology, 1883–1922*, New York: Basic Books, 1974.

Sève, Lucien, *Marxism and the Theory of Human Personality*, London: Lawrence and Wishart, 1975.

Shibutani, Tamotsu, *Society and Personality: An Interactionist Approach to Social Psychology*, Englewood Cliffs: Prentice-Hall, 1961.

Singelmann, Peter, "Exchange as Symbolic Interaction: Convergences Between Two Theoretical Perspectives," *American Sociological Review* 37 (August 1972): 414–424.

Smith, Dusk Lee, "Sociology and the Rise of Corporate Capitalism," *Science and Society* 29 (1965): 401–418.

Stack, Carol B., *All Our Kin*, New York: Harper and Row, 1974.

Stone, Gregory, et al. "On Methodology and Craftsmanship in the Criticism of Sociological Perspectives," *American Sociological Review* 39 (June 1974): 456–463.

Stone, Gregory P. and Harvey A. Farberman (eds.), *Social Psychology Through Symbolic Interaction*, Waltham, Massachusetts: Xerox, 1970.

Strauss, Anselm L., *Mirrors and Masks: The Search for Identity*, Glencoe, IL: Free Press, 1959.

Sutherland, David Earl, "Who Now Reads European Sociology? Reflections on the Relationship Between European and American Sociology," Paper presented to the American Sociological Association annual meeting, 1977.

Tiryakian, Edward A., "Neither Marx Nor Durkheim . . . Perhaps Weber," *American Journal of Sociology* 81 (1975): 1–33.

Turner, Jonathan, "Action and Interaction Theory: Some Questions of Theory-Building Strategy— A Reply," *Sociological Inquiry* 45 (1975): 65–68.

————. "Parsons as a Symbolic Interactionist: A Comparison of Action and Interaction Theory," *Sociological Inquiry* 44 (1974) 283–294.

Turner, Terence S., "Parsons' Concept of 'Generalized Media of Social Interaction' and Its Relevance for Social Anthropology," *Sociological Inquiry* 38 (Spring 1968): 121–134.

Veblen, Thorstein, "Industrial and Pecuniary Employments," *Publications of the American Economic Association* II, 1919, reprinted in *Veblen on Marx, Race, Science and Economics*, New York: Capricorn, 1909, pp. 279–323.

————, "The Limitations of Marginal Utility," *Journal of Political Economy* XVII (November 1909); reprinted in *Veblen on Marx, Race, Science and Economics*, New York: Capricorn, 1947, pp. 231–251.

————, *The Theory of Business Enterprise*, New York: Mentor, 1904, 1932.

Weinstein, James, *The Corporate Ideal in the Liberal State: 1900–1918*, Boston: Beacon, 1968.

METHODOLOGICAL AND
THEORETICAL INNOVATIONS

NOTES ON SELF GENESIS:
FROM ME TO WE TO I*

Norbert Wiley, UNIVERSITY OF ILLINOIS

The I-me problem in social psychology has not received the attention it deserves. The issue has been in the air since Kant's *Critique of Pure Reason,* which distinguishes between the transcendental and empirical egos, but it was not sharpened until William James and George Herbert Mead translated Kant's insight into the Hegelian I-me dialectic. Since Mead's treatment (especially 1913 and 1934), the issue has been neglected except for some critical discussions which, in effect, buried the issue as a false one (Kolb, 1944; Lewis, 1976). In addition, Herbert Blumer's "symbolic interaction," which is in many ways a robust development of Mead, replaced the I-me formulation with the looser notions of "communication with oneself, "self-interaction," and "interpretation" (Blumer, 1969:5).

But while this issue has become faded and blurred in the pragmatic tradition, other philosophies have shown a renewed interest in the structure of the self, though not always in the same terminology as the James-Mead-Blumer pragmatists. In particular, the phenomenologists, Edmund Husserl

Studies in Symbolic Interaction—Volume 2, 1979, pages 87–105
Copyright © 1979 by JAI Press Inc.
ISBN: 0–89232–105–9

and Alfred Schutz, have given close attention to the ego or I. And the closely related existentialists, especially Sartre (1957[1937]; 1956[1943]), have followed up on and modified Husserl.

The result is that an important issue, which declined in pragmatism and reappeared in a somewhat different form in phenomenology, is now in need of reappraisal, redefinition and synthesis. These notes will give some suggestions as to how this might be done. I will use the pragmatists, especially Mead, for examining the structure of the self, and the phenomenologists, especially Schutz, for looking at self genesis. My argument will be that the growing structure of the infant's self expands from a me to a we to an I, and that it is through Schutz's intimate "we" relationship that we first encounter the I of another and become one ourselves.

The main point of the paper, then, is that following a period in which the human baby is primarily a me, the genesis of the I is accomplished through the we experience. Before making that point, however, I will discuss the various ways the self is experienced, particularly as these experiences relate to the I-me distinction. Once the main argument—the Schutz-Mead connection—has been made, I will apply the framework to several specific, applied problems to show its general usefulness and explanatory value.

EXPERIENCES OF THE SELF

The I-me duality of the self is experienced in a number of indirect as well as direct ways. All languages appear to distinguish between an I and a me, either by using distinct pronouns for these two aspects of the self, or by using the same pronoun in syntactically different ways. Linguistically, the I is the self as subject, and the me the self as object. These distinctions are grammatical, and they do not necessarily imply that the structure of the self is psychologically experienced in this way, but they do create categories highly congruent to this self experience and they make it difficult to think otherwise.

A second indirect way the self is experienced, particularly in the European world, is in the atmosphere of law, morality, and civil liberties, all of which assume a dignified, responsible subject. Rights and wrongs are attributed to an "actor" or underlying person, not just to a physical organism or James Joycean stream of consciousness. Free will often accompanies these ideas of legal and moral culpability, but the idea of freedom should be distinguished from that of the subject or I, who performs the action and gives it human character.

A third indirect way the self is encountered is through the logical structure of experience. Kant argued that the "transcendental ego," which is the ancestor of the pragmatists's I, was a necessary "regulatory idea" which had to underlie all experience (Kant 1950[1787]:394–395). Somewhat differently, William James, in one formulation, regarded the I as an historically constructed tool, developing long after the me, though nevertheless early in the history of the species (Bayley, 1977, shows the constructionist side of James's self theory, but see Dewey, 1940, for the James of the "vanishing subject"). Both Kant and James regarded contemporary humans as logically unable to think of experience without an underlying I.

Beyond these indirect experiences of self, there are several more direct forms of encounter. Mead regarded the I as the underlying agent or actor, performing its activities in the immediate or knife-edge present. In contrast, the me was the aggregate of everything else: the body, the internalized morality and culture, the contents of memory, the self-labels and traits of a lifetime, and the entire storehouse of the personal past. As the grammar of the terms indicates, the me was the object as it has accumulated and grown until the now; the I was the subject, moving as fast as time, and giving identity to activity and the overall self. Using Mead's categories, we can experience our own selves or I's in at least two ways.

We can pay attention to and concentrate on the I through an act of reflexivity or bending-back-on-oneself, although this encounter is always somewhat distanced and indirect. Like a shadow that is seen but never quite grasped, the I of reflexivity half escapes our glance. It is as though the bending back process took a little time, and the I always escaped into that time. To stand back and look at the leading edge of the self is to simultaneously approach and retreat from the self. We approach in the act of making the I our cognitive target, but we retreat by virtue of the bending or "flexing" process of reflexive cognition. For there is always another I out there doing the reflecting. The object of reflection is inescapably seen as an object, as in the past, and as me, even though we might almost catch it in that transformative moment whereby the I slips into the me. The I that is experienced, then, in the reflexive glance of introspection is at best a brand new (layer of) me, no longer quite the I of an instant ago.

Of course, this presumes Mead's definition of the I as the actor in the knife-edge present. If we vary the categories and use William James's notion of the "specious" present (James, 1950[1890], Vol. I:608–610)—the range or band of psychological time that we experience as the "felt" present—the I is redefined as the actor in a *chunk* of time, enclosing elements of the past, present, and future in the unity of the felt now. To shift from objective to subjective time in this manner complicates things considerably, in a direction that Mead does not seem to have envisioned. I will ignore it for now, merely pointing out that the elusiveness of the I, never quite grasped as it tries to look at itself, is tied to the time categories Mead used in setting up his problem. Within that frame, the I obviously can never be directly experienced.

A second way we can experience or almost experience the Meadian I, though Mead would not accept this argument, is through a kind of peripheral vision whereby we are constantly aware of the I, though never at the center of awareness. This out-of-focus or peripheral vision, which Sartre calls a "non-thetic consciousness" (1957[1937]:46, 88) is different from outright reflection, for it does not include the distancing feature of reflexivity (Thevenaz, 1962;71–72). The contact is direct, and the I is experienced as subject rather than object. But there is another kind of distancing in the side or peripheral character of this vision. This implicit awareness of the I is always present during consciousness, no matter how much we get absorbed in the task or taken with the goal. But it is never at the core of presence. To take it from periphery to core would require an act of reflexivity, and this would be to exchange one kind of distance for another.

The distance from subject to object and core to periphery, then, constitutes the built-in limits in our ability to experience our selves. The former distance is easily conceived in Mead's pragmatic theory of reflexive cognition, though he (1913:144) and James (1950[1890], Vol. I:304) expressly denied the latter or peripheral experience of the I. One must use the cognitive categories of the phenomenologists, as I am doing, to explain this mode of self presence.

Thus far I have discussed the dual self as it shapes the institutions of language, law, morality, and logic, and as it is directly, or almost directly, encountered in reflexivity and peripheral vision. All of these brushes with the self include some degree of remoteness and distance. The only direct, immediate experience we have of the self is not with our own, but with someone else's. This was the insight of Alfred Schutz (1967[1932]:102–197; 1962:172–175), although Husserl presents a considerably more foggy version of this insight (1970[1931], fifth meditation) at about the same time Schutz first published the idea.

Schutz observes that we experience the core self or I of others in the knife-edge present and as immediately available to us. This direct, linear encounter contrasts with the indirect way we experience our own I. For Schutz, the apprehension of the other's I or ego is in the temporal present, and that of one's own self always in the past. When this encounter with the other is mutual and two-way, we have the "we" experience, in which two persons share the temporal now. In these we experiences, there is neither the distance of reflexivity nor that of peripheral vision. We do not reflect or bend back to see the other. That person's ego is immediately before us. The move is not nonlinear, as with one's own self, but linear. And the duality is not subject to object or I to me, but subject to subject or I to I. Schutz calls the we relationship one of "shared time consciousness," and in his quaint phrase, it allows the two persons to "grow old together." Of course, Schutz is not saying we experience the *content* of the other's consciousness in the same way as it appears to the other person, but that our temporal organization and flow is shared for the duration of the experience.

What Schutz is referring to is the intimate, face-to-face relationship of close communication. The lovers look into each other's eyes in the direct apprehension of selves. The friends share comforts and revelations in the immediate present. Even enemies and those in hate-filled argument experience each other's depths on the surface. The we relationship is the most privileged access to the human self.

Schutz's major emphasis is on the temporal simultaneity of the two streams of consciousness, and he is somewhat unclear about the dimension of self disclosure. At times Schutz seems to include even distant and impersonal, face-to-face interaction among his we relationships, on the grounds that the shared present always entails a sharing or exchanging of the I (1967[1932]:167–172). At other times he seems to assume a primary-like intimacy along with a shared now. But surely these are two somewhat different notions of the we relationship. The sharing of time, and the back-and-forth interactive movement through its stream, may or may not include the further intimacy of self disclosure.

Perhaps we are back to James's distinction between the knife-edge and specious or sensible present, which runs parallel to Bergson's more general distinction between objective or clock time and subjective or lived time. Earlier I mentioned that Mead's I was confined to the knife-edge present, though one could modulate the concept of the I by relocating (or rather co-locating) it in the felt or specious present. Of course, James's specious present is a *stretching out* of the knife-edge present (to several seconds, hours, years, depending on the temporal event in question), and he did not allow for the opposite possibility of the diminution or annihilation of the present. But the felt present can undoubtedly be shrunk as well as stretched, and there are certainly people so dulled to time, to the present, and to their own existence, that, psychologically speaking, they lack an I. At any rate, we can all withhold our psychological I from face-to-face interaction if the situation is meant to be an impersonal one.

I am modifying Schutz a bit, then, and suggesting that he blurs the knife-edge and specious present in his discussion of the we relationship. If we stick with Meadian categories, the self that is encountered in Schutz's we relationship is the knife-edge or existential I of the other. But if we add the James-Bergson category of felt time, we have another dimension of self contact, which may range from rich to poor, depending on what the other is willing and able to give of self. But in either case—clock or inner time, knife-edge or felt I—Schutz is presenting a striking insight in saying we experience the other more closely than the self. When I move on to the genesis of the I in the baby, I will need psychological as well as clock time, but for now it is enough to merely add Schutz's we relationship to the list of ways and manners in which we experience the human self.

I have now specified the major ways in which we apprehend the core self, I, ego, underlying subject, or knife-edge present, these terms all being roughly synonymous for purposes of this paper. The self is encountered as it is written large in social institutions, as it is contained in our own consciousness, both reflexive and peripheral, and as it is presented by another in the we relationship.

FROM MEAD TO SCHUTZ TO MEAD

To make the me-we-I argument, which moves from Mead to Schutz to Mead, we must first look briefly at Mead's general theory of meaning. Mead was trying to invent a theory of language, communication, and meaning that was more behavioristic than that of the "mentalists" and more mentalistic than that of the behaviorists. To do this, Mead had to walk a tightrope, and there seem to be times when he fell off toward one side or the other. For Mead, meanings were neither spiritual essences nor Pavlovian reflexes, but conscious tendencies to act. These tendencies or "attitudes" were abbreviated actions, and they were thus part of conduct. But they were nevertheless the stuff of consciousness, purposely and knowingly used by actors, and not blind reflexes (also see Dewey, 1972[1896]).

There seems to be an "early" Mead versus "late" Mead here, as there is for so many other geniuses who kept on thinking throughout their lives. His early papers emphasized the function or purpose of language and thought, and his later work the social genesis and thorough-going sociality of language and thought. (For a similar comment see Natanson, 1973 [1956]:1–4.) Early Mead stresses the behavioral, problem-solving function of thought; the major enemy was the mentalist or "spectator" theory of knowledge, and the central metaphor was Darwinian biology. The later Mead emphasized the social origins of thought, tracing it to the learned but non-significant gestures of animals and to the early role-taking behavior of the human infant. This led him to define the significant communication of humans in relation to the social bond, a shift in theoretical attention which caused the problem-solving or tool-using notion of thought to fall into the background.

When Mead aims his theory at the internal conversation or thought dialogue of the I and me, he presents this relationship as isomorphic with the role-taking and interaction of two separate people, though now the people are dual aspects of one and the same self. For the later Mead, then, the enemy is no longer primarily mentalism but Watsonian behaviorism, and the central metaphor has changed from evolutionary biology to relativity physics.

The early-late issue has spawned a rivalry over "what Mead said," with a more behavioristic "Iowa School" emphasizing early Mead and a more symbolic "Blumerian" school emphasizing late Mead, though this rivalry sometimes seems to stand in the way of serious scholarship.

When Mead first introduces the I-me distinction, taking it pretty much as it stands from William James (1950[1890], Vol. I, chap. 10), he is still working on the functional theory of meaning. Viewing thought as a problem-solving, Darwinian device, he realizes that the self may be one element of the problem to be solved, and that therefore the thinker must be able to mentally manipulate this object along with whichever other objects are relevant to the problem. But how can a thing conceptualize and think about itself unless you grant it the duality of the knower and known? Mead finds this duality in James's I-me distinction, and he uses it to explain how the self can at once be a tool to be used (the me), and a tool user (the I) (1964[1903]:53–55; also Cook, 1972:173–174). Actually, Mead backed himself into a corner here, because the hard science and semi-behavioristic ambience of his early thought could not comfortably tolerate the psychological status of the I as implicit subject and agent.

When Mead returns boldly to the I-me problem, ten years later in his "The Social Self" essay (1913; 1964), he is the later Mead, whose theory of truth has travelled from correspondence theory toward the more relativistic coherence theory. This change reflects his change in interest from the instrumental function of meaning to its social genesis, both in the prehistory of the species and in the infancy of contemporary human beings.

In his "Social Self" discussion, and in the later classroom lecture transcripts of Mind, Self, and Society (1934), Mead is still unable to explain the genesis of the I, though he seems unaware of this. He tries to explain it as Kant's transcendental ego, the implicit, logical assumption that Kant found underlying all thought and experience. But transcendental egos do not engage in conversations with empirical egos (the me). Mead's I is part of consciousness, and though we cannot directly stare at it (in ourselves), we can touch its empirical shadow in the acts of reflexivity and peripheral vision. Kant's transcendental ego has no such shadows, and Mead's I cannot be explained by an appeal to Kant. The I Mead is talking about is consciously though indirectly present, and it must have gotten in there somehow, unless we want to fall back on a pre-existing mind or soul. In fact, the genesis of Mead's I cannot be explained in his system at all. I think this is why we have heard so little about it from sociologists of the Meadian persuasion, both the "early" and "late" varieties. But if we add a touch of Schutz, and look at the role of the we experience in self genesis, Mead's I-me distinction can be explained and its theoretical importance appreciated.

I mentioned earlier the hypothesis that the child goes from a me to a we to an I, doing so not necessarily in pronoun use, but in the kind of consciousness and self structure it has. Schutz himself was not concerned with the genesis of self, whether me or I, for he was trying to give a phenomenological grounding to sociology, and he evidently did not regard the process of self acquisition as necessary to that task. Besides, he had the tendency of all phenomenologists, to deal with humans as fully formed grown-ups with complete and normal conciousnesses (Strasser, 1969, especially Lecture Four, is a notable exception). Though neither Mead nor

Schutz was expressly interested in the genesis of the I, they had insights which, when combined, do give a theory of self genesis.

The argument I will make is that the early self experience of the infant is that of a me without an I. This implies that role-taking, which is Mead's term for the ability to share and exchange meanings, can go on without the sense of knife-edge subjectivity which constitutes the I. Baby's first interaction with its caretakers is primarily a non-significant "conversation of gestures," like Mead's famous dog fight. The feeding, bathing, diaper-changing, and holding of baby involves a back and forth movement of postures, vocalizations and physical movements which, while causing each other, do not entail the "two-way" meaning of the significant symbol, at least not for baby. This behavioral interchange gradually elides into primitive symbolic exchanges, as gestures and cries become body language, and children begin to respond to or understand their own gestures just as the caretaker does. Facial expressions and self-styled vocalizations probably become symbolically controlled by baby before verbal language begins, but even when speech starts, there is a fairly long period before baby can use the self-referencing pronouns.

Mead is misleading on the earliness of the I because he emphasizes its role in providing novelty, innovation, and creativity. These traits develop from the impetuousness, insistence, and moral blindness of the baby's I, as he sees it. At times, he seems to be reversing my argument saying that the baby must gradually take on a restraining me to tame the uncivilized I. But Mead is mixing two things here: the novelty and unpredictability of action, and the undisciplined character of drives and instincts. Novelty can be better explained by the uniqueness of situations, which always demand something new, much as the sentences of Chomsky's transformational grammar are virtually always new sentences (Katz, 1971:52). And the push of drives and instincts can be explained biologically, without requiring a special zone of the conscious self.

Turner's concept of "non-reflexive role-taking" (1956:322), which implies the sharing of meanings without reference to the self as subject, is useful for understanding the role-taking which preceeds the I. This kind of relatively self-distant interaction is at the opposite pole from the internal, I-me interaction of thought, which assumes the ability to be and think of one's self as an I.

At some point, children become capable of an early version of Schutz's we experience, presumably with the parents and especially with the one closest at the time (the "mothering one"). My hypothesis is that this would occur in a tactile, giggly love experience in which baby and mother would share close eye contact and a flood of mutual warmth. Mother looks, smiles, caresses, embraces, and shares time in this intimate state, all the while communicating her deepest subjectivity in a way that baby can begin to receive. Baby and mother exchange meanings, largely with body language, as they have been doing right along, but they are gradually doing this in ways that bring their persons more closely together. Baby is sensing the mother, not only in her actions and discrete meanings but in her subjectivity, her I. Presumably this comes little by little, just as the earlier conversation of gestures gradually becomes symbolic role-taking, but it gets more intense during the second year. Baby's first awareness, then, that humans are subjects, as well as activities and bodies, is in encountering and being trusted with this subjectivity in the mothering one.

At the same time, baby is having another new experience, for it begins to realize that mother is relating, not only to its activities, but to a subjectivity much like the one mother has. Mother is saying you exist, you are a person, and I love the person you are (Scheler, 1973:109–110). Baby has now experienced an I in two ways: in the mother and in what he senses the mother sees in him. Up to now baby has not regarded himself as being a subject or I, but rather an object or me, without knife-edge subjectivity. But baby has now experienced the I in another and, through that other, as attributed to himself. The first sense of I, then, is encountered neither reflexively nor peripherally, but in the mirror of the intimate other.

We now have baby standing right before a self-transformative moment. Having encountered the I twice in the we experience, baby follows this up by creating a third sense of I, for it can now attribute to itself an ego or I, just as mother is doing. Baby does this through the same role-taking process of earlier interaction, although previous role-taking concerned itself primarily with specific response patterns. Now the infant shifts from discrete meanings and behaviors to the *form or totality* of the self. Baby can now take the role of being a subject, and in doing so it is engaging in the usual social learning process by attributing to itself what others also attribute to him.

Notice, I am not saying baby "grows" an I in some physical sense, as children get new hair in puberty. This new subjectivity is not something we possess independently, in the manner of an arm or leg. It is only a new way of looking at or regarding the self. Baby can now define itself as being an ego or actor, and it can do so because others so regard him, and communicate this regard in the close we experience. In this sense, the I is more a self-fulfilling prophecy than something that develops inevitably out of the organism. It is a relational or intersubjective thing, just as the earlier, less organized set of tendencies and habits we call the me. Mead does not seem to have realized that the I, for all its distance and unpredictability, was socially learned through role-taking. This is why his I dangles and seems to come from nowhere.

I will not try to guess on the biological evolution of the I, since we cannot explain the evolution of any of the distinctly human traits, but it is easy to see how a sense of being a subject is useful for this species (Bayley, 1977). But first let me repeat, I am not saying the I is an existing or physically present *thing*. It is only a way in which we look at and define ourselves, though this is true of everything about the self. Its usefulness, then, seems largely as an organizing device, a little like the way Freud's "ego" organizes the disparate tendencies of the self, although with more emphasis on cognition and less on emotion. Certainly baby can oversee and control its various tendencies more effectively with this new symbolic tool. In particular, baby can now engage in the "internal conversation," which is at the core of reasoning and higher cognitive processes, more effectively. The duality of the internal conversation—as the I and me discuss, argue, plan, and (as we will show later) play tricks on each other—has not been studied very much, since psychology dropped introspection and turned exclusively to external behavior. But it does seem to require both an I and a me. In addition, the development of conscience and moral responsibility seem to require that baby think of himself as having agency or subject-quality, in which responsibility inheres. It is true that all the higher cognitive/moral capabilities are often explained with the I, e.g., by behaviorists, but I do not think they are explained very convincingly.

I have now sketched the Mead-Schutz-Mead argument in broad strokes. This required taking some liberties with the received interpretations of both theorists, but certainly Mead would not disapprove of a little theoretical "emergence" from his thought, and Schutz all but makes my point—that the we experience creates us.

How about the distinction between the knife-edge and specious present, and what kind of I is baby getting from these early encounters? If things work out properly, baby gets both at once: the knife-edge, existential I and the psychological I of the specious present. To become the existential I is to capture a new sense of time and to locate oneself on its moving edge. To become a psychological I goes further, for the felt I is the subject as spread across a swatch of time, engaging in complex actions. The beginnings of these actions—for example, the early parts of a lengthy sentence—are temporally suspended in the felt present until their endings pronounce the action as complete (Lashley, 1951). The knife-edge I is communicated to baby by way of shared time consciousness, and it is possible for this temporally close experience to go on without true self disclosure on the part of the mothering one. This suggests trouble, and I will develop the point in a later discussion of mental illness (although I will not blame it all on mother). If, however, mother is capable of relaxed and honest self disclosure, possessing the full range of subjectivity herself and communicating her deepest sense of herself to the infant, baby will not only know itself as an I, but accept itself as a healthy, flexible self that can expand, take blows, pour into new situations, and revel in its psychological existence.

APPLICATIONS TO SPECIFIC PROBLEMS

I have now discussed the genesis of the I and the manner in which Schutz's we experience transmits the torch of subjectivity from one generation to the next. No doubt this process continues through life, and as Erik Erikson's stages of identity suggest, the I must continue to grow in dialectical relation to the developing me (Erikson, 1963: chapter 7). Similarly, social isolation or the lack of we experience can throw the I into reverse and diminish our sense of being here. It may even be possible to arrange a society in which children, or at least a suppressed caste of them, are prevented from ever having the I of subjectivity (Althussar, 1971:170–183). In fact, the hypothesis of self genesis, as outlined in this sketch, provides a new way of looking at a variety of sociological issues.

Goffman's ritual theory of self is one such issue. Goffman takes Durkheim's insight—that we create God and his attendant cognitive-moral symbols by group ritual (1965[1915])—and applies it to the ritualization of self. This appears in the early essays on "Facework"and "Deference and Demeanor" (1967), as well as in the more recent one on "Insanity of Place" (1971:335–390). As I read Goffman, he is not only saying that we shape and influence each other's selves, but that we create them out of nothing, much as we create God, via ritual, out of nothing. Now, the I-creating ritual is different from the God-creating variety, but they are formally similar in some respects. Both God and I are among Kant's "regulatory ideas," and, while Kant did not deal with their genesis in the socialization of individuals, Durkheim and Goffman do, and their analyses are therefore complementary to that of Kant. In addition, both sets of rituals—Goffman's micro and Durkheim's macro—center on a we experience, though Durkheim's we is that of the solidary tribe and Goffman's that of the face-to-face dyad. Goffman's interaction rituals, then, are not just a process by which preexisting selves joust over what they will be, but one in which they come to be in the first place.

How about Schutz? Can Goffman's interpersonal ritual be translated into Schutz's intense we experience? Are they the same thing? They do not appear to be at first glance. Schutz stresses the sharing of time and the profound sense of being together that such sharing can give. Goffman, in contrast, stresses the rites and symbols whereby we influence each other's core selves. Schutz emphasizes the unique *mode* of ego to ego contact, whereas Goffman emphasizes the uniquely ritualized *content* of this contact.

But if we grant to Schutz's we experience not only shared time but self disclosure, it becomes an intimate ritual experience, enabling people to create and maintain the sacred center in each other. Goffman's interpersonal ritual covers a wider range of self contacts, touching more on the settled qualities of the me than on the live nerve of the I, although the ritual construction of the I is also implied and it gives his overall analysis its sense of ultimacy. In contrast, Schutz's interpersonal ritual centers on the self-as-I. Neither Schutz nor Goffman, however, speak expressly of the construction of the I. One must add Mead's role-taking idea before Schutz can be used to explain self genesis, and one must press Goffman to (what I take to be) his unstated assumption: reality is open at both ends—perimeter and center—and just as Durkheim's ritual production of God explains how we give closure to the perimeter, the ritual construction of selves is our way of giving closure to the center. In addition, Goffman's approach offers a methodological advantage over Schutz's, for it makes it easier to think of the I as a "variable," rather than a constant feature of the self.

Seen as a variable, the Mead-Schutz-Goffman I is useful for a number of psychological issues, including that of mental health. Oddly, Goffman does not fit his theories of interaction ritual and madness very closely together. *Asylums* (1961) shows the insane person in the institution after he is mad. "Insanity of Place" shows the disturbed person in a family, again after the onset of madness. But how they became mad in the first place, and what role interaction ritual plays in this transition, is not made clear.

If Goffman's interaction ritual explains how the I can be a variable, it might be said that people break down partly because of the kind of I they get from interaction. Perhaps the early we experiences, or lack of them, bear on whether people can hold themselves together under stress. And the subsequent ritualization and shaping of the self—which affects both I and me—is a continuing influence on mental health. People work out their mental health together in interaction, and the result can range from a two-winner, plus-sum game to a mixed, zero-sum game, to a two-loser, minus-sum game. The most important part of the game may well be toward the beginning, where baby is being breathed into existence by the self rituals of the early caretakers.

The variable I can also be translated into the categories of the British "object-relations" psychoanalysts (Guntrip, 1971). R.D. Laing's *Divided Self* (1970) popularizes a re-thinking of Freud that has been going on for several decades, first among Hungarian and then among British psychoanalysts (especially Malanie Klein, W.R.D. Fairbairn, John Bowlby and Donald Winnicott, who are virtually symbolic interactionists). These theorists have baby acquiring an autonomous self in the second and third year, *before* the further developments of the oedipal complex. Winnicott refers to this new self as a sense of "continuity of being" (1960:590), and though his language tends to flutter between the emotional and existential planes, the later Laing goes clearly in a Sartrean, existential direction. Laing's "false self" is the person who did not get a secure I, and who therefore withholds true self from all interaction, afraid that if the I were disclosed, others would mock it into nothingness.

Erik Erikson's eight developmental stages, particularly the initial stage of acquiring trust, might also be looked at from an I-me perspective. Erikson reasons that the infant learns to trust the environment as a result of self trust, which is, in turn, acquired from a self trusting caretaker. It is not always possible to translate Erikson's clinical language into the categories of this paper, although the following passage gets quite close.

What would we consider to be the earliest and most undifferentiated "sense of identity"? I would suggest that it arises out of the encounter of maternal person and small infant, an encounter which is one of mutual trustworthiness and mutual recognition. This, in all its infantile simplicity, is the first experience of what in later reoccurances in love and admiration can only be called a sense of "hallowed presence," the need for which remains basic in man. (1968:105)

Erikson's "mutual recognition" and "hallowed presence" is a form of Schutz's we experience, and the root of trust is in a stable sense of psychological existence. This existence is a safe sense of subjectivity which the infant need not reject, hide nor mutilate. Erikson's subsequent stages of development continue the dialectic of I and me, for the me's relation to existence changes throughout the growth cycle, and the I must therefore release its existence in new ways.

A related problem, from existential psychoanalysis, is Sartre's notion of "bad faith" or "self deception," which is his way of reconceptualizing Freud's "repression" (Sartre, 1956[1943]:47–70). Sartre argues that we repress ourselves, not by burying impulses in an unconscious zone of the personality, but by splitting consciousness into two noncommunicating sectors. We consciously choose self deception, but this choice can become irreversible if the boundary between the accepting and denying spheres of consciousness can be tightly enough sealed. Sartre does not use the language of I-me (Adler, 1949:287), and his self theory rejects this distinction (Sartre, 1957[1937]:31–60), but his theory of bad faith makes excellent sense if translated into the pragmatist's terminology. Mead has the I and the me in constant communication, so to speak, and does not allow for the possibility of blind spots. Yet we are capable of acting one way and thinking that we are acting another. This inner deceit seems to be based on the conscious withholding of reflexivity, allowing us to "lie honestly" to ourselves by closing off zones of communication between I and me (Fingarette, 1969; Morris, 1976:86–89).

To relate Sartre to the pragmatic model also suggests a rethinking of his idea that the core self is nothingness (Sartre, (1956[1943]:21–45). For Sartre, the self is a special form of non-being or nothingness, which allows the person to become anything in the acts of knowing and volition. Were the self not "nothing," it would not have this ability to become anything. But Sartre could have accomplished the same end with the essence-existence distinction, as he almost does in some places (1974[1947]). If the self, specifically the I, is conceived as pure existence (subjectivity in time), it is without any limiting essence and it can do the cognitive and choice work Sartre wants of it. His bad faith, then, is the belief that the I has an essence, that it is fixed in some limiting way, and that it lacks the cognitive and choice range Sartre sees in it. To label the I with some aspect of the me is to limit and diminish its existence. This is self deceit, for the I is refusing to reflect on its autonomy from the me, and it is rejecting the possibilities of its own existence.

Not that all of Sartre can be translated into Mead (Ames, 1956), but there is enough overlap to suggest that a rethinking of the I-me problem might fruitfully take close account of Sartre.

This discussion of various forms of psychoanalysis has shown that the dual quality of the self recurs in a variety of theoretical contexts. But rather than being an emotion-based duality, the Mead-Schutz model emphasizes the duality of being, and more specifically time, in the self. This duality, and the theory of its genesis, is undoubtedly related to basic human emotions in important ways. Perhaps the I-me theory might be combined with other personality theories to show how emotional life rests on a more basic sense of being here at all.

Shifting from social psychology to social theory, Durkheim's idea of the "modern collective conscience" can be illuminated by thinking of the I as a variable—in this case an historical variable. Durkheim's movement from mechanical to organic solidarity has two main aspects: organizational and moral (Durkheim, 1960 [1893]). Organizationally, the change is from an occupational structure, in which everyone does the same kind of (primitive) work, to one in which numerous occupations fit together into a division of labor. Morally, the progression is from a society with a complex moral structure, constructed and maintained by public rituals, to one with a more simple, person-centered morality, which he sometimes called the "cult of the individual" (Giddens, 1972:23–24). Durkheim does not develop the idea of the modern collective conscience, but it seems to be rooted in the unusually intense I of modern societies. The self of mechanical solidarity is primarily a me, for social uniformity is the basis of unity, and the collective conscience (or "generalized other," in Mead's terms; see Stone and Farberman, 1967) is centered on the ritual proscriptions of the tribal me. Modern society, with its need for wide-ranging communication throughout the division of labor, has a simpler, more permissive me, but a richer and more powerful I. Durkheim's modern I, which he found reflected in contemporary law, is brought about by a variety of social processes, which Durkheim did not pay much attention to. One such process is the increased familial intimacy of modern society, maintained by Goffman's close, interpersonal ritual. This ritual process, centering on the family, transfers the sacred from God to humanity.

A full development of Durkheim's theory of social change, then, requires a clarification of the modern collective conscience and the processes that brought it into existence. I am suggesting that this can best be initiated by examining the concept of subject or I and its relation to Goffman's interpersonal ritual. I am now stringing together Mead, Schutz, Goffman and Durkheim in a loose, theoretically tandem set of processes.

There is an interesting corroboration of Durkheim in Edward Shorter's theory of the rise of the modern European family (Shorter, 1977). Historians have been using mass, quantitative data in recent years, and they are finding that the unique thing about the modern European family is not that it has gone from "extended" to "nuclear." It has been nuclear since, roughly, the late middle ages. The change, rather, is from a nuclear family of relatively impersonal emotional relations to one in which emotion has become intense.

I read Shorter as telling the story of the "two loves:" (1) the new parent-child, especially mother-child, love, appearing in the 18th century and evidenced by the rise in breast feeding (see also Aries, 1962), and (2) the new man-woman love, coming slightly later, and evidenced by a rise in illegitimacy, bridal pregnancy, and a narrowing of the age gap between men and women. The two loves do not fit together perfectly. They started at different times, of different causes, and went through the class structure in different ways, mother-child trickling down from the top and man-woman trickling up from the bottom. But for our purposes, they can be interpreted as processes by which the collective conscience changes from public to private, from God to humanity. People are now beginning to find self-realization and the meaning of life, not in the tribe, society, or community, but in the intimate relationship and the self-possession that only intimacy brings.

Shorter's research and his theoretical interpretation has not been without criticism from other historians (Tilly, 1978), and he may well be overstating his case, but he does provide a useful picture of how the Durkheimian collective conscience may have made its "about face" from God to humanity. It also suggests how the new emotional forces in the modern family might easily not find a harmony, and even sometimes grind against each other.

The clash of the two loves runs through modern psychiatric thinking, with conjugal love at times blocking filial love, and filial love at times preventing conjugal love, but it is especially noticeable in the several field studies of families that included a schizophrenic child. These four or five field studies do have methodological weaknesses, but they all find flaws in the expression of intimacy in these families (for a review article see Mishler and Waxler, 1967). Lyman Wynne's group (Wynne, et al., 1967) used the concept of "pseudo-mutuality," and all the groups came up with some similar concept. Pseudo-mutuality refers to a situation in which people are so busy talking about, ceremonializing, and insisting on their closeness that they never get around to actually approaching each other closely. In other words the distance is fenced in and lied about by a kind of second-order or would-be intimacy. The complex emotional demands of the modern family cannot be met, but they are faked, and this faking process eventually leads to a total cognitive breakdown in those children who become schizophrenic.

Translating this into the language of the present paper, the we experience in these families is false and lacked true self disclosure, the I's that were presented and affirmed were only shadow I's, and the people doing these things had an implicit awareness of the falseness. Nevertheless, they lacked firm egos, some broke down, and the cause was a faulty genesis-of-I mechanism. These studies show the modern collective conscience at its worst, for the self must be healthy if it is to sustain the holiness Durkheim ascribes to it, and the moral stability of society therefore requires an unobstructed circular flow of emotion in the nuclear family.

CONCLUSION

I have now touched on several psychological and social issues which invite the application of Mead-Schutz self theory. I have emphasized psychiatric issues because these seem so ripe for analysis, but self theory has implications for a wide range of problems in psychology and the social sciences, including the foundations of methodology.

This paper has combined elements of pragmatism and phenomenology in a new look at self genesis. When Mead spoke of the growth of self, he usually emphasized the expanding me, as the child's role-taking skills progressed from play to the game to the internalization of the generalized other. His I is a relatively silent and taken-for-granted partner alongside the developing me. In contrast, I have focused on the dialectical relation between I and me and the way in which the I comes to be. In other words, while Mead stressed the linear expansion of the me, I am pointing to the dialectical growth of an I-me relationship.

Another question for Mead, assuming his generalized other to be the same as Durkheim's collective conscience, is what happens to the form of this "other" when the collective conscience changes from "mechanical" to "organic" (or primitive to modern). The "generalized other" in the primitive case would be the collective aggregate of others in the concrete community and what they believe. In the modern case, however, staying with Durkheim, the generalized other would be the community taken distributively or individually, for the modern collective conscience represents the generalized moral inviolability of the individual. This means that the play-game-generalized other growth pattern would mean one thing in a primitive society and quite another in a modern society.

Another central point in this paper was the use of William James's distinction between the knife-edge and specious present. In applying this distinction to the I, which is a temporally defined concept, we get two I's, for we are working with two time systems. This line of thinking gives the I more structure and variation—and we might even say "intentionality"—than it has in Mead's formulation. It is the felt I in particular which invites comparison to similar ideas in Goffman, the object-relations psychoanalysts, and Sartre. One might also ask if the two time systems might not be the key to the question of self awareness, for it would seem possible for the I of the knife-edge present to reflect on the I of the specious present though Schutz thinks not: 1962, Vol. I:172–173). A somewhat similar idea s used by Bruce Kapferer in his analysis of demon possession among the Sinhalese (Kapferer, in press).

The use of Alfred Schutz, the other major source of this paper, also equired some tinkering. I had to clarify the role of self disclosure in his we relationship and distinguish between the relatively empty we relationship of he withheld I and the rich, resonant relationship in which the I is more fully shared.

My major conclusion was that the combination of Mead and Schutz explains self genesis more deeply that either can do alone. The importance of this problem is not only intellectual but also moral, for the construction of selves is related to the destruction of selves. In their most humanistic moments, Marx, Durkheim, and Weber were all concerned with protecting selves from the crushing growth of institutions, particularly those of the modern, bureaucratic world. The more that can be known about the delicate processes by which selves are created, the better the chance of preventing their systematic destruction.

FOOTNOTES

* Revised version of a paper given at the Third Annual Symposium on Symbolic Interaction, Spring, 1977, University of Illinois, Urbana, Illinois. Thanks are due to Bennett Berger, Lewis Coser, Una Creditor, Jan Gorecki, J. David Lewis and Gregory Stone for comments on earlier drafts.

REFERENCES

Adler, Franz, "The Social Thought of Jean-Paul Sartre," *American Journal of Sociology* 55 (November 1949):284–294.

Althusser, Louis, *Lenin and Philosophy*, New York: Monthly Review Press, 1971.

Ames, Van Meter, "Mead and Sartre on Man," *The Journal of Philosophy* 53 (March 15, 1956):205–219.

Aries, Philippe, *Centuries of Childhood*, New York: Vintage Books, 1962.

Bayley, James E., "A Jamesian Theory of Self," *Transactions of the Charles S. Peirce Society* 13 (Winter 1977):148–165.

Blumer, Herbert, *Symbolic Interactionism*, Englewood Cliffs: Prentice-Hall, 1969.

Cook, Gary A., "The Development of G.H. Mead's Social Psychology," *Transactions of the Charles S. Peirce Society* 8 (Summer 1972):167–186.

Dewey, John, "The Reflex Arc Concept in Psychology," pp. 96–109 in *John Dewey Early Essays*, Volume 5, Carbondale and Edwardsville: Southern Illinois University Press, 1972 (1896).

————, "The Vanishing Subject in the Psychology of James," *The Journal of Philosophy* 37 (October 24, 1940):589–599.

Durkheim, Emile, *The Division of Labor in Society*, Glencoe: The Free Press, 1960 (1893).

————, *The Elementary Forms of Religious Life*, New York: The Free Press, 1965 (1915).

Erikson, Erik, *Childhood and Society*, 2nd edition, New York: W.W. Norton, 1963.

————, *Identity, Youth and Crisis*, New York: W.W. Norton, 1968.

Fingarette, Herbert, *Self-Deception*, New York: Humanities Press, 1969.

Giddens, Anthony, *Emile Durkheim Selected Writings*, Cambridge: Cambridge University Press, 1972.

Goffman, Erving, *Asylums*, Garden City: Anchor Books, 1961.

————, *Interaction Ritual*, Garden City: Anchor Books, 1967.

————, *Relations in Public*, New York: Harper & Row, 1971.

Guntrip, Harry J.S., *Psychoanalytic Theory, Therapy, and the Self*, New York: Basic Books, 1971.

Edmund, Husserl, *Cartesian Meditations*, The Hague: Martinus Nijhoff, 1970 (1931).

James, William, *The Principles of Psychology*, Vol. I, New York: Dover, 1950 (1890).

Kant, Immanuel, *Critique of Pure Reason*, 2nd edition, London: J.M. Dent & Sons, Ltd., 1950 (1787).

Kapferer, Bruce, "Mind, Self and Other in Demonic Illness," forthcoming.

Katz, Jerrold J., *The Underlying Reality of Language*, New York: Harper Torchbooks, 1971.

Kolb, William L., "A Critical Evaluation of Mead's 'I' and 'Me' Concepts," *Social Forces* 22 (March 1944):291–296.

Laing, R.D., *The Divided Self*, Baltimore: Penguin Books, 1970 (1959).

Lashley, K.S., "The Problem of Serial Order in Behavior," pp. 112–136 in L.A. Jeffres, ed., *Cerebral Mechanisms in Behavior*, New York: John Wiley and Sons, 1951.

Lewis, James David, *The Pragmatic Foundation of Symbolic Interaction*, Ph.D. Thesis, Department of Sociology, University of Illinois, Urbana, 1976.

Mead, George Herbert, "The Definition of the Psychical," pp. 25–59 in *George Herbert Mead, Selected Writings*, Andrew J. Reck, ed., Indianapolis: Bobbs-Merrill, 1964 (1903).

————, "The Social Self," pp. 142–149 in *George Herbert Mead, Selected Writings*, Andrew J. Reck, ed., Indianapolis: Bobbs-Merrill, 1964 (1913).

————, *Mind, Self & Society*, Chicago: University of Chicago Press, 1962 (1934).

Mishler, Elliot G., and Nancy E. Waxler, "Family Interaction Processes and Schizophrenia: A Review of Current Theories," pp. 469–516 in Gerald Handel, ed., *The Psychological Interior of the Family*, Chicago: Aldine, 1967.

Morris, Phyllis Sutton, *Sartre's Concept of a Person*, Amherst: University of Massachusetts Press, 1976.

Natanson, Maurice, *The Social Dynamics of George H. Mead*, The Hague: Martinus Nijhoff, 1973 (1956).

Sartre, Jean-Paul, *The Transcendance of the Ego*, New York: Noonday Press, 1957 (1937).

————, *Being and Nothingness*, New York: Philosophical Library, 1956 (1943).

————, "Existentialism is a Humanism," pp. 171–199 in Frederick R. Karl and Leo Hamalian, eds., *The Existential Mind*, Greenwich, Connecticut: Fawcett, 1974 (1947).

Scheler, Max, *Selected Philosophical Essays*, Evanston: Northwestern University Press, 1973.

Schutz, Alfred, *The Phenomenology of the Social World*, Evanston: Northwestern University Press, 1967 (1932).

————, *Collected Papers*, Vol. I, The Hague: Martinus Nijhoff, 1962.

Shorter, Edward, *The Making of the Modern Family*, New York: Basic Books, 1977.

Stone, Gregory P. and Harvey A. Farberman , "On the Edge of Rapprochement: Was Durkheim Moving Toward the Perspective of Symbolic Interaction?" *Sociological Quarterly* 8 (Spring 1967):149–164.

Strasser, Stephan, *The Idea of Dialogal Phenomenology*, Pittsburgh: Duquesne University Press, 1969.

Thevenaz, Pierre, *What is Phenomenology?* Chicago: Quadrangle Books, 1962.

Tilly, Louise A., "The Family and Change: Two Theoretical Perspectives for Family History," *Theory and Society* 5 (May 1978):421–434.

Turner, Ralph H., "Role-Taking, Role Standpoint, and Reference-Group Behavior," *American Journal of Sociology* 61 (January 1956):316–328

Winnicott, D.W., "The Theory of the Parent-Infant Relationship," *The International Journal of Psycho-Analysis* 41 (November/December 1960):585–595.

Wynne, Lyman C., Irving M. Ryckoff, Juliana Day, and Stanley I. Hirsch, "Pseudo-Mutuality in the Family Relations of Schizophrenics," pp. 443–468 in Handel, Gerald, ed., *The Psychological Interior of the Family*, Chicago: Aldine, 1967.

TRADITIONS AND RULES AS OBSTRUCTIONS TO USEFUL PROGRAM EVALUATION*

Irwin Deutscher, UNIVERSITY OF AKRON

Margaret Gold, INDIANA STATE UNIVERSITY

. . . .I do not regard partisanship as incompatible with objectivity. The physician, after all, is not necessarily less objective because he has made a partisan commitment to his patient and against the germ. The physician's objectivity is in some measure vouchsafed because he has committed himself to a specific value: health. It is this commitment that constrains him to see and to say things about the patient's condition that neither may want to know (Gouldner, 1968a: 113).

We believe that many of the difficulties encountered in evaluating programs can be traced to the traditions and rules which are thought to characterize "good" evaluation research. The demystification of program evaluation permits the analysis of conventional rules as obstructions to

Studies in Symbolic Interaction—Volume 2, 1979, pages 107-140
Copyright © 1979 by JAI Press Inc.
All rights of reproduction in any form reserved.
ISBN: 0-89232-105-9

desired ends. In this chapter we will analyze some of the traditions which we consider partly responsible for problems in program evaluation. We will propose some unconventional solutions, describe the process through which they came about, and explain why they seem reasonable to us. In the course of developing this alternative methodology, we will use as a case our experiences in attempting to evaluate a program to improve undergraduate teaching sponsored by the American Sociological Association.

Our suggestions can be applied to the evaluation of many, but not all, types of social programs. They may be applied under many, but not all, types of conditions. It is probably true, as Martin Trow has argued (1957), that the methods we advocate are impractical for studies of large, dispersed organizations or grand programs. A comparative evaluation of the development process among two or more nations, for example, would be difficult to conduct in the manner proposed below. Furthermore, there is, as Bogdan (1978) has suggested, a tyranny of the word "evaluation." We think of our activity as program improvement. Some observers insist that we were, in fact, consultants. Whatever the case may be, if we did not use the word evaluation, we would fail to attract many readers who might find this chapter provocative. On the other hand, some people who are concerned about evaluation research will feel that the issues and arguments we are addressing are not theirs. In some instances they will be correct. If, for example, the evaluator is employed by those providing financial support for the program to provide an accounting of the extent to which the program is having the consequences it claimed it would have, our methods may be irrelevant to those concerns.

INTRODUCTION: RULES, USEFUL RESEARCH, AND THE PROJECT

Among the many traditions and rules which are commonly thought to apply to the conduct of research, and more specifically, to evaluation research, we will suggest that at least four must be broken if the research is to be useful. These four are: (1) the rule of objectivity, (2) the rule of measurable outcomes, (3) the rule of nonreactivity, and (4) the rule of the scientific report.

We do not intend to challenge the notion of "scientific objectivity" on some of the grounds which have been well covered,[1] for example, there is probably no such thing, it is a pretentious cover for explicit or implicit theoretical or political positions, etc. What we will suggest is that in applied or policy research, being objective interferes with being useful. Objectivity implies a lack of involvement in and a lack of commitment to the program. It requires that the evaluator view the program and its participants as objects to be examined with scientific objectivity. We share Gouldner's sentiments with which we opened this chapter: partisanship is not only compatible with objectivity, but is essential for a sympathetic grasp of the intentions and the problems posed by the program.

In our initial presentation of ourselves to key organizers of the ASA project on undergraduate teaching, we described our stance as one of "sympathetic skepticism." On the one hand, we sympathized with their efforts to improve undergraduate teaching in sociology and we wished them well; on the other hand, we announced our skepticism that such a massive national effort to alter basic academic values and organizational practices, undertaken by numerous committees, could hope to achieve that desirable end. To the extent that a value commitment to the basic aims of a program breaches scientific objectivity, we will argue that such objectivity obstructs useful evaluation research.

A second conventional rule of research is that of operationalization: both dependent and independent variables must be stated in measurable terms. In evaluation research, this translates into the decree that programs can be evaluated only when their goals are clearly specified in measurable terms. The means of achieving these goals must be equally specific. The logic is clear and sound: if the effectiveness of a program is to be scientifically assessed, then it must be possible to measure the extent to which the program has achieved the ends for which it was designed. "Any program which does not have clearly specified goals cannot be evaluated without specifying some measurable goals" (Rossi, 1972: 18. Cf. Brooks, 1965: 61; Greenberg, 1968: 155; Suchman, 1969: 44; Jones and Borgatta, 1972: 41). Our design for the evaluation of the project on teaching sociology deliberately breaks this rule.

Our basis for this breach derives from an earlier concern with the "goal-trap" in program evaluation (Deutscher, 1977). Its rationale includes: (1) programs do not always intend what their proposals claim; (2) program personnel cannot always articulate goals in operational terms; (3) programs may have consequences unrelated to and even of greater importance than their proposed goals. We suggest not only that programs without "clearly specified goals" ought to be evaluated, but also that there is a method for doing so.

A third rule of research is that the effects of the research and the investigators upon the situation under study must be minimized. Social research is particularly vulnerable to such effects. One recommended defense against reactivity is the adoption of unobtrusive measures and unobtrusive behavior (Webb, et al., 1966). Again, the logic is clear and sound: one ought to avoid changing what is being studied as a result of the process of studying it. We will argue in this chapter that useful applied and policy research should, by design, be obtrusive if it is to be useful.

If the evaluator is in a position to take note of activities or occurrences or events which interfere with the well-being of the project and which project personnel appear unaware of, then the evaluator may be of help to the program by bringing such things to their attention. In a more positive vein the evaluator may discover new ways by which the program can become more effective. In either case, our program improvement stance does not permit reporting of such instances after the time has passed when program people can, if they wish, take action to make changes. It is for such reasons that we argue for obtrusive research in program evaluation.

The final rule which we shall challenge is that research which is not exposed to the scrutiny of other scientists and which is not reported in such a manner that it can be fit into the corpus of scientific literature is not research at all. We consider this an essential requirement of research designed to contribute to knowledge. We also consider it as of little use in evaluation research. Our rationale is partly related to the previous rule in that a written final report is likely to come too late to be of much use. It will also be argued that a written report is not necessarily the most effective form of communication. We consider this the most dangerous of the four rule-breaking procedures we will recommend, because it removes the evaluation research from the scrutiny and criticism of the scientific community. Such scrutiny not only has scientific functions, but it provides protection which is not always otherwise available for patients, clients, students and other objects of programs

Our procedure for evaluating the project on teaching sociology deliberately breaks all of these rules. An investigator ought not to flaunt established rules of social research without explanation and justification. This chapter considers alternative logics to the one underlying the four rules and moves toward a methodology for pursuing those alternatives.

We have employed the term "useful" as a criterion of the validity of evaluation research. The primary purpose of such research is to provide information from a relatively detached observer which can be taken into account by various parties responsible for the continuation of the program. Evaluation ought to help in making decisions about the project. For the social scientists, it also provides a unique opportunity to test or to generate theories of social change (Deutscher, 1979). The latter, however, is a different purpose for a different audience, and the evaluator who intends to do both may have to deliberately induce self-schizophrenia in order to keep those two purposes from interfering with each other. The theoretical functions of evaluation research are not discussed in this chapter.

It is our position that program evaluation may often be better conceived as program improvement. Furthermore, we suspect that some of the most informative and most useful evalution studies are not seen as "evaluation" by professional evaluators and may not be defined that way by the investigators themselves.[2] Typical of such informative and useful evaluations is Alexander Leighton's study of a Japanese Relocation Center

945), Becker, Geer, and Hughes's monograph on an undergraduate col-
ge (1968), and Becker, Geer, Hughes, and Strauss's analysis of a medical
chool (1961). Such evaluations make no effort to measure the extent to
hich the organizations under study achieve certain specified goals by
ertain specified means. Not unlike those organizations, the program we
ere involved with had as its goal a cliché—the improvement of under-
raduate teaching in sociology. Its proposed means of achieving this vague
oal were fuzzy at best. By conventional standards, such a program is not
menable to evaluation.[3] We believed it was worth evaluating, although not
a conventional terms.

The methods discussed in this chapter evolved over a period of nearly
our years as we struggled to evaluate the American Sociological Associa-
on's projects to improve undergraduate teaching. This was a national
ffort directed by Hans O. Mauksch (1973). For the first three years, the
roject attempted to divide its responsibilities among three major task
roups, two of which were sub-divided into subgroups, with an adminis-
rative committee responsible for overall planning and policy. The simplest
f these (in structure) was the teacher training group, which met as a
ommittee of the whole. The curriculum group was composed of ten sub-
roups, each assigned a specific dimension of curriculum (e.g., "The First
Course," "Boundaries," "Progression of Courses," etc.). These ten sub-
roups were dispersed over the United States. Each had a convener and
nce or twice a year there was a convener's meeting. It was not until the
roject had been in motion for nearly a year and a half that the group
esponsible for the institutional context of teaching became fully operative.
That group consisted of five regional sub-groups with partially overlapping
nissions.

During the fourth year the project evolved new forms of organization.
Further description of the project will occur as it becomes necessary in our
analysis of our evaluation methods. The two evaluators became both
observers and participants, although the latter role was more circumscribed
han the former. The senior evaluator agreed to serve on the project's
administrative committee. His participation was self-consciously restrained
and limited until the middle of the fourth year, when he announced that
ield work was terminated and began to participate fully as an active
member of the administrative committee.

Participant-observation can range from the extreme of participation
found in the anthropologist who "goes native" to the extreme of observa-
ion found in the ethnographer who "fades into the woodwork." The
evaluators of the teaching sociology project were, in fact, natives, in the
ense that they were academic sociologists. We did not, however, participate
fully in the same native sub-culture as most of the project participants. We
were not as heavily committed to the role of undergraduate teacher and saw

other facets of academic responsibility as equally or more important research, scholarship, writing, publication, consulting on matters of social policy, graduate education.[4] Nevertheless, we suffered the research handicap of taking for granted many of the things our "people" take for granted. We could not observe them with the detachment of Martians since we are one of them. There are correlaries to this problem. For example, our efforts to elicit insightful criticism and suggestions from some of the best participant-observers in the discipline were disappointing. They inevitably ended up by reporting on their own experiences with teaching undergraduate sociology. They too, alas, are natives. Where then does one turn for the kind of cynical criticism of the evaluation enterprise which might ordinarily be obtained from consultants? The best has come from our graduate assistants who attempted to code and analyze portions of the data.[5]

In a sense, the problems of generating the kind of methodology we will propose in this chapter consist of walking a series of tightropes. The most difficult of these tightropes is the thin string between being helpful and being interfering. At times there was even a problem with being helpful at all. We had committed ourselves to the "program improvement" posture, yet the people involved in the program were as knowledgeable, if not more so, than we. What if we simply didn't see anything that looked helpful? Even at those times when it appeared that we could help, it was necessary to exercise extreme caution. It is dangerous for us to impose our own opinions regarding the best strategies for resolving the problems these people are trying to deal with, when our opinions have no better basis than theirs. But it is difficult to resist appeals for help (or for participation) at times such as those when only two or three members of a group show up for a meeting. With small numbers, one simply cannot fade into the woodwork. The one great advantage we had over all of the other sociologists involved with the project was our mobility. More than anyone else, we went everywhere, observed everything, and were aware of the larger complex of activities and people. Although we were not superior to individual members, we were far better situated.

In sum, we viewed conventional evaluation procedures as flawed in a number of respects. Part of our motivation for assuming responsibility for evaluating the teaching project was the opportunity it provided to generate alternative methods. Some of the problems inherent in conventional goal-oriented evaluation are:

1. It implies an experimental logic—that differences can be attributed to the project. It is, however, not always possible to obtain control groups or even comparison groups, much less randomization between them. It is, then, not possible to sort out project effects from other historical "causes" of observed changes.

2. Conventional evaluation places greatest emphasis on program output. Although sometimes attention is paid to program input, rarely is

an effort made to understand the process between the two. It becomes difficult, then, to determine why a program "works" or does not.

3. It fails to take note of consequences and processes which, although unintended, may be of great importance. It also fails to take note of consequences which, although intended, were not clearly articulated.

4. It places the evaluator in the role of judge and defines the evaluation situation as one of distrust and suspicion.

5. Results communicated in the traditional form of a final report usually come too late to be useful to those interested in making the project work. Furthermore, such reports are generally not in a form which is useful to program staff, planners, administrators, or funding agencies.

The need to overturn some conventional rules of evaluation research emerged from our efforts to correct such flaws. The following section of this chapter analyzes the creation of new rules and new roles by comparing the evaluators' and the members' definitions of the situation and the negotiated reality which resulted. The concluding section develops a rationale for breaking the four rules described in this introduction.

RULE MAKING: THE EVALUATORS' PRESENTATION OF SELF AND MEMBERS' INTERPRETATIONS

Presentation of Self. We have described the teaching projects as a program with ill-defined means for achieving vague goals. The orthodox evaluator would suspect it of being a foolish program and would insist that it could not be evaluated. Yet the program involves over one hundred teachers of sociology attempting to deal with an issue which lies within their area of experience and professional competence. If such skilled practitioners cannot define what needs to be done to achieve which ends, it is unlikely that anyone less familiar with the situation would be able to do so. It follows that the evaluators need to approach the program in an exploratory fashion in order to discover how and why its participants go about their business in the way that they do, and with what consequences.

Under these conditions, the matter of the evaluator's self-presentation becomes important. If the evaluation is to be a helpful process, it must not be perceived by program personnel as threatening. Yet the term "evaluating" implies passing judgment. It suggests that someone is assessing the worth, the skill, the integrity, the knowledge, the judgment of someone else.

At the first meeting of the Administrative Committee of the project, each of the people with major project responsibility, including the evaluator, was called upon to describe his or her role. This was a crucial point at which a public statement on the nature of the evaluation had to be made. Furthermore, it had to be made to a group which governed the project and

with which the evaluators would have to live for several years. Th
presentation of the evaluation self described below was repeated in essential
ly the same form at the organizing meetings of various project subcommit
tees, with whom the evaluators were also to spend considerable time in th
ensuing years. At initial meetings of all these groups, we told projec
personnel of our sympathetic skepticism. We also attempted to disavov
some of the connotations of "evaluation," suggesting that our view of ou
activity was one of project "improvement." It appears that we wer
sometimes successful in dissociating ourselves from traditional images o
evaluation and sometimes not.

We offered project people an alternative image by describing our primar
task as writing a social history of the project. By later backtracking throug
our detailed records, we explained, we hoped to identify differences amon
processes which had concluded more or less successfully than others. Bu
this was a vague conception. We acknowledged that we could not knov
what the eventual nature of our evaluation would be, since it would emerg
from our observations of as-yet unknown events. Furthermore, we acknowl
edged the risk involved. Suppose nothing of theoretical or practica
importance should emerge from our mass of data? At least we would hav
our "social history."[6] This self-presentation served different functions fo
evaluators and project participants. It reassured participants (all of whon
were contributing their professional services on a volunteer basis) tha
neither their selves nor their individual performances were about to b
judged. It also gave the evaluators a sense of security and overall directior
in an otherwise ill-defined enterprise.

In order to symbolize our sympathetic involvement with the project, the
senior evaluator permitted himself to be "co-opted" as a member of the
administrative committee, rather than maintaining the position of a purely
detached outside observer. To a certain extent, the evaluators showec
themselves to be part of the project, resembling in some ways an interna
program evaluation. But members of the administrative committee (and
anyone else who asked) were aware that evaluation was conducted under a
sub-contract and that the evaluator had control over his own funds, which
were administered by his own institution. Independence of the evaluation
was also established by the evaluator's insistence on freedom to publish
materials at his own discretion. The administrative committee was informed
that we would provide each of them with an opportunity to react to any
documents we might produce before wider distribution occurred. This is a
two-way street, providing the evaluators with an opportunity to discover
possible misinterpretations on their own part. The administrative committee
had assurance that we would take account of their suggestions, criticisms,
and comments. That taking of account could range from a revision of our

own analysis to an acknowledgement of the member's alternative interpretation as, for example, appears in footnote three of this paper.

A key element in our self-presentation to project members was our promise that we did not intend to quietly observe them and report at the termination of the project all of the things we thought they might have done differently. Part of our notion of project improvement was the obligation to provide immediate feedback when it seemed to us there was need for it. In effect, members were assured that there would be few if any surprises for them in whatever final report eventually appeared.

A source of variation which must be taken into account in interpreting this analysis is the fact that there are two evaluators. This resulted in two, sometimes different, presentations of self over which we had little control. We differ in several respects. One is male and the other female. The male has been an active sociologist for over a quarter of a century, and as a consequence knows and is known by many members of the discipline. The female received her doctorate during the course of the evaluation. Although somewhat older than the typical new Ph.D., she was unknown to others in the discipline and was generally perceived as the junior person on the evaluation team. We know that these differences make a difference, but we are unable to determine with any precision what kind of differences they make and what consequences they have for the evaluation. We know, for example, that when initial visits were being scheduled for group meetings, some groups were offended when it appeared that we "did not consider them important enough to send the senior evaluator."

In our early presentations, we often encountered established conceptions of what evaluators do. Despite our disclaimers, it was difficult for some people to believe at first that this experience would be substantially different. There were some expressions of concern at the prospect of being "evaluated," as in the case of the member who wrote the task group leader after the evaluator's first visit: "This was our first experience with an evaluator. I was a bit resentful and thought, why should we be evaluated when we are volunteering professional time and energy?" Apparently, the selves we attempted to present were not always the selves members perceived.

Members' Interpretations. Although we had ample opportunity to discuss the evaluation role with the three task group leaders, we sometimes encountered project participants who were unclear as to who we were. The curriculum task group was organized into ten sub-groups very early in the project's history. Each of those sub-groups had a convener and there were convener's meetings, at which we were able to describe our evolving concept of evaluation. We did not always communicate effectively. Two conveners asked us to contribute agenda items when we told them we would be attending their initial meetings. We explained that we did not wish to interfere with their agenda. On the other hand there were conveners who had a clear grasp of what we described as our role. On returning from a convener's meeting, one included the following in his written report to his group:

> Irwin Deutscher reported on his approach to evaluation. He is interested not only in assessing the consequences of the project but also in tracing the processes through which various task groups go in order to produce this product. He is hoping to identify what efforts had what kinds of outcomes. He is also trying to identify why certain things happened as opposed to others. This would include a description of the characteristics of success and failure. In terms of minimum outcomes, he hopes to (1) provide a social process history and (2) provide feedback to various task groups that might help them better accomplish what they set out to do without making any evaluations of specific individuals. (Minutes, 3/14/75/)

The deliberate obtrusiveness we planned had to be engaged in cautiously, tactfully, and selectively. Since we had no rules, we were forced to make on-the-spot decisions about the appropriateness and timeliness of an intervention. We were not always successful in implementing our decisions either to sometimes intervene or to sometimes be unobtrusive. An example of an early failure in the latter was our assumption that at a table full of academic sociologists, scribbling, doodling, taking notes, and otherwise occupied with pencil and paper, we could record our field notes without attracting undue attention. Yet, after several meetings of the Administrative Committee (ten to twelve people) and many informal contacts with its members, one member "jokingly" warned another during a discussion: "Watch out! Irwin is writing all this down." At another Administrative Committee meeting when a staff member was recording the proceedings, the recorder clicked loudly to a stop during a pause in the discussion. A member turned to the evaluator and said, "Your tape is all gone." The evaluator loudly denied ownership of the recorder, much to the surprise of several members of the committee. This incident provided us with the opportunity to make it clear that we never recorded meetings and that our tape recorders (which members sometimes saw us with in airports) were used only for dictating our notes in the privacy of our rooms.

Project members sometimes tested our disavowal of a judgmental evaluation. Relaxing over drinks after an evening work session, one member dared the evaluator to reveal what she "was really up to," adding with a hint of mischief, "I think you're a spy for the administration." A convener, on learning that the evaluator would be present during some delicate negotiations with an outsider, jokingly remarked, "I'll need you along to tell me later all the mistakes I made."

Most instances of testing date from our early contacts. Over the course of nearly four years, during which we participated with varying degrees of

1volvement, most project members grew accustomed to our presence. Some
1aim to have been undisturbed by our presence from the beginning—a
1aim which is not always supported by our observations. There is, for
xample, the extreme instance of a small group which had been ignored
ecause of its geographic isolation. They wrote a formal complaint to the
1sk group leader, protesting that the evaluators had no grounds for
eciding they were so unimportant and ineffective that they were to be
isregarded. Although this level of suspicion was unique, the majority of
1embers were, on the one hand, accepting of us, while on the other, they
vere always aware that we were evaluators. The leader of the teacher
raining task group frequently expressed sentiments like:

> I was very comfortable and am pretty sure others in task group B were too with your
> role. That at least a part of you was on the team and that all of you was with the team,
> so to speak, seemed abundantly clear to me.

1fter the evaluator became involved in a strategy discussion at a meeting of
small curriculum sub-group, a member told her, "We know you're an
valuator, but someone coming into the room cold wouldn't know it." Not
1l members approved of our emerging role. On a questionnaire which had
een sent to the project participants, one wrote:

> A major question is what are the evaluators doing! We know they are doing. We just
> haven't seen the results. . . . It is hard for an evaluator to know his/her role in a meeting.
> But I hope you evaluators discuss it. I feel there should be little talking at sessions from
> the evaluator, regardless of the quality of the comments.

Members had to account for us, to define us, to attribute a role to us, to find
n appropriate way of relating to us. Our denial of the traditional evaluation
ole made that difficult for them. One of the three major task group leaders
onsistently classified evaluation with the service component of the project.
'his is a staff-line distinction which places those who are responsible for
mproving undergraduate teaching in one category and those who support
hem in another. The latter category includes the dissemination committee,
he clerical staff, the reactor panels, the newsletter staff—and the eval-
ators! Some members saw us as advisors, consultants, communicators, as
uthorities on project policies, or as sources of information about what
ther groups are doing. In fact, from time to time we were all of those
hings. We were also asked to read and comment upon a term paper, a
hapter from a dissertation, a manuscript for publication, a research
roposal, and several questionnaire drafts. We made an effort to do all of
hose things. We were asked to help create agendas and to duplicate our
ield notes so that the group would not have to keep its own minutes. We
efused to do those things.

Members consider evaluators not only as specific persons, but also take into account their own understanding of what an evaluator is and what it means to be evaluated. Members operate on certain assumptions they make on the basis of their everyday experiences. They relate to "what everyone knows" about evaluation. In short, members respond to both denotative and connotative meanings of "evaluation." This process permits them to provide themselves with a satisfactory account of what it is evaluators do and what evaluation is. Our data suggest that most of the people we encountered in our evaluation work made one of two basic assumptions: either (1) evaluators are here to do something *to* us, or (2) evaluators are here to do something *for* us. Using case materials to illustrate, let us first examine the assumption that evaluators do things *to* people.

This assumption implies that evaluators pass judgments upon people and their activities and, as a consequence of those judgments, the people or the activities are hurt or helped. Our research-typist, an undergraduate anthropology major, took us to task for being insufficiently sensitive to this point:

> The connotation of the term evaluation . . . is not one to inspire confidence in those being observed. . . . An evaluator is there either to pass or to fail you and when an evaluator is around one tends to tread very lightly and very carefully (Barbara Bianco, Staff Memorandum, 10/29/75).

This seems to be a fair statement of a type of initial definition. It was, in fact, echoed almost verbatim a year and a half later by a newcomer to the project. He said, over a cup of coffee with the evaluator, "You really should call yourself something else besides an evaluator; it has immediate connotations of pass-fail." Later, he stated in a report that the two evaluators were discovering "some vague indicators of the project's success or failure." During the course of a project workshop, a professor at a major university said (jokingly?), "Oho, so you're an evaluator—scary!"

Some members openly expressed resentment about having their efforts evaluated, particularly when they were latecomers or had otherwise failed to be briefed:

> One of the prospective sub-group members had mentioned on the bottom of his form that he was somewhat irritated by not being told he was going to be evaluated, and why didn't they tell him that before. He had some resistance to this, to being surprisingly thrown into a guinea pig role which he didn't approve of.

Sometimes first encounters with evaluators revealed a view of us as representing authority and functioning as watchdogs. Over drinks following her first visit to a small task group, the evaluator was informed that she was seen as "the eyes and ears of the administration." The convener of the same group reminded the evaluator at the close of the meeting that they would meet again at a large convener's conference: "You'll be there in case I make any mis-statements or inaccuracies, won't you?" Another convener asked the evaluator for her view of what "they" want. The response was, "You know more about that than I do." There were, however, times when the evaluators did attempt to clarify project policy for the groups we were observing. One group, for example, found itself in opposition to the policy against promulgating any type of "orthodoxy" in the discipline.[7] Their convener asked the evaluator to discuss the dilemma they found themselves in with the project director and he did so. Some months later, the project director attended a meeting of this group and helped clarify the problem with them.

At the initial meeting of another small group, the evaluator was questioned closely by a member (the chairman of a graduate department in a large university) about the evaluation procedures. His traditional definition and her unorthodox replies clashed head on. After a series of exchanges, he finally sighed, leaned back and said, "O.K., but you don't mean evaluation research as I usually think of it . . . meaning that you're evaluating the effectiveness of our products or our actions." A contrasting view of the evaluator's role is provided by a member of another group who told the evaluator that he "seemed to the group to represent a conscience coming from the outside world—a reminder that we all have a job to do and have to keep about our business."

Participants with a judgmental perception of the evaluator do not necessarily see this as threatening. To the contrary, the vain may view this as an opportunity to perform, to shine, to score points. The assumptions of judgmental authority of course remains. The following was reported by the evaluator during the initial meeting of a small group.

> [He] is addressing much of his speech to me . . . obviously very much aware of my presence and concerned about my opinion. I'm not very happy about this clear impact of my presence upon the group, but I don't know how to avoid it or what to do about it.

One disappointed convener wrote to the evaluator who had been prevented by illness from attending this meeting: "I regret your absence because it was an excellent meeting and a model for evaluation, if I do say so myself." It was not unusual during the early days of the project for members of small groups to assume that the evaluators were responsible for helping them to organize their activities—to get "on the right track." Three of the ten curriculum group conveners and two of their five counterparts on the institutional context groups wrote or phoned the evaluators, asking what items we wanted them to have on the agenda for their first meeting.

These are the kinds of things members suspect evaluators might be doing *to* them. What do they think evaluators might be doing *for* them? Although the activities may sometimes be the same, the members define them differently: i.e., what one member sees as "doing to" another may see as "doing for." The assumption among members taking this view of evaluation is that program people can use evaluation and evaluators to further their own ends. Consider the leader who defined evaluation as a service component of the project. Even after she learned that there were certain service functions we would not perform (e.g., sending her copies of our field notes so she could see what happened at meetings she was unable to attend), she persisted in bolstering the definition some of her group leaders had of us as "Master recorders." She considered this a "good, non-threatening definition." We agreed.

Although we insisted that we would not report on or make judgments about small task groups or their leaders to project leadership, we were sometimes asked to do so. Generally, we responded to requests such as "How did the meeting in Topeka go?" with either factual information which we knew would appear in the group's own minutes ("They agreed on a product for their group and divided up the work.") or with statements about groups in general ("In many of the groups the community college representative doesn't seem to function as an equal. This may be because they are sometimes former students recruited by other members of the group, sometimes are still working on their degrees, and sometimes are younger.")

Our rule against reporting judgmentally about small groups was sometimes bent. One situation when this was likely to occur was when the responsible project administrator and the evaluator had both been present at a meeting and the administrator wanted to discuss possible lines of action to take as a result of our joint observations. Under these conditions we might be supportive, critical, suggest alternatives, or remind the administrator of possible consequences. In some cases, the decision was deliberately made to break the rule. This occurred, for example, when we informed a task group leader that the convener of one of her sub-groups was treating the women in the group as if they were his employees, telling "funny" stories about airline stewardesses, and otherwise behaving in a dictatorial and sexist manner. After observing his behavior, the leader "reorganized" the sub-group, much to the chagrin of the former convener.

One consequence of the attendance of evaluators at nearly all meetings was our usefulness as communicators. We were asked to and did carry messages, reminders, and information from their leader to the ten dispersed curriculum sub-groups. Upon visiting a task group for the first time, the evaluator was jokingly informed by members that they knew she had come to take care of all their unanswered questions. Others asked for direct advice, and one task group leader stated at the outset that he expected "political feedback" from evaluation and repeated this in the form of periodic requests throughout the life of the project. Frequently people asked, "How am I doing?" or "How are we doing?" They also wanted to

:now how other groups were doing. When project policy permitted,[8] we ;ave them information on *what* other groups were doing, although we :arefully avoided comparing groups judgmentally.

We were sometimes defined as troubleshooters or moderators or even as 'straightening out wrong thinkers." Although we did not generally see)urselves in these roles, when we were defined as performing them, the :onsequences were real enough. Thus, a group member reported to a project eader how the evaluator had taken a "troublemaking" member (one with vhom the other member had had a heated argument during their meeting) .o the bar after the session and done an excellent job of "straightening him)ut." In fact, the "troublemaker" and the evaluator both arrived early for he group's dinner and retreated to the empty bar where they were observed n animated conversation by the other member. Although the conversation vas unrelated to the group's earlier argument, the other member assumed hat it was and observed that, as a result, the "troublemaker" was much)etter behaved for the rest of the meeting.

Communication was expected not only from leadership to membership,)ut evaluators were also expected to communicate matters from the grass 'oots upward. We were often asked to facilitate matters when it appeared hat chains of authority or lines of communication had become cumbersome)r broken down. Would we, for example, go over a leader's head and tell the)roject director how urgent it was for a group to publish a product it was iitting on. One sub-group leader phoned in distress at having had no one)ut the evaluator react to a draft proposal he had submitted for funding of ais sub-group. Could we do something about the project director who was 'sitting on it." This occurred during a period of several months when the)roject hierarchy was slow in reacting to requests from members as a :onsequence of the director's distraction by family problems (lengthy erminal illness of a parent) shortly after he had assumed a new job. The)erception of evaluation as a communication and facilitation process was :onfirmed at that time by many letters and phone calls from members ısking us to find out why nothing was happening.

This communicating role was not distributed evenly among the three najor components of the project. Most of the examples are from the :urriculum task group, and that is where most of the demands were made ıpon us during the early years. This was in large part because of its)rganization into ten sub-groups which worked in almost complete isolation 'rom one another. Although the leader of the curriculum groups attempted 'rom time to time to enlist the aid of one or two others in administering her)rganization, she never succeeded and bore nearly all of the responsibility ıerself.

The task group on teaching context was not organized until the project vas well into its second year, and it consisted of only half as many sub-;roups (five) as the curriculum task group. Because there were fewer of these groups operating over a shorter period of time, fewer of our examples are derived from them. Because this group arrived late upon the scene and because of a combination of administrative difficulties, the evaluator found himself unavoidably serving a central role as communicator with its subgroups. One member remarked,

> how little communication the sub-task groups in the Institutional Context Group ever received from the project office or the task group leader. . . . This created a situation in which we were forced to quiz the evaluator in order to get even a basic understanding of what was going on. . . . The project structured you into this situational role so firmly that it would have been a major violation of your responsibility to the profession and the project for you to have failed to provide a guidance to the sub-task groups when the project's administrators were not doing so. In this situation you were co-opted into becoming a project administrator, at least in the eyes of many sub-task group members. As far as I know, people were grateful rather than resentful over this. . . . You bailed us out on more than one occasion.

The third major task group was concerned with the training and retraining of teachers. It was never subdivided, acting always as a committee of the whole. Its leader was a master communicator who spent large amounts of time and energy on the telephone and pouring out memoranda to his members and others. Demands from this group came almost exclusively from the leader himself, who was insistent on his need for feedback and grateful for whatever we were able to provide. The evaluator often returned from meetings on the same plane with this task group leader and de-briefings took place sometimes at the airport and sometimes on the plane. Communication demands became greater from this task group after the second year when it began to operate teaching workshops. Evaluators did attend these workshops and did provide feedback to the leader— frequently at his request. Workshop participants also used the evaluators to communicate upwards on occasion, but because of the *gemeinschaft* atmosphere of the workshops and the openness of communication channels, this was more often seen as something people could do for themselves. The workshop staffs also provided opportunities for participants to fill in anonymous evaluation forms.

We have reported on the evaluators' definition of the situation and on the members' definition of the situation. Apparently, these two sets of definitions did not always coincide. Like any other social reality, this one, too, ultimately resulted from negotiations between the involved parties.

NEGOTIATING THE EVALUATOR ROLE

Having created for ourselves an ambiguous situation—we will be helpful but we will not interfere—how did the evaluators and the members of the project negotiate a position which made sense to all parties?[9] Although it is not certain how successful such negotiations were, it is certain that they occurred. Our data suggest that the relationship between evaluators and members was shaped and reshaped as joint lines of action developed during the course of our day-to-day interactions. We coded our field notes for negotiative interactions according to the identification of interactions in which something of value is at stake and the outcome is settled through a sequence of proposals and counterproposals. The analysis which follows illuminates the format of negotiations, as well as the kinds of issues around which it revolves. With increasing clarity in our mutual definitions of who the parties are (roles), came increasing clarity of what constitutes appropriate behavior (rules). Although the set of behavioral rules is not the same as the set of methodological rules with which we open and close this chapter, the two are interdependent and overlapping: the rules governing evaluators' relations with members reflect and are reflected by the rules governing our research procedures. Let us consider the processes through which some of these roles and rules emerge.

Our data indicated that most role negotiations are initiated by members, largely as a consequence of the evaluators' efforts to avoid defining themselves or the vagueness of their definitions. A typical situation is one in which the member advances a definition of the evaluator in the form of a request or a proposal. The evaluator responds with an acceptance, declination, counter-proposal, or by hedging. Another style of definition by members occurred when the evaluators *appeared* to be defining their role (in our typically tentative and vague manner), and that appearance elicited an attempt at a more precise statement from the member. Both parties were seeking what Scott and Lyman describe as acceptable accounts (1968).

This "conversation of gestures" moved, then, from the evaluators' vague statement to the member's more precise reformulation, and back to the evaluators' acceptance or denial of the reformulation. If the evaluators denied the member's redefinition or refused the request for information or action, some sort of explanation was called for. A satisfactory account had to be provided (to ourselves and to members). It is at this point that rule-building occurs: "It is not that we are tired or contrary or don't like that request; it is that what you have asked for is something we do not do!" Such a refusal on the part of the evaluators invokes a rationale for subsequent refusals or requests of that order—a rule. Similarly, when the evaluators accepted a member's definition or request, an accounting had to be made and a rule formulated (not to the members but to the methodologically self-conscious evaluators themselves. One never needs to explain *acceptance* of the others' definitions to the others.)

The initial definition of the evaluation self to a member group was always vague, evoking clarification and redefinition from members. At the first meeting of the teacher training task group,

I had to say something about the evaluation and I'm sure it sounded very passive and fuzzy in defining the evaluation role. I am trying to play it down as much as possible and

trying . . . to avoid appearing threatening to these people. . . . I don't want to stifle them
or inhibit them or make them feel as if they are guinea pigs. I may be leaning over
backwards.

After completing the presentation, the evaluator observed that,

Others seem to want to support my role as a more positive one than I am describing.
Sheila pointed out that it wasn't as passive as it sounded, that I had been helpful from
time to time in one way or another and gave an illustration of that.[10]

An analysis of evaluators' acceptance or denial of members' requests
provides a picture of the fit between their efforts to define us and our
emerging definitions of ourselves. Sometimes we refused to accept their
definitions:

Harold asks me to summarize, since I am taking notes. I refuse as graciously as I can,
pointing out that . . . I'm just jotting down enough things so I can reconstruct this later
and I don't think it would be very helpful. (Small curriculum subgroup, 6/75)

Ted says to me, referring to my notes, "I hope these notes are for our use, too," and I
say "No, they aren't." (Small context sub-group, 1/76)

Even in the well-informed Administrative Committee, a member asked if
our notes could be circulated. Such events from nearly every type of group
we observed illustrate the perception of members that since the evaluators
obviously recorded whatever occurs, those records provided "minutes of the
meeting." The evaluators, on the other hand, viewed their field notes as
confidential. Although one evaluator was appalled at the inability of
sociologists to understand the privacy of such data, we never explained our
refusal on those grounds, rather insisting that our notes simply were not
much good for their purposes. The evaluators had no difficulty formulating
the rule that we did not serve as recorders, nor did we share our field notes.
Although this rule was frequently tested, it was always accepted.
We were sometimes asked to present analyses:

I am asked if I want to make a typology of the groups and I say "no" . . . each group
observed has been somewhat different . . . and we haven't seen enough to really
understand why. (Conveners of all curricula subgroups, 11/75)

Such requests highlighted the fact that the people we were observing had the
same analytic training and skills that we did. We refused such requests
generally because they were premature (we did not yet have the kind of
understanding asked of us), and because the members were as capable of
making such analyses as we were. We evolved *the rule that we would not
respond to requests to make judgments or analyses which we felt were
premature or which we otherwise defined ourselves as incapable of doing well.*
This rule was also tested frequently, and reasonably so, since members had
no way of knowing when it applied.

A final example of a type of situation where the evaluators refused to accept members' role definitions is provided by the group which was about to set up a consultation with a department in a small college which had asked for help:

> I had a call from Phil earlier in which he suggested that he might want me to go to New Orleans to serve as their advance man with the college. I think I cooled them out of that. I suggested that I really wasn't the appropriate person for that and that they should get someone else (Small Curriculum Sub-group, 11/76).

In this instance, the evaluator insisted that if the group did not feel it should send one of its own members, then either the administrator of their curriculum task group or the project director might be asked to help them. We attempted from the start to hold to *the rule that the evaluators do not actively participate in the administration or conduct of project affairs.* Although there were instances where we crossed the thin line at this point, by and large members understood this rule and did not often test it. This rule was abandoned at a meeting of the Administrative Committee in June, 1978, when the evaluator deliberately shifted to a member role with the termination of field work.

In sum, when the evaluators rejected members' role definitions, it was because we believed they were unhelpful, misleading, uneconomical, inefficient, or socially inappropriate for us. Since the members themselves were sociologists, once they became aware of an issue, their analyses were likely to be as good as and possibly better than those of the evaluators. What emerged from this acknowledgement of their skills was *a rule that evaluators should be cautious about initiating premature speculations or judgments about processes which we were only beginning to understand.* To express such observations when our data might later suggest that they needed revision would be dangerous for the project, since the evaluators' views carried considerable authority.

The distinction between our rule against responding to requests for judgments and our rule against initiating such judgments is reflected in the following two incidents which occurred in different groups six months apart:

> Jim asks me if I have any questions or comments . . . I explain my "no" as not being that I am coy or reluctant to share things with them, but I'm reluctant to say things since I don't really know what are the right and wrong directions for the group. There are many groups and one of the interesting things about this project is to find out how groups manage sometimes to succeed while others do not.

> Just before they broke, I made a comment describing my own role and my concern about feeding in my judgments. I told them what I had learned from talking with Meg [Gold] about her experience of becoming impatient with one group because of their apparent lack of progress and their wandering off on "tangents." I suggested we didn't know enough to know what a tangent was.

Although the evaluators sometimes resisted member's definitions of our role, we sometimes accepted such definitions. One such case is the role of sympathetic confidant, listener, passive therapist. Because members knew that we did not gossip and that we were thoroughly familiar with the workings and the problems of the project, they sometimes viewed us as useful sounding boards or people who would at least understand: "I notice that David seems pretty edgy and he says he really would like to talk to me about some things. I ask him if he wants me to ask Chuck to let us go on alone. He does." What was troubling David was the personal life of another member of the group. Two and a half years later, when the evaluator mentioned to David that he was occupied with writing, David expressed concern about the personal issues he had discussed years before. The evaluator assured him that, as it turned out, his observations were not relevant to understanding the project process.

Even when a mutually agreeable role has been worked out, it is not always possible to practice it effectively. The evaluators had agreed from the beginning to provide feedback, and sometimes members would demand it when we didn't have any to give:

> At the point where I was about to collapse from fatigue, Chuck said he wanted to talk to me. He told me he wanted some feedback on the meeting. He wanted some criticism on what was wrong. Did I have any advice? I was too tired to think of something and finally mumbled something to him about pushing a little too hard. Later I wished I hadn't. I was really reaching, trying to find something to say. . . . In the morning I mentioned to Chuck that this was a silly thing I had said and he really wasn't driving them too hard at all. . . . I have got to find a way of avoiding these requests for instant feedback. I don't have any! I want to gather the data; I want time to get it transcribed, look at it, consider it, think about it, organize it and see if we can't figure out what is going on—including ways in which we might at some point be helpful.

One role reluctantly accepted by the evaluator failed to materialize. During the first three years of the project, there were three requests for the evaluator to serve as a research advisor. One of these occurred when the teacher training group was about to launch a national survey:

> There is some talk of a pretest and a timing. I think they will do a pretest, and at Bob's urging (along with Chuck's encouragement), I did agree to consult with him and react to his tools and so on. Generally I would rather not be the resident research consultant, although it may be difficult to avoid that role. It was impossible in this case. So he will probably be sending me things and I will be reacting to them.

We have seen that the evaluators sometimes resisted members' definitions of their roles and sometimes complied with them. More frequently, we hedged. Our hedging derived not from a desire to be mysterious or circuitous, but from caution combined with an effort to generate rules out of project activities and our observations of them. Especially in the early days of the project, we had only the vaguest conception of what our role might be. But even as late as December, 1975, at a meeting of one of the newly organized context groups, "I try to help clarify my role, which isn't easy, since I haven't got it clarified all that well for myself."

Although the evaluators accepted a communicator role in this complex network of sometimes uncoordinated groups (at times we were probably the only ones who had knowledge of nearly everything that was happening), we sometimes hedged in that capacity too. In addition to the difficulty of responding to requests for information which we considered confidential or otherwise damaging to the donor (e.g., from a leader, "Do you think those people know what they are doing?"), there were more subtle problems of communication. What were the legitimate channels? To whom were we responsible? For example, when a memorandum was sent to the project director to be distributed by him to members of the administrative committee and he neglected to distribute it, what do we do? In the one instance when this occurred, we pursued it and discovered that the problem was one of oversight rather than the obstruction of information. Nevertheless, we adopted a policy of distributing materials directly to the administrative committee after that. In communicating project policies with which we were not necessarily in accord, we did our job of informing, but also made it clear that what happened from then on was not our business as evaluators:

> Mary asks about contacting the (other group working on the same problem). She seems to be asking *my* permission. I remind her of Sheila's request that groups working on the same issue remain independent of each other for a while—but I add that it is Mary's decision whether to go along with this or not. (Small curriculum sub-group, 11/75)

There are many instances where the evaluators mentioned project policy to a group—sometimes reminding and sometimes informing for the first time. When the evaluator warned one group to be cautious about recommendations for accreditation of sociology departments, the group leader insisted that this was an absurd policy which put his group in a double bind, and demanded that the evaluator convey the problem to the project director. The evaluator did so, and was present at a later meeting when the project director negotiated this policy with the group.

Despite our need for time in which to mutually define, test and redefine our role, we gradually came to engage in certain types of activity with increasing regularity. On occasion, we invited ourselves or asked to be included at meetings. As our rules became clearer, we also began to openly volunteer various types of information and suggestions. We frequently assumed an organizational consultant role. The second of a series of written "Feedback Memoranda" to the administrative committee appeared before the project was a year old (November, 1975). In that memo we made several suggestions (e.g., it would be helpful if the project, despite its populist ideology, could attract more prominent sociologists) and observations (e.g., the project appeared to us to be assuming many of the characteristics of a social movement and perhaps they should consider whether this was desirable, and if so, what kind of social movement they intended to become).

We attempted to rescue the abortive effort of the project to solicit and screen proposals from teachers of sociology. Following the first attempt, we conducted a telephone interview with those sociologists who had submitted proposals, analyzed the responses, and prepared a written report which included recommendations for improving the procedure the second time around. We also presented this report orally to the screening committee as it was about to begin its work. All of this was on our own initiative.

A mail survey of all project participants was undertaken after the first annual report of the project was criticized by the funding agency for failing to indicate any impact. FIPSE recognized that overall measures would not be feasible, but they wondered why it was not at least possible to learn something of the impact of the project on those sociologists who were involved directly with it. This seemed to us to be a reasonable suggestion, and "I suggested to Oscar that we could help him with some of the demands FIPSE was making on him. Specifically, their inquiry about the extent to which the project was having any impact on the participants and their institutions" (Internal memo, 4/2/76). Both quantitative and qualitative feedback reports resulted from this survey. It was repeated about a year later.[11]

The senior evaluator initiated several long, private discussions with the project director, in which the agenda consisted primarily of personal feedback to him, for example, urging him to find a leader for the unactivated task group, or pointing out to him instances of communication failure between his office and others in the project. This management consultant role was also exercised at administrative committee meetings where, for example, we warned against smugness after the group congratulated itself on the extensive organization it had built within one year. We pointed out that there was more to success than "getting organized." We also encouraged members of the administrative committee to urge the resisting project director to reorganize a major task group—and supported them in their urging.

The extent of our participation was wide and our role varied. The project director described (and titled) two remaining facets of the evaluator's role as "your finger wagging function" and "your gyroscope function." He employed these terms in response to comments made by the evaluator at administrative committee meetings in the winter and spring of 1978.

The finger wagging function evolved out of our active role as project moralists—the conscience of the project. Our field notes reflect frequent statements and gestures of admonition or disapproval. This type of activity occurred at the very first meeting we attended, when we lectured the director and staff about their obligations to the many volunteers who had traveled great distances to join this project activity. Priority, we announced, should not lie with facilitating bookkeeping procedures; rather, it should lie with repaying the volunteers for their travel expenses as quickly as possible. Many of them were people not in the habit of traveling or using credit cards and many of them were not well paid. More recently, when the administrative committee was engaged in one of its frequent discussions of how better to incorporate community college teachers into project activities, we wagged a finger and warned of co-opting and patronizing community college teachers.

The gyroscope function appeared to literally refer to our effort to bring things back into balance when they appeared to become unbalanced. We reminded them of things they intended to do but neglected. The involvement of students in the project is a case in point. After a year of talking about this without any activity on the part of the project people, the evaluators organized a student panel dealing with the project at an undergraduate sociology conference. We struggled, along with members, over the role of undergraduate students in a program which, at least indirectly, defined them as clients. After a few futile efforts to chide the project director and the administrative committee into involving students, we gave up. We gave up in part because we had done what we could, and in part because we were not convinced that undergraduate students would have a great deal to contribute to the project. Ultimately we accepted the view that teachers of undergraduate sociology formed the clientele of the project.

We also urged that pedagogical techniques be supplemented with sociological substance, that the project attempt to reach out beyond the one discipline, and reminded our friends on the project that they tended to talk selectively with sociologists who share their concerns, and that their influence may not have been as endemic as they sometimes liked to believe.

Whose side were we on? In answer to his own question, Becker (1966–67) chooses the underdog. We think we made the same choice. Our discussion on the preceding pages illustrates how we reported different kinds of things to different parties, but we never reported anything to the funding agencies or to the Council of the American Sociological Association. Ignoring these seats of power, we focused on the project itself, choosing to select for feedback those parties who could most effectively use it: a task group, the administrative committee, a proposal screening committee, an individual leader, the project director. When differences developed within the project, we were inclined to play advocate for the less powerful. Although we tended to communicate information downward through the hierarchy, we tended to communicate problems upward.

This section has been an attempt to paint a portrait of how we fumbled along in our efforts to create a definition of selves as evaluators, and how the members worked with us to begin to evolve a somewhat shared perspective on who we were and what we did—our mutual role relationships. The portrait may not illustrate the evolving set of rules as clearly as we would like, but it does illustrate the extent to which we deliberately broke the rule of objectivity, the rule of reactivity, and the rule of goal directed research. Having broken these, as well as the rule of the final report, let us close this chapter with a consideration of our rule-breaking.

RULE BREAKING: TOWARD USEFUL EVALUATION RESEARCH

The Rule of Objectivity. This paper opens with Gouldner's argument that partisanship is not incompatible with objectivity. Many social scientists do not agree with this. Following Gouldner's line of reasoning, we could argue that we have indeed been "objective" in our partisanship toward the teaching project; we will not. Following a useful distinction made by Gouldner (1968a), we have deliberately eschewed a value-free stance, but have attempted to maintain a degree of judicious detachment. Only by separating ourselves temporarily from an activity which we valued could we be helpful in ways members could not.

In spite of our deep involvement with the activities of the project and our desire for it to succeed in its efforts, and despite our difficulties in walking the thin line between interfering and being helpful, the language of the project director in describing our activities suggests that we had some success. To the extent that we were viewed as maintaining a "finger wagging function" and a "gyroscope function" for the members, there is evidence of some degree of detachment. Such detachment required constant reinforcement in order to resist co-optation. One device the senior evaluator occasionally employed was to initiate a game of "bad-mouthing." The evaluators would argue with one another, employing irreverent terms to describe the project's activities and members. These forced us to explain to ourselves why the project and its members were, in fact, not "that bad."

Another defense against co-optation was provided by our annual turnover of graduate assistants and, sometimes, research-typists, who provided a fresh and uninvolved glimpse at our activities and those of the members. Martha Beattie (1978), for example, insisted on treating the evaluators' field notes with the same skepticism that any other document deserved. A final protection for the evaluators lay in their deep commitment to traditional academic values of scholarship and research. Although we believed good teaching to be important, we also believed that good scholarship was no less so. These sentiments were not always shared by all members of the project.

Had we attempted to exercise conventional standards of objectivity, it would have been impossible to obtain the degree of trust and confidence members placed in us. Without that trust and confidence, we could not have understood the inner workings of the project as well as we did. To end the chain of reasoning, without the understanding it would not have been possible for us to be helpful or useful even in the minimal ways we were. But then, objective scientists do not generally feel any obligation to be helpful or useful. Since usefulness is, for us, the primary function of evaluation research, we suggest that scientific objectivity interferes with effective program evaluation.

The Rule of Measurable Outcomes.[12] In the introduction to this paper, we documented the fact that evaluation research, according to most authorities, can be applied only to programs with specific and explicit goals. These goals must be operationalized so that measures of their attainment can be obtained. When the goals are not clearly specified, it is argued that program people must be persuaded to make them so before evaluation research is possible. In challenging this rule, let us take a cue from organizational theory. Students of social organization, regardless of perspective or other diversity, are agreed on one thing: organizations are seldom what they pretend to be (Bogdan, 1972; Becker, et al., 1968; Gouldner, 1968b; Perrow, 1961; Blau, 1955).

The structures, processes, and goals of any organization must be assumed to vary in fact from their descriptions in form. Bogdan (1972), in explaining how "original goals become bastardized," observes that goal displacement is regarded as a key concept (Merton, 1957; Michels, 1959; Clark, 1956), while efforts to understand how organizations change their goals find the idea of goal succession most useful (Sills, 1957; Blau and Scott, 1961; Thompson and McEwen, 1958). The teaching project and its evaluation should be viewed from this organizational perspective.

The researcher's legitimate need to think in terms of measurement and to operationalize concepts can create serious problems when imposed upon program people and applied to program evaluation. In fact, the presumed requirement for clearcut goals traps the evaluation researcher into denying what he or she already knows: the "goals" which appear in proposals are designed to meet funding needs which do not always coincide with program needs. What people say they intend to do in their proposal is not necessarily what happens in their program. Furthermore, the commitment to clearcut goals contradicts knowledge derived from organizational theory about goal displacement and goal succession. Goals do change! Finally, program operators are generally trained for and experienced with efforts to help people in trouble. This kind of competence does not always entail the rigor in defining explicit goals which the researcher would like to find. Although the objectives of the ASA projects to improve undergraduate teaching are spelled out and described, the absence of clearcut goals in The Project means that by conventional standards it cannot be evaluated. We know of no way by which honest measures could be developed to provide a fair test of the effectiveness of The Project. Contrary to conventional evaluation research wisdom, we believe it is feasible to attempt to evaluate such a project. Let us consider these goal-related issues.

One way to avoid the goal trap is to recognize that goals and methods evolve and change during the lifetime of a program. The original proposal of the teaching project (Mauksch, 1973) refers to an "experimental phase" in which a program of experimentation in nine selected schools was to be initiated and evaluated. Attempts to achieve this objective ran into difficulties from the beginning. It was modified and eventually abandoned altogether. In traditional goal-oriented evaluation terms, this reflects a clear failure on the part of the project.[13] In organizational theory terms, it is a blend of goal displacement and goal succession. On the other hand, some of the project's original goals appear to have been achieved, for example, "To develop an information and resource exchange (possibly in the ASA office)," or to develop a national network of teacher-consultants.

Adaptation is usually essential to survival. Evaluation based on goals and methods immutably fixed at the program's origin ignores this fact and, in doing so, invites subterfuge, evasion, and mistrust between program people and evaluators. When the evaluator insists on specifying and retaining a fixed set of goals, program people are inhibited from learning as they go and from creating new strategies to deal with what they learn. The most "scientific" kind of evaluation research, based on measuring fixed criteria, may profoundly and adversely effect the program it evaluates. This is not the kind of reactivity we will propose below.

The evaluator may fall into a goal trap as a result of the ritual of the research proposal which demands clear definitions of means and goals. The political and public relations motivated pronouncements of program operators can be equally misleading, should the evaluator take them seriously. It is our position that evaluation is more likely to be accurate and useful if the researcher assumes responsibility for discovering what goals and strategies are in fact evolving in the program and what forces are contributing to their development.

This perspective not only shifts responsibility for goal specification to the researchers, it also suggests that a goal-seeking stance may in itself be inappropriate. We assume that any intervention in an ongoing social process will create certain consequences for certain parties. It then becomes an aim of the evaluation research to identify whatever consequences may be attributable to the program—intended or unintended, anticipated or unanticipated, desirable or undesirable. Rather than intimidating program people into specifying spurious goals, the investigator takes on the job of determining empirically what it is that program people are trying to do and how they go about it. We saw this as our central job on the ASA Teaching Project.

Such a procedure implies that evaluators and program people share the assumption that what the program attempts to achieve is worth achieving. It further assumes a modicum of integrity and competence on the part of the program people. It is assumed that they know their business and are making an effort to apply their experience and ability to altering some state of reality through the device of a "program." Our experience with the teaching project suggests that these assumptions are tenable. The fact that they may not be able to precisely state what they are trying to accomplish and by what means does not necessarily mean that they do not know what they are doing. If our subjects' behavior appears ambiguous or their goals obscure, it is up to *us* to discover the explanation.[14]

THE RULE OF NONREACTIVITY: DOING OBTRUSIVE RESEARCH

The third rule which is challenged in this chapter is that the investigator should not alter the object of study by the process of studying it. The rigorous evaluator carefully avoids interfering in the operation of the program, making the necessary measurements as unobtrusively as possible. Final assessments of the program's strengths and weaknesses are reported at the conclusion of the program or the evaluation. We believe that it is more useful for program development and troubleshooting if evaluators provide constant feedback of critical information, as we attempted to do on the teaching project. We also believe that this process helps to generate an improved program. Since such feedback is deliberately reactive in its effort to assist the program, it may also be described as obtrusive research. Such obtrusive research converts that act of program evaluation into the process of program improvement. It provides the program with a continuing assessment of what it is doing and what it is not doing, and permits program people to reassess their efforts and consider redirecting them while there is still time.

Because human beings are not passive, inert matter, they are inclined to wonder about what is happening when they are the objects of social research, and are inclined to make definitions of the event and of the relationship between themselves and the people who are studying them. This wondering and defining may alter what would otherwise be occurring. Social scientists have been aware for some time of this phenomenon of changing the object of study by the very process of studying it. Historically, we probably first took serious note of it as "The Hawthorne Effect." One of the major conclusions of the classic Hawthorne Studies was that workers became more productive as a consequence of their awareness of being studied.[15] *It was viewed as a benign effect!* Since that time, many types of research and researcher effects have been identified and labeled and

inevitably defined as malignant methodological artifacts to be eliminated
Among these are "reactivity" (Campbell, 1957), demand characteristic
(Orne, 1962), experimenter effects (Rosenthal, 1966), and various forms o
response sets (Phillips and Clancey, 1970; Weiss, 1970; Carr, 1971), includ
ing "acquiescence" and "desirability." We refer loosely to all such effects a
"reactivity."

We believe, along with Sommer (1968), that these so-called sources o
error are, in fact, intrinsic ingredients of everyday social life. As evaluators
our concern is not with their elimination or reduction; our concern is t
understand how reactivity works to either enhance or impede progran
goals. The analysis of our data from the teaching project suggests some o
the ways in which the evaluator role is negotiated. The negotiation process
although always present, becomes particularly dramatic when neither th
project nor the evaluation procedures are clearly defined. Reactivity, then
as we see it, is the process of interaction between project members and th
investigators as well as the consequences of that interaction.

There are two opposing forces which need to be taken into account as on
interprets this chapter: on the one hand, there is a common disciplinary
bond among members and evaluators. We are all sociologists. As eval
uators, we were not foreign ethnographers exploring exotic tribes o
sociologists attempting to understand social strata or social activities whicl
were strange to us. *We were natives studying our own people!* On the other
hand, there was a great deal of heterogeneity and variability in the factors
affecting interactions between them and us. The approximately 100 project
members varied in age, sex, marital status, career and disciplinary orientations, prestige within their own institutions and within the discipline, as
well as many other social, demographic, ethnic, or psychological variables.
These factors, of course, affect interaction between members and evaluators.

To further complicate this matter, there are the critical differences we
have mentioned between the two evaluators. The senior evaluator is male,
married, well-known within the discipline, and roughly contemporary in age
with the project director and other influential leaders; the associate evaluator is female, single, a recent Ph.D., and, although older than most recent
graduates, seems generally perceived as a contemporary by working members and lower level leaders within the project. If these variables affect the
ways in which members see each of the evaluators, then they also effect ways
in which each of the evaluators sees members, and certainly both of these
differential perceptions alter the mode of interaction between each evaluator
and project members.

Program improvement is indeed a form of contamination created by the
evaluators. Experimental design and the logic of experimentation are
sabotaged under such conditions. But then, experimental design is hardly

>ossible where there is no control group and not even a reasonably
approximate comparison group, where there are no pre-program measures,
where the program aims to intervene in a process which is subject to the
influence of many other factors—both known and unknown, and where
program strategy and tactics are constantly evolving. It is our contention
that this is a description of a typical program and, therefore that our
arguments and our methods are applicable to the evaluation of many social
programs. It is regrettable that, without experimental evidence, it is not
possible to attribute causation to the program as the agent of change. Since
most authorities on program evaluation agree that experimentation is
difficult, if not impossible, under program conditions, little is lost by
abandoning the effort.

Without the support of experimental logic, our efforts to attribute
causation must rest on plausible explanations which our data fail to
contradict and appear to support. If we can rule out alternate explanations,
so much the better. However, the evaluation cannot provide conclusive
evidence that the world or any part of it is different as a result of the
program.

Within the sociological tradition, participant observation and inductive
analysis offer methodological clues for the evaluation of programs whose
goals and means are difficult to operationalize and are subject to fluctua-
tions. Participant observation shares, with laboratory experimentation,
survey research, and interviewing, the reactivity problem created in the
interaction between subject and investigator. The research situation becomes defined in ways which change the behavior of both parties and may
change the outcome of the interaction—in this case, the research results.
When the purpose of participant observation is program evaluation rather
than basic research, reactivity may be viewed differently. If the purpose of
the evaluators is to help the program, then the problem of reactivity is no
longer "How can it be minimized?" The problem becomes one of distinguishing between useful and useless (or even harmful) types of reactivity.

The Rule of the Final Report. At the beginning of this chapter, we
acknowledged that scientific research which is not reported in a manner
which permits the scrutiny of colleagues is not research at all. But evaluation
research has two major functions, the lesser of which concerns scientific
knowledge. Its primary function is to provide useful feedback to those
responsible for the program. The carefully constructed scientific report is
likely to be too late to be of much use to the program and to be in a form
which is difficult to translate into program planning. For example, whatever
its faults may be, the present chapter is in the style of a scholarly report. It
is unlikely to be much use to those responsible for the teaching project.

In evaluating the teaching project, we have followed Etzioni's advice for
effective communication in policy research (1971:10): "Frequently repeated,

face-to-face exchanges seem very necessary. . . . The report itself often is not really necessary; it serves more to fulfill contractual obligation. . . ." It is not unusual for evaluation research to take the form of a ritual requirement tolerated by all parties, and for the final report to be (1) required, (2) acknowledged, and (3) ignored. To be useful, the evaluation researcher needs to develop organizational channels and lines of communication which permit him or her to reach relevant members in an ongoing and informal process. In this chapter we have attempted to convey something of the flavor of the kinds of relationships we developed and the varied kinds of feedback which ocurred throughout the project.

Etzioni suggested that one should hob-nob with congressmen and their staffs at Washington cocktail parties where much policy is formulated. We wondered how one gets invited to such parties. Fortunately, we were able to follow his principle on the teaching project, both as a member of the administrative committee and, eventually, as personal friends of all of the project leaders and many of its participants.

Effective communication requires not only an available platform, but trust and confidence between members and evaluators. We were not judging strangers as good guys or bad guys, but helping colleagues achieve ends which we shared as valuable. Our final report, an ethnography of the project which will include parts of this chapter, may be published within the next five years. That won't be much help. We hope that our continuing efforts to find useful information for members and to get it to them at the right time and in the right form—sometimes oral, sometimes written, sometimes to one group, and sometimes to another—have been of some help to project members.

We knew that efforts at experimental control would be impossible. We knew that the intricate weaving of other historical processes which focus upon the value of good teaching could not be unraveled. We knew the futility of attempting to judge an ongoing social process as a success or failure at any given point in time. When a project is a process it cannot be evaluated as if it had a beginning and an end. It is the process which demands evaluation, not the outcomes.

Some professional evaluators argue that policy makers respect hard data analyzed with precision. We see no evidence for that. In fact, many policy makers cannot interpret the masses of sophisticated statistical analyses which they frequently receive from evaluators. What the policy maker is more likely to find convincing and able to persuade others with is the touching, telling, anecdote. The researchers may have other kinds of evidence which lead them to select appropriate anecdotes, but the anecdote is the effective political weapon—not the test of significance. To the extent that policy making is a political activity, so too must policy research be a political activity.

Our efforts to be obtrusive by design were not as effective as we hoped. Although we have kind testimonials from our project friends, we cannot determine the extent to which our participation in the groups we observed has been useful to those groups. We continued to stumble along in the codification of our methods, hopefully moving toward the formation of sets of rules which can be derived from our activities.

FOOTNOTES

* Substantial criticism of an earlier draft of this chapter was provided by Martha Beattie, Howard S. Becker, Robert Bogdan, Lee H. Bowker, Charles Goldsmid, Kathleen Piker King, and Velma Pomrenke. This material will appear in part in the methodological chapter of the final report on an evaluation of a project to improve undergraduate teaching in sociology. That project, under the direction of Hans O. Mauksch, was supported in part by The Fund For The Improvement of Post-Secondary Education and the Lilly Endowment.

1. A classic statement was articulated by Max Weber at the turn of the century (Weber, 1949). The radical sociology literature and the American Sociologist in the late sixties contain frequent communications on this issue. One sequence of articles which illuminates many of the problems is Gouldner (1962), Becker (1966-67) and Gouldner (1968a).

2. A remarkable exception is found in some of the work of Robert Bogdan and his colleagues. Cf. Bogdan, et al., 1974.

3. Some members of the project disagree with this description. The argument is that a lack of specification of objectives was an intrinsic part of the design. We do not necessarily take issue with that. Our point is only that the means and ends of the project were not specified. It is also believed by some project participants that measurable outcomes are possible if we make certain comparisons before and after the project. It is our position that, because there were other forces in the society working in the same directions as the project, it is not possible to measure the extent to which any change may be attributable to the project itself.

4. It should be clear that most project participants also held some of these activities to be important and engaged in them. But with a few exceptions, project participants gave undergraduate teaching much higher personal priority on this list than did the evaluators.

5. For this service we are most grateful to Linda Lumpp, Barbara Bianco, Kathleen King, Martha Beattie, and Velma Pomrenke.

6. Even the most skillful field workers entertain an uneasy suspicion that they might not find anything. Blanche Geer has provided an essay on such discomfort (1964). Our early rhetoric of "social history" later evolved into an "ethnography" of the project.

7. This first became an issue when the Council of the American Sociological Association insisted that the discipline was too diverse for any orthodox positions—theoretical or methodological—to be prescribed. They set the elimination of any hint of orthodoxy as a condition for approval of the proposal. From that time on, this was to be a thorny issue for the project administration. Its nature and consequences will be analyzed elsewhere.

8. During the early stages of their work, sub-groups coping with the same assignments were encouraged to develop their efforts independently of one another. The evaluators felt obliged to refuse requests to communicate to such groups what their counterparts were doing.

9. Part of the evaluators' own internal rhetoric involved "walking the thin line between interfering and being helpful." It concerned us, and eventually a meeting among the four of us (graduate assistant, typist, research associate, and evaluation director) took place with the sole purpose of codifying the nature of legitimate and illegitimate interventions. This formalization at the end of our first year of field work provided the initial skeleton of the present paper.

10. Members reactions to the draft of this chapter uniformly argue that the evaluator participated more than we suggest. The distinction we attempt (and presumably they ignore) i between actively engaging in the administration or conduct of project affairs and providing feedback when it appeared appropriate. The latter type of participation was viewed as desirable by the evaluators and was engaged in whenever we thought we could be helpful.

11. A thorough analysis of these two waves of questionnaires can be found in Pamela Seubert's M.A. Thesis on this subject (in process). In mailing these feedback memoranda to the administrative committee, the evaluators deliberately excluded the FIPSE Project Officer, who was a member of that committee. The amount and kind of information to be transmitted to the funding agency were left to the discretion of the project director.

12. This discussion of goals derives from a previously published paper by one of the authors. For that more detailed treatment and associated references see Deutscher, 1977.

13. The concepts of success and failure become difficult to deal with when evaluating an ongoing organization, since they can only be applied to a specific point in the process. In their analysis of organizational success and failure of the teaching project, Deutscher and Beattie (in progress) found that a major task group, which could be defined as a failure by several objective criteria, was reorganized and began moving in new directions under new leadership at the time they were analyzing their data. It was no longer clear that the group was a failure

14. Some elements of our methodology may be found in the works of Michael Scriven who has proposed a "goal free" evaluation research (1972) and makes a useful distinction between summative and formative research (1967). The kind of analysis of a project as a social process which we are pursuing resembles Scriven's formative research, while evaluation which focuses on the end-product of the project is what he calls summative research. Others, such as Schulberg and Baker (1968), contrast the "goal attainment model," which implies experimental design, with a "systems model." They opt for the latter, primarily on the grounds of its greater usefulness and greater likelihood of being used.

15. We are aware of the lack of fit between Hawthorne data and Hawthorne conclusions and acknowledge the incredibility of the statistical findings (Cary, 1967). The effect has, however, since been detected in a variety of ways by many investigators. We accept the Hawthorne effect as a credible fact, although its extent or the precise nature of its consequences are questionable

REFERENCES

Beattie, Martha C., "Tracing a Task Force Transformation," M.A. Thesis, Department of Sociology, the University of Akron, 1978.

Becker, Howard S., "Whose Side Are We On?" *Social Problems* 14 (1966–1967):239–247.

Becker, Howard S. and Blanche Geer, "Participant Observation and Interviewing: A Comparison," *Human Organization* 16 (1957):28–32.

Becker, Howard S., Blanche Geer, and Everett C. Hughes, *Making the Grade*, New York: Wiley, 1968.

Becker, Howard S., et al., *Boys in White: Student Culture in Medical School*, Chicago: University of Chicago Press, 1961.

Blau, Peter, *The Dynamics of Bureaucracy*, Chicago: University of Chicago Press, 1955.

Blau, Peter and W. Richard Scott, *Formal Organizations*, San Francisco: Chandler Publishing Co, 1961.

Bogdan, Robert, "Organizational Goals and Success Measurement in a Job-Training Program," Syracuse University, Center on Human Policy, Mimeographed, 1972.

———, "Optimistic Evaluation Research," Syracuse: Syracuse University, Center on Human Policy, Mimeographed, 1978.

Bodgan, Robert, et al., "Let Them Eat Programs: Attendants' Perspectives and Programming on Wards in State Schools," *Journal of Health and Social Behavior* 15 (1947):142–151.

Brooks, Michael P., "The Community Action Program as a Setting for Applied Research," *Journal of Social Issues* 21 (1965):29–40.

ampbell, Donald T., "Factors Relevant to the Validity of Experiments in Social Settings," *Psychological Bulletin* 54 (1957):297-312.

arey, A., "The Hawthorne Studies: A Radical Criticism," *American Sociological Review* 32 (1967):403-416.

arr, Leslie G., "The Srole Scale and Acquiescence," *American Sociological Review* 36 (1971):287-293.

lark, Burton, "Organizational Adaptation and Precarious Values," *American Sociological Review* 21 (1956):327-336.

eutscher, Irwin, "Social Theory, Social Programs, and Program Evaluation: A Metatheoretical Note," *Sociological Quarterly* (forthcoming).

_____ , "Toward Avoiding the Goal Trap in Evaluation Research," Francis G. Caro (ed.), *Readings in Evaluation Research* (Second Edition), New York: Russell Sage Foundation, 1977, 221-238.

eutscher, Irwin, and Martha Beattie, "Success and Failure in Organizing for Change in Higher Education," in progress.

tzioni, Amitai, "Policy Research," *American Sociologist* 6, Supplementary issue (1971):8-12.

eer, Blanche, "First Days in the Field," in P.E. Hammond (ed.), *Sociologists at Work,* New York: Basic Books, 1964, 322-344.

ouldner, Alvin W., "Anti-Minotaur: The Myth of a Value Free Sociology," *Social Problems* 9 (1962):199-213.

_____ , "The Sociologist as Partisan: Sociology and the Welfare State," *The American Sociologist* 3, 2 (May 1968a):103-116.

_____ , "Organizational Analysis," in Robert Merton et al. (eds.), *Sociology Today,* New York: Basic Books, 1968b, 400-428.

reenberg, B.G., "Evaluation of Social Programs," *Review of the International Statistical Institute* 36 (1968):260-277.

nes, Wyatt C. and Edgar F. Borgatta, "Methodology of Evaluation," in Edward J. Mullen et al. (eds.), *Evaluation of Social Intervention,* San Francisco: Jossey-Bass, 1972, 39-54.

eighton, Alexander, *The Governing of Men,* Princeton, N.J.: Princeton University Press, 1945.

auksch, Hans O., *A Program of Assessment, Articulation, and Experimentation in Undergraduate Teaching of Sociology in the United States (Proposal),* Washington, D.C.: American Sociological Association, 1973.

erton, Robert K., *Social Theory and Social Structure,* Glencoe, Ill,: The Free Press, 1957.

ichels, Robert, *Political Parties,* New York: Dover Press, 1959.

rne, Martin T., "On the Social Psychology of the Psychological Experiment," *American Psychologist* 17 (1962):776-783.

errow, Charles, "The Analysis of Goals in Complex Organizations," *American Sociological Review* 26 (1961):854-866.

hillips, Derek L. and Kevin L. Clancey, "Response Biases in Field Studies of Mental Illness," *American Sociological Review* 35 (1970):503-515.

osenthal, Robert, *Experimenter Effects in Behavioral Research,* New York: Appleton-Century Crofts, 1966.

ossi, Peter, "Testing for Success and Failure in Social Action," in Peter Rossi and Walter Williams (eds.), *Evaluating Social Programs,* New York: Seminar Press, 1972, 11-49.

chulberg, Herbert C. and Frank Baker, "Program Evaluation Models and the Implementation of Research Findings," *American Journal of Public Health* 58 (1968):1248-1255.

cott, Marvin B. and Stanford M. Lyman, "Accounts," *American Sociological Review* 13 (1968)46-62.

criven, Michael, "The Methodology of Evaluation," in R. Taylor, P. Gagne, and M. Scriven (eds.), *Perspectives of Curriculum Evaluation,* AERA Monograph Series on Curriculum Evaluation, No. 1, Chicago: Rand McNally, 1967.

_____ , "Pros and Cons About Goal Free Research," Evaluation Comment: *The Journal of Educational Evaluation,* Center for the Study of Evaluation: UCLA, 3 (1972):1-5.

Seubert, Pamela, "Self Reported Changes in Attitudes and Behaviors Toward Teaching," (tentative title), M.A. Thesis, Department of Sociology, the University of Akron, in progress.

Sills, David L., *The Volunteers,* Glencoe, Ill.: The Free Press, 1957.

Sommer, Robert, "Hawthorne Dogma," *Psychological Bulletin* 70 (1968):592–595.

Suchman, Edward A., "Evaluating Educational Programs," *The Urban Review* 3 (1969):15–17

Thompson, James and William McEwen, "Organizational Goals and Environment," *American Sociological Review* 23 (1958):23–31.

Trow, Martin, "Comment on Becker and Geer's 'Participant Observation and Interviewing,' " *Human Organization* 16 (1957):33.

Webb, Eugene J., Donald Campbell, Richard D. Schwarts and Lee Sechrest, *Unobtrusive Measures: Nonreactive Research in the Social Sciences,* Chicago: Rand McNally, 1966

Weber, Max, *On the Methodology of the Social Sciences,* edited by Edward Shils and Henry Finch, Glencoe, Ill.: The Free Press, 1949.

Weiss, Carol, *Interaction in the Research Interview: The Effects of Rapport on Response,* New York: Columbia University Bureau of Applied Social Research, 1970.

MOVIDAS:

THE METHODOLOGICAL AND
THEORETICAL RELEVANCE OF
INTERACTIONAL STRATEGIES[1]

Reyes Ramos, UNIVERSITY OF CALIFORNIA,

SAN DIEGO

I once observed an encounter between an elementary school principal and Jose Perez, the father of a fourth grade student. Mr. Perez had been called to the school to discuss a broken window, which his son allegedly had broken. As I watched Mr. Perez talk with the principal, it occurred to me that he appeared to be both nervous and stupid. He spoke with broken English, and acted as though he did not understand the situation very well. Mr. Perez seemed to have stepped right off the pages of a sociological text (Grebler, et al, 1970; Moore, 1973; Penalosa, 1968). He conformed to the

Studies in Symbolic Interaction—Volume 2, 1979, pages 141–165
Copyright © 1979 by JAI Press Inc.
All rights of reproduction in any form reserved.
ISBN: 0–89232–105–9

typification of a Mexican American who speaks little English, and who can only deal with people in informal situations. But I knew differently. Mr. Perez was capable of speaking standard English, and he was able to deal with formal situations. I had seen him interact competently with a city councilman on a previous occasion. Puzzled, I asked him later why he had presented himself in such a demeaning way. Here is what he said:

> Oh, I was pulling a movida [strategy]. You know, I came on like the dumb Mexican, all lost and confused. You know how that guy thinks of us most of the time. Besides, had I come on straight, he might have held me responsible for the window Freddy broke. I am not about to pay for a window my boy broke by accident. They ought to provide a bigger play area so that kids don't break a window every time they throw a ball.

Mexican Americans, like other societal members, use strategies to cope with the practical circumstances in their daily lives. They call their interactional strategies movidas. How and when Mexican Americans create and use movidas is not known. Up to now most researchers of this ethnic group have not made movidas a topic of sociological interest, or even acknowledged their existence (Ramos, 1976). In practically all studies, social scientists describe Mexican American behavior as being culturally determined (Vaca, 1970). Recently, this claim has been criticized by some (Ramos, 1973; Romano, 1968; Vaca, 1970) who suggest that Mexican Americans do not behave solely in terms of the cultural values that have been attributed to Mexican American culture. Ramos (1973) has pointed out that Mexican Americans rely upon their commonsense knowledge of everyday life, which may or may not have anything to do with Mexican American culture, to interpret how they are to manage situations. Regardless of the position taken in this debate on whether or not Mexican American behavior is culturally determined, few have focused upon Mexican Americans as manipulators of situations and as deceivers of others. Consequently, very little is known about movidas and their use by Mexican Americans to organize and manage their daily lives.

Besides overlooking the existence and use of movidas, most social scientists in their studies of Mexican Americans also neglect to connect their data with a discussion of theoretical and methodological issues in sociology (e.g., see Heller, 1968; Grebler, et al, 1970; Derbyshire, 1969). Consequently, the literature on the Mexican American is primarily descriptive, with few discussions of methodological and theoretical issues. The purpose of this chapter is to attend to these two overlooked areas in the study of the Mexican American: the use of interactional strategies (movidas) by Mexican Americans and the sociological issues of theory and methodology which pertain to the study of movidas. First, Mexican Americans' use of movidas is documented with the presentation of two ethnographic examples. The examples are called "The Literacy Routine" and "The Authoritarian

ather." These two titles are meant to indicate the strategies used by
ndividuals in two specific instances of behavior, and are not labels for
eneral strategies. The emphasis, however, is primarily on the general idea
of movidas and their use, rather than on the identification of specific
novidas.

The discussion which follows the ethnographic data focuses on the
heoretical and methodological relevance of studies dealing with Mexican
Americans and their use of strategies. Movidas are shown to be useful in
xtending methods of data collection in order to probe further into the lives
of the people under study, and to discover how people link the ways they
tructure and manage a particular situation with the other situations which
nake up the broader social context in which they operate. This discussion
of methodology leads to a discussion of the primitive character of current
thnographic work as well as the effect primitive ethnographic work has on
any theory of social organization.

Since the primary purpose in this chapter is to show the relationship
between the study of movidas and the expansion of theoretical notions of
social organization, it is important to discuss the actual method of data
collection used and the style in which the data are presented. The two
examples used as data were collected by depth interview and participant
observation. Each example provides for both the documentation of the
existence and use of movidas, and the documentation of how strategies in
use were collected. Because the methods of depth interviewing and participant observation influence the data produced, it is important that the
researcher not be excluded from the discussion. For this reason, the data are
presented in the first person and in a "story-telling" fashion. Thus, how *I*
discovered and used the idea of the movida to guide *me* in doing the
particular depth interviewing and participant observation that I did is an
important part of understanding how theory and methodology are related.

AN ETHNOGRAPHIC ACCOUNT OF MOVIDAS

The Literacy Routine

The Trujillos are a low income Mexican American family whom I studied
for a year.[2] The Trujillos are illiterate and, like other illiterate people, they
tend to hide their illiteracy. They do so by developing and using movidas
(strategies) to make themselves appear as if they are literate. This account,
then, is on how I learned that Mr. and Mrs. Trujillo are illiterate, and how
I discovered their strategy for presenting themselves to others in ways that
make them appear as if they are literate.

During the year in which I studied the Trujillos, I visited their home many
times.[3] On one occasion, when I had gone to the Trujillos to talk with them
about the many problems they were having with community agencies, in

particular the public school, I observed how Mr. and Mrs. Trujillo managed to appear as if they were literate to a child welfare worker from the Department of Welfare.

The welfare worker had come to pick up the family's ten-year-old boy, Jimmy, who was being placed in a foster home in a neighboring town so that he could attend a school for the emotionally disturbed. Although I had gone to the home to have a general conversation with the parents, I ended up getting much more specific information than I had expected simply by witnessing the encounter between the caseworker and the family.

The conversation recorded here began when I knocked on the door and Mrs. Trujillo answered.[4] She seemed surprised to see me.

Mrs. Trujillo:	Oh, I thought you were the lady from welfare.
Ramos:	No.
Mrs. Trujillo:	Come in, come in. Honey, it's Mr. Ramos.
Ramos:	I'm not disturbing anything, am I?
Mrs. Trujillo:	No, come in and sit down. We're only waiting for the welfare. They found a place for him [Jimmy] and they said they were coming by this afternoon. Around two, I think. Two, honey?[5]
Mr. Trujillo:	I think that's what the card said.
Mrs. Trujillo:	We lost the card. Anyway, the caseworker always comes around two. So, when you knocked we thought, "Here they come."
Ramos:	If you'd like I can come back later today, or whenever you have time to talk.
Mrs. Trujillo:	That's all right. We can talk.
Mr. Trujillo:	We're just sitting here waiting.
Mrs. Trujillo:	Oh, we got up early. Didn't we, honey? We wanted to be ready. We packed Jimmy's clothes in that box and we've been ready since around noon.
Ramos:	Then it's O.K. to talk for awhile?
Mrs. Trujillo:	Oh, yes. [She said this while looking at her husband.]
Mr. Trujillo:	Why not, we might as well talk while we sit here. It'll probably make the time go faster.
Ramos:	The last time I was here with Margaret [my co-worker] we were talking about some of the problems you are having. Could we talk about that again? And do you mind if I tape our talk?
Mrs. Trujillo:	That a tape recorder?
Mr. Trujillo:	I thought it was some kind of little piano.
Mrs. Trujillo:	That's what I thought. It looks like a musical instrument.
Ramos:	Here, I'll show you how it works.

I then proceeded to demonstrate the tape recorder to them for about five minutes. I showed them the mechanics of the machine and taped their voices so they knew what to expect. As I finished and was about to start the interview, a car stopped in front of the house. Both parents looked at each other and Mrs. Trujillo got up, went to the window, and said, "It's the caseworker. No, it's not her car. It's another person."

Mr. Trujillo and I stood up while Mrs. Trujillo went to the front door. She opened the door as a young woman about thirty years old walked up the front steps.

Woman: Hello.
Mrs. Trujillo: Hello, how are you?
Woman: Fine, thank you. I am Mrs. Jones, the child placement worker. Did you get my card?
Mrs. Trujillo: Yes, yes, come in and sit down. This is my husband. This is Mr. Ramos.

After the introduction we sat down and the mother faced Mrs. Jones and smiled as if to ask, "What do we do now?" The situation was tense. At the time, I did not want to tape the conversation without permission or to interrupt by asking to tape. Since I was at one end of the room and Mrs. Jones and the parents were toward the other and not directly facing me, I took notes unnoticed.

Mrs. Jones: I know this is hard for you. But, ah, he [Jimmy] is only going to be thirty miles away and you can come up and visit on weekends. If you like, I can arrange the visits. He is a lucky boy; it's a good school, one of the best. And the family is a nice family. They have children his age and he'll be happy.
Mrs. Trujillo: [Looking down at the floor and with her hands on her lap] Well, yes, but—
Mrs. Jones: I know this is difficult, but remember the school is going to help him. Here, will you please sign this release form?

Both parents were staring at the floor but straightened up and looked at each other when she said they had to sign a form. Mrs. Jones handed Mr. Trujillo the form. He looked at it. He looked at it very seriously and nodded occasionally. He gave the impression that he was giving the paper a careful reading. After two or three minutes he looked at his wife and said, "Here, honey, you look at it."

She took the form and turned her body to one side and moved the paper to allow more light to fall on it. She held it for a while and appeared to be reading it carefully. Then she looked up.

Mrs. Trujillo: Do we sign where the "X" is?
Mrs. Jones: Yes.

Mrs. Trujillo: Does it matter who signs it?
Mrs. Jones: No, it's O.K. as long as one of you signs it.
Mrs. Trujillo: I'll sign it since I have it. Can I borrow your pen?

The mother signed the form and said, "There!" Everyone smiled. Mrs. Jones got up as the mother handed her the form and said, "I guess it's best if we leave soon." Jimmy's mother said, "Jimmy, get your box." Jimmy who had been sitting in the kitchen, walked in and picked up a little box which had Campbell Soup written on it in big red letters. His mother put her hand on his shoulder and everyone walked to the front door.

Mrs. Trujillo: This is Mrs. Jones who is going to take you to that nice
                  school we've been talking about.
Mrs. Jones: You'll like it, Jimmy.
Mrs. Trujillo: Behave yourself. [She said this as she kissed him good
                  bye on the forehead.]

It was very tense and sad. With his little box, Jimmy walked out of the house with Mrs. Jones and we watched them go to her car. She took his little box, put it on the back seat, and they both got into the front seat. We were all waving good-bye from the front door. The mother kept saying, "Bye and behave yourself." Jimmy looked at us for the first time and started to cry He put his head down on the seat and they drove off with Jimmy crying. I was very sad.

Mrs. Trujillo cried. We all just stood at the front door for about five minutes. It seemed longer than that. While we stood, I kept trying to think of faraway things so I would not start crying myself. I kept hoping that something would happen to change the situation. Finally Mr. Trujillo stopped the mother's sobbing by saying, "We'll go see him on Sunday and take him some candy. He'll be all right." "He's going to be sad," said Mrs Trujillo.

We then went back and sat down and Mr. Trujillo inquired if I was still interested in talking with them. I said yes and stressed that we did not have to if they did not feel up to it. He nodded yes and I interviewed them about some school problems. We did not discuss their literacy routine.

The occasion of witnessing the welfare worker and the parents interacting with each other was an event I had not planned on, yet it provided me with two research opportunities. First, I was able to see how the parents presented themselves as if they could read: each parent took the release form and appeared to be giving it a careful reading, before the mother asked if it mattered who signed the form and actually signed it. The way in which the Trujillos managed the signing of the form gave the impression that they had read and understood the contents of the form.

However, I knew differently. It is important to discuss how *I* learned about their illiteracy. The Trujillos, like most illiterate people I have met, did not readily tell others about their inability to read and write. They were areful and they tended to put forth great effort in hiding their illiteracy. What prompted Mrs. Trujillo to reveal their illiteracy to me was another vent I had not planned on, and one which shows why it is imperative that researcher share, as best as he can, the commonsense knowledge used by he persons he is studying to cope with their everyday life.

Several weeks prior to my witnessing the Trujillos' performance of their teracy routine for the child welfare worker, Mrs. Trujillo asked me if I ould fill out a questionnaire for them. From her I learned that their oldest on, Bobby, was in prison. They had received a questionnaire with Bobby's ame on it, but did not know how to answer it. Mrs. Trujillo said to me, 'We got a letter that looks important and it has Bobby's name on it. We aven't been able to answer it and I think we better answer it. Will you help s?" Indeed, the letter was important, as it concerned Bobby's upcoming arole hearing.

According to Mrs. Trujillo, the person who generally helped them with uch matters had gotten mad at them. Consequently, they had been earching for about a month for someone else they could trust to tell about heir son being in prison and who would be willing to fill out the questionnaire. They had been unsuccessful in their search until they asked ne. I agreed to fill out the questionnaire for them. The questionnaire, like nost written correspondence, was a form of trouble for which they had had o develop coping strategies such as their movida (literacy routine).

Had I not been asked to fill out the questionnaire, I would not have nown that both parents were illiterate and that the mother was the only ne who could sign her name. Their "reading" of the release form, then, vould have convinced me that they were literate. My witnessing this erformance was a research opportunity because I learned how the parents ctually managed a situation in which they were asked to read and sign apers in front of other people who did not know, and whom the parents lid not want to know, that they were illiterate.

The second research opportunity resulted because I used the parents' trategy of appearing as if they were literate as a research guide to help me liscover what I might want to research further, in order to understand etter the relationship between this particular family and the Department of Welfare. Thus, I took the parents' literacy performance as a cue: the arents' behavior was pointing to an area that I should study further if I vanted to find out what kinds of images others had of this family. Consequently, I made it a point to learn who, if anyone, in the welfare lepartment knew the parents were illiterate, what actions the welfare lepartment took in terms of whether or not they knew the parents were lliterate, and whether or not the parents performed this movida for veryone or just for certain people. In this way I used the coping strategies eople create to manage their affairs as a research guide.

In getting to know the family, I learned that, beyond the immediate family, only a few very close friends knew they were illiterate. For all others the parents performed a movida—they always presented themselves as if they could read and write. They were also very careful in selecting whom to tell about their inability to read and write, in both Spanish and English. This was a point of much concern to them. Indeed, the parents had to be concerned, for their inability to read and write faced them every day and they constantly had to deal with it.

From the welfare workers I interviewed, I learned that they thought the Trujillos were literate. It was not only common knowledge among the welfare workers, but it was a matter of record. When I interviewed the welfare workers, they said such things as the following:

> We've written to them, but they never answer our letters. We've even gone so far as to send our letters with self-addressed envelopes. They've never even sent those back!

The written record in the parents' folder showed the Trujillos as deviant and uncooperative parents:

> They are uncooperative. They never answer our correspondence. They appear disinterested in their children. If they cared about them, they would take the time to answer our letters.

Not once throughout a twenty page "dossier" on the family was it mentioned or even hinted at that both parents were illiterate. From reading the folder, one could easily see and understand how a new caseworker would work under the assumption that the parents were able to read and write, especially since they were very skillful in presenting their strategy. Thus, it can be concluded that the Trujillo's manner of coping with their illiteracy could and did generate trouble for them.

The Authoritarian Father

Although the "Literacy Routine" documents in part the use of movidas by Mexican Americans, another example can show the diversity and uniqueness of this behavior. The focus of "The Authoritarian Father" is on the interaction between Mr. Fausto and two of his daughters. In this case Mr. Fausto, a farm worker, managed a situation in such a way that he appeared very concerned with the quality of his and his family's work output.

The Faustos are Mexican American farm workers and ex-migrants from Texas who settled in the area where I was doing my study. I first met Mr. Fausto at the local community action center. We both went there often, or at least it seemed that way, because he was always there when I went, and I went often. Each time we met, I tried to interest him in sending his children to the summer migrant school held in the school where I worked. One evening, about the third time we met at the community action center, Mr. Fausto asked me to bring to his home the registration papers for summer migrant school, since he could not go to the school during the work day. I agreed to take them the following afternoon.

His house was out-of-town and near the sugar beet fields where he worked. Since it was late afternoon when my co-worker and I set out to make the visit to the Faustos and another family, I asked my co-worker to drop me off where I thought I would find Mr. Fausto and his family thinning beets with other farm workers in a field near their home. Indeed I found them there.

My co-worker dropped me off where the workers had their cars parked. They were parked right up to the edge of the beet field. I sat on a fender of one of the cars to wait until Mr. Fausto was done working. The group of workers were near the end of a set of rows, which ended just about where I was sitting, when Mr. Fausto started to scold his two daughters, who were working in the group, but who were behind the rest of the group. His shouting at the girls was heard by the other workers as well as by me.

Mr. Fausto: Haven't I told you to quit playing? We're here to work and you're not to engage in tomfoolery. Next time I catch you or hear that you're not working like you should, you can expect to be kicked out of the field and all the way home. Do you understand me?

Girls: Yes sir. [Said rather softly.]

Mr. Fausto: Eh!

One Girl: Yes sir. We'll do our job right.

Mr. Fausto: And you? [Said to the girl who did not answer.]

Other Girl: Yes sir.

Mr. Fausto: Don't you forget what I've said.

The two girls did not answer any more and looked as if they were embarrassed by their father's action. The situation was rather tense and the rest of the workers turned and started a new set of rows. The whole group moved away from where I was sitting and worked towards the opposite end of the field. They got there and worked back up again towards me. Then they stopped for the day on the side where I was waiting. The workers made their way towards their cars and I walked toward Mr. Fausto, who was walking toward me. We greeted each other and I asked if I could hitch a ride to his house with him, because my co-worker was to pick me up there. He said yes and we got into his car. We got into the front seat and the two girls got into the back seat. As we drove, Mr. Fausto started to talk with his two girls.

Mr. Fausto: Forgive me for having screamed at you. I didn't mean to, but I thought I didn't have any other choice.

One Girl: There is no reason to ask forgiveness.

I found Mr. Fausto's talk strange. I could not understand why he was apologizing to his daughters. After all, were they not misbehaving out in the beet field? At least Mr. Fausto made it appear as if they were by scolding them. I defined his behavior as evidence that they indeed had been misbehaving, and I supposed that other people observing him had reached the same conclusion. In addition, I took the daughter's response to mean more than a mere gesture of paying deference to her father. I felt that she knew why he did it, since her tone of voice indicated that. Their talk gave me the sense that they shared a knowledge that I did not share with them. Therefore, I concluded from the exchange that what happened out in the beet field was not what it appeared to be, but rather something else, and I decided to treat the action in the beet field as a strategy in use and to use it as my point of departure to learn more about the Fausto's life. Thus, I participated in their conversation.

Ramos: When you say you didn't have any other choice, what did you mean?

Mr. Fausto: The girls had been playing around the other day and had not been paying attention to what they were doing. Some of my friends told me the crew leader made some comments about it. So today when I saw the crew leader looking at the girls who were behind the rest of the group, I thought they were playing and not working like they should. I got after them not knowing whether or not they were playing because I didn't want the crew leader holding it up to me that my girls don't work like they should. I don't want to give him any excuses to talk to us about our work. I think he is looking for an excuse to fire me. Right now we can't afford to be out of work. We need the money. So when I saw him looking at the girls and the others looking at him and at me, I thought I had to do something right away.

Ramos: Why does he want to fire you?

Mr. Fausto: He's mad at me. He doesn't like for me to be talking about Chavez's union. I think we should have a union and I talk about it. The others are interested, but they keep quiet about it. I don't. I think the crew leader thinks he'll be better off if he runs me away. And I think we'll be better off if we stay. [He said laughingly.] We don't have a penny and we have no choice but to hold on to this job. As you know, this is the only work around here.

What Mr. Fausto had to say was rather straightforward. However, one important point needs to be made: Mr. Fausto defined the situation in terms of past and probable future events in his life. That is, he defined the situation in terms of the commonsense knowledge of the broader social world in which he operated. He did not simply rely upon his commonsense knowledge of the specific features of the situation to define it. He tied the different aspects of the situation to the other activities which made up his life and which had to be managed in ways that depended on how he managed the situation in the beet field. This aspect of how persons link events in the process of structuring and managing the events in their everyday lives is an important part of the discussion which follows.

DISCUSSION

These accounts of how the Trujillos and the Faustos used movidas to link specific events in their everyday lives to the broader social context in which they operated illustrate the fact that Mexican Americans do indeed use strategies. It is not enough, however, simply to point out this fact without delving further into the theoretical and methodological issues which arise from these accounts. This discussion will focus, therefore, on several areas, beginning first with the specific issue of Mexican American strategy usage, and broadening into a discussion of strategy usage by people in general. This involves a look at the current status of strategies in sociological literature and a consideration of the limitations of traditional sociology for the researcher who tries to find and to study strategies in use. Finally, it is proposed that ethnomethodology embodies both a perspective and some methods which can be useful in extending current theories and research on strategies in use.

Mexican Americans and Movidas

What is the theoretical relevance of finding movidas, or strategies, in studying Mexican Americans? In the first place, strategies reveal that more is going on than the normative literature reveals. Most social scientists, in their studies of Mexican Americans (e.g., Clark, 1970; Grebler, 1970; Humphrey, 1943), overlook how Mexican Americans, like Mr. and Mrs. Trujillo, and Mr. Fausto, use movidas (strategies) to link one event to another in the process of structuring and managing their daily affairs. Instead, social scientists (e.g., Clark, 1970; Heller, 1968; Grebler, 1970) generally explain Mexican American behavior in terms of Mexican American cultural norms. That is, in practically all studies on the Mexican American (Vaca, 1970), social scientists claim that Mexican Americans organize and manage their everyday affairs according to such norms as the following: present time orientation, immediate gratification, fatalism, and traditionalism. In making such an assertion about Mexican Americans, most researchers do not discover if the behavior they observe and later label "present time orientation," for example, is indeed normative behavior as specified in the literature, or something else, such as a movida, which only appears as normative behavior, but which actually is taken and defined in a totally different way by the actors (Ramos, 1973). By working under the assumption that Mexican Americans behave solely in the ways described in the literature, most researchers do not address two basic questions:

1. If Mexican Americans do indeed behave according to the cultural norms social scientists attribute to Mexican American culture, do Mexican Americans behave that way all the time?

2. If they do not, when, how, and for what reasons do they behave differently?

Because present models of Mexican American behavior are based on the notion of cultural norms, a great deal of the lives of Mexican Americans is glossed over and the discussion of strategies is missing altogether. For example, many social scientists claim that Mexican Americans generally do not use or deal with government agencies, such as the Department of Welfare or the public schools, because of their cultural orientation (Heller, 1966; Madsen, 1964; Samora and Lamanna, 1967; Rubel, 1969). That is, social scientists describe Mexican Americans as warm, friendly people who are only able to deal with others on a personal, one-to-one basis, and in an informal fashion. Therefore, when Mexican Americans do not use or deal with government agencies, most researchers conclude that they do not use them because American government agencies are run on an impersonal and formal level, a way opposite to the way Mexican Americans are said to deal with the world. This assumption is made because the data (be it qualitative or quantitative) researchers use deals only with who uses government agencies, when they do so, and how many people use government agencies, not with *why and under what circumstances* some people do or do not use government agencies.

Now, if I were to study the Trujillos in the usual fashion Mexican Americans are studied, I would only use the data gotten from the Department of Welfare, and the observation that the Trujillos do not go to government agencies. Consequently, I would only "know" that the Trujillos are literate and that they are the sort of people who do not cooperate with officials because they do not answer their mail, even when a stamped and self-addressed envelope is provided. Thus, with that sort of data, I could conclude rather easily that the Trujillos' behavior of not answering letters or filling out questionnaires conforms to the normative characteristic attributed to Mexican Americans. Furthermore, I would only have the Department of Welfare"s definition of the Trujillos, but not the Trujillos' own definition of who they are. By describing the Trujillos from the Department of Welfare's perspective, I would have to overlook that the Trujillos are illiterate, and that they create movidas in order to appear to some people as if they are literate.

If Mr. Fausto's behavior toward his daughters had been captured in a traditional ethnographic account, it, too, would appear to conform to a cultural typification, that of the authoritarian father and the submissive female, which is specified in the literature (e.g., Madsen, 1964). This typification exists because ethnographic accounts generally present only the isolated example of interaction—Mr. Fausto disciplining his daughters—with no clue as to what happened between the actors before and after the interaction. The isolated event is thus detached from the rest of the other ongoing activities which Mexican Americans create to manage their daily affairs. However, if social scientists begin to look for the strategies which underlie any given Mexican American's behavior, then the focus must shift to that Mexican American as an individual first, and as a member of an ethnic group secondly.

In addition to revealing that Mexican Americans do not behave solely in terms of cultural norms, strategies point to the fact that Mexican Americans construct everyday activities in terms of interaction with others (Mexican Americans as well as non-Mexican Americans). In the literature (e.g., Romano, 1968; Vaca, 1970), it is implied that Mexican Americans are always operating in a Mexican American world and that others, mostly Anglo Americans, as representatives of helping services such as departments of welfare and public schools, manipulate Mexican Americans (Barrera, et al, 1972; Blauner, 1972). Thus, the assumption is that Mexican Americans do not participate actively and rationally in the production of the events that make up their everyday life. To support the notion that Anglo Americans in the helping service manipulate Mexican Americans, researchers (e.g., Almaguer, 1971; Blauner, 1972; Rivera, 1970) present data, both quantitative and qualitative, which does not document what the actors take into account when producing the reported event. Consequently, the conclusion most often reached is that Mexican Americans do not actively participate in the production of the successes and failures in their lives.

I contend that Mexican Americans, like other people, do participate in the production of events. Moreover, Mexican Americans ingeniously create strategies in one situation in order to produce success in a future situation. If a researcher only records accounts of what seems to be normative performances by Mexican Americans, the researcher then glosses over how specific Mexican Americans socially construct the reality within which they operate.

The Theoretical Relevance of Strategies

In order to be useful as well as relevant, sociological theory must apply to people in general and not just to one ethnic group or another. The study of strategies is an area with implications broader than those which apply specifically to Mexican Americans. One important feature of research into strategy usage is that the social scientist can begin to assess the linkages between the immediate social context under study and the larger world in which people operate. For example, the Trujillos did not play out their lives simply within the here and now of the family. They had to deal with social institutions, such as the school and the Department of Welfare, as well as with individuals. Furthermore, the Trujillos used their knowledge of micro- and macro-settings as the raw material in creating the strategies which helped them "get through the day."

In addition to pointing out the linkages between the various social contexts in which the person under study operates, an understanding of strategies also points toward the linkages between the social settings of the actors and the researcher. By focusing on strategies, the field researcher is alerted to those aspects of the social context which the person under study considers to be relevant, and this in turn helps the researcher construct the parameters of the research setting. For example, I began my contact with the Trujillos in light of their relation to the public school. This was my initial research setting. However, their use of a strategy in order to appear literate pointed toward their relationship with other agencies, such as the Department of Welfare. This alerted me, as the researcher, to a possible avenue for further inquiry, and thus the parameters of the research setting were extended.

A virtue in discovering the parameters of the research setting is not only that we are able to discover what else needs to be studied, but also that we are able to collect data on the same people in different settings. Thus, we have data which we can compare. What the people under study tell us at one point or situation can be compared with how they perform at other times and in other places. This idea can be extended to include the comparison of data which is gathered by traditional methods (Ramos, 1976a) with data which is collected concerning strategies. It may be that in many cases the strategy-data will bring forth questions or uncertainties about the baseline-data gathered by such methods as survey research and ethnographic work. This is what happened, of course, when I suggested that the strategy-data on the Trujillos cast doubt on the notion of culturally determined norms. The Trujillos revealed that their literacy performance was created to deal with the practical circumstance of being illiterate, which had nothing to do with their cultural heritage or with the norms attributed to Mexican American culture. By extending the parameters of the research setting, then, we are forced to focus on how the people under study, and those relevant others with whom they interact, jointly create the specific social world the researcher is to study.

The Current Status of Research Strategies

It is apparent that the study of strategies can contribute to sociological theory in a number of ways, both in relation to the study of ethnic groups such as Mexican Americans, and to the study of people in general. Have sociologists exploited the study of strategies, and what is the current status of strategies-in-use in the sociological literature? To begin with, one finds strategies merely alluded to in ethnographic work. The work of Liebow (1967) and Gans (1962) can serve as an example to illustrate this. In their work, as in the work of other ethnographers (Lewis, 1951, 1959, 1961; Wax, 1971; Whyte, 1966), they tell in a generalized fashion that the people under study are calculating people who create strategies to manage their practical affairs in ways which make sense to them. This aspect of ethnographic work is one virtue of this type of sociological research: it makes it real and concrete. We can learn something about the "real" world which we do not get in quantitative studies. In doing this, Liebow (1967) and Gans (1962) underscore the importance of ethnographic work and why it needs to be further developed.

Dramaturgical sociology is another area in which sociologists have begun to use the notion of interactional strategies. Goffman, in outlining the features of presentation management, focuses on how actors in a situation position themselves and observe each other to manipulate one another (1959, 1961a, 1961b, 1963a, 1963b, 1963c, 1969a, 1969b, 1971, 1974). As Goffman writes:

> I have said that when an individual appears before others his actions will influence the definition of the situation which they come to have. Sometimes the individual will act in a thoroughly calculating manner, expressing himself in a given way solely in order to give the kind of impression to others that is likely to evoke from them a specific response he is concerned to obtain. Sometimes the individual will be calculating in his activity but be relatively unaware that this is the case. Sometimes he will intentionally and consciously express himself in a particular way, but chiefly because the tradition of his group or social status require this kind of expression and not because of any particular response (other than vague acceptance or approval) that is likely to be evoked from those impressed by the expression. Sometimes the traditions of an individual's role will lead him to give a well-designed impression of a particular kind and yet he may be neither consciously nor unconsciously disposed to create such an impression. The others, in their turn, may be suitably impressed by the individual's efforts to convey something, or may misunderstand the situation and come to conclusions that are warranted neither by the individual's intent nor by the facts. In any case, in so far as the others act *as if* the individual had conveyed a particular impression, we may take a functional or pragmatic view and say that the individual has "effectively" projected a given definition of the situation and "effectively" fostered the understanding that a given state of affairs obtains.

In pointing out the fraudulent character of human interaction, Goffman and others (e.g., Davis, 1973) have pointed out the improvisational nature of everyday life and the deceptive character of appearances. In doing this, dramaturgical sociologists have shown the importance of focusing on the production of social process and how social process tends to form those features that constitute social structure.

The Limitations of Current Strategy Research

Although Goffman's framework is comprehensive and insightful in describing strategies, and current ethnographic work does begin to point toward the use of strategies, both are just that—a beginning. What, then, are the limitations of the current sociological inquiry into strategy usage?

To begin with, traditional sociology does not deal with strategies at all. This situation occurs for several reasons, with perhaps the most important being the use of traditional research methodologies. For example, in quantitative studies of Mexican Americans (e.g., Grebler, et al, 1970), the researchers used structured questionnaires which did not lead themselves to the discovery of how people under study used strategies. The same criticism can be made of ethnographic studies, although for different reasons. The emphasis of ethnographic studies, such as the ones done by Madsen (1964) and Rubel (1969), is on the observation of isolated aspects of a person's life which are not collated into a coherent whole, and on the recording of a person's generalized account of an event without focusing upon how the person uses his commonsense knowledge to link the event to other events in his life. In other words, most researchers, in using traditional research methods, do not capture and document as concretely as possible how people create the specific social world the researcher is supposedly researching.

It is not just methodology, however, which limits the understanding of strategies in current sociological work. If we look closely at the ethnographic accounts in Liebow's *Tally's Corner,* we discover a description of how some of the men on the corner manage particular situations, but these situations are not tied into other ongoing activities which the people under study create. Thus, we are never told *why* Tally or any of the other men on the corner accept or refuse a drink from the wine bottle when it is being passed around. Could it be that a person refuses a drink because he is really supposed to be out looking for work, and since he is not, the last thing he needs is to go home to his wife with wine on his breath? Is there some other strategy at work? If Liebow were to focus on what the men on the corner take into account when they manage a particular situation, then we might learn how the men on the corner create strategies to link the particular situation of the street corner with other situations in which they find themselves.

A further limitation of current ethnographic work is the tendency of ethnographers to talk about people in general, while maintaining the posture of portraying specific details about specific people. Thus, in *The Urban Villagers,* Gans (1962) presents us with general descriptions about the working class culture, and then he documents these descriptions with ethnographic examples which give Gan's work the character of being a detailed and intimate account of the people under study. However, the accounts he presents tend to gloss over how the people under study manage their practical affairs. The people under study are discussed as if they do not have a personal history: they are without a biographical situation (Schutz, 1967), and we learn very little about what they take into account when dealing with their practical circumstances.

When Gans does discuss the way West Enders in *The Urban Villagers* manage their affairs, it is solely in terms of their group specific culture (i.e., the working class culture). The implication is that the West Enders manage their lives solely in terms of the norms which Gans attributes to "working class culture." By describing and explaining the behavior of the people under study in terms of group specific culture, Gans does not tell how the people under study create and use strategies.

Another indication of the generalization which sometimes occurs in ethnographic work lies in the use of labels for groups of people. For example, Gans talks about such people as West Enders, Caretakers, and Politicians. These are categories that Gans has created and which he uses rather conveniently to generalize about the people living in the West End. For example, in telling us about Caretakers' inability to work with West Enders, Gans (1962) writes:

> The caretakers' blindness to the nature of West End life stemmed in part from their being middle-class people who did not live in the area, but even more so from their missionary outlook. Most of the caretakers were trained professionals from middle-class backgrounds, who worked but did not live in the West End. Only a few staff members were Italian in background. Most of the caretakers, however, had worked in the West End for a long time. These were people with deep feelings of affection for the area and its people, whose interest in professional prestige or in agency growth was much less than in that of serving the West End. In fact, their feelings toward the people often were pseudofamilial in character. Many of the caretakers were single women without families. Moreover, because of their belief that wives were being neglected by their husbands, and children by their parents they were encourage to assist as quasi-family members, to sympathize with the women as quasi-siblings, and to treat the children quasi-maternally. Indeed, some caretakers talked about their youthful clients as "their children," and assumed a protective if not almost possessive attitude toward some of the women who came to them with problems.

In describing people in these abstract ways, Gans makes some gross generalizations about people working and living in the West End. First, by stating that caretakers are blind to the nature of West End life because they are middle class, Gans glosses over the problematic features of working with people. It is certainly plausible to assume that some persons who work as caretakers can deal with some West Enders quite effectively while other caretakers may not. Moreover, caretakers are not abstractions such as the "welfare worker," the "school teacher," and the "probation officer" to the people they serve. They are real people with personalities and with life histories. The same can be said about the clients. They are real people to the caretaker. And it is certainly plausible to assume that the situations that are dealt with by a particular caretaker and his respective client are constructed and managed by each actor in terms of what they know about one another and the larger social context in which the situation is embedded. It is also plausible to assume that some caretakers and some clients create strategies to help, or to hinder, the helping process. To assume, as Gans does, that trouble between a caretaker and his client results from the caretaker's middle class status is to overlook the complexities of how persons manage each other—of how they create strategies in order to manage life.

Secondly, by pointing out that some staff members of an agency were Italian in background, Gans implies that these persons could relate to the West Enders, who were mostly Italian. This in turn implies that one can communicate with others by virtue of ethnicity. Indeed, ethnicity may be a factor in establishing rapport with others, but it is not the only factor which leads to effective communication. I suggest that effective communication results from the way persons present themselves to appear as if they have many things in common and from the fact that people involved may have a vested interest in what the other has to offer.

In conclusion, perhaps the most serious limitation of ethnographic work to date is the perspective from which it is done. If the researcher collects ethnographic accounts to verify the cultural typifications which have been "found" through surveys or through other quantitative research, then it will be almost impossible for strategies in use to be discovered or used in extending knowledge of how people interact with each other and construct social reality.

What, then, of Goffman's presentation management and the whole nation of dramaturgical sociology? Although Goffman's framework does present a comprehensive model of man in society, it, too, can be seen as limited in some ways. Goffman discusses in great detail the complex features of how people manipulate one another. Indeed, it is a step forward in social science to learn what goes into defining a situation. However, he ignores the question of *why*—why people position and manipulate themselves in the ways that they do (Blumer, 1972). Consequently, he does not give attention to ". . . how concrete ongoing group activities affect the face-to-face interaction involved in them and how contrariwise, the face-to-face interaction influences the ongoing activities" (Blumer, 1972:52). Thus, interactions are abstracted from the larger social context and studied as units unto themselves. It is this limitation which makes it difficult to use the framework of presentation management in studying the interactional strategies used by Mexican Americans, or others, since these strategies must be viewed within the larger context of ongoing activities. Looking again at my data from the point of view of presentation management, I would have to exclude how the Trujillos and the Faustos use what they know about the broader social context in which they operate to structure and manage the encounters they have with others. I would also have to exclude how the people who deal with the Trujillos and the Faustos use what they know about the different aspects of their relationship with these two respective families to manage the encounters they have with the families.

To sum up the present state of research on strategy usage, it is important to point out that ethnographic work, as well as Goffman's framework, is not useless. Rather, it is simply in a primitive state which needs to be expanded. This leads, then, to a crucial point: if an understanding of the strategies people use in managing their affairs can reveal new information about Mexican Americans, and about people in general, then we must begin to refine both theory and methodology to include strategy-finding.

Ethnomethodology as a Theoretical and Methodological Alternative

How can social scientists find strategies-in-use? I suggest that what is needed is a theoretical framework which is tied to a particular methodology. I further suggest that ethnomethodology fits this requirement: it is both a theory and a methodology. What does ethnomethodology have to offer in the way of theory which can be applied to the study of strategies? First, from an ethnomethodological perspective, attention is given to specific people and their life history, to the common culture in which the people under study operate, and to the commonsense knowledge the people under study use to interpret what they are doing. Furthermore, from an ethnomethodological perspective, the commonsense knowledge the people under study use to cope with their practical circumstances is seen as the link between the way they structure and manage a particular situation and the way they structure and manage their other activities (Ramos, 1976a, 1976b, 1977).

Thus, ethnomethodology is a theoretical framework which lends itself to the study of both the micro- and macro-aspects of the social order: the focus of study is on specific persons in micro-settings, but the activities which specific people create to manage their daily lives transcend the parameters of the micro-setting. Although people tend to operate within micro-settings, it is these micro-settings in which people play out their lives which make up the features of the macro-setting.

Ethnomethodology is a methodology as well as a perspective. Two basic premises of ethnomethodology are that the familiar background features of everyday life constitute for people what there is to be known about the world in which they live, and that people work on the assumption that anybody who is a member of their small group, or circle of friends, knows the familiar background features and when they are being used. Since the familiar background features of everyday scenes are taken for granted and not readily available to a casual observer of a social scene, the observer needs to find a way to unmask or uncover what people take for granted and what people use to decide how to manage their routine affairs. Garfinkel (1967) and others (Molotch and Lester, 1972; Young and Leham, 1972) recommend that sociologists purposely make trouble for the people under study to get them to reveal their taken-for-granted world. This is an interesting and important methodological notion, but it tends to give field research an artificial character. I suggest that it is not necessary for sociologists to make trouble because people (including sociologists) make trouble for one another naturally (Ramos, 1973). Trouble occurs naturally because of the following conditions:

a. Several strata or other social locations may exist simultaneously in the social order.

b. Societal members work on the assumption that others share the world they take for granted.

c. In carrying out their daily activities, societal members interact with others who may occupy a different stratum of social reality than they do and who may view the world differently.

d. The ongoing activities that societal members create to manage their daily lives at times do not mesh with the ongoing activities of others.

e. This lack of meshing may create trouble.

I also make the following claims:

1. There is great advantage to be had in using, as an investigative device, the trouble people naturally create for one another while managing their everyday affairs.

2. Naturally created trouble, as a natural phenomenon of life, reveals what would be going on when trouble is not there, or what is expected to go on.

3. In attending to the trouble that naturally occurs, social scientists can discover how societal members go about creating the social order reality for each other.

The notion of using naturally occurring trouble as an investigative device (Ramos, 1973a) can be further extended to include any unexpected events, whether troublesome or not, which reveal the taken-for-granted world which underlies people's behavior. By unexpected events, I mean any events which are not planned or expected by a person and which conflict with the person's original idea of what is to happen. I suggest that when unexpected events occur, several things are revealed. One is the taken-for-granted world. As shown in the ethnomethodological literature, the commonsense knowledge people take into account and use as schemes of interpetation in managing their everyday affairs is taken-for-granted and not readily available to a non-member of a particular setting or group (Cicourel, 1964; Mehan and Wood, 1974; Garfinkel, 1967). Schutz (1967) and others

(Garfinkel, 1967; Ramos, 1973a) suggest that this commonsense knowledge is revealed when trouble or a problematic situation occurs. I suggest that an unexpected event, whether troublesome or not, reveals what people take into account when they cope with everyday situations. Furthermore, it is not just the occurrence of an unexpected event, but the way in which people *manage* the event, that reveals the taken-for-granted world. People's ways of coping with an unexpected event provide the researcher with data to contrast with what the researcher and the people under study themselves expected to go on, if the unexpected event had not occurred.

Unexpected events also reveal *interaction strategies.* We know that *interactional strategies* exist, and we are told about their complex features in the literature (Davis, 1973; Goffman, 1959, 1961a, 1961b, 1963a, 1963b, 1969a, 1969b, 1971). But, as I have previously stated, we are rarely told in the literature how we may find or recognize a strategy in use. Unexpected events can help us find them. Strategies can be "found" when we collect unexpected event data and compare it with baseline data.

A third aspect which the occurrence of unexpected events reveals is the different social contexts in which the people under study operate. When people manage an unexpected event, they expose what they take into account (i.e., their commonsense knowledge), which in turn reveals how they structure and manage a specific situation in terms of other past and probable future situations that they know about. I suggest that the commonsense knowledge people use to structure and manage a particular situation can be seen as the linkage between the different situations that make up a person's everyday life. Thus, in managing unexpected events, the people under study reveal not only the immediate social context in which they operate, but the "larger" social context in which the immediate context is embedded.

In order to see how the use of unexpected events as a research method for finding strategies looks in practice, I mention once again the Trujillos. I went to visit the Trujillos to discuss school problems. Soon after my arrival, however, an unexpected event occurred: the welfare worker came to pick up Jimmy. At that point I might have left with the single-minded purpose of returning to discuss school problems at some other time. Instead, I exploited the unexpected event by staying around and watching for whatever might be revealed. I was able to do this because I was already operating within the framework of ethnomethodology. I knew that there were background features which the Trujillos considered to be taken-for-granted, but which were not necessarily the same background features of my life or the welfare worker's life. I also knew that the here-and-now context of the Trujillos' living room was linked in many ways to other situations and other social contexts. It was this theoretical framework, tied in with the method of using unexpected events, which led to my discovery of the Trujillos' literacy strategy.

As unexpected events reveal the broader social context in which the people under study operate and the strategies they use in linking one context to another, they also make visible the parameters of the research setting for the researcher. In a sense, it can be said that the discovery of the broader social context in which the people under study operate is synonymous with the discovery of the parameters of the research setting. Researchers, indeed, start a field research project with some definite ideas of the types of people, places, and activities to be studied, but it takes something like an unexpected event to reveal the other relevant aspects of peoples' lives, places, and activities which are not visible or readily available to us. And if such things are visible, we as researchers may not take them to be relevant or related to what we may be studying until the people under study, in coping with an unexpected event, reveal for us the linkages that exist between the immediate context and the "larger" world in which they operate.

One further point which needs to be discussed is the role of the researcher in producing the data. Ethnomethodology focuses on the researcher as well as on the researched, because attention is given to what the researcher takes into account in making decisions about what he is doing in the data collecting process (Cicourel, 1964; Garfinkel, 1967; Schutz, 1967). This interest in the commonsense knowledge the researcher takes into account forces us to address not only how the dynamic features of the research setting affect the research process, but also how the "larger" world in which the researcher operates affects the research process. Thus, we need to look at the effect the following things have on the research process: the researcher's theoretical and methodological interests, the demands or constraints a funding agency might put on the research, the time period in which the researcher must do his research, and the researcher's familial obligations. The researcher, then, must be seen as a real person who is very much entrenched in a real world.

Although I strongly recommend ethnomethodology, both as a theoretical framework and as a methodology, for the study of strategies-in-use, I do not mean to imply that other more traditional methods should be abandoned. Ethnomethodology might be seen as the most innovative approach at present, but both participant observation and depth interviewing can lend themselves to ethnomethodological research—in fact, they are important tools when they are refined in such a way as to include the basic tenets of ethnomethodology. This means, further, that social scientists must be afforded the time to study people in particular rather than in general, and that they must be aware of the pitfalls inherent in doing participant observation and depth interviewing with the idea of confirming preconceived notions about cultural norms.

Finally, the perspective of ethnomethodology must be apparent right down to the final preparation of data for publication. For ethnomethodologist, then, there is no "caretaker" (Gans, 1962), but a real person with a name and a life history. That is, there can be Rose, the caretaker who is a mother of two children, a member in the Democratic party, a Catholic, the wife of Albert who drinks too much at parties and makes a fool of himself, and a low level employee in the agency where she works. Furthermore, there is Rose who uses her knowledge of her particular work situation and her family situation to cope with her practical circumstances in ways that conceal that her marriage with Albert is falling apart. An ethnomethodologist would be concerned with all of these aspects in the life of Rose in learning how she manages her job and her family affairs simultaneously. By failing to discover the commonsense knowledge Rose uses to create strategies in her attempt to create smoothness and the appearance of competence in her everyday affairs, we would overlook how persons in the life construct social reality for themselves as well as for others, and how people create the social order.

Since the logical conclusion to the finding of strategies is for the social scientist to publish the data for the enlightenment of others, one further caution needs to be made. Once strategies are discovered, they should not be "petrified" by premature labeling. It is all too easy to see Mr. Trujillo use his strategy in order to appear literate, and then to label it "The Literacy Routine." Then, if similar, but different, strategies used by other people are also named "The Literacy Routine," it suddenly becomes easy to gloss over the real differences which occur. Each stategy, then, should be seen in light of the specific characteristics which are peculiar to the situation and the actors involved.

CONCLUSION

The topic of strategies is a particularly fertile one, since sociological research in the area is presently in the beginning stages, and since there appears to be much to be gained, both theoretically and methodologically, from the study of strategies. Within the area of ethnic studies, knowledge of strategies provides a counter-balance to the notion of cultural norms. Thus, we see that Mexican Americans, like all others, use strategies in order to manage their daily lives. The ethnographic examples of the Trujillos and the Faustos are just two of many accounts which illustrate the use of movidas by Mexican Americans.

The study of stategies, however, is not peculiar to research on ethnic groups. There is new and important information which can be revealed when startegies are discovered. For example, strategies can reveal the commonsense knowledge people use to structure and manage their daily lives, as well as what is taken-for-granted by the actors. This knowledge points to the notion that social scientists must be concerned with broader contexts in order to see how people link past, present, and probable future events. The strategy a person uses gives new insight into the linkages made between one situation and other situations in the person's life.

Both ethnographic work and presentation management, though important in opening the way toward an understanding of strategies, are as yet primitive: there is much that is new and interesting in terms of describing strategies, but there is little which can be used methodologically for finding strategies-in-use. To this end, ethnomethodology has been suggested as a logical approach, since it combines theory and methodology in the effort to focus on specific people in specific situations. It is from this base that social scientists can begin to enlarge upon strategies and what they reveal about the ways people structure and manage daily life.

FOOTNOTES

1. I wish to thank Martha A. Ramos for her valuable comments and suggestions.

2. The names have been changed to provide anonymity. The data presented comes from a larger study I did in northern Colorado.

3. The Trujillos and I were friends. I had gotten to know them well, but this did not mean that I knew everything about them. For example, I did not know that the case worker discussed in the example was coming to the house the afternoon I was there. I point this out because it needs to be underscored that even when the field researcher has very good rapport with the people under study, it does not mean that the researcher knows everything about their lives.

4. The conversation was in Spanish and English, but mostly in Spanish. For the sake of clarity I have translated the Spanish to English in this presentation.

5. Later, I learned from the Trujillos that they guessed what was written on the card, and that they were not sure if they had guessed right. This is why they got up early and waited for the child placement worker all day. They were not really sure when she would get there.

REFERENCES

Almaguer, T., "Towards the Study of Chicano Colonialism," *Aztlan*, (Spring 1971): 7–19.

Barrera, M., et al., "The Barrio as an Internal Colony," in Harlan Hahn (ed.), *Urban Affairs Annual Reviews*, Vol. 6, 1972, pp. 465–498.

Blauner, R., *Racial Oppression in America*, New York: Harper and Row, 1972.

Blumer, H., "Action vs. Interaction: Herbert Blumer on Erving Goffman," *Society*, Vol. 19 (1972), pp. 3–10.

Cicourel, A.V., *Method and Measurement in Sociology*, New York: Free Press, 1964.

Clark, M., *Health in the Mexican American Culture*, Berkeley: University of California Press, 1970.

Davis, M., *Intimate Relations*, New York: The Free Press, 1973.

Derbyshire, R., "Adaptation of Adolescent Mexican Americans to United States Society," in Eugene Brody (ed.), *Behavior in New Environments: Adaptation of Migrant Populations*, Beverly Hills, CA: Sage Publications, 1969, pp. 275–290.

Gans, H., *The Urban Villagers*, New York: The Free Press, 1962.

Garfinkel, H., *Studies in Ethnomethodology*, Englewood Cliffs: Prentice-Hall, Inc., 1967.

Goffman, E., *The Presentation of Self in Everyday Life*, New York: Doubleday and Co., Inc., 1959.

———— , *Encounters*, Indianapolis: Bobbs-Merrill Company, 1961a.

———— , *Asylums*, New York: Anchor Books, 1961b.

_____ , *Behavior in Public Places*, New York: The Free Press, 1963a.

_____ , *Stigma*, Englewood Cliffs: Prentice-Hall, Inc., 1936b.

_____ , *Where the Action Is*, London: The Penguin Press, 1969a.

_____ , *Strategic Interaction*, Philadelphia: University of Pennsylvania Press, 1969b.

_____ , *Relations in Public: Microstudies of the Public Order*, New York: Basic Books, 1971.

Grebler, L., et al., *The Mexican American People*, New York: The Free Press, 1970.

Heller, C., *Mexican American Youth*, New York: Random House, 1968.

Humphrey, N., "On Assimilation and Acculturation," *Psychiatry* 6 (November 1943): 343–355.

Lewis, O., *Life in a Mexican Village: Tepoztlan Restudied*, Urbana: University of Illinois Press, 1951.

_____ , *Five Families: Mexican Case Studies in the Culture of Poverty*, New York: Basic Books, 1959.

_____ , *The Children of Sanchez: Autobiography of a Mexican Family*, New York: Vintage Books, 1961.

Liebow, E., *Tally's Corner*, Boston: Little Brown and Co., 1967.

Madsen, W., *The Mexican Americans of South Texas*, San Francisco: Holt, Rinehart and Winston, 1964.

Mehan, H. and H. Wood, *The Realities of Ethnomethodology*, New York: Wiley Interscience, 1974.

Molotch, H., and M. Lester, "Accidents, Scandals and Routines: Resources for Conflict Methodology," Paper presented at the August, 1972 annual meetings of the American Sociological Association, New Orleans, Louisiana, 1972.

Moore, J., "Social Constraints on Sociological Knowledge: Academics and Research Concerning Minorities," *Social Problems* 21 (Summer 1973): 65–77.

Munoz, C., "Toward a Chicano Perspective of Political Analysis," *Aztlan*, (Fall 1970): 15–26.

Penalosa, F., "Mexican Family Roles," *Journal of Marriage and the Family*, 30 (November 1968): 680–688.

Ramos, R., *The Production of Social Reality: An Ethnomethodological Study of the Making of Trouble*, Unpublished doctoral dissertation, University of Colorado, Boulder, CO, 1973a.

_____ , "A Case in Point: An Ethnomethodological Study of a Poor Mexican American Family," *Social Science Quarterly* 53 (March 1973b): 905–919.

_____ , "Data Everywhere: The Methodological Virtue of Unexpected Events in Field Research," Unpublished paper, 1976a.

_____ , "The Use of Improvisation and Modulation in Natural Talk: An Alternative Approach to Conversational Analysis," *Sociolinguistics Newsletter*, (Fall 1976b): 10–20.

_____ , "Beyond the Bilingual-Cross-cultural Classroom: The Effects of the Social Environment on the Classroom," Unpublished paper, 1977.

Rivera, J., "Chicanos: Culture, Community Role—Problems of Evidence, and a Proposition of Norms Towards Establishing Evidence," *Aztlan*, Vol. 1, No. 1 (1970), pp. 37–52.

Romano, O., "The Anthropology and Sociology of the Mexican American," *El Grito*, (Fall 1968): 9–26.

Rubel, A., *Across the Tracks: Mexican Americans in a Texas City*, Austin: University of Texas Press, 1966.

Samora, J. and R. Lamanna, "Mexican-Americans in a Midwest Metropolis: A Study of East Chicago," Advance Report 8, Mexican American Study Project, University of California, Los Angeles: Los Angeles, CA, 1967.

Schutz, A., *Collected Papers, Vol. I: The Problem of Social Reality*, The Hague: Martinus Nijhoff, 1967.

Wax, R., *Doing Fieldwork*, Chicago: The University of Chicago Press, 1971.

Whyte, W., *Street Corner Society*, Chicago: University of Chicago Press, 1966.

Young, R. and T. Lehman, "Conflict Methodology," a Paper presented at the August, 1972 annual meetings of the American Sociological Association, New Orleans, LA, 1972.

RESEARCH AND THE CONSTRUCTION OF A TEXT

Susan Krieger, UNIVERSITY OF NEW MEXICO

This article describes a research process and the construction of a text in a study of a radio station.[1] It discusses problems peculiar to that study which are also problems commonly found in participant-observation and life history types of research.[2]

The study was begun in 1972 and consisted of eleven months of interviewing persons involved with the station, obtaining documentary evidence from them and from other sources, visiting the station, and listening to it. The next two years were spent in writing a text which described a process of cooptation in the life of the station over the years 1967–72. The station had been closely associated with the Summer of Love in San Francisco in 1967. It was thought to have been the first hard rock "hippy" radio station in the country. In the five years since, it had become increasingly commercial, professional, and successful, and was frequently criticized for having sold out to the establishment. The purpose of the study was to describe and account for this change. Cooptation in the case of the station was roughly defined as a process in which an organization, once

Studies in Symbolic Interaction—Volume 2, 1979, pages 167–187
ISBN: 0–89232–105–9

viewed as new and different and at odds with prevailing practice, comes ove
time to adopt ways of a larger society which are viewed as corrupting. Th
organization is said to have sold out, to have lost some of its original virtue.

The text developed to answer the question of how this happened in the
case of the station contained four principal biases. One was that it viewec
the cooptation process as an accomplishment of individuals, an accomplish
ment guided by appropriateness to personal lives as well as to roles anc
institutions. The individuals involved are continually making ways fo
themselves as well as for the station, seeking to meet their own needs anc
objectives with the opportunities it affords.[4] A second bias was that i
viewed as formative processes in which the station's activities were madε
known to a broader public. People of the station learn of themselves a
others see them. They carry on a continuing conversation with the rest of the
world through public report and attempt to keep that report to some exten
fairly reflective.[5]

A third bias was that the process was viewed as one of negotiated gains
and concessions made in a context of growth and change. People involvec
with the station are seen as "coming to terms," learning to give in order tc
grow in a world which, over time, is increasingly large, complex, and not o
their own making.[6] A fourth bias was that the process was assumed to be
working on an intimate level, involving how people think and feel and what
they like in a world where immediate circumstances seem often more
determining than demands of a larger society. Such a view has been referrec
to in one study of a telephone company, in which it was said of customer
service representatives:

> Working in that job one does not see oneself as a victim of "Capitalism." One is
> simply part of a busy little world which has its own pleasures and satisfactions as well
> as its own frustrations but, most important, it is a world, with a shape and an integrity
> all its own. The pattern of co-optation, in other words, rests on details: hundreds of
> trivial, but human, details.[7]

These biases in part reflect personal affections for certain ways ot
thinking and in part the nature of the research and writing process in the
particular study. What follows is an account of that process and in the end
a summary of textual rules it generated and a reflection on its style and
theory.

(1) A Course of Research

I began inquiring into the history of the station in May 1972, at a time
when Tom Donahue, the man who had been the spiritual and founding
father of the station five years earlier, was finally made its general manager.
I started my research in May with his permission and encouragement. A
month later, he was fired by the President of the Radio Division ot

Metromedia, the corporation which owned the station, and the staff staged
an angry meeting, threatening to resign or walk out and take the radio
station with them. One reporter at the time described it: "Children tore their
hair, dogs ran wild in the streets." Donahue was rehired two days later;
there was said to have been premature judgment. But from May through
mid-September, when Donahue was finally appointed general manager on a
permanent basis, the staff was extremely apprehensive about what would
happen to them, and often afraid they would lose Donahue or that
Metromedia would sell the station.

It was and was not a propitious time for an outsider to start a study. It
was propitious in that Donahue's return and his temporary firing raised for
many of the staff questions concerning the meaning of their past and the
worth of their work in the present, and these were indirectly questions of
how they wanted to be viewed by the world. It was a time when the prospect
of having a history done, with its promise of an attempt to get the record
straight, might be expected to have an appeal. But it was also a time which
nourished suspicions. Over the years the station had often been covered by
journalists and the staff asked for their views on what had happened to
them. They had not liked many of the pieces written about them and
thought of themselves as having been ripped off too many times already.

a) Interviews

Individuals associated with the station varied initially and throughout in
the degree to which they were trusting or suspicious and in their receptivity
to being interviewed. The approach I took was to ask each one and make an
appointment to talk at their convenience. There were many cancelled
appointments and what seemed like too much waiting in between. But in
time, almost everyone asked for an interview gave one, people at the station
referred me to others they thought might be helpful, and most of them
expressed real interest in the outcome of the research.

In the end there were interviews with eighty-eight people. Fifty-four of
them had worked for the station at one time or another during the five years
in question. The rest were people with less central relationships to it:
advertisers, promotion men, listeners, corporate and union personnel,
accountants, lawyers, journalists. Of the interviews conducted with present
and former station personnel, most lasted two or three hours. Thirty-one of
them involved only one session of two to three hours, eighteen ran to two
sessions of two to three hours each, and three ran to three or more sessions.
There were a few exceptional cases. One was Donahue, who gave five
interviews of several hours each. Another was an engineer, who sat and
recalled all she could in one lengthy session of four and a half hours. The
interviews with non-station people were usually shorter, lasting about an
hour each, but there were several that were longer and several that ran to

two sessions. The interviews wth present station personnel were supplemented with brief periodic conversations at the station, and an attempt
was made to keep the staff informed of the progress of the research.

Most of the interviews with present station personnel took place at the
station or at people's homes, a few took place in local restaurants and bars.
With former personnel and non-station people, the interviews were usually
held at their present places of work. Seven of the eleven interviews with
advertisers were done by phone, four of the interviews with former station
personnel were done by phone long distance. Most of the present and
former station personnel were interviewed in the San Francisco area in the
first eight months of the research period, May through December. Eight
Metromedia corporate personnel were interviewed in New York City in
January. Interviews in February and March were mainly for purposes of
tying loose ends together. Along with the interviews was a continuing effort
to obtain documentary evidence, the interview situations often paving the
way for access to written reports, photographs, and tapes.

Confidentiality. The most obvious purpose of the interviews was to put
together a chronology of significant and interesting events in the history of
the station. Each person interviewed was asked how he or she first got
involved with the station, and when, and what they had done before. They
were then encouraged to talk about events of the station's history of which
they had been part, and if they had left or broken off relations or changed
in their feelings about the station, how that had come about. Much of the
conversation in the interviews resembled gossip. Individuals talked about
each other as well as about themselves, and were interested to know what
other people said and how things fit together. The interview situations were
often very intense as the conversation focused on experiences which meant
much to people. As time went on, I developed a more precise chronology of
events and fuller stories about certain ones.

As interviewer, I was willing to get as involved as I could on the level of
discussion of events, trying to piece the station's history together, treating it
as if it were in some basic respect a bewilderment, and trying to identify at
least intellectually with the feelings and circumstance of each person I spoke
with. But I was not, I think, the kind of interviewer who really breaks the
distance between self and other and I did not engage in the kinds of
sociability that might have made for brief friendships. I was, therefore,
repeatedly surprised by how much of what people told me was about their
personal lives. There were no great revelations, only small details, but I
often reflected on them and felt I had been taken too much into confidence
and was uncertain as to why.

In time I came to think what might at first seem confidence or trust in me
—that I would use what I was told with protective discretion and possibly
not at all—was not so much that, as confidence in the process of which each
interview was a part. I came to think it reflected an expectation that this

telling in the interview situation was more than to one person, it was a telling to the world at large, and not only a bid for recogniton by that world, but also perhaps for forgiveness. If this were so, I or any interviewer was relatively unimportant. The interviewer needed to do enough of the right things. In my case, I think it mattered that I was serious and persistent, apparently competent enough, and not especially threatening, but that was only part of it.

I had told each of the people I talked with that I was doing a history of the station for a doctoral dissertation in Communication at Stanford and that I expected it would also be a book. Implicit in this was the message that what people told me might "get out," and it would therefore be worth their while to consider seriously what they thought and to tell me what they felt was important. Implicit also was a word of caution. But personal life details were nonetheless brought up and I found them in documents people lent me, information about who had broken up with his wife after what, for instance, or what somewhat thought of themself or someone else when it was critical or uncomfortable and not generally known. I had not thought I had been asking for much of that kind of detail, although I had asked for some. I had asked each person about their father's occupation, for instance, in an attempt to get at class background, and I had asked for feelings each person had about themself. Yet much as it was at my prompting, I was not sure how to handle many of the personal life details I was given, as they seemed to me still private.

But two things struck me after about six months. One was that information I considered private or potentially harmful often did not seem that to the person who told it to me, and often something a person said he felt would harm him if it got out, I thought would not. I began to feel that, except in a few cases where something seemed clearly harmful or in bad taste, neither of us could really know what the consequences would be and I could not use potential harm value or conventional feelings about privacy as primary criteria for selection of relevant detail. Also, I came to feel that, in telling me what they did, the people I interviewed were irrevocably turning over to me responsibility for its use. They were not fools. They were telling me what they thought mattered and they were more or less self-consciously risking the chance that my use of it would do them harm against the hope that it would do them good. The most obvious good would be favorable recognition, but there was also the mixed good of becoming more well known and with it, the possibility of being better understood and getting, in some broader sense, one's due.

I mention all this here because sometimes in social research when interviewing is discussed, it is as if confidentality was a matter of explicitly imposing moral principle and control, and as if success in interview situations depended for the most part on techniques: on establishing rapport, structuring questions, timing, handling anxieties and objections,

and awareness of the way the interviewer affects the situation.[8] I would no
underrate the importance of being protective, or of using technique, or o
enjoyments to be found in the interview process. But it seems to me wortl
noting that part of what may make interviews work is more elusive, an
dependent in an unsaid way on some mutually shared belief in th
benignness of processes of a larger world. It is also dependent on per
mission, but that may be implicit, and rules for regulating implicit processe
are different from rules regulating others. They are not legal and they ar
not formal. They depend on trust—not absolute trust, but trust to som
degree—and persons trusted may not know the difference it makes unless o
until the trust in them fails.

Interpretation. In listening during the interviews and looking back on my
notes, a recurrent problem was that of determining the relationship betweer
what people said about past events and what those events had been like
when they originally occurred. Many things were confused. The problem
often was how to interpret from what a person said which of their comments
reflected their present circumstance and which their past, which representec
how they really felt and which how they thought they felt, and what of what
they said they believed they really believed, as if that could be discerned. Ir
recalling events of the past, a person would often be trying to justify or come
to peace with some present circumstance and would speak of the past with
reference to that, and this without intent to deceive. Sometimes the reference
was plainly stated, such as when a person had been recently fired and had
not yet come to terms with it. But more often the reference was implicit.
Statements like the following had to be assessed:

> Dusty Street said she felt one thing Tom Donahue knew was he knew what worked.
> Willis Duff did not. Duff had had crazy ideas for promotions that would never work.
> Once he wanted the staff to pose nude in a pool for a picture. They told him he was
> crazy. He said they could all stay underneath and just have their heads appear in the
> picture. Now there were some people at that station Street said she would not want to
> be naked in a pool with. About Donahue, she felt in some ways he was still in the old
> days, he thought they would do the work for love, do commercials on their overtime and
> things like that. He did not realize they were in it now for the money. Street felt one
> thing she had learned was you had to be cynical in this business, you had to be cynical
> in order to survive. You were going to be fucked in the ass and you had to take the
> pleasure you could get from it. That was better than just getting fucked and being
> realistic about it. You had to turn the joke. If you went to lunch with one of the
> salesmen to get a client, you had to think it was on them. You had to believe you were
> a free wheeling spirit even if that was not really the way it was.

Spending several hours in each interview situation, hearing a range of a
person's views and getting a sense of what they were like, helped me in
distinguishing some of the many aspects of what they had to say. Using
reports of other people also helped, although this was usually not by way of
confirming or disconfirming, but by filling out a description of the situation

o as to make questionable statements fall into what seemed an appropriate lace.[9] But try as I might to come to a definite sense of how to interpret tatements made in interviews, I could only jump to so many conclusions nd a great deal of fundamental ambiguity seemed to have to remain.

b) Documentary Evidence

The documentary evidence obtained from persons interviewed and from ther sources included station monthly reports, memos, letters, program chedules, promotion materials, legal and financial records, magazine and ewspaper articles, rating service audience estimates, and publications lealing with radio and the rock music industry. There were also, although ewer in number, tapes of programs, commercials, and meetings.

Permission. The documentary evidence presented some problems of ermission similar to those raised by the interview situations. Most of the locuments I obtained had been produced during the time in question, so here was not necessarily the complication of remembering to deal with. But ften there was, and there was the likelihood that each document had a variety of purposes, some only to be guessed at, and that each was intended or more of an audience than the one to which it was ostensibly addressed.[10] I copied most of the documentary evidence obtained from the station and rom individuals. In some cases, I had permission to see documents but not explicit permission to copy them. I took this as an invitation similar to the one I felt was implicit in many of the interview situations, one in which there was a turning over of responsibility for information without acknowledging it, thus leaving to the researcher the problem of conscience and the possibility of blame which might be associated with its use.[11]

I was not denied access to any of the evidence I requested, although some documents were inconvenient or time-consuming to obtain and some required a difficult persistence. On only one occasion did I not copy in kind a piece of evidence available to me, in this case a tape which had been the subject of controversy.

Unobtained evidence. There were several kinds of documentary evidence I knew to be available but which, for reasons of time and interest, I made no effort to obtain beyond the small selection useful for my purposes. One was logs—master logging tapes and written logs of programming—that the station was required to keep by the FCC. A second was a complete set of memos, correspondence, and advertising contracts on file at the station and in storage out at a transmitter by the Bay. A third was the many records and tapes of music played on the station over the years and, as a key to that, music lists which had been kept to compute payments to the music licensing agencies.

The music was a significant omission. I felt it was sufficient for my purposes to listen to a selection of the music as I came upon it and to learn from reading about trends of change in the concerns and style of the music over the years. But to say that what I did in a sense may have been sufficient does not acknowledge the considerable importance of the meaning of the music for many of the people involved with the station and the fact that my limited exposure did not do this aspect justice.

(c) Personal Biases

There were two important personal biases that affected the research process. One was that I never assumed a participant-observer role with respect to the radio station and never wanted to. I was, in my mind, an interviewer and a collector of evidence. I rarely passed time with anyone at the station for mainly social purposes, would on most opportunities run from it, feeling discomfort, resenting, sometimes bitterly, how much the world I wanted to know was one to which I could not belong. The second was that my attitude toward the process under study was, I felt, an amoral one. I was aware that cooptation was ordinarily used as a pejorative term to suggest that some person, society, or organization had sold out its original virtues and been corrupted or gone bad. But my intent was to consider it in a technical sense as a social process that was not necessarily any more evil than it was good.

While these biases might not obviously seem to make for problems, they were sources of distance and probably contributed to a callousness to some important concerns of the people involved. Those people, for the most part, understood cooptation as something undesirable and felt in a poignant way the loss of an earlier dream they had of building an ideal radio station. They also felt that their reality was often to be grasped in terms of its enthusiasms, in feelings of elation about the music, for example, or in terms of profound disappointment over certain sets of events. To whatever extent such things are not grasped, like evidence unobtained, the fairness of knowledge suffers. But these kinds of lacks need to be confessed because often they are less obvious. A text like the present one, which reads as intimate, is in part deceptively so.[12]

(d) Attitudes Toward Cooptation

I would tell people I interviewed, especially in the beginning, that I was interested in the station in order to understand the process of cooptation and that my interest was technical as opposed to moral, and by that I said I meant it was not to pass judgment as to whether the station had gotten better or worse over the years. But I found that my use of the word cooptation was often offensive, provoking a reaction similar to that which occurred when something I said seemed to allude to processes of payola. After a while, to avoid offense, I stopped saying I was basically interested in cooptation, unless I was asked, and just said I wanted to do a history and *ace how the station had changed over time. The idea of doing a history *emed more straight-forward and less threatening than the idea of doing a *ciological study, especially one of cooptation.[13] But I found that the *rocess called by any name was of concern to most people involved with the *tation, and they thought of it usually with moral dimension. Frequently in *onversation, I would be asked if I thought the station had really gotten *orse over time, as its critics said, and people would tell me they felt it had *nd suggest a date they thought was a turning point.

Perhaps in reaction to so often hearing that the station had gotten worse *s it had become more commercial, but more likely because the station I *new and came to like, despite a profound ambivalence, was the station of *he later period, and because I could identify with the problems people had *n the later period more easily than I could with the euphoric experience *ssociated with the earliest time, I would answer that I did not think it had *otten worse. If pressed, I would say I thought it had gotten better and *ctually was the superior station many of the staff believed it was. If pressed *urther, I would say I really meant that and that I expected the history I *vould write would turn out to reflect more kindly on the later years.

(2) Rules of a Text

*Vith the research done, my problem was to develop a text which would not *nly give back to the people of the radio station something of the life they *elt they had, but do this in a way which made a statement about how the *rocess of cooptation which had been part of it had worked. There were *:onceivably many possible styles for such a statement. The one I pursued *vas, in some respects, a novelistic style in that it used people of the station *s characters to tell a story of its changes.[14] Developing a text which did that *vas in part a process of devising a set of narrative and stylistic rules. These *vere derived not from an explicit or pre-conceived general theory, but from *a set of theoretical and descriptive preferences which seemed to me relevant *n dealing with the many particular problems which arose in converting the *esearch reports to narrative and text.

a) Creating and Peopling a World

My first task in constructing the text was to create and people a world. I *was aware this was something a novelist often did very centrally, to show a *particular attitude toward humanity or toward a group of people he or she *was depicting, but which a sociologist often did secondarily or inadvertently *as a side effect of doing something else of more central methodological or *theoretical interest. In creating and peopling the world of the radio station, *several problems seemed to me to have to be resolved in the very beginning, *in the first few chapters, so as to provide a frame of reference for the next *five years. These had to do with sensibility, characters, and naming.

Sensibility. There were at least three relevant aspects of the sensibilit‹ problem. One concerned the kind of feeling the world of the station woul have. My desire was to make it a place which could fairly easily becom‹ familiar and perhaps friendly, and so I sought to include details abou ordinary things: telephone calls, rooms in buildings, affections people ha for one another. A second problem had to do with location. I wanted t indicate that the station was to be found in different kinds of places: in th‹ building at 50 Green Street, at 106.9 on the fm band, in relations a dis‹ jockey had with a promotion man or a salesman with an advertiser, in th‹ original owner's paranoia, in the regard a benefactor had for Donahue. ‹ third and possibly more essential problem had to do with specialness. wanted the world of the station to seem peculiar, not altogether unlike othe‹ worlds, but one in which one was struck by certain things and saw then perhaps more clearly. Passages like the following therefore seemed ap‹ propriate:

> Bob McClay probably knew more about the cold cruel world of the radio and recorded music business than he did about the particulars of Bob Dylan's life in April of 1967. He was generally familiar with the way that world gave breaks to some and withheld them from others. He knew it favored the up and coming. He knew of its viciousness, yet he knew it provided certain assurances many other worlds did not. It allowed one to imagine that lives mattered, and in fact had glamour, star quality. They might be lives of records: singles, albums, or album cuts. They might be lives of people or their legends. They might be short and usually were but they could be charted. They could rise to the top or come close to it because there was a top in that world, and it had a name, number one.

It also seemed useful to have a way of listening suggest a more genera‹ orientation:

> Warren Van Orden listened to the radio in a way few people do. He noticed slight changes. He memorized formats, especially those of rock music stations. He would notice the introduction of a new line in a commercial or a jingle, an irregularity in the scheduling of a program or the style of a disc jockey, a new sound in place of an older one which, too frequently repeated, had become boring and been abandoned.

The sensibility problem, the problem of what it mattered to pay attention to and how to feel about it and evaluate its meaning, was not only an introductory one, but one which remained through the length of the text. It seemed useful periodically to recall certain sets of appreciation which pertained in this world especially. Thus, in Part III, as part of a description of the station's coverage of Altamont, a disc jockey is described in the studio:

> He felt he was expected to tell the folks out there what to think, yet he wanted instead for them to tell him what to say. For one thing, they might not be out there. For another, they were unknowable, and somewhere in Stefan Ponek was this old command he should not manipulate them. He should not tell them what to think, no matter how much they asked for it. He could not, in fact, because he did not know himself, and he

did not know them. Yet he would because he had to, and maybe he liked it. He would do it by calling attention to himself, by being there with the mike on in front of him, asking them to pick up their phones and call him. He told them he was confused about Altamont, he was stuck, they should call. They heard and they called, but they probably failed to imagine how inevitably he was stuck, all waiting, feeling them out, asking questions, commenting on what they said, most of all waiting, intensely, nervously in the half dark studio waiting. Then the Angels called in. Emmett Grogan called in. Within two days it was out in the papers.

Characters. Peopling the world of the radio station was inseparable from ·eating it, but the peopling was a more worrisome task. The people I was :scribing were alive and likely to read what I would say about them. The hallenge, it seemed to me, was to provide them with views of themselves ·hich they could recognize and which they might find interesting, but which t the same time might not be what they had expected, and this while voiding gratuitous offense. The peopling was not only to be for them, owever. My guiding questions had to do with the text and the problem of eveloping characters who would be capable of carrying its narrative. These haracters would have to be real enough to be believable, but since the urpose of the text was not a study of human personality but of a process ·hich depended on aspects of personality as one among many kinds of 1ings that mattered, I found myself accepting a sketchiness in the descrip- on of characters, and the problem then was how to do each sketch.

The nature of the research had biased what I knew about people ssociated with the station very much in terms of what they had said. I did ot feel I knew them at all well other than by what they had told me in 1terviews and left in documentary reports. So I turned to their speech, how 1ey expressed themselves and what they were concerned about, which in ach case had an apparent coherence, as the chief means of converting them nto characters. The people of the radio station thus became voices in the ext, and I was so caught up in the fact of their being voices that, but for a ew exceptions, I did not notice I had failed to give them bodies until I was ·eyond the point of thinking that would make a difference. I did think it vould make a difference to give them lives, lives with ages, roughly lesignated pasts and uncertain futures, to give them roles with respect to the adio station, and as time went on to give them histories related to the istory of the station. Also I felt it would make a difference to give them 1ames, their own personal or "real" names, as well as names indicating omething of their relationship with the station.

Naming. In a traditional history or journalistic account, it would be aken for granted that the use of personal or real names was an acceptable procedure. But in this case there was some question, both because of the ociological nature of my intent and because of the possibility of libel or ncrimination resulting from what might be said about individuals. Soci- ological case studies typically omit or change personal names, for the protection of people written about and when personal names are considered

secondary or relatively inconsequential, given that people can be referred t
in terms of class, status, role, or institutional identities.[15]

But although I considered what I was doing sociology, there were severa
reasons why I wanted to use personal names. As the subject of naming
relates to questions of protecting the privacy and the already formed
reputations and identities of individuals, I should like to present some o
those reasons here. One was that so far as I knew, most of the people
interviewed wanted to see their names in print. Many of them were used t
publicity and liked it, although some probably would have preferred
anonymity. Second was that I felt using personal names was a part of
bargain implicit in the research process. I had asked people to talk to m
and give me documents, not for purposes of contributing anonymously t
the advancement of knowledge about society, but for purposes of havin;
their history written. There were benefits which might be expected to accru
to them as a result of more public exposure, however unknown or of mixe
value those benefits might be. Their history, in a property sense, to som
extent belonged to them, and their names seemed to me one of the ways the
might claim it.

A third reason, more my own, was that I felt using the personal name
would keep me honest. I expected I might write differently if I thought I wa
saddling real, individual, living people with my statements than I would if
was once removed from doing that. It seemed to me crucial in terms o
interpreting the evidence I had obtained that I make my judgments based or
a search for particular truths, and a test of faithfulness to that search woul
be whether I would in the end be willing to stand behind what I had to say
before the people who would know and feel most intimately when and if i
was hurtful or wrong. That was a test I did not have to assume, but it wa
one I wanted and I felt it would speak to problems of research accountability.

A fourth reason for using the personal names was that I thought it was ir
keeping with the process I was studying. In that process, names, changes ir
names, and issues having to do with naming and with publicity associatec
with naming were things I considered to be of interest and consequence. I
seemed to me what I was doing would inevitably carry the process of the
radio station's cooptation one step further, and whatever protective
anonymity I might seem to be affording people by changing or omitting
their names could be penetrated by anyone who really wanted to. The
protection to be afforded by their omission would in the end be mostly for
myself and I did not feel the need of it.

(b) Describing What Goes on There

The creating and peopling of the world of the radio station was done so
as to lend to a theoretically useful description of what went on in the life of
the station over the five years in question. In that description, there were
three principal elements: time, reports, and changes.

Time. I assumed that the passing of time was integral to the possibility of ooptation and dealt with the problem of reference to it throughout by using chronological order as the main organizing device of the text. The rule I ollowed was to locate all events mentioned by date, usually by month and ear but often by day, and sometimes by day of the week and time of day. did not make an explicit or systematic attempt to indicate the logic of elations between different kinds of events in time as this, I felt, was beyond 1y knowing with any confidence. The order of association of events escribed in the text was done mainly for narrative continuity. But the ossibility of explanatory sense was something I had in mind throughout. Aany of my questions had to do with why particular events occurred as they iid and when they did, and the chronology therefore seemed worth noting n considerable specificity.

The problem of reference to time was not only a problem of dating events, ut of determining the kind of sense of the passing of time I wanted to onvey. It seemed to me appropriate to emphasize the day to day, week to veek, and month to month nature of the passing, thus calling attention to he tediousness and the persistent uncertainty experienced as part of the :ooptation process. To do this, it seemed advisable to avoid explicit oremonitions of later events in the course of the narrative. The few exceptions, usually in the start of chapters, were where introductory ummary remarks seemed likely to be helpful in clarifying subsequent equences of events which might otherwise read confusedly. It seemed ippropriate to use flashbacks throughout, however, as they would not listurb the sense of uncertainty with respect to the future. In the very)eginning, I used flashbacks to refer to events of people's lives prior to their issociation with the station. As time went on, the flashbacks were used ncreasingly for comparative purposes, recalling earlier events to indicate 1ow later ones differed and how their differences might be interpreted as neasures of change in the life of the station.

In referring to the past for comparative purposes, at least two kinds of flashback recall seemed useful. One was idealistic recall in which events of he past were brought to mind in a wishful fashion, ignoring their lisagreeable aspects. The most notable example of this was the recall of KMPX, the station of the first year, by certain of the characters in later periods as a less troubled kind of radio station than KMPX described in Part I of the text. The second kind of recall used for comparison was straight recall, in which events of the past were reintroduced later, much as they had been originally described in the text. Both kinds appear in the following passage from Part III which concerns the firing of a disc jockey in December 1968:

Bob Prescott had been one of the first to join Donahue at KMPX in the spring of 1967. He was thirty at the time and considered himself a professional radio man. He had dropped out of radio for about a year previously, disillusioned, he said, with the politics of it. The morning show had been his almost from the start at KMPX. He became operations manager in addition to morning man when Donahue went down to set up KPPC in November. It was in the living room of his apartment on Greenwich Steps that the staff of KMPX had met on March 16, 1968, and voted to go on strike. Prescott said he thought at the time their strike would be brief and Leon Crosby would take them back. When Crosby did not take them back and a group of them started at KSAN on May 21, Prescott was their morning man and their first voice on the air. It was now a year and a half after KMPX. Prescott thought his firing showed what had become of them. They had let the family fall apart.

The tense of the narrative as a whole was set in recollection. This, I felt was a way of integrating the research process with the history of the station although I kept a separation by putting the dates of interview recalls into footnotes so as not to confuse the subject time of the narrative. It was also a way of keeping faith with the evidence. It seemed to me more appropriate than would have been the alternative of relating the station's history in a present tense, or in a past tense in which events would be described without an overlay of remembering and without an accompanying sense of uncertainty as to what had really happened. A chief advantage of using recollection seemed to lie in its allowing presentation of a history of the station which was at least circumstantially, and possibly more profoundly something which survived in the memories of people. It therefore seemed appropriate to deal with the sense of recollection differently in the first period, the KMPX period, than in the later ones. Events of the KMPX period had been described by people in interviews and referred to in written reports as much more in the past than later events, as if the present and real reality began after KMPX and the KMPX strike. But although KMPX had the quality of being a distant past, it was very much present in people's minds and I wanted to convey that.

I therefore set the whole first period in a sense of present recall. It may be noted that the words "remembers" and "recalls" are used often in the first period describing events, while in the following period, Part II (Legitimacy) terms of recollection are used more infrequently. In the later parts, III (Professionalism) and IV (Renewal), where used at all, they appear more often as "remembered" and "recalled." The past referred to in Parts III and IV was still a recollected past, but it seemed more immediate in the minds of people and so it seemed fitting to refer to it usually in a direct past tense, describing events as having been said, felt, and thought by people, rather than as having been recalled.

Reports. I treated both interview and documentary evidence obtained during the research period similarly—as reports—when it came to developing the text. This was a way of dealing with the fact that much of what I had come to know about the station derived from interviews, which I thought of as personal tellings. It seemed what I knew with most confidence was that certain things had been said by someone to someone else. That some were said orally and some in writing, and some with more self-consciousness than others, seemed less helpful than the prospect that considering them all as reports would enable me to have "what had been said" as the main referent of the text.[16] Specification as to the circumstance and form of things said, and distinctions between what had been said and what might have been felt or thought by people could be included. Where a seemingly more appealing or appropriate interpretation of an event or episode came to mind, that could be introduced. But the report itself would be the main point of reference, and the rule would be to return to it repeatedly and when in doubt, emphasizing the reality of a world of talk.[17]

While treating the research evidence as reports was one way of proceeding where much of what there was to draw on was hearsay, it was also a statement about relevant reality and about one of the ways a process of cooptation might be assumed to work: what was said was assumed to affect the process as well as to be telling about it. It was at the same time a statement in retrospect about research methodology. To think of the use of research in the text as based importantly, although not exclusively, on report aspects of evidence seemed to me different from thinking of it as based only or mainly on observational or documentary aspects. If one assumed the nature of the world was such that it could make reports and thereby tell about itself, and a problem of research was to listen or get it to talk, then to carry on conversation and add to what had been said, one might expect to be faced with somewhat different issues and problems than if one assumed the world was a subject to be observed, without disturbing too much its natural state, or a place to be searched for records, which might be interpreted but could not be changed.

I dealt with the problem of converting reports to narrative in the text, in part, by techniques of paraphrase. The rule was to use what people said they remembered and thought and felt about events in a stream of consciousness fashion, in passages attributed to them but presented without quotation marks. Further attribution, whether to interview or documentary sources, would be provided in footnotes for each page as if the material had been directly quoted. The nature of the interview notes I had taken seemed to tend to paraphrase as a common form, since what people said was often not complete enough in itself in the notes or not suitable for direct quotation. In the interviews, each had discussed the history of the station in their own ways. To make a narrative that would draw on them all and space them out over time, I had to chop them up and take selections from them, and given the amount of discretion and interpretation involved, use of quotation marks, even if only for strictly textual purposes, seemed misleading.

I paraphrased many of the written reports as well as the interviews, although the written reports could have been directly quoted from. This was done in part for consistency in treating documents and interviews as selections from reports. It was also done for smoothness in flow of the

narrative and to maintain a sense of closeness to the narrative voice. Direc
quotation was used where original passages would add dimensions tha
might be destroyed by paraphrase. The quotations in such cases were se
indented in the text in accord with conventional quotation practice.

Once beyond the problem of conversion of reports to narrative throug
paraphrase and direct quotation, there was the problem of the narrativ
structure itself and its patterns of mention and association raising question
about missing evidence, seemingly contradictory reports, and multipl
interpretation. This I dealt with at times by using incidents in the history (
the station to comment implicitly on difficulties in the development of th
text. In Part III, for instance, in dealing with an obscenity charge, there is a
intent to comment on the construction of the text as well as to describe a
incident in the life of the station:

> Willis Duff's secretary Marilee Werfhorst said Tom Dougherty, when he called after
> getting the FCC inquiry in mid-December, told Duff he wanted a transcript of the
> program in Washington within a week. It was after his call they got Rona Elliott's tape
> and found it was seven or eight little reels. It was bits and pieces of the program. She
> tried to find someone who had heard the show Sunday night to help them reconstruct
> the order. That was when she called her friends and it seemed no one had heard it. Then
> she and a friend of hers named Ted and Duff and Beverly sat down one night at the
> station with Elliot's little reels and each of them typed out one or two. That was in the
> second week after Dougherty's call.
> Then they got together and put it together, they pieced it together the best they could.
> Then they timed it and they found they were missing a lot of time, maybe an hour, it
> seemed at first it was two hours. In the end maybe they lost an hour. They felt they could
> account for it by giving leeway for commercials and dead air and Eugene Schoenfeld
> speaking slowly. If a question came up they said they would say, Eugene Schoenfeld
> speaks slowly. They had a rough typed version that night. The next day another
> secretary retyped it and they standardized the language since each of them transcribing
> had done it a little differently. Where one of them had typed 'ah,' another one might
> have typed 'oh' or 'ahh' or 'uh.'

Changes. The guiding descriptive task of the text was to trace changes i
the history of the station which seemed evidence of the process (
cooptation, and to indicate with the description how these changes might b
interpreted as part of an explanation of why the process occurred as it di(
Since the changes, in order to be understood, needed context, a considerabl
amount of descriptive attention was spent on the nature and meaning (
things which did not change or which, if they did, did not seem to chang
because of cooptation. Some attention was no doubt spent on details whic
were of little or conceivably no consequence. But the question of conse
quence, of what mattered and how it mattered, could never be answere
unambiguously, and this I dealt with in the narrative, in some instances, b
raising questions of unsettled interest concerning explanatory ties whic
might be drawn between one event and others. I wanted the text to be in pa
a theoretical puzzle, a puzzle already structured to some extent, b

tructured in such a way as to admit of no one comprehensive or final olution, only of partial and tentative ones.

In order to keep the problem of explanation recurrently present, the rule followed was to include in the text statements which suggested partial xplanations of particular events along with statements which called those uggestions into question. This was done most often implicitly by the election and association of descriptive detail, but at times with explicit eference to the possibility of alternative explanation. Here, for instance, the eference is explicit:

According to the article, Edward Bear had phoned the Barb office Wednesday night to say he was canned Tuesday by the KSAN station manager Varner Paulsen. The official reason was he ran two commercials simultaneously the previous Friday. However, he told the Barb, it was really just him.

Iere the reference is implicit:

Sometime late in May, before Dave McQueen started, George Duncan, then head of the Stereo Division, came out and interviewed him at the station. McQueen said he thought Duncan made a special trip. Duff said Duncan stopped in on one of his regular visits. Duncan was uneasy about the KSAN news. He felt they had inherited a Roland Young situation at the station and it was going to require a professional as a newsman to be fair. He said he told this to McQueen when he met him and he asked McQueen where he stood. McQueen said he was completely radicalized. Duncan then asked how he thought that would affect what he put on the air as news. McQueen said he did not think it would affect it at all.

In selecting the changes to be traced and offered for explanation in the ext, my judgments were influenced by availability of evidence, personal nterest, and expectations about possible theoretical usefulness. The effort vas to focus on kinds of events which occurred regularly and frequently in he life of the station. These included monthly reports on programming and ales, advertising rate increases, references to the composition of advertisers nd audience, press coverage, changes in requirements of jobs performed for he station, backgrounds and attitudes of personnel related to circumstances f their hiring and firing or quitting, and to their remaining with the station. iuch events seemed worth following not only to note trends of change and patterns, but to encourage a continuing reconsideration of the meaning of amiliar kinds of change. I hoped to allow for the possibility that something ike increase in the monthly sales gross might be seen to have different neaning in February 1972 than it had in February 1968, such that claims about the greater importance of making money at the later date might be questioned, for instance.

The five years of the station's history over which the changes were traced vere divided into periods: Beginnings, Legitimacy, Professionalism, and Renewal. The dating of breaks between the periods was not intended to indicate clear-cut shift, but to suggest that about that time, available evidence showed a new set of concerns becoming important for people involved, and that doing something about problems posed by this new set was being thought of increasingly as necessary for the station's survival.

In the first chapter of each period, an attempt was made to say something about the nature of transition to this period from the previous one and something indicative of the nature of the new period itself. In the last chapter of each period, an attempt was made to point to changes which, seemed to have been completed since the period began. Periodically within each chapter, there were attempts to indicate how things were different by the time of this chapter than they had been in earlier ones.

(c) Summary of Rules

The following is a summary of some of the main rules of the text:

(a) Creating and Peopling a World:

1. Set up the particular world of the study through use of detail appropriate to it. Indicate with the description some of the kinds of appreciation that pertain in this world especially.
2. Introduce and identify characters. Give them biographies. Allow them to develop voices so that they may speak for themselves.

(b) Describing What Goes On There:

1. Time: Date all events as specifically as possible. Use a chronological sequence as the principal ordering device of the text. Use a tense of recollection but remain faithful to the present of the recalled experience (i.e., flashbacks are allowed, but not flashforwards).
2. Reports: Use what was said as the principal referent of the text. Transform interview and documentary reports into paraphrased statements. Describe events with these statements. Footnote sources for all evidence used.
3. Changes: Trace principal lines of change consistently. Provide context for interpreting changes (e.g., descriptions of things that do not change and comparative data on changes over time). Structure the text which describes these changes as a puzzle open to interpretation. Remember that it is the richness of the text that in the end will save the account.

(c) In General:

1. Make statements through the use of concrete detail only.

2. Make attribution as clear as possible in the text itself and further specify with footnotes.
3. Be as faithful as possible to the data: do not take leaps for dramatic effect or to construct a sense that is not a safe interpretation of reports given.
4. Write for the people of the text as well as about them.
5. Maintain an attitude of curiosity.
6. Treat everything as important.

(d) Embedded Theory

The doctoral dissertation version of the text, completed in 1975, ran to nearly 800 manuscript pages and was an attempt to describe and explain the cooptation of the station without making explicit theoretical statement. What theory there was lay embedded in the text in the pattern of its use of concrete detail.[18] Subsequent requests that more be said of a summary nature led, in 1978, to a revised version of the original which shortened its length by two-thirds and drew some generalizations from it, setting these forth in brief paragraph introductions to each chapter.[19] But the introduction to the revised version notes that these are not the only generalizations that might be drawn from the text, and the conclusion cautions that the account is "one which in its detail is more instructive than in any generalization that can be drawn from it."

Both revised and original versions reflect a commitment to the events themselves, and a suspicion that they may outlive our interpretations and that it is therefore of value simply to note them. Even patterning is heavy-handed. Yet it often seems unavoidable. One response to the manuscript after it was circulated among people of the station was a comment that: "The particular circumstances at KMPX/KSAN allowed individual occurrences to become exaggerated tragicomedies. The omnipresent clash of economics, corporations, FCC rules, and egos, combined with radical innovation, made the chaos which made the story." And this when there had not been an intent to fashion "a story."

In the text itself are many alternative explanations of why the cooptation of the radio station seemed to have to happen, why the people could not in the end have their dream, why they had to lose even what they did have in the special station of their first year. Bear says of his firing, which was part of it: "It's more like a sad, dumb joke—rather a monument to pettiness than to evil." Donahue, in the final chapter, responds to a listener on a call-in show who asks about underground radio and why it is dead: "Because life is a series of moments, man, that you live while they're happening and don't expect to constantly repeat them." Such very different interpretations as well as others stand with the text as pieces of an answer. One purpose of the present account has been to describe how a text can be made which, to some extent, allows its parts to maintain their separate authority.

FOOTNOTES

1. Susan Krieger, *COOPTATION: A History of a Radio Station,* doctoral dissertation Stanford University (Ann Arbor, Xerox University Microfilms, 1976). Passages subsequentl quoted are from this version of the text. See also: Susan Krieger, *Hip Capitalism,* Sage, 1979

2. See Howard Becker, *Sociological Work: Method and Substance* (Chicago, Aldine, 1970' Norman Denzin, *The Research Act: A Theoretical Introduction to Sociological Method* (Chicago, Aldine, 1970); Paul Diesing, *Patterns of Discovery in the Social Sciences* (Chicago Aldine-Atherton, 1971); Leonard Schatzman and Anselm Strauss, *Field Research: Strategie for a Natural Sociology* (Englewood Cliffs, Prentice-Hall, 1973).

3. The classic study of cooptation in sociological literature is also an organizational study Philip Selznik, *TVA and the Grass Roots: A Study in the Sociology of Formal Organization* (New York, Harper Torchbooks, 1966, originally Berkeley and Los Angeles, University of Californi Press, 1949).

4. In viewing the process as an accomplishment, the study shares some concerns wit ethnomethodologists. See Harold Garfinkel, *Studies in Ethnomethodology* (Englewood Cliffs Prentice-Hall, 1967); Jack Douglas, ed., *Understanding Everyday Life: Toward the Reconstruc tion of Sociological Knowledge* (Chicago, Aldine, 1970; and Roy Turner, ed., *Ethnomethodolog* (Middlesex, England, Penguin, 1974). For a recent review dealing with theoretical problems o reconciling micro- and macro-sociologies in organizational settings, see Richard Harvey Brown, "Bureaucracy as Praxis: Toward a Political Phenomenology of Formal Organiza tions," *Administrative Science Quarterly,* Sept., 1978.

5. The attempt to read and affect what is publicly known as a way of learning identity i most commonly dealt with in studies of individuals. See Erving Goffman, *Stigma: Notes on th Management of Spoiled Identity* (Englewood Cliffs, Prentice Hall, 1963): "Information Contro and Personal Identity," 41–104. For special consideration of effects of appearance, see Gregor Stone, "Appearance and the Self" in Arnold Rose, ed., *Human Behavior and Social Processes An Interactionist Approach* (Boston, Houghton Mifflin, 1962): 86–118.

6. Peter Marris, *Loss and Change* (Garden City, Anchor, 1975), deals with processes o coming to terms that have some parallel in the present case. For Marris, however, the guidin metaphor is "bereavement."

7. Elinor Langer, "The Women of the Telephone Company," *New York Review of Books* March 26, 1973; reprinted as "Inside the New York Telephone Company" in Doroth Richardson, ed., *Women at Work* (Chicago, Quadrangle, 1972): 307–360.

8. See, for example, Raymond Gordon, *Interviewing: Strategy, Techniques, and Tactic* (Homewood, Dorsey Press, 1975); and Robert Merton et al., *The Focused Interview: A Manua of Problems and Procedures* (Glencoe, Free Press, 1956).

9. This piecing together of stories to make a sensible whole produces a pattern typ explanation. See Abraham Kaplan, *The Conduct of Inquiry: Methodology for Behaviora Science* (Scranton, Chandler, 1964): "The Pattern Model," 327–336; and an elaboration in Pau Diesing, *op. cit.,* "Explanation," 157–167.

10. Many of the complexities of interpreting such documents are considered in Loui Gottschalk, Clyde Kluckhohn, and Robert Angell, *The Use of Personal Documents in History Anthropology, and Sociology* (New York, Social Science Research Council, 1945).

11. For a discussion of responsibility and copying, see Philip C. Brooks, *Research i Archives: The Use of Unpublished Primary Sources* (Chicago, University of Chicago Press 1969): 49–82.

12. Hortense Powdermaker, *Stranger and Friend: The Way of an Anthropologist* (New York Norton, 1966): "Hollywood," 209–231, discusses some similar needs for distance and possibl resultant biases. The study of show business activities may pose some peculiar dilemmas fo research.

13. Herbert Gans, *The Levittowners: Ways of Life and Politics in a New Suburban ommunity* (New York, Pantheon, 1967): xxiii, reports similar advantage when presenting a udy as a history.

14. One novel, in particular, Virginia Woolf, *The Years* (New York, Harcourt Brace, 1937), fected my thinking about overall structure of the text. It contains a saga-like treatment of ents in time and in the minds of individuals. A collection of essays, Joan Didion, *Slouching ward Bethlehem* (New York, Delta, 1968), provided a model of a narrative style in which a emingly flat presentation of particular facts is a way of indicating significance and making ore general statement.

iscussion of how a novelist's mode of writing is also a theory may be found in Wayne Booth, *e Rhetoric of Fiction* (Chicago, University of Chicago Press, 1961): 53–60. Booth is also structive generally on problems of realism.

me of the work of "new journalists" in producing non-fiction novels is also pertinent to the oice of style. See, for example, Tom Wolfe, "The New Journalism," in Tom Wolfe and E.W. hnson ed., *The New Journalism: An Anthology* (New York, Harper and Row, 1973); and onald Weber, ed., *The Reporter as Artist: A Look at the New Journalism Controversy* (New ork, Hastings, 1974): "Gay Talese: An Interview," 83–111; "Truman Capote: An Interview," 8–207.

15. Discussions of the need for anonymity are particularly conspicuous in studies of viance. See, for example, Laud Humphreys, *Tearoom Trade: Impersonal Sex in Public Places* hicago, Aldine, 1970).

16. Clifford Geertz, *The Interpretation of Cultures: Selected Essays* (New York, Basic Books, 73): "Thick Description: Toward an Interpretive Theory of Culture," 3–30, contains rtinent discussion of processes of sifting meanings in order to "inscribe" accounts.

17. The study in this regard has some affinities to oral history. See Alfred B. Lord, *The nger of Tales* (Cambridge, Harvard University Press, 1964), for a relevant discussion of ways which oral poetry is composed in performance and tradition constantly recreated through it. he interviews in the radio station case carry oral tradition as well as standing as reports. In aling with a past reconstructed from them, there is always the possibility of systematic ception. Soedjatmoko, ed., *An Introduction to Indonesian Historiography* (Ithaca, Cornell niversity Press, 1965); Zoetmiller, 326–343, contains reflection on the problem of trying to nderstand a past when one's sources of knowledge of it are the same as those which would ovide keys to it. Some related dilemmas are to be found in psychoanalytic reconstruction. See ichael McGuire, *Reconstructions in Psychoanalysis* (New York, Appleton-Century-Crofts, 71).

18. Hayden White, *Metahistory: The Historical Imagination in 19th Century Europe* (Balti- ore, Johns Hopkins Press, 1973): "Introduction: The Poetics of History," 1–42, distinguishes planations made by story and by mode of employment from those made by formal argument ways which may be helpful for interpreting the present text.

19. The generalizations drawn at the later date may be considered a kind of grounded eory. Methods for this are presented in Barney Glaser and Anselm Strauss, *The Discovery of rounded Theory: Strategies for Qualitative Research* (Chicago, Aldine, 1967). See, also, Louis ottschalk, ed., *Generalization in the Writing of History* (Chicago, University of Chicago Press, 63).

LANGUAGE AND THEORIZING IN THE HUMAN SCIENCES*

Lawrence Grossberg, UNIVERSITY OF ILLINOIS

INTRODUCTION[1]

Problems of language, communication, and meaning have become central for almost all of the disciplines within the human sciences and their paradigms. The perception of the meaningfulness of human life, experience, and communication has the potential to become a unifying theme. Different positions, however, describe and explain this meaningfulness in varying ways. Within the literature of social theory and literary criticism, explicit discussions of the nature of language and meaning are rare. More often, these terms are taken as primitives. Nevertheless, it is possible to construct readings of the various theories of meaning operative in contemporary theory.

In this essay, I shall present a classification of approaches to language analysis, describe their features and some of their proponents. I will also assess some of the current arguments for and against the utility of such approaches for social and/or literary analysis. In an essay, I can do little more than sketch and exemplify these different views. Moreover, I offer the

Studies in Symbolic Interaction—Volume 2, 1979, pages 189–231
Copyright © 1979 by JAI Press Inc.
All rights of reproduction in any form reserved.
ISBN: 0–89232–105–9

approaches themselves as ideal-types or family resemblances. While some positions will come close to the types, others will fall between them; this is perhaps the greatest weakness of the present attempt (as of all classification systems).[2] This scheme may nevertheless be useful because it reveals tensions within positions and may clarify the sympathies, alliances, and antagonisms existing among social and literary scholars.

This paper will outline six distinct views of language and meaning. Taken abstractly, these positions can be arrayed on a two-dimensional matrix. One dimension is the familiar problematic of western thought, "subjectivity" versus "objectivity." The other dimension provides three very general ways to understand the meaningfulness of language as fundamentally referential, systemic, or processual. The cross-cutting of these two dimensions produces six basic views of language and meaning: subjective and objective referential views, subjective and objective systemic views, and subjective and objective processual views. (See Diagrams 1 and 2.)

The "objective-subjective" problematic has, of course, been treated in a variety of ways. But its modern philosophic origins lie in the Cartesian tradition in which a knowing mind, an isolated consciousness, finds itself "within" but separate from a world of external, objective reality. This traditional Cartesian conception of the subject-object problematic, as we shall see, is most directly connected to what will be called referential views of language. Briefly, subjective referential views emphasize man as the architect of meaning, and meaning as the property of consciousness; objective referential views see meaning as a given property of the world, discovered by people. In either case, language is considered an instrument people use—a tool of signification, a functional system for articulation, expression, and representation; and the meaningfulness of language resides in its reference to some collection of entities (either subjective mental entities, or objective external entities).

Recent philosophy, however, has tended to see the traditional Cartesian formulation of the subject-object problematic as a stumbling block to developing a coherent theory corresponding to actual human existence and experience.[3] To escape the problems this metaphysic generates, it is generally agreed that one must move away from the traditional conceptions of subject and object. Language enters in two ways here. Not only does a move beyond the Cartesian subject-object distinction necessitate some non-referential view of language, but indeed, the treatment of language itself plays a central role in the movement to an alternative metaphysic. Instead of beginning with the metaphysics of existence, one can begin with language as a relationship between a signifier and a signified, between a material vehicle and its meaning. In this way, subjective positions are no longer bound to talking about meaning as a collection of conscious entities (to which language can refer). Instead, they treat meaning as the primacy of the signified in language. Similarly, objective positions can escape the

Diagram 1.   Alternative Conceptions of Meaning and Language*

	Conceptions of Reality		
	Entity	System	Process
Objective	Objective 1 referential (Naturalist)	Objective 3 systemic (Structuralist)	Objective 6 processual (Hermeneutic-diacritical)
Subjective	Subjective 2 referential (Mentalistic)	Subjective 4 Systemic (Interactionist)	Subjective 5 Processual (Phenomenological)

(left margin label: Locus of Meaning)

*The numbers refer to the order in which the positions are treated in the discussion.

metaphysical talk about real-world entities and instead, focus on the way the signifier, the objective dimension of language, constitutes meaning.

This movement beyond referential theories based on Cartesian metaphysics is not, however, sufficient to account for the diversity of views of language and meaning; for there are two different sorts of nonreferential views. One can understand these as divergent answers to the question: if the meaningful character of language is no longer to be conceived as residing in its reference to some collection of (subjective or objective) entities, then where does the meaningfulness of language reside? The two dominant answers in contemporary theorizing seem to be "in systems"[4] or "in processes." Discussion of the differences between these two solutions will follow.[5] For the moment, however, it suffices to see the cross-fertilization of the two dimensions—subjective versus objective, and referential versus system versus process—as resulting in the possibility of six alternative conceptualizations of the source, nature, or meaning of meaning in human life.

Unfortunately, there is another weakness in the present effort. I have a preference for one of the six positions. The chapter concludes with some preferential statements and identifies possible directions in the study of language and human life. But inevitably, my biases entered into the classification itself and into the choice of "meaning" and "language" as the key features. Nevertheless, these two terms constitute a powerful alliance because of the close relationship between meaning/language and content/form. By building both terms into my model, I can account for a number of approaches that prefer one or the other. And while these terms are redefined by each of the six views, there is a shared understanding of them in everyday discourse on which to build.[6]

The same structural differences that exist between positions on this issue exist for other related issues: for example, communication, culture, art, community, interpretation, and translation. In presenting the six views here, I shall use interpretation and translation as examples for two reasons. First, they are very closely connected to discussions of meaning and language. They both represent the attempt to understand (the meaning of) particular

Diagram 2. A Summary of the Six Positions

Conception	Sources	Current Representatives	Locus of Meaning	Language	View of Subject	Translation
Objective-Referential	Descartes, logical positivism	Charles Osgood Robert Merton Northrop Frye	referent-world	tool of information: objective locus of meaning	transcendental consciousness	paraphrase
Subjective-Referential	Descartes, idealism	Peter Berger Geneva Critics (Poulet, Starobinski)	reference— consciousness	tool of expression: objective locus of meaning	transcendental consciousness	paraphrase
Objective-Systemic	linguistics/ linguistic philosophy NeoKantian	Claude Levi-Strauss Tzvetan Todorov Harvey Sacks	system of signifieds parallel to that of	tool for defining reality; system of	transcendental speaker	structural analysis

			context intentions	defining reality; social conven- tion/language as use	scendental processes, identity	reconstruction of subjective intention
Subjective- Systemic	Wittgenstein, pragmatism	Erving Goffman Murray Krieger				
Subjective- Processual	Husserl, Heidegger	Harold Garfinkel John O'Neill Stanley Fish	intentionality, relation of identity	tool for com- municating: language as use and ideal entity	transcendental relation with other	focus on ideal rather than contextual meaning
Objective- Processual	Hegel, Nietzsche, later Heidegger	Alan Blum Michel Foucault Roland Barthes	textuality, process of difference	trace of pro- duction of reality by the articulation of opposition	determined moment of cultural textuality	creative moment of inter- textuality

linguistic texts or events. (Certainly, "communication" would be an equally good example.)[7] Second, translation may be seen as an extreme case of both interpretation and communication (parallel to the study of cross-cultural communication). The very possibility of translation assumes both that one may separate the meaning from the vehicle of language and yet that the relationship is an organic one. That is, translation raises the question of the "trans-linguistic character" of meaning.[8] Thus, any theory of translation must identify that independence of meaning from language which makes translation possible. The question of translation, then, sheds light on the relationship between language and meaning in the six views; it is a useful extreme case of the more general processes of interpretation, communication, and understanding.[9]

REFERENTIAL VIEWS OF LANGUAGE AND MEANING

A referential theorist sees language as a factual and independent entity, comparable to any other object existing in the real world. Yet, language is not *exactly* like any other object, for it is a peculiar sort of object—a collection of signs. Typically, this conception reflects an understanding of the sign originating with the Stoic philosophers: the sign is a triadic entity consisting of a material vehicle ("sign"), a reference (concept, sense), and a referent (object). Since referential positions understand language as a collection of discrete signs, each of which has its own proper reference and referent, such theories tend to be atomistic. That is, language, thought, and physical objects tend to be analyzed in terms of discrete parts functioning as independent entities.[10]

The question of whether the reference or the referent is the primary source of meaning defines the distinction between subjective and objective views in the general referential conception. Both views see meaning as an entity pointed to (referred to) in some immediate and direct fashion by linguistic signs. They differ, however, on the degree to which consciousness is considered the meaning's necessary locus. Furthermore, both positions tend to think of meaning as information—as a representation of some objective conditions —and to assume methodologically that this information is to be discovered within language itself. That is, it is the language itself which makes the meaning available to us.[11]

The Objective Referential View

Objective referential views often deny the sign's triadic structure by denying the reference's existence, that is, by denying the existence of any realm of mental entities. Such views argue that the notion of reference to a private, empirically nonverifiable entity does not make sense within the prevailing epistemology. It is, rather, reference to observable events, behaviors, and objects which constitues the dominant notion of meaning within such a view. For example, the two dominant forms of the objective referential view are representational and behavioral theories. In both of these theories, meaning is ultimately located in an objective and observable state of affairs. Behavioral theories account for meaning in terms of a series of habitually acquired mediations (which can be described neurophysiologically) resulting in a specific and physical response to the word as stimulus. Representational theories locate the informational meaning of a sign in the object to which it refers, a real object in the real world. While such theories may appeal to a mediating series of representations within the brain of the perceiver (percepts, for example), it is the objective referent which finally defines the meaning of a particular word.[12]

The Subjective Referential View

In subjective referential views, on the other hand, the sign refers to a mental entity "located" in the consciousness of the individual language users. There is a direct connection between the mental entity to be expressed and the linguistic vehicle which is its expression. But meaning exists prior to its expression in language. This prelinguistic meaning is not dependent on the existence of language, although such positions often recognize that the acquisition of language influences both the structure and content of such mental entities. Still, the meanings themselves exist within a private consciousness; the sign objectively refers to them. To be human, therefore, is to be conscious, and to be conscious entails possessing such subjective meanings (entities). The problem of the privacy of meaning is, of course, an extremely troublesome one, for if the notion of privacy is made too strong, the possibility of sharing meaning (understanding) is obviated.[13] Thus, within subjective referential positions, it is not uncommon to find a division of meaning into (1) some essential, shareable aspect and (2) some individualized, private colorations.[14]

Just as behaviorism is one of the dominant forms of the objective referential view in social theory, Schutz's Weberian program for the social sciences may be its subjective counterpart:[15]

> What concerns us is that Weber reduced all kinds of social relationships and structures, all cultural objectifications, all realms of objective mind, to the most elementary forms of individual behavior. To be sure, all the complex phenomena of the social world retain their meaning, but its meaning is precisely that which the individuals involved attach to their own acts. The action of the individual and its intended meaning alone are subject to interpretive understanding. Further, it is only by such understanding of individual action that social science can gain access to the meaning of each social relationship and structure, constituted as they are, in the last analysis, by the action of the individual in the social world.
> Never before had the project of reducing the "world of objective mind" to the behavior of individuals been so radically carried out as it was in Max Weber's initial statement

of the goal of interpretive sociology. This science is to study social behavior by interpreting its subjective meaning as found in the intentions of individuals.

Much of the contemporary work in linguistics growing out of Chomsky's earlier transformational theory provides another example of a subjective referential position. As one author has described it, "In the transformational model, language looks more like a specialized transduction system, an input-output device for converting meaning-laden messages into acoustic patterns, than as the central medium of thought,"[16] That is, Chomsky's notion of deep structure operates with a private collection of meanings prior to linguistic expression.

The Relation Of Sign And Meaning

Thus, both objective and subjective versions of the referential view see meaning as (1) an entity existing independently of language, and (2) functioning through a necessary connection between the signs of language and the domain in which meaning entities exist. The meaningfulness of language, hence, resides in the capacity of signs to refer to meaning entities.

But this description of referential positions leaves open the question of what sort of necessity connects the sign to its meaning. While language gives us information about the world or a particular subjective experience, the form of the relationship varies significantly among different theorists. One common approach postulates some causal relationship between sign and meaning. Another approach, taken by both Plato (in the *Cratylus*) and Aquinas, articulates a mimetic theory, holding that words mirror their objects. Perhaps the most prevalent approach holds that the relationship is arbitrary and, in some sense, conventional. Language is seen as built upon a "social contract," defining standardized usage in terms of the connections between signs and their meaning-objects.[17] The conventions may be understood as a set of rules requisite to competent social use of language, rules concerning how to adequately express oneself to others. Although it is possible to conceive of these rules as beliefs held in common by individuals, they are more typically located within the language itself. That is, they are publicly available to any competent speaker. As we shall see, it is the question of the relationship between signs and meanings rather than the subjectivity or objectivity of any particular version which, in the last analysis, determines the view of translation and interpretation held by a referential theory.

However, before turning to this question, two points remain. First, it is often the case that referential philosophers attempt to balance the objective and subjective views I have described. The triadic structure of the sign suggests that the sign bears a relationship to both the mental and the physical worlds. Thus, it is not necessary for a subjectivist version to deny some connection between language and physical objects. Ogden and Richards, for example, postulate a direct causal relation between the sign and its reference, and only an imputed relationship between the sign and its eferent. This latter relationship, moreover, depends upon the "more or less direct or indirect" (i.e., mediated) relationship existing between the refernce and the referent.[18] Similarly, objective positions need not deny the role f mental representations of the object in meaning processes; but it is always he referent—the real object in a real world—which is made primary as the ocus of meaning.

Second, referential theories clearly imply an instrumental or functional iew of language. It is language which enables us to share information about he world, about either a real physical world or our own private experiences. anguage is seen in essentially informational, expressive, or communica-ional terms. Thus, Ogden and Richards argue that "language, though often poken of as a medium of communication, is best regarded as an instru-nent."[19] Language is something used by the speaker or writer. The sign or vord is merely a tool, a garment which clothes or points us to some other, eal world. Language is, as Berkeley described it, "a curtain of words" vhich is to be pulled aside to reveal the meaning.[20] However, the metaphor s not quite exact, even though the objects constituting meanings exist apart rom language. For it is only in language (or some other system of signs) hat they come to exist as information, that is, as shareable and publicly vailable knowledge about the world. Meaning is thus given through anguage insofar as one knows the rules which enable him to see that to vhich the signs point.

Translation And Interpretation

The referential view of meaning can be clarified by considering the arts of ranslation and textual interpretation. Language, it must be remembered, is container which remains separable from the meaning/information it brings us. It is merely the gift wrapping to be stripped away. It is, however, necessary wrapping, for without it, there is no gift. Of course, the way in vhich one strips away the linguistic wrapping depends upon the way the sign is connected to its meaning. By postulating some form of necessary connection, most referential theories are able to see translation and interpretation as an objectively constituted, rule-governed endeavor.

For the subjective referentialist, the translation of a text involves an attempt to reconstruct the psychology of some other individual. This view of translation and interpretation has been described as "romantic" and "psychologistic."[21] Without establishing some necessary connection be-tween the language of the text and some subjective consciousness, the text remains silent. Language is void of intrinsic meaning apart from the language users' consciousness. By assuming a necessary connection between language and the meaning-object referred to, these positions avoid the reduction of translation and interpretation to a purely empathic process. Instead, it can be seen in terms of the rules governing the word-meaning relation, rules related to the competence of the interpreter as a speaker of the language.

Of course, beyond the competence of any speaker, there may also be more specialized and objective rules for particular sorts of texts. Richards's theory of criticism, for example, attempts to specify a set of rules enabling interpretation to be "scientific." Richards's view requires careful scrutiny of the words on the page and their interrelations in the particular text; the meaning is there in the words, on the page. The problem is to see that to which they are pointing—the information expressed or transmitted.[22] Because referential theories tend to be atomistic (i.e., the world is a collection of entities, the text is a product of the serial addition of words), the rules are usually concerned with an analysis of the ingredients of the text. When the critic properly pulls aside the curtain of words, the meaning of the message in the form of information about some nonlinguistic domain is revealed.

Another version of the referential view focuses on the rules governing the meanings of signs within some larger entity as the necessary starting point. Like Richards's rule system, such approaches do not see translation/interpretation involving any direct relationship to another mind except as an interpreted one in the text. Weber's theory of ideal types[23] and Frye's theory of genre,[24] for example, make the understanding of a specific text dependent upon the recognition of its appropriate class membership. The translator treats the message as an exemplification of a particular class, and assumes that the meaning of the message is crucially determined by the properties of its class. Obviously, one consequence of all such rule-mediated approaches is that "even the best translation entails a loss—perhaps not so much of the objective information as that of that intangible essence of any language—its beauty, imagery and metaphor for which there is no one-to-one translation."[25]

There are, finally, extreme subjective referentialists who maintain that even the "rules" connecting the sign and its reference are only beliefs—that is, subjective possessions—of the speaker. The appeal to mediating objective rules is cut short, and the particularity of the text demands an immediate identification with the mind of the author. Such an approach has been called for by the Swiss "phenomenological" critic, Georges Poulet, who has argued that literature must be understood as nothing more than a form of consciousness. As a result, the interpreter "dissolves the forms and structures" of language so that he can move past language to pure consciousness.[26] Such an approach seems to be present, if only implicitly, in some of the work of Alfred Schutz and more recent "existentialist" social scientists.[27] Nevertheless, in their less extreme forms, referential theories seem to dominate the social and literary sciences at the present time.

SYSTEMIC VIEWS OF LANGUAGE AND MEANING

There are serious and obvious problems with referential conceptions of meaning, and writings on the subject are replete with discussions of the weaknesses of seeing meaning as an entity. Wittgenstein and Quine are the most noted critics of such views. Quine, for example, has argued that the postulation of meaning as an entity is built upon the "fallacy of substraction," a logically fallacious move from "a linguistic expression has a meaning" to "a meaning exists."[28] Increasingly, philosophers have attempted to argue that (1) it is possible to deny that meaning is an entity (2) without denying that a linguistic text has a (determinate) meaning. Furthermore, attacks have been mounted against the radical Cartesian dualism which referential theories assume. In the present context, however, we need not concern ourselves with the details of such critiques.

Instead, we turn to a class of approaches which attempt to see meaning as an emergent and, therefore, epiphenomenal product of the relationships among the elements of language. By focusing directly on language and seeing meaning as a property of the linguistic system, such views avoid the radical separation of consciousness and world. They postulate a system of interrelated and interacting constituents of language. It is the structure of this system—the interactions among its elements—which produces that quality of experience and texts we call "meaning." Thus, while such views may talk about "process," it is always understood as interactions among preconstituted elements within a structured totality.

Language is a productive (i.e., creative) system rather than a merely passive mediator between man and world. Referential theories assume the reality of our experience both of ourselves as consciousness and of the world. Systemic views, on the other hand, examine the role language itself plays in constituting the meaning of and hence, our experience of both the self and the world. Such views divide over how to describe the linguistic system. Following Saussure's differentiation of *langue* and *parole*,[29] language may be seen either as a system of quasi-objective elements standing in a particular relationship to one another or as a system of acts of speaking performed by individuals. On this ground, I shall distinguish between objective systemic and subjective systemic approaches.[30]

AN OBJECTIVE SYSTEMIC PHILOSOPHY OF LANGUAGE[31]

Objective systemic views see meaning as the epiphenomenal consequence of the interactions of the elements constituting language as *langue*. This system has no real existence apart from the individual acts of speaking *(parole)* in which it is actualized. Nevertheless, it is this objectively describable structure which gives significance to and makes possible the successful use of language in speaking. It is this assumption of a conventional system of signs as the source of meaning which defines such positions.

In order to understand the account of meaning given within this view, we must examine the structure of the sign. The linguistic sign, on this view, cannot be conceptualized in terms of some variation of the tripartite relatio of vehicle-sense-referent. Rather, the sign is seen as a bipartite structure (signifier and signified.[32] The sign is constituted as a socially fixed relation (equivalence between a particular material signifier and its signified. Th relationship appears symmetrical so that the signifier becomes a transparer carrier of the signified. However, this appearance is only an illusion create by the systematicity of the linguistic system. Within the system, there is n necessary link between the signifier and the signified. In fact, it is only b virtue of their location within the system that this relationship of significa tion is possible. Meaning is a property of the closed system of languag which has no intrinsic relationship to any domain of objects or event outside or independent of itself. Meaning cannot, therefore, be accounte for in terms of some extralinguistic entity.

The sign, as a meaningful entity, itself exists only in the unity of its tw aspects. It is this unity which is constitutive of meaning. Furthermore, thi unity only exists in the closed system of signs. The unity of the signifier an signified is like that between two sides of a sheet of paper: the way in whic one cuts up one side of the paper (the structure of the system of signifiers– the material vehicles) will be necessarily identical to the way in which th other side (the structure of the system of signifieds—the conceptual cargo appears to be organized. Thus, what we normally think of as the mean ingfulness of language is nothing but an epiphenomenal result or emergen expression of the relationships existing between the particular elements o the system itself.

A Philosophy Of Symbolic Mediation

Thus, one can no longer talk about either a conscious self or an objectiv reality existing outside the system of signification within which we ar compelled to talk. It is not the fact of our using the system to talk that i crucial, so much as it is that the system is the origin of the meaningfulnes of *our experience* as speakers. This suggests that objective systemic concep tions do not deny the existence of something existing outside of the system On the contrary, such positions seem to require the postulation of universal and essential human nature: the language-user. In present times this transcendental subject is seen as a self-conscious person able to take cognizance of his own determination by the system of signification.[3] Similarly, the real world is not denied; it is, however, (along with the speaking subject), relegated to a position about which one can say very little The two terms become the limits of intelligible discourse. That is, Cartesia dualism is not denied, but rather is reformulated.[34] Instead of a fixed reality standing in opposition to a static, conscious self, objective systemic view see them as formless. They remain unintelligible prior to the interventio and mediation of the symbolic system. By giving meaning to our experience the system gives both the world and the subject their particular structure o eaning. The system makes them what they are to us. The "real" is nintelligible, prior to the interposition of the signification system. The ructure of our understanding of both ourselves as subjects and of the orld is determined by the structure of the system itself.

An objective systemic view, consequently, is not a philosophy of pan-ymbolism (i.e., there is no reality other than that of symbolic systems), but ather, a philosophy of symbolic mediation. And the structure of the system self is the mediating term. Since the structure is already constituted, the ystem is stable and consequently, our picture of the world and of ourselves also stable. The static quality of the system—its pregiveness—is respon-ble for the illusion of the necessary and transparent connection between gnifier and signified; this connection, in turn, fortifies our faith in the xistence of human nature and the world. As Cassirer argued, symbolic ystems create the definitions of the world for us so that when we think we re exploring reality, we are merely engaging in a dialogue with our ymbolic systems.[35] Symbols, thus, constitute our *Weltanschauung,* our way f seeing the world in which we are held prisoners by our own symbolic ystems. Such ways of talking make it clear that objective systemic views ssume that we do have some existence as subjects apart from these prisons nd that the world too exists. Otherwise, how could they be seen in a variety f ways?

A Diversity of Positions

There are, of course, a number of different objective systemic positions. he difference between them results from differing conceptions of the elationship characterizing any signification system. Let us consider briefly few examples. The most obvious objective systemic philosophy is the tructuralist movement, building off Saussure's linguistics and finding its aost famous expression in the structural anthropology of Levi-Strauss. This osition sees the relationship among the elements of the system as a set of ifferences. Thus, the significance of any element is defined by a series of ppositions: a term is what it is by virtue of what it is not. Meaning is a unction of the location or position of an element as opposed to all the other lements within the system. This position is the most radical version of bjective systemic views because meaning is explained in terms of a purely ormal set of interactions. There is, literally, no meaningfulness within the ystem apart from such formal arrangements; and there is none without.

NeoKantian philosophers—for example, Cassirer—offer a weaker ver-ion of this general position. Cassirer's view, for example, focuses less on the ormal structure of particular symbolic systems. Instead, he locates the ignificant (i.e., determining) interaction in the way the signifier and ignified are related. This results in a classification of types of symbolic ystems and ways of seeing the world. Furthermore, some theories of linguistic relativity—for example, Whorf's—see the grammatical structure of the linguistic system as determining.[37]

Finally, there are a number of analytic philosophies which can be described as objective systemic views. Lyons's recent argument that we treat meaning as a "nondetachable or syncategorematic component of such phrases as 'to have a meaning,'" is only one example of Wittgenstein's influence.[38] Wittgenstein argued that the meaning of a term is its use within a particular language game. Some recent philosophers objectify the language game into a set of determinate rules. Rule theorists, such as Winch, Searle, and Harre and Secord[39] see meaning as emerging from the structure of rules which define a particular language game. These rules reside in the language game itself (*langue*), and the language game is divorced almost entirely from the form of life—the actual historical context of language use (*parole*). The language game as a system of rules of usage defines the meaning of expressions.[40]

Translation and Interpretation

Objective systemic views raise a paradox as one examines their view of interpretation: while interpretation appears to be fairly straightforward and objective, involving a formal analysis of the text, the very possibility of translation is questionable. If translation is an illustrative (because extreme) case of the more general process of interpretation, then either the straightforwardness of interpretation or the "impossibility" of translation seems paradoxical. It is helpful to consider the problem of translation.

The particular paradox such a view raises in the act of translation is expressible in Burke's (somewhat enigmatic) use of the Augustinian doctrine, "Believe that you may understand."[41] For one is involved immediately in a circular process—how is one to know what to believe? To illustrate this problem, we can utilize Quine's theory of the indeterminacy of radical translation.[42] Imagine an anthropologist visiting a culture radically unlike our own, with a language unrelated to those of our own civilization. While walking with an informant, he sees a white rabbit running. The native points and utters "gavagai." How is the anthropologist to understand this utterance? There are a multiplicity of meaningful translations possible. For example, the native might be saying, "There is a rabbit," (or "There is a white rabbit," or "There is a running rabbit," etc.) much as we would say the same thing. But he also might be saying, "It is now rabbitting," in the same way that we describe the event of rain. Perhaps this culture does not see the world in terms of discrete objects, but rather in terms of events— "rabbitting," "manning," etc. He might also be saying, "Rabbithood is now revealing itself," similar to the way we sometimes think of abstract qualities such as virtue. The point is, according to Quine, that it is impossible to justify one decision over another. Hence, the idea of a correct translation, or of any translation, is meaningless.

Whorf's writings provide us with a further illustration of this dilemma. Whorf, at least at times, argues that the grammar of a language determines the way one sees the world. Yet this would seem to lead into Quine's paradox, for you cannot translate an utterance without knowing something outside of the language. But if the language determines all meaningfulness, translation is impossible, and Whorf's examples would seem to be unfounded. Borrowing an argument often raised against Whorf, he argues that the Hopi, because they speak of "dayness for the fourth time," do not think of days as discrete entities. Instead, they must see it as a sort of Platonic form constantly reembodying itself.[43] Now consider a Frenchman (in whose language kings are described with cardinal numbers, for example, Louis Two) travelling in America. He hears the people refer to "Louis the Second." Would he be correct if he were to think that we mean "Louis for the second time," and hence, that Americans do not think of kings as discrete entities?

A similar question might be raised about other objective systemic views; for example, on what basis is Cassirer able to justify his interpretations/translations of alternative forms of symbolic consciousness? Cassirer must claim that there is a historical evolution of such systems; furthermore, the "lower" structures never totally disappear. Thus, we are able to understand and interpret texts of mythical symbolic systems because we continue to inhabit such worlds.[44]

Once some claim is made for the interpreter's participation within the same symbolic system as the text to be translated, interpretation becomes possible. If meaning arises from the structure of the system of signs, interpretation is a description of the structure manifested within a particular text. There are actually two alternatives available: on the one hand, one can understand the message as a limited exemplification of the more general structure of the signification system. Consequently, the text must be interpreted in the context of a preceding structural analysis of that system. On the other hand, one can treat each message as its own system and seek the meaning in its own structure or in some universal symbolic structure. The first alternative is Cassirer's, the second belongs to structuralists like Levi-Strauss. In both cases, interpretation is analogous to breaking a code, and the outcome will be a structural or algebraic equation. That is, interpretation is, at its best, a purely descriptive endeavor.

Objective systemic views often claim that they have made interpretation objective and scientific. The above discussion reveals the limits of this claim. The interpreter must already understand the particular symbolic system or text he is decoding. Consequently, his own ways of seeing the world will be determined by the very structure he is attempting to analyse. This circularity is escaped only by assuming a reality independent of symbolic systems. The interpreter conceives of himself as a conscious subject able to stand outside of and above his own determination. It is precisley this assumption which will be called into question by the move from system to process. Howevei let us first turn our attention to those views which locate the systematicit of language in the interactions and relationships among the acts of speakin subjects (*parole*).

A SUBJECTIVE SYSTEMIC PHILOSOPHY OF LANGUAGE[45]

Objective systemic views see language as an atemporal code manifested onl in its concrete actualizations in language use. But this code is also, in som sense, the necessary (transcendental) condition of those very acts of speech Such positions find it difficult to account for historical change anc individual creativity because the code is static. Subjective systemic views, o the other hand, begin with the primacy of speech. The code arises out of act of speaking. Meaning emerges from and resides in the system of languag *use,* speech acts, or symbolic interactions. Hence, such views focus upor speaking as the act of a subject within a particular context with othe speaking subjects. By emphasizing the constant creation and recreation o meaning within contexts of interaction, the subjective systemic view seem to have solved the problem of accounting for change. However, sucl positions are characterized by a very real and unsolved tension betwee individual creativity (emergence) and shared understanding (communica tion) within their contextualist-orientation.[46] It is precisely this tensio which characterizes those positions labelled interactionism.

Subjective systemic positions conceive of meaning as a role or functior within a particular system of interaction. The meaning of a sign or action i publicly available and identifiable as the role it plays in the context of th natural human world of interactions in situations. Wittgenstein's concep tion of meaning as use within a language game in the context of a form o life is an influential example.[47] Another equally influential example is th pragmatist's conception of meaning as "rules for using and interpretin things, interpretation being always an imputation of potentiality for som consequence.[48] Meaning is, in such views, a natural relationship between a organism and its environment. A less naturalistic version in contemporar social theory may be found in Kelly's notion of a construct as a bipola organization of experience. Although meaning for Kelly seems to "belong to the subject in a direct sense, constructs are not some privately owne mental entities hidden from public view. They are, rather, the ver structures with which the individual's experience is organized. Consequent ly, they are available to an observer as much as to their "possessor."[49]

Creativity and Tradition

Meaning is a description of the world of human conduct, action, and interaction.[50] It exists within this public world, although precisely where it exists is a question which elicits significantly different responses. For meaning is often seen to reside, simultaneously, in the concrete speech act and in the language making possible that speech act. Within a subjective systemic conception, language is a system of conventions defining and dictating standardized usage. It has a constraining power over individuals. But the conventionality of language is constantly emerging and reemerging in the ongoing processes of social interaction and language use. It is not a static system of overlapping meanings or rules. Only by our continuing to use language in conventional ways does it continue to function as a system of conventions. The view that there is no meaning outside of actual use in interaction reflects the concern of such positions with the emergence of meaning in particular contexts. However, this does not account for the constraining power of these conventions, nor for the possibility of understanding and communication.[51] If the conventions for using language are a part of the ongoing interactions of language use, language is reducible to neither subjectively held beliefs nor to an objective system. But then, language itself must be seen as an emergent property of the ongoing system of language use. Any intersubjectively negotiated system of communication presupposes, however, some system of interpersonal interaction within which the negotiation and the requisite understanding can take place.[52] That is, subjective systemic views typically presuppose—without accounting for—the origin or existence of a shared system.

The pragmatist's view, that the meaning of a sign is its potential use, merely continues the circularity of the argument.[53] Mead's description of the sign as a collapsed act merely serves to postpone the question of the sharedness of understanding, even taken as use. This potential use must be shared prior to its actual use if understanding is to be possible. In fact, subjective systemic views rest upon an unaccounted for institutionalization of language. Such positions often argue that symbols have some sedimented meaning prior to any speech act. Different theories see this sedimentation in different forms, but such an assumption inevitably requires one to step outside of the system of ongoing interactions. Wittgenstein's view, for example, seems to suggest that language games are institutionalized within structures of social action into which the speaker is placed in the course of socialization. Pragmatism similarly appeals to the social meaningfulness of language; the individual must internalize the system if he is to successfully enter into the social processes of interaction and negotiation.

A Philosophy of Symbolic Mediation

Noting this ambivalence is not meant as a critique of such positions. Rather, it is only at this point that we are able to approach the actual conception of meaning operative within such views: subjective systemic positions see language as a mediating term between man and his environment.

Language use is the temporal unfolding of events in which the world becomes meaningful. Subjective systemic views, furthermore, presuppose a particular structure of use: by an essentially undetermined subject, of an already meaningful significatory system, in order to organize experiences and events as meaningful.[54]

Subjective systemic positions argue that both the subject and the object of the experience are given meaning in the particular interactional context in which language in used. Thus language is a mediating screen which gives meaning to a preexistent but not yet meaningfully ordered world. It also organizes the speaking subject's social identity and self-concept. The emergence of meaning is seen as a third term existing in the space between the speaking subject and his environment; this presupposes a conscious subject as the stable source of her or his own projects and interactions.

Subjective systemic positions assume the existence of universal human nature. This defines for them the nature of the subject, who stands in a particular relationship to language, objects, and other subjects, a subject who "engages in mindful, self-conscious activity" and who has his or her own "world of behavior and thought."[55] This subjective essence exists prior to the construction of a symbolic identity in language use. The pragmatists characterize it as an unknown and unknowable aspect of the human subject presupposed as the source of creativity and will. It is this "I" which relates to the world and has an identity constructed for itself (the various "me's") through the mediating processes of symbolic interaction. Nevertheless, the "I" must be endowed with certain structures of consciousness (which cannot be meaningfully ordered) enabling him/her to relate to others through language use. For example, if one describes social interaction as a process of negotiation, then that very relation (negotiation, empathy, or perspective taking) must inhere in the subject prior to the actualization of the relationship. One can clarify this point in terms of the traditional dichotomy of form and substance. A competent social actor must have a particular set of processes and the particular structures/contents (e.g., shared meanings, rules, and norms of interaction, etc.) at his or her disposal. For the subjective systemic theorist, the former is nonproblematic; it is presupposed as the possession of the subject outside of any interactional setting. When such positions are described as contextualist, it is always a context into which the subject brings himself and locates himself meaningfully.[56]

Subjective systemic positions, then, see meaning as emerging from the contextualized use or application of an already meaningful symbolic system by a subject, at least part of whose existence is universally and essentially characterizable. However, such positions often hide the fact that the position is built upon an interaction, a coming together of two already constituted and identified structures of meaningfulness. That is, such positions often fail to acknowledge their underlying mediational assumption. The Cartesian poles of subject and object are not denied; they are affirmed and related after the fact of their separation. Meaning is the structure of the relationship emerging within the context of particular acts of language use.

Subjective systemic conceptions attempt to postulate a necessary relationship between the terms of the Cartesian dualism. That relationship exists in the symbolic interactions or language uses out of which the meaningfulness of human life emerges. Such positions have increasingly come to define the major alternative to the traditional postivistic (referential) social theories. We might include within this camp, a number of diverse positions, including certain interpretations of pragmatism (e.g., Herbert Blumer's symbolic interactionism and Kenneth Burke's theory of symbolic action); some of the work in linguistic pragmatics (e.g. speech act theory); Cicourel's psychologistic ethnomethodology and cognitive-developmental theories in psychology.[57]

Systemic subjectivism constitutes a powerful and reasonable position for the social theorist at the present moment. This is due, in part, to their attempt to maintain some distance between social science and the everyday life of the speaking subject. The distinction can never be absolute, however, because of the perspectivism inherent in all of the perceptions and thoughts of the subject enmeshed in the system of interactions.[58] However, when one turns to the problem of textual interpretation and translation, the weakness of a subjective systemic philosophy as a general philosophy for the human sciences becomes more apparent.

Translation and Interpretation

Within such a view of language and meaning, the question of translation and textual interpretation is a particularly difficult one. Subjective systemic positions argue that referential views begin by distinguishing between subjective, individual meaning and objective, social meaning. Usually, one or the other of these is rejected; at best, interpretation is seen as a process in which the individual struggles to match his or her own meanings with those objectively present. The significant theoretical question concerns the possibility and accuracy of the overlaps between the contents of the two systems.

Subjective systemic positions, on the other hand, call the very meaning translation into question. The notion of meaning as emergent in interactic dictates that the meaning of a text must itself be seen as a negotiate outcome of a process of interaction among individual speaking subjects. A one author has said, "artistic productions must be seen as interaction creations, the meanings of which arise out of the interactions directed them by the artist and his audience."[59] Thus, translation and interpretatio in the conventional sense are not possible. One can attempt to reconstru the perspectives of particular individuals on a particular text, but this is n to be confused with the meaning of the text which, in the case of translatio could then be reembodied within a new language. At best, the meaning of text is to be understood as an organization of individual perspectives an interactions.

Systemic views bring to the surface a problem inherent in any attempt t articulate a general theory of meaning for the human sciences: there seem to be a significant distinction between the meaningfulness of action and tha of texts. This difference is captured in the intuitively obvious distinctio between social interaction and reading. It is obvious that context is significant variable in the former; it is not so obvious in the latter. I interaction, the other is responsive and active; in reading, the othe maintains a disquieting stance of silence. A general theory of meanin would have to account for these differences and others, as well as finding way to incorporate both into a common understanding of meaning. Thi possibility is opened up by the move into a processual view, to which I shal now turn.

PROCESS VIEWS OF LANGUAGE AND MEANING

As I have already said, systemic positions are a significant challenge an alternative to the more traditional referential theories dominating social an literary theory. Objective systemic positions have forced theorists to ex amine the internal structure of the "codes" operating in human life, whil subjective systemic views return the codes to the everyday contexts o interaction and use. Furthermore, both versions have compelled theorists t acknowledge the reflexivity of their own positions as well as of the socia world. However, insofar as such positions maintain some differentiation o their own activities from everyday life (attempting to justify the appellatio of science), they cut short the reflexive process. This is structurally expresse as a tension in their own work as they struggle to escape the Cartesiar dichotomy. Such views are generally characterized by a fundamenta assumption of the meaningfulness of human experience. However, by stil operating with a preconstituted subject, they have failed to rigorously and reflexively carry through the implications of this assumption.

A number of recent philosophical and theoretical positions attempt a
dical break with the tradition of dualism in Western thought. Such views
ake the Cartesian notions of subject and object problematic and even
dically undermine them. They argue that the fundamental structure of
uman experience is an ongoing process of the constitution of meaning
ithin which subject and object are constituted. Such views talk about a
nity, a nondifferentiation of subject and object in the processes of
gnification preceding their separation in the everyday attitude. This
elonging-together (which is the very structure of process, for the word does
ot seem to imply an agent or subject who controls the process)[60] is assumed
s the most radical point of origin, for it is out of this process in which
either subject nor object are yet differentiated that both are defined and
onstituted. It is out of this process that the subject-object dichotomy is
istalled in experience by particular interpretations. This structure is
onceptualized as a process rather than a system, for the latter presupposes
 relationship of mutual influence between entities with independent
xistences, rather than describing the relationship as one which preceeds and
 responsible for existence of the terms of the relationship. It is such
radical process views" (radical because reality itself is seen as a process)
nat we shall now consider (although it is the objective processual view
hich carries this project to its most complete expression). This view makes
he relationship of the subject to language problematic, thus calling into
oubt the very possibility of a transcendental subject. Subjective processual
iews, on the other hand, attempt to problematize the world in its relation
o the subject. Such views, therefore, can be read as explorations of the
ature of the transcendental subject assumed by previous theories.[61]

A SUBJECTIVE PROCESSUAL PHILOSOPHY
OF LANGUAGE

f, as has been argued above, subjective systemic views assume a transcen-
ental subject as the source and locus of meaning and of those processes
resupposed by actual interactions, then subjective processual views repre-
ent the complementary attempt to explore the nature of this presupposed
onscious subject. That is, such views attempt to describe the structures of
onsciousness which make meaningful experience possible. They do not call
he existence of a universal and essential human nature into question per se,
ut rather attempt to explicate what it means to talk about this transcen-
ental subject. They describe what it must be like in order to account for the
ature of our experience. In this way, language and experience are seen "as
he paired foci of the single ellipse of subjectivity."[62] However, one must be
areful not to read "subjectivity" in this instance in the traditional Cartesian
node. It is rather the processes and necessary structurings of human

existence which account for its meaningfulness. Within contemporary philosophical discourse, subjective processual views are usually described as phenomenological. However, there are a variety of phenomenological positions, including Husserl's transcendental phenomenology, Heidegger's early existential phenomenology, and Sartre's Hegelian-Marxian existentialism, all of which describe the processes and structures of the human subject.[63]

Subjectivity and Intentionality

Perhaps the most general characterization of the processual view of the transcendental subject involves the redefinition of experience in terms of the process of intentionality.[64] Intentionality—the constantly repeated conjunction of man and world—is the locus of experience and meaning. Of course different phenomenological theories will explicate the notion of intentionality in different ways. For example, in *Being and Time,* the structure of human existence is seen in terms of a process of the temporalization of existence. Human experience is defined in the three moments of man's insertion into the world: s/he is thrown into an already meaningful world; s/he is fallen into the midst of the everyday concerns of the world; and s/he is a constant projecting into as yet unrealized possibilities. The unity of these three moments describes human existence as being-there (in time).[65] However, Husserl's phenomenology of consciousness is more clearly an attempt to explicate the transcendental nature of the subject. Consequently, it seems to have had greater influence on social and literary theory.[66]

Without denying the existence or contribution of the real world to human experience, Husserlian phenomenology puts such questions aside to examine the meaningfulness of experience for consciousness. The subject, understood as a particular process definitive of transcendental consciousness, is made primary while it is denied psychological reality. To say that consciousness is intentional is to say that it always has or, more accurately, holds before itself its own objects. This intentionality is pre-explicit, that is, it exists outside the awareness of the everyday (psychological) subject. The self-consciousness which defines the Cartesian subject involves making oneself aware of this functioning-intentionality (the process of intentionality) and thus transforming it into act-intentionality (the system of intentionality).[67]

Although meaningful experience exists only in the process of intentionality, Husserlian reflection allows one to talk about the act of intending and the intended object, as if these two moments of the process were separable. Subjective processual views emphasize the primacy of the subject insofar as meanings only exist for consciousness. However, meanings are not created by the subject nor are they reducible to acts of the mind, mental experiences, or personal dispositions. While meanings are not in the mind, they are

dependent upon the processes of transcendental conciousness. These processes have a complex relation to the psychological consciousness of everyday actors.[68] Furthermore, the "intended" objects of this transcendental
consciousness have an ideal existence. They are not a private possession of
particular, individualized consciousnesses. The intended object has its own
"objectivity" insofar as it is repeatable and self-identical. An intended
object retains its sameness through the various intending acts in which it is
present to consciousness and this sameness can be identified. In summary,
these ideal entities cannot be accounted for in terms of individual consciousnesses, nor do they exist apart from the process of intentionality; instead,
they "impose themselves as necessary for any mind which would think the
world."[69]

Consequently, both the objectivity of the world and the concrete subjectivity of the human subject find their existence in the process of intentionality which is the essential structure of transcendental consciousness. This
transcendental subject is the foundation of human experience and interaction and the source of creativity.

Language and Intentionality

As such positions turn to the question of language, they usually begin,
like subjective systemic views, with the recognition that language is a system
in use.[70] By seeing language in relation to the transcendental subject, we
discover man as the creator of language as well as its user. As Mohanty
observes, "the objectivity of language is rooted in the subjective acts of the
speaker."[71] This use of language is always, at base, interpersonal and
communicative. Within such everyday uses, we do not reflect on the
transcendental constitution of meaning; consequently, we fail to recognize
the role of language in creating the subject. Language, by opening up the
realm of ideal objects, makes the possibility of thinking, imagination, and
self-consciousness available to us. In fact, it is language that creates the
psychological subject by opening up the domain of the speaker's own self-
awareness. Just as language use constitutes the speaking subject, it is also
responsible for the possibility of our having and referring to a world. Insofar
as the reference of any linguistic expression is an ideal entity (an object of
transcendental consciousness), it is indefinite; it is only in speaking that this
vague reference is channeled into a particular referent, an object or state of
affairs in the world.

Nevertheless, subjective processual views cannot be satisfied with a
description of language in use, for it must be considered in relation to the
transcendental process of intentionality. Of course, it is necessary to disrupt
this processual dimension and treat language in terms of the various
moments of the process; in the case of Husserl, as both an ideal objectivity
and as constituted by the intending acts of consciousness. In relation to

transcendental consciousness, a linguistic expression is inseparable from it meaning. Therefore, one must avoid the language of an expressive theory of meaning. Language cannot be conceived of as a physical vehicle fo meaning, since its existence as language is constituted by the unity of it meaning within the transcendental process of intentionality.

Furthermore, language requires a meaning-intending act to constitute as language in any particular speech act. Consequently, the view that linguistic expression is merely a sign, and that understanding a sign is merel the capacity to use it according to rules or conventions, is inadequate. Thus, subjective processual views both reiterate the position of systemi subjective views and go beyond it by describing the particular relatio between language and transcendental consciousness.

Similarly, subjective process views go one step further in accounting fo the sharedness of language by appealing once again to intentionality Language itself can be considered as an object of consciousness. It has a existence that can be described not only as shared, but also as ideal. It i only by recognizing the ideality of language that we can account for ou ability to understand linguistic expressions prior to or outside of any actua use of them. This ideality extends not only to the meaningfulness o particular linguistic expressions, but also to the transcendental structure which make any language possible. Thus, Husserl attempted to describe "pure a priori grammar:" "the essential meaning-forms and the a prior laws of their combinations and modifications, and no language is thinkabl which would not be essentially determined by this a priori."[73]

The preceding discussion of a subjective processual view clearly relie upon the understanding of the transcendental subject within Husserl' theory of intentionality. For example, a Heideggerian, rather than appealin; to the relationship between language and the intending acts/intendec objects of intentional consciousness, might focus on language in relation to the three moments of temporality: language as throwing man into a past enmeshing him in the idle chatter of the present and projecting him into a indefinite future. The significant point is that any subjective processua position attempts to move beyond the interactional use of language to see it relationship to a transcendental subject; the essential nature of this subject' existence—a particular process—is the necessary precondition for th meaningfulness of both the social subject and the social world.

Transcendental Social Theory

Both subjective systemic and subjective processual views are concerned to describe the locus of meaning's stability and permanence in the face of the localization and contextualization of meaning. Subjective systemic theory generally accomplishes this by accounting for the production of sharec neanings. On the other hand, subjective processual theory accounts for the existence/production of a milieu (a sense of order and stability) within which shared meanings are possible.[74] Subjective processual views have only recently entered the scene of social theory, primarily through the work of Harold Garfinkel and other ethnomethodologists,[75] as well as in discussions of universal pragmatics in the work, for example, of Habermas. While there are conflicting interpretations of this literature, it is clear that ethnomethodology rejects the notion of a stable social reality or order into which a stable social subject enters. Rather, like subjective systemic views, it explores the ways in which social order and self-identity are constantly produced and maintained in everyday life. Garfinkel, for example, attempts to identify the properties of discourse and the interactional practices which enable social actors to maintain a sense of stable order and identity (e.g., ad hoc-ing, indexicality, prospective reasoning, et cetera clause). These are not the possession or acts of the psychological subject; nor do they exist independently of the subject and his interactions. Given the influence of Schutz and Husserl on Garfinkel, it is plausible to view the findings as explorations of the transcendental subject, that is, as attempts to identify the conditions of the possibility of any social life inherent in the very structure of human consciousness.[76] Thus, ethnomethodology—at least as Garfinkel practices it—is a transcendental sociology[77] exploring the conditions which make possible the operation and existence of social and psychological reality. Garfinkel, then, has begun to examine, sociologically, the nature of that subject presupposed by all previous social theories.

Interpretation and Intentionality

Subjective processual views' potential contribution to both social theory and problems of interpretation is significant. Their focus is always on the speaker as the transcendental subject. In addition, subjective processual views are committed to an empiricism; the transcendental subject exists in and is publicly available in the texts, practices, and interactions of everyday life. But it is an empiricism tempered by interpretation, for the transcendental subject must be uncovered in the data of everyday life. Subjective processual views, then, rest upon a hermeneutic empiricism: the focus is always upon the visible, but the visible needs to be deciphered. Phenomenological criticism increasingly demands the attention of literary theorists, for it presents a theory of interpretation proper. Unfortunately, critics commonly understand phenomenological criticism to be a reading which supports and validates the particular findings of phenomenological philosophy.[78]

Transcendental reflection presents a solution to the paradox of transla-tion (and interpretation) identified earlier in this paper. Given the meaning's inherence in language as well as the contextual-interactional locus of meaning, how is it possible for any reader to understand the meaning of the text? According to subjective processual views, the key lies in the relation of the transcendental subject to language.

According to a Husserlian view, that which can be translated is the objective (ideal) meaning of the linguistic expression and not the particular concrete reference. For any expression, one can distinguish between the intended object and its possible fulfillment on the one hand and the expression's reference within the particular context of its use. Speech acts serve to channel the intended object into a particular reference. Although these two aspects of meaning are related (as the transcendental subject is related to the social-psychological subject), their separation is an important insight.[79]

Subjective processual views of translation lead our attention from the saying to the said, from the concrete, contextualized reference to the intended object of consciousness. That is, there is an aspect of meaning which exists in the text independently of context and use. While this meaning depends on the intentionality of the author, it is a transcendental rather than a psychological connection. It is the said or the enunciated (rather than the saying or the enunciation)[80] that can be repeated ideally in any language and that, consequently, defines the objective possibility of translation. The ideality of the intended object (intended by the transcendental subject and not the psychologically real and experienced subject) guarantees the repeatability and self-identity of this meaning. The possibility of translation becomes the very mark of language.

The project of subjective process views is a significant additive and corrective to systemic views. These latter assume, nonproblematically, the existence and operation of the transcendental subject. Subjective processual views, on the other hand, identify the conditions presupposed by the systems of interactions. Such views appear to be, therefore, a necessary moment in the understanding of human experience. Furthermore, they begin to make clear the significant difference between relativism (with its inherent threat to the possibility of science) and the reflexivity of all human experience.[81] In this way, they pose a significant challenge to both subjective and objective systemic views, since the process of transcendental consciousness underlies the activities of the scientist as well as of the everyday actor.

AN OBJECTIVE PROCESSUAL PHILOSOPHY OF LANGUAGE

The last three views discussed all attempt to move beyond the traditional Cartesian separation of consciousness and world and place the question of meaning at their center. The fundamental question that such position must face is how to account, within a consistent framework, for both th intersubjectivity (sharedness and constraining power) of meaning and the possibility of creativity. However, these two poles are always identified with the social and individual loci of meaning respectively. That is, by raising the question of meaning in terms of its origin or source, such positions have only transformed the Cartesian dichotomy into one of individual versus social reality. The new dualism is manifested most clearly in both the tension within subjective systemic views and in the concern with the transcendental subject. It becomes the very structure of meaning and social life.[82]

The last approach to language I will describe is the most difficult to present, since it attempts nothing less than a radical rejection of some of the most basic assumptions of Western thought. Its roots are located in writers such as Nietzsche, Hegel, Freud, and Marx. Its contemporary expressions can be seen in the "deconstructive" philosophy of the later Heidegger and of the post-structuralist ("diacritical") movement of French philosophy.[83]

Objective processual views reject the notion of a source or origin of meaning, understood as either a social or individual locus.[84] Instead, following Hegel, it is assumed that "all reality is proccess," a process constitutive of the meaningfulness and structure of experience. This process is not describable as a system or structure. It is, rather, a "structuration"[85] producing various systems or relationships capable of structural characterization. Consequently, objective processual views deny that any meaning-system can be characterized completely. Any appeal to the "totality" or completeness of a meaningful structure violates the basic assumption of process (and contradiction).

Such positions may be described as radical process views, for they postulate a process without subject or object, a process characterized only by its own movement. Such positions can also be seen as radical contextualist views, since all structures are the momentary products of this process, isolated out of the process but always requiring to be located within the totality of their contextual production. That is, every moment of experience is describable as an intertextual product; it is an intersecting point of a number of codes constantly being articulated within our cultural context.

The Process as Contradiction

Although the "traces" of this process are evident and available, it is somewhat futile to describe the general characteristics of this process. However, we must avoid assimilating this radical process view to one of interaction or mutual influence. These latter assume independently existing principles which enter into a process; the process is then defined by the characteristics of the already constituted participants. On the other hand, a radical process view sees the relationship preexisting the members of the relationship.[87] Instead of two terms entering into a relationship of mutual influence, the relationship itself is the fundamental context which positions the terms in opposition to each other. The terms "exist" only in the relations articulated in the process; their existence is nothing more than their continued presence in the "traces" of the process.

Actually, we must see this process as one of relating and of differentiating, as one which constitutes both participation and distanciation.[88] Each exists only in its struggle against the other. It is, according to such views, a process of negation or contradiction, a constantly demanded and constantly imposed distinguishing between self and other which simultaneously constitutes and relates the two; yet its only traces are the very oppositions it constitutes. It is a process of the setting-up and setting-out of relationships in which difference is the very possibility of identity.[89] Thus, creativity and tradition, subjectivity and sociality are not the terms of a relationship, but are themselves contextualized moments or products of this process.

Such objective processual views, then, are constantly undermining ("deconstructing") dichotomies while not denying them. They do not seek to overcome or transcend them, but rather, to show that the oppositions are always accomplished in the interplay of the two poles. Hence, the poles' identities are constantly being constituted in this process of contradiction. A radical process philosophy, thus, constantly problematizes the structures underlying one's thought[90] and language.

The reality of self and other is determined by their presence in a continuously constituted relationship between them.[91] This belonging-together is, finally, only comprehensible as a process of contradiction, differentiation, or negation. Our existence is a moment in a process in which the very structure of our participation (and hence, of our identity as a participant) is produced or determined. The result of such a view is that the notion of an essential human nature—for example, a stable, undetermined source of meaning—is problematic. Objective processual views do not deny either individuality or the reality of our own subjectivity in experience. They merely point to its determination in the context of the significatory practices of our culture and cultural heritage. This is not to equate the process of contradiction with practices of signification. Rather, it is in such practices—language, signification, semiosis, or "textuality"—that we find the traces of this process of the "production of radical alterity" most clearly exemplified. Further, it is in this form that it enters most significantly into the production of human life.[92] We find the constant reconstruction of our own existence as subjects in language and in the texts constituting our historical tradition.

Reading the Subject

However, we must not think of language and texts as fixed objects or structures embodying or expressing a stable set of meanings. They are rather, moments in the historical production of meaning. Similarly, meanings are not produced by the interpretive acts of subjects. "Texts" and "interpretation" are terms that carry with them the baggage of Cartesian dualism, insofar as both imply stability and unity. Consequently, objective processualists prefer to talk about the processes of "textuality" and "reading," processes which are not determined by the subject's will. In the "indefinite chain of readings" by which we live as humans,

> the subject that interprets himself while interpreting signs is no longer the *cogito;* rather, he is a being who discovers, by the exegesis of his own life, that he is placed in being before he placed and possesses himself. In this way, hermeneutics would discover a manner of existing which would remain from start to finish a being-interpreted.[93]

Heidegger, for example, sees man and world arising out of a foundational relationship of dwelling together or being-in-the-world. The possibilities for alternative structures of relationship are created and limited in *Saga,* the historical Saying of language or textuality.[94]

Our understanding of self is always the product of the reading practices present in our textuality.[95] Objective processual views deny the transparency and autonomy of the ego as the source of meaning, structure, and interpretation. Thus, they refuse any appeal to a universal human nature, including subjectivity. The subject-object dichotomy is problematized; each member exists and has meaning only in the continuous play of the contradiction between them. The world gives itself to man only as man is opened to the world. This relation is determined in the process of negation seen in the practices of reading and textual production.[96] It is in these practices that the relation of self and other is fundamentally articulated as difference. In more traditional terms, the interpretive practices of our culture already define our nature as subjects by differentiating the interpreter and the interpreted. We find ourselves as subjects and understand others (be they subjects or world-objects) only in readings. These readings are not the subject's creation. In the process of reading, the reader is a contextual product of the reading rather than a transcendental condition of the reading. "All language insofar as it says interprets. It is an interpretation at one and the same time of a reality and of the one who speaks about this reality."[97]

According to objective processual views, the human individual is always "surrendered" to its engagements with the other before its own existence as the subject of the engagement.[98] Our engagements with others, our existence in the process of readings, determine the structure of our understanding and existence. The notion of an indeterminate and uncontaminated subject (uncontaminated by the structures and structuration of our cultural textuality) is undermined. Even more radically, the assertion that the nature

and structures of this contamination are stable and describable is undermined in favor of an ongoing movement of determination. We are not in
control of our own subjectivity, of our existence as an origin of meaning.

Even in the behavioral practices of social and symbolic interactions, we
are caught up in the determinate and determinative process by which the
individual psyche is located, positioned in relation to the other.[99] Relationships are always built upon a differentiation between the self and the
other; relationships are only possible in the context of each member's not
being the other. To the extent that the available practices delimit our
possibilities, our own self-existence as subjects is constituted by our
necessary participation in those practices. These (material) practices of
relationship and differentiation, including language-use, construct our
experience as transcendental subjects. The practices are not the possession
or creation of the human subject, but rather determine the possible positions
in which the human psyche can exist in its relations with the other. For
example, Foucault has argued that the notion of an author (or subject) is a
device by which we stop the proliferation of meaning; that is, it is a
particular modern practice of closing off the possibility of an endless series
of readings.[100] It makes the various structures of our relationships nonproblematic by positioning our existence outside of them, of the determinative process of reading.[101] The notion of the subject, then, must be
transformed into one of a "subject in process,"[102] a process determinative of
the particular momentary forms of its existence. Our existence as subjects is
a contextualized product of the present moment in the historical process of
textuality;[103] it is the intersection point of the various determinative codes
operative in the present cultural context. As a result, objective processual
views often present themselves as antihumanist;[104] the Renaissance notion
of the subject, so dominant in our contemporary cultural practices, is itself
a determinate product of the readings constitutive of our particular historical tradition. Perhaps the most famous example of such a social analysis
without the use of the subject is Marx's analysis of the primary contradiction of capitalism in terms of the relations and forms of production. This
classic analysis exemplifies the possibility of replacing the human subject as
the central problematic and methodological principle with the centrality of
significatory (productive) practices.

Language and the Chain of Signifiers

Such positions avoid the vocabulary of meaning. Looking for the
"meaning" of a text suggests that there exists some stable and unified set of
signifieds hidden below the surface of the signfiers. Instead, objective
processual views talk about the chain of signifiers; meaning is on the
surface, in the system of oppositions and rules of exclusion which belong to
the discourse.[105]

Thus, language cannot be separated from this determinative process. It is not a passive object within our experience, not a filter we place between ourselves and the other. Language is not something to be used and controlled by human subjects. Language and language use cannot be separated. Language is not an object, even a symbolic one. It is an event of reading in which we find ourselves positioned (interpreted) in and with the other. We are necessarily surrendered to the process of language in which oppositions are articulated. Language opens and defines the space in which we live; it is a web of connotations that represents the most available and omnipresent trace of the process of contextualization through which our existence moves and in which it is constituted.

The subjective systemic theorist always confronts the problem of talking about our giving meaning to an already meaningful world. The objective processual theorist suggests that there is no primary act of sense-making or giving (on the part of a subject existing outside of the situation) when I enter a situation. The situation presents itself as a determinate moment in the chain of signifiers in which my existence is given. That is, the situation presents itself as already meaningful. In struggling to articulate that meaningfulness, the articulation creates both the situation and the subject. The articulation is, we might say, reflexive, for it creates the very possibility of its meaningfulness.[106] That is, both the subject and the object exist only within the particular, contextually specific configuration of the chain of texts and readings which positions each in its play of opposition with the other. Man is the speaking animal; the speaking makes man.

Language is meaningful, or more accurately, determinatively productive of meaning before it is spoken by any person. That meaningfulness does not come from individual acts of speaking subjects nor from social conventions. It is the process of contradiction, embedded in a chain of signifiers and readings, that is constantly reproducing the meaningfulness of language. Language saves the history of the readings of our existence in its significatory/interpretive practices and operative rules. Language, therefore, always does more than we are aware of, for it embodies readings that we will never and perhaps can never see. Language, is always setting up relationships through contradictions, through a web of oppositions and differences. Simultaneously, it undermines them by opening up alternative readings. It always shows a multifaceted meaningfulness to which we respond in the context of our prior determination. Thus, language is a concealing as much as a disclosing, a negative as well as a positive determination.[107]

This does not deny the reality of the individual as an active speaker of the language. For this subject, language is used to express and negotiate intentions. However, this particular experience of ourselves as subjects is itself a determined reading; the reality of the subject is a cultural-textual production. To borrow Mead's distinction between the "I" and the "me,"

objective processual theory argues that the "I" is merely another "me,'
another socially produced identity. Its uniqueness lies in its being positionec
hierarchically as a ground of all other "me's"!

Relativism and Reflexivity

Objective processual views appear to embrace a philosophy of tota
relativism, since every truth appears as nothing but another reading in the
endless chain of readings of the endless movements of texts. Given their
radical contextualist view of meaning,[108] there seems to be no ground of
appeal between competing readings; in fact, every reading would be
determined within a unique context, and so, unquestionable.

Such positions challenge the traditional epistemological principles underlying our conception of what it means to do science. They reveal the
difference between reflective and reflexive philosophy. The former is basec
upon a hierarchical value system (e.g., in which truth is higher thar
falsehood) and epistemology. The scientist is able to stand outside of anc
above his/her object of study in order to reflect on it. S/he is a transcendental subject who stands, in his/her observation, on the *terra firma* of his
own essential nature. On the other hand, reflexive philosophy refuses to
grant itself any ground; it constantly reimmerses itself in its own process of
determination. Hierarchies are refused in favor of the ongoing articulation
of oppositions.

But determination is not relativism. Relativism suggest different perspectives on some common object; it is only meaningful in a reflective
philosophy which distinguishes between the study and its object. Reflexive
positions do not deny the possibility of evaluating and criticizing readings
within the context of their determination.[109] On this basis, objective
processual positions radically challenge the authority of the particular forms
of scientific practice available to us. Reflexivity, the constant problematizing of oppositions, and the rejection of the traditional humanistic value
hierarchy result in a playfulness foreign to academic scholarship. But if the
appeal to some hierarchical value is closed, reading must at least be joyful:
it must avoid taking itself too seriously.

Reading and Interpretation

Since objective processual views make reading practices fundamental,
translation and interpretation pose few new theoretical problems. In
general, the reading of a text involves an attempt to see how the text sets up
a play of oppositions within which its significance is constituted. Critical
reading is a process of dismantling and reconstructing the system of
oppositions present in the play of signifiers; it involves one in an attempt to
identify the text as an intersection of codes following a set of rules of
exclusion.

Any reading involves, among other things, the positioning of the reader vis-à-vis the text and vis-à-vis the world opened up by the text. The text is a moment of a relationship between man and world. In that way, it opens up and closes off possibilities of existence and understanding. To interpret a text is to see the way in which this is accomplished, and this requires one to reflexively situate oneself vis-à-vis the closures of the text; this is not a circular relationship. It is not merely an interaction between the reader as a subject who brings his/her own determinations to an independently determined text. It is rather the mutual and simultaneous determination of both text and reader in a reading which is itself determined by its positioning within an historical chain of readings and practices.[111]

Translation involves a reading in which the contextuality of the text and reader are independently determined, as they are each moments of a unique historical chain of signifiers. Consequently, there is an unbridgeable gap, an inevitable distance from the text, since the two languages never constitute the identical contradictions or relationships. Translation involves the retrieval and reconstitution of two different traditions, of two different sets of possibilities and closures. It always involves us in compromise, not only of the text's language, but of the translator's as well.[112] If a translation is to work, it must attempt to bring the determinateness and the determinations of the original into a new textuality. But this new textuality cannot be absorbed within the textual tradition of the translator. If he or she is to succeed, the language of the translation must belong to the original intertextual context as well as to its own. Hence it is not surprising that we often find the most poetically innovative languages in translations.[113] Nor is it surprising that reflexive interpetations are often easier with texts which are located within a textuality different from our own.

Reading Social Life

Objective processual views have, as yet, had little influence in the domain of social theory. However, the call for a recognition of the contextual and processual nature of human life suggests the possibility of such a position. Up until now, the influence of such positions has been felt primarily in literary criticism, psychoanalytic theory, and critical social analysis.[114] However, there are some ethnomethodologists who seem to approach an objective processual view. Such writers locate the process of meaning constitution in the practices of interaction and language. Thus, one can begin to see in the work of Blum and Sandywell, et al. an attempt to deal with how the interpretive practices constituting the language-texts of our existence determine our very existence as speakers and interactants.[115] Rather than identifying language with talk or language-use, or with a set of rules, such positions seem to articulate a contextualist/processual view. They argue that the structures and forms of our existence and understanding are the determinative products of our positioning within and by the significatory practices of our cultural context. Obviously, one of the problems facing such social theories is the need to redefine scientific practice. This may account in part for some writers' hesitation to follow their insights through to their conclusion, and the hostile reception given to those who do by the community of social theorists.

CONCLUSION

This paper has attempted to present six divergent, albeit related, philosophical conceptions of language and meaning. My concern has been not with the philosophical strengths of particular views, but rather with their implications for the social and critical sciences.[116]

I offer no solution to the problem of the relationship between philosophical and scientific practice. Whether one believes in the primacy of research exemplars or of rigorous theoretical and philosophical speculation is itself a determined and determinate moment in the present context of our cultural existence. Philosophy is, as Althusser has suggested, a field without an object, the domain of the battle between various practices.[117] And as such, it will inevitably continue to assert its presence into the midst of the struggles between scientific paradigms.

As the relationships between alternative ways of doing science become more difficult to specify, it becomes increasingly necessary for social and literary theorists to be cognizant of the similarities and differences between positions. As the number of alternative theories grows and as theoretical arguments proliferate, it becomes important that we begin to try to specify the issues uniting and separating the participants. Obviously, the question of the nature of meaning and language is such an issue. The present work has attempted to contribute to a more critical awareness of the possibilities within social and literary theory.

Finally, the question of which is the most adequate conception is one that must be left unanswered. My own inclination is to favor the objective processual view, because it reunites the social and literary disciplines in a critical framework. However, subjective systemic and processual views may provide a powerful tool for social theory, since they attempt to combine a theory of human action with a philosophy of meaning. Perhaps, as Lemert and Gillan have recently argued, such positions are "texts that must be written before sociology can find its freedom from the terrible confinement of man."[118] As strange as it must sound to describe "homocentric" positions as confining for social theory, such radical theorizing may serve to reinstall academic science into the value-laden, crisis-ridden world within which we live our everyday lives.

NOTES

*Mr. Grossberg is an Assistant Professor in the Department of Speech Communication, University of Illinois at Urbana-Champaign. An early version of this paper was presented at the "Translation and Poetics" conference, Indiana State University at Terre Haute, April 3, 1976. Many people have provided valuable criticisms of early drafts, including Daniel J. O'Keefe of the University of Michigan; Jeffrey Maitland and Calvin O. Schrag of Purdue University; Peter K. Manning of Michigan State University; David Seibold, David Swanson, Jesse G. Delia, Norman K. Denzin, Charles Laufersweiler, and Cary Nelson of the University of Illinois.

1. I owe a particular debt to Cary Nelson, Daniel O'Keefe, and Peter Manning for their contributions to this introduction. This essay is not meant solely as a review article on meaning and language. First, these terms were chosen as convenient expressions of more basic "root metaphors" for talking about human existence and social life; that is, it is offered as a study in philosophical anthropology. Second, I have chosen not to follow the conventions of review articles too closely. I have been concerned with ideal types or family resemblances, rather than actual sociological or literary-critical positions, for there is a clear argumentative thrust behind the present effort. Of course, there are a number of related endeavors, for example: (1) theories of society: Ted Benton, *Philosophical Foundations of the Three Sociologies* (London: Routledge and Kegan Paul, 1977); and Werner Stark, *The Fundamental Forms of Social Thought* (New York: Fordham University, 1963); (2) theories of interpretation: Werner Pelz, *The Scope of Understanding in Sociology* (London: Routledge and Kegan Paul, 1974), ch. 3; (3) theories of language: Albert Boogmann, *The Philosophy of Language* (The Hague: Martinus Nijhoff, 1974); and Allen D. Grimshaw, "Sociolinguistics," in Ithiel de Sola Poole et al., ed., *Handbook of Communication* (Chicago: Rand-McNally, 1973), pp. 49–92.

2. Another weakness of the scheme offered here results from its focusing on *philosophical* assumptions underlying particular theories. Obviously, not all writers are concerned with articulating consistent philosophies. Nevertheless, the attempt seems worthwhile to me, if for no other reason than that "truth comes from error more easily than from confusion." R. W. Southern, "The Historical Experience," *Times Literary Supplement,* June 24, 1977, p. 771. See also Jeff Coulter, "Language and the Conceptualization of Meaning," *Sociology,* 7 (1973), 197–89.

3. Notice that the "crisis" of logical empiricism, which is constantly asserted in the social theory literature, rests to a large extent upon its acceptance of the subject-object dichotomy.

4. I include within "systems" views those positions which describe reality in terms of interactions or structures as well.

5. This movement may be seen as an historical one within the development of specific social scientific and critical disciplines: for example, the movement in linguistics from syntactics to semantics to pragmatics. See Howard Maclay, "Overview," in *Semantics: An Interdisciplinary Reader in Philosophy, Linguistics and Psychology,* eds. Danny D. Steinberg and Leon A. Jakobovitz (London: Cambridge at the University Press, 1971).

6. My own definitions are as follows: meaning is the myth of the signified, language is the myth of the signifier. This is not to say that they are not real; it implies, instead, that theoretical discourse must move beyond these concepts and the baggage they bring with them (e.g., the myth of the subject).

7. I will discuss communication in a future extension of the present work. The choice of more literary concerns reflects my belief that there is a great deal of exciting theoretical work being done by literary theorists at the present moment and by my own interest in aesthetic questions.

8. Harmon Chapman, "The Phenomenon of Language," *Phenomenology: Continuation and Criticism*, eds. Fred Kersten and Richard Zaner (The Hague: Martinus Nijhoff, 1973), pp. 14–23. See also George Steiner, *After Babel: Aspects of Language and Translation* (New York: Oxford University Press, 1975).

9. George Steiner, *After Babel: Aspects of Language and Translation* (New York: Oxford University Press, 1975).

10. Aristotle's notion of *logos* as the action of a verb on a noun within the statement provides an interesting exception.

11. See David E. Cooper, *Philosophy and the Nature of Language.* (London: Longman's 1973).

12. There is significant work currently being done within a referential framework by such people as Kripke and Putnam. See, for example, Saul A. Kripke, "Naming and Necessity," *Semantics of Natural Language,* ed. Donald Davidson and Gilbert Harmon (Dordrecht: Reidel, 1972).

13. This does not mean that a person must be or ever is overtly aware of the content of the particular meaning-entity.

14. For example, Suzanne Langer's distinction between concept and conception. Of course, there are a diversity of views of the nature of this mental entity: propositions, images, concepts, intentions, projected acts, etc.

15. Alfred Schutz, *The Phenomenology of the Social World,* trans. George Walsh and Frederick Lehnert (Evanston: Northwestern University Press, 1967), p. 6. I have described Schutz as a subjective referentialist because, unlike other theorists who build upon his work (e.g., Garfinkel), Schutz seems to make no provision for intersubjective or shared meaning; consider the difference between Schutz's ideal types and the ethnomethodologist's normal forms. The latter are intersubjective structures in the talk, while the former are subjective structures which enable us *to assume* that our private meanings are shared.

16. Roger M. Keesing, "Transformational Linguistics and Structural Anthropology," *Cultural Hermeneutics,* 2 (1974), p. 248. Obviously, this is not an adequate description of the whole of Chomsky's work. It is meant only to characterize Chomsky's Cartesian view of meaning-input into the transformational system.

17. See David K. Lewis, *Conventions: A Philosophical Study* (Cambridge, Mass.: Harvard University Press, 1969).

18. C.K. Ogden and I.A. Richards, *The Meaning of Meaning: A Study of the Influence of Language Upon Thought and of the Science of Symbolism* (New York: Harcourt, Brace and World, 1923).

19. *Ibid.,* p. 98.

20. Obviously, my use of Berkeley at this point is somewhat misleading since he is most commonly seen as a subjective idealist; however, insofar as he postulated ideas in the mind of God, there is little doubt that his is a representational theory. For example, in *Alcophon,* the world is understood as God's language, his attempt to communicate with us.

21. Paul Ricoeur, *Interpretation Theory: Discourse and the Surplus of Meaning* (Fort Worth: Texas Christian University Press, 1976).

22. See, for example, I.A. Richards, *Principles of Literary Criticism* (New York: Harcourt, Brace and World, 1925).

23. See, for example, Max Weber, *The Protestant Ethic and the Spirit of Capitalism,* trans. Talcott Parsons (New York: Charles Scribner's, 1959).

24. See, for example, Northrop Frye, *Anatomy of Criticism: Four Essays* (Princeton: Princeton University Press, 1957).

25. Paul Watzlawick, *How Real Is Real?,* (New York: Random House, 1976), pp. 8–9.

26. Richard Macksey, "The Consciousness of the Critic: Georges Poulet and the Reader's Share," in *Velocities of Change: Critical Essays from MLN,* ed. Richard Macksey (Baltimore: Johns Hopkins University Press, 1974), p. 336.

27. For example, Jack D. Douglas and John M. Johnson, eds., *Existential Sociology* (London: Cambridge University, 1977); Alfred McClung Lee, *Toward Humanist Sociology* (Englewood Cliffs: Prentice-Hall, 1973); and Ian Craib, *Existentialism and Sociology* (London: Cambridge University, 1976).

28. See Willard Van Orman Quine, *Word and Object* (Cambridge, Mass.: M.I.T. Press, 1960).

29. See Ferdinand de Saussure, *Course in General Linguistics,* trans. Wade Baskin (New York: McGraw Hill, 1966) and Jonathan Culler, *Saussure* (Hassocks, Sussex: Harvester, 1976).

30. I will not discuss the appropriate categorization for either general systems theory or Marxism, because the number of radically diverse interpretations co-existing under these rubrics makes the task too large for the present essay.

31. I have united, under the rubric of objective-systemic philosophy, a number of separable positions: European structuralism, theories of linguistic relativity, and critical idealism (post-Kantian). Furthermore, while it is difficult to identify contemporary research arising directly out of the latter two schools, their ideas are often cited in a variety of contexts.

32. This description of an objective systemic view of the sign is obviously based on the narrower example of structuralist philosophy. This, I hope, is nevertheless fair, given the similarities between the various views within the general category. See Paul Ricoeur, *The Conflict of Interpretations,* ed. Don Ihde (Evanston: Northwestern University Press, 1974).

33. Jacques Derrida, *Of Grammatology,* trans. Gayatri Chakravorty Spivak (Baltimore: Johns Hopkins University Press, 1976). I use the term "transcendental subject" to refer to any postulation of some absolute subjective origin or locus of meaning and knowledge; "absolute" in the sense that its existence is both the necessary condition for all meaning and, furthermore, that such a subject must be taken as free of all entanglements with some other which may have the power to determine it. That is, although a particular relationship with the world is mediated or determined by a structure of meaning so that one no longer talks about "things-in-themselves," talk about a transcendental subject rests on the assumption that at least some part of our experience of our "inner lives" is not mere appearance but some "consciousness-in-itself." See Friedrich Nietzsche, *The Will to Power,* trans. Walter Kaufmann (New York: Vintage, 1968), especially Book 3, sections 1, 3.

34. I do not offer this as a criticism, merely as a description/interpretation of what such positions are doing.

35. Ernst Cassirer, *An Essay on Man* (New Haven: Yale University Press, 1944).

36. Claude Levi-Strauss, *Structural Anthropology,* trans. Claire Jacobson and Brooke Grundfest Schoepf (New York: Basic Books, 1963). There are a number of excellent introductions to structuralism: Culler; Robert Scholes, *Structuralism in Literature* (New Haven: Yale University Press, 1974); Terence Hawkes, *Structuralism and Semiotics* (London: Methuen, 1977); Philip Pettit, *The Concept of Structuralism: A Critical Analysis* (Berkeley and Los Angeles: University of California Press, 1975). See Edmund Leach, *Culture and Communication* (London: Cambridge University Press, 1976), p. 16 for an illustrative view of communication.

37. Ferrucio Rossi-Landi, *Ideologies of Linguistic Relativity* (The Hague: Mouton, 1973).

38. John Lyons, "The Generation of Meaning," *Times Literary Supplement,* July 8, 1977, p. 827. See also Ludwig Wittgenstein, *Philosophical Investigations,* trans. G.E.M. Anscombe (New York: MacMillan, 1953), p. 518.

39. Peter Winch, *The Idea of A Social Science and Its Relation to Philosphy* (New York: Humanities Press, 1958); John R. Searle, *Speech Acts: An Essay in the Philosophy of Language* (London: Cambridge at the University Press, 1969); H. Harre and P.F. Secord, *The Explanation of Social Behavior* (Totowa, N.J.: Littlefield, Adams, 1973); Malcolm Coulthard, *An Introduction to Discourse Analysis* (London: Longman, 1977).

40. Similarly, speech act theories which locate the illocutionary force of an utterance within the utterance itself belong in the present category. One proponent of this "performative

hypothesis" is Jerrold Saddock, *Toward a Linguistic Theory of Speech Acts* (New York: Academic Press, 1974). I am grateful to C. Laufersweiler for having pointed out that the work of conversational analysts—Sacks, Schegloff, Jefferson, etc.—fits an objective systemic description; the burden is placed on a system of structural preferences defined in terms of pair-parts. See Jim Schenkein, ed., *Studies in the Organization of Conversational Interaction* (New York: Academic Press, 1978).

41. Kenneth Burke, *Language as Symbolic Action: Essays on Life, Literature, and Method* (Berkeley and Los Angeles: University of California Press, 1966), p. 23.

42. Quine.

43. Cooper, ch. 5.

44. This coexistence is premised upon Cassirer's hierarchical conception of symbolic systems. Such an assumption also underlies recent stage theories of psychological development.

45. Subjective-systemic philosophy is, for me, the hardest to characterize for two reasons. First, of the six views, this one is the most eclectic. It is weighted toward pragmatism as opposed to, for example, Wittgenstein; therefore, it is the most debatable of the ideal types. Second, it is the most powerful philosophy of human action yet articulated in my opinion, although it also suffers from the greatest internal tensions.

46. This tension is, I think, a significant improvement over more traditional expressions of this opposition in terms of the debate between methodological individualists and methodological socialists. See John O'Neill, ed., *Modes of Individualism and Collectivism* (London: Heinemann Educational Books, 1973).

47. See Ragnar Rommetveit, *On Message Structure: A Framework for the Study of Language and Communication* (New York: John Wiley and Sons, 1974); and Karl-Otto Apel, *Analytic Philosophy of Language and the* Geisteswissenschaften, trans. Harold Holstelilie (Dordrecht: Reidel, 1967).

48. John Dewey, *Experience and Nature* (1925; 2nd ed., La Salle, Ill.: Open Court, 1929), p. 148.

49. George A. Kelly, *A Theory of Personality: The Psychology of Personal Constructs,* 2 vols. (New York: W.W. Norton, 1963), see especially p. 55. Nevertheless, such positions frequently talk about meaning in terms of private intentions, either through an appeal to the internalization and manipulation of publicly available meanings or through some attempted synthesis with a subjective referential position.

50. The use of the word "natural" is meant here to suggest (1) the public availability of meaning and (2) the possibility of accounting for the emergence of meaning without postulating a new metaphysical principle standing in opposition to "natural" processes.

51. Jeffrey Maitland of Purdue University has, in personal conversation, made the following argument against views which see language as conventions: From the statement that conventions are a necessary condition for language use, it does not follow that language is nothing but conventions (i.e., that conventions are both the necessary and sufficient condition of language). Without denying that language is grounded upon social conventions, one can deny that language is nothing but conventions or that it is reducible to these. To say, for example, that art requires conventions if we are to recognize and understand a particular work of art as a work of art is not a warrant for asserting that art is nothing more than conventions.

52. Charles Taylor, "Interpretation and the Sciences of Man," *Review of Metaphysics,* 25 (1971), 3–51.

53. David L. Miller, *George Herbert Mead: Self, Language and the World* (Austin: University of Texas Press, 1973).

54. A common criticism raised against such a position is that it has too narrow a conception of use, seeing it only in naturalistic and technical terms. While this seems less true of Wittgenstein, it may apply to some of his followers.

55. Norman K. Denzin, *Childhood Socialization: Studies in the Development of Language, Social Behavior, and Identity* (San Francisco: Jossey-Bass, 1977, pp. 15–27).

56. Ibid. We might also see this position as a "process" view in which process is conceptualized as the temporal interconnectedness of acts, as an *unfolding* movement through time rather than—as in later views—as constitutive of temporality itself.

57. Herbert Blumer, *Symbolic Interactionism: Perspective and Method* (Englewood Cliffs: Prentice-Hall, 1969); Rommetveit; Aaron Cicourel, *Cognitive Sociology: Language and Meaning in Social Interaction* (New York: Free Press, 1974); Peter Cole and Jerry L. Morgan, eds., *Syntax and Semantics 3: Speech Acts* (New York: Academic Press, 1975); Heinz Werner and Bernard Kaplan, *Symbol Formation* (New York: John Wiley and Sons, 1963). See also David R. Maines, "Social Organization and Social Structure in Symbolic Interactionist Thought," *Annual Review of Sociology,* 3 (1977), pp. 235–59; and Jerome S. Bruner, "From Communication to Language: A Psychological Perspective," *Cognition,* 3 (1975), 255–87.

58. Such positions, following Thomas S. Kuhn, *The Structure of Scientific Revolutions* (2nd ed., Chicago: University of Chicago Press, 1970), are consequently forced into some form of relativism, since the only way to escape is to separate the subject's contribution from that of the world or other. One not uncommon solution given to the need to defend "science" is to adopt certain quasi-scientific (e.g., quantitative) methods. On the connection between such views and Kuhn, see Richard Bernstein, *The Restructuring of Social and Political Theory* (New York: Harcourt Brace Jovanovich, 1976).

59. Norman K. Denzin, "Problems in Analyzing Elements of Mass Culture: Notes on the Popular Song and Other Artistic Productions," *American Journal of Sociology,* 75 (1970), 1035.

60. Obviously, I am not using the term "process" in the traditional sense, although I believe the notions of (1) a lack of subject and (2) a movement in which the independent existence of related terms is denied are operative within the tradition, especially in more radical expressions of the position. For an interesting analogy, see Lewis Thomas, *The Lives of a Cell* (New York: Viking, 1974). The alternative would have been, as in some of the authors to be discussed, to redefine or simply create a term, one which may not be meaningful outside its use in the particular texts. The problem of talking about "process views" is significant: "The language that . . . [has] evolved has no common theoretical context with anything that exists in English. To transfer it bodily—simply to anglicize the words, which is not difficult—produces a wall of opacity that blocks all curiosity at the start. To adapt, to paraphrase, which can also be done and often looks inviting, runs the risk of denaturing the original and reducing disconcerting ideas to acceptable common places." Stephen Heath, cited in G. Hough, "The Importation of Roland Barthes," *Times Literary Supplement,* December 9, 1977, p. 1443.

61. The argument could have been presented in terms of a dialectical position, as well. See Frederic Jameson, *Marxism and Form: Twentieth Century Dialectical Theories of Literature* (Princeton: Princeton University Press, 1971) and Lawrence Grossberg, "Dialectics and Rhetoric as Modes of Understanding," *Quarterly Journal of Speech,* forthcoming (October, 1979).

62. Don Ihde, "Language and Experience," in *New Essays in Phenomenology: Studies in the Philosophy of Experience,* ed. James M. Edie (Chicago: Quadrangle Books, 1969), p. 52.

63. The best introduction to phenomenology is still Herbert Spiegelberg, *The Phenomenological Movement,* 2 vols., (The Hague: Martinus Nijhoff, 1971).

64. Notice that intentionality, as a phenomenological concept, has nothing whatsoever to do with intentions as a psychological description.

65. Martin Heidegger, *Being and Time,* trans. John Macquarrie and Edward Robinson (New York: Harper and Row, 1962). See also Paul Ricoeur, "Phenomenology and Hermeneutics," *Nous,* 9 (1975), 85–102.

66. Maurice Natanson, ed., *Phenomenology and the Social Sciences,* 2 volumes (Evanston: Northwestern University Press, 1973); Paul Filmer, Michael Phillipson, David Silverman and David Walsh, *New Directions in Sociological Theory* (Cambridge, Mass.: M.I.T. Press, 1973); George Psathas, ed., *Phenomenological Sociology* (New York: John Wiley and Sons, 1973). For literary theory, see Michael Murray, *Modern Critical Theory: A Phenomenological Introduction*

(The Hague: Martinus Nijhoff, 1975); and Robert R. Magliola, *Phenomenology and Literature: An Introduction* (West Lafayette: Purdue University Press, 1977).

67. This is a crucial distinction, often ignored, because it allows the phenomenologist to deal with "meanings not intended."

68. See Paul Ricoeur, *Husserl: An Analysis of His Phenomenology* (Evanston: Northwestern University Press, 1967); Joseph J. Kockelmans, *Edmund Husserls' Phenomenological Psychology: An Historico-Critical Study* (Pittsburgh: Duquesne University Press, 1967); Amedeo Giorgi, "Phenomenology and the Foundations of Psychology," in *Nebraska Symposium on Motivation: 1975 Conceptual Foundations of Psychology,* ed. William J. Arnold (Lincoln: University of Nebraska Press, 1976).

69. James M. Edie, *Speaking and Meaning: The Phenomenology of Language* (Bloomington: Indiana University Press, 1976), p. 22.

70. Remy C. Kwant, *Phenomenology of Language* (Pittsburgh: Duquesne University Press, 1965).

71. J.N. Mohanty, *Edmund Husserl's Theory of Meaning* (The Hague: Martinus Nijhoff, 1969), p. 64. See also Ragner Rommetveit, *On Message Structure* (New York: John Wiley and Sons, 1974).

72. Ibid., p. 42.

73. Edmund Husserl, *Formal and Transcendental Logic,* trans. Dorion Cairns (The Hague: Martinus Nijhoff, 1969), p. 49. Note the similarity to Chomsky's position, which once again affirms the difficulty in describing his position adequately within such a scheme.

74. One can see a complex "hierarchical" relation among and between the variety of subjective processual and systemic views as follows:
Garfinkel: behavioral practices establish an intersubjective sense of order.
Cicourel: "deep" interpretive assumptions establish an individual sense of order.
Symbolic interactionism: recurrent processes and issues establish a process of the social production of shared meanings.
Cognitive psychology: individual structures and processes establish individual and social meanings.
Ethnography: shared cultural structures establish contextualized/localized meanings.

75. Harold Garfinkel, *Studies in Ethnomethodology* (Englewood Cliffs: Prentice-Hall, 1967); D.L. Wieder, *Language and Social Reality* (The Hague: Mouton, 1974); Hugh Mehan and Houston Wood, *The Reality of Ethnomethodology* (New York: John Wiley and Sons, 1975); Anthony Giddens, *New Rules of Sociological Method: A Positive Critique of Interpretive Sociologies* (New York: Basic Books, 1976); Thomas A. McCarthy, "A Theory of Communicative Competence," *Philosophy of the Social Sciences,* 3 (1973), 135–56.

76. I am grateful to D. Lawrence Wieder for this insight, in personal conversation.

77. The distinction between transcendental and phenomenological sociology is rarely made, but it is part of the problem underlying the attempt to define phenomenological sociology as the conflict between Husserl and Schutz. See John O'Neill, *Making Sense Together: An Introduction to Wild Sociology* (New York: Harper and Row, 1974).

78. Too often, phenomenological critics interpret a text as revealing, for example, the temporality or finitude of the protagonist. In the meantime, questions of critical practices are rarely raised.

79. Mohanty, p. 53. For a theory of interpretation built upon this distinction, see E.D. Hirsh, Jr., *Validity in Interpretation* (New Haven: Yale, 1967).

80. Paul Ricoeur, "The Model of the Text: Meaningful Action Considered as a Text," *Social Research,* 38 (1971), 532.

81. See Calvin O. Schrag, *Experience and Being* (Evanston: Northwestern University Press, 1969), pp. 276–82.

82. This suggests the possibility of continuing to reconceptualize the fundamental issue of social theory: from individual versus social to creativity versus tradition (or intersubjectivity) to the dialectic of immanence and transcendence. See Lawrence Grossberg, "Dialectical Hermeneutics and the Human Sciences: Foundations for a Cultural Approach to Communication," unpublished diss., University of Illinois at Urbana-Champaign, 1976, ch. 6.

83. I include under this label a variety of authors all of whom, I believe, express a tendency toward a materialistic philosophy which they oppose to their reading of the later Heidegger as still idealistic: Derrida, Barthes, Lacan, Althusser, Kristeva, etc. Of course, the texts of these authors are significantly different, but they are, as a group, becoming increasingly influential in post-structuralist and Marxist theorizing. Good discussions related to this group of texts may be found in Samuel Ijesseling, *Rhetoric and Philosophy in Conflict: An Historical Survey* (The Hague: Martinus Nijhoff, 1976); Rosalind Coward and John Ellis, *Language and Materialism: Developments in Semiology and the Theory of the Subject* (London: Routledge and Kegan Paul, 1977); and Charles Lemert and Garth Gillan, "The New Alternative in Critical Sociology: Foucault's Discursive Analysis," *Cultural Hermeneutics*, 4 (1977), 309–20.

The distinction between Heidegger's later work and the diacritical philosophers is an important one, and points to Heidegger's continuing assumption of the text as a unity. The diacritical position, with its emphasis on contradiction, focuses on the text as a disunity, as constantly dislocating itself. It begins, then, with the "structured absences" of the text. See Editors, *Cahiers du Cinema*, "John Ford's *Young Mr. Lincoln*," in *Movies and Methods*, ed. Bill Nichols (Berkeley and Los Angeles: University of California Press, 1976), pp. 493–528.

Two obvious lacunae in the present text should at least be acknowledged: (1) There is no systematic explanation of materialism as used in the present context, partly because it is a term "in process." For the present context, materialism may be understood as a revolutionary philosophy of the primacy of practices within social formations (and not a reductionistic philosophy of "matter in motion"); (2) although those texts which are a part of this "materialist diacritical" view reject the hermeneutic tradition, my own inclination is to be more sympathetic to it—especially to the later works of Heidegger (e.g., *Identity and Difference, On Time and Being, The End of Philosophy, The Question Concerning Technology*) and parts of the work of Gadamer, recognizing the remnants of utopian and idealistic language in these texts—as an important attempt at the "decentering of the home of significations, a displacement of the birthplace of meaning." (Paul Ricoeur, *Freud and Philosophy: An Essay on Interpretation* (New Haven: Yale University Press, 1970), p. 422).

Finally, I must acknowledge my debt to others who have helped me begin to understand the issues raised in an "objective processual" view. I am aware that, often, the best and clearest expressions of the position in the present work are themselves expressions of my own intertextual existence. Therefore I would like to thank the members of the Criticism study group at the University of Illinois, Gayatri Spivak of the University of Iowa, Calvin O. Schrag of Purdue University, and especially Cary Nelson of the University of Illinois.

84. See Michel Foucault, "Nietzsche, Geneology, History," in Michel Foucault, *Language, Counter-memory, Practice*, ed. Donald F. Bouchard (Ithaca: Cornell University Press, 1977).

85. I take the term from Roland Barths' *S/Z*, trans. Richard Miller (New York: Hill and Wang, 1974). It is important to note that the contemporary expressions of objective processual philosophy are not metaphysical descriptions of the world. Cf. Friedrich Nietzsche, *The Will to Power*, trans. Walter Kaufmann and R.J. Hollingdale (New York: Vintage Books, 1967).

86. Such systems may be described, using a marxist/psychoanalytic metaphor, as "economies."

87. To describe it in these terms is obviously to use structural terms. Actually, the preexistence of the relationship is not a temporal one but a praxical or significatory one.

88. See Paul Ricoeur, "Phenomenology and Hermeneutics."

89. Heidegger's *Ereignis*—eventing or the event of approporation. Derrida's *differance* and Althusser's ideology are all attempts to specify this "process," which is not to deny significant distinctions between them. Of course, each of these positions would see these distinctions as traces of the process they attempt to identify.

The principle of contradiction is parallel in some ways to Nietzsche's will to power. On a more political note, it seems obvious that contradiction or opposition is the primary characteristic of our age. Because this view is reflexive, it moves towards its own negation. Contradiction determines its own response which is itself a manifestation of contradiction. One might consider the various expressions and experiences of violence—in action and art—as contradiction. But violence, like contradiction, is not an overcoming or resolution which leads to a dialectical *aufhebung* to peace and calm. Thus objective processual views represent a nondialectical philosophy of contradiction.

90. That is, the transcendental conditions.

91. This relationship cannot be described in empirical (psychological or sociological) terms. It is an ontological or textual one.

92. "The interplay of distance and proximity, constitutive of the historical connection, is what is brought to language rather than what language produces." Paul Ricoeur, "Can There Be A Scientific Concept of Ideology," unpublished manuscript, University of Chicago, 1974.

93. Ricoeur, *Conflict*, p. 11.

94. These possibilities are neither created nor brought to realization by the subject. Thus "chance" and determination become significant categories for such positions.

95. Note that the terms "reading" and "textuality" are used for processes of structuration, all significatory practices productive of cultural codes. By using these terms, objective processualists attempt to avoid assuming a text/interaction dichotomy.

96. Burke's insight of the importance of the negative is a crucial one. See *Language as Symbolic Action: Essays on Life, Literature, and Method* (Berkeley and Los Angeles: University of California Press, 1966).

97. Paul Ricoeur, cited in Don Ihde, *Hermeneutic Phenomenology* (Evanston: Northwestern University Press, 1971), p. 89.

98. This paragraph owes a great debt to conversations with Gayatri Spivak of the University of Iowa. Note the similarity between this view and the pragmatists' belief in the primacy of relationships. Both argue that identity is determined by interactions.

99. At this point, we can understand the relevance of Freud and Marx to objective processual views. If textuality (contradiction) produces reality, then the position of the psyche is determined in part by the self/other oppositions set up in family and economic life. In fact, these are obviously major determining codes.

100. Michel Foucault, "What is an Author," *Partisan Review*, 4 (1975), 603-14.

101. Heidegger sees it as a trace of the *Gestell* or technological frame, Derrida as a trace of the myth of the presence of an ultimate signifier and signified (Logocentrism), and Althusser as the result of determinative ideological domination.

102. See Coward and Ellis.

103. Of course, this is true not only of the subject, but of any term whose existence is constituted within the play of (binary) oppositions. Nevertheless, it may be appropriate at this point to raise the problem of the necessity of a "privileging of the self." My own view is that this is unavoidable unless one adopts either (1) a negative "theology" which denies the self or (2) a constant and hence playful problematizing of the self, as in Derrida. It is toward the latter that I would move, although allowing a certain privileged moment as a necessary and determined one within a reflexive philosophy.

This privileging results from the attempt to decenter without denying the subject as an active moment in practice, a moment which requires acknowledging the structuration of the unconscious (desire) in textuality. See John Ellis, "Ideology and Subjectivity," *Working Papers in Cultural Studies*, no. 9 (1976), 205-18; also, Part 3: "Subjectivity and Individuality," 'orking Papers in Cultural Studies, no. 10, (1977), 201–64; and Diana Adlam, et al., Psychology, Ideology and the Human Subject," Ideology and Consciousness, no. 1 (1977), -56.

104. This suggests transforming the problematic of social theory from either individ- al/social or creativity/tradition to text/context.

105. For an extreme statement of the rejection of meaning and interpretation, see Gilles eleuze and Felix Guattari, Anti-Oedipus: Capitalism and Schizophrenia, trans. Robert Hurley, elen R. Lane and Mark Seem (New York: Viking Press, 1977).

106. Examples of this experience may be seen in one's finding the mot juste, or in the artist 'ho is aware that his or her text opens possibilities of which they themselves are not cognizant.

107. One can think of language, following Borges, as a labyrinth. It involves the unsaid and ue unsayable as well as the said and the sayable.

108. That is, reality is produced by and exists as the ongoing moment of an intersection of ɔdes.

109. Roland Barthes, Critical Essays, trans. Richard Howard (Evanston: Northwestern Jniversity Press, 1972), esp. pp. 255–60; Louis Althusser, Essays in Self-Criticism, trans. iraham Lock (London: New Left Books, 1976).

110. See Friedrich Nietzsche, The Gay Science, trans. Walter Kaufmann (New York: 'intage Books, 1974); and David B. Allison, ed., The New Nietzsche: Contemporary Styles of nterpretation (New York: Delta, 1977). For current examples of this attitude, see Roland arthes, The Pleasure of the Text, trans. Richard Miller (New York: Hill and Wang, 1975); and acques Derrida, "Limited Inc.," Glyph, no. 2 (1977), 162–254.

111. At this point, there is a close connection with phenomenological hermeneutics. See effrey Maitland, "Identity, Ontology, and the Work of Art," The Southwestern Journal of 'hilosophy 6 (Fall, 1975), 181–96; and Ricoeur, Interpretation Theory.

112. See Hans-George Gadamer, Truth and Method (New York: Seabury Press, 1975); and :ary Nelson, "Reading Criticism," PMLA, 91 (Oct. 1976), 801–15.

113. See Steiner.

114. The work of Paul de Man, J. Hillis Miller, Daniel Lafferiere, Cary Nelson, and Edward aid is illustrative. Journals such as Diacritics, Sub-Stance and Semiotexte (in literary riticism), Cine-tracts and Screen (in film theory), Ideology and Consciousness, and Working 'apers in Cultural Studies, (in social theory) are major sources of such contemporary work.

115. See Alan Blum, Socrates: The Original and Its Image (London: Routledge and Kegan 'aul, 1978); Barry Sandywell, David Silverman, Maurice Roche, Paul Filmer, and Michael 'hillipson, Problems of Reflexivity and Dialectics in Sociological Inquiry: Language Theorizing)ifference (London: Routledge and Kegan Paul, 1975); John B. O'Malley, Sociology of Meaning (London: Human Context Books, n.d.); Charles Lemert, The Twilight of Man: Homocentricism and Discourse in Sociological Theory (Carbondale: Southern Illinois University 'ress, forthcoming).

116. My use of the term "philosophical" is obviously problematic in this context, since there s little clear agreement as to how one even carries on philosophical criticism and debate. However, it seems clear that such practices, whatever they might be, are different in kind from he analogous theoretical practices. See Louis Althusser, For Marx, trans. Ben Brewster (New York: Vintage Books, 1970).

117. Althusser, Essays in Self Criticism. "Practice" is not the same as method. It might be ɪnderstood, in a preliminary way, as how particular methods (analytic tools) are used. Ɔbviously, to complexly interpret a position, one must look, not only at their theoretical statements, but also at their research practices. These latter embody a theoretical stance as well. What must be left unanswered is what happens when theory and research practice conflict.

118. Lemert and Gillan, p. 313.

THE SOCIAL SERVICES
AND LABELING THEORY

SYMBOLIC INTERACTIONISM AND THE STUDY OF SOCIAL SERVICES*

Carole Joffe, BRYN MAWR COLLEGE

The subject of this essay is the contribution that a symbolic interactionist perspective can make to our understanding of the social services.[1] My intention is not to develop a theory of the services, nor is it to review thoroughly the voluminous, multidisciplinary literature on the topic. Rather, I want to argue that most writing on the services leaves us with a somewhat flat, one-dimensional view of the subject that fails to grasp the richness and complexity of social service institutions in the current period. In contrast, I will suggest that an interactionist approach—which stresses the subjective meaning of the services to all categories of participants, the many-leveled negotiations transpiring within and around the services, and the ever-changing nature of the services—is a necessity if we are to correct for this limited view. I believe that the close examination implied by an interactionist analysis can not only lead to a deepened theoretical understanding of the services, but also, on a more practical level, might help

Studies in Symbolic Interaction—Volume 2, 1979, pages 235–256
Copyright © 1979 by JAI Press Inc.
All rights of reproduction in any form reserved.
ISBN: 0–89232–105–9

answer the perennial question of why some service programs seem to "work" and others do not. Before specifying further what an interactionist analysis would entail, I will briefly review and critique some of the dominant approaches to the services.

TRADITIONAL APPROACHES

In recent years, a vast literature has emerged that explores the relationship between social policy and social services (Hirschorn, 1977, 1978; Kahn, 1973; Kammerman and Kahn, 1976; Rein, 1970; Titmuss, 1968; Wilensky and Lebeaux, 1958). Generally, social services are seen as the concrete programs through which social policy is implemented. Kahn's attempted definition (1969: p. 179) is fairly typical of much writing on the subject:

> Social services may be interpreted . . . as consisting of programs made available by other than market criteria to assure a basic level of health, education and welfare provisions, to enhance communal living and individual functioning, to facilitate access to services and institutions generally, and to assist those in difficulty and need.

More specifically, the social policy/social service literature focuses on three different issues. The first is the emergence of services through the legislative process, as social policy develops out of many-sided conflicts among diverse interest groups. Secondly, there is extensive discussion of the interorganizational arrangements and funding mechanisms through which services are delivered to consumers. Thirdly, considerable attention has been focused on a discussion of the broad purposes and philosophical underpinnings of the social services, with some arguing, as in the statement of Kahn, that services should be understood as playing a benevolent integrative role, while a minority claim that services should be seen as manipulative institutions that serve to bind together an oppressive social order (Galper, 1975).

Despite the important contributions of all of these lines of inquiry, they share in common a tendency to focus on what services are *for,* rather than analyzing what they are *like.* A focus on the actual content of social service organizations that grasps the way services are experienced by participants is not an important part of these approaches. In fact, when such issues are raised, they are usually dismissed by involving the abstract conception of service institutions as being "human service organizations" (Hasenfield and English, 1974). But the type of formal organizational analysis suggested by that phrase is equally far removed from the experience of participants; it simply offers a particular form of an organizational model as a way of understanding this special type of social organization.

In sum, much of the existing social policy literature on social services makes the actual character of the services nonproblematic. The issue for these writers is generally service creation: whether particular services will be socially and legislatively approved, what functions they might serve, how hey will be organized. Even the detailed descriptions of "service delivery systems" by writers such as Kammerman and Kahn (1976), with their emphasis on funding mechanisms and interorganizational networks, still concentrate on events external to the service setting itself. For most of these writers, in short, the most interesting part of the story seems to end with the creation of a service program. The further attention that is given to services after their creation usually takes the form of general reflective efforts to account for a particular program's failure or success, still with little attention to the actual service setting.[2]

There have been, of course, some general exceptions to this general pattern. Some writers have seen that not only are there strains at the broadest societal level about the purposes of social services, but that those strains also come to shape the character of face-to-face interactions within the service agency itself. And these strains within the institution can have a profound impact on the service's effectiveness. Martin Rein (1964), in an early and important essay of the "Social Service Crisis," points to the existence of conflicting definitions of the situation in any service context, and shows the critical importance of the capacity of aspiring professionals to impose a definition of the situation that fits with their own needs. He talks, for example, of how the "good client" for service professionals is one who "will deliver all the rewards that professionals and agencies need or want," so that agencies become organized to maximize contact with good clients, while avoiding "bad" ones. More recently, Hirschorn (1978) has argued that the modes of interpersonal behavior now characteristic of service settings—professional rigidity and withdrawal, client cynicism and hostility—are both consequences of larger political economic processes and further causes of service failure.

While the insights of Rein, Hirschorn, and others writing in a similar vein are important, they still do not go far enough in exploring systematically the content of the service setting. Such a detailed focus strikes me as a crucial component of policy analysis for the simple reason that even when a service is "mandated," what it will ultimately consist of is seldom clear. Suppose, for example, that a new program is proposed with the general aim of "reducing isolation among the elderly." In studying this program, the relevant issues are not only—as conventional approaches would suggest—whether such a program is officially approved, and at what level it is to be funded. We would want to know if the thrust of such programs is to be recreational, vocational, or something else entirely; whether the programs would be staffed by one or another of competing professional groups, by the aged themselves, or by still another group. And even if such decisions about staff and program had been predetermined by planners, we would have to examine how such decisions were received by various relevant constituencies, including the potential clients themselves. The struggles which might well emerge over the original definitions imposed by planners could result in

such services being used avidly by certain sectors of the aged population, bu
shunned by others. Similarly, we might see a transformation in the purpose
of such programs: for example, services which had a rather broad goal o
"reducing isolation" among a quite large targeted population might fin
that they are serving, quite specifically, as a vocational training base for a
fairly small number of clients. Thus, staff positions which had been
allocated to physical therapists or recreational specialists may now have to
be shifted to career counselors. In the absence of such kinds of staff re
adjustments on the part of administrators, the vocationally-motivated
clients may withdraw their patronage, and the programs would be left with
virtually no constituency. As this very brief example suggests, the actual
contribution of a new service to a particular policy goal can hinge in
considerable part on the outcomes of internal struggles over the shape of the
service.

My quarrel, then, with most mainstream approaches to social policy and
social services is that the events transpiring within service institutions are
not taken seriously as inputs into the overall creation of "policy." Symbolic
interactionism, as I suggested earlier, provides us both with a framework for
examining these internal events and for linking these observations to larger
issues of social policy.

SYMBOLIC INTERACTIONISM, SOCIAL PROBLEMS, AND SOCIAL SERVICES

Although I will not attempt here a full exposition of the symbolic
interactionist perspective,[3] the following brief statement by Herbert Blumer
will serve as a useful guide:

> Symbolic interaction involves *interpretation*, or ascertaining the meanings or remarks of
> the other person, and *definition*, or conveying indications to another person as to how
> he is to act. Human association consists of a process of such interpretation and
> definition.

> This dual process (of definition and interpretation) operates both to sustain patterns of
> joint conduct and to open them to transformation. Established patterns of group life
> exist and persist only through the continued use of the same schemes of interpreta-
> tion. . . . Let the interpretations that sustain them be undermined or disrupted by
> changed definitions of others and the patterns can quickly collapse. . . . In the flow of
> group life there are innumerable points at which the participants are redefining each
> other's acts. (1969: pp. 66–67, emphasis in original).

Thus, the symbolic interaction perspective emphasizes the central place of
interpretation in social life, the conflicting meanings that are held by
different actors, and the transformations in the social order that result from
the negotiations of these different meanings.

Social Problems

In spite of a number of interesting case studies, writers in the interactionist tradition have not devoted much attention, on a theoretical level, to the social services. But the substantial body of interactionist literature on social problems (Becker, 1963, 1966; Blumer, 1951, 1971; Kitsuse and Spector, 1973; Spector and Kitsuse, 1973, 1976) gives us a helpful base upon which to build.

In brief, interactionist writers argue that social problems cannot be understood in terms of "objective" social factors; rather, such problems are rooted in "processes of collective definition" (Blumer, 1971: p. 298). As Kitsuse and Spector have put it, somewhat more concretely, social problems are "the activities of groups making assertions of grievances and claims to organizations, agencies and institutions about some putative conditions" (1973: p. 415). Blumer (1971) and Spector and Kitsuse (1976) have both suggested a natural history of social problems—a succession of stages through which society responds to the emergence of a set of issues. Though each of the natural history models is somewhat different, both have as central components a popular mobilization around a perceived problem, and the inevitability of negotiations between official agencies and "claim-makers." Both models recognize that official responses to social problems are shaped and reshaped as a result of ongoing activity by different social groups—the original "claim-makers," as well as subsequent constituencies, such as professional groups, taxpayers, and so forth.

This focus on the negotiated character of social problems has two important implications for the understanding of social services. First, the official response to claim-making activity often involves the creation of new social services, so services must be understood as an integral part of the process of societal handling of social problems. Secondly, services are often (though not always) the locus in which further claim-making activity takes place. Hence, new social problems will emerge within existing service organizations as social groups demand that those services respond in new ways to their particular needs. Each of these points reinforces the idea that both established and newly created social services must be viewed as arenas in which different social actors attempt to impose their own definition of reality on the situation.

The first point—that services are often created as "official responses" to collective mobilization—does not mean, of course, that those who are mobilizing get what they have asked for. Even when a new service is established in response to direct demands, as, for example, when a rape crisis center is created in response to feminist groups, there still will remain questions of who will control the center, how it will be staffed, and so on. Bureaucratic procedures themselves, as Emerson and Messinger (1977) have recently argued, can impose definitions according to their own logic, hence leading to programs different than those visualized either by recipients or authorizing agency. Often, moreover, the official response to mobilization involves a conscious distortion of the initial demands. The Headstart program might be taken as an example of this. In the 1960s, urban black unrest centered around demands for significant government response in the areas of jobs and housing. Officials, however, redefined the problem of the urban black poor as the inability of black children to take advantage of educational opportunity, which was argued to be the critical determinant of economic progress (Kraft, 1966). The result was that one of the major (and most durable) of all anti-poverty programs was Headstart. In Blumer's terms, "the official plan constitute(d) the official definition of the problem (1971: p. 304). There are many other examples where the impetus behind the creation of new social services appears to be the control of troublesome populations. This is how one might analyze the development of community mental health centers in the urban ghetto in the same period (Kenniston, 1968), and this is how some have interpreted the extension of compulsory schooling in the nineteenth century (Katz, 1968).

The second point—that existing services are often the arena in which social mobilization by claim-making groups takes place—provides a context for understanding the growing importance of conflicts between clients and service providers. Many of the social conflicts of recent years fit within this framework: students demanding reforms of educational institutions; prisoners organizing for change in institutional practices; welfare recipients organizing to put pressure on the welfare system. All of these social conflicts revolve around differing conceptions of how a particular social service should be organized. On this, of course, hinges broader notions of how the larger society should be organized or reorganized. By locating social services within the process by which the society defines and resolves social problems, we highlight the growing importance of the services as a focal point of social conflict and change.

AN INTERACTIONIST APPROACH TO THE SERVICES: THE CASE OF ABORTION

What does it mean to examine concretely a particular service, from an interactionist perspective? An interactionist approach, as the above discussion has suggested, implies, first, seeing most facets of the service in question as problematic: the designated content, staff, clientele, funding sources, and so forth, of a particular program have emerged out of a set of negotiations among relevant actors and are always subject to further negotiations. An interactionist approach, secondly, dictates a view of the service setting itself as a prime arena for further social mobilization around the problem area in question. Although these characteristics are as true of established services as of emergent ones, it is with newer services that we can most strongly see the problematic character of the services. Using a quite new service area, abortion, as a case in point, let us examine the types of questions than an interactionist study would involve.[4]

For purposes of discussion, I will divide the material into three groupings: the legitimation of a problem and subsequent creation of new services; the institutionalization of such services; the various types of "careers" that emanate from such services. Though these categories overlap somewhat with the natural history models of social problems cited above, here I am concerned specifically with events surrounding the creation and development of service institutions. Furthermore, though the three categories suggest "stages" of a process, in reality they must be understood as circular —that is, developments in category #3 can lead to awareness of altogether new social problems, and hence new forms of service programs.

Legitimation of the Problem/Innovations of New Services

For many years, the abortion "problem" was conceptualized in terms of legality. The problem, at least from the standpoint of abortion advocates, was that the illegality of the procedure denied abortion services to many, and drove thousands of others to "back alley" facilities which often resulted in injury and death. The legalization of abortion would presumably solve the problem; abortion services would be safe and accessible. Accordingly, the predominant activity of the pro-abortion movement was oriented toward securing legalization. *Roe* v. *Wade,* the landmark Supreme Court decision of 1973, might be seen as the "official response" to collective mobilization on behalf of abortion.

However, the Court's decision on abortion serves as a prime example of the pitfalls of equating legal rulings with "social policy." For not only did the decision itself leave certain crucial legal issues unresolved (e.g., the "viability" of the fetus, confidentiality for minors), more importantly, it said very little about what abortion services actually should be like. From an interactionist standpoint, therefore, the most compelling part of the abortion story begins *after* the Court decision, with the coming together of a range of diverse actors seeking to create an abortion policy. Certainly the most dramatic of these varied efforts are those of the Right-to-Lifers, whose notion of an abortion policy is to overturn the Court's decision and to once again make abortion illegal. But while the attempts of anti-abortion forces to overturn or weaken the 1973 decision have dominated media attention, and are to be taken very seriously, just as important, from the standpoint of this paper, is the fact that among those who favor abortion, there is not agreement as to what an abortion policy should be.

Some of these ambiguities refer most directly to "technical" matters: for example, the medically safest technology at various stages of a pregnancy, or the desirability of inserting an IUD directly after an abortion. Other questions relate to the perceived needs of the abortion client: even in an era of legality, for example, what precautions should hospitals and clinics take to insure confidentiality? Is the client entitled to a "counselor," someone who will act as the patient's general advocate/therapist, and accompany her through the procedure? If such counselors are to be available, as the general consensus seems to be (American Public Health Association, 1973; Planned Parenthood, 1976), then should such counselling be *required* of all potential clients prior to receiving an abortion?

Still other unresolved issues of abortion policy speak more directly to the concerns of abortion personnel. In view of the apparent distaste that some medical staff have for abortion work (Bourne, 1972; Kane, 1973; Kibel 1972; Such-Baer, 1974), what should be the response of health care administrators? Should such work be made optional? If required, should such work involve frequent rotations? Should hospitals and clinics provide specialized support services for abortion staff, such as liaison therapy?

The routinization of abortion work, additionally, leads inevitably to difficult "ethical" problems for which a policy must be developed. What are the obligations, for example, of medical staff if, in the course of a late saline abortion, the fetus is born live? How should clinics manage the task of discreetly disposing of accumulated fetuses, without offending either community sensibilities, or placing too much of an unpleasant burden on staff?

Furthermore, though I have spoken of each of these sets of policy dilemmas as separate entities, in real life, of course, they overlap considerably. "Medical" or "technical" matters become inevitably entwined with nonmedical considerations. Frequently the decision made about the locale of an abortion—hospital, clinic, or doctor's office—is based upon the funding arrangements that obtain in a particular situation. Similarly, the choice of a method used in a particular abortion may not only be determined by "medical" considerations, but also by the discomfort implied for staff. A comparison of the two most prevalent methods of late abortion —the saline method and dilation and evacuation—illustrates the different, and opposing, needs of doctors, nurses, and clients. The saline method, which involves induced labor and the delivery of a stillborn fetus, is typically both physically and emotionally quite unpleasant for the client, but puts relatively little burden on the doctor. In contrast, the dilation and evacuation method, which involves scraping out the woman's uterus and a confrontation with fairly developed fetal parts, can be quite trying for doctors, but usually far less upsetting to the client than the saline method.

The Institutionalization of Services

The "institutionalization" of abortion services emerges from the resolution of the many problematic aspects of abortion policy, such as those mentioned above. A strategy for making sense of these resolutions, suggested by interactionist theory, would be to first note the relevant actors in the above situations and ascertain what "meaning" abortion has for them. For example, in questions pertaining to the organization and delivery of abortion services, we would identify such actors as doctors, nurses, other medical personnel, state and county health departments, insurance agencies, present and potential abortion clients, and particular interest groups such as Right-to-Lifers and abortion rights groups. In assessing the "meaning" that abortion has to each group or individual within it, we would likely find that, although in some cases the "meaning" is quite clear-cut—with some Right-to-Lifers, for example, being unalterably opposed to the delivery of abortions anywhere—in most cases, the meanings held will be ambiguous: a doctor may be personally opposed to abortion, but feels as an employee of a public hospital, it is his/her duty to perform them; a hospital board member may personally approve abortions, but worry about the consequences to the hospital's image; a client may both desire an abortion yet feel immense shame and guilt; feminist groups may be "pro-abortion" yet very troubled by the profit motives of certain forms of private clinics.

These ambiguities suggest the usefulness of distinguishing among different kinds of "meaning" in the abortion context. At a minimum, it seems reasonable in this case to differentiate between "legal," "moral," and "experiential" aspects of abortion. The legal meanings would encompass both the rights and formal constraints facing each actor: the obligation of certain facilities, such as public hospitals, to perform abortions; the procedures to be followed in late pregnancy; the rights of minors and married women to confidentiality, and so on. "Legal meanings" should not of course be reified. As in other new social policy areas, laws about abortion are themselves ambiguous, in flux, and most importantly, selectively attended to and enforced. This is most strongly shown by the number of public hospitals refusing to perform abortions in the period immediately following the 1973 decision.[5] But legal meanings are nevertheless useful for our purposes because they offer a framework which at least partially circumscribes the movements (and perceptions) of our relevant actors.

The second category of meaning, "moral," speaks of how various participants abstractly *feel* about abortion. Here the range of meanings might be expected to range from those who think abortion is synonymous with murder, to those who think it "unfortunate" but necessary, to those who consider the only relevant moral issue to be a woman's right to control her body, to those who argue that abortion is as reasonable as any of the other presently available means of contraception. Of course, the various moral stances taken toward abortion will not only vary from group to group, but within each group as well: it is perfectly possible to imagine, for example, a doctor or nurse holding each of the above positions. Thus, negotiation of meaning has to be explored not only as it occurs across various groups, but internally as well.

Finally, by "experiential" meanings, I attempt to refer to the *consequences* for various actors of different policy choices being made: that is, what does it "mean" for doctors, nurses, clients, and so on, if abortions are delivered in a certain way? As indicated already, the choice of a particular method for a late abortion has different consequences for doctors and clients. Similarly, Bourne (1972) explains the variation in staff response to abortion work in terms of assigned duties: nurses, according to this argument, have the most negative reaction to this work because their task is narrowly confined to the medical aspects of the procedure; social workers have a more favorable attitude toward abortion work because of greater interactional opportunities with the patient. These examples suggest that the full "meaning" of any social policy cannot be understood without taking into account the *activities* that various actors are called upon to perform.

"Change," a central concern of symbolic interactionists, is also relevant to our consideration of meaning. For example, change in the nature of a pregnancy—passage from an early one to a late one, a "normal" pregnancy suddenly becoming a hazardous one—has definite consequences for the legal, moral, and "experiential" meanings people have of abortion. Legally, the more advanced a pregnancy is, the greater the likelihood of state intervention, as the issue of fetus "viability" becomes more explosive. Morally, many persons, both those directly involved and the general public, are seemingly less troubled by early terminations than later ones, and similarly more approving of abortions of "at-risk" pregnancies than of normal ones. In "experiential" terms, we have seen that late abortions involve a kind of "dirty work" (Hughes, 1971) for professionals and an unpleasantness for clients that earlier ones do not.

The Negotiation of Meaning

After meanings, however tentative, have been established, the task of the interactionist is to explore the negotiation of these meanings and their subsequent translation into "policy" (Strauss et. al. 1963). A consideration of "negotiation," of course, immediately confronts one with the issue of power. In social service institutions, as elsewhere, the differential degree of power held by various actors shapes the character of possible negotiations. In the abortion clinic, doctors hold a position of formal authority over other medical personnel, the clinic director has the power to hire and fire lower level staff, licensing regulations dictate certain matters and presumably put them out of the realm of "negotiations," and so forth.

The limitations on negotiations that are imposed by "social structure" are real, and the point of an interactionist analysis is not to indiscriminately see "everything" as subject to negotiation (Maines, 1977).[6] Rather, the strength

f an interactionist analysis is to show that certain features of institutional
fe—seemingly bound by hierarchy and rules—are, in fact, much more fluid
aan conventional organizational analysis would have us believe. The
roblematic nature of "rules" governing institutions and the *informal*
ources of power within them are two of the creative contributions of
iteractionists studying institutions—both with obvious relevance for the
ervices.

From an interactionist standpoint, a crucial aspect of "rules" is whether
r not they can be broken, without sanction, by various actors. For
xample, an individual abortion clinic is subject to a vast number of rules
nd guidelines, emanating from a number of different sources: national
amily planning and health organizations, local and state health depart-
nents, internal clinic committees composed of Board and staff members.
ome of these rules—for example, that a qualified physician must perform
n abortion or that a pregnancy must be verified before the abortion
ommences—are never deliberately broken; if they were, the clinic would
xperience a "crisis." Other clinic rules, such as the policy that counselors
ust speak to all abortion recipients about birth control before the latter
ave the clinic, are more laxly monitored and enforced. A comparison of
ie relative seriousness with which each of the above rules is taken points to
uch further useful lines of inquiry as: the dominant conception clinic
ianagers have of abortion (foremostly, a "medical" procedure, and only
econdarily a "social" one); the most relevant outside constituencies for the
linic (health departments and insurance agencies); and managerial dif-
culties in specifying and monitoring tasks of counselors, a new occupation
rhose boundaries have not yet been firmly established within the clinic
ivision of labor.

The abortion counselor also serves as an interesting example of informal
ower within a service organization. The concept of an abortion counselor
riginated within the feminist health movement in the period before the
videspread availability of legal abortions; the counselor acted as the client's
dvocate, which meant guiding her to appropriate facilities, explaining the
rocedures, exploring the client's feelings about the upcoming event, and in
ome cases, accompanying her through the procedure. Since national
egalization in 1973, this form of abortion counseling has been incorporated
nto many facilities offering abortion. My observations have suggested that
hese counselors, fairly low paid and usually without professional degrees,
ften have considerable leverage in negotiating some clinic decisions:
eneral policy matters, the choice of medical staff, and especially, certain
ssues concerning individual patients. For example, one of the major
nstances of counselor discretion in first trimester abortions is deciding
vhether clients are able to adequately handle the abortion procedure, which
s done under a local anesthesia. This is not a "medical" judgment, but a

"psychological" one: the counselor attempts to identify those who would, as counselors put it, "freak out on the table" during the abortion. The counselors' recommendations in such cases, typically accepted by supervisors, is for the potential client to go to a hospital, where an abortion can be received under general anesthesia. Another manifestation of the counselor's power, which also takes place at the pre-abortion "options counseling" session, is collaboration in a decision-making process which sometimes results in the client choosing not to proceed with any form of abortion. In these ways, therefore, counselors act as gatekeepers to clinic services.

In seeking to account for these forms of informal power held by counselors, the answer seems to be at least partly due to the stigmatized character of abortion, in spite of its legality. Medical professionals directly involved in the delivery of abortions are well aware of public apprehension about their activities, and to a certain extent, are themselves troubled by what they are doing. Thus counseling serves both important rhetorical and practical functions. The visible presence of counselors in a clinic serve as testimony to the larger community that abortions are not lightly decided upon, but undertaken only after a process of "counseling." The counselor also serves as buffer between the clinic and the client. Potentially troublesome clients (and/or family members) are either screened out, or, more usually, soothed. Hence the possibilities of potentially damaging action against the clinic, legal or otherwise, are reduced. Finally, external threats aside, the activities of the counselors help reassure conflicted abortion personnel that, indeed, the procedure being done is what the woman "really" wants.

Clients, too, often exert a certain amount of informal power in service settings. In the abortion context, the precarious social standing of many facilities, in spite of legality, makes for a considerable vulnerability to disgruntled clients—particularly those who are threatening to go "public," either with lawsuits or simply exposés of allegedly bad service. Thus, in spite of the precautions clinics take with consent forms and so forth, we might speculate that the hostile atmosphere surrounding many clinics leads to an attentiveness to clients—for example, assiduous follow-up on problems by phone calls—that may not be present in more secure organizations.

In a more social-psychological sense, client powers are also exhibited in face-to-face interaction with service professionals. For clients, as Hughes has argued (1971: pp. 338–347), have considerable abilities to confirm or deny a desired professional identity. This is especially true in relations with newer "marginal" professionals, whose sense of "professionalism" is quite weak. In the case of abortion counselors, as I have written elsewhere (Joffe, 1978), the demeanor shown by abortion-seeking clients and their receptivity to the counselors' therapeutic skills are major determinants of counselors' responses to abortion work.

Finally, client powers can be manifested through organized groups of "service consumers." An organized clientele can be most helpful to a new service through its willingness to testify on behalf of the service's usefulness, and to lobby for continued funding. Abortion services generate this type of client mobilization only to a limited degree: though there have been some notable exceptions,[7] most recipients shun a public identity as "abortion clients"; also, involvement with an abortion facility is typically very brief, involving one or two visits. But in other services, that is, childcare, services to the blind and aged, where the relationship to the service institution is more stable and where identity as a service consumer is viewed more positively, self-conscious organization among clients is far more common. And it is in these situations that we can see most clearly the internal consequences of the external powers of clients. In return for lobbying favors, clients are able to extract certain concessions from professionals. In the case of childcare, for example, minority clients have demanded, with some success, that professionals shift from their historic emphasis on social development to a more cognitive program (Joffe, 1977).

"CAREER" ASPECTS OF THE SERVICES

The provisional character of the services—their always changing and developing character—is best captured by the notion of "career." Career, as interactionists have used the term, is applied not only to individuals, but to groups and institutions as well. In our analysis of abortion services, the relevant career lines to follow would be, at a minimum, the career of abortion itself as a social problem, those of new occupational groups emerging within abortion facilities, and the careers of organized client groups and oppositional groups.

Abortion as a Social Problem

The career of abortion as a social problem refers to the ways in which abortion is responded to, by various publics, at various stages of development. These developments, in turn, are shaped by events occurring in such relevant spheres as law and medicine. The 1973 Supreme Court decision becomes further elaborated and refined by various judicial bodies; Congress and state legislatures continue to wrestle with the abortion issue. Medical advances in abortion technology and procedures have consequences not only for those directly involved, for example, staff and clients, but for the general public's perception of abortion. For example, one possible scenario for a future abortion policy involves the separation of a fetus from its mother, and the maintenance of the fetus in an artificial life-support system until the fetus reaches maturity (Remsberg and Remsberg, 1976). Such a policy, if it came to pass, would quite possibly make abortion more palatable to many, though obviously leaving some on each side of the issue further alienated. Similarly, developments—or lack of them—in related areas of medicine affect the career of abortion. The increasing sophistication within the genetic counselling field, especially the ability to detect birth defects during pregnancy, presumably creates a greater legitimacy of abortion among some. In similar fashion, the inadequacies of available contraceptive methods—and in particular the medical dangers associated with the leading methods—also might cause a higher acceptance of abortion.

Social, as well as legal and medical, changes would be part of the study of the career of abortion. Here, for example, we would be concerned with understanding the anti-abortion movement in the fullest possible sense: we might come to understand the movement as not only expressing narrow anti-abortion sentiments, but also a widespread discomfort with current attempts to alter family life (Easton, 1978). We would want to examine how the abortion issue becomes affected by official recognition of other new social problems, such as teenage pregnancy. We would want to investigate, finally, how changes in attitude toward abortion might be occurring simply because of the passage of time, and the consequent "normalization" of abortion. For some, abortion might now seem less sinister and "wrong;" for others, the very fact of routinization, with much media attention given to the volume of abortions performed, might be cause for new anti-abortion feelings (Remsberg and Remsberg, 1976).

Careers of New Professions

The new services institutions, established in response to the creation of social policy in a new area, become increasingly important arenas of career developments. One of the most crucial of these careers is the launching of new human service professions. The proliferation of new services means that some people now occupationally identify as abortion counselors, rape prevention specialists, battered wives' advocates, childbirth educators, and so forth. Without getting into the issue of whether these new occupational groups sociologically qualify as "professionals," the relevant point rather is that these workers *act* to some degree as if they were indeed professionals. They argue that these new kinds of services require specialized training and supervision; they make pronouncements—as "professionals"—on what should be public policy in the new field; they seek to upgrade the conditions of their work, including a quest for increased decision-making powers.

Several implications flow from service institutions being the staging ground of new professions. First, it is usually workers lower down in the agency hierarchy who seek such "professional" status, as those higher up, that is, doctors and managers in the abortion case, already have stable professional identities. Thus the new human service professions in creation re unlikely to go beyond the status of "weak" or marginal professions. This n turn has consequences for relations with both clients and supervisors. Clients may be less inclined to take the claims of the new professionals eriously, and indeed, argue strongly against attempts to professionalize the ervice in question. In services that have a strong tie to an active social movement—such as the relationship of abortion and rape services to the women's movement—client and movement activists both argue that the riterion for staffing should not be "professional" credentials, but rather the act of real life experience: that is, the best abortion or rape counselor is one who herself has experienced abortion or rape.

From the perspective of dominant professionals, the new human service professions are (sometimes) conceded to have a certain legitimacy, and, as n the case described of abortion counselors, are sometimes granted decision-making powers that seem to exceed their formal status. Yet the fullest professional aspirations of these new occupations are not, of course, completely accepted, and exacerbated tensions over the appropriate division of labor becomes part of the work situation. In a family planning clinic, for example, a staff worker might convert a routine fifteen-minute medical history interview into an hour-long session when the client reveals she is having sexual problems. The interviewer feels justified, if not compelled, to do so because her own professional self-image is that of a "sexuality counselor." The clinic manager in charge of scheduling and the doctor waiting in the examining room become furious, both because of the delay involved, and because of the inappropriateness of turning a contraceptive interview into a "therapy session."

Professionalization attempts within service settings thus mean that "personal" concerns get entwined with "impersonal" ones. Staff will have impulses not only to do what they think objectively is "best," but also what s best for them. For example, workers seeking to further professional skills and experience might seek out the most "interesting" cases, be impatient with the "routine" ones, or perhaps convert a routine case into a "special" one. This dynamic partially explains the disaffection abortion counselors feel toward clients who repudiate offers of in-depth counseling (Joffe, 1978). n short, the fact that services are a staging ground of new professions implies the creation of specialized interests—these interests may, or may not, coincide with the needs of clients.

Finally, as the careers of new professions unfold, members of these groups are not only in potential conflict with superiors and clients, but also with each other. "Segments" of the emerging professions disagree over the way to further the new group's aims (Bucher and Strauss, 1961). Among abortion counselors, for example, there is a split between those who see as a first priority additional training in therapeutic skills and those who argue instead for increasing medical knowledge. Among contemporary midwives, who are in the midst of a spectacular comeback in the United States, there are splits between those who favor credentialing and absorption into mainstream health care systems, and those who favor autonomous—if necessary, semi-clandestine—careers.

Client Careers

The institutionalization of services also implies opportunities for client careers. The careers of individual clients may change, in predictable ways, through repeated encounters with the service setting: a second-time abortion recipient is likely to respond differently to clinic services—being less needful of counseling, for example—than a first-timer; parents of a second child may be more assertive with obstetrical, pediatric, and day care personnel.

But changes in client careers occur on a more collective level as well. In the past ten years, there has been particularly intensified organization among service clientele. Gartner and Riessman (1974) argue that for many persons, social service settings are replacing occupational ones as primary sources of social identification.

As suggested above, when clients organize, they may come to question some of the practices of professionals; in particular, they may challenge some of the new professionals' claims to expertise, and demand some staffing positions for themselves. In some service areas, Headstart programs for example, a successful career as a parent-client very often does lead directly to a staff position;[8] indeed, in the Headstart case, such upgrading of clients into staff has come to be defined by program planners as a formal goal of the program.

Just as increasing professionalization opportunities ultimately lead to splits among service workers, so, too, do increased political powers of clients lead to factionalization. Sometimes these splits are along tactical lines: "militants" will urge sit-ins and other forms of disruption at the service site or agency headquarters, while "moderates" will urge "working within the system." Sometimes the splits are along racial, ethnic, class, or sexual lines: the War on Proverty programs, for example, frequently led to bitter competition among various racial and ethnic groups; more recently, middle class groups have argued that service programs should not only benefit the poor; affirmative action programs are frequently accused of pitting Third World males against white women. Most commonly, perhaps, conflicts within client groups emerge as specialized interest groups within the same broad service area come to recognize that they have different, often opposing, agendas. This point is vividly illustrated by a recent statement of a spokesman for the blind:

> There's a tendency of managers to want to generalize everybody, to say that all handicapped people have the same needs. . . . But, in fact, the problems are not the same. We have no more in common with a bunch of wheelchair guys than we have with

a bunch of black guys. Wheelchair groups want the curbs out; we want them in. (N.Y. *Times,* Oct. 24, 1977 p. 24)

Opposition Careers

The institutionalization of services also has consequences for the careers of oppositional groups. After the legalization of abortion in 1973, anti-abortion forces expanded their activities to include a specific attack on the practices of abortion clinics. Thus, in addition to extensive legislative lobbying, currently a major activity of anti-abortion groups is mobilization at actual clinic sites: facilities are picketed, clients and staff are verbally harassed, and increasingly, there are incidents of disruption and vandalization of clinics.

Oppositional groups, too, split into various factions. In the abortion case, we can see tactical splits between those favoring confrontation action vs. those choosing legislative activity. And within each of these two groups there are of course further splits: the confrontationalists dividing according to how much violence is sanctioned; the lobbyists according to which issues should get priority. Another split within anti-abortion forces is whether the movement should remain strictly a one-issue campaign, or join with a coalition of other oppositional groups, such as various anti-ERA and daycare groups.

CONCLUSION: SOCIAL SERVICES AND THE RENEGOTIATION OF SOCIAL LIFE

The above thus represents the types of issues an interactionist would take into account in a study of a new social service. I have argued that in the analysis of these issues, a prime consideration must be the differing interpretations and, therefore, subsequent negotiations among different actors. I now reiterate that such a view of services as a "negotiated order" cannot, in itself, do justice to *all* aspects of the services. For example, a purely interactionist approach cannot adequately analyze the political economy of the services, and in particular, the current fiscal crisis which is necessitating severe cutbacks in service funding. (Though, to be sure, certain features of this fiscal crisis could be examined fruitfully from an interactionist perspective.[9]) My argument at the outset of this paper was not that symbolic interactionism could provide a total theory of the social services, but rather that the perspective allowed us to see particular aspects of the services in a richer way. In the concluding section of this paper, I will summarize what I believe to be the primary contributions of the perspective for the study of the social services.

I submit that the advantges of an interactionist approach to the services fall into two categories: first, a deepened understanding of the internal life of service institutions; second, a guide to the part played by services in the "renegotiation" of social life at the broadest levels. With respect to the former, the symbolic interactionist tradition encourages us to examine the face-to-face encounters between relevant actors in the services, and offers a framework with which to make sense of these observations. The conflicts that we see, for example, between intake worker and client over appropriate client demeanor in an income maintenance office, between doctor and counselor over whether an abortion procedure should take place, among rape workers as to the costs and benefits of a close alliance with the local police force, between county health officials and free clinic staff members over the issue of record keeping and patient confidentiality, all become comprehensible. These conflicts occur because actors come to the service setting with different conceptions of what the services actually "are," and with different personal and political agendas for their transformation.

This view of professional/client relationships and division of labor issues as conflicting, even antagonistic, is, I believe, one of the most important overall contributions of the interactionist school (Hughes, 1971; Becker, 1951, 1970; Freidson, 1961, 1968; Goffman, 1961), one with an obvious relevance to the services. This is a view that differs sharply from more conventional sociological views of the services, in which professionals and clients and various levels of professionals are seen to exist harmoniously in a system of clear-cut roles and expectations (Parsons, 1951; Wilensky and Lebeaux, 1958). But such a static view simply does not do justice to the various events now transpiring within the services: the extraordinary rise in client "consumerism," perhaps most strongly seen in the radical and feminist health movements, in which not only professional autonomy, but also professional expertise are profoundly challenged; the number of unpleasant, sometimes violent, incidents at welfare offices, community mental health centers, and schools; the ongoing confusion over the proper use of "community" people in staff positions in service institutions; the upward mobility strivings of a host of new "human service professionals." The interactionist position, on the other hand, does offer a meaningful explanatory framework for such events. Seemingly disparate events can be seen as part of a larger pattern, and we can start to move toward a unified conception of contemporary service institutions.

Finally, in a more macro-sociological sense, an interactionist approach can enrich our understanding of the larger social role played by the services. The interactionist emphasis on meaning and the negotiation of meaning is here used in the broadest sense to look at the transformation of society. As an example, let us consider briefly the realtionship between the services and "family life." One way of understanding the development of services generally is to see them as a gradual assimilation of various functions once performed by the family: AFDC payments replace a male wage earner; child

care centers share in child-rearing tasks; intimate discussions about sexuality now take place in Planned Parenthood centers; old people spend their last
years, not with kin, but in nursing homes; and so on. This phenomenon of
the content of family life spilling over into institutional settings—with an
attendant erosion of the authority of individual family members—has
generated considerable comment, and it has recently become fashionable,
from the left as well as from the right, to bemoan the usurpation of family
functions by "experts" (Lasch, 1977).

While not denying the validity of specific instances of punitiveness,
racism, and intolerance in various social policies toward the family, I believe
an interactionist viewpoint allows for a more subtle understanding of the
family/services relationship than the rather simple nostalgia for the self-
sufficient family expressed by Lasch (1977) and others. An interactionist
sees the family and social services existing in a *dynamic* relationship, with
services not only imposing changes on family life, but also responding to
desired changes. To fully understand the implications of the rise of service
institutions that encroach on family life, we have to examine not only the
motives of the helping professionals and social scientists, but also the
meaning of these events to family members. It may well be that *some* family
members—for example, women—welcome some of these developments to a
greater degree than other members, for the reason that traditional modes of
family organization are no longer experienced as tenable. This kind of
thinking casts the possible relationship of services and families in a different
light. For if we consider such events as are now occurring in the services—
the linguistic shift among service officials, from "broken home" to "single
parent family;" the designation of "displaced homemakers" as a new social
category, requiring specialized services; the changes in adoptive policies,
granting adoptive rights to singles, homosexuals, and poor persons; the
extraordinary speed with which "battered wives" services are being absorbed into mainstream service networks—they all point to the role that the
services are playing in the erosion of the nuclear family (male as wage
earner, woman at home with children) as the "official" national model of
family organization.[10] Unevenly and ambivalently to be sure, the services
are nonetheless assisting members in fleeing "bad" nuclear families, and are
conferring legitimation on new forms of families. Again, I do not want to
minimize the historical or contemporary regressiveness of much family
policy: the AFDC "bedchecks" and inadequate stipends, the means tests for
various services and their resulting stigmatization, the forced sterilizations,
and so on. But we must recognize the services for the locus of contemporary
social change that they are, and see that for some, the services contain
genuinely liberating possibilities. In fact, it does not seem too grandiose to
say that there seem to be virtually no important areas of social life in which
struggles over their "meanings" are not being played out in the services.

Traditional ways of giving birth, and of spending one's first hour of life, are under significant challenge, as natural childbirth enthusiasts, "birth without violence," and homebirth advocates confront the practices of obstetricians and hospital maternity ward personnel; at the other end of the life cycle, there are similar confrontations over the most appropriate organization of death, as a coalition of euthanasia, hospice, and "death at home" advocates challenge traditional medical practices. In sum, the services appear to be the arena of some of the most basic events occurring now in post industrial society, and symbolic interactionism facilitates a way to comprehend these events.

FOOTNOTES

*I would like to thank Fred Block, Patricia Bourne, Norman Denzin and Ann Swidler for their comments on an earlier draft of this paper.

1. By "social services," I refer in the broadest sense to health, education, and welfare programs, both publicly and privately funded.

2. I should clarify that I am not including in my discussion a consideration of "evaluation research"—a tradition that does, narrowly speaking, focus on what programs are "like," but, obviously, not in the sense intended in this paper.

3. Readers not familiar with symbolic interactionism are urged to read Blumer (1969) for the classic statement on this perspective, as well as Meltzer et. al. (1975), for a useful summary of different tendencies within the perspective, as well as the leading internal and external critiques.

4. Much of the data that follows are drawn from a year-long participant observation study that I conducted of a family planning clinic that includes an abortion service. A preliminary report of this research is found in Joffe (1978).

5. In the face of legal ambiguities about the obligations of facilities receiving public funding to perform abortions, public hospitals "have been the slowest to respond to the mandate involved in the Supreme Court decision. Of 2,144 public hospitals identified by the American Hospital Association in 1972, only 17% (363) provided abortions during 1973 and the first quarter of 1974." Institute of Medicine (1975, p. 31).

6. However, I am in strong sympathy with Maines's (1977) recent contention that there is nothing inherently incompatible between the interactionist perspective and considerations of social organization and social structure. Maines points to a number of recent studies which show a renewed interest among interactionists in larger-scale negotiations.

7. One of the most notable examples of client activism on behalf of abortion has been the publication of statements, both in the United States and Europe, of prominent women (writers, political figures, actresses, and so forth) acknowledging that they have had illegal abortions.

8. Upwards of 10,000 Headstart parents have been estimated to have used these programs as stepping stones to careers, within Headstart itself and similar programs elsewhere. N.Y. *Times,* June 8, 1975.

9. For example, an interactionist would want to examine public reaction to service cutbacks, the possible incidents of consumer protests against the cutbacks, and changes in the official definitions of "permissible funding levels" in view of any such popular mobilization.

10. Recent estimates of the numbers of American families living in the "official" nuclear mode—male as wage earner, female at home with children—typically fall below 20%. See, for example, the N.Y. *Times,* May 22, 1978, p. D2.

REFERENCES

American Public Health Association, "Recommended Program Guides for Abortion Services," Washington, D.C., 1973.

Becker, Howard, *The Outsiders*, N.Y.: Free Press, 1963.

————— , "The Professional Dance Musician and His Audience," *A.J. of Sociology*, 57 (1951): 136–144.

————— , *Social Problems: A Modern Approach*, N.Y.: John Wiley, 1966.

————— , "The Teacher in the Authority System of the Public School," in *Sociological Work*, H. Becker, ed., Chicago: Aldine, 1970.

Blumer, Herbert, "Collective Behavior," in A.M. Lee, ed., *New Outline of the Principles of Sociology*, N.Y.: Barnes and Noble, 1951.

————— , "Social Problems as Collective Behavior," *Social Problems* (Winter, 1971).

————— , *Symbolic Interactionism: Perspectives and Method*, Englewood Cliffs, N.J.: Prentice-Hall, 1969.

Bourne, Judith P., "Health Professionals' Attitudes Toward Abortion," in Sarah Lewitt, ed., *Abortion Techniques and Services*, Amsterdam: Excepta Medica, 1972.

Bucher, Rue and Anselm Strauss, "Professions in Process," *A.J. of Sociology* (January, 1961).

Easton, Barbara, "Feminism and the Family," *Socialist Review* (May/June, 1978).

Emerson, Robert and Sheldon Messinger, "The Micro-Politics of Trouble," *Social Problems* (December 1977).

Freidson, Eliot, "The Impurity of Professional Authority," in *Institutions and the Person*, H. Becker et. al., ed., Chicago: Aldine, 1968.

————— , *Patients' Views of Medical Care*, N.Y.: Russell Sage, 1961.

Galper, Jeffrey, *The Politics of Social Services*, Englewood Cliffs, N.J.: Prentice-Hall, 1975.

Gardner, Alan and Frank Riessman, *The Service Society and the Consumer Vanguard*, N.Y.: Harper and Row, 1974.

Goffman, Erving, *Asylums*, N.Y.: Doubleday, 1961.

Hasenfeld, Yehaskel and Richard A. English, *Human Service Organizations*, Ann Arbor: U. of Michigan Press, 1974.

Hirschhorn, Larry, "Social Policy and the Life Cycle," *Social Service Review* (September, 1977).

————— , "The Theory of Social Services in Disaccumulationist Capitalism," *International Journal of Health Services*, forthcoming, 1978.

Hughes, Everett, *The Sociological Eye*, Book Two, Chicago: Aldine, 1971.

Institute of Medicine, *Legalized Abortion and the Public Health*, Washington, D.C.: National Academy of Sciences, 1975.

Joffe, Carole, *Friendly Intruders: Childcare Professionals and Family Life*, Berkeley: U. of California Press, 1977.

————— , "What Abortion Counselors Want from their Clients," *Social Problems* (October, 1978).

Kammerman, Sheila and Alfred Kahn, *Social Services in the United States*, Philadelphia: Temple University Press, 1976.

Kahn, Alfred, *Social Policy and Social Services*, N.Y.: Random House, 1973.

————— , *Theory and Practice of Social Planning*, N.Y.: Russell Sage, 1969.

Kane, F.J., et. al., "Emotional Reactions in Abortion Service Personnel," *Archives of General Psychiatry* (March, 1973).

Katz, Michael, *The Irony of Early School Reform*, Cambridge, Mass: Harvard University Press, 1968.

Kenniston, Kenneth, "How Community Mental Health Stamped out the Riots (1968–78)," *Transaction* (July–August, 1968).

Kibel, Howard D., "Staff Reactions to Abortion," *Obstetrics and Gynecology*, 39 (1972): 128–133.

Kitsuse, John and Malcolm Spector, "Toward a Sociology of Social Problems," *Social Problems* (Spring, 1973).

Kraft, Ivor, "Headstart to What?," *The Nation* (September 5, 1966).

Lasch, Christopher, *Haven in a Heartless World: The Family Besieged*, N.Y.: Basic Books, 1977.

Maines, David, "Social Organization and Social Structure in Symbolic Interactionist Thought," *Annual Rev. of Sociology*, 1977.

Meltzer, Bernard, et al., *Symbolic Interactionism: Genesis, Varieties and Criticism*, London: Routledge and Kegan Paul, Ltd., 1975.

Parsons, Talcott, *The Social System*, Glencoe, Ill.: The Free Press, 1951.

Planned Parenthood, "Recommended Standards for Abortion Counselling," N.Y., 1976.

Rein, Martin, *Social Policy*, New York: Random House, 1970.

————— , "The Social Service Crisis," *Transaction* (May, 1964).

Remsberg, Charles and Bonnie, "Second Thoughts on Abortion," *Good Housekeeping* (March, 1976).

Spector, Malcolm and John Kitsuse, *Constructing Social Problems*, Menlo Park, CA: Cummings, 1977.

————— , "Social Problems: A Reformulation," *Social Problems* (Fall, 1973).

Strauss, Anselm et al., *Psychiatric Ideologies and Institutions*. N.Y.: Free Press, 1964.

Wilensky, Harold and Charles Lebeaux, *Industrial Society and Social Welfare*, N.Y.: Russell Sage, 1958.

LABELING THEORY AND MENTAL DISORDER:

A SYNTHESIS OF PSYCHIATRIC AND SOCIAL PERSPECTIVES*

William C. Cockerham, UNIVERSITY OF ILLINOIS

For over 25 years, labeling theory has been a major sociological approach to the study of deviant behavior. Moreover, according to Cole's (1975) analysis of citations of deviance research published between 1950–1973 by four leading American sociology journals, labeling theory has emerged as the dominant theoretical orentation toward deviance.[1] Yet, as evidenced by the so-called "Gove-Scheff controversy" (See Gove, 1970a, 1970b, 1975a, 1975b, 1976; Clancy and Gove, 1974; Gove and Howell, 1974; Scheff, 1970, 1974, 1975a, 1975b) and several other critiques (for reviews, see Gove, 1975a; Conover, 1976; also see Gibbs, 1966, 1971; Bordua, 1967; Gove, 1970a, 1976; Davis, 1972; Manning, 1973), the utility of labeling theory for accounting for deviant behavior in general and mental disorder in particular has been seriously questioned.

Studies in Symbolic Interaction—Volume 2, 1979, pages 257–280

In rebuttal, proponents of labeling theory have pointed out that some of the criticism has imputed ideas to them which they themselves have not formulated, thus prompting Lemert (1976:244) to observe that "labeling theory seems to be largely an invention of its critics." Becker (1973) has explained that labeling theory should not be considered the sole explanation for what deviants actually do, and Schur (1969, 1971) has argued that labeling theory is not a self-contained theory but should be regarded in relation to other theories. Scheff (1974) claims that the weight of the evidence is clearly on the side of the labeling perspective.

Nevertheless, some critics have maintained that labeling theory is exhausted (Manning, 1973) and should be either abandoned or modified (Kirk, 1974; Gove, 1975a). It is the purpose of this paper, accordingly, to investigate the major criticisms of labeling theory as they pertain to mental disorder, and suggest a synthesis of sociological and psychiatric perspectives where appropriate. The discussion will be centered around schizophrenia, the most commonly diagnosed mental disorder.

LABELING THEORY REVISITED

The central position of labeling theory is that social groups create deviance through making rules whose infraction constitutes deviance (see Lemert, 1951; Erikson, 1962; Becker, 1973; Lindesmith, Strauss and Denzin, 1978). Both deviant behavior and the deviant person become "deviant" because they are labeled as such by the social audience who is witness to the rule-breaking behavior. However, labeling theory holds that responses to deviance are not always uniform; instead, such responses can be problematic in that what is regarded as deviant by one person or social group may not be so regarded by other persons or social groups. Moreover, as Becker (1973) observes, responses to deviance can vary according to when the act is committed, who commits the acts, who feels harmed by it, and so forth. Thus, deviance is not a quality of the act a person commits, but is a consequence of the responses of others to that act.

Labeling Theory and Mental Disorder: Scheff's Position

When mental disorder is considered, however, mere rule-breaking in Western society is not in itself enough to cause others to respond to the rule breaker as mentally ill. Scheff (1966) has, therefore, added the notion of residual rule-breaking to the labeling approach to mental disorder. Residual rule-breaking is based upon the notion that most social conventions are fairly clear and understood; yet there is a residual area of social convention which is assumed to be so natural that it is part of "human nature." These residual conventions include such behaviors as looking at the person you are talking to or responding to someone who calls your name. To violate these residual conventions goes beyond just violating norms; it involves acting "unnatural." In certain circumstances, the basis of this unnatural behavior may be mental illness.

If a person is labeled "mentally ill" as a result of residual rule-breaking and society responds toward that person in accordance with that particular label, Scheff contends that a deviant has been created by society. This rule-breaker becomes constrained by others to behave as a crazy person in conformity to the prevailing stereotype learned in childhood of how crazy persons are supposed to act. While Scheff does not specify what this stereotype is, he implies that it consists of acting bizarre or violent or some combination thereof. The person actually labeled "mentally ill" is rewarded, claims Scheff, for accepting the label (i.e., regarded as a "good" patient), or punished if he or she attempts to return to a normal role (i.e., rejected by others, removed from that role, pressured to admit to being mentally ill).

Scheff further suggests that virtually everyone at some time engages in behavior that might be construed as mental illness. But once these behaviors become full public knowledge, and if they continue, it is likely that the individual in question will be referred to some authority, such as a psychiatrist, and perhaps eventually the court. Whether this happens, however, will depend upon the nature of the act committed, the amount of tolerance for the act, the status and power of the rule-breaker, and the availability of alternative explanations for the act which will deny ("normalize") the rule-breaking by ignoring or rationalizing it. If denial fails and a person enters a community's formal system of social control for mental disorder, Scheff believes it is probable that the person will be processed and sent to a mental institution largely as a matter of routine. When this occurs, that person "is launched on a career of 'chronic' mental illness,"that is, the person is irreparably stigmatized as a mental patient.

From his approach to mental disorder, Scheff (1975a:9–10; also see Scheff, 1966:31–54) has derived a series of nine hypotheses which he believes demonstrate the applicability of labeling theory for mental illness. These hypotheses are:

1. Residual rule-breaking arises from fundamentally diverse sources (that is, organic, psychological, situations of stress, volitional acts of innovation or defiance).
2. Relative to the rate of treated mental illness, the rate of unrecorded residual rule-breaking is extremely high.
3. Most residual rule-breaking is "denied" and is of transitory significance.
4. Stereotyped imagery of mental disorder is learned in early childhood.
5. The stereotypes of insanity are continually reaffirmed, inadvertently, in ordinary social interaction.
6. Labeled deviants may be rewarded for playing the stereotyped deviant role.

7. Labeled deviants are punished when they attempt to return to conventional rules.
8. In the crisis occurring when a residual rule-breaker is publicly labeled, the deviant is highly suggestible and may accept the label.
9. Among residual rule-breakers, labeling is the single most important cause of careers of residual deviance.

Labeling Theory and Mental Disorder: Gove's Position

Gove has been the leading critic of Scheff and the labeling approach to mental illness (for a summary, see Gove, 1975a). For example, Scheff (1966:129) has stated that "the status of the mental patient is more often an ascribed status, with conditions for status entry and exit external to the patient, than an achieved status with conditions for status entry dependent upon the patient's own behavior." Gove takes this statement and uses it to emphasize that Scheff views mental disorder as being primarily dependent on conditions external to the individual. These "conditions," of course, are the responses of others who interpret and define the behavior they observe; they base their actions toward the person in question upon the label which results from their interpretation. Thus, Gove (1975a:67) states: "The labeling perspective does not view the deviant as someone who is suffering from an intrapersonal disorder, but instead as someone who, through a set of circumstances, becomes publicly labeled a deviant and who is forced by societal reaction into a deviant role." Gove goes on to cite research involving genetic propensities toward mental illness, comparisons of psychiatric symptoms between mental patients and nonpatients, and the effects of recent experiences of critical life events to suggest that those who become labeled as mentally ill are different from those not so labeled in a manner inconsistent with the labeling perspective (Gove, 1975a:48–51).

However, Gove's major point of attack against labeling theory is not on the inherent nature of mental disorder. Instead, Gove (1976) directs his criticism primarily toward two issues: (1) the social characteristics of those labeled and (2) the consequences of being labeled.

The strongest argument against labeling theory, in Gove's view, concerns the issue of *who* is most likely to be hospitalized. Labeling theory suggests that it is the individual who is marginal (and least likely to be able to resist labeling) to society who is most likely to be committed to a mental hospital. Gove (1975a:67) argues, in contrast, that "it is the individuals with the most resources who are the most likely to enter the role of the mentally ill," and he feels this is "perhaps the most telling evidence" against Scheff. He bases this argument on research which indicates that lower class persons are slower to recognize psychiatric symptoms (Hollingshead and Redlich, 1958; Myers and Roberts, 1959), that lower class persons tend to delay seeking psychiatric treatment (Hollingshead and Redlich, 1958; Gove and Howell,

1974), and that middle class families are less willing to tolerate mental disorder among family members (Freeman and Simmons, 1959).

The second major argument advanced by Gove questions whether labeling results in being accorded a deviant status on a more or less permanent basis, subsequently stabilizing the deviance. Gove argues (1) that stabilized deviant behavior occurs prior to labeling, (2) that most forms of deviance do not persist after labeling, and (3) that labeling results in a decrease rather than an increase in the amount of deviant behavior because of society's active intervention to treat the deviance (Gove, 1976:225–226). Furthermore, Gove (1975a:68) claims that in most cases the stigma of being a former mental patient does not appear to greatly affect that person's performance in the community. He supports this contention by citing research showing improved relationships with spouses (Sampson et al., 1961; Gove and Fain, 1973), increased employment (Gove and Fain, 1973), and the feeling among ex-mental patients that stigma will pass with time (Cumming and Cumming, 1965; Gove and Fain, 1973). In citing his own data, Gove (Gove and Fain, 1973:500) states that it was his impression, based upon interviews with former patients, that "a substantial minority of the ex-patients were initially somewhat embarrassed and uncomfortable about having been in a mental hospital, but they did not perceive the stigma of hospitalization as having any serious or long-term effects."

Scheff's Reply to Gove

If we reduce Gove's argument to its central points, we find that he does not directly attack Scheff's nine hypotheses pertaining to labeling theory and mental illness. Instead, Gove's objections appear to stem largely from findings contained in studies based upon the labeling perspective. Thus, Gove's objections can be summarized as follows: (1) those persons on the margin of society are not necessarily those most readily labeled as mentally ill, (2) being labeled as mentally ill does not result in stigma of a lasting nature, and (3) persons who are mentally ill have an inherent mental condition quite apart from how they are labeled.

In reply, Scheff (1974, 1975a, 1975b) points out that a majority of studies (13 out of 18) explicitly relating to labeling theory and incorporating systematic research methods provide supportive evidence for his views over the arguments advanced by Gove. Research by Scheff (1964), Wilde (1968), Wenger and Fletcher (1969), Linsky (1970a, 1970b), Rushing (1971), and Greenley (1972), among others, showed that the social characteristics of patients determined their eventual fate independent of their psychiatric condition. Especially noteworthy was the work of Linsky and Rushing who utilized an index measuring the ratio of involuntary to voluntary hospital admissions; a common finding in both studies was the strong relationship between powerlessness and commitment. As for the consequences of being labeled mentally ill, Scheff did not address this point in his 1974 article, bu research by Phillips (1963) and Whatley (1959) clearly indicates the powerfu effects of stigma upon the lives of former mental patients.

Gove's argument, however, is also weakened by the fact that some of hi work (Gove and Tudor, 1973; Gove and Howell, 1974) has been called int question for using limited and misleading statistics, failing to deal witl trends over time, and omitting data for certain categories of menta problems, such as personality disorders (see Dohrenwend and Dohrenwend 1976). Two other particularly significant criticisms of Gove's work i general are that he fails to adequately distinquish between voluntary an involuntary hospital admissions (Krohn and Akers, 1977) and that h misrepresents the work of labeling theorists (Scheff, 1974, 1975a, 1975b Lemert, 1976). Lemert (1976:244–245), for example, states:

> When I first read Scheff's demurrer that Gove misrepresented his writings, I thought that he—Scheff—was being normally testy about his cherished ideas or showing some mild academic paranoia (Scheff, 1974). My impression changed when in a recent paper Gove stated that in my 1951 book I said: "Those labeled as mentally ill do not differ markedly from those who are not labeled and it is those on the margin of society who are most readily labeled" (Lemert, 1951). Curious after 24 years to see again what I said, I reread the designated pages not once but four times. I found no such statements in them.[2]

Labeling Theory and Mental Disorder: An Assessment

At present, the Gove-Scheff controversy is unresolved. Evidence exist which supports both sides. Scheff claims his position is more secure in view of the findings rendered by a majority of studies, but this is a questionabl assumption, as additional research is forthcoming. For instance, Clauser and Huffine (1975:415) have recently observed that if a former menta patient manages to function well on the job and in the family, feelings o stigma will diminish. Other work, like that of Olmsted and Durham (1976) suggests that lay persons tend to accept the authoritative judgement o "experts" that an ex-mental patient has recovered. Thus, it can be arguec that the findings concerning the consequences of labeling for menta patients are inconclusive.

As for the significance of the social characteristics of mental patients a extrapsychiatric variables intervening on psychiatric conditions, the liter ature strongly supports Scheff. The recent review of the literature by Krohn and Akers (1977) helps to place this issue into perspective. Although some of the studies reviewed contain methodological and conceptual inade quacies, Krohn and Akers were able to construct a general conclusion tha extrapsychiatric factors were more significant than psychiatric factors (defined as the nature and severity of the disorder) in determining menta hospital admissions and discharges of both a voluntary and involuntary ype. This finding clearly runs counter to Gove's position, which emphasizes he importance of psychiatric factors. Krohn and Akers found that extrapsychiatric variables—specifically, those of social class, family influence, marital status, legal status, and challenges to psychiatric decisions—were strongly related to admitting and discharging mental patients, even when judgments about the nature and severity of the mental disorder itself were controlled.[3]

Not only are Gove's views not substantiated, but it appears that he is emphasizing the wrong criticisms. If Gove were correct, that it is those persons with the greatest resources who are the most likely to be hospitalized, the direction of labeling theory would be in question rather than a negation of the existence of the labeling process. And, furthermore, if Gove were correct that mental patients are not irreparably stigmatized, that does not detract from findings pertaining to the powerful effects of labeling in temporary circumstances (cf., Rosenhan, 1973). While the social characteristics of those labeled and the consequences of being labeled are important issues to be clarified, the primary channel of inquiry should be to investigate a more fundamental issue, which is that of the inherent nature of mental disorder itself. Although Gove raised this issue, he has not given it the focus t deserves. Yet it is upon this point that most mental health professionals disagree with labeling theory (Kendell, 1975).

For example, Krohn and Akers also note that existing research shows that individuals are not randomly or capriciously singled out and labeled mentally ill, even though psychiatric diagnoses and categories may sometimes be vague and inconsistent. Regardless of the theory involved, inferences of mental disorder are made from verbal and nonverbal behavior. These behavioral cues indicate what must be done about hospitalization or release in the first place. They serve as indicators of the ability of the person in question to affect or react to the situation. A schizophrenic person may attempt to carefully select ambiguous cues which later may be denied or provided alternative explanations. This process may nevertheless lead the recipient to question the candor or genuineness of the cues. Thus, in trying to establish an ambiguous situation, the schizophrenic person may promote definitions of abnormality about himself or herself—a process Bateson (1956) terms as the "double-bind." Therefore, what seems apparent is that prior to the onset of labeling, there exists a troubled mind independent of the labeling process. Once the individual who possesses that troubled mind expresses his or her internal state to others, extrapsychiatric factors then intervene to influence the external responses and decisions made about the individual in question.

This situation represents the single most important weakness in the application of labeling theory to mental disorder. *Labeling theory does not explain what actually causes mental disorder other than societal reaction to residual rule-breaking, nor does it explain why certain people become mentally ill and others do not in the same social circumstances.* If we return to Scheff's nine hypotheses about labeling theory and mental illness, we find that hypothesis 1 takes note of the fact that residual rule-breaking arises from diverse sources, which include organic and psychological factors. But hypothesis 9 states that *labeling is the single most important cause of careers of residual deviance.* And it is upon this latter hypothesis that the merit of labeling theory for explaining mental disorder is adversely affected. Labeling does not cause careers of residual deviance; residual deviance brings about labeling.

THE ETIOLOGY OF SCHIZOPHRENIA

Space precludes anything more than a cursory discussion of the genetic, biochemical, and psychological aspects of mental disorder, but if we briefly consider only some of the evidence about schizophrenia—the most commonly diagnosed disorder and what Scheff (1975a:8) calls the "residue of residues"—we will find points of relevance for our discussion. The American Psychiatric Association's *Diagnostic and Statistical Manual of Mental Disorders* (DSM-II) defines schizophrenia as a psychosis characterized by disturbances in mood, thinking, and behavior, manifested by distortions of reality, particularly delusions and hallucinations. The impaired psychological functioning of a schizophrenic person results in an inability to handle personal stress and to cope with everyday problems.

Theories of Schizophrenia

Although there is no one theory adequately explaining the cause of schizophrenia, some general statements can be made (for a review, see Weiner, 1975). First of all, there is increasing evidence, particularly from studies of concordance rates for schizophrenia in monozygotic and dizygotic twins reared in different environments, which shows that a general tendency or predisposition toward schizophrenia is inherited (Rosenthal, 1971; Kaplan, 1972; Kety, 1975; Weiner, 1975). While the specific genetic factors important in the transmission of schizophrenic tendencies have not been identified nor are fully understood at present, the existing data do provide a partial explanation of why certain people appear to be prone to schizophrenia and why schizophrenia tends to be prevalent in certain families and not in others.

Other approaches emphasizing developmental (psychoanalytic), psychophysiological (disturbances in psychological functioning, i.e., learning, perception, attention), environmental (especially family pathology), sociocultural (i.e., social class), physiological, and biochemical theories have, at present, failed to produce data as strong as that found in genetics in accounting for the cause of schizophrenia. In medicine, for example, much of the recent emphasis has been to focus upon the biochemistry of the central nervous system. One result is that a number of drugs derived from the phenothiazine and butyrophenone biochemical groups have been found effective in the treatment of schizophrenia. These drugs are thought to be able to block the action of dopamine, a neurotransmitter whose hyperactivity may be significant in the production of paranoid delusions and auditory hallucinations. While this approach in itself does not explain what causes schizophrenia, it may offer important clues. It may also be one of several possible genetic bases of the disorder (see Snyder, 1977). On the other hand, certain drugs may have certain effects on the brain, regardless of whether or not they play a role in causing a particular mental disorder. Biochemical theories of schizophrenia have yet to demonstrate a precise cause and effect relationship.

The strongest biologically based evidence remains in genetics, but genetic factors alone cannot fully explain why certain people become schizophrenic and others do not develop the disorder. While most investigators agree that twin and adoption studies show that genetic factors are important in the etiology of schizophrenia, they have not shown how significant genetic factors are in comparison to social environmental factors (see Clausen, 1968: Kohn, 1972; Dohrenwend, 1975; Townsend, 1978). According to Weiner (1975:887): "The most likely model of schizophrenic illness is that given a genetic predisposition, which may very likely be polygenic, stressful life events elicit schizophrenia." The notion, therefore, that environmental factors in the form of stressful life events act as a "trigger" for schizophrenia in genetically susceptible persons is a highly promising line of inquiry in producing an explanation for the onset of schizophrenia.

Schizophrenia and Stress

Several studies (cf., Rogler and Hollingshead, 1965; Brown and Birley, 1968; Pollin, 1972; Brenner, 1973; Hudgens, 1974; Paykel, 1974) have provided evidence that acute episodes of schizophrenia may follow the experience of stressful life situations. Rogler and Hollingshead (1965) compared a matched set of 20 "well" families to 20 "sick" families (defined as having either the husband or the wife or both spouses diagnosed as schizophrenic) of lower class status in Puerto Rico. Based upon the recall of life events by the subjects and involving no genetic analysis, it was found that there were no significant differences in the family lives of the normals and the schizophrenics during childhood and adolescence. All of the subjects were exposed to the same conditions of poverty, family instability, and lower class socialization. There was also a lack of difference in their respective adult lives, except that for those persons who became schizophrenic, there was a recent and discernible period, *prior to the appearance of overt symptomatology,* where they were engulfed by a series of insoluble and mutually reinforcing problems. Schizophrenia thus seemed to originate from being placed in an intolerable dilemma brought on by stressful life events.

Brown and Birley (1968) studied a group of 50 schizophrenic patients suffering from either an onset or relapse of schizophrenia compared to control group of 377 normal persons. The major difference between the two groups was that 60 percent of the mental patients, as opposed to 19 percent of the control group, experienced at least one significant change in their lives during the three weeks prior to the study. This finding could not be explained away by the argument that mental patients tend to cause more trouble than normal people, since the relationship between stressful experiences and being a mental patient also held for those experiences which the patients had no control over and therefore were unable to affect the outcome.

We find further evidence when we consider the work of Brenner (1973). Brenner compared rates of first admissions to state mental hospitals to cycles of economic activity in New York from 1914 to 1967. The data supported his hypothesis that mental hospitalization increases during economic downturns and decreases during upturns. Regardless of the number and combination of factors that predispose a person toward mental illness, the question Brenner attempted to answer was why does mental disorder appear *when* it does. He believed that an inability to fulfill one's social role frequently results from downward shifts in economic activity and that the stress resulting from this experience is a precipitating factor in the appearance of mental illness. By finding significantly higher rates of mental hospital admissions during economic recessions and depressions, he suggested that a substantial proportion of all stress factors that precipitate mental disorder is economic in origin. Schizophrenia was included among those disorders which matched economic downturns more sharply than other diagnostic categories.

Schizophrenia and Problems in the Interpretation of Symptoms

The impact of stressful life events upon the etiology of schizophrenia is not surprising in view of the growing literature on stress and health problems in general (see Dohrenwend and Dohrenwend, 1974; Cockerham 1978). What is indicated here for our discussion is not only the significance of stress as a causal factor in schizophrenia, but also that these events *precede* the appearance of symptoms of schizophrenia. And it is the overt expression of symptoms which provide the basis upon which an individual is labeled. While the exact cause or causes of schizophrenia is/are unknown and most likely involves the complex interaction of a combination of factors, psychological and physiological as well as genetic and social, the point to be made is that labeling does not cause careers of residual deviance the case of mental disorder. The acting out of symptoms is what is labeled y others as mental illness; labeling, of itself, does not constitute the cause. However, this situation has not been overlooked by Scheff. In discussing is views, Scheff (1975a:8–9) has stated:

> These remarks should not be taken to suggest that there is no internal experience associated with "symptomatic" behavior; the individual with symptoms *does* experience distress and suffering, or under some conditions, exhilaration and freedom. The point is, however, that public, consensual "knowledge" of mental illness is based, by and large, on knowledge not of these internal states but of their overt manifestations. When a person runs down the street naked and screaming, lay and professional diagnosticians alike assume the existence of mental illness within that person—even though they have not investigated his internal state. Mental health procedure and conceptual apparatus of the medical model posit internal states, but the events actually observed are external.

True, the events observed are external, but the events in which symptoms re demonstrated are not the cause of the disorder; they are the conse-uences. Consider, for example, the definition of mental disorder developed y Spitzer. Spitzer (Spitzer and Wilson, 1975:829) defines mental disorder as ollows: (1) it is a condition that is primarily psychological and involves lterations in behavior, including changes in physiological functioning if the hanges can be explained by psychological concepts, such as personality, otivation, and conflict; (2) it is a condition which, in its "full-blown" state, regularly and intrinsically associated with subjective stress, generalized npairment in social functioning, and also includes voluntary behavior the erson would like to stop because it is associated with threats to physical ealth; and (3) it is a condition distinct from other conditions and responds treatment.

Of the three criteria described by Spitzer, the first separates psychiatric om nonpsychiatric conditions; that is, it clearly defines mental disorder as problem of the mind and recognizes that it may have an accompanying hysiological component. The second criterion specifies that the disorder ay be recognizable only in a later stage of its development ("full-blown"), nd requires that its identification depend upon consistent symptomatology "regularly associated with"). *Spitzer also maintains that the disorder must rise from an inherent condition and not from the manner in which society eacts to the condition.* He adds that the impairment in functioning not be mited to a single form, such as not being able to have a sexual relationship vith a member of the opposite sex, but must include an inability to function n several social contexts ("generalized impairment in social functioning"). riterion two also includes "voluntary behavior," such as compulsive eating nd smoking as a form of mental disorder if it threatens one's health. The hird criterion places the definition within the confines of the medical model s a distinct condition that is treatable.

This definition of mental disorder obviously clashes with Scheff's per-pective. Scheff maintains that the medical model refers to a culture-free process that is independent of the public order. A case of pneumonia or syphilis, he argues, is pretty much the same in New York or New Caledonia. Mental disorder, conversely, is seen by Scheff as not being culture-free. Instead, it is culture-bound in that it arises from symptoms that are offenses against implicit understandings of particular cultures. Thus, each society or social group should be able, if Scheff is to be taken literally, to arbitraril define mental disorder in its own distinct manner according to its own unique cultural views.

Therefore, as Murphy (1976) points out, information about cultures that are markedly different from Western society should support the theory. They would be expected to have their own unique cultural interpretation of insanity. This was not the case in Murphy's research with Eskimos in Alaska and Yoruba tribesmen in Nigeria. Both groups had explicit labels for insanity that described mentally disturbed behavior as emanating from the mind of an individual. Although influenced by cultural beliefs, Murphy found a consistent pattern, composed of hallucinations, delusions, disorientations, and behavioral abnormalities pertaining to what is commonly recognized in Western culture as schizophrenia, that appeared to identify the idea of "losing one's mind." Murphy (1976:1027) concluded: "Rather than being simply violations of the social norms of particular groups, as labeling theory suggests, symptoms of mental illness are manifestations of a type of affliction shared by virtually all mankind." Other research supports the contention that while mental disorders are likely to carry some local interpretation, there are no essential differences in mental conditions resembling schizophrenia between Western and non-Western cultures (Kaplan and Johnson, 1964; Schmidt, 1964; Ciba Foundation Symposium, 1965; Kiev, 1972). In every society, Western clinical categories of schizophrenia and effective psychoses are recognized and considered aberrant (Townsend, 1978:68). Kendell (1975:22–23) puts it this way:

> For the foreseeable future, the usefulness of the concept of schizophrenia is amply established by the universal occurrence of the behavioral and experiental anomalies to which the term refers, irrespective of differences in language and culture; by the biological disadvantage associated with these anomalies, again irrespective of language and culture; by the evidence that these abnormalities are, at least in part, transmitted genetically; and by the influence on them of drugs which lack analogous effects on other people.

This is not to say, however, that the term "schizophrenia" refers to an obdurate clinical or social reality. Since there is no demonstrable organic pathology, even experts of similar cultural backgrounds disagree at times about its symptoms. A study often cited in this regard is that of Kendell et al. (1971), who showed videotaped interviews of eight mental patients to audiences of approximately 200 American and British psychiatrists. There was substantial diagnostic agreement on three of the patients who exhibited classical textbook symptoms of schizophrenia and general agreement about schizophrenia on three other patients with schizophrenic and affective symptoms. For the other two patients, there was serious disagreement. On one of these latter patients, 69% of the Americans diagnosed schizophrenia compared to only 2% of the British psychiatrists who diagnosed a neurosis or personality disorder. Additional comparisons between American, British, and Canadian psychiatrists and between American psychiatrists in New York, Illinois, and California likewise found some levels of disagreement (Sharpe et al., 1974; also see Kendell, 1975). American psychiatrists, especially those in New York, generally appeared to be more prone to diagnosing schizophrenia. In attempting to account for such diagnostic differences, Kendell (1975) suggests that American and British psychiatrists may ascribe different meanings to the same diagnostic stereotypes, may require different degrees of correspondence between symptoms and stereotypes or may perceive abnormalities differently while observing the same behavior.

Therefore, as Townsend (1978) points out, although schizophrenia and the other major psychoses are found universally, their diagnosis is not always clear-cut or simple. While the general characteristics of schizophrenia may be culture-free, the content of those characteristics is culture-bound and subject to variance in interpretation. Thus, Scheff is only partially correct when he argues that schizophrenia is culture-bound. The general characteristics of schizophrenia (i.e., withdrawal from reality, delusions, hallucinations) are pretty much the same in New York or in New Caledonia, but the *content* of schizophrenic delusions, hallucinations, and distortions of reality may differ somewhat in New York and in New Caledonia and be perceived differently by some witnesses as well. What schizophrenia represents is a general and abstract set of agreed-upon understandings and clinical assumptions that float from New York to New Caledonia and is subject to occasional modification, depending upon the judgment, training and experience of those involved.

LABELING THEORY AND MENTAL DISORDER: A REFORMATION

As noted, the basic weakness in labeling theory as it applies to mental disorder is that it does not explain the cause of mental disorder other than societal reaction to residual rule-breaking, nor does it explain why certain people become mentally ill and others do not in the same social circumstances. These deficiencies in the theory stem from a failure to adequately consider nonsocial factors in mental disorder, a criticism which Scheff may have anticipated. For Scheff (1975b) states that while he had hoped that his

work might have some effect on psychiatry, its principal aim was to sugges
that there are processes which are distinctly social that are involved i
madness and that these processes can be studied in their own right. Schef
(1975b:257) says:

> Like suicide, madness occurs in a social context. As I have suggested in everything I
> have ever written about madness, the purpose of a purely sociological model is not to
> replace the psychiatric perspective, but to serve as a corrective to the exclusive emphasis
> of the medical model on the isolated individual. Although in my recent work I have
> become interested in integrating individual processes, such as the dynamics of emotion,
> with collective processes, I believe that as long as the prevailing psychiatric and
> psychological views are atomistic, we will also need purely social models of behavior to
> help establish a balanced view of the real world.

What is needed, accordingly, to strengthen labeling theory is to integrat
psychiatric factors into the concept to balance its sociological one-sidednes
(a similar argument can be made for balancing the one-sidedness of medica
and psychological models). With that view in mind, let us return to Scheff'
nine hypotheses regarding the applicability of labeling theory to menta
disorder.

1. *Residual rule-breaking arises from fundamentally diverse sources (tha
is, organic, psychological, situations of stress, violitional acts of innovation o
defiance).* For schizophrenia, strong evidence indicates that its onset i
related to stressful life events and that a genetic component is likely to b
involved for some persons. Other sociocultural, biochemical, psychophysiological, and environmental factors may be involved in its etiology
Similar arguments can also be advanced for many other types of menta
disorders (see Freedman et al., 1975). Yet all of this assumes that menta
disorder is a form of residual rule-breaking and Scheff never really defines
in any precise fashion what he means by residual rules. He assumes there i
such a thing, but does not specify what it is nor how it differs in regard to
mental illness, law violations, or the expression of physical symptoms—al
of which might be regarded as unnatural. More clarification is needed on
what constitutes residual rule-breaking.

2. *Relative to the rate of treated mental illness, the rate of unrecorde
residual rule-breaking is extremely high.* The argument can be made that
practically everyone, at some time or another, acts "crazy" (Goffman,
1971). Furthermore, while studies of the "true" prevalence (both treated
cases and untreated cases in the general population) of schizophrenia and
other mental disorders have been subjected to extensive methodologicaℓ
difficulties, Dohrenwend (1975) has noted that in over 80 such investigations conducted throughout the world since 1900, a consistent result has
been that the greatest number of "cases" have not been in treatment. Thus,
if mental disorder is a form of residual rule-breaking, it may be that much
of it is unrecorded and presumably substantial.

3. *Most residual rule-breaking is "denied" and is of transitory significance.*
ince rates of "true" prevalence suggest that most cases of mental disorder
re untreated, it appears that many such persons are able to deny their
esidual rule-breaking through remedial action. Remedial action constitutes
n effort to modify what has happened and avoid denunciation by others
see Garfinkel, 1956, on degradation ceremonies). It consists of accounts
apologies, excuses, or justifications) rendered by the rule-breaker to explain
he unanticipated or untoward behavior and to help restore order and
ationality to a disrupted scene (see Scott and Lyman, 1968). Successful
emedial action would allow the deviance to remain primary rather than
econdary as conceptualized by Lemert (1951).

4. *Stereotyped imagery of mental disorder is learned in early childhood.*
Vhile recognizing that no substantiating studies exist in this area, Scheff
aintains that the literal meaning of "crazy" is grasped by children at least
y the early years of elementary school. The grossest stereotype resulting
rom childhood, claims Scheff, is the notion of the so-called "boogie man."
)pie and Opie's (1969) study of children's games does describe "daring"
ames (like knocking on the door of a house in which a "crazy" person
ives) or "ghost" games which contain some idea of craziness. Still, this
ypothesis is in need of further study and is an unproven assumption at best.

5. *The stereotypes of insanity are continually reaffirmed, inadvertently, in
rdinary social interaction.* Assuming that hypothesis 4 is sound, Scheff
uggests that stereotypes of insanity are continually reinforced in the mass
nedia and during ordinary conversation (especially slang references:
'flipped," "screwy," "screwball," "loony," "nut," "off the deep end,"
'batty," "off your rocker" and so forth. Since *everyone* in society, according
o Scheff's (1966:80) analysis, learns the symptoms of mental disorder, this
magery is available to residual rule breakers to guide their behavior and
inderstand their experience.

Unfortunately, Scheff does not define what stereotypes pertain to mental
llness, nor what psychiatric symptoms are structured by these stereotypes.
Townsend (1975), in a study of American and German high school students,
nental patients and mental hospital staffs, has pointed out that a coherent
`olk-model of mental illness has not been demonstrated among urban
populations. Moreover, Townsend found that the two most common
stereotypes suggested by Scheff's discussion (uncontrolled violence and
delusional personalities) did not effectively shape symptoms of mental
patients (nor were these stereotypes reinforced by mental hospital staffs).
Townsend did find, however, that certain cultural conceptions of mental
disorder existed and that these did apparently influence patient perceptions
and coping tactics. Thus, Scheff's fifth hypothesis is also in need of
clarification.

6. *Labeled deviants may be rewarded for playing the stereotyped deviant
role.* Even though the stereotyped deviant role is not clearly defined, some

studies of mental patients suggest that patients are initially encouraged and rewarded for conforming to the hospital staff's concept of being mentally ill The "good" patient is expected to recognize that he or she is mentally ill and needs treatment (cf., Goffman, 1961; Denzin, 1968). The reward the patient receives is positive attitudes and feedback from therapists and other staff members; it is not likely to be mental and physical comfort, as the patient is still subjected to therapy in the form of drugs, electric shock treatment, and so forth.

7. *Labeled deviants are punished when they attempt to return to conventional roles.* This hypothesis refers to the stigma that is ascribed to mental patients when they attempt to resume normal roles. As previously discussed, certain studies indicate that these persons are more or less permanently stigmatized and other research studies disagree. Hence, the evidence is inconclusive. It would appear that the ease of return to conventional roles would be contingent on the relational networks that surround the person (see Miller, 1971). Scheff's model does not account for active, interpretative selves nor for networks of significant others, anchored others (representative of normality or insanity), and collusive others (as communities of patients or normals). In addition, while labeling theory is supposed to explain who and how one gets labeled, it seems logical that it should be able to explain who and how one gets unlabeled. Labeling theory does not do this; it assumes the label "sticks" and this may be false.

8. *In the crisis occurring when a residual rule-breaker is publicly labeled, the deviant is highly suggestible and may accept the label.* Scheff suggests that when insane persons intitially begin to realize that they cannot control their actions or have sensed they have reached a "breaking point" in their efforts to sustain normality, they will seriously consider that they are mentally ill or will be likely to entertain suggestions to that end. This process of realization will be assisted by the person's knowledge of the stereotyped imagery available in his or her society of being insane. While research, such as that by Rogler and Hollingshead (1965), supports this hypothesis, it is not at all clear that this is a generalizable experience in view of the tendency of many mental patients to deny their condition (cf., Goffman, 1961; Townsend, 1976). In fact, Townsend (1976) argues that it may not be an empirically useful question to define exactly what a mental patient thinks of his or her condition at any one time, in that the patients themselves may not accurately interpret or report their feelings, admit their suspicions, or believe anything is wrong with them.

When Scheff's first eight hypotheses are considered, hypotheses 2 and 3 appear to be essentially correct and hypotheses 1, 4, 5, 6, 7, and 8 are in need of more extensive investigation. While questionable, and in need of clarification, there is some supporting evidence for these latter hypotheses. Obviously, additional data are needed to determine their accuracy. Hypothesis 9 *(Among residual rule-breakers, labeling is the single most important cause of careers of residual deviance)* is a different matter, however, and needs to be reformulated. The basic problem with hypothesis 9 is that labeling is a consequence rather than a cause of the overt expression of mental abnormality. Therefore, it is proposed that Scheff's ninth hypothesis be reformulated and replaced by two other hypotheses:

9. *Among residual rule-breakers labeled as mentally ill, the critical variable which distinguishes them from those not so labeled is their inability to cope normatively with stressful conditions. Mental disorder, thus, becomes a response to their environment.*

10. *Once labeled, the "career" of the residual rule-breaker is determined by factors external to the mental condition (i.e., social class, family influence, marital status, challenges to psychiatric decisions) with the nature and severity of the disorder providing relevant cues as to what action is appropriate under the circumstances.*

What this reformulation accomplishes is that it offers an explanation for the onset of insanity (arises from diverse sources, including exposure to stressful life events), and helps to explain why certain people become mentally disordered (through their inability, perhaps genetically predisposed, to contend with stressful circumstances) and others do not in the same social situations. Very clearly, an exception to this would be insanity induced by senility, injury, or a disease process like syphilis or cerebral arteriosclerosis. This reformulation thus helps to blend concepts prevalent among both psychiatrists and sociologists in regard to mental disorder in such a manner that the concepts can be shared and acted upon by both. Furthermore, it removes the major objection to labeling theory (which is not that, as suggested by Gove, of whom is most likely to be hospitalized in terms of their respective resources). The major objection is that labeling is the single most important cause of careers of residual deviance.

This reformulation still allows labeling theory (1) to recognize the problematic aspects of reaction to mental disorder, (2) to explain how people labeled as mentally ill may be forced to play a deviant role because of the manner in which other people respond to them, (3) to show how systems of social control are activated to deal with the mentally ill, and (4) to describe how control activities become institutionalized modes of response to the insane (cf., Kitsuse, 1975; Schur, 1975; Lemert, 1976). Because of its utility in accomplishing the above, labeling theory should not be abandoned, nor is its contribution to our understanding of human behavior exhausted. Instead, the reverse can be argued: that the full potential of the labeling perspective has yet to be drawn.

CONCLUDING COMMENTS: RESEARCH STRATEGIES

As a final note, some comment should be made concerning appropriate data collection strategies designed to empirically confirm the reformulation

proposed in this paper. While most of Scheff's hypotheses demand clarification through additional research, the focus of this paper has been upon
the reformulation of hypothesis nine, and this discussion of research
strategies will be limited to that particular hypothesis. There are numerous
research strategies, i.e., participant observation, surveys, interviews, life
histories, and so forth, but a review of past studies bearing on similar
subjects (especially that of the 1965 Rogler and Hollingshead study) and the
requirements of this particular research question suggest that the life history
method is an appropriate mode of data gathering for confirmation of the
proposed reformulation. The reader, however, is invited to consult Denzin
(1978) for a thorough discussion of the strengths and weaknesses of the
various forms of data collection and analysis. As for the research problem
at hand, the author proposes the following along the guidelines suggested by
Denzin (1978:229–248):

Step 1: Identify persons in the community who have experienced
schizophrenia. You may wish to consider ex-patients or current patients, or
some combination thereof, providing they have similar social characteristics
and experiences and are able to relate those experiences. If both ex-patients
and current patients are interviewed, you should account for any significant
differences between the two groups. The most likely source of finding such
persons would be a local community mental health center. The cooperation
of the mental health center is essential not only in identifying a relevant
population, but also in obtaining permission from that population to
participate in the study. The preferred approach would be to have the
community mental health center contact its patients to see of they will agree
to participate in the study. Lists of those agreeing to participate would then
be made available to the researcher. This list would be the basis upon which
a sample would be drawn. While such a sample might contain bias in that
it would include only those persons who agree (for whatever reason) to be
subjects and who therefore might not be typical, such a measure is necessary
to conform to regulations pertaining to Protection of Human Subjects.
Other sources of identifying potential respondents would be area mental
hospitals, psychiatric clinics, and private practices of psychiatrists and
clinical psychologists. Again, the rights of the patients would need to be
protected.

Step 2: Once an appropriate population is identified, the next step would
be to draw the sample by selecting individual patients on a random basis.
The usual method would be to employ a table of random numbers for this
purpose. If the patient population is small, the researcher might consider
including the entire population in the study. In order to fully assess the
labeling process, relational networks of significant others should also be
included in the sample.

Step 3: After having selected a sample of mentally ill persons for study,
a normal, nonschizophrenic sample should be selected for purposes of

omparison. The sample should be similar in numbers and social character-
tics (age, sex, education, income, occupation, social class, location of
esidence, etc.). Ideally, this sample would be selected randomly, but the
verall choice of the population to be studied would be guided by how well
s social characteristics matched the sample of mentally ill persons.

Step 4: While the sample is being identified and selected, the form of the
fe history method should be determined. Use of a questionnaire as a "life
istory guide" (Denzin, 1978:229) would allow the researcher to ask those
uestions considered relevant to the study and assist the respondent in
rganizing his or her replies in line with that same relevance. An important
imension of this questionnaire would be that of allowing the respondent to
xpress his or her own personal thoughts and social realities in relation to
ie questions asked. Thus, the format of the questionnaire should be
iggestive rather than forced-choice and allow for open-ended responses. In
rder to obtain such responses, the questionnaire should be administered in
face-to-face interview between the researcher and the respondent so that
romising lines of inquiry can be pursued in depth. The specific questions
1ould be designed to obtain responses relevant to the reformulation of
cheff's hypotheses. A pretest should be conducted to assess the clarity and
elevance of the questions and the amount of time needed to conduct the
iterviews.

Step 5: The questionnaire should be constructed in such a way as to
rovide for the reporting of the "natural history of events over time"
Denzin, 1978:231). The questionnaire would consist of five parts: 1) personal
nd social data pertaining to age, education, social class, etc.; 2) family
istory of mental disorder intended to assess possible genetic factors
particularly relevant would be experiences of twins or adopted children);
) record of objective events and experiences in the respondent's life;
) accounts of recent life events, paying particular attention to stressful
onditions as reported by the respondent; and 5) statements of the re-
pondent's subjective interpretation and assessment of objective experiences
nd events in the order in which they took place.

Step 6: Following interviews of both mentally ill and normal re-
pondents, interview other individuals who comprise the respondents' social
ietwork to gain their interpretation of events, to verify respondent reports,
nd to ascertain the effect of the labeling process. This is an especially
mportant step in regard to judging the accuracy of the reports and
tatements made by the mentally ill persons.

Step 7: Check all reports in terms of internal and external validity and
riticism. The use of analytic induction should free the study from any
|uestion of external validity, because analytic induction requires each
iegative case collected to force a revision of any emerging hypothesis. The
esearch should not end until all cases adequately support any general-
zations or can be explained as specific exceptions. As for questions of

internal validity, such as respondent mortality, bias, or maturation, the effect of general historical events taking place during the study or the effect of the interview situation need to be taken into account. For appropriate strategies in this regard, see Denzin, (1978:236–247).

Step 8: Resolve the validity and establish the priority of sources for the testing of the reformulated hypotheses (hypotheses 9 and 10).

Step 9: Test the hypotheses by seeing how well they fit the accounts rendered by the respondents, paying particular attention to significant differences between the comparison groups of normals and mentally ill. The presence or absence of significant differences would determine whether the hypotheses should be accepted or rejected.

Step 10: Search for negative cases which might affect the findings.

Step 11: Accept, reject, or modify the hypotheses upon the basis of the evidence.

Step 12: Write an initial draft of the life histories of all respondents and have the respondents verify their accuracy.

Step 13: Incorporate any verified inaccuracies into the data and modify conclusions if appropriate.

Step 14: State the findings by writing the final report.

If the life history method is employed in accordance with the above guidelines, it should provide data accounting for the progressive experiences of the respondents leading up to the onset of their mental disorders and the aftermath of that event. It will allow the researcher to delineate those stressful conditions in terms of the respondent's ability to handle them in a normative fashion, thus indicating both the nature of the stress and the strategies utilized by the respondent until such time as those strategies failed and mental disorder itself became the response to problems. By including information obtained from others in the relational network, the researcher will also be able to ascertain the effects of labeling upon the "career" of the respondent as a mentally ill person. Moverover, the life history method will allow the researcher to investigate the interplay of micro- and macro-forces as they impinge upon the lives of individuals and aggregates (for an example of this approach, see Denzin's 1977 study of the American liquor industry).

In sum, it is the position of this paper that labeling theory needs to account for psychiatric perspectives if it is to fully explain the world of the mentally ill as outlined by this discussion on schizophrenia. In doing so and in moving beyond the Gove-Scheff controversy, labeling theory holds the promise of being much more than a sensitizing concept. It can explain the entire status passage of the person from being normal to being mentally ill by recognizing genetic predispositions and possibly other physiological factors as contributing to the disorder when triggered by stressful life events. The expression of symptoms thus becomes the basis of labeling, and labeling then takes effect in the labeled person's life, influencing that person's experiences and interpretation of self.

FOOTNOTES

*The author would like to express his appreciation to Lawrence E. Cohen and Norman K. Denzin for their helpful comments on an earlier draft of this article.

1. The journals were the *American Journal of Sociology, American Sociological Review, Social Forces,* and *Social Problems.*

2. The pages in question are 392–398 (Lemert, 1951).

3. Even though Krohn and Akers find stronger evidence in favor of the labeling approach, they suggest that the behavior of both patients and those who provide treatment might best be viewed from the standpoint of a learning model (i.e., rewarding and punishing consequences shape behavior). Whether or not a learning model offers a better approach to explaining mental illness than that of labeling theory, however, has not been empirically demonstrated.

REFERENCES

Becker, Howard S., *Outsiders: Studies in the Sociology of Deviance,* 2nd ed., New York: Free Press, 1973.

Bordua, David J., "Recent trends: Deviant behavior and social control," *Annuals of the American Academy of Political and Social Science* 359 (January 1967): 149–163.

Brenner, M. Harvey, *Mental Illness and the Economy,* Cambridge, Massachusetts: Harvard University Press, 1973.

Brown, G.W. and J.L.T. Birley, "Crises and life changes and the onset of schizophrenia," *Journal of Health and Social Behavior* 9 (September 1968): 203–214.

Ciba Foundation Symposium, *Transcultural Psychiatry,* Boston: Little Brown, 1965.

Clancy, Kevin and Walter Gove, "Sex differences in mental illness: An analysis of response bias," *American Journal of Sociology* 80 (July 1974): 205–216.

Clausen, John A., "Interpersonal factors in the transmission of schizophrenia," pp. 251–263 in D. Rosenthal and S.S. Kety (eds.), *The Transmission of Schizophrenia,* London: Pergamon Press, 1968.

Clausen, John A. and Carol L. Huffine, "Sociocultural and social/psychological factors affecting social responses to mental disorder," *Journal of Health and Social Behavior* 16 (December 1975): 405–420.

Cockerham, William C., *Medical Sociology,* Englewood Cliffs, New Jersey: Prentice-Hall, Inc., 1978.

Cole, Stephen, "The growth of scientific knowledge: Theories of deviance as a case study," pp. 175–220 in L. Coser (ed.), *The Idea of Social Structure; Papers in Honor of Robert K. Merton,* New York: Harcourt, Brace and Jovanovich, 1975.

Conover, Patrick W., "A reassessment of labeling theory: A constructive response to criticism," pp. 228–243 in L. Coser and O. Larsen (eds.), *The Uses of Controversy in Sociology,* New York: Free Press, 1976.

Cumming, John and Elaine Cumming, "On the stigma of mental illness," *Community Mental Health Journal* 1 (Summer 1965): 135–143.

Davis, Nanette J., "Labeling theory in deviance research: A critique and reconsideration," *Sociological Quarterly* 13 (Autumn 1972): 447–474.

Denzin, Norman K., "The self-fulfilling prophecy and patient-therapist interaction," pp. 349–358 in S. Spitzer and N. Denzin (eds.), *The Mental Patient: Studies in the Sociology of Deviance,* New York: McGraw-Hill, 1968.

———, "Notes on the criminogenic hypothesis: A case study of the American liquor industry," *American Sociological Review* 42 (December 1977): 905–920.

———, *The Research Act,* 2nd Ed., New York: McGraw-Hill, 1978.

Dohrenwend, Barbara Snell, and Bruce P. Dohrenwend (eds.), *Stressful Life Events: Their Nature and Effects;* New York: John Wiley, 1974.

Dohrenwend, Bruce P., "Sociocultural and social psychological factors in the genesis of mental disorders," *Journal of Health and Social Behavior* 16 (December 1975): 365–392.

Dohrenwend, Bruce P. and Barbara Snell Dohrenwend, "Sex differences and psychiatric disorder," *American Journal of Sociology* 81 (May 1976): 1447–1454.

Erikson, Kai T., "Notes on the sociology of deviance, *Social Problems* 9 (Spring 1962): 307–314.

Freedman, Alfred M., Harold I. Kaplan, and Benjamin Sadock (eds.), *Comprehensive Textbook of Psychiatry*, Vols. 1 & 2, 2nd Ed., Baltimore: Williams & Wilkins, 1975.

Garfinkel, Harold, "Conditions of successful degradation ceremonies," *American Journal of Sociology* 61 (March 1956): 420–424.

Gibbs, Jack, "Conceptions of deviant behavior: The old and the new," *Pacific Sociological Review* 9 (Spring 1966): 9–14.

————— , "Issues in defining deviant behavior," pp. 39-68 in R.A. Scott and J.D. Douglas (ed.), *Theoretical Perspectives on Deviance*, New York: Basic Books, 1972.

Goffman, Erving, *Asylums*, New York: Doubleday, 1961.

————— , *Relations in Public*, New York: Basic Books, 1971.

Gove, Walter A., "Societal reaction as an explanation of mental illness: An evaluation," *American Sociological Review* 35 (October 1970a): 873–884.

————— , "Who is hospitalized: A critical review of some sociological studies of mental illness," *Journal of Health and Social Behavior* 11 (December 1970b): 294–304.

————— , "Labeling and mental illness: A critique," pp. 35–81 in W. Gove (ed.), *The Labeling of Deviance: Evaluating a Perspective*, New York: Halsted, 1975a.

————— , "The labeling theory of mental illness: A reply to Scheff," *American Sociological Review* 40 (April 1975b):242–248.

————— , "Deviant behavior, social intervention and labeling theory," pp. 219–227 in L. Coser and O. Larsen (eds.), *The Use of Controversy in Sociology*, New York: Free Press, 1976.

Gove, Walter A. and Terry Fain, "The stigma of mental hospitalization: An attempt to evaluate its consequences," *Archives of General Psychiatry* 28 (April 1973): 494–500

Gove, Walter A. and Patrick Howell, "Individual resources and mental hospitalization: A comparison and evaluation of the societal reaction and psychiatric perspectives," *American Sociological Review* 39 (February 1974): 86–100.

Gove, Walter A. and Jeannette F. Tudor, "Adult sex roles and mental illness," *American Journal of Sociology* 78 (January 1973): 812–835.

Hollingshead, August B. and Frederich C. Redlich, *Social Class and Mental Illness*, New York: John Wiley, 1958.

Hudgens, R.W., "Personal catastrophe and depression: A consideration of the subject with respect to mentally ill adolescents and a requiem for retrospective life-event studies," pp. 119–134 in B.S. Dohrenwend and B.P. Dohrenwend (eds.), *Stressful Life Events: Their Nature and Effects*, New York: John Wiley, 1974.

Kaplan, Arnold R., (ed.), *Genetic Factors in "Schizophrenia,"* Springfield, Illinois: Charles C. Thomas, 1972.

Kaplan, Bert and Dale Johnson, "The social meaning of Navaho psychopathology and psychotherapy," pp. 203–229 in A. Kiev (ed.), *Magic, Faith and Healing*, Glencoe: Free Press, 1964.

Kendell, R.E., *The Role of Diagnosis in Psychiatry*, Oxford: Blackwell Scientific Publications, 1975.

Kendell, R.E., J. Cooper, A. Gourley, and J. Copeland, "Diagnostic Criteria of American and British psychiatrists," *Archives of General Psychiatry* 25 (1971):123–130.

Kety, Seymour S., "Biochemistry of the major psychoses," pp. 178–187 in A. Freedman, H. Kaplan, and B. Sadock (eds.), *Comprehensive Textbook of Psychiatry*, Vol. I, 2nd Ed., Baltimore: Williams and Wilkins, 1975.

Kiev, Ari, *Transcultural Psychiatry,* New York: Free Press, 1972.

Kirk, Stuart A. "The impact of labeling on rejection of the mentally ill: An experimental study," *Journal of Health and Social Behavior* 15 (June 1974): 108–117.

Kitsuse, John I., "The 'new conception of deviance' and its critics," pp. 273–284 in W. Gove (ed.), *The Labelling of Deviance: Evaluating a Perspective,* New York: Halsted, 1975.

Kohn, Melvin L., "Class, family and schizophrenia," *Social Forces* 50 (March 1972): 295–304.

Krohn, Marvin D. and Ronald L. Akers, "An alternative view of the labeling versus psychiatric perspectives on societal reaction to mental illness," *Social Forces* 56 (December 1977): 341–361.

Lemert, E.M., *Social Pathology,* New York: McGraw-Hill, 1951.

——— , "Response to critics: Feedback and choice," pp. 244–249 in L. Coser and O. Larson (eds.), *The Uses of Controversy in Sociology,* New York: Free Press, 1976.

Lindesmith, Alfred, Anselm Strauss, and Norman Denzin, *Social Psychology,* New York: Holt, Rinehart & Winston, 1978.

Linsky, Arnold S., "Community homogeneity and exclusion of the mentally ill: Rejection vs. consensus about deviance," *Journal of Health and Social Behavior* 11 (December 1970a): 304–311.

——— , "Who shall be excluded: The influence of personal attributes in community reaction to the mentally ill," *Social Psychiatry* 5 (July 1970b): 166–171.

Manning, Peter K., "On deviance," *Contemporary Sociology* 2 (March 1973): 123–128.

Miller, Dorothy H., "Worlds that fail," pp. 102–114 in S. Wallace (ed.), *Total Institutions,* Chicago: Aldine, 1971.

Myers, Jerome and Bertram Roberts, *Family and Class Dynamics in Mental Illness,* New York: John Wiley, 1959.

Murphy, Jane M., "Psychiatric labeling in cross-cultural perspective," *Science* 191 (March 12, 1976): 1019–1028.

Opie, Peter and Iona Opie, *Children's Games in Streets and Playgrounds,* Oxford: Clarendon Press, 1969.

Paykel, E.S., "Life stress and psychiatric disorder: Application of the clinical approach," pp. 135–149 in B.S. Dohrenwend and B.P. Dohrenwend (eds.), *Stressful Life Events: Their Nature and Effects,* New York: John Wiley, 1974.

Phillips, Derek L., "Rejection: A possible consequence of seeking help for mental disorders," *American Sociological Review* 28 (December 1963): 963–972.

Pollin, W., "The pathogenesis of schizophrenia: Possible relationships between genetic, biochemical and experiential factors," *Archives of General Psychiatry* 27 (1972): 29.

Rogler, Lloyd H. and August B. Hollingshead, *Trapped: Families and Schizophrenia,* New York: John Wiley, 1965.

Rosenhan, David L., "On being sane in insane places," *Science* 179 (January 19, 1973): 250–258.

Rosenthal, D., *The Genetics of Psychopathology,* New York: McGraw-Hill, 1971.

Rushing, William A., "Individual resources, societal reaction, and hospital commitment," *American Journal of Sociology* 77 (November 1971): 511–526.

Sampson, Harold, Sheldon Messinger, and Robert Towne, "The mental hospital and marital family ties," *Social Problems* 9 (Fall 1961): 141–155.

Scheff, Thomas J., "The Societal reaction to deviance: Ascriptive elements in the psychiatric screening of mental patients in a midwestern state," *Social Problems* 11 (Spring 1964): 401–413.

——— , *Being Mentally Ill,* Chicago: Aldine, 1966.

——— , "Letter to the editor," *Journal of Health and Social Behavior* 11 (September 1970): 247–248.

——— , "The labeling theory of mental illness," *American Sociological Review* 39 (June 1974): 444–452.

————, *Labeling Madness*, Englewood Cliffs, New Jersey: Prentice-Hall, Inc., 1975a.

————, "Reply to Chauncey and Gove," *American Sociological Review* 40 (April 1975b): 252–257.

Schmidt, K.E., "Folk psychiatry in Sarawak: A tentative system of psychiatry of the Iban," pp. 155–189 in A. Kiev (ed.), *Magic, Faith and Healing*, Glencoe: Free Press, 1964.

Schur, Edwin M., "Reactions to deviance: A critical assessment," *American Journal of Sociology* 75 (November 1969): 309–322.

————, *Labeling Deviant Behavior*, New York: Harper and Row, 1971.

————, "Comments," pp. 285–294 in W. Gove (ed.), *The Labelling of Deviance: Evaluating a Perspective*, New York: Halsted, 1975.

Scott, Marvin B. and Stanford M. Lyman, "Accounts," *American Sociological Review* 33 (February 1968): 46–62.

Sharpe, L., B.J. Gurland, J.L. Fleiss, R.E. Kendell, J.E. Cooper, and J.R.M. Copeland, "Some comparisons of American, Canadian and British psychiatrists in their diagnostic concepts," *Canadian Psychiatric Association Journal* 19 (1974): 235–245.

Snyder, Solomon H., "Biochemical factors in schizophrenia," *Hospital Practice* 12 (October 1977): 133–140.

Spitzer, Robert L. and Paul T. Wilson, "Nosology and the official psychiatric nomenclature," pp. 826–845 in A. Freedman, H. Kaplan, and B. Sadock (eds.), *Comprehensive Textbook of Psychiatry*, Vol. I, 2nd Ed., Baltimore: Williams and Wilkins, 1975.

Townsend, Marshall J., "Cultural conceptions, mental disorders and social roles: A comparison of Germany and America," *American Sociological Review* 40 (December 1975): 739–752.

————, "Self-concept and institutionalization of mental patients: Overview and critique," *Journal of Health and Social Behavior* 17 (September 1976): 263–271.

————, *Cultural Conceptions and Mental Illness*, Chicago: University of Chicago Press, 1978.

Weiner, Herbert, "Schizophrenia: Etiology," pp. 866–890 in A. Freedman, H. Kaplan, and B. Sadock (eds.), *Comprehensive Textbook of Psychiatry*, Vol. I, 2nd Ed., Baltimore: Williams and Wilkins, 1975.

Wenger, Dennis L. and C. Ritchard Fletcher, "The effect of legal counsel on admissions to a state mental hospital: A confrontation of professions," *Journal of Health and Social Behavior* 10 (June 1969): 66–72.

Whatley, Charles D., "Social attitudes toward discharged mental patients," *Social Problems* 6 (1959): 313–320.

Wilde, William A., "Decision-making in a psychiatric screening agency," *Journal of Health and Social Behavior* 9 (September 1968): 215–221.

POLITICS, PRESIDENTS
AND POWER

THE PRESIDENCY AND IMPRESSION MANAGEMENT*

Peter M. Hall, UNIVERSITY OF MISSOURI—COLUMBIA

INTRODUCTION

The focus of attention in American politics has for many years been on the presidency, its incumbents, and those who desire and aim for it. That focus is easily found in the works of political scientists and historians, in the products of the graphic and video media, in the anticipations and observations of the citizenry, and in the responses of foreign leaders and countries. It seems almost unnecessary to add that that attention has been magnified and concentrated since the tragedy of United States involvement in Vietnam, the deceptions and abuses of power of Lyndon Baines Johnson and Richard Milhous Nixon, Wategate, the White House tapes, impeachment hearings, and the ultimate resignation of Nixon.

While there is a great deal of writing and rethinking about the presidency by political scientists, much of it relates, necessarily, to normative and constitutional concerns, to the personal character of the president, or to the organization of the office and its interorganizational and interinstitutional

Studies in Symbolic Interaction—Volume 2, 1979, pages 283–305
Copyright © 1979 by JAI Press Inc.
All rights of reproduction in any form reserved.
ISBN: 0-89232-105-9

relationships. Few political scientists are utilizing theoretical perspectives to examine the processes of the operation of the presidency and the activities of the president.

Despite this focus by political scientists, the media, and the public, sociologists who are interested in politics and political systems have not examined the president or the presidency with little more than superficial concern. The primary concerns of political sociologists have been with public opinion, voting behavior, distributions of power, and governmental bureaucracies. At least one notable exception to the above is the drama-turgical analysis of the Nixon White House by T.R. Young (1976). One general point of this paper is that sociological perspectives and particularly symbolic interaction can be extremely useful in analyzing, explaining, and understanding activities of the presidency.

Several years ago, I presented and developed the concept of political impression management as a means of partially understanding political processes in the United States (Hall, 1972). Impression management means that control over the conduct of others for one's own interest is achieved by influencing the definition of the situation in which all are involved. This is accomplished by acting in such a way that an image is created of the actor (and related objects) that leads others to voluntarily act as the actor wishes them to act. Control over others is accomplished by getting others to accept as reality the propounded definitions (Goffman, 1959:3-4). Impression management is concerned not only with what is said but what appears. It is concerned not only with what is said but also not said. In other words, impression management refers to what conclusions people draw from appearances and actions (partially nonverbal) and also what controls are placed upon the inward and outward flow of information. For my past purposes, I had divided political impression management into (1) informa-tion flow control—the gathering of intelligence, the maintenance of secrecy, the planning and rehearsing of performances; and (2) symbolic mobilization of support—the use of symbols, verbal and nonverbal, in various settings and forms to maintain or strengthen the position of the actor. Political impression management, then, represented two processes of power.

Rosabeth Moss Kanter, while recognizing the insights and utility of applying symbolic interaction to political matters, was critical of its limitations.

> Symbolic manipulation is a relatively mild political weapon compared to some. Power politics also involves the use of force, the bringing to bear of great financial resources, the withholdings of resources and decisions, or the invoking of legitimized authority to control others. Negotiating, bargaining, and impression management give way quickly to guns, bombs, and huge sums of money. A Howard Hughes or a Rothschild does not gain or lose influence by the kind of impression he makes or the symbols he invokes. If a policeman points a gun at a Black Panther, that weapon is more than a symbol and certainly takes precedence over any other "definition of the situation." Bureaucrats can control and sanction welfare mothers not by symbolically manipulating them or

bargaining with them but by invoking the "rules" to prevent them from obtaining their payments; sanitation inspectors, similarly, can close communes, merely by utilizing their legitimate authority and without any negotiation (Kanter, 1972:86–87).

Kanter's criticism, on the surface, appears obvious and damning. We all grew up yelling and/or hearing "sticks and stones can break my bones, but names can never hurt me." However, the criticism neglects the structure, the norms, the day-to-day realities of the American political system, the relationship of the United States to the rest of the world, and the significance of domestic and international communication.

In terms of the American political system, it must be remembered that, constitutionally and normatively, we are a republic, a representative democracy, where elected officials are supposed to make decisions based upon open, reasoned, rational discussion, where they are theoretically obliged to seek support from the people and explain their actions, where there is a free press for purposes of informing the people, and where the people have the right of free speech, assembly, and organization. Such forms, together with the heterogeneity of the population, its diverse and potentially conflicting interests, the seriousness of the consequences of political decisions, and the distance of most people from the actual political events all point to the utility of political impression management.

Kanter's criticism also ignores more theoretical implications of multiple audiences for single events and the simultaneous or consecutive use of multiple processes of power. The kinds of events described by Kanter will either require secrecy, further justification, or they will already have had the appropriate symbolic foundation developed. They might also be intended to be viewed or known about as an example to others in the audience or in other audiences. We must also keep in mind that in real situations, in the context of interactions in relationships, authority, coercion, threat of coercion, eavesdropping, secrecy, bargaining, organizing, appealing, and persuading may all occur in conjunction with one another.

The purpose of this paper will be to demonstrate the relevance and consequences of political impression management by analyses of the presidencies of Nixon and John F. Kennedy. Their foreign policies based upon credibility in conjunction with their views of world communism, their conceptions of the presidency and a concern with toughness, their elitist conceptions of the people, and their de-emphasis of domestic politics necessarily required and utilized impression management. The paper will conclude with a general discussion of the presidency and impression management.

THE NIXON YEARS

The assertion that the Nixon administration had an obsession with impression management should be no surprise.[1] Lack of access to the

President, illegal wiretaps and break-ins, the Watergate cover-up, the shadowing of Ted Kennedy, and the proposed merger of intelligence agencies all reflect control of information flow. The conscious staging of rallies, campaigns, conventions, speeches, and surprise announcements of trips abroad were clearly for symbolically mobilizing support and defining political reality. Many key members of the administration had public relations backgrounds and others were quick to learn. Schell states that Nixon's administration was a new form of rule "in which images were given precedence over substance in every phase of government" (Schell, 1976:51). As a result, the Nixon years are filled with incredible contradictions.

In the 1968 campaign and the early presidency, Nixon gave us little specific information. He was able to convince many, including Walter Lippman, that there was a new Nixon. He promised to (1) bring us together, (2) have an open administration, (3) do more for the Negroes than any other president, and (4) have peace with honor. His administration promised solutions to problems through action and organization instead of talk. Only peace came, but not for four long years and with some unexpected actions.

With reference to the peace plan for Vietnam, one of Nixon's first actions was to order the secret bombing of Cambodia in March of 1969. While we were being told that the war would end soon, it was being widened. In a similar vein, the following spring the President announced success in pacification, Vietnamization, peace in sight, and the withdrawal of 150,000 troops over the next year. But ten days later, he announced the ordering of U.S. ground forces into Cambodia along with statements that this action was a test of character and will, and if the people at home failed to rally behind the President, it would be catastrophic. He also said, "If we fail to meet this challenge, all other nations will be on notice that despite its overwhelming power, the United States, when a *real* crisis comes, will be found wanting" (emphasis mine). Further apparent contradictions of withdrawal and de-escalation countered by increased military intensity can be seen in the Christmas bombing of 1971 and that of Christmas, 1972, when we were told the negotiations were 99% complete. While Nixon was visiting China, military action continued. More dramatically, the activity concurrent with the planning and taking of the trip to the Soviet Union indicated a world of opposites. The mining of North Vietnamese harbors and the bombing of railroad lines was seemingly accepted by the Soviets in return, perhaps, for trade deals. But at the same time Nixon was addressing the Soviet people on television, the American military was conducting a heavy massive bombing of North Vietnam. Peace, of sorts, did eventually come on January 27, 1973, but not without many twists and turns which on the surface appear quite perplexing.

Much of the attention of the administration during these years when we were being brought together was focused on opponents of the war and, therefore, of the President. Student protesters became an early target with the indictment of the Chicago Eight, pressure by the administration on colleges to deny aid to students convicted of crimes in campus disorders, and the speech at General Beadle State College which claimed that our fundamental values were under bitter and violent attack from protestors.

The media, because they were presumed to be anti-Nixon and supportive of the anti-war movement, the Democrats, and liberals came under attack and manipulation. On November 3, 1969, Nixon made a major speech on Vietnam, emphasizing the avoidance of defeat and humiliation, preserving confidence in American leadership, an honorable peace, a secret peace plan, the negative consequences of minority opposition, and the need for support from the silent majority. Vice-President Agnew had earlier been turned loose on the "effete corps of impudent snobs," but he now, in a speech polished by Nixon, lambasted the networks for "instant analysis and querulous criticism" for their comments on the November 3 speech which was, in Agnew (-Nixon)'s words, "one of the most important of our decade."

The congressional campaign of 1970 became another instance of what Agnew termed "positive polarization." The Democrats were portrayed as being extremists, of being like or supportive of the protestors—excusing disorders, tolerating crime, apologizing for our wealth, undercutting the President's foreign policy, and being radical liberals who bus children. Nixon used demonstrators as foils in that campaign and presented it as a battle against those who would destroy our society.

Daniel Ellsberg became an important target in the summer of 1971. Interestingly, the aim was not so much to have him convicted for leaking the Pentagon Papers but to try him in the media, discredit him, and tie him to the anti-war movement and the Democratic party. At the same time, the Administration used the leaked papers, which they allegedly did not want open, to attack their Democratic predecessors.

Dealings with other branches of government reflected the opposite of an open administration or acknowlegement of the proper structure of the Federal government. When the defeat of Nixon's nomination of Carswell for Supreme Court Justice appeared imminent, he argued that the Senate was frustrating the *authority* of the President to *name* Supreme Court Justices. One can only surmise that he never heard of "advise and consent." In general, to Nixon *any* opposition would cripple the authority of the President. In order to prevent this, reorganizations were designed to move control from the Cabinet and federal bureaucracies to the White House. Attempted centralization of intelligence agencies was part of this plan also. The cutting of federal spending and the tactic of impoundment were not for the manifest reason given by the administration, but rather to curtail the power of Congress.

Domestic policy was not particularly important to Nixon. Its purpose was primarily to develop a supportive political base with which to conduct foreign policy. Much of what occurred, then, was "symbolic." For example, in the area of civil rights, the administration publicly took conservative stances but failed to follow up with normal political lobbying. They did not attempt to actually succeed, but rather to deceive the Southern segregationists and shift political onus to the courts and Congress. In crime policy, Nixon knew he could only exercise "vigorous symbolic leadership," so the D.C. Crime bill was introduced with provisions (preventive detention and no-knock entry) that the D.C. police chief did not want or need, which would signal a red light to criminal forces. The administration did not expect this bill to pass. It was designed as "political law-and-order" to enhance images. They wanted to blame Congress for being "soft" on crime. To their surprise, Congress passed it. Finally, Nixon's support of Moynihan's Family Assistance Plan was perplexing. It substantively had a liberal core. Nixon made a minor part of it—penalty for nonworking recipients—seem like a major plank to appeal to conservatives. They were not fooled, but the liberals were and they opposed it. The program failed to pass, but it did not receive much activity on the part of the administration at all. Nixon, however, is alleged to have told Moynihan that Tory men and liberal policies are what have changed the world. Behind these kinds of contradictions and inconsistencies lie the basic separation between word and deed.

THE KENNEDY YEARS

John Kennedy believed in the power of facts, the need to be tough, cool, and objective, and was interested in results and action.[2] He disdained abstractions, theories, emotion, and ideology. He basically accepted American society as given and had few social change goals or saw his role as educator or mobilizer. He did, however, want to be a hero, and this could be done by acting tough and courageous in crises which could best be found in the international realm. Because of his view of history, which saw monolithic Communistic expansion, Kennedy could find his heroic role in standing opposed to the ubiquitous challenge of the Russians. Every international conflict was a crisis, a test of will and nerve. Any wavering or retreat would only encourage our enemies.

Kennedy was concerned with the maintenance and extension of presidential power. He believed that it was of a relatively fixed quantity, so one should not squander its capital on questionable issues. Domestic issues meant, then, dealing with entrenched interests and offices with whom one could, if necessary, bargain or otherwise allow their way. But the President should deal only with these elites and not with representatives of the aroused masses or respond on their terms. Major issues were sophisticated and technical and required expertise and deliberation. At the same time, efforts were taken to increase the efficiency of the executive branch to reflect concerns with action through reorganization and the establishment of ad hoc task forces.

Kennedy believed that he could derive strength in his battle with Communism from a healthy, expanding economy. He believed that business prosperity and a warm government-business alliance were necessary to contribute strength to the presidency. Consequently, under Kennedy, the government assumed greater responsibility for guaranteeing markets and underwriting risk-taking. In return, he wanted a subordination of group or class conflict to national purpose. The government would provide practical neutral management of the economy. In order to bring this about, Kennedy made numerous concessions to business. Labor received few relative benefits because Kennedy was not in favor of redistribution, only enlargement of the economic pie. But such expansion was for the purpose of giving weapons to the president and decreasing internal problems which would lessen total resolve and collective purpose.

Civil rights is an area where Kennedy is believed to have been involved and active. In fact, Kennedy did not "feel" the depth of the movement or the issue, nor regard it as a moral question. It was simply another political issue that competed for his attention. What bothered Kennedy was the unpredictability of the actions of the movement and their intrusions upon *his* agenda. Civil rights bothered him because he could not control it. Kennedy's response to the movement was to reassert the dominance of pragmatic, elite politics, and of his own dominance of that brand of politics. Miroff states:

> . . .we can observe a pattern of slighting the significance of the civil rights movement, criticizing civil rights demonstrations, and claiming primary credit for his own administration for civil rights accomplishments (Miroff, 1976:227).

Indeed, in the search for power, heroic courage, and global supremacy, Kennedy's one great nagging fear was loss of control. Whether in Berlin, Cuba, Vietnam, with steel executives, or the movement, at issue was being on the defensive or being impotent.

Kennedy began his presidency with the belief that it was "the hour of maximum danger." It was his belief that the nation needed to overcome the soft sentimentalism of Eisenhower with vigilance and toughness. To stop the Russians, we needed a step-up of military spending, particularly in missiles, the improvement of mobility and versatility of weapons and armed forces for effective and swift intervention in limited wars, the meeting of every Russian challenge to demonstrate the determination and will of America, the government, and the President. By carrying this out and failing to respond to conciliatory moves from the Russians, Kennedy created his own history by making his theory about the Russians become a reality. Spiraling defense expenditures on both sides, the Bay of Pigs, the failure of the Vienna

Summit, the tense situation in Berlin, Russian resumption of atmospheric nuclear testing, and the Cuban missile crisis are all part of this scenario.

A brief examination of the Cuban missile crisis is helpful here. The U.S. government deliberately let the Russian government discover, in 1962, that they knew the actual deployment and small number of Soviet nuclear missiles. Our government had also changed our nuclear strategy so the Russians feared a possible U.S. first strike. Their defensive strategy was to secretly place some intermediate range missiles in Cuba. This was reckless, because we had an election coming and Cuba was already a Kennedy soft-spot. When Kennedy became definitely apprised of the presence of offensive missiles, he gathered a group of his advisors and experts to design strategies and responses.

According to Sorenson, five major theories were suggested:

(a) Cold War politics—It was a Soviet probe of United States will, expecting little response, and consequently the United States would look impotent.

(b) diverting trap—the real target was Berlin and the Soviets wanted the United States to take its eye off Berlin and attack Cuba.

(c) Cuban defense—the Soviets were determined to defend at any cost their satellite in the Western hemisphere.

(d) bargaining barter—Krushchev wanted to use missile sites as chips for a deal on Berlin or United States withdrawal from overseas bases.

(e) missile power—It was designed as the swiftest and cheapest means of increasing the number of missiles directed against the United States (Sorenson, 1966:762–764).

Kennedy, we are told, did not buy (b) or (d), and did not think (c) or (e) had sufficient support. He leaned, as we should expect, toward (a). It certainly fit *his* theory. The debate focused around the appropriate U.S. response. Sitting tight or restrained responses were rejected because they suggested weakness in the face of an aggressive challenge. Stevenson's suggestion of using political machinery was ignored. The general debate was over what kind of *military action* should be taken. As we know, invasion and an air strike were discarded in favor of a limited, low-level action of a blockade which allowed for flexibility and the control of the pace of escalation. On October 22, Kennedy announced to the nation (and to the Soviets) that he knew of the presence of the missiles and that we were taking steps to compel their removal. Eventually they went, but it was a week of great tension and peril. While Kennedy may have wanted a showdown, Krushchev did not and so, eyeball to eyeball, the Russians blinked.

Kennedy really did not believe the missiles were a military threat. He saw it as a political challenge.

> They were planning in November to open to the world the fact that they had these missiles so close to the United States; not that they were intending to fire them. . . . But it would have politically changed the balance of power. *It would have appeared to, and appearances contribute to reality* (Kennedy, Public Papers, 1962, p. 898). [Italics mine.]

It was, in essence, a test of reputation, prestige, credibility, determination, or will. For the sake of political appearance, Kennedy got the victory he desired. He showed his toughness and overcame Vienna, Bay of Pigs, and the Berlin Wall.

It would be unfair to portray Kennedy's foreign policy only in terms of Cuba. His Alliance for Progress and the total Vietnam policy indicate an interest in social reform, economic development, and the growth of democratic institutions while at the same time attempting to control revolutionary movements. In Vietnam, there was the initial praise for and expectations of Diem as a member of the elite who would institute reform. The development of strategic hamlets were ostensibly for isolating the Vietnamese from the Communists and serving as centers of reform. The use of counterinsurgency, the Green Berets, and later larger numbers of American soldiers was an extension of the necessity to forestall Communist wars of national liberation. Pressure for democratic reform, however, took second place to curbing Soviet expansion.

THE DOCTRINE OF CREDIBILITY AND IMPRESSION MANAGEMENT

Despite their obvious differences, there are some strong similarities between the men. They both considered foreign affairs more important than domestic issues. They tended to perceive the world-wide Communist threat in the same way. They tended to identify the presidency as the epitomé of American society. They both were preoccupied with toughness and strength and with surviving what they defined as personal crises through tests of will. They were both bothered by a fear of loss of control and potential impotence of presidential authority. They both lacked a conscious ideology or a conception of a changed society. In a way, they were both conservatives, although Kennedy would probably be seen as more enlightened and moderate. They were both elitists who saw no real role for the public to play in a democracy, save support their actions. However, a major difference was that Kennedy basically accepted the limits of the broader institutional system and worked within them, while Nixon ignored some of the boundaries and in the process destroyed himself and almost much more.

The links between them and between each of them and their policies can be found in the connections between the assumptions of U.S. foreign and military policy, the conception of the presidency, and the strategy of credibility—a form of impression management. The foreign policy of the United States from Kennedy until the present is based upon the calculated doctrine of credibility. It emerged in reaction to the Dulles-Eisenhower foreign policy of brinkmanship and massive retaliation. That policy meant that every time the Russians or their satellites moved aggressively, we would rattle our nuclear weapons and threaten to blow up the world, ourselves included. The proponents of credibility (Kissinger, Kennedy, and Maxwell Taylor) believed that the Russians would not believe us, that they would not be deterred by our threats and would call our bluff. Consequently, there was a need to develop a strategy that would take a middle course between total extinction and totalitarian expansion. Credibility meant that the impression would be created in the minds of the leaders (and their peoples) throughout the world that the United States not only *possessed* great power but also had the *will* to use it. This led to the strategy of the limited war, which meant that the United States would use a number of flexible military strategies (but primarily utilizing conventional nonnuclear forces) to offensively stop Communist expansion while defensively maintaining our nuclear deterrent to stop a potential Soviet first strike. The limited war was presumed to be a short-term action which would demonstrate the resolve of the United States to use force. Given its flexibility and use of conventional forces, it allowed for the principle of escalation to indicate the extent to which we were willing to use force until the enemy desisted.

It seems obvious that the doctrine of credibility is one of appearance and the creation of images that a nation is strong and resolute. Schell observes that the strategists become preoccupied with questions of how to demonstrate determination and toughness and how to avoid appearing soft, weak, and indecisive. Kissinger said, "Soviet reactions to what we do will depend not on what we intend but on what the Soviet leaders think we intend" (Schell, 1976:354). Taylor adds, "It must be clear to the aggressor that we have the will and the determination to use our retaliation power without compunction if we are attacked. Any suggestion of weakness or indecision may encourage the enemy to gamble on surprise" (Schell, 1976:352–353). The proponents of credibility believed, because of Communist expansionism, that we would have numerous and continuing instances where the United States would have to use the limited war strategy to show that we would not allow them to undermine the "free world." Should we fail to demonstrate our will and resolve, the middle ground would be destroyed. Therefore, if they resisted, then we would have to boost our use of force one notch, and so forth. It was absolutely necessary that we demonstrate our willfulness not to be pushed around. Kennedy's beliefs about the Soviet

Union, his responses to the Bay of Pigs and Krushchev in Vienna, and his failure to respond to conciliatory moves, all logically culminate in the Cuban missile crisis. As Kennedy said, we had to respond strongly because it would have *appeared* to alter the balance of power.

The doctrine of credibility and the strategy of limited war place a great onus on the actions of the president. According to Schell, the impression management requirements of the policy demand centralization. The president must be totally free of constraints and be able to command obedience and response. The president stands for and is the entire society because his every action places the prestige of the United States on the line. Given this premise, we can understand why Kennedy and Nixon, independent of their psyches, were so preoccupied with toughness and being seen as strong. We can understand why they were so concerned with political defeats or avoiding involvement in domestic political issues. Any loss would be seen, according to the theory, as lessening the reputation and prestige of the president and of weakening his ability to contend with the major enemies. At the same time, one can see why reorganization of the executive branch and increasing the power of the president were so important to the incumbents. They saw this as a means of maximizing their ability to maintain and increase the image of their strength and to limit the ability of their domestic opponents to constrain them. We can also see why the aura of secrecy, the obsession with leaks, and attempts by all the presidents of this era to control and manipulate the media occurred. The emission of discrediting information would disfigure the image of the president. Given this notion of the presidency and the dangers of world communism, the elitist nature of both Nixon and Kennedy is explicable. They needed to feel or believe that they were in control and that they determined how the society responded. To be seen as democratically responsive to the people or passive to the discussion of others would allow the Communists or even our allies to believe the president could not do what he said he could do. Kennedy's claims of being responsible for civil rights progress and not giving credit to the movement may be partially explained in this light. In general, the lack of concern by Nixon and Kennedy with domestic issues may be due to the fact that the political forces are possibly more articulate, entrenched, and relatively pluralistic in these areas.

Credibility and impression management have a number of important consequences in action and in analysis. Our involvement in Vietnam was calculated according to this doctrine. Vietnam became a laboratory to test a theory-limited war and counterinsurgency to rebuff a Russian-inspired war of national liberation. The application of general and abstract theory failed because it ignored context and history, but it was no accidental quagmire. It was rationally calculated to demonstrate our willful resolve. The quagmire resulted from the continuing commitment to a poorly conceived theory. Defeat, loss, humiliation, withdrawal would mean a major loss of credibility. Examination of the Pentagon papers and other documents reveal that Vietnam, *per se,* was not strategically important, nor were we that concerned about the freedom of the Vietnamese, the domino theory, or even wars of national liberation as the war progressed. Rather we were fighting to preserve our reputation as guarantor and our effectiveness in the rest of the world. Even a bloody loss (deaths and casualties) was better than a simple retreat because it demonstrated our willingness to sustain losses. The "symbolic" quality of the war far exceeded its material purpose.

Given this thesis, the Johnson-Nixon concern about public opinion, demonstrations, and the anti-war movement becomes more comprehensible. The appearance of division and dissent encourages our enemies, discourages our allies, distracts the president, and restrains our united energies to support decisive action. It clearly shows that the president is not in complete control so necessary to pursuing credibility. Opposition limited the ability of the president to convey images of strength, determination, and risk, not so much for its own sake then, but in a continuing dangerous future. In this context, we understand why Nixon said on April 30, 1970, about Cambodia:

> If we fail to meet this challenge, all other nations will be on notice that despite its overwhelming power, the United States, when a *real* crisis comes, will be found wanting [emphasis added].

Many of the contradictions during the Nixon years regarding Vietnam become clarified. Given the overall assumptions of Communist expansionism and the doctrine of credibility, withdrawal and peace mean weakness and defeat. To compensate and counter, the United States must give a show of force to prove powerful will and willful power. Therefore, the United States bombed or invaded Cambodia at the time of announcing troop withdrawals. The Christmas bombings were reminders that although peace was near, the United States still had muscle and would use it. Also, if the United States was engaging in detente with Russian or China, perhaps a sign of weakness, military action represented a simultaneous demonstration of toughness. Of course, if such actions are erratic or unpredictable, that can increase the appearance of power.

The easy conclusion is that actions of force and killing are intended literally and figuratively as messages beyond their immediate impact. Acts do not simply speak for themselves. Indeed, as Norman Denzin said, the meaning of Vietnam is that "it is better to destroy a small nation state than it is to lose symbolic face in the world and local arenas of political interaction" (personal communication). That hardly seems like a "relatively mild political weapon."

PRESIDENTS, PROBLEMS, POWER, AND IMPRESSION MANAGEMENT

On the day that I sat down to write this section, the morning paper had a headline in the middle of the front page saying, "Powell accuses press of 'witch-hunt'." A column by Mary McGory on the opinion/columns page said that the conclusion to be drawn from the Bourne affair is that Carter is " . . . once again exposed as a man who can't find people who know how to handle power, the most powerful drug of all." (Kansas City Times, July 24, 1978) In the furor about Bourne, drugs, prescriptions, aides, one might ask what does all this have to do with the president, politics, and the important issues of the country and the world. Surely the president is more interested in them than nagging trivial issues about whether White House aides smoke pot or snort cocaine.

All of this, however, must be put in the context of a president stymied in terms of international dealings, forced to continually compromise, and even accept defeat, in dealings with the Congress. Newspaper reports of statements about the Russians portray the President as waffling between hard and soft or harder and softer. The impression is that he is indecisive. The dollar continues to fall in value as Congress is unable to pass energy legislation. The United States economy continues to suffer "double digit" inflation and the papers are filled with stories of tax revolts and growing support for Proposition 13 measures. Meanwhile, the popularity of the President, as measured by the various polls, shows a lack of support, having declined fairly continuously since he took office. Those polls supposedly measure his *performance* in office, or at least measure the perception of performance. The polls are matched by the continuous evaluation by the media of how the President is doing. There seemingly is no time to rest, no celebration of successes or gains, no place to relax. Indeed, what seems to have infuriated Jody Powell, aside from the hypocrisy of press people who also smoke and snort, is that the President was caught offguard backstage, literally and theoretically, by an intruder who did not announce his professional identity. Here is a President, who is just back from what is being presented as a successful foreign trip, and who cannot take advantage of that alleged success. It is, of course, well-known that foreign trips can be used, and have the effect of focusing positive attention upon the president, to improve, at least temporarily, his popularity.

To some extent, Jimmy Carter is being hoisted on his own petard. The Democratic nomination-seeker who came out of Georgia, from almost nowhere, to become the candidate and then the President, did it very heavily by his organization's, his family's, and his ability to use the media and create successful images (Auletta, 1976). This, then, is the President who proclaims openness in government but complains about "leaks" and takes steps to stop them. The President who promised not to lie has a new official photograph which makes him look realistically older and more serious. Untouched, unlike the first one, the wrinkles are there to be seen and to convey the weight of office and the concern by the President with governing. So much so that the famous grin is gone and only 7, count them, 7 teeth show instead of 10 as on the first official photograph. This is the consequence of bringing his media person, Gerald Rafshoon, into the White House and putting him on the payroll to improve the image and increase public support as measured by polls.

We could, if we took the time, examine Gerald Ford's problems with image and being President, and with his strong concern for effective use of the media to communicate with the people. However, we must keep in mind that he restored integrity to the office (which Carter has apparently continued). The presidency then appears as an institution of incompetent integrity. But beyond that, the more basic issue involves an examination of the presidency and its relationship to impression management. What is there about the role, its incumbents' perception of its power and its resources, the expectations "the people" have of it (and the perception of those expectations by the administration), the nature of American society and politics, and intermediary relationships of the media to both the president and the people that inevitably involves the office in the use of political impression management?

The issues here are relative, because any person in a position of responsibility and leadership who requires some degree of responsiveness from his or her subordinates will try using the aura of legitimacy and authority, persuasive appeals, or information release before giving up tangible resources or utilizing force, all other things being equal, because the former are easier and more plentiful forms of power. In other words, political impression management is part of *any* relationship among unequals.

Our concern is then a matter of emphasis. Why is there more of a preoccupation with presidential use of symbol manipulation and information control? Why are presidents more concerned about public relations and information leakage? Why, then, is political impression management of increasing importance, and under what kinds of social conditions is it likely to be used and used more frequently? Answers to these questions can only be made in an exploratory and relatively brief fashion. They involve a number of different and complexly interrelated dimensions.

As a result of the New Deal, World War II, and the emergence of the United States as a major world power, there has been an incredible expansion of the federal government and of the responsibilities and activities of the president. Expectations developed, very much based upon the model of Franklin D. Roosevelt and his government, of the interest, ability, and responsibility of the presidency to solve all major problems. The general consensus on the presidency was what Thomas Cronin (1975:25–49) called the "textbook presidency," which exaggerated the omnipotence and moralistic benevolence of the president.

Much of the recent work on the presidency has made an attempt to revise this view of presidential omnipotence. Empirically, normatively, and theoretically, the role of Congress is being reasserted as a separate institution sharing powers. Much is being written on how difficult is is for the president to control the federal bureaucracy (Mullen, 1976). The power of special interest groups to veto policies that affect them is pointed to by Cronin (1975:99). Even the president's own staff is seen as bloated and given to layering, overspecialization, communication gaps, and inadequate coordination (1975:120). The consequence is that there is a concern that the president cannot get good information or advice for planning and deciding, nor is he presumed to have the resources and time for implementing and monitoring (Hargrove, 1974). Presidential frustrations then become a much discussed point by presidents, aides, and scholars. As Neustadt says:

> What Presidents do every day is make decisions that are mostly thrust upon them, the deadlines all too often outside their control, on options mostly framed by others, about issues crammed with technical complexities and uncertain outcomes (1976:34).

Thus, we have a situation where, according to the scholars, the expectations cannot be met, where performance cannot match demand. In fact, President Carter in his 1978 State of the Union address told the people to expect less from government and, obviously by implication, the President. The United States, he said, was going to have to accept problems, learn to live with and manage them, rather than expect government to do away with them. The degree to which the attempt to lower expectations by governments and scholars will be successful is yet to be seen, but it is obviously worth watching.

In an earlier discussion of American politics, I suggested that personalities and issues outweighed ideology and parties, and that issues themselves often became personalized (Hall, 1972:60,66). Richard Sennett (1977), in a brilliant and controversial book, argues that Western society has an obsession with personality matched by the decline of a public life of debate about significant issues. The consequence of having no real public life is that

> A political leader running for office is spoken of as 'credible' or 'legitimate' in terms of what kind of man he is, rather than in terms of the actions or programs he espouses (Sennett, 1977:4).

In the United States, that preoccupation with personality can be seen in observations, concerns, and analyses of the president. The workings of the government are said to be dependent upon the character of the president.

Past presidents are erected as national heroes of courage, bravery, honesty, and myths are constructed of their lives which are engrained in the youthful citizenry. Presidents who failed or who were not "great" are said to lack those individual characteristics. Most recently, psychohistories have been written to examine the personality development of presidents and why they failed or succeeded. Barber (1974) represents that genre and argues that those who failed had negative personality characteristics.

Concerns with the actions, style, character of the president dominates the public space of the society and receives undue amounts of media attention. This can be seen in the nonpolitical concerns with the presidents' families, with their marital interaction, with their leisure activity, with their popular tastes. It can also be seen in the definition of politics as presidential drama. American politics becomes a series of episodes detailing *his* battles, struggles, and challenges and *his* victories and defeats. Miroff (1978) has nicely demonstrated who and how this dominance is accomplished. The consequence of this dominance is an inhibition of participatory democratic politics as the president is transformed into the surrogate of the people and the symbol of the nation. Presidential domination of public space and the personalization of the presidency obviously become inducements for and tools of impression management. Much of presidential public relations is designed to create or reinforce images of character.

How that is done and whether it can be done successfully, even if divorced from the context of "real" situations and "actual" actions and results, is not a simple matter. There are opponents and skeptical groups with which to contend, but there are many ambivalent dualities in our political culture about government vs. politics and statesmen vs. politicians (Hall, 1972:53). A successful president will want to be viewed as a statesman, not a politician. He will want to be remembered historically as resolute, courageous, decisive, in charge, and in control—all of which might come under the heading of "appearing presidential." Presidents, most of all, do not want to be seen as weak, unconcerned, abdicating responsibility, overtly manipulative, or excessivly involved in political wheeling and dealing. Cronin (1977) has explicated and elaborated these dualities in terms of what he calls presidential paradoxes—logically contradictory expectations that people have for the president. Some of these include: 1) being gentle and decent but also forceful and decisive; 2) being programmatic but also pragmatic; 3) being innovative and inventive but also majoritarian and responsive; 4) being inspirational but not promising more than can be delivered; 5) being above politics but involved in politics; 6) being a common man who gives an uncommon performance. Since they cannot be met, Cronin says, they invite two-faced behavior (1977:69). The president, in this case, represents an example of the classic dilemma of inadequate role definition under conditions of conflicting expectation by an actor under tremendous surveillance. These kinds of conditions, with the resources available to the president and with access to the media, are tailor-made for impression management in the absence of the ability to compartmentalize audiences or to withdraw backstage.

It goes without saying that one of the factors to consider in regard to impression management and the presidency is the role of the media and particularly television. The most potent and dramatic medium is television. Because of its widespread access, the maxim that seeing is believing, and the belief that one is seeing the total being, television has gained predominance. It has changed the style of campaigning, perhaps even the kind of candidates, the mode of presidential contact with the people, and the nature of news and news reporting. Media values emphasize action and actors and not complex background or even verbalization. Thus, the media becomes willingly caught up in portraying politics as presidential drama.

The relationship between the president and the media is a complex one. Some of their interests are convergent and others are divergent, but they both need each other in order to do their jobs as they define them. As Miroff states:

> Portrayal of national politics as a drama of presidential character has become so much a commonplace that the media appear reluctant to depart from it. Beneath much of the disappointment in Jimmy Carter can be heard the complaint that so far this main character is undramatic and this story unexciting. Presidential drama is *expected* to fill up the public space; presidential dominance over visible public action is now as much demanded by the media as it is sought by the President. (1978:5).

While the president can go directly to the people, that is not done too often to avoid overexposure. Consequently, much of the contact between the president and the people will be mediated. The president and his aides, therefore, want consciously to use the media to get their chosen image and message across. The media representatives, on the other hand, are aware of administration intents and may strive to counter such intentions by uncovering misdeeds, creating conflict and controversies, making news by discrediting presidential actions, finding "scoops" that reveal intentions before preparations have been completed for public unveiling. In handling these conflicting interests, while seeking to dramatize its actions and humanize its character, the presidency seeks to restrict access to the backstage and to control information flow. The latter, by the way, is often difficult because members of the federal bureaucracy and Congress do not identify with the president nor share his goals or values.

Some years ago, Richard Neustadt (1960), while not focusing upon most of the presidential problems we have listed so far, did raise the question of how the president could ensure the success of his actions over obstacles. He suggested that, in order to overcome the constraints upon the office, the president had to calculate what were *his* personal stakes in any situation and he had to make choices or avoid making choices which could utilize and benefit *his personal* power. According to Neustadt (1960, 1976) the formal powers of the presidency were insufficient to get things done. The president had to learn how to use to his advantage his reputation within the Washington community of legislators, bureaucrats, political observers and writers, and his prestige or popularity among the people. Personal presidential power, drawing upon formal powers, resources, reputation, and prestige, was the power to persuade and the power to bargain. To Neustadt persuasion and bargaining were the same. I view them as separate, but the point is that Neustadt, recoiling against Eisenhower's passivity, Truman's failures, and believing in the consummate political skill and desirable goals of FDR, is urging that presidents adopt the style of the forms of power that stress manipulation. Neustadt sought or desired a president who was a power-seeker and a power-maximizer. It seems clear that the personalization of the presidency and the emphasis on calculation, bargaining, and persuasion were internalized quickly by Kennedy, Johnson, and Nixon. There is a useful critique of this approach by Sperlich (1969), and Neustadt (1976) himself notes that he undervalued Eisenhower and that Johnson and Nixon became obsessed with power. Nevertheless, I think Neustadt's perspective became accepted practice in Washington. Such an approach to the presidency begets impression management. Doris Kearns's study of Johnson spells this out in great detail (1976). The consequence of what Neustadt was suggesting is that the president avoid situations where he would lose, where he would not look good, where he would be engaged in long-term ambiguity, where he would not, in essence, appear presidential. Aaron Wildavsky (1966) coined the term "the two presidencies" to refer to activity 1) in foreign policy and defense and 2) in domestic affairs. In the former the president has generally achieved greater successes than in the latter. The concept, Peppers (1975) argues, is somewhat fuzzy because of the numbers of issues that cut across both areas. An additional problem, because of when he was writing, was that the presidency had some setbacks from Congress and abroad in the areas of foreign and military policy. Nevertheless, the obstacles in Congress and the bureaucracy, and from the organized special interests allegedly inhibit presidents from pressing for reforms in domestic problems. This is to be contrasted with Leonard Garment's comment to Theodore White,

> In foreign policy you get drama, triumph, resolution—crisis and resolution so that in foreign policy Nixon can give the sense of leadership. But in domestic policy, there you have to deal with the whole jungle of human problems (1973:52).

Cronin (1975:251-259) adds aggregate economics to the two areas of foreign and domestic and six types of presidential activities—symbolic eadership, priority setting and program design, crisis management, legislaive and political coalition building, program implementation and evalation "follow-through," and oversight of government routines. Presidents eem to concentrate on foreign affairs most, aggregate economics second, he domestic policy third, and on the first three of the activities most, and levote decreasing amounts to the other three. If we ignore structural onsiderations for the moment, this is because those areas are subject to ;reater presidential control and those activities are easier, more rewarded, nd appear more presidential. Cronin's evaluation is that the presidency cquires an empty, self-serving, swollen character, often neglecting what is mportant by following the incentives of area and activity.

The swelling of the presidency, i.e., the huge increase in the numbers of >eople on the White House staff directly responsible to the president, has mportant implications for impression management. A number of these >eople have direct responsibilities for that kind of activity—speech writers, >ublic relations specialists, press secretaries, pollsters, advance men, communication specialists. That in itself can help measure the preoccupation. There is something, however, of deeper significance. This swelling of staff means that there are more people between the president and the outside world. Secondly, as reports continue to demonstrate, such people tend not to question the president or disagree with him. Thus there develops a distortion and narrowing of perspectives. Thirdly, presidents can easily, and certainly Johnson and Nixon did, come to be deceived by their own illusions of their importance, correctness, and omnipotence. They tend to downgrade the value of "the people" and of opposing viewpoints. They come to believe that they are the nation and that those who oppose them are parochial, stupid, or subversive. Given the assumption that there are people out there who want to do them in (and there actually are—as the sign on my office door says, even paranoids have real enemies), the president and his aides attempt to calculate the tactics (and maybe even strategies, if time permits) designed to facilitate their goals. It is a maxim that in circumstances with oppositions and spectators, impression management will be contemplated and utilized if the actors have any degree of sophistication.

One of the observations that has emerged since presidents have had their performances monitored and measured using public opinion is that the longer they are in office, the less they are liked. One of the causes of this phenomenon is that, to some extent, the office has been demythologized. The decline of the imperial presidency under Johnson and Nixon gave way to the cry that the emperor had no clothes. Ford and Carter do not inspire the same awe, nor do they try to, at least not in the same way. Interestingly, Jimmy Carter is trying to add the pomp back in, as exemplified by the reintroduction of "Hail to the Chief." But the point is that what support the president has is less total and solid. He has less of a reservoir of trust. Also, as Kernell, Sperlich, and Wildavsky (1975) demonstrate, the nature of the public has changed with a decrease in the numbers of the kinds of people who gave automatic and total approval to the president. The contemporary public is more knowledgeable, skeptical, critical, and sophisticated.

Political scientists who have tried to explain the decreasing popularity of the president have devised several explanations. John Mueller (1973) argues that it is a result of the disappointment of intense minorities eventually overwhelming lukewarm majorities. Brody and Page (1975), on the other hand, dispute Mueller and argue that popularity declines correlatively with bad news. If presidents and their aides can perceive this, then we can easily understand why they are concerned about the media, about personalization and the attribution of responsibility, about withholding discrediting information, and in staging *their* dramas and getting *their* message out in the form chosen by them.

Wildavsky, in his introductory comments about the Brody and Page piece, raises an interesting question, but then gives the wrong answer.

> I would suggest that if the popularity of presidents shows a long-term decline—so that it hardly seems to matter who the president is or what he does—the reasons are likely to be of a systemic nature, concerning the gap between what citizens expect of him and what he can do, rather than the attributes of particular personalities. Putting it another way, if presidential popularity declines because the news is bad, *how does it happen that the news is always so bad or that presidents can do so little to make it better?* (1975:8) [emphasis added].

CONCLUSION

The answers to those questions lie outside the gap between expectations and capabilities, outside the tension between the press and the administration, and even outside the structure and norms of the government of the United States. While all of the factors discussed in the previous sector do hamper the president and create circumstances which, from the perspective of that office, lead to the use of impression management, there are factors beyond the government which lead to those circumstances. While it is true that the lowering of expectations would ease the job of the president and government, that strategy deals only with symptoms and not with causes.

The answers are to be found in a world which has changed over a period of 30 years and is less subject to control and domination of the United States. The answers are to be found in a socioeconomic order which is experiencing problems in the United States and around the world which were not supposed to occur and for which no solutions seem forthcoming, promising, or legitimate. The answers are to be found in the exhaustion of interest group liberalism or corporate liberalism as political responses to unstable economic conditions and the threat of the Left. The answers are also to be found in consequences of the tragedy of Vietnam.

Maurice Duverger (1974) has recalled most clearly that during the post-World War I period, governments and leaders were criticized for impotence, instability, incompetence, corruption, and extravagent expenditures which were then supposed to be responsible for economic problems. Duverger demonstrates that the problems were initially economic and only derivatively political. The economies were organized in such a way that governments could not deal with their consequences. I would suggest that same line of reasoning holds today.

Historical changes, structural rigidities, tremendous disparities of wealth and power, and conventional and confused thinking have all contributed to the guarantee of bad news. Sophisticated analyses of these dilemmas can be found in O'Connor (1973), Wolfe (1977), and Wright (1978). Indeed, as Block (1977) states, the system may be "out of control." Presidents are in a no-win situation. Even if they are and the press got along, even if the president had a good character, even if past reforms were legislated and implemented, and even if reforms were instituted to make government more open and more efficient, governments and presidents would face bad news and would "fail" as long as they continue conventional thinking, maintain taken-for-granted reality, and support and are supported by the existing socioeconomic structure. What this means is that as long as the power and resources of government are not used to redistribute the tangible resources of the society to increase the extent of legitimacy, trust, and satisfaction, as long as coercion is unused or used only sparingly, as long as the people remain organizationally unmobilized and dependent upon the media, as long as the forms of liberal democracy are maintained, presidents will use the manipulative aspects of impression management to try to simulate consensus, establish legitimacy, overcome dissatisfaction, transcend opposition and the frustrations of office, and neutralize insoluble problems.

Symbols can be used in a number of different ways to elicit a number of different activities, e.g., from narcotization to killing to revolution. In the context of politics in the United States, current use of impression management is designed to induce acquiescence, a certain response on a public opinion poll, or a vote at the next election from a desired, generally passive, audience. The dominant contemporary rhetoric of politics does not urge organization, mobization, or mass action. Participation is not a real element of the political process. As long as participation is inhibited by elitist conceptions of representative democracy with primary focus upon a single figure, with the willing assistance of the media, attempts at impression management will flourish.

We are likely to see emphases upon symbolic reassurance and lowered expectations, the creation of enemies and scapegoats, stylistic activity and promised successes, finding and appearing to be the RIGHT leader. The foreseeable future does not seem to suggest brightness and success. The extent of disillusionment, cynicism, and lack of trust do not seem likely to decline. One might ask, how long can this go on? People have been able to endure deprivation for many years. They have also been able to accept and tolerate injustice and wide gaps between ideals and reality. The acceptance of those gaps is obviously made easier when it happens to someone else and when the victims themselves can be blamed. Much of the reason for enduring deprivation derives from a lack of resources, organization, consciousness, and hope. Much of the acceptance of the inevitability of those gaps or basic social problems like inequality and poverty can be found in the consequences of the extant symbol systems.

Murray Edelman's (1977) latest work theorizes that our political language contains contradictory beliefs that create ambivalence and, ultimately acceptance of major social problems. If such problems are insoluble and inevitable, then managing and coping seem reasonable strategies. To the extent that United States citizens lead segregated lives, experience problems from a distance, and reject structural theories and solutions, then acquiescence seems a likely response. If more people become affected, if they come into cooperative contact with others similarly affected, and if they develop alternative perspectives and futures, they might then act to deal with those problems. No analysis of impression management can neglect the context, the nature of the audience, and the available symbols.

Finally, there are a number of paradoxes involving impression management. First, it is a relatively easy and cheap form of power but one which, if exposed, could lead to stigmatization and illegitimacy. Secondly, it is a form of power which could be used to inform, to inspire, to motivate, but which, as normally practised, is designed to pacify, deflect, confuse, and seduce. Thirdly, it is a form of power used by the powerful, but it is also a sign of weakness because it is used in lieu of positive action and ultimate ends. It is, like Cronin's views of the presidency, "always too powerful and yet it is always inadequate." (1977:84).

FOOTNOTES

* A revision of a paper presented at the 1977 American Sociological Association Meetings Chicago, Illinois

1. The substance of this section comes from a book by Jonathan Schell, *The Time of Illusion.* New York: Random House (Vintage), 1976.

2. A book by Bruce Miroff, *Pragmatic Illusions,* New York: McKay, 1976, provides the material for this section.

BIBLIOGRAPHY

Auletta, Ken. "Covering Carter is like playing chess with Bobby Fischer," *More,* October 1976, 12–21.

Barber, James David. *The Presidential Character,* revised edition, Englewood Cliffs: Prentice-Hall, 1977.

Block, Fred. "Beyond corporate liberalism," *Social Problems,* 24:3 (February, 1977): 352–361.

Brody, Richard A. and Benjamin Page, "The impact of events on presidential popularity: the Johnson and Nixon administrations," in *Perspectives on the Presidency*. Aaron-Wildavsky, ed., Boston: Little, Brown, 1975:136–148.

Cronin, Thomas E. "The presidency and its paradoxes" in *The Presidency Reappraised*, second edition, Thomas E. Cronin and Rexford G. Tugwell, eds., New York: Praeger, 1977:69–85.

————, *The State of the Presidency*, Boston: Little, Brown, 1975.

Duverger, Maurice. *Modern Democracies: Economic Power versus Political Power*, New York: Holt, 1974.

Hall, Peter M. "A symbolic interactionist analysis of politics," *Sociological Inquiry*, 42, 3–4 (1972): 35–75.

Hargrove, Erwin C. *The Power of the Modern Presidency*, Philadelphia: Temple University, 1974.

Kanter, Rosabeth M. "Symbolic interactionism and politics in systemic perspective," *Sociological Inquiry*, 42, 304(1972): 79–92.

Kearns, Doris, *Lyndon Johnson and the American Dream*, New York: New American Library, 1976.

Kernell, Samuel. Peter W. Sperlich, and Aaron Wildavsky, "Public support for presidents" in *Perspectives on the Presidency*, Aaron Wildavsky, ed., Boston: Little, Brown, 1975:148–181.

Miroff, Bruce. "Monopolizing the public space: the presidency as a barrier to democratic politics," Paper presented at the 1978 Southwestern Political Science Association meetings.

————, *Pragmatic Illusions*, New York: McKay, 1976.

Mueller, John E. *War, Presidents, and Public Opinion*, New York: Wiley, 1973.

Mullen, William, *Presidential Power and Politics*, New York: St Martin's, 1976.

Neustadt, Richard E. *Presidential Power*, New York: Wiley, 1960.

————, *Presidential Power with Reflections on Johnson and Nixon*, New York: Wiley, 1976.

O'Connor, James. *The Fiscal Crisis of the State*, New York: St Martin's, 1973.

Peppers, Donald A. " 'The two presidencies': eight years later" in *Perspectives on the Presidency*, Aaron Wildavsky, ed., Boston: Little, Brown, 1975:462–471.

Schell, Jonathan. *The Time of Illusion*, New York: Random House, 1976.

Sennett, Richard. *The Fall of Public Man*, New York: Knopf, 1977.

Sorenson, Theodore. *Kennedy*, New York: Bantam, 1966.

Sperlich, Peter W. "Bargaining and overload: an essay" in *Presidential Powers in the Presidency*, Aaron Wildavsky, ed., Boston: Little, Brown, 1969:168–192.

White, Theodore. *The Making of the President, 1972*, New York: Atheneum, 1973.

Wildavsky, Aaron. "The two presidencies," *Trans-action*, 4, 2 (December 1966): 7–14.

Wolfe, Alan. *The Limits of Legitimacy*. New York: Free Press, 1977.

Wright, Erik O. *Class, Crisis, and the State*, London: NLB, 1978.

Young, T.R. "Critical dimensions in dramaturgical analysis. Part II: backstage at the White House," Paper presented at the 1976 American Sociological Association meetings.

POLITICAL CRIME
IN THE UNITED STATES

Julian Roebuck, MISSISSIPPI STATE UNIVERSITY

Stanley Weeber, MISSISSIPPI STATE UNIVERSITY

INTRODUCTION

This paper presents an empirical typology of political crime in the United States from 1960 to 1976. Though some lawyers, journalists, historians, and a few sociologists have produced a vast literature related to political crime, most of their productions take a reportorial form which reflects an amorphous mass of complex political events. Unfortunately, these materials are not ordered for systematic analysis. The extant body of criminological literature on political crime likewise illustrates the amorphous nature of this type of criminal behavior. Criminological writings may be roughly classified into a descending order of theoretical abstraction: studies of crime in a political perspective (Quinney, 1970, 1974, 1975; Reasons, 1974; Galliher and McCartney, 1977); conceptual definitions of political crime and political criminals (Schafer, 1974; Minor, 1975; Turk, 1975); cross-cultural

Studies in Symbolic Interaction—Volume 2, 1979, pages 307–329
ISBN: 0–89232–105–9

studies (Ingraham and Tokoro, 1969); development of new concepts flowing from recent social movements (Hancock and Gibbons, 1975); trans-historical analyses of political criminals (Engquist and Coles, 1970); case studies of political crime (Mouledoux, 1967); studies of corrupt or violent police conduct (Stoddard, 1967; Stark, 1972); and descriptive studies of social and personal characteristics of incarcerated war resisters (Gaylin, 1970).[1] The few systematic works by criminologists have either compared political crime with other forms of criminal behavior (Clinard and Quinney, 1973) or have focused upon specific types of political deviancy, e.g., subtypes of police corruption (Roebuck and Barker, 1974). No attempt has been made to delineate types of political crimes based upon dimensions appropriate to their special nature.

This typology is based primarily upon the action patterns of the offender, thus recognizing that political offenses are expressed in complex behavior patterns. The question has been raised concerning the appropriateness of typological analysis for studying political crime (Reasons, 1974:6). In short, a typology may not specify what it is about a certain category of behaviors (and offenses) that make them "political" in nature.

Criminologists have traditionally identified political criminals as nonconformists rather than aberrant deviants. Political criminals, in contrast to conventional criminals, announce their intentions publicly; challenge the very legitimacy of laws or their application in specific situations; aim to change the norms they are denying; do not have personal gain as a goal; and appeal to a higher morality by pointing out the void between professed beliefs and actual practices (Merton and Nisbet, 1971:829–832). These offenders have a moral commitment to a "higher social order" different from that which presently exists (Cavan, 1964:239; Clinard and Quinney, 1973:161). Unfortunately, this assessment is limited to offenders against the state, such as traitors, anti-war demonstrators, and draft resistors. Should one desire to study state lawlessness (e.g., that displayed by the CIA, the White House, and the federal regulatory agencies), then these assumptions are hardly applicable. Governmental offenders, for example, may wrap their true intentions in a cloak of secrecy; uphold their legitimacy as agents of the government; aim to maintain in public the very norms they may privately violate; may or may not seek personal gain; and may extol their moral virtues while deceptively broadening the gap between their professed beliefs and their actual practices. As Clinard and Quinney (1973:154) suggest, these offenders are committed to the preservation of the particular social and political order of which they are a part.

The evidence thus underscores the need to distinguish between the illegal action patterns of government agents and those of citizens acting against the government. Though this typology is sufficient for the purposes at hand (i.e., to construct types based upon action), the issue of definition must be dealt with. Reasons (1974:101) recently called for a more radical perspective which would emphasize the fundamental role of "power, politics, and people" in political crime. Following his suggestion, we offer a number of assumptions concerning political crime[2] which emphasize the goals of the offenders as they relate to the existing social structure. We suggest that the structural nature of income, wealth, and political power shape the offender's actions toward certain desired economic goals. Our assumptions enable us to conceptualize political crime as political action. The five assumptions are as follows:

1. The American social structure is characterized by an extreme differential distribution of personal income and wealth (Kolko, 1962; Domhoff, 1967) and a consequential unequal distribution of political power (C. Anderson, 1974; Domhoff, 1970). This unequal distribution of wealth and power is not the result of economic competition, but rather the lack of it. The ever-increasing monopolistic tendency in the United States is illustrated by the rise and proliferation of the multinational corporation, among other things (Barnet and Muller, 1974).

2. Political power stems from economic power and upholds the structural inequality. The power is realized when the ruling class uses political means to maintain its economic advantage. As many political historians have noted (Foner, 1977), the law and its interpretation is a direct expression of corporate interests. Some leading agents of government play an active, collusive role in this endeavor. Members of the executive branch, the courts, the police, government lawyers, senior Congressmen, and heads of regulatory agencies occupy positions which allow them to appropriate, distribute, or protect large sums of capital. Obviously, the ruling class is interested in cultivating these contacts, and often this is easily accomplished, since some agents of government are themselves members of the ruling class. Collusion benefits both groups that are already partially amalgamated. Corporate campaign contributions get favorable politicians elected (Mintz and Cohen, 1971:151–178; *New York Times,* 1976b, 1976e, 1976f; J. Anderson, 1976a; Alexander, 1976). Politicians direct favorable appointees to the regulatory bureaucracies (Sherrill, 1974: 205–206). Politicians and bureaucrats consult corporate executives and lawyers in formulating laws, regulations, and public policies. This last favor is accomplished by calling these executives and lawyers to testify before Congress; having them serve as consultants to the regulatory agencies and other governmental committees or commissions; and by cooperating with them in such policy-planning organizations as the Business Council, the Council on Foreign Relations, and the Council on Economic Development (Quinney, 1974: 60–75; Domhoff, 1970: 134–137, 156–250).[3] These various consultations are enhanced by the rapid movement of corporate lawyers and executives in and out of government positions (Kolko, 1969; 17; *Commercial Appeal,* 1976a). Moreover, in some cases the political-business bond is strengthened by a network of social clubs and intermarriage. Finally, the collusive arrange-

ment comes full circle when politicians solicit reelection funds by threatening to withhold business favoritism (Sherrill, 1974: 147; Cockburn, 1974: 8).
3. The ruling class is the social manifestation of these tendencies. It is made up of the owners and managers of large banks and corporations who share many economic and political interests as well as many conflicts with ordinary working people. Comprising about 1 percent of the total population, members of this class own 25 to 30 percent of all privately held corporate wealth, receive 10 to 20 percent of the yearly income, direct the large corporations and foundations, and dominate the federal government. Members of this group form a socially cohesive national upper class, that is, they are part of interlocking social circles which perceive each other as equals; belong to the same clubs; interact frequently; and intermarry (Domhoff, 1974:82–91).

4. The ruling class therefore controls the political process that determines who gets the greatest share of economic rewards. Conflict ensues between those possessing political power and those seeking access to it. Agents of government want to maintain the *status quo*, or the existing relations of power, so that they may remain in their positions of authority. The powerless (the politically and economically dispossessed) seek a "higher order" contingent upon drastic structural changes which will allow them and others to participate in political decision-making.

5. Political crimes are therefore committed in order to *maintain* (crimes by government) or to *change* (crimes against government) the existing structural relations of power. Several points must be clarified at the outset. Political crime falls into two major categories:

(1) Acts committed by government or capitalist agents which are defined as criminal by sectors of the government's own people, even though these acts are not necessarily illegal as defined by the government. Marcuse (1969:67) has summarized the issues in his *Essay on Liberation.*

> It seems that the continued functioning of the society is sufficient justification for its legality and its claim for obedience, and "functioning" seems defined rather negatively as absence of civil war, massive disorder, economic collapse. Otherwise anything goes: military dictatorship, plutocracy, government by gangs and rackets. Genocide, war crimes, crimes against humanity are not effective arguments against a government which protects property, trade, and commerce at home while it perpetuates its destructive policy abroad. And indeed, there is no *enforceable law* that could deprive such a constitutional government of its legitimacy and legality.

Thus political crime by the government would fall into at least the following categories: (a) actions by the government (and/or capitalist agents) which are not illegal in its criminal code but are illegal in the criminal code of a foreign government; (b) actions by the government and/or capitalist agents which are in violation of international law (e.g., fishing within the territorial waters of another nation); (c) government and/or capitalist agents' actions which are deliberately designed *not* to enforce existing statutes (e.g., the failure of regulatory agencies to regulate big business); (d) government and/or capitalist agents harmful actions which are beyond recognition by the people, either because of secrecy (e.g., violations of the law by the CIA and FBI), or because such acts are not yet definable in the criminal codes (e.g., pollution control). In all of these cases, the state escapes the criminal label for political reasons and reaffirms its control over the economy.

(2) Sectors of a government's people that are defined as criminal by law for acts which these sectors define as political. Again, Marcuse (1969:67) summarizes:

> . . . there is no (enforceable) law other than that which serves the *status quo,* and that those who refuse such service are *io ipso* outside the realm of law even before they come into actual conflict with the law.

Several points are of importance here and may be delineated as follows: (a) acts which are clearly definable as criminal on the surface (e.g., the bombing of banks), but are committed for purely political reasons (e.g., not to rob the bank, but to "liberate" the people from the dominance of capitalism); (b) illegal acts committed by the state for political reasons against dissenting sectors of the people (e.g., the harrassment of Martin Luther King); (c) situations defined as criminal by the state which are not of themselves illegal (e.g., the very existence of some political groups, like the Weather underground).

A TYPOLOGY OF AMERICAN POLITICAL CRIME

The present typology is empirical in that it attempts to construct types of political crime from characteristics amenable to reliable observation. These characteristics appear as dimensions of study which serve to differentiate the types from one another. Four dimensions are utilized: action patterns, the goal of the offender, the legal status of the offense, and the nature of the offense.

I. Action Patterns. Political crimes occur as fluid and complex behavior patterns. Offenders are members of groups who are constantly attempting to improve or to maintain their relative positions vis-a-vis that of other groups. Therefore, political crimes are a natural part of an on-going social process (Vold, 1958:203–219). The action patterns of agents of government are likely to help maintain the structural relations of power, while those of competing and dissenting groups are likely to strive for a change in these structural relations.

II. Goal of the Offender. The "convictional" nature of the political offender has long been recognized (Schafer, 1974:145–154). The offender, for reasons which are not personal, seeks a higher social order different from that currently existing. Those in power may also be "convictional" offenders, in that they desire to maintain the particular social order of which they are a part. The offender is therefore interested in maintaining or changing a set of structural conditions. However, it is also possible that some political offenders act for reasons that are purely personal.[4]

III. Legal Status of the Offense. Political offenses are *illegal* when the participant actors violate established legal codes. Or, these offenses may be *surrogate-illegal* when selected legal codes are applied solely for purposes of punishment or castigation. There may be nothing inherently criminal in the act, but the actor is criminalized when persons in power attach the illegal label to his behavior. For example, this occurs when political dissenters are arrested for petty crimes such as criminal trespass, parading without a permit, or for more serious crimes such as treason, sabotage, or espionage. Because the "real" crime, political action, cannot be punished (the American legal system does not officially recognize political crime), the actor is instead punished for legalistic substitutes. Finally, actions may be *para-legal.* One acts with authority derived from a system of executive power, such as an executive committee or agency appointed by the President. This authority may appear to have a legal base (it is derived from the executive branch of government), but it does not in fact have any legislative determination or definition since it is beyond Congressional control. Such a situation exists in the secret deliberations of executive committees where there may be no Congressional oversight whatsoever[5] (Borrosage, 1975:73). As might be expected, para-legal actions are usually taken by the government against the people. Both ordinary citizens and agents of government are likely to act illegally. For purposes of this paper, actions that are illegal, surrogate-illegal, or para-legal will all be considered as *criminal* acts.

IV. Nature of the Offense. The offender's illegal actions may be violent or nonviolent, secretive or unconcealed (Minor, 1975:385, 389). The forthcoming typology delineates four types of political crime: (1) intervention, (2) surveillance, (3) confrontation, and (4) evasion and/or collusion. It has been previously noted that it is necessary and desirable to distinguish between crimes by government and crimes against government. Therefore, *crimes against government* are realized in attempts to protest, express dissatisfaction with, or alter in some way the existing structural relations of power. This category would include violations of the criminal law as well as acts which are made criminal by the state in an effort to block political dissent.

On the other hand, *crimes by government* consist of criminal violations by agents of government. These violations typically are actions designed to maintain the *status quo,* or the existing structural relations of power.

The typology is presented as follows. First, the major type (intervention, surveillance, etc.) is discussed in a general introduction. Second, the two sub-types (crimes against government and crimes by the government) are presented. When each sub-type is examined, the dimensions of study will guide the discussions in the text in the order in which they were given above: action patterns (with documentation of those patterns); the goal of the offender; the legal status of the offense; and the nature of the offense.

I. INTERVENTION

Intervention designates illegal attempts to change the domestic affairs of a sovereign nation (political and/or economic) in a manner that will produce favorable results for the changer. The changer(s) may be agents of the United States government desiring certain alterations in a foreign nation, or they may be individuals or groups attempting to make changes in the American structure. Regardless of who the changers are, they affect same through the systematic manipulation of events. In some cases, manipulation takes the form of penetration or infiltration of agents into the institutional life of the target nation. Penetration is subsumed under manipulation and could ideally be considered as preparatory to a planned manipulation. The line between the two is difficult to establish. Manipulation might constitute direct actions, such as war-making or para-military operations. Penetration, on the other hand, might refer to financial support and technical assistance to political parties; support of private organizations, including labor unions and businesses; and covert propaganda.[6]

Crimes by Government

American conduct in the Vietnam War exemplifies manipulative state action as an instrument of corporate policy. Notwithstanding the evidence that the war was unconstitutional, or that innumerable American war crimes were committed there (Quinney, 1975:152–156), participation continued as part of a global strategy for pursuit of certain raw matrials badly needed by American corporations (Kolko, 1969).

Penetration, followed by manipulation, is characteristic of CIA intervention. In Ecuador (which was to become the model for CIA intervention in the sixties) this agency funded labor organizations, the press, and anti-communist factions that in concert disposed of the Arosemena regime in 1963 (Morris, 1975:76–77). The same pattern is amplified by the CIA's record in Chile. The agency spent $20 million in the 1964 Chilean elections to boost Eduardo Frei, a friend of America's ITT, into power. When it appeared likely in the 1970 elections that the Marxist candidate Allende would nationalize ITT's holdings, ITT together with the CIA and the White House developed plans to block Allende's candidacy. After Allende was elected, more elaborate plans were operationalized, including economic sabotage and the fomenting of labor violence. CIA funds were funneled into

Chile to "destabilize" the Allende regime and to arrange the military *coup* that eventually ousted Allende in 1973 (Petras and Morley, 1975:x). In addition to Allende, the CIA is suspect in two other assassination plots involving heads of states and made concrete attempts against the lives of five others (*New York Times,* 1975f). Intervention has not ceased, as witnessed in recent CIA activity in Angola, Italy, and Portugal. The agency was also an accomplice in Lockheed's payoffs to foreign government officials, supplying information to the corporation that helped it to illegally secure contracts (*Washington Post,* 1975: Anderson, 1976b).

For the past 20 years, the CIA has funneled money to foreign government officials and private citizens both to secure intelligence information and to enhance American capitalist interests (e.g., King Hussein has received $750,000 in 10 years for information that could be gathered from the news media) (*New York Times,* 1977c).

By the end of 1976, more than 250 companies had confessed to making illegal payments, including so-called facilitating payments and suspicious commissions as well as outright bribes to foreign officials. Two dozen of these companies have been sued by the SEC. The Lockheed Aircraft Corporation, for example, spent over $25 million in questionable attempts to sell its planes (*New York Times,* 1977a).

The goal or purpose of these actions appears to be perpetuation of corporate capital. The aftermath of CIA intrusions into Ecuador, Chile, Zaire, Brazil, Somalia, Indonesia, Iran, and other nations has left a trail of poverty, social chaos, and political repression (*New York Times,* 1976h; Baraheni, 1976; Anderson, 1976d), but above all, regimes receptive to American businesses. Morris (1975:77) notes that ITT, Dow Chemical, and other U.S. interests account for 60 percent of the holdings of foreign investors in Ecuador as a result of CIA intervention. In Chile, the changes occuring after the 1973 *coup* were more dramatic:

> The military regime discarded completely the Allende government's nationalist foreign policy, became unconditional supporters of U.S. policies and business interests, and outlined a new development strategy designed to encourage foreign capital investment. . . . The vast majority of foreign and domestic enterprises intervened in or nationalized during the preceding three years would . . . be returned to their original owners, and the junta agreed in principle to paying compensation to the U.S. copper companies (Petras and Morley, 1975:140).

All of the foregoing interventions by government are illegal. These violations infringe upon the United Nations Charter which protects the political independence of sovereign states.[7] Despite the illegalities involved, offenders are not very likely to be brought to trial, nor is there usually any consideration of this possibility. Foreign covert operations by the CIA (particularly those related to violence, assassination, and the overthrow of existing political regimes) may be considered para-legal as well as illegal. Authority for the CIA operations is derived from a series of secret National Security Council directives handed down since 1948. These directives appear to have a legal base, since they are approved by an executive committee of government; but since their secret deliberations are beyond the reach of Congress, the directives do not in fact have any legislative determination or definition (Wise, 1975:28).

The nature of government intervention may be violent or nonviolent, secret or open. As capitalist interests are increasingly threatened, there is an increasing likelihood of violent intervention by the state in order to protect these interests. Interests of capitalists may openly conflict with those of workers, and thus the state must shroud its interventions in secrecy— although this is not always true. The Vietnam War, for example, was carried on openly, despite the fact that the national consensus on the legitimacy of the war had dissolved (Kolko, 1969). Additionally, the U.S. government permits U.S. companies to bribe and pay-off officials in foreign countries to do business.

Crimes Against Government

Offenders against the state resort to direct manipulation to actualize what they term class interests when it is evident that these interests cannot be achieved through the existing political system. Such groups as the Symbionese Liberation Army and the Black Liberation Army have assassinated civic leaders and city policemen, have kidnapped wealthy individuals as a lever for economic change, and have engaged in terror tactics, such as bombing the offices of Gulf Oil, Shell Oil, and other large corporations. In Mississippi, the Republic of New Africa attempted through violence to establish a sovereign Black nation. The Weather underground emerged in 1970 to wage violent struggle against the establishment, as evidenced by several bombings.

The rationale for direct intervention is baldly stated as a desire to completely restructure the existing distribution of wealth, property, and political power. The public policies dictated by the capitalist class are viewed as oppressive, exploitative, and morally unjust. The doctrine of the radical collective amounts to nothing less than a declaration of war against capitalists, as this announcement by the SLA illustrates:

we of . . . the SLA *do not* under the rights of human beings submit to the murder, oppression, and exploitation of our children and people and do under the rights granted to the people under the Declaration of Independence of the United States, do now . . . by force of Arms and with every drop of our blood *declare revolutionary war* against the Fascist Capitalist Class, and all their agents of murder, oppression, and exploitation (emphasis in the original, *Berkeley Barb, 1973*).

Similarly, the Black Liberation Army has stated its goals, and its identity as well:

> ... we are small urban guerilla units, waging armed struggle against the agents of death —the United States government. ... We view guerilla war as an embryonic form of the National Liberation Army. ... In other words we are the embryonic form of the people's army (National Committee for the Defense, 1972).

The actions of the offender become defined as illegal, and the statutes are applied vigorously since the actions call into question the legitimacy and necessity of the state. The actions are characteristically violent, and occur as open manipulations to serve as inducements for change.

II. SURVEILLANCE

Surveillance is the accumulation of information which is commonly referred to as intelligence gathering. Intelligence is designed to reflect events presently occurring at a given location, to discover past events of a sensitive nature, or to estimate when and where future events may be expected to occur. Unlike intervention, which attempts to change certain conditions, surveillance is intended only to monitor them. Systematic accumulation of information is reached by electronics or by classical espionage. Electronics refers to the full range of technology applied to the search for information, and includes bugs and wiretaps. Classical espionage, on the other hand, employs human rather than electronic means of collection. Human spies serve as monitors, informers, or infiltrators who gain access to certain bodies of information. They may also perform petty criminal offenses in the course of information gathering (e.g., burglary and robbery).

Crimes by Government

The government employs both electronic and human agents to gather information about its citizens. From 1969 to 1971, President Nixon placed wiretaps on 13 ranking Administration officials and newsmen. Later, in 1972, the White House bugged the Democratic National Committee (U.S. House of Representatives, 1975:212–218; U.S. Senate, 1974:84). Electronic surveillance was also used by the Army, which kept files on 100,000 American dissidents. The CIA kept 7,200 similar files plus 100 more on organized radical groups. The IRS had political intelligence files on 8,000 individuals, freely trading its information with the CIA and the FBI. Millions of private communications between the United States and foreign countries from 1947 to 1975 were scanned by the National Security Agency. By far the most wide-reaching intelligence campaign was reserved for the FBI. The Bureau collected 500,000 intelligence files, and compiled a list of 26,000 persons to be jailed in the event of a national emergency. FBI agents subjected many private citizens to secret harassment. The repertoire—which is still being adhered to (*New York Times*, 1976c)—called for burglaries, buggings, wiretappings, anonymous letters, and the use of informants. Most all of these tactics surfaced in the smear campaign against Dr. Martin Luther King. The FBI harassed and attempted to discredit Dr. King for six years. Among other things, the bureau tapped his phone and bugged various rooms where he was present; sent him anonymous threatening letters; and sent his wife a tape recording which supposedly revealed an extra-marital affair of Dr. King's (*New York Times*, 1975e). Other targets of abuse, besides Dr. King, were women, socialists, youth (in short, any and all working class groups attempting to develop class consciousness or striving to pursue class goals). The FBI has demonstrated a pattern of break-ins, buggings, surveillance, and mail openings over a number of years, which, in view of the investigating Senate committee, violated the rights of thousands of U.S. citizens—many of whom had committed no crimes at all (*New York Times*, 1977b).

Securing a political victory and monitoring dissent (see *Clarion-Ledger*, 1975) constitute the objectives behind surveillance by government. This subtype of surveillance is illegal. Domestic activities by the CIA, whether by electronic or human agents, violate the National Security Act which states that the CIA "shall have no police, subpoena, law enforcement, or internal security functions." Unwarranted wiretapping of any kind violates the Fourth Amendment in most cases, even when directed toward "subversives" allegedly threatening the national security (*Vanderbilt Law Review*, 1971). Covert data collection on American citizens violates sections of the Right to Privacy Act (U.S. House of Representatives, 1974). The nature of government surveillance is nonviolent and covert.

Crimes Against Government

Agents collecting information on the American government have made use of both electronic and human agents. Though the Soviet KGB did bug the American Embassy in Moscow (Marchetti and Marks, 1974:214), classical espionage cases such as Butenko and Ivano in 1964, Whalen in 1966, and Ellsberg and Russo in 1971 have appeared more regularly. These cases pertained to retention or transmission of secret military information (*New York Times*, 1964, 1971; Marchetti and Marks, 1974:212–214). Butenko and Ivanov, for example, were charged with conspiracy to commit espionage for retaining documents related to the Strategic Air Command. Similarly, Whalen was charged with passing defense secrets to the Soviets. The Ellsberg-Russo case was unusual in that the defendants did not reveal their secrets to a foreign government but rather to an American newspaper. Ellsberg turned over the *Pentagon Papers* to the press as a personal protest against U.S. involvement in "a hopeless war."

Surveillance against government is undertaken to aid a foreign government (e.g., the Whalen case) or to protest a specific issue, such as the Vietnam War. Espionage is illegal (according to 18 U.S.C. 793:798) or surrogate-illegal. An example of the latter is the trial of Ellsberg and Russo, where the espionage statutes were apparently used as legalistic substitutes applied for the purpose of castigating an Administration opponent. The specific sections on which the government based its case had never before been implemented; the government was, in effect, asking the court to establish a precedent which would criminalize *ex post facto* the defendants' actions (*Columbia Law Review*, 1973:935). The nature of surveillance against government is nonviolent, covert, and in Ellsberg's unusual case, overt.

III. CONFRONTATION

While intervention and surveillance are concerned with one group's changing or monitoring the conditions of another group, confrontation represents two groups who are in conflict with one another. Patterned confrontation may take two forms. One form is a personal, face-to-face contact with other persons within the context of controversy over a specific issue or a cluster of closely related issues. A second form, which also occurs within the context of controversy, is symbolic contact. Here the conflicting parties need not meet face-to-face. Terrorists, for example, do not arrive bomb-in-hand to execute their deeds. The dividing issues are represented by an action (e.g., a bombing) which symbolizes conflict.

Crimes by Government

Two groups of government agents, the police and National Guard forces, have on numerous occasions committed offenses of the "personal, face-to-face" variety. These agents killed students at Kent State, Jackson State, and other campuses. Nearly 700 protestors and innocent bystanders were beaten and jailed by police at the Democratic Convention at Chicago in 1968. That same year police battled protestors at Columbia University and San Francisco State College, and in 1969 a similar "police riot" took place at People's Park in Berkeley, California.

Confrontation crimes by government are motivated by the desire to quash dissent. Such offenses violate criminal law ranging from robbery and burglary to murder. The nature of these offenses runs the full spectrum of possibilities in terms of violence and secrecy.

Crimes Against Government

Action patterns representing this sub-type are personal, face-to-face, and symbolic. Large scale protests and mass demonstrations, such as the Free

Speech Movement at the University of California in 1964, the anti-war demonstration at the Pentagon in 1967, and May Day demonstration in Washington, D.C., in 1971 all illustrate this type of confrontation. Though these events were for the most part peaceful, most were marred by some violence. Following the 1969 Vietnam Mobilization in Washington, D.C., for example, splinter groups fought police and destroyed property (*New York Times*, 1969). In the 1970s, more symbolic forms of confrontation were on the increase. Karber (1971:523) reported 1,425 terrorist bombings between January, 1970 and March, 1971. Kidnapping as a form of political terrorism (in America, at least) is a recent development. The first case emerged with the abduction of Patricia Hearst by the SLA.

The goals of these various confrontations included the desires for symbolic communication (terrorism); protesting specific issues; and changes in the structural relations of power (protests and mass demonstrations). The second goal appears in selected events, such as the Sproul Hall incident at Berkeley and the 1969 Vietnam Mobilization, where one dominant issue served as a catalyst for action. The "structural change" goal was evident at such political trials as the Chicago 8 and New York 21 trials. A principal argument of the defendants was that power does not belong to the people, but to a minority of elected officials who do not respond to the will of the majority. This theme waŝ expressed in testimony which focused upon a number of issues resulting from actions of the power structure, e.g., chemical warfare, pollution, racism, poverty, and the oppressive nature of law and the judicial system (Clinard and Quinney, 1973:163).

Confrontation against government is illegal where destruction of property occurs, or where the civil rights of protesting groups are violated (*New York Times*, 1975a). However, most instances are surrogate-illegal. Protestors are usually not arrested on the basis of their intent or motivation (because American law does not officially designate dissent as a crime), but for legalistic substitutes instead. For example, 208 protestors were arrested not for protesting, *per se,* but for failing to honor the parade permit expiration deadline following the 1967 march on the Pentagon (*New York Times,* 1967). Conspiracy laws may also be considered as substitutes. These laws (18 U.S.C. 2101-2102) stipulate that the conspirators need not be proven to have planned any activity, but only to have said something to each other. Defendants at the Chicago 8, Oakland 7, Harrisburg 7, Boston 5, and Gainesville 8 trials were tried under these statutes (Quinney, 1975:63).

These offenses by nature are violent or nonviolent. All are overt. Conspiracy laws to the contrary, the evidence suggests that the "conspirators" act in an open and announced manner, at least *prior* to the trial (Sternberg, 1974:197).[8] Even terrorists, who do plot secretly, wish for their actions to be recognized and to communicate a message (Karber, 1971:527).

IV. EVASION AND/OR COLLUSION

Evasion, unlike other types of political crime, involves a disavowal or retreat from a condition that the participating actors define as undesirable. There are two kinds of evasion: denial of responsibility and flight in order to escape prosecution. The former means that persons disclaim knowledge of or responsibility for an accountable action. Tied in with this sub-type of evasion is collusion between governmental agencies and big business, which these agencies are required by law to regulate. In our opinion this collusion, which in effect permits big business to regulate itself, designates the most significant and insidious form of political crime.

The latter form of evasion, flight, indicates a physical displacement or escape from the United States. This sub-type deals primarily with draft evaders.

Crimes by Government

High government officials, especially presidents, have denied complicity in questionable events which they had previously approved. President Nixon repeatedly denied for two years any involvement in the Watergate break-in and cover-up. Nixon has not yet fully conceded his involvement, even though it is documented that he was in command of the facts pertaining to the Watergate break-in almost immediately after it occurred, and that he orchestrated (especially after March 21, 1973) a cover-up plan to protect many of his aides who had planned or initially covered-up the break-in (U.S. House of Representatives, 1975:39, 60–69, 120–123, 134–140, 151–168, 174–175, 177–178, 182–197). Moreover, the sworn statements of Secretary of State Kissinger, when compared with his behind-the-scenes manipulations, strongly indicate that he lied to Congressional committees about the CIA's role in the Chilean *coup* of 1973 (Petras and Morley, 1975:xi., 131–137).

Government evasion and collusion is also evident in the deliberate actions and non-actions of federal departments and regulatory agencies. The Justice Department, for example, allowed Exxon to expand its operations into Iran in 1952 despite carefully documented evidence that the expansion involved extensive anti-trust violations (Sampson, 1975:121–126). Twenty years later, the Justice Department allowed ITT to undertake the largest merger in American history by virtue of a $400,000 campaign contribution by ITT to President Nixon's reelection committee (Anderson and Clifford, 1974). This trend of nonenforcement is also characteristic of the independent regulatory agencies whose mission is to regulate business. It is well known that the regulated businesses have come to dominate their regulators.

Gulf Oil was recently charged by a House Subcommittee for failing to deliver contracted amounts of natural gas to 16 states. Moreover, the

Political Crime in the United States

Federal Power Commission was accused of a six-year regulatory failure in its dealings with Gulf (*Clarion-Ledger*, 1977b). As another case, the FPC allegedly has permitted Texaco to withhold 500 billion cubic feet of natural gas this winter that was tapped to ease the energy shortage (*Clarion-Ledger*, 1977a).

In a recent timely book, *The Control of Oil* (1977), John Blair documents that the anti-trust laws and several regulatory agencies, including the Federal Trade Commission and the Federal Energy Administration, render no effective controls over the seven largest oil corporations in the world. The seven sisters (Exxon, Mobil, So-Cal, Texaco, Gulf, Royal Dutch Shell, and British Petroleum), through and by a collusive symbiotic relationship with private, local, state, and federal governmental agencies, maintain a monopoly over the crude oil industry from the time the oil is mined, refined, transported, and retailed on domestic markets. This control results in an absence of free markets, free enterprise, and political accountability.

The Office of the Comptroller of the Currency is responsible for regulating competition among the 4,700 national banks in the Federal Reserve System. The Office's functions are, among others, to supervise bank mergers and to determine the scope of permissible banking activities. The interests of working class citizens are to be looked after. However, the supervisory policies of the Office are formulated by the National Advisory Committee to the Comptroller, a group comprised of representatives from the largest national banks. In the 1960s the Comptroller, with help from the advisory committee, was unusually lenient in policing bank mergers. In fact, it was by far the most lax of the federal agencies whose authority touched upon bank mergers, even though all the agencies were interpreting the same statutes (Leinsdorf and Etra, 1973:280).

The enormous costs of nonenforcement are bared by a review of the Federal Communication Commission's "regulation" of long distance telephone rates. In 1953, the FCC determined that utility companies could establish charges on interstate calls yielding no more than a 6.5 percent rate of profit. But American Telephone and Telegraph proceeded to charge its customers more than it was supposed to—at times yielding as much as a 7.9 percent profit rate. Between 1955–1961, AT&T reaped $985,000,000 in unauthorized profits due to the overcharges. When the FCC finally decided to do something about the overcharges, they ruled in AT&T's favor by raising the acceptable rate of profit from 6.5 percent to 7.5 percent (Mintz and Cohen, 1971:249–250).

The chronicle of bureaucratic inactivity could extend almost endlessly, and we can mention only a few additional cases. Recent revelations have indicated the inadequate regulation of pesticide use (*Clarion-Ledger*, 1976a); discrimination in the granting of home loans (*Clarion-Ledger*, 1976b); discrimination in the hiring practices in the building trades and trucking unions (*Clarion-Ledger*, 1976c); "clear-cutting" (i.e., massive denuding of physiologically immature trees) in the natural forests (*New York Times*, 1976a); environmental pollutants (Anderson, 1976c); and tax violations by large corporations (*Jackson Daily News*, 1976). Trends such as these continued under the Ford Administration's deregulation programs, which had the effect of loosening already lax controls on corporate behavior, thus allowing corporations greater freedom to pursue illegal activities (*New York Times*, 1976d).

Some other cases relate to cabinet level departments of the executive branch, and to special departments created in response to specific needs. An example of the latter is the Special Watergate Prosecution Force. The Special Prosecutor failed to bring any charges in 60 percent of the investigations initiated by his office, thus leaving many of the Watergate crimes to gather dust in the Watergate transcripts, the Senate Watergate Report, and other sources (Sale, 1975:8).

Police corruption represents still another example of evasion and collusion. The police fail to enforce many laws and often break the laws that they are supposed to enforce. Officers fail to uphold the law and, when confronted, characteristically deny any wrongdoing. However, it has been documented that police officers have received payoffs in return for protecting gamblers, prostitutes, and burglars from arrest. They have systematically engaged in theft, shakedowns, casefixing, and other offenses (Roebuck and Barker, 1974:427–437). These crimes are personally lucrative to the officer. There is evidence, also, that police corruption may be but a portion of a larger system of relationships which are pursued for profit. Chambliss discusses the organization of criminal vices in Seattle. The vices, he claims, are

> organized around, run by, and created in the interests of economic, legal and political elites. . . . The cabal that manages the vices is composed of important businessmen, law enforcement officers, political leaders, and a member of a major trade union. Working for, and with, this cabal of respectable community members is a staff which coordinates the daily activities of prostitution, gambling, bookmaking, the sale and distribution of drugs, and other vices. Representatives from each of these groups . . . meet regularly to distribute profits, discuss problems, and make the necessary organizational and policy decisions essential to the maintenance of a profitable, trouble-free business (1976:162–163).

Corruption by elected public officials parallels police corruption in many ways. Elected officials and their aides also face situations of personal gain. Bobby Baker and Thomas Dodd were among those convicted in the Sixties for using their positions to gain unauthorized profits (Green et al., 1975:76–78, 180–184). In 1973, Vice-President Agnew acknowledged that he awarded government contracts to Baltimore County engineers in return for $100,000 in kickbacks from 1962 to 1972 (*New York Times*, 1973). Richard

Nixon received unlawful government funds for his private residences and avoided paying a portion of his income taxes for 1969–1972 (U.S. House of Representatives, 1975:17–18, 316–320, 462–463). In the past fifteen years, numerous U.S. Congressmen received kickbacks from the South Koreans for rigging grain and defense contracts (*Commercial Appeal,* 1976b). These corrupt practices, much like police corruption, are linked to a larger system of organized corruption that is pursued for profit. Evidence shows, for example, that the profitable exploits of Nixon and Agnew are not simply blotches on the records of these individuals, but rather are integral to a larger system of official favors and backscratching (Sale, 1973; Quinney, 1975:159–161).

Protection of both executive authority and national security were the issues leading to the presidential crimes. The executive authority rationale is illustrated in the Watergate cover-up. One of the President's tape recordings best summarized the purpose of the cover-up, quoting Nixon as saying ". . . we're going to protect our people [i.e., the White House staff], if we can" (U.S. House of Representatives, 1975:147). Eisenhower and Kennedy, on the other hand, cited national security reasons for lying to the public. Given the early Sixties Cold War atmosphere, such a rationale is realistic. Structural maintenance is a second major goal of evasion. The failure to regulate big business, criminal vices, and official corruption, which costs consumers millions of dollars annually, is probably the most pervasive mechanism that now exists to maintain the distribution of wealth and power in the United States.

Evasion by agents of government is clearly illegal in executive, administrative, and police crimes. In the case of Watergate, for instance, the House Judiciary Committee drew an article of impeachment which charged President Nixon with plotting "to cover-up, conceal, and protect those responsible" for the Watergate break-in (U.S. House of Representatives, 1975:2). Eight of the President's aides were convicted of conspiracy, obstruction of justice, or defraudation of the United States for their roles in the cover-up (*Time,* 1975). Kissinger's actions were also illegal, amounting to perjury. The collusion between governmental regulatory agencies and big business is likewise clearly illegal. All such acts are nonviolent; some are overt and some are covert.

Crimes Against Government

Persons evading specific laws and government regulations may flee to a jurisdiction outside the United States or escape to the underground. Some 10,000 draft evaders, for example, emigrated to Canada each year from 1965 to 1970. Underground evaders may have accounted for most of the 15,310 Americans listed as "delinquent" by the Selective Service in 1968. These men were primarily draft registrants who fled to ghettos, communes, or other areas where no questions were asked or where they could find friendly refuge (Roebuck and Friery, 1974: 6, 13–14).

Evasions characteristic of this sub-type were engaged in for personal reasons.[9] Emigrant draft evaders lost faith in the American government because of its conduct in the Vietnam War, and considered draft resisters to be "fools in an un-worthy, sinking ship" (Roebuck and Friery, 1974:19). Neither emigrants nor undergrounders attempted to "change the system;" instead, they followed their own independent judgments and abandoned the system altogether. Evaders used illegal means to escape prosecution. They employed nonviolent tactics, and beyond a handful of helpful intimates, utilized overt means to avoid the draft.

SUMMARY AND CONCLUSIONS

This paper has delineated four types of political crime: intervention, surveillance, confrontation, and evasion and/or collusion. Intervention involved attempts to change the domestic affairs of a sovereign nation in a manner desirable to the changer. Surveillance designated the monitoring of events through intelligence gathering. Confrontation was realized in group conflict, and evasion referred to a retreat from a condition or situation which the participating actors defined as undesirable. Prior to presenting the typology, we set forth a number of assumptions about the nature of political crime which provided the theoretical frame on which the typology was based. The typology indicates a number of points for future research: (1) Contemporary political crime cannot be understood without adequate consideration of its economic base; (2) Class conflict, relating to economic and political inequality, generates political crime; (3) Total reliance on strictly legal definitions of political crime is incomplete and unreliable; (4) Political crime in the United States must be viewed in a global perspective (i.e., the activities of multinational corporations and some governmental agencies overlap with those of many foreign nations by design).

In connection with all these points, we found evasion and/or collusion to be the most significant form of political crime in the United States. Finally, our analysis indicates the possible need for statutes defining political crime and political criminals.

FOOTNOTES

1. Because of lack of space, this literature review is necessarily limited. For further reading, see the bibliographies in Clinard and Quinney (1973), Reasons (1974), and Minor (1975).

2. Ferdinand (1966:48) criticizes empirical typologies: ". . . although they are defined directly in terms of observations, those who have made use of this approach in social science have generally done so with an implicit theory of human nature in mind. Consequently, the resultant typology almost always reflects certain ill-defined assumptions regarding the causes

of behavior. This bias means essentially that the researcher will be particularly attentive to certain trends in his data but peculiarly blind to others." In this paper, we attempt to overcome a portion of this bias by indicating our assumptions concerning political crime prior to presenting the typology. Our analysis does "take sides" (Becker, 1967); our data are reliable only to the extent that another researcher, operating under similar assumptions, would arrive at findings which are similar to ours.

3. To supplement these relationships, corporations may bribe politicians or may form business lobbies, such as the Business Roundtable (*New York Times,* 1975d), to solicit the enactment of self-serving legislation.

4. That is, given a set of structural conditions, the actor may opt to commit a political crime for personal reasons. See especially the discussion below (pp. 20–21) concerning political corruption.

5. For reasons to be made explicit later, the activites of the CIA provide the best examples of para-legal actions.

6. These penetration tactics are among those employed by the CIA in its covert operations. For a brief overview of these tactics, see Marchetti and Marks (1974:63–74).

7. See Falk (1975) for a discussion of CIA violations of international law.

8. The 1960s radicals ("conspirators") conducted themselves in a quite open manner. They wrote often, and spoke frequently to large gatherings as a means to gathering support for their cause. Ironically, it was not until long after the so-called "harmful" or "conspiratorial" actions that any kind of real conspiracy existed. Not until the radicals were indicted and given a group identity (e.g., Chicago 8, New York 21) did any conspiring proceed, such as the "Bobby Seal Birthday Cake Incident," "The Great Bathroom Debate," and other courtroom disruptions.

9. See note 4 above. In this case a structural condition—the Vietnam War—was viewed as intolerable, and the evaders violated the law for personal reasons, given this condition.

REFERENCES

Alexander, Herbert, *Financing the 1972 Election,* Princeton, N.J.: Citizen's Research Foundation, 1976.

Anderson, Charles H., *The Political Economy of Social Class,* Englewood Cliffs, N.J.: Prentice-Hall, 1974.

Anderson, Jack, (United Features Syndicate, Inc.), "Political Payoffs Are Documented," March 22, 1976a.

————— , "The Power of the Multinationals," March 23, 1976b.

————— , "Government Ignoring Health Standards," July 27, 1976c.

————— , "Dictatorships Receive U.S. Backing," October 11, 1976d.

Anderson, Jack and George Clifford, *The Anderson Papers,* New York: Ballantine, 1974.

Baraheni, Reza, "Terror in Iran," *New York Review of Books* 23 (October 28, 1976): 21–25.

Barnet, Richard and Ronald E. Muller, *Global Reach,* New York: Simon and Schuster, 1974.

Becker, Howard S., "Whose Side Are We On?" *Social Problems* 14, 3 (Winter 1967): 239–247.

Berkeley Barb, "Declare War," August 21, 1973:3.

Blair, John, *The Control of Oil,* New York: Pantheon, 1977.

Borrosage, Robert, "Secrecy vs. the Constitution," *Society* 12 (March/April 1975): 71–75.

Cavan, Ruth, "Underworld, Conventional, and Ideological Crime," *Journal of Criminal Law, Criminology, and Police Science* 55 (1964): 235–240.

Chambliss, William J., "Vice, Corruption, Bureaucracy, and Power," pp. 162–183 in W. Chambliss and M. Mankoff (Eds.) *Whose Law? What Order?* New York: Wiley, 1976.

Clarion-Ledger (Jackson, Mississippi), "CIA Reportedly Opened, Read Mail of Americans," September 25, 1975:8.

————— , "Agency's Inaction on Pesticides Told," February 12, 1976a:C1.

————— , "4 Agencies Discriminate on Loans, Suit Claims," April 27, 1976b:4.

————— , "Panel: U.S. Still Discriminating," May 12, 1976c: C5.

————— , "Investigators Say Texaco Withholding Natural Gas Production," February 23, 1977a: A1, 20.

————— , "Panel: Gulf Broke Law, Withheld Gas," February 24, 1977b: A1, 24.

Clinard, Marshall B. and Richard Quinney, *Criminal Behavior Systems*, New York: Holt, Rinehart, and Winston, 1973.

Cockburn, Alexander, "Sweet Mysteries of Watergate," *New York Review of Books* 21 (November 28, 1974): 8–16.

Columbia Law Review, "The Espionage Statutes and Publication of Defense Information," Volume 73 (May, 1973).

Commercial Appeal (Memphis, Tennessee), "Federal 'Conflicts' Draw Interest," October 31, 1976a:14.

————— , "Korean Influence-Peddling Sparks Variety of U.S. Probes," November 15, 1976b: 1 and 6.

Domhoff, G. William, *Who Rules America?* Englewood Cliffs, N.J.: Prentice-Hall, 1967.

————— , *The Higher Circles*, New York: Random House, 1970.

————— , *The Bohemian Grove and Other Retreats*, New York: Harper and Row, 1974.

Engquist; Virginia and Frances S. Coles, " 'Political' Criminals in America: O'Hare (1923); Contine and Rainer (1950)," *Issues in Criminology* 5 (Summer 1970): 209–220.

Falk, Richard A., "CIA Covert Intervention and International Law," *Society* 12 (March/April 1975): 39–44.

Ferdinand, Theodore N., *Typologies of Delinquency*, New York: Random House, 1966.

Foner, Eric, "Get a Lawyer!" *New York Review of Books* 24 (April 14, 1977): 37–39.

Galliher, John F. and James L. McCartney, *Criminology: Power, Crime, and Criminal Law*, Homewood, Illinois: The Dorsey Press, 1977.

Gaylin, Williard, *In the Service of Their Country*, New York: Random House, 1970.

Green, Mark, Bruce Rosenthal, and Lynn Darling, *Who Runs Congress?* New York: Bantam, 1975.

Hancock, Kelly and Don G. Gibbons, "The Future of Crime in American Society," Unpublished manuscript, Department of Sociology, Portland State University, 1975.

Ingraham, B.B. and Kazuhiko Tokoro, "Political Crime in the United States and Japan," *Issues in Criminology* 4 (Spring 1969): 145–170.

Jackson Daily News (Jackson, Mississippi), "Nader Group Says IRS Soft on Audits," November 15, 1976:14.

Karber, Phillip A., "Urban Terrorism: Baseline Data and a Conceptual Framework," *Social Science Quarterly* 52 (December 1971): 521–540.

Kolko, Gabriel, *Wealth and Power in America*, New York: Praeger, 1962.

————— , *The Roots of American Foreign Policy*, Boston: Beacon, 1969.

Leinsdorf, David and Donal Etra, *Citibank*, New York: Grossman, 1973.

Marchetti, Victor and John D. Marks, *The CIA and the Cult of Intelligence*, New York: Dell, 1974.

Marcuse, Herbert, *Essay on Liberation*, Boston: Beacon, 1969.

Merton, Robert and Robert Nisbet, *Contemporary Social Problems*, New York: Harcourt Brace Jovanovich, 1971.

Minor, William M., "Political Crime, Political Justice, and Political Prisoners," *Criminology* 12 (February 1975): 385–398.

Mintz, Morton and Jerry Cohen, *America, Inc.*, New York: Dial, 1971.

Morris, Roger, "The Aftermath of CIA Intervention," *Society* 12 (March/April 1975): 76–80.

Mouledoux, Joseph C., "Political Crime and the Negro Revolution," pp. 217–231 in M. Clinard and R. Quinney (Eds.), *Criminal Behavior Systems*, New York: Holt, Rinehart, and Winston, 1967.

National Committee for the Defense of Joanne Cheismard and Clark Squire, "Break de Chains," Pamphlet, New York City, 1973.

New York Times, "Butenko and Ivanov Guilty in Spy Case," December 31, 1964: 1.
————— , "Protestors Defying Deadline Seized in Capital," October 23, 1967:1.
————— , "Tear Gas Repels Radicals' Attack," November 16, 1969: 1, 60.
————— , "Ellsberg Yields, Is Indicted; Says He Gave Data to Press," June 29, 1971:1.
————— , "Evidence Shows Gifts to Agnew," October 11, 1973: 1.
————— , "The Illegal Arrests," August 3, 1975a: E16.
————— , "Antitrust Bill Stopped by a Business Lobby," November 16, 1975b: 1, 62–63.
————— , "FBI Tried to Kill Reverend King's Reputation," November 23, 1975c: A1.
————— , "Senate Details, Deplores CIA's Murder Plots," November 23, 1975d: A1.
————— , "Timberland Rules Tighten," February 8, 1976a: F4.
————— , "Business Builds Its Political War Chests–Legally," March 28, 1976b: F2.
————— , "Excerpts From Senate's Intelligence Report," April 29, 1976c: 31–33.
————— , "Mr. Ford's Plan to de-Regulate," May 16, 1976d: E3.
————— , "G.F.'s Campaign Chest," May 16, 1976e: F1.
————— , "Where the Corporate Money Goes," May 16, 1976f: F5.
————— , "The World's Political Jails," October 3, 1976g: E2.
————— , "Payoffs: Are they Stopped or Just Better Hidden?" January 9, 1977a: NES 23.
————— , "Secrecy and Abuse of Power," February 13, 1977b: D1.
————— , Questions on Hussin," February 27, 1977c: E17.
Petras, James and Morris Morley, *The United States and Chile,* New York: Monthly Review, 1975.
Quinney, Richard, *The Social Reality of Crime,* Boston: Little, Brown, 1970.
————— , *Critique of Legal Order,* Boston: Little, Brown, 1974.
————— , *Criminology,* Boston: Little, Brown, 1975.
Reasons, Charles E., *The Criminologist,* Pacific Palisades: Goodyear, 1974.
Roebuck, Julian B. and Thomas Barker, "A Typology of Police Corruption," *Social Problems* 24, 3 (1974): 423–437.
Roebuck, Julian B. and Rodney N. Freiry, "A Typology of Objectors to Military Conscription," Unpublished manuscript, Department of Sociology, Mississippi State University, 1974.
Sale, Kirkpatrick, "The World Behind Watergate," *New York Review of Books* 20 (May 3, 1973): 9–15.
————— , "Laying the Dust," *New York Review of Books* 22 (December 11, 1975): 5–9.
Sampson, Anthony T., *The Seven Sisters,* New York: Viking, 1975.
Schafer, Stephen, *The Political Criminal,* New York: Free Press, 1974.
Sherrill, Robert, *Why They Call It Politics,* New York: Harcourt Brace Jovanovich, 1974.
Stark, Rodney, *Police Riots,* Belmont: Wadsworth, 1972.
Sternberg, David, "The New Radical-Criminal Trials: A Step Toward a Class-for-Itself in the American Proletariat," pp. 189–208 in C. Reasons (ed.), *The Criminologist,* Pacific Palisades: Goodyear, 1974.
Stoddard, Ellwyn, "The Informal Code of Police Deviancy: A Group Approach to 'Blue Coat' Crime," *Journal of Criminal Law, Criminology, and Police Science* 59 (1968): 201–213.
Time, "A Fateful Trial Closes a Sorry Chapter," January 13, 1975: 9–16.
Turk, Austin T., *Political Criminality and Political Policing,* New York: MSS Modular Publishers, 1975.
U.S. House of Representatives, *Access to Records,* Washington: U.S. Government Printing Office, 1974.
————— , *Impeachment of Richard M. Nixon, President of the United States,* New York: Bantam, 1975.
U.S. Senate, *The Senate Watergate Report,* Volume 1, Pinebrook: Dell, 1974.
Vanderbilt Law Review, "Warrantless Wiretapping of Suspected Domestic Dissident Group's Conversation Violates Fourth Amendment," 24 (1971): 1289–1295.
Vold, George, *Theoretical Criminology,* New York: Oxford University Press, 1958.

Washington Post, "U.S. Aided Lockheed Dealings," September 12, 1975: 1.
Wise, David, "Cloak and Dagger Operations: An Overview," *Society* 12 (March/April 1975): 26–32.

Typology

Differentiating Characteristics	*Intervention*	
	By Government	Against Government
I. *Action Patterns*	1. manipulation (e.g., war crimes in S.E. Asia); 2. penetration (e.g., CIA in Ecuador and Chile, CIA assassination plots).	1. manipulation (e.g., the Symbionese Liberation Army)
II. *Goal of the Offender*	1. structural maintenance	1. structural change
III. *Legal Status of the Offense*		
A. Illegal	yes	yes
B. Para-Legal	yes	no
C. Surrogate-illegal	no	no
IV. *Nature of the Offense*		
A. Violent/Nonviolent	Violent and nonviolent	Violent
B. Overt/Covert	Overt and covert	Overt

Differentiating Characteristics	*Surveillance*	
	By Government	Against Government
I. *Action Patterns*	1. electronics (e.g., bugging and wiretapping by Nixon, CRP, Army, and CIA); 2. espionage (e.g., spying by CIA, FBI, IRS, and Army).	1. electronic (e.g., KGB bugging); 2. espionage (e.g., Whalen and Ellsberg cases).
II. *Goal of the Offender*	1. political victory; 2. monitoring dissenters.	1. aid foreign government; 2. protest specific issues.
III. *Legal Status of the Offense*		
A. Illegal	yes	yes
B. Para-legal	no	no
C. Surrogate-illegal	no	no
IV. *Nature of the Offense*		
A. Violent/Nonviolent	Nonviolent	Nonviolent
B. Overt/Covert	Covert	Overt and Covert

Typology (*continued*)

	Confrontation	
Differentiating Characteristics	By Government	Against Government
I. *Action Patterns*	1. personal, face-to-face contact (e.g., police violence);	1. personal, face-to-face contact (e.g., mass demonstrations, war resistance, urban riots): 2. symbolic contact (e.g., terrorism).
II. *Goal of the Offender*	1. quashing of dissent.	1. symbolic communication; 2. structural change; 3. protest specific issues.
III. *Legal Status of the Offense*		
A. Illegal	yes	yes
B. Para-legal	no	no
C. Surrogate-illegal	no	yes
IV. *Nature of the Offense*		
A. Violent/ Nonviolent	Violent	Violent and nonviolent
B. Overt/Covert	Overt	Overt

	Evasion and/or Collusion	
Differentiating Characteristics	By Government	Against Government
I. Action Patterns	1. denial of responsibility (e.g., Watergate cover-up, bureaucratic malfeasance and police corruption).	1. flight (e.g., draft evasion).
II. *Goal of the Offender*	1. Protect executive and administrative authority and private interests; 2. structural maintenance.	1. personal escape.
III. *Legal Status of the Offense*		
A. Illegal	yes	yes
B. Para-legal	yes	no
C. Surrogate-illegal	no	no
IV. *Nature of the Offense*		
A. Violent/Nonviolent	Nonviolent	Nonviolent
B. Overt/Covert	Overt and covert	Overt

THE KMPX STRIKE
(MARCH–MAY 1968)

Susan Krieger, UNIVERSITY OF NEW MEXICO

This is a chapter from a life history of a radio station. It is offered as an ethnographic-journalistic account of one phase in the early development of an organization. The larger study from which it is taken[1] is concerned with the cooptation of the station, a process defined as one in which an organization once viewed as new and different, and at odds with prevailing practice, comes over time to adopt ways of a larger society which are viewed as corrupting. The organization is said to have sold out, to have lost some of its original virtue. The particular station studied had been closely associated with the Summer of Love in San Francisco in 1967. It was thought to have been the first hard rock "hippy" radio station in the country. In the five subsequent years, it became increasingly commercial, professional, and successful and was frequently criticized for having sold out to the establishment.

Toward the end of the station's first year, trouble developed between the staff and the station's small businessman owner, resulting in a strike. One

Studies in Symbolic Interaction—Volume 2, 1979, pages 331–355
Copyright © 1979 by JAI Press Inc.
ISBN: 0–89232–105–9

outcome of the strike was the movement of the staff to a new station under different ownership. The story of the strike is of special interest because of its dramatic quality. It was a way people involved with the station could assert a commitment to their past—the ideal radio station they had to leave —and at the same time take steps toward a very different future—that with a media conglomerate. One purpose of an account like this is to show some of the ways drama enables change by providing opportunities for exploring limits and for acting in ambivalent situations. The strikers are able in the end to make a move they were not capable of initially, despite the fact that, as one of them says, "It was tucking their tails they went. They were selling out going over there and they knew it."

It may be helpful to view the events of the strike on two levels. One is in terms of the talk about them, in particular the rhetorics used by the strikers —at first a rhetoric of liberation, then of negotiation, then disillusionment, and finally defeat. These rhetorics enable interpretation of a situation so as to make it seem familiar and acceptable. At the same time, on a second level, there is a drama of change which produces a move which to some extent is unconscionable.

Summary of Events: (March) staff quittings, pre-strike meeting, final broadcast on KMPX, demonstration in front of 50 Green Street, negotiations with owners, reaction to scabs, benefits, community support, publicity; (April) Superball benefit, harassment of scabs, April 18 negotiation meeting, disillusionment, search for new station; (May) negotiations with Metromedia in New York, individual buy-off attempts, negotiations with KSAN in San Francisco, final strike meeting, first KSAN broadcast.

Cast of Characters: Donahue (program director and founding father); Crosby (owner); Hunt (sales manager and assistant to Crosby); Melvin, Laughlin, Towle, Harris (salesmen); Bear, Prescott, Pigg, McClay, Miller, Voco (disc jockeys); Ickes (scab disc jockey); Johnson, Street (engineers); Huges (record librarian); Boucher (chief engineer); Avery (benefactor and part owner, KPPC); Graham (rock entrepreneur); Gleason (journalist); Weinberger (advertiser); Sullivan (president, Metromedia Radio Division); Ponek (disc jockey, KSAN); Dunlop (salesman, KSAN); Leath (general manager, KSAN).

THE STRIKE

March

Donahue ignored Crosby's offer that he take one station. He felt arbitrarily relieved of his duties. Whether he had brought it on or not, he did not care. Crosby had just taken back what was not his to reclaim. The world for a moment collapsed. Donahue walked out of the office and left 50 Green Street. A while later he talked with Melvin. They decided to go on strike.

They did not think of going to another station. They did not want to kill this one. They wanted to keep it from being destroyed. You do not kill what you love, Donahue said.

Before his meeting with Crosby on Wednesday, Donahue recalled thinking he and Melvin were fighting to keep the stations together until Avery could get on his feet. Avery was part owner. It was now no longer a question of that. On Thursday, March 14, Melvin resigned his position as station manager of KPPC and word got out that he and Donahue had left. At 50 Green Street, Crosby and Hunt tried to assure the remaining staff they wanted to keep them on.

The weekend before, late Saturday night and early Sunday morning, Johnson and Donahue's eldest daughter had stayed up and dubbed about forty-five small tapes in the KMPX record library. These were the stations's collection of original recordings by Dylan, Joplin, Kaukonen, and other local musicians. Toward the end of the week, after Donahue and Melvin had left, the station's record librarian stayed up two nights from midnight to 6 a.m. and read into a tape recorder names of the titles and distributors of all the records in the library. She recalled there were between three and four thousand. According to a Federal regulation, they were property of the station owner.

On Thursday, March 14, Prescott replaced Donahue as program director at KMPX. Prescott understood that Crosby had at first told Donahue he would be relieved of his duties at one of the stations and later, on Thursday, had fired him. Prescott said he was then asked by Crosby and Hunt to take Donahue's place as program director. He had doubts but agreed to do it. He wanted to keep the station from going into instant crumble. He wanted to talk to Donahue at the time but could not. He thought Donahue must have gone home after he walked out of Crosby's office, done whatever he did to recover, and then decided with Melvin to leave.

Friday, March 15, was payday at KMPX. Prescott said everybody knew on Friday that Donahue and Melvin had left. Donahue came into the station to pick up his things. People were walking around stunned. They talked about having a meeting Saturday. Many of them thought Donahue had been fired. When he walked out of Crosby's office on Wednesday, Donahue had shaken his head and said something Johnson thought could only mean he was fired. He may have felt he was fired. He felt he was forced to resign. Crosby said he quit. Crosby said Donahue did not say yes or no about taking one of the stations. He did not name the one he wanted. He just walked out.

On Friday, March 15, Johnson set about to quit her job as an engineer at KMPX. She felt she had had enough. She was tired of coming into the station and getting yelled at. She wrote a letter to Crosby saying that since he had fired Donahue, she could not work there anymore. On her way to mail the letter at the Rincon Annex post office in San Francisco Friday night, so it would have a Friday postmark and she would not have to work that night, she stopped off at Donahue's house and told him. After mailing the letter, she stopped by the station. Someone else was doing her shift. The next morning, Donahue called her at home and told her there was going to be a meeting at Prescott's that afternoon.

At midday on Saturday, March 16, twenty-nine members of the staff of KMPX met in the living room of Prescott's apartment on Greenwich Steps, up Telegraph Hill behind 50 Green Street. Donahue proposed they go on strike. Crosby had made their situation at KMPX unworkable. Melvin concurred. The staff discussed it and voted to go on strike. They would let their troubles out. They agreed to a starting time of 3 a.m. on Monday, March 18.

There was debate about the starting time. Some thought they should take the station off the air at peak audience time Sunday night. Others thought they should play it to the end at three o'clock Monday morning, when the transmitter would ordinarily be turned off for three hours so engineering maintenance work could be done. One salesman voted against the 3 a.m. starting time, but in the end the staff agreed to convey a build up to the audience Sunday night. In the early hours Monday morning, they would give details of their planned strike. At three o'clock they would split.

Among the twenty-nine people present in Prescott's living room, there were doubts about the desirability of taking the station off and walking out on strike. But there was a general will to do it and an expectation that their absence would be brief, they would not be out for more than a week, maybe for only a few days. They would demonstrate their value to Crosby. He would realize he could not stand their loss and would take them back and stop trying to restrict their conduct. Prescott recalled he thought the staff could intimidate Crosby, that the logic of making money would get to him. Prescott felt the initial idealism they had at KMPX had turned into a working situation by the time the staff met in his living room. Their voting to go on strike was a way of reaffirming that idealism, a way of saying the whole thing was more important than anyone's job, and that it was necessary it not fail. They still had a long way to go, and what they were about to do could not legally be called a strike. It was only a walkout. The staff were not members of any trade union. They formed a union of their own for purposes of the strike: the AAFIFMWW, the Amalgamated American Federation of International FM Workers of the World, Ltd., North Beach Local No. 1. The FM could stand for frequency modulation or free men.

On Friday, March 15, the Friday after Donahue left and before the staff voted to strike, Hunt had accompanied some of the staff to the bank to make sure their checks would not bounce. He went for a beer with Crosby afterwards and remembered saying to Crosby, for the first time he could see the way to their making a buck. The financial situation was actually getting better. Expenses were leveling off, the rent was covered, the ratings were good. Then Sunday night, the strike hit. Donahue wanted to take it over. Hunt said he could see Donahue had been frustrated during the past few months because of power struggles. If you are a Hitler, you are frustrated if you cannot take over the country. Hunt went to bed at home in Pleasant Hill at 11 p.m. on Sunday night. Crosby phoned him after twelve and said he had been listening to the station and there was something going on down there. Hunt thought Crosby was not too concerned, that Crosby felt it was a lot of crap, but he did not like it going on the air and he asked Hunt if he would go look into it.

Hunt got out of bed, dressed, and drove the twenty-six miles from his home in Pleasant Hill to the station at 50 Green Street. When he got there he found bands out front, a crowd of people, signs, pickets, a light show, The Dead were playing. He was flabbergasted. He went inside. He came out. He talked with Donahue. They hashed over some of the problems. He did not call Crosby for several hours. He did not want him to find out more. He knew Crosby had a hearing to attend in court at nine the next morning, a lawsuit filed against him by one of the Portuguese program producers who had been on KMPX before the format change and had a political dispute with another of the Portuguese producers.

Hunt stayed at 50 Green Street and talked with the strikers outside. He read their list of demands and thought they were fruitless. They would let Crosby retain ownership, he could keep his managership, and the employees would run the place. Hunt said he agreed with the strikers that the station was the people. However, it was property and owned. The owner was responsible to the FCC, he had to run the station. Hunt felt the staff had been insulting to Crosby for months before the strike. They had tried to keep him out and had not given him a say. It was true Crosby blew up at the wrong times and did not handle it well, but he was the owner. Hunt stayed at 50 Green Street and continued to talk with the strikers in the early hours of the morning. He tried to get a few of them to go inside and go back on the air but they refused. Later in the morning, Crosby came over. He and Hunt went for coffee. Crosby then left for his hearing and Hunt went back to the station. He remembered he talked and talked but he got the feeling, despite what they said, the strikers were not going to negotiate a bit. They had played their hand and that was all they were going to do. They even asked him to go on strike with them.

When Crosby got back from his hearing, he called a labor law firm. The labor lawyers advised him not to talk to the press. They told him something in the National Labor Relations Act forbid him from interfering with a strike and that publicizing his side would be doing that. Hunt said he thought the labor lawyers had in mind a normal factory strike where the workers did not try to kick out the management and take over the plant, they just wanted better conditions. He told the labor lawyers he thought there was a difference, but they could not see it. They advised against publicity.

When Crosby came back from his court hearing and sat down with Hunt on Monday, Hunt thought Crosby was just plain mad. He was not realizing the future. He simply wanted to fire them. Hunt said he told Crosby he thought they should talk to the strikers, for the sake of the station's image. Crosby agreed. He said they would try to negotiate the reasonable demands. Some of the money ones would have to be met, but not the others.

Johnson was a member of the negotiating group representing the strikers which talked informally with Crosby and Hunt on Monday. She had not wanted to go on strike at first because she had already quit. She told the others Saturday at Prescott's house that she did not want to go, but they had her join them. They said they were all a family and they made her a member of their negotiating group. Shortly before midnight on Monday, the negotiating group had an informal meeting with Crosby and Hunt at the station. Johnson remembered Hunt and Crosby kept saying, "You can't do this to us, you can't do this to us."

Hunt said he and Crosby thought Donahue's walking out the previous week was probably done on purpose to bring on the strike.

The KMPX staff had announced their plans to strike on the air on KMPX on Voco's program between midnight and 3 a.m. Monday, March 18. Bear had made the initial statement:

Bear: As you know more or less, we've been talking of splitting and leaving and that is indeed what we're doing. If you haven't picked that up directly, the entire staff, and that means just about the entire staff from secretarial help on through everybody, is going out on strike at three o'clock this morning when we normally go off the air. And the reason we're going out on strike is not because there's so much black plague running around but that it seems kind of apparent to all of us that the ability to have creative growth here has been so limited to the point that the foreseeable future is grim.

This does not mean the present is that awful. You have, we have all been enjoying a groovy thing, I think, for quite some time. But the management and the creative staff are truly at odds, simple as that. And I'm sure most people know that Tom Donahue, more responsible than anybody for the existence of KMPX, I expect, quit last week. The entire strike has to do with that. It would be nonsense to say that it didn't. This is in sympathy with Tom. With the same conditions that he had to quit, well, so are we all.

And I really got mixed feelings. My head is in a strange place because I really feel sad, and at the same time rather hopeful that the reason that we're doing this all is so that there can be creative freedom, so that there can be truth, be it in the music or what we say or whatever in broadcasting. What a good thing in communications that it can be truthful. At the moment we're getting crimped and I hope you don't, I hope you don't feel abandoned, for a lot of people who have spent a lot of time with us. Because that's not the whole thing. Anyway, we wanted to let you know we are going out on strike and we have a bunch of things, I don't know if I should—We're called, by the way, the Amalgamated American Federation of International FM Workers of the World, Ltd., North Beach Local No. 1. That's us. We have at the moment about thirty members and we all work here at KMPX, until three o'clock, and then we're out on strike. We have eleven things that we want considered, and say I'm not to the point of airing them at the moment, but they're things to allow for that freedom.

Yeah, it's crazy. Anyway, so we're going out on strike, at three o'clock. We're going to have, I don't know, did the Dead say they're definitely coming, Voco?

Voco: Right.

Bear: Anybody else?

Voco: The Dead will be here, Almond Joy will be here.

Bear: Anyway, there's going to be a dance.

Voco: The cops are going to crash.

Bear: It's going to be chilly outside. If somebody would like to bring some barrels or some firewood, that'll really be nice, and we could have some fires out here maybe. I don't think we're going to get hassled from the heat because they're aware that something's going to happen. There have been announcements in the Fillmore and the Carousel and the

Avalon, for people if they want, if they care about the
station, if they want to, anything from be curious to come
for support, hang out at about three o'clock. There will be
music. There will be us all picketing. And like that.

Music: We shall overcome. . . .

Hammond: Good evening. This is Phil Hammond. The moon is in
Scorpio until 10:21 p.m. Monday night. The great sphinx
looks with scorn upon our station. He has watched while
our motives were murdered and our talent wasted. To his
mighty disgust, white sheep have been sacrificed to our
sponsors with averted face, and hordes of black scorpions
overrun our controls. Tonight Pluto, the god of death,
dripping crimson, stands atop our broadcast tower to
signal our redemption. With a face on either side of his
head, he looks on the disappointments of our past and
urges us to command our own future. The great sphinx
stirs at his coming. He knows death is near and his giant
wings, unused for centuries, begin to throb and tingle with
anticipation. Soon he will fly in the sunlight.

[Statements by Voco, McClay, Street, interspersed with music]

Voco: Hey, make it here at KMPX, 50 Green Street. There's a
light show going on downstairs. The people, the groovy
people from The Family Dog, the Avalon Ballroom,
brought their light show. The Ace of Cups are here,
missing one, one ace. Denise, if you're nearabouts and
you'd like to fall on by, the girls are here and they'd dig to
play. The Dead are going to be here and Blue Cheer is
going to be here. Yeah. They're going to rush the Ice
House. We're going to have crushed ice next door, baby,
this is Voco, and if you want to hear me anymore it won't
be here on KMPX for a while. But I'll be on KPFA in
Berkeley tomorrow night at midnight on the King Biscuit
West, I think that's the name of the show. I'll be there at
midnight so, I gotta play the blues somewhere, baby. . . .

McClay: They're here! They just walked in with their cannons.

Voco: Beautiful, man, come on in. Play it. Play James Brown.

Voice: This is radio free San Francisco.

Voco: Hey, that's about it folks. We're going to split downstairs. The Grateful Dead are here. Ace of Cups are here. The light show from The Family Dog, we're all here. Hurrah!

Voice: Hurrah!

Indian Warwhoop.

Hammond: The time has come again for KMPX to take a brief rest while our team of technical tinkerers tear away at our tiny transistors for the next six hours. KMPX broadcasts on an assigned carrier frequency of 106.9 megacycles with 80,000 watts of power authorized by the Federal Communications Commission. We will return to the air at 6 a.m. with a reading from the I-Ching.

Music: "...I shake my head and walk away, walk away.... Sometimes I wanna stay here, then again I wanna leave.... I just can't make my mind up, I shake my head and walk away...."

Voice: Okay. This is now radio free San Francisco. Everybody is free to do as they please.

Music: "...I just can't make my mind up, I shake my head and walk away...."

Hammering Noises.

Voice: Let's go.

Sound of record playing in grooves.

Sound of a switch flicked.

  By the time the last of the KMPX staff walked downstairs and out of the building at 50 Green Street shortly after 3 a.m., there were about 500 people assembled in the street outside. Some were listeners who had heard about the walkout on the air, some were people in the music business who had gotten word before. Some, like the bands, had been asked specifically to come. Creedence Clearwater Revival started playing at 3:05 a.m. Blue Cheer, the group Voco produced for Mercury, was there. The Grateful Dead set up their instruments and played. A group of people associated with the Dead wanted to take over the transmitter and free the airwaves. They tried to get Boucher to let them but he wanted to leave the station operational and did. A group from The Family Dog had a light show going. People were dancing near the pickets walking in the street. Green Street was not a wide street. It was shouldered by warehouse buildings. Looking up, one saw Coit Tower on Telegraph Hill. The bands played loud and the music carried up. Residents up the hill complained about the noise and after about twenty minutes police arrived and ordered the crowd to disperse. They tried to relocate at Pier 10 on the Embarcadero but failed to. Someone forgot to carry over the amplifiers. By 4 a.m., the bulk of the crowd had gone. Pickets remained.

The *Chronicle* reported on the walkout briefly on March 18 and said KPPC in Pasadena was out on strike in sympathy. The AP ran an item on it the same day. On Tuesday, March 19, the *Chronicle* ran a feature describing the scene outside the station Monday morning which began by mentioning that Owsley the Acid King had been there and that while the bands played, joints were passed around, acid taken, the wealth shared. On March 20, *Variety* in Hollywood reported that the staff of KPPC had gone on strike in Pasadena and that KMPX in San Francisco had joined in sympathy.

Once off the air, the striking staff of KMPX started printing up announcements about their activities. In an office on the sixth floor of the Columbus Towers building at Columbus and Kearny, over the hill from 50 Green Street, McClay had a duplicating machine and paper he used in turning out the Tempo newsletter. He donated these to the KMPX group for running off strike literature. The first widely circulated piece they ran off was a notice listing eleven demands the striking staff was making of Crosby-Pacific. The first was that Crosby's lawyer have no authority over supervision of employees, the second that Donahue and Melvin be reinstated, the third that Donahue have complete control of programming, the fourth that Melvin have complete control of sales. The fifth demand was that Boucher have complete control of engineering, the sixth that Blue have complete control of traffic, the seventh that employees share in the increase in profits of the radio station, the eighth that employees be paid in full for time on strike, the ninth that there be wage increases to be agreed upon. The tenth demand was that no employee be discriminated against for reasons of union activity, and the eleventh that all the conditions herein named be agreed to in writing before the strike be considered settled.

Hunt remembered putting KMPX back on the air at 5 or 6 p.m. Monday evening. He did not worry about it back on earlier since he thought the strike would be over by the end of the day.

The KMPX strike, begun on Monday, March 18, lasted until Monday, May 13, eight weeks. The striking group maintained a picket line in front of 50 Green Street the entire time. Volunteers joined them. Crosby and Hunt recruited new staff to put the station back on the air and keep it going. Advertisers withdrew their accounts from the station. Rock groups requested their music not be played. Local bands appeared in concerts to benefit the striking staff. There were formal negotiation meetings between Crosby and Hunt and the strikers. There was publicity, press coverage, and good weather. KPPC, the sister station in Pasadena, was also out. The board of directors of Crosby-Avery Broadcasting met and voted among themselves. Five weeks into the strike, on April 18, a large negotiation meeting was held in the New Committee theater, chaired by Bill Graham and attended by several hundred people. Crosby spoke at that meeting and said he had been a hippy before any of them were hippies and it seemed apparent he would not take back the striking staff. Donahue and Melvin traveled across the country in search of another station for the staff to move to. On May 21, a group of them moved to KSAN, a Metromedia station with studios in downtown San Francisco. Their strike on KMPX was never settled.

By the time the strike was over, Crosby felt irreparably damaged. Hunt felt the station was dead and that the strikers had killed it. Avery was voted off the Crosby-Avery board. McClay thought maybe it was the first time in history people managed to shut down a business that had to operate. He believed the strike was a success in that respect but that it failed because the goal was to go back. The staff for the most part felt defeated, especially when, on May 21, they walked into KSAN on Sutter Street, their new home, and the first thing they saw was Metromedia wallpaper. Johnson drove away from the strike line during the sixth week and did not come back. She thought the striking group was doing horrible things they were not conscious of. She thought the others held it against her for pulling out, and she thought they all changed during the strike, but none of them would admit it.

On Wednesday, March 20, at 11 a.m., members of the striking staff of KMPX held a press conference on the ferryboat San Leandro tied up by the Ferry Building at Mission and Embarcadero. The strikers had run off several notices for distribution at the press conference and on the picket line in front of 50 Green Street with AAFIFMWW appearing as letterhead on each. The main notice was one which said the strikers of KMPX and KPPC were a "tribe of people" who had brought the new music to San Francisco and Los Angeles: "When these two stations were teetering on the brink of collapse," the notice said, "management had been content to have long-haired, barefoot, and beaded employees." But when the stations became successful, management had seen fit to remove some of the people who created them. Donahue and Melvin had been forced to resign. They then joined the staff on strike. "We love these stations," the notice read, "not as a collection of chairs, desks, tubes and turntables, but as the living idea of a loving group of people. We love our work and wish only to be allowed to do it as we have in the past. For the present, KMPX and KPPC are on the air—the idea is on the street."

On Wednesday, March 20, in the evening, The Family Dog held a benefit concert for the KMPX strikers in the Avalon Ballroom. Eight local bands performed: the Grateful Dead, Blue Cheer, Jeremy Steig and the Satyrs, Kaleidoscope, Charlie Musselwhite Southside Sound System, Santana Blues Band, Fruminous Bandersnatch, and the Clover. $2,400 was reportedly raised for the strikers.

On Friday, March 22, the strikers held a press conference at the Avalon. According to a release they distributed, several recording artists and groups had expressed their support by requesting that KMPX not play their records on the air during the strike. Among them were the Grateful Dead, Blue Cheer, Mimi Farina, and Joan Baez, Jerry Garcia of the Dead was said to have walked into the station at 50 Green Street and asked for return of the Dead's latest single. Country Joe and the Fish and The Jefferson Airplane subsequently asked that their records not be aired. The Rolling Stones sent a cable from England on March 21: "We want you to know that we support your battle against the bureaucracy. We believe in KMPX and KPPC and will keep the faith over here. Love, Mick, Keith, Brian, Charlie, Bill."

On Saturday and Sunday, March 23 and 24, a street fair was held in a parking lot near 50 Green Street. The fair was originally planned for in front of 50 Green Street but the site was changed when the San Francisco police refused to grant the strikers a permit for closing off the street. Nine bands were scheduled to appear. Bill Graham sent over food each day. The New Orleans House sent ham on Saturday.

Within twenty-four hours after the strike began, all but a few of the advertisers who had accounts with the station withdrew them. Starting the morning of the day the strike broke, the KMPX salesmen now on strike telephoned and went door to door speaking with the advertisers, explaining their situation, saying they did not expect to be off for more than a week and felt they needed the advertisers also to leave in order for the strike to succeed. They requested that the advertisers stay off the air until the strike was settled. Thirty of the advertisers formed a committee in support of the strike. On Sunday, March 24, the advertisers' committee held a dinner for the striking staff, their families, the advertisers, and the press. It was reported to have raised $1,000 for the strikers.

Laughlin was in charge of maintaining the strike line in front of 50 Green Street seven days a week, twenty-four hours a day. The first week the weather was good, it did not rain. The nights were San Francisco spring nights, foggy and chilly. Laughlin said he and Hughes, his old lady, scheduled the striking staff and volunteers they recruited to walk the line, day and night, in shifts. They parked Laughlin's Chevy van by the side of the street and organized from there. They served food from the van, monitored the line from the van, and distributed pamphlets and benefit checks from it. On occasion the van was used as a whorehouse.

Shortly after the start of the strike, Hughes spent several days in Voco's Mercury office transcribing the list of record titles and distributors she had read into the tape recorder in the KMPX library a few days before the strike was called. With the list written up, she could send away to record companies and stock a library anywhere just like the one they had at KMPX. She felt it was shitwork transcribing the list, but it was for revolutionary radio and that made it bearable.

By 6 p.m. the first day of the strike, although Hunt had the station back on the air, there was a problem in finding staff. Hunt knew Crosby had run the station before as a radio school. A day or two after the strike began, he and Crosby went out to local colleges: San Francisco State, the College of San Mateo, and one school in Fremont, and recruited students from broadcasting classes, telling them here was an opportunity to get professional experience.

When the striking staff found out that Hunt and Crosby had the station back on with the help of students from broadcasting schools, they were furious. Several of them went out to the colleges. They went, Melvin said, to explain their side of the situation. The students might not have realized there was a strike on or what it meant. They tore down signs Crosby and Hunt had posted on bulletin boards and told students in broadcasting classes if they came to work at KMPX, they would be treated as scabs. Laughlin told a reporter for the San Francisco State *Daily Gator* that he and Johnson and some other strikers had driven down to the College of San Mateo on Thursday, March 21, and literally blitzed the place. The radio and television department was shipping its kids out to the station and he felt they had to stop them. The whole point of the strike was to prove to Crosby that the original staff was invaluable. The scabs coming on proved they were replaceable. Melvin said when the scabs came on was the first time that thought had struck him. Then the scabs claimed the music was more important than a certain bunch of people's jobs. They said Donahue and the strikers were on an ego trip, that the strike was a power play, that they, the scabs, were keeping the station alive.

Hunt thought in the first week of the strike he must have gone through 150 disc jockeys. He went through disc jockeys like they were going out of style. Some he recruited would not come in when they got to the station and had to face the strikers out front. Some would come once and not return. Some were really bad on the air. For the first two weeks after the strike began, Hunt thought he stayed at the station just about twenty-four hours a day. Crosby remembered Hunt befriended him. Hunt slept on the floor there in the building with him when the strikers made it so bad he did not dare leave. Hunt said he felt everything seemed to fall to him as the strike continued. He had to take care of Crosby, since Crosby was not up to it and had problems with his girl friend at the time. He had to get money to pay the day-to-day jocks. He had to stall off the long-term payments. The advertisers had gone off because of the strikers' threats. The strikers had even gotten to the factoring service and asked them not to collect. He finally sold time to an Italian program again.

April

During the second week of the strike, the last week in March, the strikers began planning a benefit to be held on Wednesday, April 3, at Winterland. Being April, a year since the month Donahue started on KMPX, this could be called their first birthday benefit. They advertised it as such and gave it the name Superball. Bill Graham donated Winterland and a half dozen bands volunteered their performances: The Grateful Dead, The Jefferson Airplane, Electric Flag, It's a Beautiful Day, Malachi, and Moby Grape. The Superball was scheduled to run from 6 p.m.–2 a.m. with an admission charge of five dollars a seat. Crosby saw an advertisement for it which appeared in the *Barb* of March 29 showing a couple nude balling and got mad. He thought it typical of the strikers' tactics. It was illegal pornographic use of the call letters of his station. The Superball was a benefit for them, the strikers, it was not for him. It was not for KMPX.

The Superball was the most lucrative of the KMPX strike benefits, raising between seven and nine thousand dollars. Street wrote out the checks giving the proceeds to the striking staff. The engineers got $200 each, what they made in a month at KMPX, they said. Donahue and Melvin got $1,000 each. The staff had agreed that the two of them needed funds for flying around the country in search of a way to help settle the strike. Street remembered there was grass and booze provided for the bands at Winterland and the Superball came off well, although Bear, who was supposed to be in charge, disappeared three days before and other people had to do the work. Bear reappeared the night of the show and took a bow with the others. He felt he had done the groundwork by the time he left but it got too much for him near the end, so he took off to the mountains for a few days for a rest.

While most of the staff were over at Winterland, Harris walked the strike line in front to 50 Green Street. Gleason stopped by with a bottle of wine and told him he thought that was where the story would be. But apparently it was not. Gleason went on over to Winterland and in his column on Friday described the turnout there. He said he had gone and found it a delightfully varied scene. Mingling with the hippies were auto salesmen and executive types, all friends of KMPX. Miller was there with his white hat, one of the heroes of the night. At midnight, the entire KMPX staff filed across the stage, including Tom Dominant, which Gleason said was what the Congress of Wonders called Tom Donahue. It was like a family reunion. Some of the management of KMPX was there. More bands were present than got a chance to play. The bands who did, played with their hearts in it. The Dead set off cannons and cherry bombs in one of their pieces.

In the audience at Winterland was one young man who earlier in the day had turned in his draft card in an anti-war demonstration outside the Federal Building in San Francisco. He had grown up in Los Altos, near Palo Alto, gone to college in Los Angeles, dropped out, and in the summer of 1967 come back up to San Francisco. He began listening to KMPX then, thinking the music the station played merged political and cultural consciousness and made it one, as he believed it should be. He thought in terms of media, KMPX was somewhere between what a college was and a newspaper was. At the Superball, he went up and asked Dusty Street to announce what had happened at the anti-war demonstration he had attended that afternoon. About 500 people had shown up and a fourth of them had turned in their draft cards. Street did not announce it. The next day, he heard on the radio at a friend's house that Martin Luther King had been killed. He thought it must have been on another station than KMPX that he heard it, since he and his friends felt listening to KMPX during the strike was scabbing.

From the first week in April through the third, what was done in private meetings, public and community meetings, and negotiation sessions all seemed unsatisfactory to those among the striking staff who wanted to reach agreement on some version of their demands. In mid-April, they still felt justified in their demands, but it seemed to Johnson they were losing their ability to imagine the strike could be settled.

By mid-April, a disc jockey by the name of Larry Ickes had been doing the morning shift on KMPX for three weeks. In the eyes of the strikers, he was a full-time scab. Ickes said when he started, the strikers called him over and asked if he realized what he was doing. They said they would not be out for long. Donahue came up to him and said they would really appreciate it if he did not go in and that he was hurting their cause especially because he was a professional. He went in nonetheless and came back regularly and crossed the line. The strikers called him scab and other names he felt were abusive. Within two weeks, the line for him became a gauntlet. By about the second week in April, the strikers were threatening him physically and saying things like, "Wait until we give your name to the Hell's Angels. We're not responsible for what may happen to you. We haven't tried anything physical yet." They posted his home phone number with instructions for people to call him twenty-four hours a day with musical requests, and drove a spike through the door of his Jaguar XKE and wrote "scab" on top of it.

By mid-April, Ickes was convinced he was on the right side. He felt Crosby and Hunt were being ganged up on by the strikers and that most people would see that if they talked with Crosby and Hunt personally. He felt if he had not talked with them personally, he would not have come to work at the station, but once he did and then got treated as he did by the strikers, he had to work there. It seemed to him Crosby and Hunt had the press against them in addition to the strikers. He noticed they did not comment to the press and he never understood why.

On Tuesday, April 16, Ickes recalled Donahue came up to him in front of 50 Green Street and told him they were having a meeting on Thursday at the New Committee Theater and he thought the strike would be settled then. The meeting would be open to the public. Graham was going to chair it. For several days before, the strikers had been calling former advertisers, the press, and others concerned about settling the strike, asking them to attend the meeting to show support. Graham recalled he may have initiated the meeting. It seemed to him that by mid-April, the strike was hurting all of them in the music community. It was hurting his dance hall business. Weinberger of Mr. Broadway's remembered he was called by one of the strikers and asked to come to the meeting April 18 to show his support. Whoever called him said the advertisers had a vested interest in getting the station on the air again. Weinberger said of course he would come, advertising on KMPX had totally changed his business.

When Weinberger got to the meeting Thursday night, several hundred people were already there. Many of the former KMPX advertisers had come. Weinberger thought that meeting brought them together and made them realize they were a community. The meeting itself had the feel of a theatrical event more than a strike negotiation session, although there were two sides, the tables were set up to face each other, and Graham chaired it in a serious manner. The New Committee Theater was packed. In the course of the meeting, people cheered and catcalled. Johnson thought Graham was the only one there who was really intent on settling the strike. The owner and manager of Music City said he was told by the person who called him and asked him to come that he could speak his piece at the meeting. He went but he found it boring and left. Van Orden set up equipment to record the meeting for KPFA, the noncommercial station in Berkeley. Someone held the microphone for the KPFA recording in plain view of the audience, but the proceedings either never made it to the tape or the tape was lost or somehow or other disappeared.

Graham remembered at that meeting the hip types were nice to him for once. Their anti-capitalist accusations went Crosby's way instead of his. Donahue spoke on behalf of the strikers. So did Harris and several of the others. Donahue was asked at one point whether he had been fired from KMPX in March or quit. Harris thought that was the first time Donahue admitted in public that he had not formally been fired. Johnson thought even then it was not clear what had happened. It was not clear if Donahue had manipulated them to get them to leave or not. It was not clear if the strike really had to happen.

Then Crosby spoke. Harris recalled Crosby said he would be willing to have the strikers back if they treated him reasonably but they did not. He said he knew sometimes when you were in business, your partners did things you did not like, but they were still your partners. He referred to his early days in radio as a country disc jockey and said he had been a hippy before any of them were hippies, or he was the first hippy, or words to that effect.

When Crosby spoke at the meeting he was convinced it was stacked against him. The tables were set up so Donahue faced the audience and could speak to them directly while he was sideways to them. The meeting proceeded like a kangaroo court. People were heckling. He expected Hunt would do the talking for him but Hunt was a country boy and got up there and got afraid. He could hardly open his mouth. He was mumbling. They were making fun. So, Crosby said, he spoke. He told them Donahue had hired so many people he could not meet the payroll.

By the time of the meeting of April 18, Crosby felt they were holding a gun behind his head. He had received an eviction notice at 50 Green Street earlier in the day. He felt he had been starving with the station all these years, he was finally about to make it, and these guys came up and said they were taking the station whether he liked it or not. They had kicked the elevator door in the building in. The night he was supposed to go to KPFA in Berkeley to tell his side of the story, they let the air out of his tires. The articles in the papers were all partial to Donahue. Gleason had been on the station for a while before the strike. But when it came, he wrote articles partial to Donahue. Crosby thought he might have talked to Gleason, but Gleason never called him. Caen never called him. The demands the strikers were making were unreasonable. It would have been suicide for him to take them. They were killing him. But he felt he had to stay in it, he had to keep the station.

Graham remembered toward the end of the meeting, he proposed that Crosby and Donahue sit down in private with whoever they needed and man to man work it out, they should take the pimple and squeeze it. He offered to put them up at the Highlands Inn in Carmel for however long it would take to settle the thing. He thought they should once and for all find out if the two of them could work together. Crosby refused. Graham thought then there was no hope. He told Crosby he would never advertise on his station again.

Johnson felt that meeting was the last ditch. After it, the staff all realized the strike was going to be a failure. She began thinking it was a result of their taking drugs and being on fantasy trips. So many of them thought the world would be transformed by drugs. After that meeting, she began to feel bad about herself for what the strikers were doing. It seemed to her their tactics were sadistic and it was clear Crosby would not have them back. Sometime the following week, she drove away from the strike line in front of 50 Green Street and never came back. She thought the others held it against her for pulling out. McClay called her, she thought it was shortly before she left, and said another station, KSAN, was sending out feelers to some of the staff. He was thinking of taking a job there, getting himself established, then doing something. She recalled she told him it was every man for himself now and then she hung up.

Melvin said he felt some of the staff's ugliest moments came out in meetings during the strike. He felt the strike was a negative thing while the station had been positive, and you could not keep people going that long on a negative thing. He thought the group of them fell apart during the strike. Street remembered their meetings were demoralizing. As time went on, people individually left. Johnson, she felt, was burned by the strike.

After the April 18 meeting, the question of where the staff might go became urgent for Donahue. In the end of April, he and Melvin went to Chicago to meet with the vice-president in charge of radio for ABC. They stayed in a motel on Michigan Avenue for four days waiting to see him, feeling duty bound, Donahue said, not to spend more of the strikers' money than they had to. So they ate candy bars and played gin rummy in the motel. They finally met with the vice-president and the man was tempted. He could see the format had been successful in Los Angeles as well as San Francisco, but a deal did not work out.

In late April, on his own, prompted by the outcome of the Graham meeting, McClay called a friend of his who was program director at a Metromedia station in Philadelphia. During the first week of the strike, McClay remembered the staff had drawn up a list of all the fm stations in the Bay Area and gone through it considering alternatives. One was the Metromedia fm in San Francisco, a classical music station. So far as McClay knew, nobody talked to anybody about it then. After the April 18 meeting, he called his friend and asked him who was in charge of radio for Metromedia. His friend said it was John Van Buren Sullivan, Jack Sullivan, and he would call and tell Sullivan there was a group from KMPX in San Francisco with a proposal. McClay then spoke to Sullivan on the phone himself. McClay thought he must have been on the phone to Sullivan two or three days a week for two weeks in late April and early May. At first he explained to Sullivan the goal of the strike was for the staff to go back to KMPX. However, should that become impossible, the group would want to go to another station. Then he had to tell Sullivan it did not look like they would get what they wanted.

May

On the evening of Saturday, May 4, Crosby sent a telegram to Avery informing him that a meeting of the board of directors of Crosby-Avery

Broadcasting would be held on Monday, May 6, at 2 p.m. in the office of Crosby's lawyer in San Francisco. On Monday, May 6, in an outcome of that meeting, Crosby sent a telegram to Avery informing him that he had been removed as president and general manager of Crosby-Avery Broadcasting.

Months later, when Crosby finally asked his lawyer to resign from the board, he thought maybe he should have taken him off earlier instead of taking Avery off. But at the time they were in the midst of a strike. The strike was technically against Avery's interests as well as his own and Avery was acting as if it was not. There had been one meeting of the board where the next day Donahue did things indicating he had known what went on. Crosby said he precluded then that Avery was the culprit, but it might have been his lawyer. Crosby liked Avery.

Stefan Ponek had feelings for neither of them. In May 1968, Ponek was a disc jockey on KSAN, previously KSFR, the Metromedia fm in San Francisco. He knew the KMPX strike was on. In April he felt he had started being opportunist about it when he convinced the KSAN general manager to let him do more of what the strikers had been doing on KMPX by extending the length of a rock music program he did on Saturday nights. He had started the program in January in a style like that of KMPX, calling it the Underground Sunshine show. It ran for an hour each week. In April, with the KMPX strikers out, Ponek felt there was advertiser support for him to extend the program to four hours.

Doug Dunlop, a salesman with KSAN, sold the time on Ponek's show. When the staff of KMPX went on strike in March, one of their initial publicity handouts had been a list of the names, addresses, and phone numbers of advertisers who had gone off the air on KMPX in support of their strike. They urged people to patronize these advertisers. Dunlop said he got hold of a copy of the list and started calling on the advertisers asking them to place buys on Ponek's show. By late April, he had done so well selling Ponek's show that its expansion was possible. The station manager, Reid Leath, was for it. Other than on rare occasions, he said, the station had not before received requests for time by advertisers.

Dunlop wore three piece suits when he went out selling time on Ponek's program in April and May. The merchants he had gotten from the KMPX list were mostly hip types. He knew he looked straight but he felt the fact he was young helped him. He was twenty-two. Also he was enthusiastic. When he sold time to the Middle Earth clothing store on Stanyan Street, the manager said he reminded her of her son. Several of the former KMPX advertisers called Harris and asked if it would be all right with him for them to advertise on Ponek's show. Harris recalled telling them okay, that KSAN was the best thing going in town.

Ponek remembered in April inviting the KMPX strikers to appear as guests on his show. He extended an invitation to all of them but Prescott and Bear were the only ones who came. Probably in the end of April, he suggested to Leath that they hire some of the striking staff from KMPX. Leath said he was worried about trouble with Metromedia since the station was not making money and he did not want to do it. Then one Monday, probably Monday, May 6, Ponek said Leath called him into his office and asked him what he would do if he were in his position. What would he do if he had to hire a group of people he could not control? Ponek said he told Leath he would take them but buy them off one at a time. Leath said to go ahead and do that, go ahead and hire them and he could be program director. He also told him it had to be a secret.

The day he talked with Ponek, Leath had just come back from New York where he had gone for a managers' meeting with Sullivan. He had previously talked with Sullivan about expanding Ponek's show and about possible combinations of rock and classical programming on the station. But after this meeting, he knew they were going to change the format of his station and they were going to change it entirely. It was only a matter of setting the date and making the local arrangements.

Leath did not know at the time that earlier in the first week of May, Donahue had been to New York and talked with Sullivan. McClay had gone East on vacation and had set up an appointment for himself and Donahue, following on his phone conversations with Sullivan. Donahue flew East, joined McClay, and met with Sullivan at 975 Park Avenue. Donahue recalled their meeting was brief. They got along well and concluded it all in one day. He was impressed that Sullivan had really listened to the music.

The proposal resulting from their meeting was that Metromedia would take some of the staff from KMPX onto KSAN and change the KSAN format from classical and lively arts to rock. Donahue would come on as program director. The present KSAN air staff would all be dismissed except for Ponek, who would stay on as a disc jockey. Donahue did not like the prospect of Ponek's staying on, as that would leave the KMPX staff short one man, and he did not like it that KSAN was a combo operation with the disc jockeys doing their own engineering. That meant there would be no positions for the engineers.

When he returned to San Francisco, Donahue talked with Melvin. Sullivan had not made a formal offer, but it was likely. They talked about how the strike had been getting hard and how they would have a problem splitting shifts if they went to KSAN.

McClay, not yet back, was also disappointed by Sullivan's reluctance to take the whole staff. Sullivan seemed to want to pick off the cream. But he had an enthusiasm for KMPX. Sullivan felt KMPX was exciting, like WNEW had been in New York in the late 1940s when he first went to work there. To Sullivan, it made eminent sense to take the staff from KMPX when Donahue and McClay came to him in May. He felt you learned in this business there were damn few really original personalities as opposed to imitators and realness was important. Knowledge of music and records did not mean anything without it. What had made WNEW was that people listening could really identify with the air people. That was also what made KMPX. The people in San Francisco were into the new music and it was right for their life style. It did not have to be Sullivan's life style for him to see it had appeal. When he met with Donahue, he liked him. He was high on Donahue. He liked his philosophy, he thought Donahue was the gospel father of progressive rock radio. He felt good about the whole thing. Then he had to tell the president of Metromedia he wanted to change the format on KSAN by hiring the group from KMPX. The president of Metromedia had reservations. He said what in hell did Sullivan think he was doing?

Sullivan said all he could tell him was this was for San Francisco and for that market it was right. He had been hammering away at the 20–29 age demographic for all their stations, so had the corporation's research department. He felt the president of Metromedia had reservations not because it was bad marketing to change the format, but because it was new and different.

The president of Metromedia was an investor, not an operator in radio stations, so of course he would not understand. He had originally been in food brokerage, representing grocery manufacturers to supermarket operators, had bought into Metromedia in 1958 when it was the Metropolitan Broadcasting Corporation, and had become its president in 1959. In the nine years since, Metromedia had developed a reputation as a fast growth company which bought red ink and made money off it. In May 1968, the company owned a dozen radio stations, half of them am, half fm, and four television stations, all in major markets. Their other principal holdings included Foster & Kleiser, the nation's largest outdoor advertising company, a transit advertising company, a direct mail advertising company, a documentary film company, The Ice Capades, and Playbill, a theater magazine. In January 1968, *Forbes* magazine quoted the president of Metromedia as saying the whole idea was to reach the customer where they could.

In San Francisco, after Leath gave him permission, Ponek started trying to buy off members of the KMPX group individually. One of the first he approached was Pigg. Pigg remembered meeting with Ponek and telling him he could not make a decision without consulting the group. Bear remembered Ponek contacted him that second week in May and asked him to keep their meeting a secret. Ponek seemed nervous about it. Bear said he wanted badly to go back to work, to go back on the air after all this time, but he told Ponek he could not come without the group. Melvin recalled meeting with Ponek in a Foster's restaurant near KSAN. Their meeting was supposed to be secret. Ponek brought the KSAN sales manager with him and the two of them wanted to know what kind of business the KMPX group would bring.

Melvin said he told them all the accounts would follow. That knocked them out. Ponek suggested a group of them come without Donahue, that he would be program director. Melvin said he told them they would all have to come together. In the end, they agreed to set up a meeting with Leath to see what could be arranged.

Ponek made offers to Pigg, Bear, Melvin, McClay, and Prescott. It seemed to him each of them was afraid of being a bad guy in the eyes of the others. Ponek felt he was putting his own neck out to do it. He had to keep his advances secret from the classical staff at KSAN. So far as he knew, he and Leath were the only ones at the station expecting the format change. When it came, the classical staff would be canned and they would hate him for his complicity. He told Leath he had been turned down by each of the KMPX strikers he approached, that they each said they had to check with the group. Leath said he felt it was blackmail.

Probably on Thursday, May 9, the KMPX staff still on strike held a meeting. Pigg recalled he was the first to say he had been approached by Ponek for Metromedia. Then the others spoke up. Bear thought each of them said they had told Ponek yes, but they could not come without the group, and that at that meeting they agreed it was all of them or none. Bear remembered that meeting especially because he spoke out against Donahue. He felt the strike morale was ready to fall apart and that it was time for the staff to go back to KMPX. He told them he had been talking with Crosby and Crosby was willing to take some of them back. They had gone out initially because of Donahue but now they had been out too long. He said for himself he was ready to go back, he did not need a Big Daddy.

Donahue recalled at that meeting Bear announced he had been talking to Crosby and that Crosby wanted to take some people back. Donahue thought it was at the same meeting they worked out a package to go to KSAN. They had to decide on a group since they could not all go and they would be short a man because of Ponek's staying. They agreed that Bear would not be in the package. It seemed he did not want to come.

It seemed to Leath that for a small station, KMPX had one of the biggest staffs he ever heard of. They came and asked him to take their heavyweights and offered to give him the rest for free. But he knew people did not work for nothing. He told them he could take only a selection. Then in all the commotion, word go out and people assumed there would be a format change on his station before he formally announced it.

Ponek thought Donahue probably went to New York after Leath went there, that he must have gone after he found out they were making offers to buy off his staff individually. He must have arranged in New York to get himself put in as program director and then came back and talked with Leath to work out details. That must have been why Leath told Ponek he would keep him on as a disc jockey but that Donahue would be program director. It was only after that Ponek first met Donahue.

Ponek attended the last meeting of the KMPX strike on Monday, May 13, where Donahue announced that the staff could move to KSAN and that it was arranged for the following Tuesday, May 21, Donahue's fortieth birthday. The assembled group moved and voted to end their strike and divided up what remained of the strike fund. Johnson came back for the meeting. She remembered Donahue told them KSAN was not set up for combo operation so they would not have positions for the engineers, but that he would talk them into setting it up for engineeers and then rehire them. She did not believe him. She told him at the meeting, "I don't believe you," then said she was just going to leave and do her own thing. She felt the pressure of the drug scene was too much, and she felt she had been used by Donahue. Street said she felt Donahue had led them to believe the whole family would go on to greater heights. Then it seemed he said fuck the whole family, eight of us are going back to work. It was arranged for five of the disc jockeys and three of the salesmen to start at KSAN full-time on May 21. Some of the others would come on weekends. There was a suggestion that the engineers and a few of the rest form a company of their own to produce commercials.

Prescott recalled feeling good about the prospect of going to KSAN because he got a job. He would be morning man on KSAN as he had been on KMPX. Nonetheless, he felt the move to KSAN was second best. The staff had wanted to go back to KMPX. Part of the dream was to be independent, to work for themselves and not be interfered with. They had wanted to get rid of what interference they had from Crosby at KMPX. In retrospect that seemed not much. A big corporation would be worse.

Melvin thought they were caught at a disadvantage by the Metromedia offer. They wanted so much to go back to work. But it was tucking their tails they went. They were selling out going over there and they knew it. The justification for it was it would be better than the streets. Just Thursday of the week before, he had gone on the air on KMPX as a guest, reviewing the strikers' grievances once again and arguing against the side of the scabs who were on the air. He told them they would not escape the problems the first staff had. Melvin had been offered a management job at *Rolling Stone* during the strike and had turned it down. He would be a salesman at KSAN.

The KMPX strike was over. The underground press reported it toward the end of the week of May 13. The *Barb* said when word got out, Miller announced on the air on KMPX: "Well now they have their own station, we have our own station, and you have your radio." The *Barb* also reported on a showing of the Beatles' film "Magical Mystery Tour," May 12 and 13, in the Straight Theater on Haight Street. The showing was a benefit for the striking staff of KMPX, arranged some time before. It was their last strike benefit. The turnout was impressive but the film reviewer for the *Barb* was not sympathetic. The poor could march on Washington, he said, but the heart of this community was with people who complained they were not getting enough bread for playing records. The KMPX strikers had wanted creative freedom, and what that amounted to, he said, was freedom to play cut three side B, instead of cut five side A.

Crosby felt relieved that the strike was over. He would hang on, although people were urging him to sell the station. The strikers would be happy somewhere else. It was ridiculous, he thought, Donahue had tried to make him look like a wealthy man. Donahue had told people he was a rotten capitalist so-and-so. He had not said much in reply, he did not want to tell everyone his problems. Now Donahue was going to Metromedia, a giant corporation. Crosby believed in capitalism within reason. He did not believe in giant corporate capitalism or huge inheritances. He thought if the strikers were really looking for independence, they had it at KMPX. Going to a huge corporation there would be no freedom at all. It was money they were after.

FOOTNOTES

1. Susan Krieger, *Hip Capitalism*, Sage, 1979.

THE DRAMA OF CHANGE

March	April	May
Pre-strike meeting	Later strike meetings Picket line Strike benefits Publicity	Final strike meeting
	Superbowl	Final strike benefit
	Negotiation sessions Community meetings Crosby–Avery meetings	
	April 18 meeting	Removal of Avery
	Scabs on station	
	Harrassment of scabs	
	Trips in search of new station	
	Contacts with Mm	Mm negotiations, N.Y. Individual buy-off attempts KSAN negotiations, S.F.
Final broadcast on KMPX	Expansion of rock programming on KSAN	First broadcast on KSAN

rhetoric of liberation ——— rhetoric of negotiation ——— rhetoric of disillusionment ——— rhetoric of defeat

☆☆☆ The KMPX Strike ☆☆☆

Small scale ownership ——————————————— Large corporate ownership

SOCIABILITY, INTERACTION AND SOCIAL EXCHANGE

SOCIABILITY AND PUBLIC BEHAVIOR IN A MID-SIZED CITY*

Patricia T. Clough, FORDHAM UNIVERSITY

Because the middle class is considered to be dominant in our society and cosmopolitanism to be extensive throughout society, public behavior in general and sociability in particular are characterized as being egalitarian in nature. Further, status appraisals underlying such behavior are assumed to be based completely on appearances, since anonymity pervades social life. The research reported here questions the generality of these assumptions by examining the egalitarian nature of middle class sociability as it is exhibited in a public drinking place which is located in a mid-sized community. An ethnographic study of this bar, called The Lantern, provides evidence for the following propositions. First, segmentation within the middle class is systematic and serves as a structure for relations in public. The segmentation is based on vertical cleavages in a local status structure. Relationships between segments are not hierarchically arranged, although the status structure is unstable and there is a tendency toward hierarchy. Therefore, while relationships between segments are not hierarchically ordered, the

Studies in Symbolic Interaction—Volume 2, 1979, pages 359–376
ISBN: 0–89232–105–9

tendency toward hierarchy results in nonegalitarian relationships. Secondly, the status arrangement is based on status appraisals which rely on reputation as well as appearances. Further, it is suggested that the approach to a study of public behavior within dramaturgical or phenomenologically oriented sociologies must be revised to take into account reputation as distinguished from appearances in the status structure underlying social relations exhibited in public places. Methodologically, this is approached by considering a public place as part of a larger community, that is, as part of the community's institutional matrix. This is equivalent to analyzing both the way in which participants define the boundaries of public gatherings and the internal structures thus generated.

In 1953, Form and Stone noted that there is a "conspicuous contrast in modes of appropriation and assignment of status" within a small town and a large urban area. Further, this contrast suggests that methodological techniques must vary in the study of the local manifestation of status differentiation, depending on whether the community is small and status appraisals rely on known reputation or whether it is large and anonymous, where appraisals depend on appearance or the manipulation of symbolism (504). It is now often assumed that in the two decades since these remarks were formulated, there has been an invasion of cosmopolitanism into every corner of society and that mass society tampers with the isolation symbolically associated with the physical boundedness of smaller towns and cities.

If relations of sociability are based on appraisals of shared social status (Weber, 1946:186–187), one result of assuming that cosmopolitanism exerts influence on most members of society is that the dynamics of interpersonal status rituals can be reduced to a compendium of strategies for handling and manipulating appearances in social interaction. Erving Goffman's work on public behavior is an outstanding example of this assumption (1971; 1967; 1963; 1961; 1959). There may be reason to question this position, however, in that the evolution of the new middle class has not proceeded in the radical manner once expected (Giddens, 1973). This is important, since the internal structure of the middle class as well as its position in the urban environment and larger social structure are relevant to the contemporary view of social relations in public. Riesman, Potter, and Watson (1960), for example, argue that egalitarianism characterizes the sociability of the new, urban middle class, while Goffman (1963:163) argues that a relatively egalitarian use of public places results from the dominance of the middle class in our society. Goffman concludes that the rules of public order tend to be symmetrical (1967:53). The rules of public order, therefore, assume a homogeneous, urban middle class.

It follows that the situational manipulation of status is considered to be possible in anonymous, large urban centers and it is probable that the status appropriated is that of the middle class. This is because the middle class fails to monopolize specific status symbols (Stone and Form, 1953). But if, within the middle class, an old middle class persists, and if a localite life style resists change, or segmentation within the class is systematic, the assumptions that either status appraisals pertain only to appearances or that egalitarianism pervades the sociability of the middle class may not hold. At least within smaller cities, or even in enclaves within large cities, appraisals of status may well rely on reputation and/or symbol manipulation.

Therefore, the relationships of middle class persons are relevant because of the significant role these play in formulations concerning sociability and behavior in public. In questioning these formulations, the generality of assumptions concerning sociability is challenged. This study, then, is concerned with status assignment and appropriation *within* a local middle class and gives some examples of the way in which these are displayed in behavior in public places. Continuous prestige models are more often part of middle class imagery (Ossowski, 1963; Giddens, 1973), so that within the middle class, fine distinctions of marginal status differentiation are expected. Although marginal, status differentiation among segments of the middle class may be relevant to middle class persons, and may underlie the structure of sociability in public places. It is the purpose of this paper to support this suggestion with data collected during a thirteen-month study of a regulars' bar, called The Lantern, which is located in a college town in a mid-western state.[1] Further, it is argued that in smaller cities, the appraisals of social status refer to reputation as well as manipulation of appearances. Considering a group of public places as a set of stratified units is one way in which appearance and reputation co-interact, contributing to local status differentiation.

CIRCUMSTANCE AND SITUATION

Commenting on Riesman's description (1952) of the social struggle between the members of the same but vastly increased and differentiated middle class, Stone and Form (1953) suggest that the way in which this struggle is exhibited at the local level remains unclear. I have already hinted that the contemporary approach to public behavior has limited the possibility of using ethnographies of situated activity for investigating the manifestation of status differentiation at the community level.

This is because approaches to situated activity which emphasize interpersonal interaction are often critical of conventional variable analysis, in that categories such as social class, status, etc., are viewed as variables independent of the actors' definitions of them. But carried to extreme, an interactionist position can become equivalent to a naive voluntarianism, where actors are seen to always and willingly give meaning to an otherwise absurb "reality," or interactional forms are treated as universals, not contingent on status or class differentiation. Thus, while there have been attempts to highlight the actor's taking account of culture in terms of interpersonal interaction (Scott and Lyman, 1968; Hall and Hewitt, 1970; Hewitt and Stokes, 1975; Goffman, 1967, 1971), these studies are not utilized to detail the features of the social structure; that is, culture is treated as monolithic. Stone and Farberman offer a moderate approach which is at once concerned with interaction and differentiation within social structure:

> . . . there are social worlds of sex, age, ethnicity, and status, but . . . these worlds are variously permeable and are undergoing transformations over historical time. Consequently conventional variable analysis may not be the most appropriate model to use in social psychological study. The outstanding problem of interpretation now seems to narrow on the situation as distinguished from circumstance. The matter of boundaries —their formulation, maintenance, change, loss and reconstitution—is of overriding importance (1970:212).

The important implication embedded in these remarks, however, is that since social worlds of class, status, age, sex, etc., are permeable, the boundaries of situations are also permeable and are not merely identical with physical barriers. Therefore, a circumstance is seen to:

> . . . envelop the act. For whatever reason, escape from or redefinition of the circumstance lies outside the range of possibility. From the standpoint of the observer, the acting one is trapped, ensnared, fated (Stone, 1970:235).

Status, for example, is a circumstance when it constitutes "a network of life fate," and it is a phenomenon of the situation when, through the staging of appearances, it can be manipulated from situation to situation.[2] Just as conventional variable analysis may be an inappropriate model, a model which assumes the physical containment of situations whereby forms of social interaction can be observed isolated from the circumstances of actors is also limited.

Unfortunately, in studies of situated activity, it is frequently assumed that situations are physically contained. Goffman, for example, recognizes the role of status, age, or sex in situated behavior, but he does not relate these variables to the subject's establishment and maintenance of boundaries. Nor does he give any priority to any one of these variables. He, as many other micro-analysts, is a pluralist in that he gives as much weight to ". . . noise, fatigue, or facial disfigurations" as to socio-economic factors in face-to-face interaction (1961:80). Frequently, Goffman's work implies that structure-based features do not generalize to informal settings (Archibald, 1976). Most often, he focuses on behavior patterns which are routinely expected in given settings and which are independent of the changing population. This allows him to relax his investigation of the circumstances of particular actors. Cavan (1966), for example, in applying Goffman's framework to a study of public drinking places, reduces the investigation to the summation of numerous but brief observations of interaction. The sociability of particular actors is not considered over time, and at the same time, barrooms are considered places cut off from the community's institutional matrix. It is for these reasons that the framework for study of situated activity must be modified in a direction which facilitates description of the interdependence or distinction of circumstance and situation, reputation, and appearance. These modifications, which are embedded in the following definitions, allow for a relationship of situated behavior, social identity of the actor, and context of relevance, such as a local community.

DEFINITIONS FOR THE STUDY OF SITUATED ACTIVITY

A situation is defined as a context in which objects, events or persons are positioned or placed as social objects through social relationships. The boundaries of a situation may be or may not be the physical and temporal limits of a setting or a gathering.[3] The *setting* refers to the "furnished frame," that is, those configurations of physical materials such as walls, floor, seats, etc. (Goffman, 1971:284–285). The *gathering* is an event where the members "include all and only those who are at the moment in one another's immediate presence" (1963:18). *Situated activity* refers to any event occurring in the gathering and is comprised of an intersection of circumstantial and situational aspects.[4] The *situational aspect of situated activity* is the part which could not occur outside the gathering, being intrinsically dependent on the conditions which prevail therein. A *circumstance* is that which envelops the act, and may refer to the status, class, age, ethnicity, etc., of the participants. The *circumstantial aspect of situated activity* is the part that occurs in the gathering without necessarily being intrinsically dependent upon it. For an individual or collectivity, a circumstance may be considered a transsituational aspect of situated activity.

The notion of circumstance refers to a structural variable as it emerges in the definition of the boundary of a situation, linking the individual's social identity to a larger community. Given some influence of mass society on community life, the boundaries established for public sociability may be one of the few indications of community stratification when a community is caught between social relations based on reputation and relations based on situational manipulation of status. For example, when Lantern regulars describe The Lantern, they not only indicate to what extent they see their social status, broadly defined as middle class, as their circumstance, but they describe the community in terms of a stratified set of drinking situations (see Stone for a similar finding). The following are the remarks of some of the regulars:

> They may think all types come in here, but in no way is this a laborer's bar. A worker's bar is tough. Not only the language, the general behavior. This is a socially accepted bar among the upper middle class. If some of these guys went into Timmy's or Honey's or

the old Shoeshine [all local taverns], the people in there would say, "What's he becoming, an alcoholic," or "What's he after," if he brought some woman in there.

This is a good bar for me. I couldn't go to Christie's [local]. I mean, it's working class. I wouldn't mind being there but eventually my clothes, my style—I wouldn't be comfortable; they wouldn't.

When I first came to town as a young professor, I went to this tavern; I enjoyed it. You're with real honest to goodness people but I'm established now. I wouldn't do that anymore.

The social statuses of regulars are taken account of by them in choosing The Lantern as their drinking place, that is, in establishing the boundary of the situation. The discrimination against laborers, for example, can be seen as the members' way of shoring up the flimsy bottom barrier to membership in the middle class. To label the bar "a middle class drinking place," however, also refers to the interaction of circumstantial and situational aspects which characterize activity *within* the situation. Our focus here shifts to the emergence of circumstance as aspects of on-going activity, which aspects I have called circumstantial. The Lantern regulars define the boundary of the situation in terms of middle class social status with respect to other status strata in the community. But within their gatherings, the circumstantial aspects of activity refer to the internal structure of the middle class as a status level.

STATUS SEGMENTATION AND THE LANTERN

That there are distinct segments within the middle class is suggested by Mills's distinction of old and new middle class (1953, 1946), Riesman's inner and other directed characters (1952), and Merton's local and cosmopolitan influentials (1957:387–420). It has also been suggested that within the middle class, there may be a series of diverse groups related to occupation rather than dichotomized groups (Stone and Form, 1953:157). Certainly the middle class is best described as ". . . a mixture of heterogeneous elements, some in undisguised conflicts" (Kaufman, 1952:436).

The regulars of The Lantern represent three segments of the middle class, each distinguished by occupational status and aspects of life style. The regulars see this segmentation as reflecting the community's status arrangement. Two regulars explain:

Bill: There are three kinds of people in this town. The professors, the professionals—doctors and lawyers—and the streetpeople [he nudges the other regular] like us.

Steve: And they're all in The Lantern.

Since this is a less than accurate picture of Carsdale-Roseville,[5] Bill's view of the community is lopsided, but Steve's view of The Lantern is not. Still, Bill's view of the community is confirmed and, perhaps, Steve's is learned with their attendance at the bar. In this sense, The Lantern status arrangement and the community one are interrelated. A professional/businessman states, "The Lantern is in cliques because the whole town is in cliques."

The local segmentation of members of the middle class differs from a "segmentary system" as found in slum areas (Suttles, 1968).[6] Inclusion in segments is not mutually exclusive, although members of different segments do little or no socializing together (The Lantern being one important exception). The segments are not oppositional units, but antagonistic or competitive cooperators. The segments are not equivalent; there is a tendency toward hierarchy. Finally, the segments are not strictly socio-spatial units, if we mean that a defined territory in the community is claimed by one segment at the complete exclusion of the others. There is rather a status arrangement among these members of the middle class. The term arrangement implies instability, in that an arrangement is not uni-dimensional or hierarchical, although the instability can be observed as a dynamic tendency toward hierarchy (Stone and Form, 1953:149n). In the case of the regulars, the arrangement is marked by vertical cleavages and differentiates life style and occupational prestige, and there is tendency toward hierarchy.

The status differences between the segments of regulars—the professors, the streetpeople, and the businessmen—are not specific enough to close one segment completely to the others. The differences which are relevant have been carefully managed so that the complete breakdown of interaction can be avoided, but the limits to interaction across segments are sometimes tested. Among Lantern regulars, the streetpeople see other segments as more ensnared by their statuses than they. A streetperson tells me:

> The Lantern is a middle class tavern. It's just like a tavern but for these kinds of people. I go to other bars where there are working class people but I can handle it. Nobody pushes me around. These guys, they wouldn't like it; they [he points to some of the professors and businessmen] couldn't take it.

Some of the streetpeople do not feel that there is a well-defined barrier between themselves and the working class. Yet, they do not see themselves as working class. The same streetperson states, "I think of myself as a professional. I am a professional; I'm just not bourgeois." It is these persons who feel at times that they are at the bottom of a status hierarchy and it is these men who will attack the gathering when they feel that they are being treated in a way that is inferior to the others. Interestingly, it is the streetpeople who will differentiate the segments in terms of financial resources for life style:

> The regulars are mostly middle class, but some you might say are just middle class. The difference between those and others is some have to keep working, not that they're waiting for their paychecks. Then there are those who can live just the way they are from now on. [Streetperson]

This suggests that underlying the unstable status arrangement is an unstable class or economic system.[7] Other segments only recognize a tendency toward hierarchy with respect to status:

> The businessmen, well, they can only talk about what they know, what they do. That's understandable, but I'm usually bored to death. We can speak abstractly, but some of the regulars can't. [Professor]

> I don't see the professors outside the bar; after all, I'm just a dentist. [Businessman]

The tendency toward hierarchy is unstable in that usually the status arrangement among the segments is marked by vertical distinctions. Evaluations take place with regard to a local/cosmopolitan divergence:

> Professors can't be involved in the community. You have to really live in the community. You have to be invested in it. It matters to your life. Even people who work here in goods and services, maybe not their own businesses, they've got that interest. The professors don't have that relationship to the community. [Businessman]

> Well, the professors have been here a long time, but you can't think of them as old families.[8] Their kids don't stay. I mean, you can't produce a string of little professors. What do you leave to your kid, if you're a professor? [Streetperson]

The local/cosmopolitan distinction cross-cuts age levels. The local businessmen are in their fifties or sixties; the local streetpeople are in their thirties and early forties. The cosmopolitan professors are in their fifties or sixties.

The streetpeople are not all professionals, as are the businessmen. Among the latter, there is a dentist, an architect, an accountant, a funeral parlor director, an owner of a real estate firm, and a pharmacist. The streetpeople include a middle manager of a nonlocal food consulting firm, a Protestant minister, an owner of a printing shop, an owner of a house painting operation, the foreman of the city's disposal operation, and a reporter. Except for one streetperson who has a Ph.D., these regulars have not completed college, as some of the businessmen have. The streetpeople distinguish themselves by their involvement in local politics, either as a city council person, a city desk reporter, a manager of campaigns, or as an employee of the city, and in being from old families. One of the businessmen, who had been mayor of Roseville, says of his friendship with the streetpeople, "Well, you know, I've known their families for a long time." On the other hand, the professors who have lived in the community for more than ten years belong to no local organizations, including the country club.

The segmentation of the regulars refers also to their political preferences. The professors consider themselves liberal, while the businessmen, conservative. A local Republican politician describes the businessmen as "conservative, a little right of center. Let's say they think welfare is a necessary evil. If not directly involved in politics, they are supporters." The streetpeople are politically cynical, whether expressed in liberalism, conservativism, or even radicalism. Although localites, broad cultural trends—divorce, the Viet Nam war, alienation from organized religion—have affected nearly all of the streetpeople.

THE DESIGN OF THE GATHERING

The barriers between segments, which crystallize around the status each segment holds in the community, are observable as circumstantial aspects of their barroom behavior. The regulars' interpretations of their statuses are fixed, underwriting routine behavior, so that their public gatherings can be observed as designed. The ethnographer of situated behavior has the goal of delimiting this design or the context in which objects, events, and persons are positioned or placed as social objects. Regarding the situational aspects of activity, the concern is with the setting along temporal and ecological dimensions, obdurate or fixed props, and modifiers of props such as light, heat, and sound (Bennett and Bennett, 1970:190–196). Situational aspects refer also to behavior routine to a setting, such as drinking in a bar, and to overall cultural expectations concerning a particular setting, such as the freedom of activity often attributed to a public drinking place (Roebuck and Frese, 1976:48–49). But the way in which these situational features are interpreted by the actors involves their evaluations of their statuses and the extent to which status is circumstantial. Since it is not the purpose to give a full account of The Lantern's social order, I will only briefly consider the ecology of the bar, a graphic and simple example of how circumstantial and situational aspects of activity interact.

THE ECOLOGICAL ORDER OF THE LANTERN

The ecological order refers to the regulars' arrangement in space with respect to others and to each other and to the corresponding spatial divisions of The Lantern. The regulars think of the whole of the bar as theirs, a home territory (Cavan, 1966:205–233), and those whom the regulars call "foreigners" are not acceptable co-participants. With regard to these persons, regulars try and are usually successful in dominating space. Most often persons whose social identities misfit them for the bar (e.g., laborers) are treated as foreign. These acts of home territory defense, most often carried out by streetpeople, comprise a class of acts which pertain to the symbolic definition of the boundary of the situation.

Within the home territory, however, the ecological arrangement is further refined to accomodate the internal and distinctive structure of the group of regulars. The bar proper, which is four-sided and square shaped, is divided into segment territories. The streetpeople claim what is called the north end, the professors claim seats on the east side nearest the north end, and the businessmen claim seats on the east side nearest to the south end of the bar. The choice of a seat within the bar pertains to physical aspects—lighting, comfort, task locations. The younger men, for example, prefer stools on the north end; the older men prefer chairs, some of which are on the east side. The south side is not a segment's territory because a buffet lunch is served at this side of the bar. However, according to regulars, the seating arrangement also refers to a talking arrangement. Persons sit with those they feel comfortable with. The barely distinguishable physical separation of segments keeps open interaction between segments by cutting down opportunities for one-to-one interaction across the segments. Within the ecological arrangement, there are mechanisms for managing both the relative lack of openness between segments and the relative freedom of the setting.

The ecological arrangement is a territorial arrangement rather than a dominance order, the former referring to control over space, the latter, to control over space by intimidating others out of or into less space. Dominance is a hierarchial arrangement (Sommer, 1969:12-13). However, just as the instability in the regulars' status arrangement reveals a tendency toward hierarchy, the seating arrangement, which is for the most part territorially organized, is unstable; there is a tendency towards a dominance hierarchy. Examples of this instability are evidenced in the symbolic references to each side of the bar and the uses and defense of each of the territories by the respective segments. For example, a streetperson invites a waitress to eat lunch beside him at the north end, "Come on, sit here. They put all the workers on this side of the bar." On another occasion, two streetpeople are arguing with the bartender:

Streetperson: He [bartender] gives us shit, but these "nurdhead" east siders [points to a professor] get all the god damned service.

Occasionally a professor or a businessman will be standing at the north end when no seats are vacant at other sides. In such an event, it is by no means rare for a streetperson to offer his seat. Just as often the bartender will say, "Are you going to let this old man stand?" In a joking manner, the bartender arranges for a seat for a businessman or professor. For this relative lack of control over their place, the streetpeople compensate by being the most audible and visible persons in the bar. They often express annoyance with the hierarchy of service.

The professors generally react to the regulars' claims on seats as "rather amusing": "Aren't we all incredibly silly; everybody with a seat?" Rarely do the professors engage in territorial defense, and usually they appear amused or embarrassed when others do. More often, businessmen do engage in territorial defense, albeit indirectly. Other regulars protect their territory for them by avoiding it; the bartender also helps to keep their seats vacant. When a businessman takes a seat on a side other than his, as soon as his seat becomes available, he will move to it. One regular says:

> If one of the businessmen sits down next to me, I know he's going to move to be with the others as soon as a seat opens up on his side. That's the way it is.

Among the segments, the interactional barriers are accepted by all sides, in some cases willingly, in others begrudgingly.

This brief description of the ecological order of The Lantern emphasizes that situated activity is comprised of situational and circumstantial aspects. It also indicates that both reputation and appearance are at work in status differentiation at the bar. Segmentation among the regulars depends on reputation.

The Lantern regulars are not anonymous members of a large urban center. They are among the leading residents of a mid-sized community. They are, as The Lantern manager describes them, ". . . people with scratch in the community." Membership in Kiwanis, Chamber of Commerce, country clubs, and Elks are not beyond their reach, and many regulars do sustain such memberships. In fact, many of the regulars complain of being "saddled with a great deal of social interrelationships." For the most part, each segment of regulars comes to the bar to relax from daily interactional obligations. However, it is not anonymity the regulars seek, and if it were, The Lantern would be an inappropriate setting. They come for relaxation in the style which is comfortable for them and to which they have grown accustomed. Many of the regulars feel they have earned The Lantern. The bar is a place where the regulars can cash in their occupational success for social esteem and acceptance. Not surprisingly but ironically, the obligations taken on with the privileges of status are designed into the interactions of regulars.

The segments, while remaining distinct, cooperate in each segment's use of some other as an audience to its status. Each segment looks at the other for and at the same time avoids the others' judgments. Although the regulars have drunk together for many years, the competition between the segments and the sustained social distance result in the regulars' relationships being between friendship and familiarity without warmth, as one regular explains:

> There's no owning of mutuality in The Lantern. It's a substitute for primary relationships but it's not primary relations. There's no responsibility. No one wants

tension. Everything is kept implicit and there is a tremendous resistence to making it explicit. . . . If it's communal, it's like the out-group, in-group kind of thing. Everyone keeps their distance and the caring is not deep but still, when Ray's had too much to drink, John or Bill will follow him out to the car. They want to make sure he hasn't passed out. They'll pull the key out—maybe just that. . . . The complete acceptance in the bar is a neutral acceptance.

The limited emotional involvement of the regulars can be viewed as underscoring the importance of status in one's being accepted as a regular. Being "really friendly" will not be enough to offset a misfit of social identity. A professor explains, for example:

If you can't be engaged in conversation with a great deal of sophistication, you just won't make it in here. It's not that a fellow may not be intelligent or may not have something to contribute; we don't seem to give him a chance. I've seen people come in here, be real friendly but not sophisticated and leave kind of frustrated. I often think, that fellow's thinking, "I won't be back."

A businessman explains:

I could sit down at some bar next to a guy—a truck driver. He says, "Hey, give me another beer," and he closes his newspaper. We say a few things. I leave; there's nothing there, even if I tried.

Because many of the regulars are involved with the workings of city government and because the mayor of the town often frequents the bar, talk about city politics occurs at The Lantern. Matters of consequence are discussed—decisions of the city council, the mayor's attitude toward some policy, budget issues, the interrelation of different features of city government. Therefore, besides the atmosphere of sociability which city-involved persons may enjoy in the bar, regulars purposefully seek each other out to apply oil to the city machine. Riesman, Potter, and Watson have repeated Mill's suggestion that:

In many studies of small town social structures, the country club looms as the locus of power. No doubt this mixture of play and power is very American (1960:324n).

While The Lantern may not be *the* locus of power in Roseville, it is certainly one meeting place for persons of influence, reputation, and city clout. For this reason the bar takes on an atmosphere of play mixed with power. The regulars can monitor happenings in city government, the university, and business. Frequenting The Lantern regularly allows one to display social position; it reinforces a claim to social position. The claim, however, must be justifiable, not only by apparently appropriate behavior at the bar, but also by a reputation which can be validated over time, that is, the worth of past careers and future expectations can be assessed by others. Perhaps there is no better example of this than the regulars' rejection of a would-be regular.

A FAILED ATTEMPT AT BECOMING A REGULAR

A thirty-one year old man, named Troy, started to frequent The Lantern shortly after returning to his native Roseville. He had just lost his job at a university on the west coast, where he was working as a computer analyst. He was nearly finished with his course work for a masters in business. Troy let it be known at The Lantern that he was out of a job and was looking for one. But he did not project that he was down and out. He wore slacks, shirt, tie, and jacket. He spoke in what the regulars called "an affected tone" of education, sophistication, and intelligence. He passed himself off as having a masters and he often talked about his certainty of getting a job with the city or university. Troy told me:

I like The Lantern because it is a stimulating environment. It has a professional dimension. Conversations are intelligent and sophisticated. I find interchange active.

When I first came to The Lantern, I thought it was one group of regulars, then I saw distinctions. I placed myself with the professors because I wanted to be there. I see myself as there.

I come here because I'm unemployed. Coming here is important. It gives me something to do. Something to do everyday. It gives me something to do that makes me feel that I'm still working. And, I'm not unaware of the influence these people have.

The streetpeople soon rejected Troy for what they viewed as "his affectations." "I don't like him. He's not friendly; it's his voice. What crap that guy gives off; he's too much." Troy usually sat with the professors and he did tell them his problems. He told me:

I come here because I'm lonely. My wife has left me a year now and I have no job. I come here because I'm lonely, but I don't think that's how it is for the others.

The professors were civil, but their feelings were rejecting of the young man. One told me:

We have this guy, Troy. He wants to tell everyone his personal problems. This is the last place I would bring my problems or expect to have to listen to problems.

The businessmen were even less accepting of Troy. One told me the following story:

I was sitting here one day; Sandy [bartender] had stepped out. This guy Troy calls out "Would you like a drink?" I don't know who the hell he is but I say, "O.K." He makes it and sits down. Then he says, "What's your name?" I said, "Well what's yours?" Then we exchanged names. He says, "What do you do?" I wanted to say, "What the hell is it of your business." I said, "Well, what do you do?" He says "Well, you may need my services" and he gives me his card. I said, "Fine, but there's no address on it." He says, "Well, I move around; I'm unemployed." Imagine that; imagine him telling me I could use his services when he doesn't even have a job. When he was talking to you yesterday, I was just about to say, "Excuse me, but who are you, without a job?"

Troy stopped coming to The Lantern just about at the same time he took a job as a bartender at a local restaurant, eight months after his first visits to the bar. The regulars' rejection of Troy was based on their perceptions of a discrepancy between his appearances and his reputation. The discrepancy either embarrassed or irritated them. Troy had seen The Lantern as a place to establish social position and had failed to see that regularity only confirms an established social status.

DISCUSSION

The findings of this study suggest that outside of large urban areas, anonymity is not pervasive throughout social life. In smaller cities or within enclaves in larger cities, sociability in public places relies on status appraisals based on reputation, although appearances also play a role. For example, in distinguishing themselves from the working class, Lantern regulars make reference to apparent characteristics of social strata such as communicative strategies, interactional looseness, clothing, etc. However, the distinctions made among the segments of the middle class, itself, are often based on reputation. In fact, basing social relations on reputation may be characteristic of the middle class in smaller communities, but it may be that it is only within the middle class that appeals to reputation actually play a relevant role in interaction. Thus, the systematic status contentions and competitions between segments of the middle class can be related to the structure of situated activity, in particular, sociability. In this study, I have shown that there is a relationship between the boundary of a situation as established by the actors and their interpretations of situational features such as decor, services, clothing, etc. In the case of The Lantern, regulars define both themselves and the features of the bar as middle class. For example, regulars have told me:

> Maybe I'm more of a snob than I think, but I like nice things. I'm used to the right kind of environment. I like The Lantern, the leather, the carpeting.

> I've never been in any bar that was so sophisticated. It's middle class. A guy who came in here in work clothes would only last one beer.

There is also a correspondence between the boundary of a situation and the internal structure of situated activity in that the definitions of boundaries by different segments of regulars reveal the status hierarchy which is maintained within the gathering of regulars. Those who see themselves (streetpeople) as being closest to the working class are those who most readily and overtly display territoriality. Those (professors and businessmen) who feel the most distinct from the working class are those who see the exclusion of the latter from the bar as inevitable, so that they are less overt in denying access to their gatherings to those working class people who may occasionally come to the bar.

Second, this study suggests that the relatively egalitarian use of public places is not assumed within communities which are outside large urban areas. In fact, a set of public places, such as the local drinking places in a community, can be viewed as a stratified set of public situations, in which case the observations of public behavior with respect to defining boundaries may be one important tool in uncovering status stratification and its role in social interaction. The circumstantiality of class, status, sex, etc., depends not only on the individual's perception of himself, but on his or her social identity where the latter is considered to be based on a relationship of a person to a community or a set of community institutions. In other words, when status is circumstantial, not only are persons observed as being trapped, but the observer can also observe the set or sets of traps.

It follows that if social identity is not bound within a single organism, then the identities of situations are not entirely defined by physical boundaries. Rather, situations are comprised of both situational and circumstantial features. It is when we consider the possibility of circumstantial features in situated activity that we can question the assumption of the egalitarian nature of middle class sociability. In communities outside large urban areas, the middle class may be significantly and systematically segmented, and segmentation may provide a status arrangement upon which relationships are based.

Finally, viewing The Lantern as part of the institutional matrix of the community offers some interesting suggestions toward a revised view of alcohol consumption. Although drinking has often been studied as deviant behavior, there have been those studies which have investigated alcohol consumption as normal behavior, at least from the perspective of the drinker. The latter emphasize the positive functions of drinking in public, especially for those who live in the large cities. Supposedly, the isolation, depersonalization, or impersonalization of the urban environment are alleviated in public drinking houses which offer a substitution for primary relations or a means to maintain relationships (LeMasters, 1975; Warren, 1974; Samuels, 1970; Richards, 1963; Gottlieb, 1957; Moore, 1897). On the other hand, the bar is sometimes viewed as providing the overly socialized urban man or woman a time-out from information and interactional overload (Roebuck and Frese, 1976; Cavan, 1966). Most often, the working class person is viewed as using the bar in the former way and the middle class person in the latter (Listiak, 1974; Gottlieb, 1957).

The study of The Lantern suggests that, while urbanites in large cities may make use of public drinking places in the ways indicated above, these uses do not necessarily represent universal standing patterns of behavior within bar settings, as it is so often assumed. Indeed, at The Lantern, regulars relax from the interactional obligations of family and work, but drinking at the bar as a regular is only accessible to those of a certain community status. Therefore, social status becomes an important aspect of drinking behavior at the bar. Status distinctions, obligations, rights and duties are all maintained at the bar. "Letting go" can only be done in a limited manner, one that is appropriate to the social status of the drinker. Restraint is evident in the decorum, language, and common understandings about alcohol consumption.

Further, The Lantern does support social relationships among regulars, but not because alcohol necessarily reduces the barriers to friendliness. Rather, it is the maintenance of interactional barriers among the segments which supports and allows for the regulars' social relationships. Thus, if these relations are pseudoprimary ones, they are less so because they are formed in a public drinking place and more so because segmentation within a class prevents group formation expressed either as class consciousness or status closure. Alcohol consumption neither assures a democracy of drinkers nor is it an indication of drinkers' avoidance of community-based expectations and obligations. Rather, it is a socially defined activity. Attitudes and behavior directed toward that object refer to the social identity of the drinker in relation to a local community. Perhaps the most salient feature of alcohol consumption is that drinking style bears on the social status of the drinker and the social status of the drinker bears on the drinking style.

FOOTNOTES

* The data reported here are fully detailed in, The Lantern: Patterns of Public Drinking in a Middle Class Bar, Unpublished Doctoral Dissertation, University of Illinois, 1977.

1. The population of approximately 92,000 actually comprises the citizenry of twin cities, Carsdale (59,000) and Rosevile (33,000).

2. Status is conceived, in the Weberian sense, as distinguishable from class and party. However, Weber assumed that status referred always to the components of life fate. He designated as status ". . . every typical component of life fate . . . determined by a[n] . . . estimation of *honor*. . . . In content, status honor is normally expressed by the fact that above all else a specific *style of life* can be expected from all those who wish to belong to the circle" (1946:186–187). In contrast, Stone is assuming the possibility of the situational manipulation of status.

3. Goffman, on the contrary, defines *situation* as ". . . the full spatial environment anywhere in which an entering person becomes a member of the gathering, that is (or does then become) present" (1963:18). Stone's definition of identity (1970a:399) has influenced my definition of situation.

4. Goffman defines the *situated activity* as ". . . any event occurring within the physical boundaries of the situation" (1963:21).

5. The white population of the community consists of 78,468 males and 71,870 females. The black population consists of 10,644 persons of which half are males; persons of other non-white races number 2,666. Of the employed population, 8.8 percent is in manufacturing, 60.5 percent is in white collar occupations, and 38.9 percent is in government. In the urban center, 8.4 percent of the employed is in manufacturing, 66.2 percent in white collar occupations, and 43.8 percent is in government. The state university employs, of the cities' population, 234 administrators, 7,572 academics, and 10,291 nonacademics. The median income is $10,147, while 23.6 percent of the population is earning $15,000 or more, and 7.2 percent of the population is below the poverty level.

6. The features of such a system are: "First, each group is a socio-spatial unit. Second, inclusion in these groupings is mutually exclusive. Third, opposition is between 'equivalent' units. Fourth, the order by which groups combine preserves the equivalence of oppositional units" (Suttles, 1968:31).

7. Wiley suggests that status instability is an expression of an underlying class inconsistency (1964:538).

8. Thielbar points to the possibility of a cosmopolitan being less oriented to mobility when he is attached to a cosmopolitan institution such as a large university (1970:266–274).

REFERENCES

Archibald, W.P. "Face-to-face: the alienating effects of class, status and power divisions," *American Sociological Review* 41 (1976):819–837.

Bennett, D. and J. Bennett. "Making the scene," pp. 190–196 in G. Stone and H. Farberman (eds.), *Social Psychology Through Symbolic Interaction,* Massachusetts: Ginn and Company, 1970.

Cavan, S. *Liquor License,* Chicago: Aldine Publishing Co., 1966.

Giddens, A. *The Class Structure of the Advanced Societies.* New York: Harper Torchbooks, 1973.

Goffman, E. *Relations in Public,* New York: Harper Colophon Books, 1971.

———, *Interactional Ritual,* New York: Amchor Books, 1967.

———, *Behavior in Public Places,* New York: Free Press, 1971.

———, *Encounters,* Indianapolis: The Bobbs Merrill Company, Inc., 1961.

———, *The Presentation of Self in Everyday Life,* New York: Doubleday Anchor Books, 1959.

Gottleib, D. "The neighborhood tavern and the cocktail lounge: a study of class differentiation." *American Journal of Sociology* 62 (1957):550–560.

Hall, P. and J. Hewitt. "The quasi-theory of communication and the management of dissent," *Social Problems* 18 (1970):17–27.

Hewitt, J. and R. Stokes. "Disclaimers," *American Sociological Review* 40 (1975):1–11.

Kaufman, H. "An approach to the study of urban stratification," *American Sociological Review* 17 (1952):430–437.

Le Masters, E.E. *Blue Collar Aristocrats,* Madison: The University of Wisconsin Press, 1975.

Listiak, A. " 'Legitimate deviance' and social class: bar behavior during grey cup week," *Sociological Focus,* 7 (1974):13–44.

Merton, R. *Social Theory and Social Structure,* Illinois: The Free Press, 1957.

Mills, C. Wright. *White Collar,* New York: Oxford University Press, 1953.

———, "The middle classes in middle-sized cities," *American Sociological Review* 11 (1946):520–529.

Moore, E. "The social value of the saloon," *American Journal of Sociology* 3 (1897):1–12.

Ossowski, S. Class Structure in the Social Consciousness. New York: The Free Press, 1963.

Riesman, D., et al. *The Lonely Crowd,* New Haven: Yale University Press, 1952.

Riesman, D., R. Potter, and J. Watson. "Sociability, permissiveness and equality: a preliminary formulation," *Psychiatry* 23 (1960):323–340.

Richards, C. "City taverns," *Human Organization* 19 (1963):17–27.

Roebuck, J. and W. Frese. *The Rendezvous,* New York: The Free Press, 1976.

Samuels, F. "The negro tavern," Unpublished doctoral dissertation, University of Illinois, Urbana, 1970.

Scott, M. and S. Lyman. "Accounts," *American Sociological Review* 33 (1968):46–62.

Sommer, R. *Personal Space,* New Jersey: Prentice Hall, Inc., 1969.

Stone, G. "Sex and age as universes of appearance," pp. 227–237 in G. Stone and H. Farberman (eds.), *op.cit.,* 1970.

———, "Appearance and the self," pp. 394–414 in G. Stone and H. Farberman (eds.), *op.cit.,* 1970a.

Stone, G. and H. Faberman (eds.) Social Psychology Through Symbolic Interaction, Massachusetts: Genn and Company, 1970.

Stone, G. and W. Form. "Instabilities in status: the problems of hierarchy in the community study of status arrangements," *American Sociological Review* 18 (1953):149–162.

Suttles, G. *The Social Order of the Slum,* Chicago: The University of Chicago Press, 1968.

Thielbar, G. "On locals and cosmopolitans," pp. 259–275 in G. Stone and H. Farberman (eds.), *op.cit.,* 1970.

Warren, C. Identity and Community in the Gay World. New York: Wiley Interscience Publication, 1974.

Weber, M. "Class, status and party," pp. 180–195 in H.H. Gerth and C. Wright Mills (eds.), *From Max Weber: Essays in Sociology,* New York: Oxford University Press, 1946.

Wiley, N. "America's unique class politics: the interplay of labor credit and commodity markets," *Amercian Sociological Review* 32 (1964):529–541.

BARGAINING, ECONOMIC
EXCHANGE, AND CIVILIZATION

Carl J. Couch, UNIVERSITY OF IOWA

ABSTRACT

Exchange theory has been offered as a formulation for the detection of basic features of social life. This statement advocates the necessity of examining economic exchanges as instances of minded and cooperative behavior, that a dyadic level of analysis is required, and that economic exchanges are complex social activities involving little commitment on the part of the participants. The study of economic exchange activity cannot account for the emergence of minds and selves. However, if the study of economic exchanges is properly conceptualized, then it may be possible to develop a theory that provides an explanation of one way complex (civil) societies may arise.

The construction of an economic exchange presumes two social units acting with intentionality, interdependently, with some autonomy, and at the same time cooperatively. The consequence of the completion of an economic exchange is that A receives services or goods that are dependent upon B and B receives services or goods that are dependent upon A. At the minimum,

Studies in Symbolic Interaction—Volume 2, 1979, pages 377–398

the analysis of economic exchanges requires attending to a dyad, two units capable of acting independently of one another who construct an interdependent act, an act which produces a condition at time two different from that present at time one for each of them.

Economic exchanges are but one of several ways that can result in the distribution of services and goods. Others include theft, sharing, gift exchange and taxation. Theft is an autonomous act requiring only the presence of a victim or the victim's possession and the ability of the recipient to extract the goods. Sharing need not involve any anticipation of reciprocity. Gift exchange, while typically involving reciprocity, need not. Further gift exchange occurs within a context of reciprocal obligations that extend beyond the immediate transaction such that the gift given is not contingent on the gift received. Economic exchanges are often limited to the immediate context; no shared past nor anticipated shared future need be involved. Taxation is typically within a context of indirect economic exchange, but need not be. When it is extracted as tribute, it is a form of theft.

The fact that economic exchanges are an instance of cooperative activity does not assure that they are symmetrical, that the participants are equals. If one participant has a monopoly on a service or good and the other is competing with several other units in offering services or goods to the monopolistic unit, the relationship may be highly asymmetrical.

Not all instances of economic exchange are conducted within an interactive and cooperative context. We go to the store, note the price of an object, and decide to make the purchase. In such instances we do not interact with the person who owns the item. In such encounters, copresent cooperation is not an integral part of the exchange transaction. The transaction is mediated by money, credit cards, representatives, and clerks. Such transactions involve extremely complex social relationships. To simplify the analysis, attention will be restricted to those instances of exchange that occur within a copresence context and are not mediated by money, credit cards, or third parties, namely, the analysis will be restricted to bartering. Even so, copresent economic transactions are relatively complex social activities.

The simplest form of cooperative activity requires at the minimum: (1) the establishment of reciprocally acknowledged attention, (2) mutual responsiveness, (3) the projection of congruent future lines of behavior, (4) a shared focus and (5) a social objective. For example, for two persons to move a log that is too heavy for either of them to move alone, they must attend to each other's activity, be responsive to each other' on-going activity project to the other what each is going to do next with the other detecting the projected line of activity, share a common focus—that is be attending to the same log, and have a social objective. They must agree that they are going to move the log to the left. If they do not agree on the objective—if one plans to move it to the right and the other to the left—they may act with respect to each other but they will not be successful in producing a unit of cooperative behavior. (See Miller, Hintz, and Couch [1975] for an extended discussion of the basic elements of cooperative behavior.)

The simplest form of cooperative action is *solidary* action (Sehested, 1975). In *solidary* action there is minimal or no differentiation of self from other. Participants attend to each other and are responsive enough to each other so as not to get in each other's way as they take similar or identical actions toward a shared focus to produce a social objective. The acquisition of symbol systems (minded behavior) is based upon the construction of solidary action. The primary way we become embedded with each other is through constructing units of solidary action. Human beings are capable of constructing complex units of solidary action long before they can construct economic exchanges. Before they can construct economic transactions, they must be able to engage in minded behavior, to be able to imaginatively construct the completion of a social act.

Further, before they engage in economic transactions, they require a history of participating in accountable interaction sequences. Accountable social action differs from solidary action in that, in accountable social action, the participants differentiate themselves from each other and produce differentiated lines of individual action toward a shared focus. A takes one course of action while B takes a second course of action, while at the same time the two of them fit their behaviors together to produce what they recognize as a unit of social action. When two persons cooperate to play a basketball game, with one being the ball handler and the other the shooter, they are constructing a course of accountable social action. They have differentiated themselves but still cooperate. Further, they are still attempting to achieve the same social objective, winning the game. It is more complex than solidary action, since it requires the fitting together of differentiated lines of behavior.

"It is through engaging in solidary forms of activity that persons acquire symbols; it is through the objectifications of differentiated actions that persons acquire selves" (Weiland, 1975:89). Before persons can participate in economic exchanges, they must have acquired a mind and a self. Furthermore, cooperative action requires the projection of a shared future, whether the future be for a second, for example, the moving of the log, or for decades, for example, the establishment of a lifelong business partnership. "Without a shared future the organization of behavior by human beings becomes chaos, i.e., panic, apathy, or war on all. The most complex social relationship possible under this condition is that of predator-prey" (Hintz and Couch, 1975:45).

ELEMENTS OF EXCHANGE

The production of an economic exchange act requires that we have different but compatible interests. For example, I want blue marbles and have red ones, while you have red marbles and want blue ones. The construction of an economic exchange act also requires each of us to project the shared future of the possibility of constructing a transaction that results in the cooperative change in control over specific marbles. If one of us is not interested in making a transaction, no economic exchange can occur. If I am not interested in trading marbles, you may steal mine, but such an act does not constitute an economic exchange, even if you leave me one of your marbles in return.

The construction of an economic exchange act, then, presumes you control something of interest to me and I control something of interest to you. This condition does not assure that an exchange transaction will occur. Children develop attractions for services and goods long before they acquire the ability to complete an exchange. They demand services and appropriate goods long before they participate in exchanging them.

The exchange of services and goods are constructed within a context of expected mutual benefit. However, children and other animals can construct relations that are mutually beneficial before they can produce an exchange. Two children may huddle together for warmth in a cold bed without participating in an exchange act. Mutually beneficial acts simply require that organisms act together, not that one acts in terms of the other's interest. Mutual benefit may occur simply because while one is benefitting himself, he is benefitting another.

The exchange of services is much simpler than is the exchange of goods. The phrase "I'll scratch your back while you scratch mine" encapsulates the exchange of services. The exchange of services is fundamentally an exchange of experiences. The exchange of simultaneous services, for example, I'll scratch your back *while* you scratch mine, is simpler than the exchange of sequential services, for example, the parent who indicates he will play with the child at some later time in exchange for a few moments of peace and quiet. In the exchange of services, the interdependence is that of each other's experience depending upon the behavior of the other. The construction of an exchange of services requires a recognition of differentiation of self and other, and that the actions one takes can be satisfying or dissatisfying to another as well as to oneself.

To exchange goods, it is necessary that each participant acknowledges and accepts the idea of ownership, or at least control, at a moment in time. Before children can meaningfully participate in an exchange of goods, they must be capable of recognizing the significance of me and mine, not only for self but for others as well (that is you and yours). Once the idea of ownership has been acquired, then it is possible for a person to acquire the idea that ownership may be willingly relinquished under certain conditions.

Before an exchange of goods can be constructed, A must recognize B has control of X and may be willing to relinquish control of X if at the same time A is willing to relinquish control of Y to B. In many discussions of exchange in the sociological literature, the emphasis has been on the exchange of objects; but an exchange may be one of experiences or an exchange of control of an object for an experience. The exchange of objects presumes the awareness of and acceptance of relationships between human beings and other objects, or the presence of categorical identities.

Exchanges of experiences (services) require only the presence of functional or "doing" identities. I will help you with your school work if you will clean my room. In such transactions there is only the specification of congruent functional identities. We complete the exchange in such cases by doing something *for* each other. By doing things for each other, we presumably achieve more satisfying experiences than we would have if the exchange was not consummated. There is no question of ownership with respect to functional identities. What I do is always an expression of me, but what I do may have consequences for you.

The presence of ownership requires the presence of categorical as well as functional identities. A categorical identity is the specification of what someone *is*. One form of categorical identities is that of ownership. "He owns the red car" is a specification of a relationship between someone and a specific car. In an exchange of objects, then, the exchange is a redistribution of categorical relationships. Once you have traded the car for my house, each of us now has a different categorical identity than we had prior to the exchange. As with the exchange of services, the presumption is that the consummation of an exchange results in greater mutual benefit than if no exchange has occurred.

Obviously, not each and every instance of exchange results in greater mutual benefit. Often one or the other feels they got a raw deal, and on occasion both may wish after the fact that the exchange had not occurred. But in general, "exchange is just as productive, as creative of values, as is so-called production" (Simmel, 1971:47). On occasion when we attempt acts of production, we find we have also wasted our time, for example, the farmer who plants a corn crop and is struck by a drought.

Simple cooperative action requires the presence of only a single shared focus, for example, the log. Exchange acts require that the participants manage at least two foci. Both A and B must attend to what A has to offer and both must also attend to what B has to offer. Exchange acts can, of course, involve far more than two foci.

Furthermore, in the construction of an exchange act, there are at least three distinct futures: (1) the shared future that the two of them may be able to consummate an exchange, which is typically a short range future; (2) the future consequences of the act for A by A; (3) the future consequences of the act for B by B. Commonly, there are also two other futures present within an exchange, namely, A's anticipation of the future consequences of the exchange for B, and B's anticipation of the future consequences of the exchange for A. The latter two need not be present. Each may be concerned only about his own future and they will still be able to make an exchange. Therefore, both shared and contingent futures are an integral part of each exchange. The participants share the short range future of completing the act. At the same time, each individual's future is contingent upon the activity of the other person. If you will not trade me one of your jaw breakers for my marble and if no one else is around with jaw breakers, you in part control my future. I will not be able to experience the joy of chewing a jaw breaker. The degree of contingency present within any given exchange is highly dependent upon conditions external to the immediate dyad. If there are other used car dealers readily available, then my future is much less dependent upon you than if you are the only one in town and I find myself in need of a used car.

The exchange act then is an extremely complex form of social activity. In addition to the elements present in all forms of cooperative action, the exchange act requires the presence of the following elements: (1) mutual benefit as an imaginable outcome of the transaction, (2) differentiated but compatible interests, (3) multiple foci, and (4) contingent futures as well as a shared future. The exchange of goods requires the additional element of ownership (mine versus yours) and an awareness that ownership can be acquired and relinquished through interacting with another.

When economic exchanges are commonly practiced, then, there are three additional elements present in most cases: (1) the assessment of A's sacrifice versus his gain; (2) the assessment of B's sacrifice versus his gain; and (3) the differences between these two differences. If one gains far more than he sacrifices, while the difference for the other is slight or even negative, then the assessment may be made that an unfair transaction has occurred. Once persons begin making assessments of the differences between sacrifice and gain, differences of opinion are going to arise, so what is a fair exchange is never established in any absolute manner. However, as the community participates in these discussions, a standard of distributive justice can arise. Such a standard is not likely to arise if only those directly involved in the transaction participate in the discussion. The assessment of fairness requires some degree of agreement that each person's relative sacrifice and gain was comparable to the other's.

Many exchanges are far more complex than indicated. With the introduction of a medium of exchange (money or credit), the processes of constructing an exchange act can become exceedingly complex. For our purposes, we shall restrict attention to bartering. Even then, it is apparent that the exchange act is an extremely complex one in comparison to some other forms of cooperative behavior. One of the unique features of it is its complexity in the absence of any commitment.

BARGAINING

Bargaining refers to that sequence of activity beginning with one person indicating to another that he is interested in the two of them making an exchange. Bargaining ends when an agreement is reached on what will be exchanged for what. There can be extensive bargaining without the production of an exchange act. Conversely, exchanges can be consummated without any explicit bargaining, for example, a merchant displays his wares with a price attached, which when noted can be purchased or not purchased.

Exchange refers to the rendering of services and the transfer of control of goods. When there is a time period between the reaching of an agreement and the actual exchange of services and goods, then there must be an element of trust within the relation. If the exchange is made simultaneous with the agreement, as is commonly the case in bartering, then there need be no trusting of the other, only confidence in one's ability to assess the value of the other's services or goods.

In modern societies, we participate in little dyadic bargaining. What is not commonly recognized is that within most tribal groups that depend primarily on hunting and gathering, there is also relatively little bargaining. This is not to say that distribution of services and goods are not generic processes in both modern and tribal societies; they are. Distribution is simply accomplished differently. In modern societies, if large numbers cease purchasing a given item, then that item may be changed or disappear from the market, for example, the Edsel. We reify such processes into laws of supply and demand, often forgetting that changes in what is offered at the market place are the cumulation of innumerable individual decisions to buy or not buy a given product. The bargaining that underlies these events is indirect or mediated.

Sharing and gift exchange are common distributional procedures in tribal societies. Within hunting and gathering societies, for the most part, production is for immediate consumption, if not by the individual, by the immediate social unit. The feasts and famines of Eskimos and other hunting and gathering groups are legendary. Many societies have elaborate gift exchange networks. An appreciation for some of the distinctive qualities of bargaining can be obtained by comparing it with gift exchange.

On the basis of observing the transactions, we are usually capable of distinguishing exchanges that are the result of bargaining from those of an exchange of gifts. This is the case even if the participants are the same and the objects exchanged are the same. When gift exchanging and bargaining are extensively practiced within the same society, there are two different sets of words used to designate the activity. For example, among the Troborian islanders, the Kula ring was a gift exchange network. Among the same people, the term Ginwali referred to bargained exchanges.

Within these two networks, there were marked differences in behavior. Exchanges within the Kula ring were conducted in a highly circumscribed fashion. The participants do not exchange with just anyone, but with someone previously designated. Bargaining within the Ginwali network could be and was conducted with anyone available.

When gifts are exchanged, expressions of appreciativeness are given; to express a concern with the "market" value of the gift would be to demonstrate one's crudeness. At the same time, not to bargain for the best deal in the Ginwali network would demonstrate one's foolishness.

These same distinctions between gift exchanges and exchanges consummated by bargaining appear to be present in all societies. When bargaining, the value of the object offered by self is routinely exaggerated and the value of that being offered by the other is minimized. When persons exchange gifts, if any reference is made to the value of the gifts, the opposite occurs. The person offering a rug at the market place routinely stresses its worth; the same person offering the same rug as a gift will depreciate it. To haggle within the context of a gift exchange is to demonstrate one's lack of proper upbringing.

In some contexts, gift givers exaggerate the worth of a gift. Such activity was common among some Northwest coast Indians. However, both in the Northwest coast example and other similar situations, such exchanges are not constructed to acquire wealth, but to acquire personal prestige. The primary concern was with the relationship between the giver and the receiver, with the giver publicly demonstrating his superiority to the receiver. It can serve as a means of distribution, as Harris (1974) notes, but it is not an exchange consummated by negotiating with the other about what he will give to you in return for what you are offering him.

The exchange of gifts always includes an element of shared history and/or an anticipated shared future. We do not exchange gifts with strangers. We commonly bargain with persons we have never met before and never expect to see again. Gift exchanges may be part of a first encounter, for example, the first meeting of heads of state, but only in the context of an anticipated shared future. Friends upon parting may exchange gifts. Usually, when gifts are exchanged, both a shared past and future are integral parts of the encounter.

Bargaining may be conducted within a context of both a shared history and future, but they are not necessary features of the transaction.

To work toward an exchange, a shared future must be projected by one and acknowledged and accepted by the other; but the shared future projected may be limited to the immediate context. A person interested in making an exchange may approach another and say, "What do you want for your two geese?" In doing so, he is projecting a future of bargaining with the other, but he is not projecting a future that requires an exchange, only that he is willing to work toward an exchange. To make a commitment to make an exchange prior to bargaining would severely restrict one's options.

No bargaining may occur in the above example. The owner of the geese may indicate he is not interested in relinquishing control of his geese. Before bargaining can occur, both must express some minimal interest in the possibility of an exchange. Then and only then can they bargain. Upon entering into bargaining activity, each retains his autonomy while recognizing that cooperation may result in greater mutual benefit. Each person can break off the encounter at any moment. It takes two to construct bargaining but, as in any other instance of cooperative activity, only one to bring it to a halt.

The fact that each has the ability to bring the bargaining to a halt does not necessarily mean that they participate as equals. Variation in external factors, for example, number of other geese owners available, and variation in internal factors, for example, competence and experience, may give one an advantage over the other.

Bargaining, like mutuality (Weiland, 1975), then, is a highly present centered activity. The shared future extends only until they make the exchange or until one indicates a lack of interest. Bargaining can be fun in and of itself, for bargaining, in contrast to exchange, need have no future consequences for the dyad or either member of it.

The individual futures that are present within the bargaining may be short or long ranged. The person may be interested in purchasing geese because he intends to spend the rest of his life specializing in raising geese and needs breeding stock. Or, the individual future may be short ranged. He may be interested in the geese only to offer a feast to his friends. The long range future, to the extent it enters the bargaining, is that of individuals, not that of the dyad, although each participant may take the other's long range future into account while bargaining. If I know you plan to become a competitor, it might make quite a difference in how I behave, the price I will ask.

While bargaining is a very complex activity, it is an activity that for the most part is conducted within a context of minimal commitment. When we begin bargaining, my only commitment is to treat you as an equal and attend to your counter-offers. Bargaining can occur within a committed context, as when a seller promises to make good on the purchase if the buyer is dissatisfied. However, it only requires the commitment that, if we can reach an agreement, then and only then will A surrender control of Y when B surrenders control of X. No other shared or contingent future is necessary.

Even when participants anticipate having future contact with each other, no commitment need be present, only a concern with one's reputation. Such a concern, of course, does operate as a constraint. Traders who continue to do business in the same location are far more constrained than are those who move from place to place. A reputation of dishonesty can severely restrict one's future opportunities.

To engage in any form of cooperative behavior, each participant must assess the other's standpoint if they are to produce a course of joined behavior. If we cannot determine what the other is attending to, we cannot anticipate what he is going to do. This reciprocal assessment of standpoint need not be completely accurate, but if it is completely inaccurate—for example, I thought you planned to move the log left when you wanted to move it to the right—then we cannot cooperate. We can only act toward each other, not with each other.

In bargaining activity, the same restrictions apply. We both must assess correctly that each is interested in bargaining. However, in the bargaining there is a premium on accurate assessment of each other's standpoint. If you think I am indifferent about obtaining the geese when in fact I want them desperately, I have an advantage over you if you are interested in getting the best price possible.

Consequently, one of the primary activities present within bargaining contexts is each participant attempting to make an accurate assessment of the standpoints the other takes toward the two or more foci of concern. By participating in extensive bargaining, persons soon learn that if they can prevent the other from making an accurate assessment of their standpoint, they may have an advantage. Accurate assessment or even any assessment of the value the other attaches to the foci is not a necessary element for the production of an exchange act. However, accuracy of assessment of the other's values and inaccurate assessment of one's own values by the other facilitates at least the short range promotion of the individual's welfare.

As persons bargain, they commonly put on a performance in an effort to deceive the other. Each can be engaged in this activity. One result of this is that it produces a highly complex social act. They are engaged in cooperative behavior, that is, bargaining to work toward an exchange, while at the same time each is attempting to deceive the other.

Not all bargaining involves deceit. Bargaining can occur within an open awareness context, wherein each recognizes that an exchange will be to their mutual benefit. The possibility of deceit and cooperation at the same time gives bargaining an ambivalent feature. The concept mixed motive is one attempt to characterize this ambivalent feature of bargaining.

When persons assess each other's standpoint, they may then adopt the other's standpoint. As we act together to produce a protest march or build a house, we not only assess each other's standpoint toward the shared focus, but often come to adopt each other's standpoint. If, in a bargaining context, one person adopts the other's standpoint, he then will, in part, see the consequences of the exchange in terms of the other's welfare. To adopt the other's standpoint and experience concern with his welfare, of course, makes one more vulnerable to deceit. From an individualistic and short ranged point of view, the most effective bargainer is the one who can treat the other as an object, as an instrument that can be used to promote one's own welfare. However, from the point of view of the dyad or the community, in the long run the most effective bargaining is that which is based upon the open recognition of mutual benefit flowing from the exchange.

IMPLICATIONS

Most "exchange theorists start with the simplest assumptions of behavioral psychology and elementary economics" (Simpson, 1972:1). One of the cardinal rules of scientific inquiry is to develop the simplest system possible when offering an explanation. However, attempts to apply a system of thought that is incapable of recognizing the complexity of the phenomenon under examination can stifle the development of explanations.

Behavioral psychology takes as its unit of analysis the individual in an environment; some classical economists also take the individual in an environment as the unit of analysis. Such an orientation does not allow for a fruitful conceptualization of the exchange. At the minimum, the unit of analysis must be a dyad, two persons, to some degree cooperating with each other within an environment in an effort to produce an exchange.

Many of the studies of exchange by social psychologists are conducted within a context that denies the possibility of the emergence of mutual benefit, that is, within a zero-sum context. When one person benefits within a zero-sum context, another person must lose an equal amount. By restricting the interaction to this context, a condition is created whereby the successful one is the one most deceitful. It does not allow them to join their behavior in a way that results in mutual benefit.

The world of human beings is not restricted to contexts equivalent to zero-sum games. Bargainers commonly recognize that exchanges are creative of services and goods. In fact, in many situations the opposite is the case; when there is no exchange, both lose.

This is not to say that useful knowledge about social life cannot be generated within a carefully controlled zero-sum context. It may be. But it will not be knowledge capable of giving us an understanding of exchanges that occur within a context where participants anticipate mutual benefit. To develop an understanding of the exchange act, it will be necessary to study exchanges within such a context.

Many exchange theorists approach the act as the most primitive or basic human action. To the extent other forms of social interaction are given attention, they are viewed largely as a neutral forum for the consummation of exchanges. They tend to view "interaction as . . . a forum for gaining rewards" (Abbot, Brown, and Crosbie, 1973:505). The position taken here is that an understanding of exchange requires acceptance of the proposition that human beings must communicate and think before they can construct exchange acts.

The exchange act appears both phylogenic and ontogenic after human beings have acquired the abilities to engage in symbolic activity. Social interaction is not a neutral medium for the emergence of mind; it is out of interaction that mind arises (Mead, 1934; Hintz, 1975). The fact that persons can subsequently act as if interaction is a neutral medium once they have acquired minds and differentiated themselves from others does not allow one to conclude that exchange can be examined in a context that denies the cooperative and minded nature of the act.

The study of exchange, either economic or gift, cannot provide us with an explanation of those features that make us human beings, for example, minds, identities, selves. However, a thorough examination of the exchange act will allow for the development of knowledge about certain facets of modern society. Specifically, it appears that (1) the emergence of economic exchanges as a common procedure for persons to relate to each other is one way for civilization to arise and (2) economic exchange underlies the rise of complex societies with democratic political institutions.

EARLY CIVILIZATIONS

Jacobs (1970) developed the theory that the rise of cities rested upon the establishment of exchange as a major way of persons relating to each other. Using the evidence of Mellaart (1967), she demonstrates that centers of exchange (markets) have existed far longer than agriculture, that is, domesticated plants and animals; that contrary to the traditionally accepted sequence, human beings first traded with others outside their immediate group, then domesticated plants and animals.

The traditional formulation stresses the improvement of productive means. Implicitly, the traditional formulation presumes the critical activity is the improvement of production, through greater and greater specialization, followed by persons becoming involved in exchange acts as a result of the increase in production; that first there is specialization and the creation of surplus, then the development of exchange networks. Jacobs claims that both Marx and Adam Smith accepted this sequence of development. She may be correct in her characterization of Marx. However, she is less than completely accurate in her characterization of Smith. As Smith (1937:17) stated it, "it is the power of exchanging that gives occasion to the division of labour, so the extent of this division must always be limited by the extent of that power, or in other words, by the extent of the market."

Some nebulous form of bargaining toward economic exchanges can probably be found in all human groups. However, this mode of distribution appears to play a relatively minor part in the internal distribution in most hunting and gathering groups. Further, it plays a relatively minor part in the distribution within any social unit, wherein one of the primary ways of persons relating to each other is on the basis of functional solidarity. Within such groups, sharing is the prevailing mode of distribution. Within a family or any other unit that has a high level of solidarity, persons do not commonly bargain over who will get what for what.

We share with those we are embedded with and with those we are obligated to. Sharing is based upon extant relationships and anticipated consequences for the relationship. To focus on due value when sharing with kin and friends, or even when making a gift exchange, is almost universally regarded as immoral. Exceptions might be those groups where the trading mentality is so entrenched that most social activities are evaluated on the basis of economic exchange. The Phoenicians and the Venetians appear to have approached this norm.

The embeddedness that is pervasive in most hunting and gathering groups would prevent the rise of rationalistic economic exchanges. When such exchanges do occur, they are constrained by other considerations.

Participation in economic exchanges does not ensure the development of a civil society. There is extensive evidence from around the world of persons having a long history of participating in economic exchange acts without the activity being associated with civil societies or leading to the development of civil societies. Examples range from the Ginwali trade of the Troborian Islanders, to that between the tribes of the American Indians, to the bartering between the pygmies and others in Africa.

It appears that before a civil society, such as that detected by Mellaart at Catal Huyuk, can arise, more than reciprocating exchanges between two units must be present. When the trade is restricted to two units routinely exchanging with each other in a historical context, it is unlikely that a surplus sufficient for the development of a civil society will be accumulated.

One of the key ingredients for the rise of a sufficient market for the development of a civil society appears to be that the exchanges must be between "strangers." The development of markets and urban life in pre-classical Greece and in medieval Europe was closely associated with aliens. In these instances, almost without exception the early merchants were foreigners or outsiders who dealt with each other and the local population (Finley, 1967; Pirenne, 1925). The merchant class of ancient Athens was dominated by metics (aliens) and slaves. The trade centers of medieval Europe were populated almost entirely by aliens.

Further, in these cases where there is evidence available, the local inhabitants who became involved in trade were not persons who were embedded in the local community. Rather, most of the local residents who became involved with the market place during the developmental phase of the market were poverty stricken or in some other way marginal persons. In the rise of markets in ancient Greece and in medieval Europe, the local elite, almost without exception, looked down upon traders. Aristotle regarded trading as husterism written large (Finley, 1967).

The conclusion that is warranted by these data is that persons who are embedded with each other do not participate in extensive bargaining with each other. The rise of markets, then, is associated with persons somehow coming to bargain and exchange with outsiders, persons who are not members of one's own community.

What appears to have happened at places such as Catal Huyuk and other early urban centers based on trade is a substantial proportion of the local community became involved with trading with outsiders, strangers. These trade centers then became known to surrounding populations as places where one could go and exchange goods. The local residents, through extensive participation in bargaining, would acquire two features essential for the rise of a civil society—complex thought and surplus. Both can result from participating in bargaining and exchanging.

Complexity of thought arises from the bargaining process and surplus arises from making profitable exchanges. And the greater the complexity of thought developed within the bargaining process, the more likely a person is to make profitable exchanges, that is, acquire surplus.

Complexity of thought among traders is in part generated by the very complexity of the social act that bargaining and exchanging entail. To be effective, the trader must make an accurate assessment of the two goods under consideration, not only an accurate assessment of their worth now, but what will be their worth in the future. To be effective requires that a concern with the future be an integral part of the immediate transaction. The future or course is that of the individual trader, not that of the dyad.

If the exchange act is restricted to dyadic encounters, it will not provide the complexity of thought sufficient for the rise of civil societies. When exchanges are restricted to A providing B with X and B providing A with Y and B consumes X and A consumes Y, no great complexity of thought need arise. However, when the exchange is potentially triadic, that is, one of the participants has the opportunity to select between two or more others which he will exchange with, there is a qualitative difference in the social relations that facilitates the development of complex thought.

For example, if A has obsidian and exchanges it with B for turkeys, it is a relatively simple activity. However, if A discovers that C is also interested in obtaining some obsidian and has pigs to exchange for it, then A has alternatives to weigh. As he enters into each of these relationships, the other possibility is a viable part of the encounter. While participating in any given transaction, he can imaginatively participate in the other. Unless there is more than one trader with obsidian, this possibility is denied those with turkeys and pigs to barter.

Through participating in such activity, the owner of the obsidian may begin a bidding war between B and C that will work to A's advantage. Such a state of affairs is likely to result in A accumulating a surplus. The surplus can then be used for other purposes, namely, the accumulation of personal possessions that have little utilitarian value, that is, luxuries.

The rise of the early urban centers based on trade involved members of a local population exchanging some local good for a variety of goods with outsiders. At Catal Huyuk, the good controlled by the local population was obsidian. Within such a context, the local traders become professionals dealing with amateurs. Both the professionals and amateurs will develop complexity of thought based upon making a part of the distant future part of the immediate context. However, the professional will develop far greater complexity. Most, in their dealings with outsiders, will use that complexity of thought to their own advantages. This same relationship still exists today in enounters between traders and country bumpkins.

Not only is there the generation of complex thought within the bargaining process itself, but contacts through trade will make the participants aware of alternative life styles. Again, this will occur for both the professional trader and the amateur. When the outsider first comes to the market he is impressed with the variety of goods that are available. However, as the professional trader has a greater range of contact than the amateur, the greater awareness of variety will operate to the professional's advantage.

The less embedded a trader is in relationships with others, the more effective he can be in his bargaining. Effective participation in bargaining requires that the person be self-centered. It requires that one be concerned primarily with the consequences of his action for his own future welfare. If the trader is concerned with how his family or clan will respond to his exchange, it operates to constrain his behavior. Those who participate as amateurs and as representatives of some larger unit then are at a double disadvantage. The amateur participates to acquire goods for their utilitarian or entertainment value; the professional participates in the interest of acquiring a surplus (capital).

While the earliest cities based on trade appear to have developed in locales where the local population had access to some resource valued by others, this does not appear to be a necessary feature for the rise of urban trade centers. The prototype of such a civil society is Venice during the Dark Ages. Without fields, mines, or any other sources of production, Venice became a wealthy city (Cox, 1959). The essential thing is simply that a group of persons establish a location that comes to be recognized as a place where one can go and engage in exchange. It is among those who constitute the local population that a civil society can arise.

MORALITY

The development of trade has often been charged with the destruction of community solidarity and morality. That it has had that consequence for amateurs cannot be denied. In some ways, it probably has the same general consequence for the relationships extant among the professional traders. That is, extensive trade within a community probably undermines a form of communal solidarity. What is overlooked by many critics of trade is that it also is a major procedure that lead to the destruction of authoritarian systems. The defenders of capitalism, of course, see the destruction of authoritarianism as a major consequence of trade.

Those living in a state of primitive solidarity or authoritarianism live within a "taken for granted social world" over which they have little or no control. Persons who extensively participate in bargaining with outsiders learn, in the process of acting, that at least part of the world is a negotiated order, something constructed by human beings, and that what was the case yesterday need not be the case tomorrow. Those who form units based upon similarity of interest can recognize that social systems are relationships that can be controlled, and are therefore subject to discontinuation and re-negotiation. This attitude is, for the most part, absent in societies based primarily on some combination of primitive solidarity or authoritarianism. It is also lacking in societies that are based on long range centralized programming (Couch and Hintz, 1977).

The fact that bargaining and exchanging involve individuals projecting their futures and attempting to produce the desired future through their own efforts informs persons that their welfare is something that is, in part at least, in his own hands. It is something one can attempt to control. One is not completely at the whims of higher powers or the community. Especially those who achieve a modicum of success in the market place are likely to view their future as something over which they could intentionally exercise considerable control.

When bargaining is conducted within a context where there is more than one source of any given goods, it also promotes a sense of independence. One learns that one is not dependent upon a centralized authority, but upon self in relation to a variety of others. To the extent markets are monopolistic for the participant, they do not facilitate the development of independence and autonomy.

While the market does undermine primitive solidarity and morality, it at the same time provides a base that allows for the emergence of a different kind of solidarity and morality—at least among the professional traders. The impact upon the amateur participants is often quite different.

The autonomy associated with bargaining provides the foundations for the rise of the integrity of the individual. The market place is one of the major sources of a morality based upon individual liberty and freedom of choice.[1] As one of the inscriptions that has come down to us from ancient Babylonia states it, "even a dog is free when he enters the city" (Oppenheim, 1964:121). Throughout history, traders have received a bad press. The Greeks regarded the Phoenicians as despicable characters as did the Romans. Pirenne, who has made as insightful an analysis of the part trade played in the rise of modern Europe as anyone, made the following observation, "No scruple had any weight with the Venetians. Their religion was the religion of business men. It mattered little to them that the Moslems were the enemies of Christ, if business with them was profitable" (Pirenne, 1925:86).

Why not look at this in a somewhat different manner? Implicit in Pirenne's standpoint is that the Christians were engaged in a moral act, fighting and killing the Moslems. If other social units wish to kill each other off, those societies infused with a trading mentality have often been quite willing to trade with both sides. That those at war wish to use the benefits achieved in trade for destructive purposes is their affair, from the trader's point of view. For, after all, the mentality of the trader is one that recognizes the autonomy of all.

Any market that lasts for any length of time does generate within it a communal organization that is quite different than that based on primitive solidarity or authoritarianism. They form associations that recognize their interdependence while at the same time respecting each participant as an independent unit. They consciously form social units for their mutual benefit. They construct a communal solidarity based not upon fate, but upon individual choice.

Nor are traders particularly warlike groups. Not that societies infused with the trading mentality have not engaged in warfare, but war has largely been to protect their trade networks. They typically do not engage in wars of conquest. While Western European history glorifies the Roman Empire and belittles the trading empire of the Phoenicians, most external units of that day and age, if they had their choice, would rather have dealt with the Phoenicians.

One of the distinctive features of trading civilizations of the past is their relatively unwarlike character. Their warfare was largely that of defense. They built walled cities to keep the uncivilized out. Their very wealth was such a temptation to surrounding units that they were attacked again and again, many suffering the fate of Jericho.

The impact of participating in trade for the amateurs is quite different than it is for the professionals. When amateurs participate in exchanges, it is often quite destructive of their prior relationships. Further, the destruction of the extant patterns of relationship are not replaced with a new set of relationships. In the process of bargaining and exchanging, the amateurs become unembedded and autonomous individuals also.

When the amateur begins participating in exchanges, he learns that one can produce, not for immediate consumption or for sharing with other members of his social unit, but with the intention of exchanging with outsiders. Once the Eskimo learns he can exchange furs for rifles, he may then hunt to accumulate personal wealth to be exchanged. He then no longer hunts simply for the necessary food and clothing. In doing this, the individual acts not on the basis of immediate needs and wants, but on the basis of a relatively long range want. He relates a distant future to his immediate activities.

Hunting then becomes a much more individualistic activity. The hunter seeks prey not because his family or clan need food, but because he as a person desires a rifle. Whereas before the hunter took it for granted he would share with others, he now thinks in terms of what are the implications of this activity for himself. In the process, of course, he may destroy both the resources of his natural environment and the extant social relationships within his society.

The amateur is also at a disadvantage due to the simple fact that when he enters the market, he often finds himself confronted with a monopoly, a monopoly of only one trader or a monopoly based upon price fixing. The professional traders simply have far greater opportunity to coordinate their stance vis-a-vis the amateurs than the amateurs do vis-a-vis the professionals. The amateur then can come to find himself in a highly dependent position.

It is this facet of trade that Polanyi viewed with dismay and found destructive of human institutions. And it is a feature of the market that has caused much human suffering. It also has resulted in the accumulation of centralized wealth, which can then be used in turn to hire others, ranging from mercenaries to intellectuals, to act on the behalf of the professional trader to control the behavior of the amateurs.

Defenders of the market place have long maintained that it is the source of many desirable human institutions. Critics of it have focused on the evils associated with the market place. The more reasonable position is that both are correct. The defenders for the most part have limited their attention to the developments that occur among the professional traders; while the critics have focused their attention on what the market place does to the amateurs. Each has looked at only one half of the relationship.

ALTERNATIVES

The market is not the only way that civil societies can emerge. The Egyptians of the old kingdom developed a civil society of considerable complexity in which exchange played a minor, if any, part—at least exchange with outsiders. They had no word for merchant or trader until the time of the middle kingdom. Then, during the middle kingdom when they traded with outsiders, the trade was conducted by representatives acting in behalf of the ruling elite. Internal redistribution of goods was largely under the control of a centralized bureaucracy. The civil society of the Old Kingdom, and others like it, appears to have developed on the basis of elaborate timekeeping procedures, centralized programming, and storage of goods. (See Couch and Hintz, 1977.)

Civil societies based upon centralized programming have an entirely different bias than those based upon the market place. One of the primary concerns of such societies is order. The Egyptians were extremely concerned with Maat (order), everything in its place and no loose ends. Civil societies with an exchange base, in contrast, take disorder and fluidity as normal state of affairs.

Within civil societies based primarily on centralized programming, there is a complex set of accountable relationships that focus upon a central authority. Each member of the society is accountable to that central authority. Such a system does not engender the rise of autonomous individuals nor a concern with personal freedom. Duty is the primary concern.

Within civil societies based primarily on exchange networks, concern with personal freedom can come to the fore. In the market place, the contacts one makes and who he will act with are not controlled by commitments but by what is available. The contacts are not controlled by a system of relationships external to the market place. Consequently, from the point of view of those embedded in a programmed society, the activity within a market place appears to be essentially random and chaotic.

Both trade and centralized planning are procedures that enable the rise of complex thought, produce disembeddedness from primitive solidarity, and surplus, all of which appear to be necessary developments of a civil society. Both activities can and do occur within the same social units. Within the United States, we have both long range social programmers and persons who organize themselves within the market place primarily in terms of their individualistic long range interest. In fact, this is the major ideological conflict present in contemporary American society. In the process of making the decisions as to how much each orientation is to be stressed, it would appear to be reasonable to attempt to ferret out the consequences of each. That there is an inherent conflict between the two need not lead us to conclude that one must be abolished in favor of the other.

CONCLUSION

Exchange theory has been offered by some sociologists as a formulation that will allow us to detect the basic elements of human life, with the further promise that once this has been accomplished it will provide the base for the development of a comprehensive theory of society. Hopefully, it has been demonstrated that such an approach is chauvinistic; that the exchange act cannot underlie all other forms of social life, rather that cooperative and minded behavior precedes the rise of the exchange act.

Nonetheless, exchange theorists have provided a useful antidote to much of sociological theorizing by reminding us all that we do have bodies that demand food if we are to survive, that we are flesh and blood organisms with needs and wants that can only be satisfied by entering into commerce with others.

However, the future development of "exchange theory" will rest upon a willingness to recognize that exchange acts are minded activities, involve at the minimum a dyad, and are often productive of mutual benefit. Any studies of exchange directed toward the ferreting out of general implication of the exchange for human existence that denies these qualities cannot provide us with findings that allow an understanding of consequences of participating in economic exchanges.

If the complexity of the act is recognized and closely analyzed, then beyond a doubt, careful and systematic studies of exchanges will provide us with insights into some of the more complex features of civil social structures that at the present are only dimly perceived. The insights of the classical economists and Simmel appear to be a much firmer base upon which to build a theory of exchange than are those of rat or pigeon psychology.

FOOTNOTES

*Presented at the conference of society for the Study of Symbolic Interaction, Urbana, IL, 1977

**The comments and suggestions of Robert Hintz, Frank Kohout, Gayle Scriven, Mike Katovich, Joel Rudd, Mary Jo Rudd, Bruce MacMurray and Mark Wardell are gratefully acknowledged.

1. McLuhan (1962) developed the thesis that the rise of individual autonomy and democratic institutions were based upon popular literacy. He marshalls a wealth of data supporting his position. His position is not incompatible with one that would see their foundation in the market place. Both the development of popular literacy and markets facilitate individuals behaving autonomously. Those in control of centralized programmed societies usually attempt to control both the flow of information and the rise of markets.

When there is widespread literacy and a free flow of information, persons can engage in extensive autonomous acts wherein they select from a variety of sources the ideas they will expose themselves to. Literacy and the free flow of information make it possible for persons to be exposed to alternative thought, as does the market place.

One difficulty of sorting out the significance of the market place as opposed to literacy for the rise of democratic political systems is that the two developments have been closely intermingled. The ancient Greeks, who were the first to concern themselves extensively with democratic institutions, were exposed to both market relations and a variety of ideas on the basis of written material. Iceland, which has the oldest continuous elected parliament, was settled by persons who were both literate and had a history of trade. The concern with democratic institutions that developed after the Dark Ages in Europe was also closely associated with the spread of markets and written material. Their respective contributions appear to be impossible to sort out at this time.

REFERENCES

Abbot, Charles W., Charles R. Brown, and Paul V. Crosbie, "Exchange as Symbolic Interaction: For What?" *American Sociological Review* (August 1973): 504–506.

Adams, Robert McC., "The Emerging Place of Trade in Civilization Studies," in Jeremy A. Sobloff and C.C. Lamberg-Karlovsky (eds.), *Ancient Civilizations and Trade*, Albuquerque, N.M.: University of New Mexico Press, 1975

Baudin, Louis, *Socialist Empire: The Incas of Peru* (translated by Katherine Woods), New York: D. Van Nostrand Company, Inc., 1961.

Blau, Peter M., *Exchange and Power in Social Life*, New York: J. Wiley, 1964.

Couch, Carl J. and Robert A. Hintz, "Timekeeping, Social Programming and Civilization," Paper presented at 1977 Conference of Symbolic Interactionists, 1977.

Cox, Oliver C., *The Foundations of Capitalism*, New York: Philosophical Library, 1959.

Culbert, T. Patrick, *The Classic Maya Collapse*, Albuquerque, N.M.: University of New Mexico Press, 1973.

———— , "The Maya Downfall at Takal," in T. Patrick Culbert (ed.), *The Classic Maya Collapse*, Albuquerque, N.M.: University of New Mexico Press, 1973.

Dalton, George, *Economic and Anthropology and Development*, New York: Basic Books, Inc., 1971.

"Karl Polanyi's Analysis of Long-Distance Trade and His Wider Paradigm," in Jeremy A. Sobloff and C.C. Lamberg-Karlovsky (eds.), *Ancient Civilization and Trade*, Albuquerque, N.M.: University of New Mexico Press, 1975.

Finley, Moses, *Studies in Land and Credit in Ancient Athens, 500–200 B.C.*, New Brunswick, N.J.: Rutgers University Press, 1967.

Hammon, Nicholas G.L., *A History of Greece of 322 B.C.*, Oxford: At the Clarendon Press, 1967.

Harris, John R., *The Legacy of Egypt*, Second Edition, Oxford: At the Clarendon Press, 1971.

Harris, Marvin, *Cows, Pigs, Wars, and Witches: the Riddles of Culture*, 1st Edition, New York: Random House, 1974.

Herm, Gerhard, *The Phoenicians*, New York: William Morrow and Company, Inc., 1975

Hintz, Robert A., "Foundations of Social Behavior," in Carl J. Couch and Robert A. Hintz (eds.), *Constructing Social Life*, Champaign, Ill.: Stipes Publication Co., 1975.

Hintz, Robert A. and Carl J. Couch, "Time, Intention and Social Behavior," in Carl J. Couch and Robert A. Hintz (eds.), *Constructing Social Life*, Champaign, Ill.: Stipes Publication Co., 1975.

Homans, George C., *Social Behavior: Its Elementary Forms*, New York: Harcourt, Brace and World, 1961.

Innis, Harold A., *The Bias of Communication*, Toronto: University of Toronto Press, 1951. *Empire and Communication*, revised by Mary Q. Innis, Toronto: University of Toronto Press, 1972.

Jacobs, Jane, *The Economy of Cities*, New York: Random House, 1970.

Lamberg-Karlovsky, C.C., "Third Millenium Modes of Exchange and Modes of Production," in Jeremy A. Sobloff and C.C. Lamberg Karlovsky (eds.), *Ancient Civilization and Trade*, Albuquerque, N.M.: University of New Mexico Press, 1975.

Marshack, Alexander, *The Roots of Civilization*, New York: McGraw-Hill, 1972.

McLuhan, Marshall, *The Gutenberg Galaxy*, New York: New American Library, Inc., 1962.

Mead, George Herbert, *Mind, Self and Society*, Chicago: University of Chicago Press, 1934.

Mellaart, James, *Catal Huyuk*, New York: McGraw-Hill Book Co., 1967.

Miller, Dan E., Robert A. Hintz, and Carl J. Couch, "The Elements and Structure of Openings," in Carl J. Couch and Robert A. Hintz (eds.), *Constructing Social Life*, Champaign, Ill.: Stipes Publication Co., 1975.

Oppenheim, A. Leo, *Ancient Mesopotamia*, Chicago: University of Chicago Press, 1964.

Pirenne, Henri, *Medieval Cities* (translated by Frank D. Halsey), Princeton, New Jersey: Princeton University Press, 1925.

Renfrew, Colin, "Trade as Action at a Distance: Questions of Integration and Communication," in Jeremy A. Sobloff and C.C. Lamberg-Karlovsky (eds.), *Ancient Civilization and Trade*, Albuquerque, N.M.: University of New Mexico Press, 1975.

Sahlins, Marshall D., "On the Sociology of Primitive Exchange," in Sahlins, *The Relevance of Modes of Social Anthropology*, Praeger, 1965.

Sehested, Glenda J., "The Evolution of Solidarity," in Carl J. Couch and Robert A. Hintz, Jr. (eds.), *Constructing Social Life*, Champaign, Ill.: Stipes Publication Co., 1975.

Service, Elman R., *Origins of the State and Civilization*, New York: W.W. Norton & Company, 1975.

Simmel, George, "Exchange," in Georg Simmel, *On Individuality and Social Forms* (translated by Donald N. Levine), Chicago: The University of Chicago Press, 1971.

Simpson, Richard L., *Theories of Social Exchange*, New York: General Learning Press, 1972.

Smith, Adam, *Wealth of Nations*, New York: The Modern Library, 1937.

Sobloff, Jeremy A. and C.C. Lamberg-Karlovsky, *Ancient Civilization and Trade*, University of New Mexico Press: Albuquerque, N.M., 1975.

Thibaut, John W. and Harold Kelley, *The Social Psychology of Groups*, New York: Wiley, 1959.

Weiland, Marion W., "Forms of Social Relations," in Carl J. Couch and Robert A. Hintz (eds.), *Constructing Social Life*, Champaign, Ill.: Stiper Publication Co., 1975.

NESTED IDENTITIES*

Saul D. Feldman, CLEVELAND OPERA THEATER

INTRODUCTION

The idea that individuals have multiple identities is one of the cornerstones of symbolic interactionist thought. Individuals have identities relating to many spheres of their lives, such as occupational, political, and familial identities (Gordon, 1976:407). According to Goffman (1961:90), "It is a basic assumption of role analysis that each individual will be involved in more than one system or pattern, and therefore, perform more than one role. Each individual will, therefore, have several selves, providing us with the interesting problem of how these selves are related." It is not surprising that considerable attention (e.g., Goffman, 1959; Strauss, 1959; and McCall and Simmons, 1969) has been paid to examining the situation under which one identity rather than another is involved, as well as the conflict resulting because individuals have this "simultaneous multiplicity of selves" (Goffman, 1961:132). The focus of most research on multiple identities has been on the differences *between* these often disparate identities. This paper proposes that there is another type of multiple identity pattern—multiple

Studies in Symbolic Interaction—Volume 2, 1979, pages 399–418
ISBN: 0–89232–105–9

identities *within* one sphere of life, and that identities may be as diverse within this one sphere of life as between spheres.

Sociologists do not always agree on the meaning of the concepts they use. For example, there are a variety of definitions and interpretations of such basic concepts as community (Sutton and Munson, 1976), deviance (Feldman, 1978:1–58), and social class (Gordon, 1950:1–20). This too is the case with the concept of *identity*. I shall use this term as it appears to be understood by those in the symbolic interactionist tradition.[1] According to Stone (1962:93),

> Almost all writers using the term imply that identity establishes *what* and *where* the person is in social terms. It is not a substitute for the word "self." Instead when one has identity he is *situated*—that is, cast in the shape of a social object by the acknowledgement of his participation or membership in social relations. One's identity is established when others *place* him as a social object by assigning him the same words of identity that he appropriates for himself or *announces.*[2]

Stone (1962:94) further states that through identity, we "situate the person as a social object" by bringing him or her "together with other objects so situated, and at the same time to set him or her apart from still other objects." Thus identities are shared with others and set apart those with a common identity from those who do not share this identity.

Travisano (1970:597) links the concept of identity to another term which appears to have a multiple meaning—role. He feels that identity "is a signal in interaction for the mobilization of specific role expectations. Identities are, so to speak, the labels or names on the scripts of various situationally specified programs of behavior which make up the abstract totalities we call roles. Identities tell people what to do and what to expect during a given interaction."

Klapp (1969:5) operationalizes and defines identity simply as "any generally satisfactory answer to the question, Who am I? (Who are you?)" As others do, he emphasizes the changeable nature of identities, feeling (1969:6) that it is "to some extent arbitrary, challengeable, and changeable." Because identities are not fixed but are changeable and situational, he feels (1969:6) that identity "is factually a fragile mechanism whose equilibrium needs constant maintenance and support from the proper environment, and it is quite easy for something to go wrong with it." To Klapp (1969:39), identity is a "functioning system of three basic variables: (1) what a person thinks about himself introspectively; (2) what he projects or sees imaged or accepted in the eyes of others (his social identity); and (3) his feelings, validated when 'real to me' and when shared with others."

Following the notions of Stone, Travisano, and Klapp, I interpret identity to be a socially situated (social) placement which links an individual with others because of some significant commonality. At the same time, this social placement sets those so identified apart from others who do not share this identity. People with common identities act more alike (and are expected to act more alike) than those who do not share this identity. Identities are not immutable. They are constantly being subjected to change and challenge and therefore require social support and social validation. Identity may be imposed upon an individual by others, or it may be part of an image that an individual holds of himself or herself. Identities are probably strongest when an individual accepts the same identity that others have of him or her, that is, receiving self and social support (McCall and Simmons, 1969:79) for this identity.

Individuals have multiple and often unrelated identities. At the same time, a person may have an occupational identity, religious identity, familial identity, deviant identity, etc. Sometimes these identities remain separate, sometimes they conflict with other identities, and sometimes they may complement each other. These multiple identities are from divergent spheres of life, with different sets of significant others, different expectations, different types of social relationships, and differential levels of identity salience and identity prominence (McCall and Simmons, 1969).

It is no wonder that this web of identities is a focus of considerable attention by many sociologists, but there can be as much diversity within one identity as between identities. For instance, I have an occupational identity, but I am sometimes identified (and identify myself) as a college professor in general, a college professor at my university, a sociologist, a member of a sociology department at my university, or as part of an identifiable clique of sociologists within my department. Similarly, Jews may be identified as part of the community of monotheistic western organized religions, sometimes as Jews (or non-Christians), sometimes as Jews holding a particular philosophy within Judaism (e.g., orthodox, Conservative, Reformed), and sometimes as a member of a different congregation. All of these multiple identities are part of religious identity. In the largest generic sphere of identity (in these cases occupational or religious), there are smaller, meaningful, identifiable subunits. Under some conditions, the salient identity is with the larger unit, while at other times the salient identity is part of the smaller unit. Identities which have this component of larger and smaller units I have termed *nested identities.* Like Russian nesting dolls in which there are dolls within dolls within dolls, many identities are nested so that within a given sphere of life, there may be identities within identities within identities.

CHARACTERISTICS OF NESTED IDENTITIES

In examining nested identities, five characteristics should be noted.

(1) Nested identities are situational. It is generally accepted by sociologists that particular identities are shaped by the setting or social context (Meltzer et. al., 1975:94–95). This is equally true for nested identities. What

is taken for granted in one situation may be the key basis for identity in another situation. At a national meeting of sociologists, most people share the identity of sociologist. One may be sharing this identity with thousands of people, most of whom are strangers. Most people at such meetings have very little in common with other attendees. There are many people with different social characteristics and intellectual interests who call themselves sociologists. People tend to feel isolated and alienated in such large settings and may reduce their anxieties by identifying with a smaller part of the nest of sociological identities, such as being a Ph.D. from a particular graduate department, a faculty member at a given institution, a person with interests in a subfield (symbolic interactionism, demography, race relations), or as part of a caucus or special interest group within the field (teaching specialists, feminists, etc.). Members of particular departments may socialize with each other at meetings thousand of miles away from home with an intensity that you would never see in their home territory. A common identity is invoked, an insider-outsider (Becker, 1963:79–119) definition of the situation is reinforced, and anomie is reduced.

At a large meeting, certain individuals are physically recognizable to each other, although neither party may know the other's name ("familiar strangers" in Milgram's (1974) terminology). If these two people happen to meet away from this large grouping of sociologists, for example at a meeting of behavioral scientists, they are in this setting more likely to interact and invoke their common identity as sociologists. Identity from a different component of the professional identity nest has been invoked.

When common identities are shared, the identities invoked are from a smaller part of the nest rather than the larger unit. In the larger setting, many share a common identity but few are part of the smaller nest. The inner nest is most salient when many share the larger identity. People rarely approach one another at sociology meetings and attempt to engage in interaction because "we are both sociologists," but they are more likely to do this with a familiar stranger in other situations "because we are both sociologists in a sea of economists and political scientists."

(2) Nested identities are generally evoked as shared identities. The importance of membership in a smaller nest generally does not occur until one goes to a larger unit. What often evokes this identity is meeting a similarly nested other outside the larger identity nest. At Morley University (an urban private midwestern university), the sociology and the history department are in separate buildings about 100 yards apart; however there is very little interaction between members of these departments. Few Morley sociologists personally interact with their historian colleagues. However, a member of the Morley sociology faculty was driving through a state 500 miles away and stopped for gasoline. The gas station attendant saw the Morley parking sticker on the car and said, "My son teaches history at Morley and is now visiting us for the Christmas holidays." He immediately

phoned his son so that the two could speak. Had the Morley sociologist stopped for gasoline in her home city, the attendant would not have noticed her Morley parking sticker and the interaction between the historian and the sociologist would not have taken place. The nest was invoked because both shared a significant identity out of its normal social context.

The smaller the part of the nest, the more individuals have in common. The closer they are located in the identity nest, "the more accurately they can take the role of the other and the more correspondence they will have in their respective role-taking accuracies" (Kohout, 1977). We have more direct and accurate information on the other person and do not have to rely on stereotypes or make inferential leaps for efficient role taking.[3]

(3) Although all identities are potentially nestable, not all identities are nested. For any individual, some identities appear as part of a nested hierarchy and some do not. *The most salient identities for any individual are those that are most likely to be nested.* Others may identify me as a poor tennis player and I may incorporate these views as part of my self-concept; for me, at least, these are not part of an identity nest since I rarely play tennis. For an avid tennis player, there may be many identity nests—as an athlete, a tennis player, a member of a particular tennis club, as part of a regular tennis foursome, etc. As one devotes more and more time, interest, and attention to an activity, one can make finer and finer gradations and see significant distinctions that an "outsider" may not see. These gradations make a hierarchical relationship more salient, and hence facilitate the awareness of identity nests.

(4) Identity nests differ as to the number of components within. Some spheres of identity, such as geographical identity, may have ten or more components. On the other hand, the family probably can be considered to have three nests—an extended family, the nuclear family within, and similar roles (spouses, siblings) within the nuclear family. There appears to be no relationship between the number of components within the nest and the salience of the overall identity sphere.

(5) Although common identities are more "similar" in the smaller parts of the nest, larger parts of the nest may also be highly salient for identity. Several sociologists (e.g., Glock and Stark, 1965:263–288; and Thielbar, 1970) have distinguished between local and cosmopolitan orientations among college and university faculty members. Locals identify with their own school and/or department, while cosmopolitans identify with their discipline. The central professional reference group for locals consists of colleagues at their university, no matter what their department, while the reference group for cosmopolitans consists of members of their disciplines, no matter what their school. Locals and cosmopolitans each have a professional identity, but their most salient identity is at different places in the nest. On the other hand, a given circumstance may dictate that the locals identify or be identified as members of their discipline, while cosmopolitans

must sometimes identify or be identified as part of their department or college/university. Thus, in one case, a different aspect of professional identity was evoked by going further up the nest, while in another case, it was evoked by going further down the identity nest.

IDENTITY NESTS: SOCIOLOGICAL AND JOURNALISTIC OBSERVATIONS

Although this paper appears to be the first explicit delineation of the concept of nested identities, I have found descriptions of nesting in both the sociological literature and in journalistic observations of different social settings. The notion of nesting is implicit in studies and observations of such diverse groups and people as orthodox Jews, San Francisco homosexuals, Green Berets, military academy students, United States Senators, and the family of the President of the United States.

A newspaper article describing Jimmy Carter's family (Shawn and Cimons, 1977:28) sees three significant competent to their identity nest:

> As with all families, relationships within the Carter family consist of circles within circles.
>
> From his public and private statements and the comments of those close to him, the President seems to view himself and Rosalynn at the core of an inner family circle consisting of their 10-year old daughter, Amy, their three grown sons and their wives, and their two grandsons.
>
> Surrounding this is another circle, dominated by Miss Lillian, Billy Carter and the President's two sisters. Beyond lies still another circle populated by an assortment of aunts, uncles, nieces, nephews, cousins and in-laws.
>
> It's from the outer two circles that most rumblings of discontent are heard. But there clearly has been trouble within the inner circles, too.

The largest generic identity for our elected federal legislators would be *member of the United States Congress*. The next largest identity nest would be a significant one—member of U.S. Senate or member of the House of Representatives, and within each house, smaller nests such as members of the same political party or people from the same state or region. A journalist (Ungar, 1977:31) has noted the growth of caucuses in the House. Some are based on common political interests, but others are to invoke other common shared identities within the larger organization. Ungar states:

> In place of strong parties and committees new caucuses and subcaucuses sprout like desert flowers. There is a Rural Caucus, a Northwest-Midwest Economic Advancement Coalition, and a New England Caucus; a Black Caucus and a Hispanic one; a Congressional Clearinghouse on Women's Rights and one of "the Future." There is now even an Italian Caucus, whose chairman, Frank Annunzio of Chicago, has been heard to say, "We don't do anything very controversial; we just get together to eat." And a Blue Collar Caucus, organized by second-term Congressman Edward Beard of Rhode Island, a former house painter.

San Francisco has probably the largest, most active, and visible homosexual community in the United States. For many individuals in this city, sexual preference is an important basis of identity. For homosexuals, gay identity is reinforced by participation in homosexual organizations and by participation in the active gay community. But for many of the participants, homosexual identity is nested. Gold (1977:94, 96) notes some of the smaller significant identity nests in San Francisco:

I have counted more than 30 gay organizations working on political action in San Francisco. G.A.I. (Gay American Indians), and the Jewish Lesbian Gang—which assaulted a group of Nazis in a memorable encounter—are some of the specialty organizations. There are the Gay Asians, Gay Latinos and Join Hands, a gay prisoner organization. The Black Gay Caucus supports gay blacks in South Africa: "This is our outreach program." The Tavern Guild succeeded in "gaycotting" Florida orange juice in its bars. The Lesbian Mothers Union fights legal battles to protect two-women-plus-children families. The Coalition to defend Gays in the Military. The Pride Foundation. SIR. Third World Gay Caucus. Effeminate Caucus.

It is safe to assume that within these nests are additional nests, perhaps of leaders, subcaucuses, etc.

But journalists are not the only people to have observed the nesting phenomenon. Sociologists too have been implicitly aware of identity nests. For example, Heilman (1976) studied an Orthodox synagogue which was part of a larger, well-organized, orthodox community supporting such orthodox institutions as a Jewish day school, kosher butchers, and a ritual bath. Although all identified as Jews, and as Orthodox Jews, the central basis of identity was the individual synagogue. There were many such shuls within the Orthodox community, with people not only praying together but engaging in other activities together. For Orthodox Jews, the shul was the most important component of the religious identity nest. However, within the shul, there were also significant identity nests. People tended to sit in the same place for each religious service. According to Heilman (1976:38):

The newcomer signals his newness by changing his seat from week to week. Eventually he finds his group and seats himself accordingly. Yet at times it becomes difficult to ascertain whether seats and seating patterns reflect or account for friendships. In truth, the relationship must be described as synergetic: people sit with friends and thereby confirm and intensify that relationship. Worshiping side by side, chatting, and generally touching one another, seat neighbors share a literal and symbolic vantage point. Indeed, a knowledge of seating patterns reveals much about the network of relations within the community.

Heilman (1976:41) described a nesting phenomenon which occurs on Simchas Torah, a holiday in which all congregation members must be called up to read from the Torah.

At such times separate prayer services are set up in various locations, among them the men's foyer. Such services ensure that everyone will be called in the shortest possible time. During these readings the shul seems in effect to be made up of separate congregations, divided by closed doors, and each operating with its own rules of behavior, its own gabbai, chazan, Torah scroll reader, and even status hierarchy, reflected in the dispensation of kibbudim.

In the end, of course, all the separate shuls come together again at one large minyan in the sanctuary for the final reading, thus latently reaffirming the solidarity of the entire Kehillat Kodesh [4] community, while manifestly coming together for the reading of the final chapters of the Pentateuch.

The final reading does solidify membership in the shul community, but at the same time membership is also solidified in the Orthodox community and in the Jewish community, major larger components of the religious identity nest.

Several sociologists studying military institutions have also uncovered the nesting phenomenon. Members of the military have a different identity than civilians, and within the military, members of different military branches have distinct identities. Members of the Navy, Army, and Air Force are all members of the military, but their own branch of the service creates a major identity nest. Within the Army, the Special Forces have their own strong identity, setting themselves apart from members of other divisions of the Army (Cockerham, 1977). In fact, there is a real symbol of their identity since they wear and are known as Green Berets. Charles Moskos (1970:24) states: "There is a picture of a pervasively shared identity among members of Special Forces which results in invidious definitions of all others as outsiders. Thus, the image of the Green Berets coming through in all accounts whether favorable or not is a total institution within a total institution."

Dornbusch (1955) was a cadet at the United States Coast Guard Academy for ten months. He later wrote a retrospective description of life at the academy, and we can find in his description nested identities. Students at the academy all have that identity, but there are many important smaller (and larger) nests. For instances, all feel that they are a part of the Coast Guard itself, but identify as regular members of the Coast Guard (rather than the reserve for whom they have disdain). They also identify as officers rather than enlisted men. As students, there is strong identity by class. There are unequal rights and obligations by year in school, and each new class will first undergo a hazing process (which creates ingroup solidarity), while in later years the class will do the hazing to others. Dornbusch also found a further identity nest of Jewish cadets, the first minority group to be admitted to the academy.

The observations of nesting just discussed were done in an unstructured manner. The investigators noticed nests, discussed them, but were not aware of the phenomenon *per se*. In the next two sections, I will discuss systematically two diverse types of identity nests—geographic identity and identity patterns among students at a conservatory of music.

NESTED GEOGRAPHIC IDENTITIES

Although they are not a central component of most people's identities, nested geographic identities illustrate some important aspects of the operation of nested identities. Geographic identities are most often invoked when one is outside a component and in a higher unit or with people from a number of different places. At some points, we are identified as being from a neighborhood, and sometimes as being from a city or from a country; yet all are parts of geographic identity. To illustrate the principles of nested geographic identities, I will begin with reference to my own current living situation as a resident of a high-rise apartment in a highly urbanized suburb of Cleveland, Ohio.

1. Resident of the twenty-second floor. Studies indicate that life in urban middle class high-rise apartments is generally anonymous (Zito, 1974). In a building, in a fairly small portion of a city block, are stacked 24 stories of apartments with each floor containing twelve different dwelling units. (An even smaller component of geographic identity would be the apartment itself, but this geographic unit is not shared with strangers). The general common meeting ground for floor residents is by the elevator on their floor. Interaction here tends to be superficial, with most neighbors not even knowing others' names. Still, in other parts of the building, people identify one another as sharing a residence on the same floor. (Occasionally, floor residents may band together to deal with common problems such as troublesome neighbors. This would tend to strengthen their common identity as residents of the same floor.)

2. Resident of an apartment house. Since high-rise living tends to foster anonymity, individuals rarely interact simply because they live in the same building. Interaction among most residents is rare even in public places within the building such as the lobby, elevators, laundry area, parking lot, and recreational facilities; yet these same individuals may meet outside the apartment setting and at that point acknowledge each other, thus reinforcing their common geographic identity.

3. Resident of a particular neighborhood. Lynn Lofland (1973:119) has noted that:

> The city is a world of strangers simply because its population is so large that anyone living in it cannot possibly know personally everyone else living in it. Even the individual who works very hard at acquiring acquaintances will never succeed in getting to know more than a minuscule proportion of the city's total population. Nevertheless, urbanites can and do arrange things such that their encounters with the personally-unknown when they are out in public are minimized and their encounters with the personally-known are maximized.

One way that this urban anonymity can be countered is with identification with a smaller identity nest—the neighborhood. In many cities, neighborhoods are easily identifiable by specific names and offer common public meeting places such as stores, parks, and a delineated territory (Jacobs, 1961:112–140). Common neighborhood identity is manifested in such diverse manners as attendance at neighborhood schools, representation in elective government by individuals associated with the neighborhood, and in some cases, the presence of subcultural expressions utilized only in particular neighborhoods or parts of the city. For instance, a children's game of street handball in certain neighborhoods of Philadelphia is known as "chink," while in other neighborhoods it is known as "wall ball" (Lebofsy, 1970). Two neighborhoods in a city may share similar ethnic and social class characteristics, but if they are distinctive entities in different parts of the city, their individual character gives rise to meaningful neighborhood identity.

4. *Resident of a particular suburb.* I am a resident of a relatively small suburb in an area filled with many small, interconnected, and indistinguishable urban communities. Differently colored street signs are often the only indication where one community ends and another begins. At its borders, the City of Cleveland is indistinguishable from its suburbs, and surrounding communities are small enough so that there are few real neighborhoods outside the parent city of Cleveland. Within the confines of the urban area, people come to be identified either as a resident of the City of Cleveland (and of a particular neighborhood) or as a resident of a particular suburb. Residence, in this instance, coincides with a political boundary, so that common residents share the same government and common urban services such as libraries, public recreation, and police and fire protection. People may be most aware of this common identity at election time. The neighborhood may be the locus of *social* geographic identity, but the city is the basis of *political* geographic identity.

5. *Resident of the east side of the Cuyahoga River.* The city of Cleveland is divided in two by the Cuyahoga River. The city and its suburbs are found on both the east and west banks of the river. Residents (whether from Cleveland or its suburbs) are identified as east or west siders—depending on which side of the river they live on. The east side houses most of Cleveland's cultural institutions and has most of the city's blacks and Jews. East siders stereotype people from the west side as being working class and acultural; thus the Cuyahoga River represents a social as well as a physical barrier. East siders tend to interact with other east siders and west siders tend to interact with other west siders. Side of the river represents a strong part of geographic identity and residents maintain that crossing the river often brings them the feeling that they are in a different city. To outsiders, communities may appear alike, but to a resident within, there are very meaningful community distinctions. Thus, to a west side Clevelander, there it is meaningful that one lives in western suburb X rather than western

suburb Y, but to an east sider, they are all indistinguishable entities. What is important is the side of town on which it is found.

6. *Resident of the Cleveland SMSA.* Whether I live on the east side or west side or whether I live in the city or a suburb is unimportant to a non-Clevelander. To an (American) outsider, the important aspect of my geographic identity is that I live in Cleveland. When they are outside of their SMSA, urban residents tend to be identified with the principal city of their SMSA[5]. Although certain cities have identifiable suburbs (such as Cleveland's Shaker Heights, Los Angeles's Beverly Hills, or New York City's Scarsdale), the principal city is the most meaningful identity nest to outsiders. Within the SMSA, common city identity is maintained through such factors as media utilization (the circulation of urban newspapers and the signals of urban radio and TV stations go beyond city borders and serve the entire SMSA) and identification with sports teams bearing the city's name. (The home of Cleveland's National Basketball Association team is in another county about 20 miles from the Cleveland city limits.)

City identification can be problematic for people who grew up in one urban area and move to another. There may be confusion in city identity between SMSA of current residence and a person's original home town.[6] For some people, the question "Where are you from?" may be answered by current city, while for others, by original home town. Urban identity may be most salient among people who grew up in one city and move to another. They are more likely to compare the two cities and may feel conflicting urban identities. Many sports fans identify with the sports teams they grew up with rather than the teams of their current city.

7. *Resident of a state.* State residence is the next highest unit, although in some states there are meaningful distinctions *within,* such as "upstaters" vs. "downstaters." Like city residence (and county residency, which is not very salient in Cleveland), state residency is bound up in the political sphere. State identity is reinforced when one votes for a senator or governor, or when one deals with the state bureaucracy (taxation, welfare, university, licensing, etc.) Some states, such as Texas, California, or Maine, conjure up the notion of a distinctive life style and are thus probably more an important part of individual identity. Other states, such as New Jersey (Flanagan, 1973), Delaware, or North Dakota, offer little in the way of distinctive state identity. The west coast of the United States has many individuals who originally came from midwestern or southwestern states. Original state identity is invoked in annual state picnics in which migrants reaffirm their identity as being originally from another state, setting them apart from natives of their adopted state.

8. *Resident of a region of the country.* Whatever their city or state, individuals are often identified as part of a region. Regional differences (Feldman and Thielbar, 1974:183–222) are fostered by the influence of

geography, history (including migration), and are manifested in regional life styles. Regions differ in such areas as the pace of life, customs, foods, as well as in the presence of regional terms and regional accents. Despite Census Bureau attempts at categorizing regions, it is often difficult to know where one region ends and another begins.[7] Clevelanders feel themselves to be midwesterners. People in Iowa also consider themselves midwesterners, and often consider Clevelanders easterners. To a resident of Seattle, going "back east" often means just going to Spokane or Idaho

9. National identity. To Clevelanders, it is meaningful whether one comes from the east side or west side of town and to Americans it is meaningful that one comes from Brooklyn, New York, rather than the Cleveland suburb of Brooklyn, Ohio, but to non-Americans, the important fact is that this individual is an American. Common national identity is believed to be an important part of all Americans' lives, but since our nation is so large and heterogeneous, there is more meaningful identity within smaller components of the nest. Despite these meaningful internal distinctions, there is belief among many (e.g., Mencken, 1922; Martindale, 1963; and Reisman, 1967) that there is a distinct and readily identifiable American national character.

Like most nested identities, American national identity is heightened when individuals are outside of the identity nest. Two Americans in a foreign land, who would never interact in the U.S. simply because they are both Americans, interact and reinforce their common identity outside the borders of their country—especially if they are in a remote part of the world.

There are many programs in this country and others trying to increase a sense of national identity. Recently Italian leaders expressed dismay over the fact that Italians first think of themselves as Northerners or Southerners, then as associated with a city, and finally as Italians. National identity, like all identities, is situational and may become strongest in times of national emergencies such as wars.

10. Continental identity. Continental identity is rarely in the active identity sphere of most individuals, but there are common problems which residents of continents face which may reinforce such an identity. Despite vast national differences, Europeans are part of the Common Market nations, and Africans may share a feeling of being overly dominated or neglected by the United States. Continents are such large entities with a potential for fission or unity (Merton, 1957b:316–317) that they may have real effects of world events.

Some continents are more accessible to Americans than others. While most Americans see meaningful distinctions between European nations such as France and Italy, they do not see such distinctions in more remote continents such as South America. Few Americans can make meaningful distinctions between nations such as Argentina or Peru. A woman from

Bogota, Colombia, states: "Americans are always asking me if I know their relative in Rio or Buenos Aires. It is farther from Bogota to these cities than it is from Bogota to New York and there are millions of people living in Rio and Buenos Aires. Why should I know them?"

Some nations even have a continental identity crisis. Costa Rica is bordered by Nicaragua on the north and Panama on the south. Residents of this country insist they are from Central America (and Costa Rican license plates also state this). North Americans, however, define Costa Ricans as South Americans, while South Americans define Costa Ricans as North Americans.

11. Planet identity. Few individuals have as part of their geographic identity the fact that they are residents of the Planet Earth. This identity is associated with world planners or environmentalists who are aware of the world-wide impact associated with pollution, overpopulation, energy use, etc. However, it is very likely that we will someday be in contact with residents of other planets and at that point, planet identity may be more salient than it is now.

NESTED IDENTITIES AMONG MUSIC CONSERVATORY STUDENTS

In my role of participant as observer (Gold, 1958), at the Forest City Institute of Music I discovered the strong presence of nested identities. FCIM is an independent (i.e., not affiliated with any college or university) institution solely devoted to the training of musicians (from young children to doctoral students). FCIM has many distinguished faculty and alumni, and in prestige rankings would probably fall in the second stratum of music conservatories. Students at the baccalaureate level (and above) enter the Institute already proficient in music and already thinking of themselves as musicians. The conservatory is a place where they can increase their skills and obtain the necessary credentials (Kadushin, 1969). In many ways, the conservatory is a vocational school with almost all classes and instruction geared toward producing a professional musician. Although it is autonomous, the Forest City Institute of Music is located on the campus of Morley University, a medium-sized, private, urban university. Through a cooperative arrangement, students at FCIM may register for courses at Morley, where they are made aware of their first (outer) nest of student identities.

1. Student at Forest City Institute of Music. Although all students at FCIM identify as musicians, they are also aware that they are students. Their main interest is their specialty (instrument, composition, etc.), and they devote most of their time to this endeavor; however they must also take required courses outside of their specialty. Their awareness of their student status is enhanced by the bureaucratic life of students everywhere—school regulations, degree requirements, tuition payments, etc. Students identify with the school itself, since it has a good reputation and they know their degree will be meaningful to potential employers or graduate schools. While taking courses at Morley, FCIM students are made even more aware of their identity with their school. FCIM students see themselves as quite distinct from students at Morley; FCIM students tend to sit together when they take classes at Morley. Morley has a music department offering degrees in music education and performance, but even though the Morley music building is across the street from FCIM, there is little contact between the students at the two institutions. FCIM students thus set themselves apart from all other students. They feel that they are venturing outside their own territory when they take their Morley liberal arts courses.

2. *Theoreticians vs. Performers.* Students at FCIM are either students of a particular instrument or are involved in the nonperforming aspects of music (theory, composition, history, education). A professor of music education describes the gap between theoreticians and performers as a "chasm." On the outside and at Morley U., all are just students at the Institute, but within, their worlds are entirely different. Performers share many common problems—all must give public recitals, must memorize music, and must work with other performers in ensembles. Performers complain about music history and music theory courses because these courses take them away from practice time with their instrument. Conversely, nonperformers must take courses geared toward performing and resent these courses. They feel that theirs is not a world of performance but a world of ideas. They are the intellectuals while the instrumentalists are not.

3. *Performance specialty.* The most salient aspect of the conservatory student's identity nest is his or her specialty, that is, instrument. Performers associate with each other more than with nonperformers and performers of a given instrument associate with one another more than with other performers. This occurs for a variety of reasons. The key to a musician's self image is generally not that they are musicians but that they are clarinetists, pianists, singers, etc. They enter the Institute as students of their instrument and already know much of the music for their instrument. They are constantly comparing themselves to each other. Piano recitals are mainly attended by pianists, voice recitals by singers, etc. There are classes (which are really large recitals) in which all students of a given instrument meet to hear each other. Also, they are more likely to perform with one another in ensembles (singers in operas, string players in chamber ensembles, etc.), and again get to compare themselves. In addition, students may also be part of the larger local community of their instrument. For example, singers, whether they are nonstudents, students at FCIM, or students elsewhere, may meet at concerts, may compete with other local singers for jobs in churches, for parts in locally produced operas, and for acceptance at

national voice training apprenticeship programs. But even in the local musical community of their instrument, they are identified and set themselves apart as instrumentalists from FCIM.

The salience of instrument as a basis of identity is made very evident in each semester's performance of a full scale (costumes, sets, orchestra, paying audience, etc.) opera. This involves bringing together many singers and the school's large orchestra. For the singers, the opera is a major event, with a great deal of competition for choice roles. Weeks before the opera is cast, rumors fly as to who will fill what part. Students aim toward principal roles and are most unhappy if they are cast in the chorus.[8] Much time goes into the voice student's preparation for the student opera role. For graduate students, performance in a major role may be counted as fulfilling the requirements for one of the two mandatory master's recitals. For weeks before the opera, voice students talk about the quality of the production, its problems, and its prospects.

As much as a voice students look forward to operas, instrumentalists hate it. For them, it is being placed in the orchestra pit below the stage, and as such being invisible to the audience; therefore, most instrumentalists wear jeans and not concert attire. Orchestra members tend to treat opera accompanying as a required but unimportant duty and try to do what they can to amuse themselves. This may involve practical jokes among each other and attempts to distract the singers.

In one student production, the orchestra was placed on the stage itself. Orchestra players resented this since they would have to dress up. At a coffee break, the division between the two groups was very evident. Singers walked off stage talking with each other, totally ignoring the instrumentalists, who were also behaving in a similar manner. It was as if each group did not really exist for the other. Interestingly enough, the instrumentalists are identified by the singers as "the musicians," a label which they use to distinguish themselves from the instrumentalists.

The only instrumentalists who really know performers of other instruments are pianists. Piano is one of the largest majors at FCIM and there is a large pianist subculture. Pianists, however, as part of their degree requirement must accompany other students. In this task they get to know and enter the world of other instrumentalists. There are several pianists who are opera lovers and make accompanying singers their specialty. They identify as both pianists and as a functioning part of the singers' community.

4. Students of a particular teacher. Instruction among students is carried out in a variety of settings—required performing ensembles, standard classroom situations, and most importantly, in private instruction with a teacher of the student's major instrument. Some come specifically to FCIM to study with a particular teacher, others randomly choose or are assigned teachers, while still others audition to be accepted by a particularly well-known teacher. Instrumentalists become known as a part of a particular teacher's "studio." Some studios are more prestigious than others and some produce "better" students than others. (Quality is often measured by performing career after the student leaves school.) People within a studio tend to strongly identify with their teacher and their fellow students. In recitals and competitions, they are identified as a student of their teacher often disregarding the fact that some in a studio may level. This gradation is not that important at FCIM since there is often no relationship between year in school and talent. Studios may differ greatly in philosophy and technique. One voice studio may emphasize tone production through body tension, another may emphasize no body tension, while in a third the emphasis may be on a philosophy of breath control. Students tend to embrace the philosophy of their teacher and feel most comfortable with others who also embrace this philosophy. Each studio has sessions in which all of its students meet formally or informally. Within the conservatory, there are often open try-outs for performers in operas, chamber ensembles, etc. If a certain studio's students are disproportionately chosen, it is considered a victory for the studio. People within a studio strongly identify with one another, and see each other socially. At events within the Institute, students from a given studio tend to sit with one another and tend to reserve their strongest in-group feelings for members of their studio. One graduate student in voice described her friendship with another student by saying, "We can only be good friends up to a point because she studies with _____." Ingroup feelings by studio may be so strong that there may be overt or covert hostility toward students in other studios. Attendance at recitals of students from other studios is encouraged but not required, while attendance at recitals of students within the same studio is almost considered mandatory and serves to reinforce common identity.

At the student opera production discussed previously, there was strong identity among singers by their studio. At some breaks, students of one studio would congregate together, usually to disparage people from other studios who were in the production. They would also constructively criticize each other's performances. Warming-up is a very important activity for any singer, but the norms dictate that this is an individual responsibility. For opening night, one voice teacher had his students congregate in his studio and warmed up all of his students as a group. This solidified the belief that they were his representatives in the production.

5. *Student within a studio having a particular specialization.* Although students may share the same teacher, they may not have the same specialization. A voice teacher may have students at various voice ranges, each singing a different literature. Although all singers have similar

problems, and may solve the problems using their teacher's philosophy, each voice part has its unique problems. A soprano would compare herself to other sopranos and not to tenor students of her teacher. She would compare herself to the universe of sopranos at FCIM but most especially to other soprano students of her teacher. They are assigned many of the same pieces so that they hear others perform the same composition utilizing the same technique. Since not all instruments are as specialized as voice, specialization may not be an important part of other identity nests.

We have examined five components of the identity nest of students at Forest City Institute of Music. The general sphere of identity is that of music student, but within, there are a variety of major components to this nest. In classes at Morley University, squabbles between studios are unimportant and whatever their specialty, FCIM students stay together. Within FCIM, students of one instrument set themselves apart from others. There are even stereotypical beliefs about certain instrumentalists, maintaining barriers and enhancing insider-outsider feeling. There is the belief that singers are dumb, not very musical people who are constantly making funny noises to warm up their voices. Among singers, there is the strong division by studio, and disputes as to technique, while important to singers, are unknown to other instrumentalists. (Likewise, singers have stereotypical views of other instrumentalists and are generally unaware of their performing problems.)

The Forest City Institute of Music is small enough so that the students at the Institute constitute a real subculture. Although they may venture out to an occasional class at Morley, their lives are centered at FCIM. They may enter FCIM at 9:00 A.M. and not leave until the building closes. The strongest subcultural identification is by instrument and by teacher, with both being a lasting part of the student's musical identity after he or she leaves school. Nested identities at conservatories are far from insular. Student musicians may be part of others nests and other subcultures in the musical world but as students, the nest of student identities is an important part of their lives.

PERSONAL NOTE AND SUMMARY

I am no longer an active sociologist. At the time I wrote this paper I was a survey researcher and am not a symbolic interactionist by training or inclination. I was aware of the importance that symbolic interactionists placed on multiple identities. The symbolic interactionist literature is rich with studies of how people cope with their many selves. I recently attended a concert with a friend. A man came up to her and asked, "Are you Pepper Bullard?" She was not, but I knew Pepper, a costume designer, and had seen her about two minutes before. I said to him, "You mean the costume designer?" He said, "She's not a costume designer. She's a medical librarian." Pepper had both identities and this man was not aware of her multiple selves; but within both of these diversent identities, there is a whole set of significant nested identities—costumer for a particular show, competitor with other costumers, librarian at a particular institution, graduate of a particular library school, etc.

This paper results from my observation of multiple identities within one sphere of life. My purpose in this paper was to point this out as a social phenomenon, state some of its salient characteristics, and give examples of its operation through my observations as well as through others. Some have described the concept of nesting as "a minor insight worth twenty minutes in a lecture and a paragraph in an undergraduate text." Others have felt it is a real contribution to the symbolic interactionist literature. I do not know. If it is of value, hopefully others will discover other examples of nesting and show its importance to an understanding of the very problematic notion of identity.

FOOTNOTES

*I wish to thank the following for their helpful comments: Carl Couch, Norman Denzin, Frank Falk, Sharon Guten, Frank Kohout, Michal McCall and Richard Travisano.

1. Hewitt (1976:80) states that "frequently 'identity' is used interchangeably for *identity* and *situated identity,* and sometimes also for *social identity* and *situated social identity* and one must infer from context which of these is actually intended."

2. Emphasis is in the original.

3. I would like to thank Frank Kohout for bringing the points in this paragraph to my attention.

4. This is the name of the congregation he studied.

5. Different cities create different external images to outsiders. For a good discussion of city images, see Strauss (1961).

6. I would like to thank Connie Prener for reminding me of this point.

7. In an attempt to discover where the region of the south really is, Reed (1976) counted the number of listings for the word "Dixie" in telephone white pages, finding that he could delineate a distinctive southern as well as a "Dixie" territory. For an extended study of the uniqueness of the south, see Reed (1972).

8. Among singers, there is a nesting of identity within a given opera. All are singers in an opera and identify as a member of the cast; within, there are identity nests between chorus members and principals. Among principals, there may be common identity nests among people who appear in many of the same scenes and thus are more likely to rehearse with each other. A further common practice involves invoking identity with past productions. Singers may recall past common experiences that they shared, invoking their solidarity, common identity, and showing that they are more experienced since they appeared in other productions.

REFERENCES

Becker, Howard S., *Outsiders,* New York: Free Press, 1963

Cockerham, William C., "Green berets: social cohesion in a closed society," pp. 27–38 in Arthur B. Shostak (ed.), *Our Sociological Eye,* Port Washington, N.Y.: Alfred, 1977.

Dornbusch, Sanford, "The military academy as an assimilating institution," *Social Forces* 33 (May 1955):316–321.

Feldman, Saul D. and Gerald W. Thielbar (eds.), *Life Styles: Diversity in American Society,* 2nd ed., Boston: Little, Brown, 1975.

Feldman, Saul D. (ed.), *Deciphering Deviance,* Boston: Little, Brown, 1978.

Flanagan, Terrence J., "Guess what state's initials are N.J.?" *The New York Times* (February 21, 1973).

Glock, Charles and Rodney Stark, *Religion and Society in Tension,* Chicago: Rand McNally, 1965.

Goffman, Erving, *The Presentation of Self in the Everyday Life,* Garden City, N.Y.: Anchor, 1959.

————, *Encounters,* Indianapolis: Bobbs Merrill, 1961.

Gold, Herbert, "A walk on San Francisco's gay side," *The New York Times Magazine* (November 6, 1977):67–69 and 94–114.

Gold, Raymond, "Roles in sociological field observation," *Social Forces* 36 (1958):217–233.

Gordon, Chad, "Development of evaluated role identities," in Alex Inkeles (ed.), *Annual Review of Sociology:* Volume Two, 1976, pp. 405–434.

Gordon, Milton M., *Social Class in American Sociology,* Durham, N.C.: Duke University Press, 1950.

Heilman, Samuel C., *Synagogue Life: A Study in Symbolic Interaction,* Chicago: University of Chicago Press, 1976.

Hewitt, John P., *Self and Society,* Boston: Allyn and Bacon, 1976.

Jacobs, Jane, *The Death and Life of Great American Cities,* New York: Random House, 1961.

Kadushin, Charles, "The professional self-concept of music students," *American Journal of Sociology* 75 (1969):389–405.

Klapp, Orrin E., *Collective Search for Identity,* New York: Holt, Rinehart, Winston, 1969.

Kohout, Frank J., Personal Communication, 1977.

Lebofsky, Dennis S., "The Lexicon of the Philadelphia Metropolitan Area." Unpublished doctoral dissertation, Princeton University, 1970.

Lofland, Lyn H., *A World of Strangers,* New York: Basic Books, 1973.

Martindale, Don, *Community, Character and Civilization,* New York: Free Press, 1963.

McCall, George J. and J.L. Simmons, *Identities and Interactions,* New York: Free Press, 1966.

Meltzer, Bernard, John W. Petras and Larry T. Reynolds, *Symbolic Interactionism,* London and Boston: Routledge and Kegan Paul, 1975.

Mencken, H.L., *Prejudices,* Third Series, New York: Alfred Knopf, 1922.

Merton, Robert K., *Social Theory and Social Structure,* rev. ed., New York: Free Press, 1957.

Milgram, Stanley, "The frozen world of the familiar stranger—a conversation with Carol Tarvis," *Psychology Today* (January 1974):71–80.

Moskos, Charles, *The American Enlisted Man,* New York: Russell Sage, 1970.

Reed, John Shelton, *The Enduring South: Subcultural Persistence in Mass Society,* Lexington, Mass.: Heath, 1972.

————, "The heart of Dixie: an essay in folk geography," *Social Forces* 54 (June 1976):925–939.

Riesman, David, "Some questions about the study of American Character in the twentieth century," *The Annals* 370 (1967):36–47.

Shawn, Gaylord and Marlene Cimons, "The first family," *The Cleveland Plain Dealer* (November 13, 1977) Section Four: 28–30.

Stone, Gregory P., "Appearance and the self," pp. 86–118 in Arnold Rose (ed.), *Human Behavior and Social Processes,* Boston: Houghton Mifflin, 1962.

Strauss, Anselm, *Mirrors and Masks,* New York: Free Press, 1959.

———— , *Images of the American City,* New York: Free Press, 1961.

Sutton, Willis A. Jr. and Thomas Munson, "Definitions of community: 1954 through 1973," Paper presented before 1976 annual meetings, American Sociological Association, New York, 1976.

Thielbar, Gerald W., "On locals and cosmopolitans," pp. 259–275 in Gregory P. Stone and Harvey Farberman (eds.), *Social Psychology Through Symbolic Interaction,* Waltham, Mass.: Ginn-Blaisdell, 1970.

Travisano, Richard, "Alternation and conversion as qualitatively different transformations," pp. 594–605 in Gregory P. Stone and Harvey A. Farberman (eds.), *Social Psychology Through Symbolic Interaction,* Waltham, Mass.: Ginn-Blaisdell, 1970.

Ungar, Sanford J., "Bleak house: frustration on Capitol Hill," *The Atlantic* 240 (July 1977):27–38.

Zito, Jacqueline M., "Anonymity and neighboring in an urban, high-rise complex," *Urban Life and Culture* 3 (1974):243–263.

DYING AS A STATUS PASSAGE AND THE ORGANIZATIONAL CAREER:
A STRATEGY FOR RESEARCHING ORGANIZATIONAL ENVIRONMENTS*

Raymond L. Schmitt, ILLINOIS STATE UNIVERSITY

Ricky Gorshe, ILLINOIS STATE UNIVERSITY

Sandra Lindberg, ILLINOIS STATE UNIVERSITY

ABSTRACT

A naturalistic strategy was used to study the interrelationships between the organizational careers of 50 corporate executives and managers and dying as a status passage. This linkage promised to be more subtle than linkages between previously researched passages. The youngest males reacted to a death study stimulus in terms of their organizational careers, viewing it as nonfunctional or dysfunctional for organizational activities. The oldest males reacted to the stimulus in terms of dying as a status passage, perceiving it as having a death

Studies in Symbolic Interaction—Volume 2, 1979, pages 419–456
Copyright © 1979 by JAI Press Inc.
All rights of reproduction in any form reserved.
ISBN: 0–89232–105–9

education benefit for them and their loved ones. The females, although similar in age to the youngest males, did not view death study negatively or in relation to their organizational careers. But unlike the oldest males, the younger women described the value of death study in more general death education terms. These results underscore the following: (1) The passagee is the *fundamental* link between the organization and its environment; (2) Sociologists have underestimated the types of environments that influence organizations; (3) The reciprocal influences between the occupational career and environmental status passages can be employed as a link to study the interrelationships between the organization and its environment.

A strategy for studying organizations as processual systems that requires additional attention is to approach the organization through the passages of its members. Individuals experience multiple passages during their lives (Glaser and Strauss 1971). Some of these passages are bound to organizations, such as bureaucracies and mental institutions, and are frequently labeled careers. Others, such as aging and marriage, are not so intimately tied to entities deemed organizational by sociologists, and are more commonly called status passages. Organizational or nonorganizational, however, passages involve both an "objective" and a "subjective" component. Faulkner (1973, p. 334), for instance, has stressed this dual aspect of passages in his observations regarding organizational careers. "On the one hand, careers are made up of systems of positions, their relation to one another, and typical sequences of movement within and through them. On the other hand, members acquire ways of thinking, feeling, and believing about these arrangements; they orient themselves, positively and negatively, emotionally and intellectually, toward the roles they are paid to perform and the routes they are constrained to pursue."

Some sociologists are urging innovation in organizational analysis (Benson 1977), emphasizing that the role of individuals and interaction in organizations must be given more emphasis (Manning 1977). Organizational careers, however, are "a neglected topic in most sociological analyses and descriptions of organizations. The focus of explanations of behavior is typically upon goals and work expectations, authority and power structures, rational decision-making, efficiency demands, and working conditions" (Glaser 1968, p. 2). Organizational careers underscore the *processual* aspects of organizations, including career flow, recruitment and replacement, training modes, attachment and severance, timing in status passages, multiple routes and switching, climactic periods, interdependence of organizational careers, the changing work world, and personal identity (Becker and Strauss 1956; Blankenship 1973; Faulkner 1973).

But organizational careers offer another avenue for the study of organizations. Because individuals go through more than one passage at a time (Glaser and Strauss 1971, p. 142), organizational careers can be used to explore the linkages between the organization and what is typically identified as the organization's environment. The organization and its environment can both be conceptualized in terms of the passages of its members. The analytical separation of the organization from its environment is not an easy matter, and an arbitrary element may always be involved. Homans (1950, p. 87) indicates that this is partly because the investigator "determines" the boundaries of a social system through the very designation of the social system to be studied. We suggest, however, that a more basic reason for the analytical difficulty in distinguishing the organization from its environment is because interactions, both symbolic and overt, and passages are not always sharply differentiated as organizational and environmental in the everyday world. However, in one sense, *the organization can be conceptualized as those interactional and symbolic encounters in which the organizational-based passages of its members are most prominent and are structurally related.* These passages would include organizational careers and any other *organizationally* anchored passage as well. On the other hand, *the organizational environment can be conceptualized as including those interactional and symbolic encounters in which the other status passages of its members are most salient.* The organizational member's passage through his families of orientation and procreation would be an illustration of this, as would be the member's passage through various fraternal groupings and the individual's history of friendships.

Although there is some research regarding the multiple passages of organizational members, as discussed in this paper (also see Wilensky 1960; Roth 1963), "Clearly the facets of organizational careers that relate to society are in need of much research and theory development" (Glaser 1968, p. 16). This inattention is explainable. (1) Our knowledge of organizational careers and status passages has only recently been significantly extended (see particularly Glaser 1964; Strauss et al. 1964; Becker et al. 1968; Glaser 1968; Olesen and Whittaker 1968; Glaser and Strauss 1971; Strauss 1971; Strauss 1975). (2) Given the emphasis of sociologists on the structural features of organizations (see Benson 1977), it would have been unlikely that an individual-based strategy for linking organizations to their environments would have much appeal. (3) In addition, such a linkage would have been regarded as irrelevant by most sociologists because the environment being tapped would have been classified as a "personal and idiosyncratic," rather than as a systematic, source of influence. The complexity of organizational environments, however, has been underestimated by sociologists. Haas and Drabek (1973, p. 17, our italics) have recommended:

> First, rather than continuing with the concept of one organizational environment, it is far more productive to structure the analysis in terms of environments, for there are *many levels and types of interaction with a multitude of environments* that must be differentiated.

The position taken in this research, as should now be clear, is that one of these "environments," to use Haas and Drabek's terminology, is the status passages of the organizational members. (4) The methodology appropriate for the study of the relationship between organizational careers and other status passages is a vexing issue. Every passage not only includes the individual's covert view of it, but the *linkages between* passages may frequently be as covert as they are overt. The detection of the symbolic and overt linkages between passages that are being "worked out" over time and that frequently reflect personal and sometimes sensitive experiences is a difficult task.

THE ORGANIZATIONAL CAREER AND ENVIRONMENTAL STATUS PASSAGE LINKAGE

One of the more puzzling aspects regarding the relationship between the organization and its environment concerns the dynamics of this linkage. Azumi and Hage (1972, p. 27) have concluded that "There is as yet no definitive work that states precisely what it is about the environment that has an impact on the organization and what processes are actually involved in it." Because the individual goes through more than one status passage at a time, we have already hinted that the actor's status passages are part of the environment having such an impact. The assumptions implicit in our premise that the organization and the environment are interrelated through the linkage of the actor's organizational career and other status passages follow.

(1) The passagee is the crucial link between the organization and the environment. That person is the common denominator because he or she physically and symbolically moves between passages and joins them symbolically through interpretations and interactionally through associations. Organizations do not move, or interpret actions. Environments do not move, or interpret actions.[1] Organizations and environments represent different settings where individuals meet and where distinctive passages are emphasized. As Blumer (1962, p. 182) has stressed in his classic discussion of society as symbolic interaction, "The human individual pieces together and guides his action by taking account of different things and interpreting their significance for his prospective action. There is no instance of conscious action of which this is not true." We stress that this observation is as true of individuals moving from place to place or from passage to passage over long periods of time as it is for persons in brief interaction encounters.

(2) The organizational career provides a viable index of the individual's experiences within the organizational setting because it reflects (a) the meanings that the individual holds about (b) his organizational position.

We have already explained this assumption and traced it to the work of Hughes, Becker, Glaser, Strauss, and others. The individual is merged with the organization through his organizational career.

(3) Status passage provides a viable index of the individual's experiences within the environmental setting because it reflects (a) the meanings that the individual holds about (b) his important environmental positions. Status passage, simply put, refers to the more important passages and their "turning points" (Strauss 1959) that occur in all our lives. Individuals not only come to attribute meanings to their organizational careers, but to their other status passages as well.

(4) The reciprocal influence between the occupational career and environmental status passages can be employed as a link to study the interrelationships between the organization and its environment. Because individuals experience these passages simultaneously, this assumption, or conclusion, logically flows from the first three assumptions. If the passagee is the common denominator between the organization and its environment, and if organizational career and status passage tap some of the more meaningful experiences of the individual in the organization and the environment, respectively, it follows that (a) he may come to symbolize his "work world" and his "nonwork world" in overlapping and related terms, and that (b) behavioral changes may be manifested in either world as a result of this overlap.

We emphasize that the extent to which symbolic and behavioral influences exist between the organizational career and a given status passage is a matter for empirical study. However, it seems there are a limited number of ways in which two passages can be linked. It is, of course, advantageous to be aware of these alternatives. (1) There simply may not be a meaningful linkage between two passages. (2) There may be certain "unique" connections between passages, linkages that are not characteristic of all passagees. Such linkages should not be dismissed as trivial. Although distinctive, unique linkages may be *common* occurrences and, in fact, reflect a generic or formal type. Persons, perhaps particularly in mass societies, experience many enduring passages. It is to be expected that such experiences would result in unique blends. (3) There may be a linkage between two structurally related passages that tends to hold for all passages. Strauss et al. (1964) found linkages between the passages of individuals who were pursuing organization careers within the hospital and professional careers in medically-related fields. These passages were structurally interrelated because both passages evolved about the "world of health." The way in which passages are structurally interrelated needs to be more fully considered. Still, even in the instance of highly structured passages, the passages are *also* intertwined within the passagee. The manner in which structurally interrelated passages are manifested or viewed by its passagees will, of course, not be identical.

Passages must always be considered from a social psychological, as well as a sociological, perspective. (4) There may be a linkage between two structurally distinct passages that tends to hold for all passagees. In this instance, the passage is the primary link between the passages. Olesen and Whittaker (1968), for instance, found that the nursing careers of young student nurses were linked to the status passages that pertained to becoming a young woman. This type of linkage has been given the least attention, and it is the focal point of our research.

DYING AS A STATUS PASSAGE

If the linkage between the organization and its environment was to be investigated, decisions had to be made regarding the environmental status passage(s) to be considered. This matter could have been resolved entirely through the data-gathering process. Our subjects, however, were approached with a particular status passage—dying—in mind. Status passage research has been criticized on the grounds that it has been limited to the participants' views, and frequently to the views of only a few participants (Day and Day 1977, pp. 133–134). Our approach enabled us to systematically estimate the views of 85 corporate employees, who were members of a clearly defined category. We further observe, in regard to this methodological criticism, that the actor's view of his passages is paramount, that the employees were approached in a nondirective manner so that the types of meanings that could be attributed to dying and to the organizational career would emerge through the research, that independent information was used to assess the employees' organizational positions and other personal characteristics, and critically, that the employees' reactions were analyzed sociologically. Critics of areas rooted in interactionism are confused on the latter point. The interactionist does not equate the "everyday world" of the actor with the "scientist's interpretations" (see Denzin 1970, pp. 9–10; Schmitt 1974, p. 455).

Given the paucity of knowledge regarding the linkage between organizational careers and status passages, it was not an easy task to determine what status passage to study. Dying was selected for several reasons. (1) Dying is a status passage. "Dying may be viewed sociologically as a career involving a passagee (the dying person) and, in some cases, others who accompany him or who control aspects of his status passage" (Marshall 1975, p. 349). (2) Dying is an inevitable status passage (Glaser and Strauss 1971, p. 4). All employees will experience it. (3) Given that most Americans die later in life, the employees will be at different points in this passage. Dying is a complicated status passage, being intertwined, often, with the life cycle process. Although the unscheduled aspects of dying have been skillfully studied among those close to death in hospitals (Glaser and Strauss 1964, 1965, 1968) and facilities for the aged (Marshall 1975), this status passage is not limited to those "moving out of it." Persons usually take initial steps *toward* their status passages. They are not simply thrust into them. We believe that the temporal aspects of status passages (Glaser and Strauss 1971, pp. 35–56) include *anticipations and early, probing actions.* There is evidence, for instance, that various types of experiences make death more or less salient for individuals (Vernon 1970, pp. 23–30). (4) The linkage between dying as a status passage and the organizational career promises to be more subtle than the linkages beween previously researched status passages. Such subtleties deserve attention. In regard to breavement, for example, Marris (1974) has found provocative similarities between "different" status transitions. (5) The properties (Glaser and Strauss 1971, pp. 4–5) associated with dying and the organizational career are quite distinct. Dying, for instance, is inevitable and nonrepeatable, while an occupational career is not inevitable and is repeatable.

THE ORGANIZATIONAL CAREER: CORPORATE EMPLOYEES

Our research involved 50 high status employees of a large international corporation. A recent information booklet distributed by this corporation states that "Today we operate 300 individually managed profit centers employing approximately 400,000 men and women in some 80 countries, making us one of the world's largest employers. . . ." The 50 employees were rather homogeneous in that they all worked for the same corporation, had at least a master's degree, with one exception were all married, and were all members of the corporate staff. According to the information booklet, "Corporate Staffs advise the Chairman and President on corporate matters within functional areas of responsibility." A computer bank supplied information concerning the variable characteristics of the employees including age, sex, salary, religious affiliation, city and region, and organizational position (see Table 1).

The 50 corporate employees are most appropriately classified as executives and managers (see Hall 1969). This highly educated group occupied prestigious and well-salaried organizational positions, generally had authoritative roles, and helped to set policy for the corporation. The fact that they were all members of the corporate staff is, itself, evidence of their prestige and involvement in the policy-making system. Although there have been some exceptions, sociological research has contributed little to our understanding of executives, being "content to accept descriptions of executives developed by such journalistically oriented writers as William H. Whyte, Jr. or, of all people, Vance Packard" (Hall 1969, p. 139). Executives and managers constitute "a group which also has received relatively little systematic attention from social scientists" (Hall 1969, p. 163).

R.L. SCHMITT, R. GORSHE and S. LINDBERG

TABLE 1. 50 Corporate Employees: Age; Sex; Salary; Religion; City and Region; Organizational Position; and Reaction to Death Stimulus*

AGE	SEX	SALARY	RELIGION	CITY AND REGION	POSITION	REACTION
27	M	A	L	Omaha[N]	Assistant Sales Manager	-
28	M	A	L	Dallas[S]	Assistant Sales Manager	+
29	M	A	C	Philadelphia[E]	Assistant Comptroller	-
29	M	B	B	Detroit[N]	Assistant Sales Manager	N
30	M	B	L	Dayton[N]	Sales Manager	-
30	M	B	L	Cincinnati[N]	Assistant Sales Manager	-
31	F	A	C	New York[E]	Company Secretary	+
31	M	B	L	Kansas City[N]	Assistant Sales Manager	-
31	F	B	C	Dallas[S]	Computer Components Buyer	+
31	F	A	C	New York[E]	Company Secretary	+
31	M	A	B	Laredo[S]	Assistant Sales Manager	-
32	F	A	C	New York[E]	Company Secretary	+
32	M	B	L	Minneapolis[N]	Computer Analyst	-
32	F	B	C	San Francisco[W]	Comptroller	+
33	M	B	N	Des Moines[N]	Assistant Sales Manager	0
36	M	B	L	San Antonio[S]	District Sales Manager	N
36	M	B	N	Pittsburgh[E]	Sales Manager	0
36	M	B	B	Columbia, MO[N]	Sales Manager	-
36	F	C	C	Myrtle Beach, SC[S]	Sales Manager	+
36	M	B	B	Chicago[N]	Sales Manager	N
36	F	B	C	New York[E]	Company Secretary	+
38	M	C	L	Dallas[S]	Sales Manager	-
38	M	B	L	Little Rock, AR[S]	Sales Manager	-

TABLE 1 (continued)

AGE	SEX	SALARY	RELIGION	CITY AND REGION	POSITION	REACTION
38	M	B	C	Boston[E]	Assistant Sales Manager	+
39	F	C	C	New York[E]	Assistant Medical Physician	+
40	M	B	M	Dallas[S]	Comptroller	−
40	M	B	L	Portland[W]	Sales Manager	N
41	M	B	C	Phoenix[W]	Sales Manager	+
43	M	C	B	New York[E]	Chief Electrical Engineer	N
43	M	D	C	New York[E]	Company Physician	+
45	M	B	L	Dallas[S]	Sales Manager	N
45	F	B	C	New York[E]	Company Buyer	+
45	M	B	C	Boston[E]	Regional Sales Manager	+
47	M	C	N	New York[E]	Director of Affairs	O
50	M	C	C	New York[E]	Assistant Personnel Manager	N
52	M	B	L	Chicago[N]	District Sales Manager	N
53	M	C	C	Des Moines[N]	Sales Manager	+
53	M	C	C	New York[E]	Motivational Counselor	+
55	M	C	C	Chicago[N]	Sales Manager	+
55	M	C	C	New York[E]	Psychiatrist	+
56	M	C	C	Seattle[W]	Regional Sales Manager	+
56	M	B	C	New York[E]	Chief Buyer Supervisor	+
57	M	C	C	Highlands, NM[W]	Regional Sales Manager	+
57	M	C	C	New York[E]	Personnel Supervisor	+
57	M	C	C	Minneapolis[N]	Marketing Research Manager	+
58	M	D	B	New York[E]	President	−

TABLE 1 (continued)

AGE	SEX	SALARY	RELIGION	CITY AND REGION	POSITION	REACTION
58	M	C	C	Cincinnati[N]	District Sales Supervisor	+
59	M	D	C	Chicago[N]	Comptroller	+
60	M	C	C	New York[E]	Regional Buyer	+
61	M	C	C	Chicago[N]	Regional Sales Manager	+

[*]Sex: F = Female, M = Male; Salary: A = $15,000-19,999, B = $20,000-29,999,

C = $30,000-39,999, D = $40,000 and above; Religion: C = Catholic, B = Baptist,

L = Lutheran, M = Methodist, N = None; Region: E = East, N = North, S = South,

W = West; Reaction: - = Negative, + = Positive, N = Neutral (see text), 0 = None.

The focal point of the corporate employees' organizational career was their organizational positions. According to Glaser (1968, p. 1), it is a specific entity offered by the organization to the people working in it. Although this component of the employee's organizational career was easily identified, the actor's meaning, or subjective view (see Stebbins 1970), of the organizational position was a much more difficult variable to tap. The *essence* of an organizational career hinges on the meaning of the organizational position to the actor. As Hughes (1958, p. 63, our italics) observed in his discussion of career and office, "Subjectively, a career is the moving perspective in which the person sees his life as a whole and interprets the *meaning* of his various attributes, actions, and the things which happen to him." As discussed below, a naturalistic strategy was used to elicit the meaning of the organizational position to the employees.

A NATURALISTIC STRATEGY

Although a naturalistic or emergent approach to research has been criticized (Huber 1973; Day and Day 1977), we employed this strategy. The naturalistic method (see Denzin 1971) is consistent with the symbolic interactionist assumptions that characterize the status passage literature, and it has proved effective in the study of organizational careers (Strauss et al. 1964; Heyl forthcoming) and dying (Glaser and Strauss 1964; 1968). It should also be recalled that certain of our primary research decisions were made in response to some of the alleged weaknesses of status passage research.

While the emergent-type strategy employed in this research has been described in various ways, including grounded theory (Glaser and Strauss 1967), the naturalistic method (Denzin 1971), and the methodological principles of empirical science (Blumer 1969, pp. 21–47), the heart of this method is that *the investigator goes to the empirical world* to resolve his research questions. As Blumer (1969, p. 32) has observed:

> Very simply put, the only way to get this assurance is to go directly to the empirical social world—see through meticulous examinaton of it whether one's premises or root images of it, one's questions and problems posed for it, the data one chooses out of it, the concepts through which one sees and analyzes it, and the interpretations one applies to it are actually borne out.

More specifically, however, rooted in symbolic interactionism, we take the major features of a grounded or naturalistic approach to be that the method (1) goes directly to the empirical world and attempts to understand it through inspection and exploration (Blumer 1969), (2) generates through an inductive, or emergent, and comparative method grounded substantive theories (Glaser and Strauss 1967) and grounded formal theory (Glaser and Strauss 1971), (3) employs various forms of methodological and theoretical triangulation (Denzin 1970), and (4) discovers and verifies the covert and overt aspects of behavior within natural contexts (Denzin 1971).

The emergent or inductive component that is so germane to the naturalistic method was included in our research by anchoring our interviews with the corporate employees in their everyday or natural worlds, and through the use of an indirect and open-end stimulus. Although our contact with our subjects was not as extensive as in previous status passage research, we believe that the emergent component was successfully implemented.

The views of the corporate employees toward their organizational careers and dying were prompted through a single indirect and open-end stimulus. The stimulus was indirect in that the employees were not directly asked about their views of dying or their organizational careers. An indirect approach was used because both organizational careers and dying apparently represent taboo areas for many Americans. Although people do talk about many of their careers (Glaser and Strauss 1971, p. 2), with regard to organizational careers, Glaser (1968, p. 1) believes that "generally speaking, people do not like to talk about their careers or to be asked about them in everyday conversations with many or unknown people." Tausky and Dubin (1965, pp. 726–727) phrased their questions about business careers as choices about other persons because of their concerns in this regard. Similarly, various writers have concluded that death is a taboo topic for many Americans (e.g., Ariès 1974). Our stimulus was presented within the natural context of the employees' everyday world in order to further alleviate any sensitivities that might be present in regard to the two status passages being studied.

As will be shown in the following section, "Approaching the Corporate Employees," the indirect stimulus applied both to the employees' organization and to death in general. We felt that such a stimulus would provide the opportunity for the corporate employee to tell us about any meaningful linkages between their organizational careers and dying. We did know that this type of stimulus would be able to elicit views in the area of death. The senior author has recently been using varied data-gathering approaches to investigate reactions to death-related topics in different populations. The results indicate that there are clear advantages in *unexpectedly querrying individuals about the study of death in a face-to-face and everyday context.* Reactions obtained under these conditions seem to possess spontaneous, distinctive, and genuine qualities. The senior author has now had 82 students in four Sociology of Death classes approach over 2000 persons in a primarily open-end and indirect manner, and these spontaneous qualities have been elicited irrespective of the interviewee's age, social class, sex, religion, occupation, relationship to the interviewer, or the situation.

The genuine reactions to death cues that are inserted into the actor's everyday world are probably elicited because Americans are not accustomed to discussing death (see Vernon 1970, pp. 166–167), and when the topic is presented, its uniqueness attracts the individual's true feelings. For example, one student would bring up the fact that he was taking a university course on death with the customers in a Radio Shack while he was writing up their bills. Illustrative negative and positive reactions follow:

Negative Reactions:	"I don't think that you should study death. It's natural, like the facts of life. It's gonna happen someday and that's that."
	"Can't you people leave anything alone? Christ sake, if God wanted you to know, he would have told you."
	"You're sick, talking about dead things to an old man. Son, you've got a lot to learn about people."
Positive Reactions:	"Good idea. It should go over good."
	"People don't have any idea about death. A course like this might help."
	"I'd like to take it. Cancer runs in my family."

These reactions, however, are frequently reflected in a nonverbal as well as a verbal manner. Persons not only say what they are thinking, but the inflection in their voices, the looks on their faces, and their bodily movements also denote their feelings. This dual response facilitates the observer's evaluation of the subject's reaction.

The stimulus that was presented to the corporate executives also had an open-end rather than a forced-choice format. This type of format has recently been shown to be effective in a study of nurse's meanings toward death (Bakshis et al. 1974) as (1) it allowed the nurses to rather completely describe their views of death, and (2) it did not direct the nurses to a given mental set. The senior author has also found these same characteristics present in the reactions of persons who were verbally presented with an open-end death stimulus that had been introduced in their natural domain. One of the older women to have taken the death course, for instance, brought up the course with one of her friends, a 63-year-old retired teacher, while visiting with her. The teacher's positive reaction to the course is a good illustration of how an open-end stimulus is capable of eliciting nondirected meanings that relate to the *subject's* everyday world.

> Mary, that really sounds interesting. I think I know my views on death, but I'd be interested to find out how other people view death. You know, Ma was born and raised a Catholic. She had such a bad heart at the last I'd tell her, "Ma, don't do that wash, I'll do it after school!" Well, I'd come home and she'd have it done and I'd say, "Ma, you shouldn't do that." "Listen," she'd say, "when that grim reaper comes, I'm ready," and you know, Mary, she was. Pa, that was different. He never did go to church. After Ma died, he was so lonely and then, of course, he got sick too. For a while there he had a lot of pain. I'd say, "Pa, pray." He said, "Daughter, I don't know how to pray. I don't know any prayers." I said, "Dad, you don't have to use formal prayers with Him, just talk to Him." Some of my family said near the end, "You know, Dad seems to have accepted his illness so much better lately." I think I know why. Maybe a course like that would help people understand.

It should be emphasized that the value of the volunteered responses to open-end questions has been argued in several contexts. Becker et al. (1961, pp. 43–45) contend that volunteered responses are more valid than directed responses in participant observer studies, and Kuhn has made this same type of argument in terms of studying the self (Kuhn and McPartland 1954), reference groups (Kuhn 1964), and other social objects (see Bakshis et al. 1974). Given the possible sensitivities of persons in regard to organizational careers and dying and the paucity of knowledge about the linkage of organizations to their environments, these characteristics of an open-end strategy were particularly desirable in our work.

APPROACHING THE CORPORATE EMPLOYEES

Eighty-five corporate employees met for an annual business conference in Chicago in the spring of 1977. These employees were required to stop at an office upon their arrival, register, obtain certain materials, and determine their conference agenda. By prearrangement, the second author was in charge of these duties. After they had been discharged, each person was asked the question, "Do you feel that it would be practical for a corporation such as _____ to offer a course on death?" None of the employees knew that they were being studied for other purposes and assumed that the questioner was an employee of their corporation. At a point early in the conversation, it was mentioned that a nearby university offered a course on death and the employee was shown one of the death books that was used in this course. Almost all of the employees went straight to the index and looked at the topic headings. It will be recalled that they all had at least a Master's degree. Fifty of the corporate employees were interviewed; 25 interviews took place each day. It was necessary to spread the interviews out due to the duties that had to be performed, and we wanted to interview each employee privately. Although the rate at which the employees appeared at the office influenced the interviewee selection, the interviewees were more or less randomly selected. Due to their small number, however, all of the women employees were interviewed.

Almost all of the corporate employees were very willing to share their time and ideas regarding the proposed sociology course. Most of the employees became very interested in the question and said that they had never talked to anyone before about death. These individuals seemed to undergo some catharsis and may have been experiencing the effects of what Kübler-Ross (1969) has referred to as "the door-opening interview." The interviewer said very little during the course of the interviews once the stimulus had been introduced. He found it best to be a listener, as the employees usually had extended comments or stories to tell. The low-key nature of the interviewer made him ideal for the listener role. As anticipated, in responding to the death question, the employees related the death course to their experiences and feelings about death and dying, their loved ones, their chronological age, their aspirations, and their positions within the organization, and provided a range of reactions to the death inquiry.

A *QUANTITATIVE* ANALYSIS OF THE CORPORATE EMPLOYEES' REACTIONS: THE DETECTION OF DYING AS A STATUS PASSAGE

The reactions of the 50 employees are presented in Table 1 along with their other previously described characteristics. These reactions were classified into four categories: (1) Positive reactions indicated a basic approval of the course; (2) Negative reactions indicated a basic disapproval of the course; (3) Neutral reactions indicated an indifference to the course or involved both positive and negative feelings toward it; (4) No response referred to those few instances in which the employees did not respond to the stimulus. The senior author and one other person coded 48 and 49 of the 50 reactions, respectively, in the same way as the interviewer.

The individual reactions of the corporate employees, however, had no meaning as separate items. If these reactions were in any way indicative of a dying-related passage, it was necessary to demonstrate that some sort of pattern existed among them. A passage, of course, implies some sort of "a becoming." We did not know *a priori* that such a passage existed. A quantitative analysis of the reactions was initially conducted in order to determine if there was any evidence of a dying-related passage. This analysis was supplemented with a qualitative analysis of the interview materials generated in response to the death stimulus to see if they would provide any insights into a dying-related passage.

The zero order relationships between the employees' reactions to the study of death and age, religious affiliation, sex, salary, and geographic region are depicted in Table 2. Various passages have been found to evolve about age, sex, religious affiliation, and salary (as it is conceptualized here). Our strategy, then, was to determine *if there was a pattern to the death reactions by linking them to other variables that are known to be reflective of passages.* With regard to salary, we interpret it as *an indicator of the prestige of the corporate employee's position within the organization.*[2] The significance of salary as a more general indicator of social class position within the community is later dismissed on logical and other grounds. While some passages do involve geographic movement, for various reasons, region is used as a control variable in this research to see if it influenced any of the examined linkages.

The magnitude and consistency of the percentage differences in Table 2 indicate a significant relationship between the reaction to death variable and age, salary or prestige of organizational position, sex, religious affiliation, and geographic region. Although the validity of the correlations between the independent variables and the death reaction variable is yet to be considered, *the ordering of the death reactions certainly suggests that a dying-related passage is being tapped!* The fact that all five independent variables are correlated with the reactions is not surprising because the independent variables are "block-booked" (Rosenberg 1968, pp. 26–27). Age and salary are positively correlated with the reaction variable and females, Catholics, and persons from the East and West tend to be more positive than their counterparts. Fifty-four percent of the 50 employees expressed a positive reaction toward the proposed course. Although the percentage of individuals favorable to the study of death may have been considerably less in the past, the proposed course was still not universally acceptable to the employees in our sample. Importantly, as is discussed later, only one person indicated that death was a taboo subject.

We were interested in what would happen to the relationships between the reaction variable and each of the other variables depicted in Table 2 when more than one of the latter variables was considered. The method of

TABLE 2. Zero Order Relationship—Reactions of 50 Corporate Employees to Death
          Stimulus by Age; by Salary; by Sex; by Religious Affiliation; by
          Geographic Region

		Reaction to Death Stimulus				
		Positive	Negative	Neutral	None	
Total Sample		54%	24%	16%	6%	50/100%
Age	20's	25%	50%	25%	0%	4/100%
	30's	43%	38%	10%	10%	21/101%*
	40's	44%	11%	33%	11%	9/99% *
	50's	79%	7%	14%	0%	14/100%
	60's	100%	0%	0%	0%	2/100%
Salary	$15,000-$29,999	40%	33%	20%	7%	30/100%
	$30,000 and above	75%	10%	10%	5%	20/100%
Sex	Male	44%	29%	20%	7%	41/100%
	Female	100%	0%	0%	0%	9/100%
Religious Affiliation	Catholic	93%	4%	4%	0%	28/101%*
	Non-Catholic	4%	50%	32%	14%	22/100%
Geographic Region	East	70%	10%	10%	10%	20/100%
	North	38%	38%	19%	6%	16/101%*
	South	33%	44%	22%	0%	9/99% *
	West	80%	0%	20%	0%	5/100%

*Rounding Error

elaboration (Rosenberg 1968) was used to help answer this question and,
although we did not have a large N, it did provide additional insights into
the effects of sex, age, and geographic region on the reaction variable. The
dispersions of the salary and the religious affiliation distributions prevented
us from learning more through this method about the effects of these two
variables on the reaction variable. Most of the older males were Catholic,
with salaries in excess of $30,000, while the younger males tended to be non-
Catholic and had lower salaries.

The relationship between the reaction to the death stimulus and sex by age is shown in Table 3. The age range was trichotomized in this and all the following tables.[3] The zero order relationship between sex and reaction (see Table 2) held up among the corporate employees in the 27 to 39 age category (Table 3). All eight of the women were positive, while only 12% of the males were positive and 59% were negative (Table 3). As there was only one woman above 40 years of age, a sex comparison could not be made in the other two age categories.

The relationship between reaction and age by sex can be observed by comparing similarly placed percentages across the rows in Table 3. The positive relationship between age and reaction that was observed at the zero order level (Table 2) holds for males (Table 3). Twelve and 59%, 30 and 10%, and 93 and 7% of the men in the 27 to 39, 40 to 52, and 53 to 61 age categories had positive and negative reactions, respectively. The relationship between age and the death reaction could not be examined among the women.

While it was not possible to include religious affiliation and salary in the first order analysis, the relationship between reaction and geographic region by age for males was considered. These results, however, are not presented in table form.[4] As six of the females were from New York City, the relationship between reaction and region was not examined among the females. Although the n's are small, or nonexistent in some instances, it appears that age has more influence on the reactions variable than region. Irrespective of region, for instance, the youngest males, generally, did not make a positive response, while the oldest males were all positive except one. Perhaps, most convincingly, in the Northern region, where the n's are relatively more adequate, 68% of the youngest males had a negative reaction while 100% of the oldest males had a positive reaction. These results for the Northern region are particularly interesting in that the Eastern and Western regions had the highest percentages of employees with positive reactions in the zero order analysis (Table 2). Of course, the six women from the East are not included in this analysis. There is also a tendency for the males in the 40 to 52 age category to be neutral across all the regions.

The quantitative analysis has shown that (1) younger females are notably more positive than younger males in their reaction to death study, and that (2) age is positively related to reaction among the males. The latter relationship seems to hold with geographic region controlled. The two variables presented in Table 1 that could not be considered in our first-order analysis are salary and religious affiliation. Based on a logical criterion, we believe that the relationship between salary—if conceptualized as income level or as a general index of class position—is a spurious one (see Rosenberg 1968). Although the salaries of the employees do vary, their salary is sufficient in all instances to be positively correlated with some of

TABLE 3. Reactions of 50 Corporate Employees to Death Stimulus and Sex by Age

	AGE														
	27 to 39					40 to 52					53 to 61				
	Reaction					Reaction					Reaction				
	Positive	Negative	Neutral	None		Positive	Negative	Neutral	None		Positive	Negative	Neutral	None	
SEX Female	100%	0%	0%	0%	8/100%	100%	0%	0%	0%	1/100%	0%	0%	0%	0%	0/100%
Male	12%	59%	18%	12%	17/101%*	30%	10%	50%	10%	10/100%	93%	7%	0%	0%	14/100%

*Rounding Error

436

the death-related variables that are known to be related to salary, such as level of medical care, access to medical services, and motivation to use these services (see Goldscheider 1971). Salary is also a component of social class. Other components of this *global* variable include occupation and educational level (Rosenberg 1968, pp. 40–45). The corporate employees are similar in these respects. On the other hand, the relationship between the prestige of the organizational positions occupied by the corporate employees, of which salary was taken to be an index, and reaction to the death variable was not considered in the quantitative analysis. As is discussed below, the qualitative analysis indicates that the mens' views of their organizational positions were indeed linked to their reactions to the death stimulus. In other words, there was a linkage between organization career and dying as a status passage among the men.

We also believe that religious affiliation is spuriously rather than directly related to the reaction variable. Evidence for this contention comes from the interview data. As will be shown, religious symbols never came up during the interviews. Although a counterargument can be made, we find it unlikely that religious affiliation could be significantly accounting for the variation in responses to the death stimulus and not have been mentioned in some form during the interviews.[5] The interview data also lends further support to the relationship between age and reaction.

A *QUALITATIVE* ANALYSIS OF THE CORPORATE EMPLOYEES' REACTIONS: THE DETECTION OF DYING AS A STATUS PASSAGE

The interview data from the 47 corporate employees who responded to the death inquiry were content-analyzed. The interviews were not difficult to categorize into meaningful classifications, as the employees had provided distinctive reactions to the interviewer's stimulus. These classifications and the frequency with which they were mentioned are considered in relation to age and sex, the two variables that proved to be the most significant in the quantitative analysis. The three coders classified all but one of the negative reactions into the same category; 24 of the 27 positive reactions were coded in the same way.

The results of the content analysis of the 12 male negative reactions are shown in Table 4. The two modal reactions described the study of death as irrelevant because the employee's death was so far in the future or because death study would interfere with some more important activities. One reaction contained both of these modal responses. The following reaction of the president should illustrate the interference category. The president was the only male above 52 to be negative toward the death course.

I am very surprised to see a university starting to teach unimportant courses. People should live each day to the fullest and not worry about depressive thoughts such as death. Those who think about death are putting themselves in a position where they begin to go downhill as far as life is concerned, instead of fighting for success and letting death come when it comes. State colleges should get rid of useless courses and have more positive life motivation courses.

One of the younger executives who had an interference reaction said that there were more important things to do in life, and "if he was going to be further educated, he would take a business course."

Two employees said that they were not in favor of the death course because there was nothing that could be done about death. One individual put it this way.

Don't feel the course can be of any help. People know they will die, so why worry about something that we have no control over?

On the other hand, one person argued that he didn't need a death course, "because the way our technology is going, by the time I am old enough to die, there will be some type of medicine to help me live forever." The interviewer was convinced that this "faith in technology" reaction was not a "put-on," and that this employee, who had a background in chemistry, was absolutely serious. Shneidman (1974, pp. 85–86) has observed that some

TABLE 4. Content Analysis of Corporate Males' Negative Reactions to Death Stimulus and Age (in frequencies)

	AGE			
Negative Reaction	27 to 39	40 to 52	53 to 61	Total
1) Study of death as interference	3	0	1	4
2) Personal death not imminent	3	0	0	3
3) Death cannot be controlled	2	0	0	2
4) Study of death as interference and personal death not imminent	1	0	0	1
5) Death is taboo topic	0	1	0	1
6) Science will negate death	1	0	0	1
	10	1	1	12

people are "death-disdainers," and do not believe that death can happen to them. The one person who gave a taboo type reaction shook his head and had a very distasteful expression on his face. He didn't think that "humans should study the unknown."

The negative reactions are particularly significant *because they clearly relate to both the corporate employees' organizational careers and to dying as a status passage.* While there is independent evidence regarding the elements in the employees' reactions that pertain to organizational careers and to dying as a status passage, these reactions constitute some of the clearest and most convincing documentation of an *interrelationship* between these two passages. The reactions, in other words, show a link between the younger employees' experiences in the organization and in the environment. With regard to the death-related component of the employees' reactions, there is independent evidence of a relationship between the achievement-success value aspect of the American value structure and Americans' views of death and dying (see Howard and Scott 1965–1966; Spilka 1967; Vernon 1970, pp. 80–81). Vernon (1970, p. 81, first italics ours) has observed:

> The influence of the achievement-success value definitions upon interpretations of death is evident in those who evaluate death *negatively,* since it brings an end to achievement and success. Death is seen as infringing upon what is considered to be the *right* to life, liberty, and pursuit of happiness. To the extent that success-achievement incorporates such things as practicality, adaptability and efficiency, and hard work, death may be seen as destroying desirable behavior patterns. Death has no place in the scheme.

Vernon's description reflects precisely the feelings of the youngest employees in our study. Their reactions indicate that at this point in their occupational careers, "death had no place in their world of work."

There is also independent evidence of the achievement-success orientation of high-status organizational personnel. The organizational literature indicates that the major personality traits of executives frequently include high drive and achievement (Henry 1949), dominance (Harrell 1961, pp. 172–173), and a strong orientation toward the immediate and the practical (Henry 1949). There is also evidence that young men who seem to be progressing rapidly toward executive positions have a strong positive desire to become an executive (Dill, Hilton, and Reitman 1962). Etzioni (1975, p. 429) has implied, however, that certain traits may have been too universally attributed to executives. We, ourselves, found no evidence of mobility aspirations among the oldest males.

Death study was viewed in a negative manner by the youngest corporate employees because it was perceived to be *nonfunctional or dysfunctional to their occupational careers.* Some of the negative reactions indicate that death study was simply seen as being nonfunctional for their occupational careers. It is perhaps understandable why an autonomous individual would not be interested in an area over which it is thought "no control could be exerted," or if he believed that "his own death was not an imminent status passage." It can even be contended that the person who said that "science will negate death" viewed death study as nonfunctional. On the other hand, some employees saw death study as a threat to their success because such study would bring about a defeatist or passive view of life. "Death would interfere" with their occupational careeers. With regard to both the nonfunctional and the dysfunctional reactions, it must be emphasized that the success orientations of these young male employees was *tied to their occupational careers*, and that it was this standard that was used in the negative evaluations of the death study course. The employee who was interested in taking more business courses is a prime example of this. The business course was seen as a success vehicle.

The results of the content analysis of the positive reactions to the proposed death course are recorded in Table 5. These reactions were primarily made by the oldest men and the youngest women. All 27 reactions were classified as death preparation reactions, since they all referred to the capacity of a death course to enhance the ability of an individual to cope with a death-related situation. There were, however, eight different types of death preparation reactions. The differences between these categories centered on the nature of the time frame and the individual described in the reaction.

The first two categories (A and B) in Table 5 refer to the employees' imminent and future deaths, respectively. One middle-aged male said that "he was dying of cancer and only had six months to live." Three of the oldest males indicated "that they were getting old and should learn more about death." Three categories (C, D, and E) pertained to the death of a loved one within different time frames. Three employees described the past death of a loved one, for example, "I wish I would have had such a course when my daughter died." One of the two males under 39 to give a positive reaction said that "my father is on his death bed," while four employees referred to the future deaths of their loved ones. Another category (F) contained five reactions that described the future deaths of the employee and of his loved ones. The final two categories (G and H) were more general. Six employees indicated that "a death course would help others prepare for death." Four employees simply indicated that "it would be helpful to learn more about death."

A comparison of the positive reactions of the oldest males and the youngest females in Table 5 indicates more differences than similarities. The oldest males viewed death preparation more *specifically* in terms of their own future deaths or the future deaths of their loved ones (categories B, E and F), while the youngest females tended to view the death course *generally* as helpful for others or as just helpful (categories G and H). This difference is explainable, as death is more of an imminent status passage for the oldest

TABLE 5. Content Analysis of Corporate Employees' Positive Reactions to Death Stimulus and Age by Sex

Positive Reaction	MALE Age			FEMALE Age		
	27 to 39	40 to 52	53 to 61	27 to 39	40 to 52	53 to 61
1) Preparation for death						
A) Subject's imminent death	0	1	0	0	0	0
B) Subject's future death	0	0	3	0	0	0
C) Loved one's past death	0	0	1	2	0	0
D) Loved one's imminent death	1	0	0	0	0	0
E) Loved one's future death	0	2	1	1	0	1
F) Subject and loved one's future deaths	1	0	3	0	1	1
G) Help others prepare	0	0	2	4	0	4
H) Helpful to learn more about death	0	0	3	1	0	3
	2	3	13	8	1	9

males. Fifty-four percent (7 out of 13) of the oldest males and 12% (1 out of 8) of the youngest females reacted in terms of specific deaths (categories B, E, and F) while 38% (5 out of 13) of these males and 62% (5 out of 8) of these females described the value of a death course in much more general terms (categories G and H).

As was true of the negative reactions, the positive reactions suggest a link between the oldest employee's experiences in the organization and in the environment. A *different* type of link, however, pertains to these older men. From the perspective of a linkage between organizational careers and dying as a status passage, the positive reactions of the males reflect three critical themes. (1) Dying was seen by some of these men as an imminent status passage both for them and for their significant others. Such concerns were not reflected in the negative reactions of the youngest men. (2) Significant others were discussed. These others never came up in the interviews with the youngest men. It is pertinent that the older corporate employees mentioned their loved ones (wife, children, and relatives) rather than their work associates. (3) Reference was never made to any nonfunctional or dysfunctional dimensions of death study for their occupational careers. Such concerns were the focal point of the youngest males' negative reactions. As is discussed below, the absence of such mentions suggests that the "career anchorage" (Tausky and Dubin 1965) of the oldest males is in the past rather than in the future.

Given the significance of the difference between the positive and the negative reactions of the youngest and the oldest males, the themes contained in these reactions are depicted and compared in Figure 1. This figure also depicts the themes involved in the males' neutral reactions. These reactions, it will be recalled, were largely made by the individuals in the 40-to-52 age category, and, as is shown in Table 6, they tend to reflect the nonfunctional and dysfunctional elements that typified the youngest male employees' negative reactions (see categories 2, 3, 5, and 6 in Table 6) and the death preparation element that characterized the oldest male employees' positive reactions (see categories 2, 5, and 6).

Critically, as was the case with the negative reactions, independent evidence exists regarding the themes that characterize the positive reactions. But the corporate employees' positive reactions provide some of the clearest evidence available that these themes are involved in a linkage between organizational careers and dying as a status passage. With regard to the discrepancy between the youngest and the oldest mens' emphasis on dying as a status passage, Kastenbaum (1977, pp. 188–192) has alerted us not to stereotype the relationship between age and death-related behavior. Age, as death, is a complex variable, and it has no necessary or intrinsic meaning to the actor (Hochschild 1975). However, there is a variety of evidence showing a correlation between age and certain death-related variables (see particularly Dumont and Foss 1972, pp. 89–92). Sudnow (1967) and Glaser and

FIGURE 1. Themes in Corporate Males' Negative, Neutral, and Positive Reactions to the Death Study Stimulus

| Male Corporate Employees | | Themes in Negative, Neutral, and Positive Reactions* | | |
Age	Modal Reaction to Death Study	Death Study Nonfunctional or Dysfunctional for Organizational Career	Preparation Function as Status Passage of Dying in Family Other's Future	Preparation Function as Status Passage of Dying in Employee's Future
27 to 39	Negative	X	O	O
40 to 52	Neutral	X	O	X
53 to 61	Positive	O	X	X

*X = Prominent in interviews

O = Absent in interviews

443

TABLE 6. Content Analysis of Corporate Males' Neutral Reactions to Death
Stimulus and Age (in frequencies)

		AGE		
Neutral Reactions	27 to 39	40 to 52	53 to 61	Total
1) Indifferent	0	1	0	1
2) Death cannot be controlled but death study good for elderly	1	0	0	1
3) Study of death as interference but good for security seekers	0	1	0	1
4) Individual matter	1	1	0	2
5) Death not relevant now but useful later on	0	2	0	2
6) Not useful except for death-related positions	1	0	0	1
	3	5	0	8

Strauss (1964) have shown that younger persons receive better treatment
than older persons in some hospitals precisely because the latter are seen as
having less social worth to the society. Hertz (1960, p. 85) believes that,
whatever the explanation, death seems to be more acceptable to the aged
than to younger persons. The *fact* that the status passage of dying is
experienced by most Americans at a given interval during their later years
should be emphasized. Parsons (1963), for one, in responding to the death
denial literature, doubts that this fact generally goes unnoticed in as
scientifically-orientated a society as America.

The variation in the mentions of family others by the youngest and the
oldest males can be approached in two ways. With regard to dying as a
status passage, it is now a truism among those who study death that death
is a "two-way street." Toynbee (1968, p. 267) has observed that "There are
always two parties to a death; the person who dies and the survivors who are
bereaved." Shneidman (1974, p. 4) has emphasized the following about
death preparation: "Death work imposes a two-fold burden: intraphysic
(preparing oneself for death) and interpersonal (preparing oneself in
relation to loved ones and, simultaneously, preparing the loved ones to be
survivors). Shaffer (1970, pp. 169–170) has even criticized the courts for
assuming that the dying forget about their loved ones.

The absence of family references among the youngest male employees is consistent with our knowledge of organizational careers. Discussions of the interdependence of careers indicate that the actor's identities and significant others change with different career phases (Becker and Strauss 1956; Glaser 1964, pp. 74–84).While these discussions have focused on the interdependence of organizational careers, there is also evidence that organizational careers relate to significant others in the environment. Hall (1969, p. 341), for instance, has observed that "deep involvement in an occupation can lead to withdrawal from the family. Such involvement is particularly likely among high status occupations. . . ." Conceivably, younger corporate employees, particularly strivers, may be more actively involved in the organization and be more prone to this deep involvement. Scanzoni (1967), in reacting to Parsons' notion of a "uniform family," argues that the complexity of the American society should be reflected in the family as well as in other areas, and delineates five different family types. Even more pertinently, Glaser observes, in his discussion of the temporal or changing aspects of mobile careers, that the *same* family members may deliberately juggle the time at their disposal. Strauss (1971, p. 198) notes that:

> What makes juggling a less than overwhelming problem is that most people do not expect forever to be juggling exactly the same balls, for juggling is related to expectations about phases in life. Thus a young physician can promise his wife, and himself, that after his time-consuming internship and residency he can spend more time with her and the children. He may be wrong about that expectation, but at least he acts on it. An ambitious young scientist can confidently proceed on the assumption that he must "work his ass off" until he has a secure reputation, then he can coast a little.

Somewhat ironically then, loved ones may be temporarily juggled out of an actor's life—given a lesser priority in his scheme of things, precisely because the loved ones are significant. This may have been what was happening in the lives of some of the youngest male employees in this study.

Tausky and Dubin's (1965) innovative and important research on "career anchorage" bears a striking resemblance to our finding that the youngest and the oldest males differed so dramatically in their view of death study as being nonfunctional and/or dysfunctional for their organizational careers. Tausky and Dubin (1965, p. 730) found that "Age is probably the most crucial factor in the career-long stability of orientations." The younger managers and specialists in their study were upwardly mobile in their career anchorage, while the older employees were downwardly mobile. The younger individuals were looking ahead to their *future* occupational accomplishments while the older persons were anchored in their *past* in terms of their prior organizational accomplishments. The older managers and specialists, however, were not "skidders" in Wilensky's terms, but rather, as Tausky and Dubin put it, "resters." Similarly, in our study, the reactions of the younger males indicate that they, too, were upwardly mobile. If they were not concerned with their future organizational careers, why would they be worried that death study would be nonfunctional or dysfunctional for them? We reemphasize that these reactions were elicited indirectly. At no time did the interviewer ever quiz the person about his ocupational aspirations. Moreover, the lack of similar reactions among the oldest males to the *identical* stimulus certainly suggests that they were "resters." At least, none of them gave any evidence of being concerned about their future mobility, and their present organizational positions makes it doubtful that many of them were "skidders."

Goldman's (1973) research that merged "career anchorage" with the earlier work of Dubin (1956) and others on "central life interests" also relates to our findings. Central life interests basically refer to the person's primary interests. Goldman dichotomized these into work and nonwork interests and found that the upwardly oriented middle managers and specialists in his study had more work interests than the downwardly oriented workers. If one takes the family references in our interviews as an index of nonwork interests, and family items are an integral part of the CLI questionnaire that Goldman and others have used, we show an identical result. Our upwardly oriented males did not mention their families. Our "downwardly" oriented males did mention them. Given the fact that all but one of the oldest males in our study viewed our death stimulus positively, it should be stressed that it is not unusual for even high status employees to have many of their central life interests in nonwork areas (see Goldman 1973).

The reactions of the nine women in our study should be reviewed in light of our attention to the males' mobility aspirations. The women are an anomoly in that they are generally similar in age to the youngest males, but yet they all reacted positively to the death stimulus. Presumably, because dying is not yet an imminent status passage for them as it is for the oldest males, they did not as often relate the value of death study to their own death or the future deaths of their significant others (Table 5). Although two of the women had lost loved ones through death, and one woman was a medical assistant, it is curious, in light of the youngest males' reactions, that none of the women gave even a slight indication that death study was potentially dysfunctional or nonfunctional for their organizational careers. Given the recent movement of women into new occupations, and the interest of social scientists in these changes, there are two possibilities that merit further study. (1) The women may define their organizational positions differently than the men. In other words, their organizational careers may not be the same. Perhaps there simply isn't as much room for advancement. Four women are company "secretaries." The women may be more reliant on their spouses than the men, or they may be "resters." Although young, given the traditional expectations regarding the female in the market place, these women may be satisfied with their achievements. Epstein (1967) has also convincingly argued that, for a variety of reasons, the work situation is different for women than for men. (2) The women may have been socialized differently in regard to the status passage of dying. There is some evidence, for instance, that under some conditions, women fear death more than men (Vernon 1970, pp. 204–205; Dumont and Foss 1972, p. 87). If this were true of the women in our study, the proposed death course might have been perceived as functional for these fears.

MOBILITY, DYING AS AWARENESS, AND NEGOTIATION

What has been learned about the relationship between organizational careers and dying as a status passage through our quantitative and qualitative analyses? While recognizing the cross-sectional nature of the data, our open-end strategy, grounded in the everyday world of the corporate employees, enabled us to begin to understand, particularly among the men, (1) the organizational careers of these persons, (2) the subtleties of the awareness passage that was being experienced in regard to their eventual deaths, and (3) the linkage between these two passages.

The organizational careers of the corporate employees did involve an "objective" and a "subjective" component. Objectively, the employees occupied different organizational positions. Not unexpectedly, the prestige of these positions was positively correlated with age. Subjectively, the open-end stimulus confirmed that the employees felt differently about their organizational positions. Age was also a factor in this regard. The younger men, in particular, defined their organizational positions as encompassing. The older men gave little evidence of holding such a view.

The evidence for a dying-related status passage is as convincing as that for the organizational career, but the make-up of this passage is not as easy to grasp. This is not surprising, however, as such a passage has not previously been detailed in precisely this manner. We believe that the dying-related passage being experienced by the corporate employees can *now* best be described as *a death awareness passage*. Glaser and Strauss (1965) have underscored the existence of death trajectories among dying patients. These trajectories are, in effect, passages attributed to the dying passagees by others, including doctors, nurses, wards, and hospitals. The corporate employees were also becoming increasingly aware of death. Their awareness, however, was (1) *an actor-based awareness* and (2) *it was an awareness that preceded the more immediate onset of death*. This is in the very nature of passages; they extend over time, perspectives change, objects become more or less salient, and future aspects of passages may be anticipated before they are experienced.

Subjectively, it was clear that the men felt differently about death. The older men were receptive to a death course. The younger men were not. The objective component of the dying awareness passage is less clear, but it involved age and the organizational careers of the corporate males. While age and organizational career were too tightly "block-booked" in our sample to distinguish their effects quantitatively, the totality of our results indicate that both variables were "in some manner" tied to dying preparation as a status passage. This issue is further complicated by the interpretation that is given to age. As Hyman (1955, p. 196) notes in his discussion of time order in the method of elaboration:

> They (variables) may be indices of more than one phenomenon, so that the time order, rather than being fixed, is determined, by the particular problem being considered. Age is perhaps the most typical example of such "ambiguous variables."

If one views age as an index of chronological age, an argument can be made that age, organizational career, and the dying-related status passage were involved in a "causal sequence" (see Rosenberg 1968). Not only does our data indicate that age was positively related to the organizational career, but quite clearly chronological age is antecedent to organizational career in time. Similarly our data showed that organizational career was positively related to the dying-related status passage, and the qualitative responses suggest that experiences in the career preceded the dying awareness. The younger men were not open to death preparation. The older men were. It should also be recalled that there was increased awareness of death among the older men due to the actual or potential loss of significant others through death. This awareness can be related to increasing chronological age.

On the other hand, if age is viewed more as a locational type variable (see Hochschild 1975), a slightly different explanation emerges. Here the impact of age depends more on the social context in which individuals grow old. Hochschild, for instance, posits that the impact of growing old for disengagement depends on the social context in which the person is located. She states, for instance, that "access to work, under certain conditions, determines the likelihood of working in old age, and this affects the character of engagement" (Hochschild 1975, p. 565). Relatedly, although perhaps more subtly, and with regard to the dying awareness passage, the segment of the organizational career passage through which the younger employees were passing was not conducive to an increased awareness of death. However, the apex of the career passage through which the older employees were passing was more conducive to such an awareness.[6] It should be noted that our results support Hochschild's view that individuals do not necessarily disengage as they grow older. Psychologically at least, the older corporate males exhibited an awareness of death and a readiness to prepare for it in an active and mature manner.

Irrespective, however, of whether age is viewed as chronological or locational, or in some other manner, if age is to be linked to a dying awareness passage (and it need not be), this linkage must be manifested through some other social, historical, or interactional variable(s). In our study, this linkage evolved about the organizational career. What do we now believe was the nature of this linkage? Glaser (1968, p. 1) has observed that an organizational career is one that is *offered* to the employee. The corporate employees seemed to have taken this offer seriously. Some things, however, had to be given in return for this offer. Our data indicates that the young males, implicitly or explicitly, had agreed to focus their time and energy on their organizational careers in return for promotions and the other success symbols that accompany mobile careers. Given this context, death and death study would indeed be defined as interference and nonfunctional. Among the older males, the nature of the bargain had apparently changed. Either the bargain had been fulfilled or the employee now had attained a much stronger bargaining position. Strauss (1975) has recently emphasized the role that negotiations play in organizational contexts and stresses that these negotiations are frequently complex and novel. Our data certainly tends to coincide with this observation.

We believe that it can be argued that the linkage between the death awareness passage and the organizational career was "symmetrical." Among the younger males, the organizational career seems to have inhibited the employees from coming to grips with the passage of death. In this respect, we would stress that *it is just as significant to understand the forces that inhibit status passages from acting on the organization as it is to understand the forces that facilitate such influences.* Among the older males, it is more likely that the dying awareness passage was influencing their organizational careers in a more direct manner. Our argument is inferential at this juncture, because no evidence was generated regarding specific behavioral changes within the organization. There was clear evidence, however, that the older males were more susceptible to becoming aware of death. It is not unlikely that this increased awareness, even if partly or largely prompted by the corporate employees' mobility patterns, also, in turn, influenced the corporate activities of these men.

MULTIPLE PASSAGES: TOWARD FORMAL THEORY

Glaser and Strauss' work, *Status Passage: A Formal Theory,* directs attention to a number of interrelated variables, provides a framework for their study in relationship to passages, is grounded in the empirical world, and is moving toward formal theory. A directive of utmost significance points to multiple passages. This directive has been fundamental to our research and enabled us to emphasize the usefulness of multiple passages for the study of organizational environments. Perhaps, however, new insights were to be expected. Two substantively different passages were compared through grounded research. This is the prime strategy for generating formal theory (Glaser and Strauss 1971, pp. 176–195).

Although Glaser and Strauss (1971, pp. 4–5) have delineated twelve significant properties of passages, our research indicates that other properties of multiple passages have not been conceptualized in as explicit a form as possible. These properties are shown in Figure 2. As some investigators, however, have been concerned with these properties in their research, illustrative examples are noted in Figure 2. (1) Multiple passages may involve one or more than one passagee. The focus of our work was on the solo actor involved in more than one passage. Even here, however, the complex interrelationships of these passages with the passages of others was apparent. The deaths of significant others had a bearing on the employees' view of our death stimulus and it was suggested that the womens' organizational careers may have been more closely tied to their spouses than the younger males. It is this type of "interdependence," as it has been called, between the passages of different persons that has been emphasized in the literature. (2) Multiple passages can be conceptualized in terms of the settings with which they are primarily linked. While this could be done in various ways, our research shows the value of an organizational and a nonorganizational classification. (3) The direction of the influence between passages varies. Given two passages, the direction of the influence may be (a) symmetrical, (b) asymmetrical in the direction of the first passage, (c) asymmetrical in the direction of the second passage, (d) nonexistent, or (e) varied, depending on such factors as time period, situation, and the nature of the influence. Only asymmetrical influences are shown in Figure 2.

Glaser and Strauss' work has been criticized on the grounds that while "it may be true, as they contend, that negotiation is present in all social situations, the structural problem is to grasp *the relations between situations —the ways in which some negotiations set limits upon others"* (Benson 1977, p. 12, our italics). Our research begins to address this issue by drawing attention to the need for sociologists to broaden their conception of the types of environments that influence organizations, by underscoring that mutiple passages do represent a viable strategy for tapping these environments, and that passages should be studied in such a way that the analyst does not contaminate what he is studying. In the latter regard, some (e.g., Day and Day 1971) have criticized the interactionist assumptions in Strauss and other's work for failing to reflect the role of power and history in organizational behavior. Interactionists are giving more attention to these matters, but an unfortunate implication of this criticism has been the position that power and history always play a predominate and constant role in organizational affairs. Such a stance represents an overreaction. The role of any variable or process for a designated piece of organizational behavior—and history is no exception—must be grounded in research and not be prejudged by the scientist.

Although our research will be a directive to others, it only marks a beginning in the more systematic study of multiple passages. Other proper-

FIGURE 2. Examples of Three Additional Properties of Asymmetrical Multiple (Two) Passages: (1) Passagees, (2) Direction of Influence, and (3) Context

	Passagees			
	Actor Passagee in both Passages		Actor Passagee in One Passage	
	Passage* As Source of Influence		Passage* As Source of Influence	
Direction of Influence and Organizational Context	The Organization	The Organization's Environment	The Organization	The Organization's Environment
Passage As Object of Influence The Organization	Employee's corporate associate relationships influence his power position within the corporation (Kanter 1977).	Extent of perceived recognition from external professional sources influenced scientists' organizational careers (Glaser 1964, pp. 41-63).	The independent nature of the careers of contemporary prostitutes has a considerable influence on the career of the madam of a house of prostitution (Heyl forthcoming).	Dying as a status passage related to saliency of family others among 50 corporate employees (this study).
The Organization's Environment	Truman's position as President influenced his private life (Klapp 1964, p. 15).	The poolroom hustler's view of marriage as dysfunctional for his occupation inhibits him from getting married (Polsky 1967, p. 83).	Army officer's rank and years of military service influence the level of role conflict and role strain present in certain recurring interactions among their wives (Stoddard & Cabanillas 1976).	First generation immigrant and ethnic families' sacrifices influence mobility of second generation child within American life (Strauss 1971, p. 97).

*First passage cited in example is the source of the influence. Several of the illustrations are probably symmetrical but only one of the asymmetrical influences is depicted in these instances.

451

ties of passage (see Glaser and Strauss, 1971, pp. 3–6) should be considered, and as ours is not a longitudinal study, the variation in the employees' reactions could be argued to be a function of different generational experiences rather than a function implying individual changes over time. We believe, however, that if this study had been longitudinal, it would have shown that the reactions changed as the men grew older, an interpretation that is most consistent with the passage concept. The consistency of the changes in our data by age moved us toward this alternative. Tausky and Dubin (1965, p. 730) used precisely this criterion to resolve the generational question in their work. The extent to which both our positive and negative reactions could be corroborated by independent evidence involving both organizational careers and dying as a status passage was found to be additional and persuasive confirmation.

Our research did not go as far as it might in showing the behavioral effects of the two passages on each other. We have, however, (1) identified two pertinent passages for the individuals studied and (2) provided evidence of a *reciprocal, changing* and *complex* influence between them. With regard to the former point, the obligation of sociologists to identify the pertinent passages in which persons are involved should not be taken for granted. It should not be assumed that we are knowledgeable about all passages. Some may be much more subtle than they are now believed to be. The Social Science Research Council (1977, p. 14) has recently underscored the need for more fundamental knowledge about organizational careers.

> Many basic questions have yet to be adequately and systematically addressed; for example, how and when to conceptualize a sequence of jobs as a "career"; what are the social and psychological forces that shape career lines; and what aspects of job sequences are relevant to adult personality development.

There is also the task of identifying the pertinent passages of particular individuals. This is not always done. The retirement literature indicates that "Upper-status job-holders . . . are reluctant to retire, seek to avoid information on retirement, and in fact, because they are accustomed to manipulating the environment to achieve goals, often seem to need little formal preparation for retirement" (Atchley 1976, p. 32). Our evidence suggests that if high status workers are counseled in relation to dying as an awareness passage, instead of the retirement experience, they would be more receptive and may have a need for knowledge about how to face death. The awareness passage of dying may also be having some effect upon the high status employees' retirement reactions. Mitchell (1972, p. 201) has stressed that "there is no more reason to associate retirement with aging than there is to regard a sabbatical year as aging."

We have not adequately stressed the significance of the linkage between organizational careers and nonorganizational careers for the understanding of the enviroment external to the organization. The varied reactions of the corporate employees to the study of death, for example, should be of interest to those concerned with death-related behaviors. Some feel that the increased academic interest in death is evidence of a more favorable and less inhibited view of death (Shneidman 1976, p. xxii), but one must be cautious of overgeneralizations in this area (Lofland 1975). Our evidence indicates that, in some instances, the study of death is viewed in relation to one's ongoing careers in other areas and found to be nonfunctional and dysfunctional for them. Rapoport and Rapoport (1965) have also emphasized the need to study the interrelationships between work and the family and, in fact, argued that status transitions are a vehicle for this purpose.

Perhaps the most notable aspect of our research involving the influence of dying as an awareness passage on the employees' corporate careers is the changing and complex nature of this influence. The significance of the family members for the oldest males was at least partially a function of their growing old together, while dying was not yet an imminent status passage for the youngest males. On the other hand, the more intense mobility aspirations of the youngest males seems to have accounted for their negative reactions. The absence of such aspirations did not provide a similar basis of perception among the oldest men.

The reciprocal, changing, and complex qualities of the interrelationships that probably exist between many multiple passages should make this vehicle attractive for those interested in the study of organizations and their environments. As Benson (1977, p. 11) recommends, a process-oriented approach must attend "to the micro-processes continuously occurring within the organization and its environment within a particular period of time, that is, the ongoing interactions that continuously reproduce the organization and/or alter it." Passages generally reflect the long-range and significant experiences of the individual. The entire passage is important, not just the passage's "turning points."

FOOTNOTES

* Appreciation is expressed to Norman K. Denzin, William Erbe, Anselm Strauss, and Glenn Vernon for their sage observations.

1. For a discussion of the organization as a reification, see Silverman (1971).

2. Salary was a convenient index of the prestige of the organization career. However, the clear linkage between reactions to the death stimulus and organizational career, per se, can be observed by examining the Position and the Reaction columns in Table 1.

3. The trichotomization formed was used consistently in Tables 3 through 6. These particular limits were selected in an attempt to categorize persons of "similar" chronological ages together and to disperse the frequencies somewhat equally across the three categories. There were more younger than older males and all but one of the women were under 40. Moreover, given the preceding criteria, reasonably different categorizations of the age variable in Tables 3 through 6 do not lead to appreciably different results. The data in Table 1 can be used to verify this for Tables 3 and 4. It is also clear from Table 2 that the relationship between age and the reaction to the death stimulus is not dependent on the manner the age variable is cut.

4. The results discussed in this paragraph can be generated from the information contained in Table 1.

5. It should also be noted in this regard that our indirect and open-end stimulus was capable of generating religious reactions from subjects. The students in the Sociology of Death classes frequently found that this happened in their work with the stimulus. The conversation that was discussed earlier between the older student and the 63-year-old retired teacher illustrates this.

6. As writers, psychoanalytic and others (see Sheehy 1976, p. 11), frequently stress that orientations toward dying, such as fear, influence social behavior, we underscore that, in our research, the younger males' social experiences shaped their orientation toward dying.

7. Symmetrical refers to a reciprocal or two-way influence between two passages.

REFERENCES

Ariès, Philippe, *Western Attitudes Toward Death: From the Middle Ages to the Present*, translated by Patricia M. Ranum, Baltimore: Johns Hopkins University Press, 1974.

Atchley, Robert C., *The Sociology of Retirement*, Cambridge, Mass.: Schenkman, 1976.

Azumi, Koya and Jerald Hage, *Organizational Systems*, Lexington, Mass.: D.C. Heath and Company, 1972.

Bakshis, Robert, Michael Correll, Myra Duffy, Stanley E. Grupp, James Hilliker, Thomas Howe, Gail Kawales, and Raymond L. Schmitt, " 'Meanings' Toward Death: A TST Strategy," *Omega: The Journal of Death and Dying* 5 (Summer 1974): 161–179.

Becker, Howard S. and Anselm L. Strauss, "Careers, Personality, and Adult Socialization," *The American Journal of Sociology* 62 (November 1956): 253–263.

————, Blanche Geer, Everett C. Hughes, and Anselm L. Strauss, *Boys in White*, Chicago: University of Chicago Press, 1961.

————, David Riesman, and Robert S. Weiss., eds., *Institutions and the Person*, Chicago: Aldine, 1968.

Benson, Kenneth J., "Innovation and Crisis in Organizational Analysis," *The Sociological Quarterly* 18 (Winter 1977): 3–16.

Blankenship, Ralph L., "Organizational Careers: An Interactionist Perspective," *The Sociological Quarterly* 14 (Winter 1973): 88–98.

Blumer, Herbert, "Society as Symbolic Interaction," pp. 179–192 in Arnold M. Ross (ed.), *Human Behavior and Social Processes: An Interactionist Approach*, Boston: Houghton Mifflin, 1962.

————, "The Methodological Position of Symbolic Interactionism," pp. 1–60 in Herbert Blumer (ed.), *Symbolic Interactionism: Perspective and Method*, Englewood Cliffs, N.J.: Prentice-Hall, 1969.

Day, Robert and JoAnne V. Day, "A Review of the Current State of Negotiated Order Theory: An Appreciation and a Critique," *The Sociological Quarterly* 18 (Winter 1977): 126–142.

Denzin, Norman K., *The Research Act: A Theoretical Introduction to Sociological Methods*, Chicago: Aldine, 1970.

————, "The Logic of Naturalistic Inquiry," *Social Forces* 50 (December 1971): 166–182.

Dill, William R., Thomas L. Hilton, and Walter R. Reitman, *The New Managers*, Englewood Cliffs, N.J.: Prentice-Hall, 1962.

Dubin, Robert "Industrial Workers' Worlds: A Study of the Central Life Interests of Industrial Workers," *Social Problems* 3 (January 1956): 131–142.

Dumont, Richard G. and Dennis C. Foss, *The American View of Death: Acceptance or Denial?* Cambridge, Mass.: Schenkman, 1972.

Epstein, Cynthia F., "Woman's Place: The Salience of Sex Status in the Professional Setting," Paper read at the 62nd Annual Meeting of the American Sociological Association, San Francisco, August 1967.

Etzioni, Amitai, *A Comparative Analysis of Complex Organizations: On Power, Involvement, and Their Correlates,* New York: Free Press, 1975.

Faulkner, Robert R., "Career Concerns and Mobility Motivations of Orchestra Musicians," *The Sociological Quarterly* 14 (Summer 1973): 334–349.

Glaser, Barney G., *Organizational Scientists: Their Professional Careers,* New York: Bobbs-Merrill, 1964.

_____, ed., *Organizational Careers: A Sourcebook for Theory,* Chicago: Aldine, 1968.

_____ and Anselm Strauss, *Awareness of Dying,* Chicago: Aldine, 1964.

_____, "Temporal Aspects of Dying as a Non-scheduled Status Passage," *The American Journal of Sociology* 71 (July 1965): 48–59.

_____, *The Discovery of Grounded Theory,* Chicago: Aldine, 1967.

_____, *Time for Dying,* Chicago: Aldine, 1968.

_____, *Status Passage,* Chicago: Aldine, 1971.

Goldman, Daniel R., "Managerial Mobility Motivations and Central Life Interests," *American Sociological Review* 38 (February 1973): 119–126.

Goldscheider, Calvin, *Population, Modernization, and Social Structure,* Boston: Little, Brown and Company, 1971.

Haas, J. Eugene and Thomas E. Drabek, *Complex Organizations: A Sociological Perspective,* New York: Macmillan, 1973.

Hall, Richard H., *Occupations and the Social Structure,* Englewood Cliffs, N.J.: Prentice-Hall, 1969.

Harrell, Thomas Willard, *Managers' Performance and Personality,* Cincinnati: South-Western, 1961.

Henry, William E., "The Business Executive: The Psychodynamics of a Social Role," *The American Journal of Sociology* 54 (January 1949): 286–291.

Hertz, Robert, *Death and the Right Hand,* Aberdeen, England: University Press, 1960.

Heyl, Barbara Sherman, "House Prostitution in the Seventies: Negotiating Survival," in David R. Maines and Norman K. Denzin, eds., *Work and Problematic Situations: The Structuring of Occupational Negotiations,* New York: Thomas Y. Crowell, forthcoming.

Hochschild, Arlie Russell, "Disengagement Theory: A Critique and Proposal," *American Sociological Review* 40 (October 1975): 553–569.

Homans, George C., *The Human Group,* New York: Harcourt, Brace and Company, 1950.

Howard, Alan and Robert A. Scott, "Cultural Values and Attitudes Toward Death," *Journal of Existentialism* 6 (Winter 1965–1966): 161–174.

Huber, Joan, "Symbolic Interaction as a Pragmatic Perspective: The Bias of Emergent Theory," *American Sociological Review* 38 (April 1973): 274–284.

Hughes, Everett Cherrington, *Men and Their Work,* Glencoe, Ill: Free Press, 1958.

Hyman, Herbert, *Survey Design and Analysis,* Glencoe, IL: Free Press, 1957.

Kanter, Rosabeth Moss, *Men and Women of the Corporation,* New York: Basic Books, 1977.

Kastenbaum, Robert J., *Death, Society, & Human Experience,* Saint Louis: C.V. Mosby, 1977.

Klapp, Orrin E., *Symbolic Leaders,* Chicago: Aldine, 1964.

Kübler-Ross, Elisabeth, *On Death and Dying,* New York: Macmillan, 1969.

Kuhn, Manford H. "The Reference Group Reconsidered," *The Sociological Quarterly* 5 (Winter 1964): 5–21.

_____, and Thomas S. McPartland, "An Empirical Investigation of Self-Attitudes," *American Sociological Review* 19 (February 1954): 68–76.

Lofland, Lyn H., "Toward a Sociology of Death and Dying: Editor's Introduction," *Urban Life* 4 (October 1975): 243–249.

Manning, Peter K., "Rules in Organizational Context: Narcotics Law Enforcement in Two Settings," *The Sociological Quarterly* 18 (Winter 1977): 44–61.

Marris, Peter, *Loss and Change,* New York: Pantheon, 1974.

Marshall, Victor W., "Organizational Features of Terminal Status Passage in Residential Facilities for the Aged," *Urban Life* 4 (October 1975): 349–368.

Mitchell, William L., "Lay Observations on Retirement," pp. 199–217 in Frances M. Carp, ed., *Retirement*, New York: Behavioral Publications, 1972.

Olesen, Virginia L. and Elvi W. Whittaker, *The Silent Dialogue*, San Francisco: Jossey-Bass, 1968.

Parsons, Talcott, "Death in American Society—A Brief Working Paper," *American Behavioral Scientist* 6 (May 1963): 61–65.

Polsky, Ned, *Hustlers, Beats, and Others*, Chicago: Aldine, 1967.

Rapoport, Robert and Rhona Rapoport, "Work and Family in Contemporary Society," *American Sociological Review* 30 (June 1965): 381–394.

Rosenberg, Morris, *The Logic of Survey Analysis*, New York: Basic Books, 1968.

Roth, Julius A., *Timetables*, Indianapolis, Ind.: Bobbs-Merrill, 1963.

Scanzoni, John, "Occupation and Family Differentiation," *The Sociological Quarterly* 8 (Spring 1967): 187–198.

Schmitt, Raymond L., "SI and Emergent Theory: A Reexamination," *American Sociological Review* 39 (June 1974): 453–456.

Shaffer, Thomas L., *Death, Property, and Lawyers: A Behavioral Approach*, New York: Dunellen, 1970.

Sheehy, Gail, *Passages: Predictable Crises of Adult Life*, New York: E.P. Dutton and Company, 1976.

Shneidman, Edwin S., *Deaths of Man*, Baltimore: Penguin, 1974.

————— , ed., *Death: Current Perspectives*, Palo Alto, Calif.: Mayfield, 1976.

Silverman, David, *The Theory of Organizations*, New York: Basic Books, 1971.

Social Science Research Council, "Occupational Careers and Social Support," *Items* 31 (March/June 1977): 14–15.

Spilka, Bernard, "Death and Cultural Values: A Theory and a Research Program," Paper read at American Psychological Association, Washington, D. C., September 1967.

Stebbins, Robert A., "Career: The Subjective Approach," *The Sociological Quarterly* 11 (Winter 1970): 32–49.

Stoddard, Ellwyn R. and Claude E. Cabanillas, "The Army Officer's Wife: Social Stresses in a Complementary Role," pp. 151–171 in Nancy L. Goldman and David R. Segal, eds., *The Social Psychology of Military Service*, Beverly Hills: Sage, 1976.

Strauss, Anselm L., *Mirrors and Masks: The Search for Identity*, Glencoe, Ill.: Free Press, 1959.

————— , *The Contexts of Social Mobility*, Chicago: Aldine, 1971.

————— , "Organizational Negotiations," pp. 267–273 in Alfred R. Lindesmith, Anselm L. Strauss, and Norman K. Denzin, eds., *Readings in Social Psychology*, Hinsdale, Ill.: Dryden, 1975.

————— , *Professions, Work and Careers*, New Brunswick, N.J.: Transaction, 1975.

————— , Leonard Schatzman, Rue Bucher, Danuta Ehrlich, and Melvin Sabshin, *Psychiatric Ideologies and Institutions*, Glencoe, Ill.: Free Press, 1964.

Sudnow, David, *Passing On: The Social Organization of Dying*, Englewood Cliffs, N.J.: Prentice-Hall, 1967.

Tausky, Curt and Robert Dublin, "Career Anchorage: Managerial Mobility Motivations," *American Sociological Review* 30 (October 1965): 725–735.

Toynbee, Arnold, *Man's Concern with Death*, Highstown, N.J.: McGraw-Hill, 1968.

Vernon, Glenn M., *Sociology of Death: An Analysis of Death-Related Behavior*, New York: Ronald Press, 1970.

Wilensky, Harold L., "Careers, Life-Styles, and Social Integration," *International Social Science Journal* 12 (Fall 1960): 553–558.

Studies in Symbolic Interaction

A Research Annual

Series Editor: **Norman K. Denzin, Department of Sociology, University of Illinois.**

The essays in this annual series consist of original research and theory within the general sociological perspective known as Symbolic Interactionism. Longer than conventional journal-length articles, the essays wed micro and macro sociological concerns within a qualitative, field-method empirical orientation. International in scope, this series draws upon the work of urban ethnographers, phenomenologists, ethnomethodologists and critical theorists. The emphasis is on new thought and research which bridge links to an emergent theory of self, socialization, interaction, social relationships, social organization and society.

Volume 1.   Published 1978   Cloth   352 pages   Institutions $ 26.50
ISBN 0-89232-065-6   Individuals $ 13.50

CONTENTS: Forward. *Norman K. Denzin.* **Social Unrest and Collective Protest,** *Herbert Blumer, University of California - Berkeley.* **Organizational Crime: A Theoretical Perspective,** *Edward Gross, University of Washington.* **Crime and the American Liquor Industry,** *Norman Denzin, University of Illinois.* **A Social World Perspective,** *Anselem Strauss, University of California.* **Toward a Symbolic Interactionist Theory of Learning: A Rapproachement with Behaviorism,** *Edward Gross, University of Washington.* **The Social Psychology of Sexual Arousal: A Symbolic Interactionist Interpretation,** *Jeffery S. Victor, State University of New York.* **The Social Construction and Reconstruction of Physiological Events: Acquiring the Pregnancy Identity,** *Rita Seiden Miller, Brooklyn College, CUNY.* **The Meditation Movement: Symbolic Interactionism and Synchronicity,** *Richard Bibbee and Julian B. Roebuck, Mississippi State University.* **Bodies and Selves: Notes on a Fundamental Dilemma in Demography,** *David R. Maines, Center for the Study of Health Services, Yale University.* **Tyranny,** *Dan E. Miller, University of Dayton, Marion W. Weiland, Wichita State University and Carl J. Couch, University of Iowa.* **The Sociology of Female Artists,** *Michal McCall, Case Western Reserve University.* **The Use of Improvisation and Modulation in Natural Talk: Alternative Approach to Conversational Analysis,** *Reyes Ramos, University of California - San Diego.* **Index.**

A 10 percent discount will be granted on all institutional standing orders placed directly with the publisher. Standing orders will be filled automatically upon publication and will continue until cancelled. Please indicate with which volume Standing Order is to begin.

JAI JAI PRESS INC., P.O. Box 1678, 165 West Putnam Avenue, Greenwich, Connecticut 06830.

Telephone: 203-661-7602   Cable Address: JAIPUBL

OTHER SERIES OF INTEREST FROM JAI PRESS INC.

Consulting Editor for Sociology: Rita J. Simon, Director, Program in Law and Society, University of Illinois

COMPARATIVE SOCIAL RESEARCH
(Formerly: Comparative Studies in Sociology)
Series Editor: Richard F. Tomasson, University of New Mexico
POLITICAL POWER AND SOCIAL THEORY
Series Editor: Maurice Zeitlin, University of California—Los Angeles
RESEARCH IN COMMUNITY AND MENTAL HEALTH
Series Editor: Roberta Simmons, University of Minnesota
RESEARCH IN LAW AND SOCIOLOGY
Series Editor: Rita J. Simon, Director, Program in Law and Society, University of Illinois
RESEARCH IN RACE AND ETHNIC RELATIONS
Series Editors: Cora B. Marrett, University of Wisconsin, and Cheryl Leggon, University of Illinois—Chicago Circle
RESEARCH IN SOCIAL MOVEMENTS, CONFLICTS AND CHANGE
Series Editor: Louis Kriesberg, Syracuse University
RESEARCH IN SOCIAL PROBLEMS AND PUBLIC POLICY
Series Editor: Michael Lewis, University of Massachusetts
RESEARCH IN SOCIAL STRATIFICATION AND MOBILITY
Series Editor: Donald J. Treiman, National Academy of Sciences
RESEARCH IN SOCIOLOGY OF EDUCATION AND SOCIALIZATION
Series Editor: Alan C. Kerckhoff, Duke University
RESEARCH IN SOCIOLOGY OF KNOWLEDGE, SCIENCES AND ART
Series Editors: Robert Alun Jones, University of Illinois, and Henrika Kuklick, University of Pennsylvania
RESEARCH IN THE INTERWEAVE OF SOCIAL ROLES: WOMEN AND MEN
Series Editor: Helena Z. Lopata, Center for the Comparative Study of Social Roles, Loyola University of Chigago
RESEARCH IN THE SOCIOLOGY OF HEALTH CARE
Series Editor: Julius A. Roth, University of California—Davis
RESEARCH IN THE SOCIOLOGY OF WORK
Series Editor: Ida Harper Simpson, Duke University, and Richard Lee Simpson, University of North Carolina, Chapel Hill
STUDIES IN COMMUNICATIONS RESEARCH
Series Editor: Thelma McCormack, York University—Toronto

OTHER SERIES OF INTEREST FROM JAI PRESS INC.

Consulting Editor for Sociology: Rita J. Simon, Director, Program in Law
and Society, University of Illinois

STUDIES IN SYMBOLIC INTERACTION
Series Editor: Norman K. Denzin, University of Illinois

*ALL VOLUMES IN THESE ANNUAL SERIES ARE AVAILABLE AT
INSTITUTIONAL AND INDIVIDUAL SUBSCRIPTION RATES.
PLEASE ASK FOR DETAILED BROCHURE ON EACH SERIES.*

A 10 percent discount will be granted on all institutional standing orders
placed directly with the publisher. Standing orders will be filled automatically upon publication and will continue until cancelled. Please indicate
with which volume Standing Order is to begin.

 JAI PRESS INC.
P.O. Box 1678
165 West Putnam Avenue
Greenwich, Connecticut 06830
(203) 661-7602   Cable Address: JAIPUBL